STATS™ 1992 BASEBALL SCOREBOARD

John Dewan, Don Zminda, and STATS, Inc.

Foreword by Bill James

Illustrations by John Grimwade

Statistical Compilations by Robert Mecca
with Dr. Richard Cramer and David Pinto

STATS, Inc. (Sports Team Analysis & Tracking Systems, Inc.) – Chicago

STATS™ 1992 Baseball Scoreboard. Copyright © 1992 by STATS, Inc. All rights reserved. Printed in the United States of America. No part of this book may be used or reproduced in any manner whatsoever without written permission except in the case of brief quotations embodied in critical articles and reviews. For information address STATS, Inc., 7366 N. Lincoln Ave., Lincolnwood, IL 60646-1708. phone: (708)676-3322.

STATS is a registered trademark of Sports Team Analysis and Tracking Systems, Inc.

First Edition: February 1992

Cover Design by John Grimwade

ISBN 0-9625581-4-1

Dedication

To John Dewan Sr., thanks for all the bat day doubleheaders, Dad!

and

To Gene Zminda, who taught his son who Nellie Fox was.

ACKNOWLEDGEMENTS

This book is the culmination of a very busy off season here at STATS. It's the fourth and last book that we work on between baseball seasons. But it's definitely not the least. The *Scoreboard* is my favorite of them all because it answers baseball's toughest questions — questions whose answers were mere speculation before now.

Literally hundreds of baseball devotees contribute to this book each year. I can't list them all on this page, but I can tell you a little about some of those people who went far beyond the call of duty.

First, there's Don Zminda, my co-author on this book. Don and I have been working together for quite some time now, and yes my opinion is biased, but I believe Don to be one of the most talented baseball analysts and writers in our field. Most of the writing you see in this book originates from Don's keyboard. Nobody does it better.

You also can't get any better than the work of John Grimwade. From Day One when we started working with John through *Sports Illustrated*, I told myself that we ought to find a way to work more closely with him. Fortunately, we did. His artistic skills make what could be just another chart of numbers explode right off the page.

As we approached our publishing deadline, Bob Mecca and I took turns locking the office door on our way out after each long day . . . evening . . . and night working on this book. Bob is simply awesome in his ability to get the most amazing information out of the STATS computer.

Steve Moyer joined STATS less than a year ago, but in that short time his contributions to improve our publications, and specifically the book you're holding in your hand, have been fantastic. Jonathan Forman has also been with us a short time, but his valued computer skills had a direct beneficial impact on many different essays in this book.

Dr. Richard Cramer, founder and Chairman of the Board of STATS, continues to be an inspiration to us all. He designed the basis for the STATS computer system over ten years ago, and it's still the state of the art.

David Pinto has been very instrumental in keeping us at the cutting edge with both his baseball and computer knowledge.

Arthur Ashley, Bob Meyerhoff and Sue Dewan make up the core management group at STATS. I can't say enough good things about them. Not only does their professionalism show in everything they do, but they make certain that every STATS product is top notch.

Thanks to the rest of the STATS organization and our associates who do innumerable things to help keep STATS operating: Michael Canter, Mike Cieslinski, Matt Greenberger, Tom Hilgendorf, Tom Horowitz, Nadine Jenkins, Chuck Miller, Marge Morra, Jim Musso, Suzette Neily, Rob Neyer, Bud Podrazik, Ross Schaufelberger, Bob Wirz, Craig Wright, and the whole reporting staff throughout the country.

Finally, without Bill James, STATS would probably not exist today.

— John Dewan

Table of Contents

FOREWORD ... 1

INTRODUCTION ... 3

I. GENERAL BASEBALL QUESTIONS ... 5

- HOW DOES THE WIND AFFECT RUN-SCORING AT WRIGLEY? ... 6
- WAS SCORING POSITION THE KEY FOR THE TWINS AND BRAVES? ... 8
- WHO DOES WHAT THE MOST? ... 11
- WHAT'S THE FUTURE HOLD FOR CAL RIPKEN? ... 14
- WHY THROW TO FIRST? ... 16
- AL WEST: HOW DID THE WEST BECOME THE BEST? ... 18
- AL EAST: HOW IMPORTANT IS AN ACE? ... 20
- NL WEST: FROM WORST TO FIRST TO . . .? ... 22
- NL EAST: CAN THE LITTLE GUYS COMPETE? ... 24
- DOES A HOT START MEAN A HAPPY FINISH? ... 26
- HOW WOULD PYTHAGORAS PREDICT THE PENNANT RACE? ... 28
- DOES SWITCHING SKIPPERS IN MIDSEASON EVER WORK? ... 30
- WHO TAKES 'EM, WHO SWINGS AT 'EM, WHO FOULS 'EM OFF? ... 32
- HOW MUCH DIFFERENCE DOES THE UMPIRE MAKE? ... 36
- WHY DON'T THEY PRINT LINEUPS ON SCORECARDS ANY MORE? ... 38
- WHY DID MITCH LOVE TO PITCH LAST AUGUST? ... 40
- ARE THE BEST TEAMS GOOD LATE-INNING TEAMS? ... 42
- WHO ARE THE SLOWEST STARTING BATTERIES? ... 44
- WHAT KIND OF TEAM CAN'T RALLY IN THE NINTH? ... 46
- ARE THE BRAVES AND ANGELS TOO LOADED WITH LEFTIES? ... 48

II. QUESTIONS ON OFFENSE ... 50

- WHY WAS WILL CLARK'S 116 RBI BETTER THAN CECIL FIELDER'S 133? ... 51

WHO WAS BASEBALL'S BEST CLEANUP HITTER IN '91?	54
IS WADE, RICKEY, PAULIE OR BRETT NO. 1 AT NO. 1?	56
WHERE WILL WE FIND THE NEXT JOHNNY BENCH?	58
CAN WE GO AHEAD AND SAY JOE CARTER IS A CLUTCH HITTER?	61
DO WE REALLY KNOW "WHO CAN POP IN THE CLUTCH"?	64
WHY DOES JOE CARTER LOVE SKYDOME... AND PAUL O'NEILL THE RIVERFRONT?	67
WHY PLAY FOR ONE RUN?	70
IS PITTSBURGH'S BUNT-IN-THE-FIRST STRATEGY WORTH IT?	72
WHO'S THE BEST BUNTER: BELL, BUTLER, CUYLER, FINLEY OR NIXON?	74
WHO ARE BASEBALL'S TABLE SETTERS?	76
FOR WHOM DOES CRIME PAY?	78
ARE SOME BASERUNNERS SIMPLY TOO AGGRESSIVE?	80
ARE POWER HITTERS PULL HITTERS?	82
WHO HAS THE BEST "HEART OF THE ORDER"?	84
WHO WENT TO THE MOON IN 1991?	86
WHY SHOULD YOU TAKE A SECOND(ARY) LOOK AT ROB DEER?	88
WHO ARE THE "HUMAN AIR CONDITIONERS"?	90
WHAT KIND OF HITTERS HAVE BIG PLATOON DIFFERENTIALS?	92
WHY DON'T MORE CLUBS PLATOON?	94
SHOULD KEVIN McREYNOLDS BE KNOWN AS "MR. AVERAGE"?	96
WHAT'S AN AVERAGE LINEUP (1991 VERSION)?	98
CAN AGGRESSIVE BASERUNNING HELP WIN CHAMPIONSHIPS?	101
DOES PATIENCE LEAD TO SLUGGING?	104
IS PATIENCE A VIRTUE?	106
CAN YOU BE AN MVP, AND YET NOT CREATE RUNS?	109
WHO ARE THE ROSES AND AARONS OF TOMORROW?	112
HOW IMPORTANT ARE GOOD PINCH HITTERS?	114
WILL THE ORIOLES DRIVE MERCEDES TO A WINNING RECORD?	116
IS HE THE NEXT VINCE COLEMAN... OR THE NEXT DONELL NIXON?	119

WILL THE LINEOUTS OF '91 BECOME THE LINE HITS OF '92? 122
IS McGWIRE UPPERCUTTING HIMSELF TO OBLIVION? 124
DO CLUTCH HITTERS GEAR UP WITH RUNNERS IN SCORING POSITION AND TWO OUT? 127
WILL COMISKEY BE "THE HOUSE THAT FRANK BUILT"? 130
WHO ARE THE BEST TWO-STRIKE HITTERS? 132
WHAT KIND OF HITTERS MAKE "PRODUCTIVE" OUTS? 134
WHO ARE THE RALLY KILLERS? 136
WHERE HAVE YOU GONE, JOE DiMAGGIO? 138
WILL THE REAL ALAN TRAMMELL PLEASE STAND UP? 140
WHO WINS THE "GAME OF THE STATES"? 142
IS THERE SUCH A THING AS A "TURF HITTER"? 144

III. QUESTIONS ON PITCHING   147

DO MINOR LEAGUE STRIKEOUT KINGS MAKE GOOD MAJOR LEAGUE PROSPECTS? 148
WHOSE HEATER IS THE HOTTEST? 151
WILL THEY KEEP 'EM OFF BASE IN '92 LIKE THEY DID IN 1991? 154
WHO PITCHED BETTER IN 1991 — BILL GULLICKSON OR FRANK VIOLA? 156
CAN ANYONE HIT NOLAN RYAN — NOW OR EVER? 158
HOW IMPORTANT IS IT TO "HOLD THE FORT"? 160
WAS BILL SWIFT THE BEST "TOTAL RELIEVER" OF 1991? 162
DID LEE SMITH TAKE A SHORT CUT TO THE SAVE CROWN? ... 164
WILL MIDDLE RELIEF BE THE WHITE SOX' HIDDEN ADVANTAGE AGAIN IN '92? 167
HOW IMPORTANT IS IT TO GET THE FIRST BATTER? 170
WHY DID ATLANTA BUY 'LECKI (AND HIS 4.46 ERA)? 172
WHICH SOUTHPAWS EAT LEFTIES? 174
IS IT EASIER TO STEAL OFF A LEFTY? 176
WHERE WILL WE FIND THE NEXT DON ROBINSON? 178
IS THE NEXT BOB LEMON SOMEWHERE IN YOUR OUTFIELD? . 180
WHO ARE THE HIDDEN RELIEF STARS? 182
CAN YOU PITCH YOURSELF INTO A HOLE BUT STILL SURVIVE? 185
DO WORKHORSE STARTERS STILL EXIST? 188
DID CLEMENS SACRIFICE SOME QUALITY FOR QUANTITY? 190

DO PITCHERS COAST WITH A BIG LEAD? 192
ARE CLEMENS AND GOODEN ON THE TRACK TO
IMMORTALITY? 194
IS FADING IN THE STRETCH A FATAL WEAKNESS? 196
HOW IMPORTANT IS GOOD CONTROL? 199
WILL IT BE DR. TREVOR . . . OR MR. WILSON? 202
DID MORE THROWS TO FIRST HELP DWIGHT GOODEN? 204
IS HOLDING RUNNERS OVERRATED? 206
IS "UNEARNED RUN AVERAGE" A LEADING INDICATOR? 209
WHICH STARTING STAFFS STAR, AND WHICH RELIEF STAFFS
REEK? 212
WHY DO THE METS LET THEIR ACES THROW SO MANY
PITCHES? 216
WHO'S WORST IN THE FIRST? 218

IV. QUESTIONS ON DEFENSE   220

DO GOOD-THROWING CATCHERS INTIMIDATE
BASERUNNERS? 221
WHAT DO YOU SACRIFICE FOR A GOOD-THROWING
CATCHER? 224
CAN A CATCHER HELP A PITCHER'S ERA? 226
SHOULD YOU GUARD THE LINE IN THE LATE INNINGS? 228
WHO LED THE LEAGUE IN FUMBLES? 230
WHO'S BEST IN THE INFIELD ZONE? 232
WHO'S BEST IN THE OUTFIELD ZONE? 236
WHO ARE THE PRIME PIVOT MEN? 238
WHICH OUTFIELDERS HAVE THE CANNONS? 240
WHAT MAKES FOR AN EFFICIENT DEFENSE? 242

APPENDIX   244

About STATS, Inc.   334

Index   336

FOREWORD

By **Bill James**

This book is one of the undiscovered annual treasures of the American Sports Library. It is my basic theory of writing that the discriminating reader wants to know something at the end of each paragraph that he didn't know at the beginning of the paragraph. My most fundamental criticism of sportswriting and broadcast journalism in general is that a great deal of what we see and hear is merely an attempt to lend personal style and new credibility to words pulled off the shelf of common knowledge, bound with standard opinions.

This is a book of uncommon knowledge.

The *Baseball Scoreboard* is rich in specific information — new specific information, specific information which did not exist until this book was published. The *Scoreboard* is made up of specific information like who the best hitting pitchers in baseball today are, which managers platoon the most, and pulled together with discussion of and information about specific questions like how artificial turf affects hitters and how the catcher affects the ERA of the pitching staff.

It's a wonderful thing to have access to that kind of informaton — not that every dribble of it is interesting, you understand, but that it's wonderful to be able to draw on these charts to discuss not only the issues that STATS has raised, but other related and cross-related notions. In many ways, this is the book that I wanted to do when I started the *Baseball Abstract* fifteen years ago. I wanted to ask simple, specific questions, and go find the answers to them.

Of course, I wasn't able to do that, so I compensated by doing what could be done at the time, and it worked out great. With limited access to game accounts and no computer skills, what I could do was brainstorm a lot. If you could study the relationship of this to that, here's what it might show.

If we had multi-year, systematic information about how players had hit against left-handed and right-handed pitchers, here's what it might show. If we had systematic information about how players had hit with runners in scoring position, here's what I think it would tell us.

The *Abstract* did great anyway, because it came along at the right time. The absence of data led the *Abstract* into a lot of long-winded statistical gerrymandering to try to cover the gaps in the information. This stuff is pretty irritating, read in retrospect, but I got by with it because at the time there was a great hunger to know these things. I couldn't exactly find out how many bases were stolen against Gary Carter and how many were stolen against Manny Sanguillen, but I could come pretty close, and at the time that was good enough.

Well, I know in my heart that this is in many ways a better book than the early *Abstracts*. The difference here is, you can take out the ifs. John and Don and their associates can actually check and see what the data is and check the side effects to see what it means, rather than doing little test studies for partial data, and then speculating about what it means.

I don't think I'm telling any tales out of school, but this book hasn't been a great success in the market place. STATS is a well-run company, and a good percentage of the things they do work out alright on the bottom line, but it's been a struggle to get this book to work out. The problem is, quite simply, that the *Scoreboard* came along at a difficult time, when there were so many stat books fighting for a spot in the market that it is difficult for any of them to find their spot. In the early eighties publishers were so anxious for baseball stat books that several books were able to get published that really weren't well thought-out or well researched. By 1988 major publishers had decided that there were too many stat books out there, and they by and large didn't discriminate between good new stat books and bad new stat books — and by so doing, have declined to publish the best new stat book in the last five years, which is this one.

So we can't really say, at this time, whether this is the third edition of a book that's going to run for fifty years and eventually reach a wide audience, or whether this is it, and whether these books will be sort of collector's items, prized by baseball afficianados twenty years from now the way 1968 press guides are prized now by people with an insatiable thirst for baseball knowledge.

INTRODUCTION

Welcome to the third edition of *The STATS Baseball Scoreboard*. For those of you who have read our previous editions, we're sure you'll agree this is the best *Scoreboard* ever. If you're a first-timer, we think you're in for a treat.

We at STATS like to think of ourselves as students of the game. Any good student is going to ask a lot of questions, and we structure this book in question-and-answer form, 101 of them each year. A lot of the subjects are perennial favorites, like the pitchers with the best (and worst) run support or the list of the best bunters. But we try to come up with at least 30 new questions each year, and we think you'll like the subjects we're exploring for the first time in 1992. For example, most people are familiar with "pitchers' parks" and "hitters' parks," but what are the best home run parks for left- and right-handed hitters? We provide the data. We always hear that some players are "great artificial turf hitters," but is there really any such thing? The answer might surprise you. The Chicago Cubs like to say that the image of Wrigley Field is all wrong, that it's tough for hitters when the wind blows in. Are they right? We provide the data, and the discussion.

Many of you loved the old Baseball Abstracts, and we think you'll like the fact that we continue to provide many of the stats Bill James made famous. This year we revive the "Defensive Efficiency Rating," a unique and effective way of identifying the clubs who play the best defense. Last year we ran an article using "The Favorite Toy" — statistical projections on players' chances to reach milestones like 3,000 hits — and it was so well received that we've updated the list this year. Leaders in runs created, offensive winning percentage and secondary average are all here, along with many other James favorites.

As STATS expands, we're able to delve into new subjects. We now have a minor league database, and this year we have three articles on minor league prospects. Our historical database also continues to grow, and as that happens we increase our ability to answer questions about baseball's past. Want to know which manager was the master of the "midseason takeover"? You'll find it here. Interested in how Dwight Gooden and Roger Clemens compare with pitchers of the past at the same age? That's another question we explore.

There's lots more, with many of the articles embellished by John Grimwade's insightful illustrations. One thing we love about John's work is that it's FUN as well as informative. As always, we hope you'll feel the same way about our entire book.

John Dewan and Don Zminda

I. GENERAL BASEBALL QUESTIONS

HOW DOES THE WIND AFFECT RUN-SCORING AT WRIGLEY?

The Chicago Cubs play in what most fans consider one of the classic parks in baseball history. Yet even the Cubbies can get defensive in talking about their ball yard. It was Keith Moreland, we think, who complained that people considered Wrigley a great hitters' park — but that when the wind blows in (as it often does), it is an entirely different place. The Cubs themselves have come out with statistics that indicate that poor Ryne Sandberg is lucky that he hasn't been blown off second base, across home plate, and right over Harry Caray's broadcast booth onto Clark Street (Holy Cow!) . . . the wind blows in that hard, and that frequently.

Statistics provided by major league teams are often fascinating, but they can be prejudiced by the fact that clubs want to make themselves and their players look good, and tend to stick to numbers which will do just that. If the Moreland/Cub theory is right, Wrigley Field would probably be a pitchers' park — favoring hitters when the wind blew out, favoring pitchers when it blew in . . . as, they say, it usually does. We all know this is nonsense. Wrigley Field is perennially one of the best hitters' parks in the majors, ranking near the top in its positive effect on batting average, home runs and runs scored.

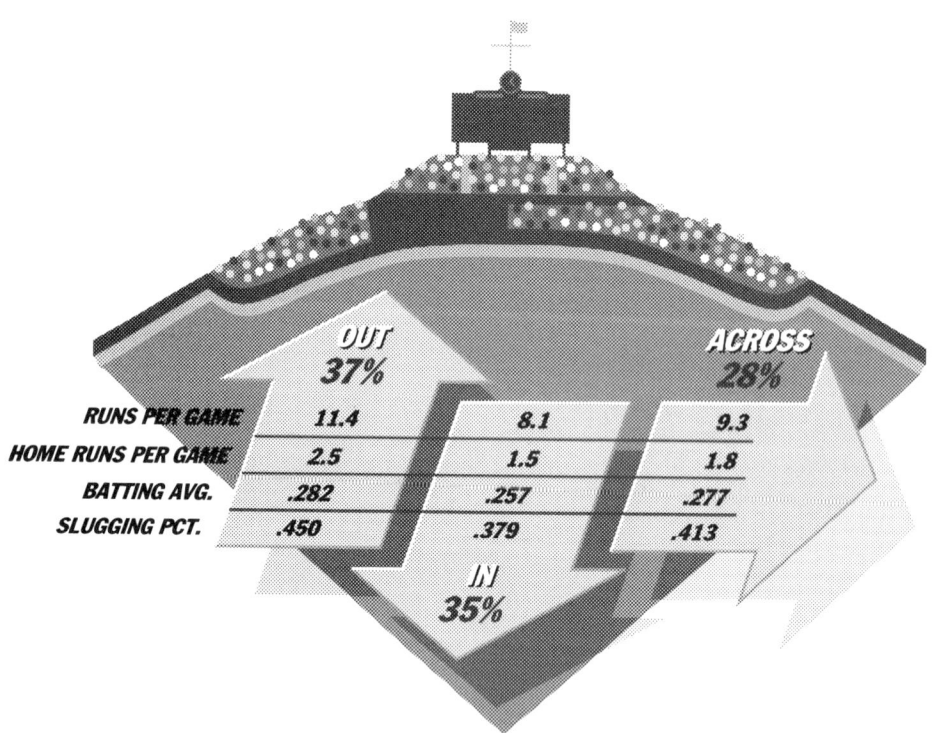

	OUT 37%	IN 35%	ACROSS 28%
RUNS PER GAME	11.4	8.1	9.3
HOME RUNS PER GAME	2.5	1.5	1.8
BATTING AVG.	.282	.257	.277
SLUGGING PCT.	.450	.379	.413

But while the Cubs may overestimate the net effect of the wind, they are absolutely right about one thing: Wrigley is a very different park when the wind blows in. As the graphic shows, the Cubs and their opponents hit 25 points higher (.282 to .257), score over three more runs per game (11.4 to 8.1), and hit 67 percent more homers per contest (2.5 to 1.5) when the wind blows out than they do when it blows in (based on the 1990 and 1991 seasons). There's only a slight exaggeration in measuring the frequency of various wind directions — it blows in (35 percent of the time) about as much as it blows out (37 percent).

However, these numbers greatly need to be put into context. To begin with, the wind often blows neither in nor out, but across — from left field to right, or from right to left. Our stats indicate that this occurs about 28 percent of the time, a significant amount. And when there's a cross wind, the park definitely favors the hitters, ranking well above the National League average in terms of batting average (.277), runs per game (9.3) and homers per contest (1.8). Thus Wrigley is a decided hitters' park well over 60 percent of the time.

And there's this fact, one the Cubs never note: even when the wind blows in, Wrigley is no worse than a neutral park by National League standards. Over the past two seasons, the National League batting average has been .253; that's four points below Wrigley's wind-blowing-in average of .257. Over the same time, the league has scored 8.3 runs per game, just slightly over the North Side figure of 8.1 when the wind blows in. And during that period, the league has hit 1.5 homers per game, exactly the same total as at Wrigley with the wind blowing in.

The conclusion? When the wind blows out, Wrigley is a **great** hitters' park; when it blows across, it's a very good one; when it blows in, it's a neutral park. Anyone want to break the news to Keith Moreland?

A complete listing for this category can be found on page 246.

WAS SCORING POSITION THE KEY FOR THE TWINS AND BRAVES?

Batting

This is one of those glamorous "clutch" categories, one that our friends from Elias insist is all-important — the final exam of performance under pressure, although maybe that's with runners in scoring position **and** two outs. So call it the semi-final exam. Anyway (get your pencils and papers ready) which American League clubs were best on offense with runners in scoring position last year? Here they are:

American League
Batting with Runners in Scoring Position

Team	Avg	OBP	Slg	R	HR
Kansas City	.290	.374	.422	592	30
Milwaukee	.283	.362	.438	683	38
California	.275	.344	.387	526	24
Texas	.274	.359	.435	626	48
Chicago	.272	.368	.409	592	35
Seattle	.265	.352	.387	542	28
Boston	.264	.356	.400	592	34
Minnesota	.262	.343	.400	599	37
Oakland	.261	.357	.419	596	47
Detroit	.257	.352	.422	577	48
New York	.257	.334	.389	512	33
Cleveland	.254	.322	.347	473	16
Baltimore	.252	.338	.391	488	32
Toronto	.247	.337	.373	524	27
AL Average	**.265**				

If you rated offenses strictly on the basis of batting with runners in scoring position, who would be the tops? Why the Kansas City Royals, of course, with that gaudy .290 average. And how many total runs did those mighty Royals score in 1991? Why, 727 (applause, applause)! And how many runs did the average American League club score in 1991. Why, um, 727. So let's say this category is **something**. Let's not say it's everything.

Here is the National League offensive data:

National League
Batting with Runners in Scoring Position

Team	Avg	OBP	Slg	R	HR
Atlanta	.285	.367	.427	594	36
St. Louis	.272	.360	.376	558	10
Pittsburgh	.270	.355	.413	609	36
San Diego	.267	.347	.412	515	36
Los Angeles	.259	.354	.382	545	33
New York	.256	.345	.362	503	22
Cincinnati	.255	.337	.393	504	32
Houston	.255	.341	.367	508	21
Chicago	.249	.318	.398	522	41
Montreal	.244	.328	.343	459	19
San Francisco	.243	.326	.359	476	27
Philadelphia	.239	.314	.362	493	28
NL Average	**.258**				

This is a little more logical. The NL champion Braves have the best batting average, and the clubs which scored the most runs from scoring position were the division champion Pirates and Braves. More importantly, the top two clubs in runs scored overall last year were Pittsburgh and Atlanta. We told you this category meant something.

Pitching

Stopping the opposition with runners in scoring position is an often-neglected category. Not by us. Here's the American League data:

American League
Pitching with Runners in Scoring Position

Team	Avg	OBP	Slg	R	HR
Minnesota	.236	.318	.358	375	30
Seattle	.246	.351	.360	420	25
Toronto	.247	.337	.374	364	34
Boston	.253	.345	.395	411	33
California	.253	.336	.406	358	38
Texas	.254	.350	.379	498	35
Chicago	.257	.342	.396	367	37
Kansas City	.262	.340	.380	440	27
Cleveland	.273	.344	.403	461	31
Oakland	.279	.370	.435	414	38
Milwaukee	.280	.352	.421	428	40
New York	.280	.357	.441	424	41
Detroit	.288	.380	.418	487	31
Baltimore	.303	.379	.460	439	37

The best American League club in terms of lowest batting average allowed, lowest on-base percentage and lowest slugging percentage was the world champion Minnesota Twins. We told you this category meant something.

Here is the National League pitching data:

National League
Pitching with Runners in Scoring Position

Team	Avg	OBP	Slg	R	HR
Los Angeles	.232	.325	.320	332	17
Philadelphia	.240	.337	.366	428	29
Montreal	.248	.341	.387	402	33
San Diego	.251	.327	.361	337	25
New York	.255	.327	.372	371	31
Atlanta	.259	.341	.405	346	34
Houston	.259	.359	.399	434	35
St. Louis	.266	.343	.407	362	29
Pittsburgh	.268	.334	.389	345	27
Cincinnati	.270	.351	.379	426	21
San Francisco	.273	.358	.402	406	29
Chicago	.276	.353	.409	451	31

The starring club in this category is the Dodgers — lowest in all five categories. Dodger Stadium plays a part, of course, but that's impressive. All they have to do is hit a little better.

A complete listing for this category can be found on page 247.

WHO DOES WHAT THE MOST?

We keep track of everything — the good, the bad, the indifferent stats. Some are serious, some are just fun. If you're interested in finding out things like who grounded out the most times last year, read on; if not, you'll never know, will you? Here are the major league leaders for 1991 in just about every conceivable category:

Play	No.	Leader	
Run Scored	18,127	Paul Molitor	133
Single	25,766	Brett Butler	162
Double	6,499	Rafael Palmeiro	49
Triple	894	Ray Lankford	15
Home Run	3,383	Cecil Fielder	44
		Jose Canseco	44
Game-Winning RBI	1,952	Ron Gant	23
Sacrifice Hit	1,519	Jay Bell	30
Sacrifice Fly	1,243	Howard Johnson	15
Hit by Pitch	905	Jeff Bagwell	13
Walk	12,755	Frank Thomas	125
Intentional BB	1,229	Fred McGriff	26
Strikeout	24,311	Rob Deer	175
Stolen Base	2,767	Marquis Grisson	73
Caught Stealing	1,545	Brett Butler	28
Ground DP	2,999	Kirby Puckett	27
1B/Interference	16	Paul Molitor	3
1B/K+Wild Pitch	54	7 tied with	2
1B/K+Passed Ball	25	25 tied with	1
1B/Failed FC	164	5 tied with	3
1B/Error	1,420	Cal Ripken	15
2B/Error	262	Dan Pasqua	6
3B/Error	21	21 tied with	1
4B/Error	1	Juan Gonzalez	1
1B/SacBunt+FC	45	3 tied with	2
1B/SacBunt+Err	60	5 tied with	2
1B/Ball Hits Runner	16	Tony Phillips	2
Flied Out	22,749	Harold Reynolds	134
Foul Fly Out	503	3 tied with	6
Ground Out	32,422	Steve Sax	209
Line Out	5,939	Tony Gwynn	44

Play	No.	Leader	
Bunt Out	541	Otis Nixon	23
Pop Out	6,619	Howard Johnson	54
Foul Pop Out	3,088	Ron Gant	33
Force Out	4,385	Lance Johnson	36
Bunt/Force Out	171	7 tied with	3
GDP on Bunt	22	Bob Scanlan	3
Bunt Fly DP	20	Rafael Belliard	2
Line DP	323	Jeff Bagwell	6
Ground Triple Play	4	4 tied with	1
Line Triple Play	1	Tony Gwynn	1
Bunt Fly Out	261	Brian McRae	8
Fly DP	87	Tim Wallach	4
Double Steal	230	Rickey Henderson	7
SB + Error	123	Otis Nixon	6
CS + Error	22	Julio Franco	2
SF + Error	6	6 tied with	1
Pickoff	204	Ozzie Smith	5
Out Advancing	846	Tony Pena	9
		Roberto Alomar	9
Advance-No Play	79	7 tied with	2
Pick Off Error	146	Ray Lankford	7
Advance on Throw	542	Harold Reynolds	10
Advance on Error	947	3 tied with	11
Error-Foul Fly	58	Rafael Palmeiro	3
Batter Obstruction	18	18 tied with	1
Out on Obstruction	7	7 tied with	1
Advance on Obstruction	2	Roberto Alomar	1
		Gary Redus	1

A few comments on this momentous data:

1. Neither the Yankees nor the Mets had very good years in either 1990 or 1991. But in both seasons, Steve Sax led the majors in ground outs, while Howard Johnson was the top man in pop outs. We couldn't help noticing that HoJo is the toast of New York these days, while Sax escaped the New York jungle with his trade to the White Sox. Note to Steve: try hitting the ball in the air a little!

2. Forget that boring World Series. The most thrilling contest of 1991 was the race for the fly-out championship among Harold Reynolds (134),

Kevin McReynolds (132), Rafael Palmeiro (128) and Don Mattingly (126). You did us proud again, New York . . . but of course you disappointed us in the end. (No wonder the Mets traded McReynolds.)

3. Pitcher Bob Scanlan is the "Babe Ruth of the bunt." We wish we could say that was a compliment. Unfortunately, Scanlan bunts the ball so hard that, three times in 1991, he bunted into a double play. What did Harry Caray have to say about that?

4. White Sox outfielder Dan Pasqua is no gazelle, but he reached second base on an error six times last year. The Sox rewarded Pasqua with a lucrative free agent contract at the end of the year. If Pasqua doesn't defend the title, will it be because of the pressure, or just another case of free agent complacency?

5. Tony Gwynn led the majors in lineouts last year, defending his crown from 1990. And who, pray tell, was the hitter on the majors' only lineout-triple play? None other. If Gwynn was in a bad mood last year, he had his reasons.

6. You'd think the leader in "most times picked off" would be some dumb rookie. Sure. The 1990 leader was Rickey Henderson; the 1991 leader was that inexperienced youngster, Ozzie Smith.

7. We're not supposed to be keeping track of the "game-winning RBI," but the 1991 leader was Ron Gant with 23 game-winners. You have to promise not to tell anyone.

8. You know the saying "Every silver lining has a cloud" (or is it the other way around)? Well, Tony Phillips had an excellent season. But he led the major leagues in a dubious category: base hits where he nailed a baserunner with his batted ball causing the runner to be called out.

WHAT'S THE FUTURE HOLD FOR CAL RIPKEN?

Cal Ripken seems to enjoy fooling people. From 1983 through 1990, Ripken's offensive numbers were in a fairly steady decline, and it was easy to conclude that his consecutive game streak was wearing him down. Ripken felt otherwise, and in 1991 he proved his critics (us included) wrong. Though he turned 31 in August, Ripken had what was arguably the best season of his career, and won his second Most Valuable Player Award in the process.

We know what Ripken has done in the past; is there a way to project what he'll accomplish in the future? To some extent there is. Along with STATS, Bill James has designed a projection system based on past performance; we use that system to estimate the next season's offensive numbers in our annual **STATS Major League Handbook**. While the projections are obviously only reasonable estimates, they've proven to be very accurate the vast majority of the time.

Since the system includes age adjustments, you can also use it to project the rest of a player's career. Bill James started doing that several years in what he originally called the Brock2 (later Brock6) system; the current projection system is an offspring of Brock6. Naturally, it's far easier to make an accurate prediction of what a player will do in 1992 than what he'll do in 2002. We know, as a general rule, what age does to a player's offensive performance; it's a leap of faith to predict what it will do to **this** player's performance. In Ripken's case, the playing streak adds complications because it may well accelerate Cal's aging process. Nonetheless, and just for fun, we asked the computer to predict the rest of Ripken's career. Here is what it came up with:

Computer Projection for the Rest of Cal Ripken's Career

	G	AB	R	H	2B	3B	HR	RBI	BB	SO	SB	CS	Avg
1992	162	635	84	175	34	2	25	96	66	62	4	2	.276
1993	161	616	82	169	31	2	34	100	67	62	8	4	.274
1994	162	624	81	171	33	6	26	92	62	64	4	2	.274
1995	162	618	78	166	39	0	22	85	65	60	8	0	.269
1996	163	622	76	162	28	1	30	84	66	63	5	8	.260
1997	162	627	70	159	30	5	19	87	65	65	4	3	.254
1998	162	615	76	154	28	0	25	76	73	66	2	2	.250
1999	73	253	27	67	9	1	3	33	27	32	0	0	.265
2000	158	593	64	145	30	1	15	76	63	65	1	1	.245
2001	153	564	59	135	21	0	20	63	68	64	0	0	.239
2002	147	537	52	127	20	1	9	69	60	72	0	0	.236
2003	140	513	50	120	19	0	11	55	58	64	0	0	.234
2004	87	300	27	68	9	0	4	28	33	39	0	0	.227
Total	3,530	13,422	1,796	3,580	671	52	502	1,886	1,461	1,525	64	46	.269

This is wild, isn't it? Some comments on the projections:

1. The first thing you'll probably notice is that Cal is projected for only 161 games in 1993. We are NOT NOT NOT predicting that Ripken will take a day off in '93; almost every year one or more clubs plays fewer than 162 games due to unplayed rainouts, or more than 162 because of a tie. Ripken, while maintaining the streak, played only 161 contests in 1985, 1988 and 1990. That's what the computer's saying about 1993.

2. The second thing you'll notice is that the computer predicts that Cal's streak will go well beyond 1995, when he would pass Lou Gehrig's 2,130. The projection is that it would continue into 1999 when an apparent injury strikes. At the start of the '99 season, Ripken would have played 2,707 consecutive games, or nearly 600 more than Gehrig. This is extremely unlikely, of course; the odds are overwhelming that Ripken would begin taking some days off once he's passed Gehrig's records. The computer doesn't make that sort of assumption; it has him continuing to play every day, based on the fact that he's done it for so many years in the past. The important thing is that the computer does predict that he'll break the consecutive-game game streak.

3. If the computer is right, Ripken will keep playing until 2004 (see it at your local theater — "2004: A Ripken Odyssey"). At the end of that season, he would be 44 years old. This is certainly possible, but there's a strong chance that the string of predicted .230-ish seasons toward the end of his career would persuade Cal to hang 'em up before then. If the projections are right and he keeps playing, however, he would retire fifth on the all-time hits list and fifth in doubles as well. Ripken would also rank second in lifetime at-bats, behind only Pete Rose.

4. You may notice that the computer predicts Ripken to wind up with 502 homers; in our article on The Favorite Toy, he's given less than a 10 percent chance to reach 500. How is this so? Simple. The Favorite Toy is based on all players; this formula is more Ripken-specific, taking into account Ripken's unusual durability. The odds are still pretty long that he'll actually reach 500, since we have him barely over that total.

5. If you read our book last year, you're surely aware that the computer is much kinder toward Ripken's future than we were last year. We still think there's a danger in continuing to play him every day, a danger of lost production from a tired player. But after what he did in 1991, we have to give Ripken the benefit of the doubt. As they say in the NFL: After further review, we have a reversal!

Though the final numbers might be off, the projection makes perfect sense: a magnificent career, one of the greatest in baseball history. We'll save some time in 2004, Cal, to be part of that final standing ovation.

WHY THROW TO FIRST?

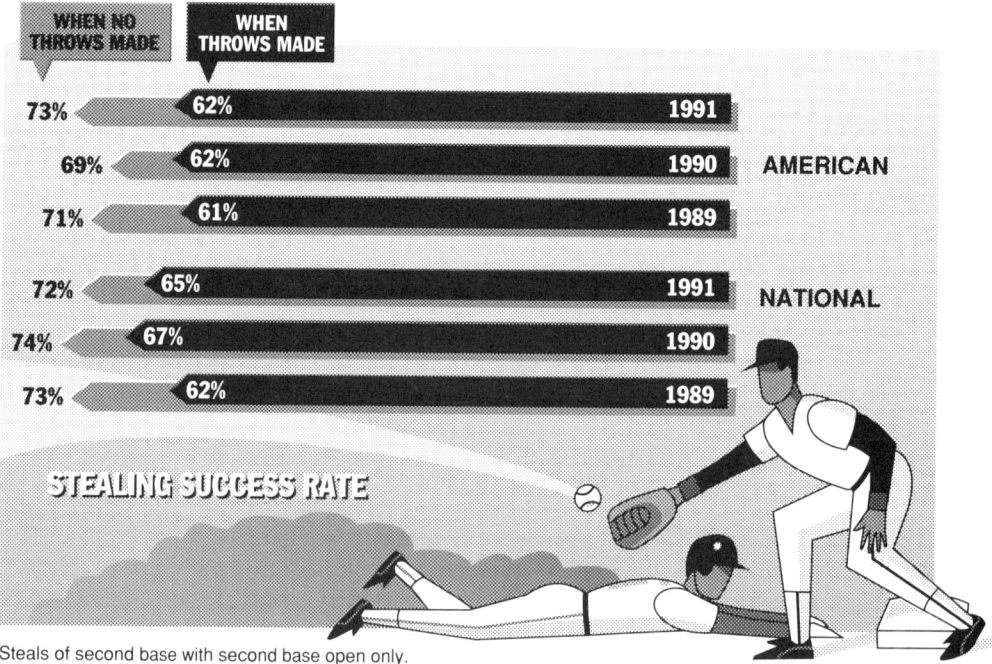

Steals of second base with second base open only.

We've been studying the effects of pitchers' throws to first for several seasons now, and we have to admit the results have been a lot more significant than we imagined they would be. One simple study we made for the first edition of this book involved comparing situations when a runner tried to steal but no throw to first was made, to situations where the runner attempted to steal with at least one pickoff toss. If throwing to first were essentially meaningless, one would expect to find little difference — or random year-to-year variations — between the two situations.

The numbers, though, have been remarkably consistent. In each of the three seasons we've studied the issue, throwing to first has helped cut down on the stolen base success rate. The figures haven't varied much, ranging from a 7-to-11 percent improvement over each of the three seasons. The chart above gives you an idea of just how consistent those numbers have been. Here are the complete figures, with both leagues combined, for the three seasons (steals of second base only):

	1989			1990			1991			Three Years		
	SB	CS	%	SB	CS	%	SB	CS	%	SB	CS	%
No Throws Made	1401	526	73	1422	560	72	1436	560	72	4259	1646	72
Throws Made	1175	681	63	1321	721	65	1255	786	61	3751	2188	63

But while the overall numbers have stayed consistent, one variance we did notice last year came among the top base stealers. In the first two years of our study, throwing to first worked even better against the top stolen base men than it did against runners in general. This was not quite the case in 1991, though pickoff throwing still proved to be an effective strategy (note — figures are for steals of second base only):

	No Throw Made			Throws Made		
Baserunner	SB	CS	Pct	SB	CS	Pct
Marquis Grissom, Mon	21	5	81	37	9	80
Otis Nixon, Atl	24	4	86	35	15	70
Rickey Henderson, Oak	24	3	89	13	9	59
Delino DeShields, Mon	13	7	65	35	11	76
Roberto Alomar, Tor	15	6	71	17	4	81
Tim Raines, WSox	27	4	87	22	11	67
Luis Polonia, Cal	17	7	71	14	12	54
Ray Lankford, StL	15	4	79	26	13	67
Barry Bonds, Pit	12	5	71	21	7	75
Milt Cuyler, Det	12	3	80	19	6	76
Totals (Top 10)	180	48	79	239	97	71

Among the ten players who stole 40 or more bases, throwing to first cut down on the success rate by an eight percent margin — three percent less than against runners overall. There was some player-to-player variance, of course; the throw to first worked a lot better against Rickey Henderson and Luis Polonia than against Roberto Alomar and Delino DeShields. The big picture is pretty clear, however: there seems to be little doubt by now that throwing to first is effective strategy.

Hey, maybe that's why they do it (and why we study it).

A complete listing for this category can be found on page 248.

AL WEST: HOW DID THE WEST BECOME THE BEST?

Once described by Bill James as "the Third World of baseball," the American League West has gradually become the best division in baseball. Last year all seven AL West clubs finished at .500 or better, the first time that's ever happened. The West didn't stop there. In the championship series the Twins easily handled East champion Toronto, making it the fifth straight season a Western club had won the playoffs; in those five series, Eastern teams have won a grand total of three games. Minnesota went on to win the World Series, the third time in five seasons the AL West has produced the world champion.

As we stated a couple of years ago, the West's ascendancy has been a gradual progression. As recently as 1986, West clubs were winning only 45 percent of their interdivisional games with the East. By last season, the West's winning percentage was almost 100 points higher:

**AL West vs. AL East
1986-91**

Year	Win %
1986	.456
1987	.478
1988	.497
1989	.535
1990	.533
1991	.551

How did this happen? You could cite a number of reasons, but a big key was the way Eastern and Western clubs handled the draft during the 1980s. At the end of the 1981 season, the best club in the American League was the Yankees, with two world titles, four pennants and five division championships in the previous six years. Free agent signees like Catfish Hunter, Reggie Jackson and Dave Winfield had helped make the Yanks a dominant club. New York continued to work the free agent market throughout the decade, but with diminishing returns. It's still not completely understood that when you sign a top level free agent, you lose a top draft choice. And no one lost more draft choices than the Yankees:

Year	Top Yankee draft choices lost
1982	First (to Reds for signing Dave Collins)
1983	First (to White Sox for signing Steve Kemp)
	Second (to Reds for signing Bob Shirley)
	Third (to Angels for signing Don Baylor)
1985	First (to Padres for signing Ed Whitson)
1986	First (to Angels for signing Al Holland)
1987	First (to Rangers for signing Gary Ward)
	Second (to Brewers for signing Rick Cerone)
1988	First (to Cardinals for signing Jack Clark)
	Second (to Astros for signing Jose Cruz)
	Third (to Mets for signing John Candelaria)
1989	First (to Dodgers for signing Steve Sax)

Even granting that top draft choices in baseball are far more hit-and-miss than they are in any other sport, doesn't it seem ludicrous to sacrifice your first three picks to get Steve Kemp, Bob Shirley and Don Baylor? Or your first two to get Gary Ward and Rick Cerone? Or a second pick for 40-year-old Jose Cruz, who would bat 80 times for the Yankees (hitting .200) before retiring?

Stranger still, the Baltimore Orioles — like the Yanks, one of baseball's best clubs well into the eighties — decided to copy the Yankee system. In 1985, the O's gave up their first three draft choices in order to sign Fred Lynn, Lee Lacy and Don Aase. In '86 the Orioles sacrificed their first pick in order to get 36-year-old Juan Beniquez. Is it such a mystery that the Orioles and Yankees eventually slid to the bottom of the standings?

While that was going on, AL West teams were making much more intelligent decisions. In 1984 and '85, the Athletics picked up Walt Weiss and Mark McGwire in the first round; in 1987 the Mariners snagged Ken Griffey Jr.; in 1988 the Angels' top pick was Jim Abbott; from 1987 to 1990, the White Sox' first-round picks were Jack McDowell, Robin Ventura, Frank Thomas and Alex Fernandez. West clubs made their share of mistakes, also, but no Western club was as short-sighted as the Yankees or Orioles were. The West used the draft to its advantage, and it's now prospering.

AL EAST: HOW IMPORTANT IS AN ACE?

To say the least, the Toronto Blue Jays are feeling frustrated. Since 1985 the Jays have been hearing that they have "the best talent in baseball" — a heavy trip to lay on anybody — but all they have to show for it are three measly division championships. (Any number of teams would love to trade places.) Theories have abounded about why Toronto couldn't get over that hump. A year ago, the Blue Jays decided that the problem was that they were flunking Chemistry 101. Over the winter they got rid of those guys who were cracking jokes in the back of the classroom, and all season long we heard about how this was a different Toronto team. Different, yes, but no better, as it turned out; after five quick playoff games, it was time to develop a new theory.

Call this one the "staff ace" theory. "You've got to have an ace in the hole," sings George Strait, and when the playoffs arrived last year, Minnesota had Jack Morris — veteran number-one starter and former World Series hero — all primed and ready. The Jays countered with Tom Candiotti, a knuckleballer who'd never started a postseason game. Candy got rocked, and Morris went on to pitch the Twins all the way to the world championship. So for 1992, the Jays have signed Morris to a free agent contract. Now, when a big game arrives (regular season, playoff or World Series), Toronto will have one of the best all ready to go.

It's an interesting idea, and one which has some merit. Since the late forties, at least, one characteristic of the best teams has been a dominant starter — a Cy Young-type who thrives on pressure. Through the seventies the great teams, the ones who won back-to-back pennants and at least one world championship, always seemed to have a pitcher like that, sometimes more than one. The ones who didn't, like the Dodger clubs of 1949-53, found themselves falling short, just like the Blue Jays. Here's a roll call:

Team	Staff Ace(s)
49-53 Yankees	Allie Reynolds, Vic Raschi
55-58, 60-64 Yankees	Whitey Ford
57-58 Braves	Warren Spahn, Lew Burdette
63, 65-66 Dodgers	Sandy Koufax, Don Drysdale
64, 67-68 Cardinals	Bob Gibson
69-71 Orioles	Jim Palmer, Dave McNally, Mike Cuellar
72-74 A's	Catfish Hunter
77-78 Yankees	Ron Guidry

Through all that time, the only team that won multiple pennants without a dominant starter was the Cincinnati club of 1970-72-75-76. The others fit the profile, winning titles on the pitching of their aces.

Since 1978, only one club has managed back-to-back pennants: the 1988-90 Athletics. Sure enough, the A's had an ace in Dave Stewart. Other clubs have won one flag, and usually a dominant starter was instrumental: Steve Carlton (1980 Phillies), Fernando Valenzuela (1981 Dodgers), Morris (1984 Tigers, 1991 Twins), Bret Saberhagen (1985 Royals), Frank Viola (1987 Twins), Orel Hershiser (1988 Dodgers). Why have these clubs failed to repeat? Often because the staff aces failed to have great years back-to-back. Many of them have come down with arm trouble; others, like Roger Clemens and Dwight Gooden, even in their great seasons, have worn down by the time September arrived. Though they don't pitch as many innings as their predecessors, today's top starters are expected to go all-out from the first pitch to the last. It takes its toll.

Morris has been a magnificent clutch pitcher, and Toronto is happy to have him. But he will be 37 this year, and hasn't had back-to-back winning seasons since 1987-88. During the off-season the Jays lost Candiotti, and their chief rivals, the Red Sox, added an ace of their own in Viola, who should take some of the strain off Clemens.

It certainly is important for a modern-day team to have an ace, but it isn't everything. While listening to all that talk about their "great talent," the Blue Jays have developed some holes in their lineup: catcher, shortstop, left field, first base (unless John Olerud develops). Though they play in a hitter's park, the Jays were 11th in the American League in runs scored last year, and Jack Morris won't solve **that** problem. The Red Sox will provide formidable competition again, as will whoever wins the West. It's quite possible that, a year from now, the Blue Jays will be expounding a new theory about why they haven't won a pennant.

NL WEST: FROM WORST TO FIRST TO...?

Worst to First — Lord, we heard enough of **that** phrase last fall, didn't we? By now, even your baseball-hating grandmother knows that the Minnesota Twins and Atlanta Braves finished last in 1990, first in 1991, and then hooked up in an epic World Series. But what can we expect from Atlanta in 1992, and in the next few years?

To get a handle on this, you first have to understand that what the Braves achieved last year was a much greater accomplishment than what the Twins did. Minnesota had been a good club in the very recent past: world champs in 1987, 91 wins in 1988. Even when they finished last in 1990, the Twins' record was unusually strong (74-88) for a cellar dweller. The Braves, though, had been hopeless for years:

The Braves — 1985-1991

Year	Record	Finish	
1985	66-96	5th	
1986	72-89	6th	
1987	69-82	5th	
1988	54-106	6th	
1989	63-97	6th	
1990	65-97	6th	
1991	94-68	1st	(improved by 29 games)

Since 1900, there's really been only one other club which has had this same pattern — hopeless doormats for years, then a sudden breakthrough to a pennant. You probably know what team that was. After finishing last or next-to-last in each of their first seven seasons, the New York Mets won it all in 1969:

The Mets — 1962-1970

Year	Record	Finish	
1962	49-120	10th	
1963	51-111	10th	
1964	53-109	10th	
1965	50-112	10th	
1966	66-95	9th	
1967	61-101	10th	
1968	73-89	9th	
1969	100-62	1st	(improved by 27 games)

There are more than a few parallels between these two clubs. Both the Mets and Braves had strong young pitching staffs (Seaver, Koosman, Gentry, Ryan, McGraw for the Mets; Glavine, Avery, Smoltz, Stanton, Mercker for Atlanta). The Met pitchers had better ERAs, but a lot of that is the difference between Shea Stadium and Fulton County; these Atlanta guys can pitch. Both the Mets and Braves carefully added some veteran pitchers to add stability (Cardwell, Taylor; Leibrandt, Berenguer/Pena). Each club brought in a veteran leader to play first base (Clendenon, Bream), juggled a hitter and a fielder at second (Boswell/Weis; Treadway/Lemke), played a light-hitting glove man at short (Harrelson, Belliard), and had two brilliant young outfielders (Jones, Agee; Gant, Justice). The Braves didn't have a pitcher quite as good as Tom Seaver was in 1969, but the Mets didn't have a Terry Pendleton, either. All in all, it's an interesting match.

Can the Braves expect to continue to play winning ball? If the Mets are any precedent, they can; New York was over .500 in six of the next seven years, and reached the World Series again in 1973. But there was no Met "dynasty," and in those seven years the best Met record was 86-76. It seems pretty clear now that they were playing over their heads in 1969. Seaver, Koosman, and McGraw were the real thing, but Gary Gentry wasn't, and the Mets foolishly traded away Nolan Ryan before he could develop. Cleon Jones and Tommie Agee, both 26 in 1969, showed only flashes of brilliance in future years.

In modern baseball history, there's one other club (along with the Mets) which reasonably parallels the '91 Braves. After finishing eighth, seventh, eighth, ninth and ninth in the ten-club American League from 1962 to 1966, the Boston Red Sox improved by 20 games and won the pennant in 1967, surprising the baseball world as much the Mets and Braves later would. That Boston club also had a core of brilliant young players: Carl Yastrzemski, George Scott, Rico Petrocelli, Tony Conigliaro, Jim Lonborg, etc. Like the Mets, the Sox played winning ball for years afterwards, but Boston wouldn't win another pennant for eight more seasons.

Our conclusion: it's reasonable to expect Atlanta to win 85 games or so this year. This is a good, well-rounded team, with better hitting than the '69 Mets and better pitching than the '67 Red Sox. A repeat pennant, however, is a very tall order.

NL EAST: CAN THE LITTLE GUYS COMPETE?

Let us now observe a moment of silence for those poor Pittsburgh Pirates: "Alas, poor Bucco, I knew him well." Two-time defending National League East champions, the Pirates have already been buried by critics who feel they won't be able to survive the free agent departure of Bobby Bonilla this year, and (presumably) Barry Bonds next year. In the modern era, we're told, the small-market clubs can't compete.

Is this a valid assessment? It's tempting to say yes. This year the Pirates have lost one of their best players, Bonilla — and to a key rival, the New York Mets. The assumption is that the Pirates will be weaker, the Mets stronger. Yet the history of free agency indicates that it's always been something of a desperation move, and one which often backfires.

Look at clubs which have heavily invested in the free agent market since 1977: the Yankees from the late '70s to the late '80s; the Angels of the late '70s and early '80s; the Braves, Padres, and Rangers of the late '70s; the Orioles of the mid-'80s; the Royals in 1989-90. While the Yankees unquestionably found early success with Reggie Jackson, Goose Gossage, etc., what most clubs got were debts and a lot of frustration. It's true that last year's Twins and Braves worked the free agent market successfully, but mainly to embellish the talent which was already in place. Most other teams signed free agents for a basic reason: they couldn't develop their own talent, so they opted to sign someone else's.

Meanwhile clubs which **could** develop their own players — clubs like today's Pirates — found that they could lose star players through free agency and not only survive, but thrive:

Stars Lost Through Free Agency

Club	Player(s) lost	Results
1977 Orioles	Bobby Grich, Reggie Jackson	2nd in 1977; pennant 1979
1978 Pirates	Goose Gossage	2nd in 1978; pennant 1979
1979 Reds	Pete Rose	Division title 1979
1983 Dodgers	Steve Garvey	Division title 1983, 1985
1985 Cardinals	Bruce Sutter	Pennant 1985, 1987

The reason these clubs were able to survive the losses was that they had replacement players — usually not stars of the level of the players lost, but adequate replacements — in their farm system. What people often don't consider is that baseball is, and always has been, a young man's game. Players generally have their greatest seasons when they're around age 27 or so; in most cases that means they're still with their original clubs. Beyond that, they begin to decline, slowly at first and then more rapidly as they get into their thirties. Thus a club which loses a free agent has already had the best years of his career, while a club which signs one is getting a player who is past his prime. That's a subtle thing, but it's one reason why clubs are often able to withstand free agent losses.

One man who understood this idea, though in a very different era, was Branch Rickey. In the years long before free agency, Rickey built the rag-tag St. Louis Cardinals into a powerhouse. St. Louis, like Pittsburgh today, was decidedly a "small market," and in the early twenties, a lot of people felt that it was impossible for the Cardinals to compete with the mighty New York Giants. But Rickey had a keen eye for talent, and his solution was to sign as many good young players as possible, usually at very cheap prices; the Cardinals would carefully nurture that young talent, keeping the players they liked and selling the excess to other teams at big profits. With his eye always on the bottom line, Rickey was also unafraid to trade away players he had developed into stars, replacing them at regular intervals with younger, cheaper players. Through it all, St. Louis kept winning.

Under today's rules, a Rickey-style operation is no longer possible. But a lot of his principles — sign your own talent, stock your roster with younger players, don't be afraid to deal away a player in his prime — still apply. It's not easy for small market clubs to compete; they have to be smarter, and sometimes willing to make unpopular decisions (like letting a free agent go). But some clubs can pull it off . . . the small-market Twins, after all, are the world champions. It's too early, we think, to give up on the Pirates.

DOES A HOT START MEAN A HAPPY FINISH?

"Well begun is half done," my old English teacher, Father Carrico, used to say. That's good advice, particularly for those of us who are inclined to postpone writing those last 98 essays until the night before the book is due. But how does the concept apply to baseball? Every year a few clubs seem to roar out of the starting gate, often to the amazement of almost everybody. Does a hot start portend a strong season, or is a club that is hot in April just as likely to fade in June?

Let's look at the evidence. Over the last five seasons a total of 14 clubs have won more than two-thirds of their games in April, posting winning percentages ranging from .682 (the 1987 Reds) to .857 (the 1987 Brewers). Here they are, and here's how they wound up:

Team	April		Finish		
1987 Brewers	18-3	.857	91-71	.562	3rd
1990 Reds	13-3	.813	91-71	.562	1st
1989 Rangers	17-5	.773	83-79	.512	4th
1990 Athletics	14-5	.737	103-59	.636	1st
1988 Pirates	16-6	.727	85-75	.531	2nd
1988 Indians	16-6	.727	78-84	.481	6th
1988 Mets	15-6	.714	100-60	.625	1st
1988 Red Sox	14-6	.700	89-73	.549	1st
1990 Pirates	14-6	.700	95-67	.586	1st
1988 Yankees	16-7	.696	85-76	.530	5th
1988 Athletics	16-7	.696	104-58	.642	1st
1987 Giants	16-7	.696	90-72	.556	1st
1989 Athletics	18-8	.692	99-63	.611	1st
1987 Reds	16-7	.682	84-78	.519	2nd

Does a hot start mean something? It sure does. Eight of the 14 clubs wound up winning their division, and two more finished second. Only one finished with a losing record — the 1988 Indians started out 16-6, but wound up in sixth place with a 74-88 record. (Well, Cleveland's always been the joker in the major league deck.) Even including the Tribe, however, these clubs averaged 91 victories, which is good enough to win a lot of pennants.

The 1988-90 Oakland A's were probably the best example of a team which had its act together from the start of the season. In each of those three campaigns the A's got off to a hot start, and though they always hit a slump at some point during the season, Oakland had enough momentum to easily push on to a championship.

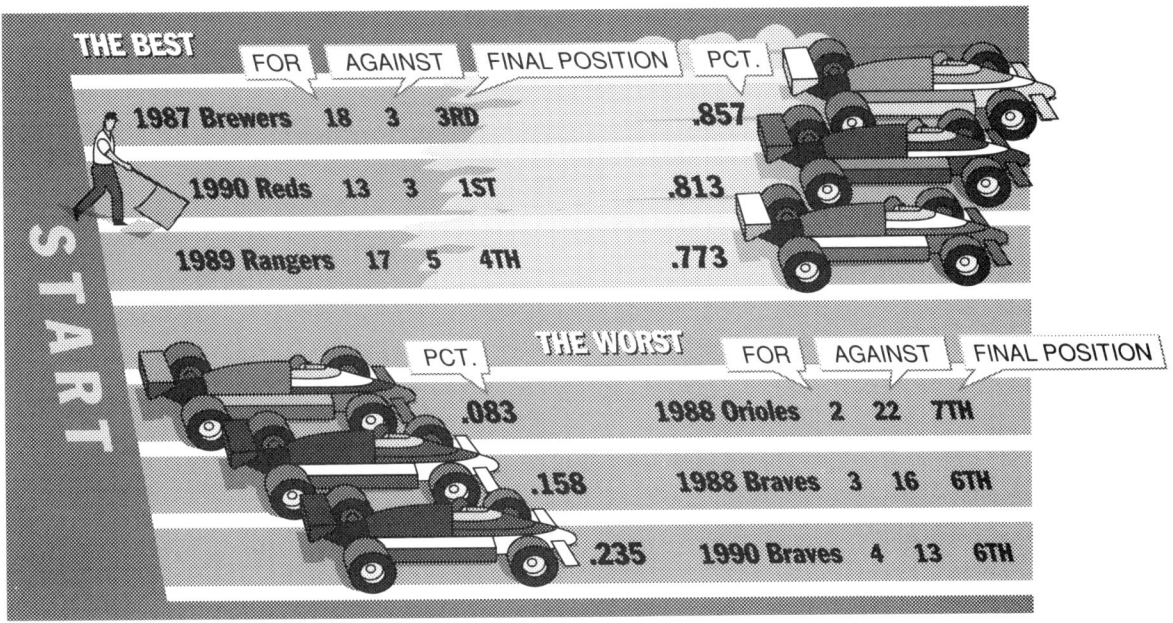

Curiously, the model didn't work very well in 1991. The NL East champion Pirates got off to a strong start (13-7) last year. But the Blue Jays finished April 12-9, and the pennant-winning Twins (9-11) and Braves (8-10) were both under .500. But that's hardly enough evidence to make us doubt our conclusions.

How about clubs which get off to a really **bad** start? That's significant, too. Over the past five seasons, seven clubs managed to lose two-thirds or more of their April games. None of them could recover:

Team	April		Finish		
1988 Orioles	2-22	.083	54-107	.335	7th
1988 Braves	3-16	.158	54-106	.338	6th
1990 Braves	4-13	.235	65-97	.401	6th
1987 Padres	6-17	.261	65-97	.401	6th
1991 Orioles	6-12	.333	67-95	.414	6th
1987 White Sox	6-12	.333	77-85	.475	5th
1990 Royals	6-12	.333	75-86	.466	6th

The '88 Orioles and Braves, the two worst clubs of recent years, showed their true colors right away (particularly those legendary 0-21 O's). Hmm, given their recent history, the Braves probably thought their 8-10 beginning last year **was** a hot start!

A complete listing for this category can be found on page 249.

HOW WOULD PYTHAGORAS PREDICT THE PENNANT RACE?

Those of you who are Bill James fans are undoubtedly familiar with the Pythagorean Theorem. What it does is project a club's won-lost percentage based on its runs scored and runs allowed. The formula:

$$\frac{\text{Runs squared}}{(\text{Runs squared}) + (\text{Opposition Runs squared})} = \text{Won-Lost Percentage}$$

As we noted last year, the formula usually works very well. Last year, for example, the Red Sox scored 731 runs and allowed 712. The formula would predict a record of 83-79; their actual record was 84-78. Generally the formula will come within three wins of the club's actual record.

It's when the theorem is off that things become interesting. There are many reasons why a club would perform better than expected, but a big one is luck. And when a club is lucky, or unlucky, in year one the pendulum tends to swing back in year two. The 1990 Blue Jays won only 86 games, seven fewer than one would expect according to their runs scored and allowed. In '91 Toronto figured to have a more normal run of luck, and they did; predicted to win 89 games by the formula, they won 91. The White Sox were the opposite extreme; in '90 the overachieving Sox won seven more games than the formula said (94 instead of 87). Teams seldom do that sort of thing two years in a row, and the White Sox were no exception. Last year Chicago's runs scored/allowed projection was 90 wins, but the Sox were below the mark with only 87 wins. Overachievers no more . . . or more likely, just not so lucky as they were in 1990.

			Actual		Projected		
AL East	R	OR	W	L	W	L	Diff
Blue Jays	684	622	91	71	89	73	2
Red Sox	731	712	84	78	83	79	1
Tigers	817	794	84	78	83	79	1
Brewers	799	744	83	79	87	75	−4
Yankees	674	777	71	91	70	92	1
Orioles	686	796	67	95	69	93	−2
Indians	576	759	57	105	59	103	−2
AL West	R	OR	W	L	W	L	Diff
Twins	776	652	95	67	95	67	0
White Sox	758	681	87	75	90	72	−3
Rangers	829	814	85	77	82	80	3
Athletics	760	776	84	78	79	83	5
Mariners	702	674	83	79	84	78	−1
Royals	727	722	82	80	82	80	0
Angels	653	649	81	81	81	81	0

The chart above shows the American League for 1991 — runs scored and allowed, actual won-lost record, the won-lost record projected by the Pythagorean theorem, and the difference between the two.

As usual, the formula's projections were very close to the actual won-lost figures. This is more stability than you usually see, in fact; the only clubs off by more than three wins were the Brewers (four fewer wins than expected) and the A's (five more). What would Pythagoras say? That Milwaukee figures to be luckier in 1992, while Oakland may be in for a long season. The numbers also indicate that the Twins definitely did **not** luck into a championship last year. However, the White Sox would figure to pose a stiffer challenge than they did in 1991. It should be a good race.

			Actual		Projected		
NL East	R	OR	W	L	W	L	Diff
Pirates	768	632	98	64	97	65	1
Cardinals	651	648	84	78	81	81	3
Phillies	629	680	78	84	75	87	3
Cubs	695	734	77	83	77	85	0
Mets	640	646	77	84	80	82	-3
Expos	579	655	71	90	71	91	0
NL West	R	OR	W	L	W	L	Diff
Braves	749	644	94	68	93	69	1
Dodgers	665	565	93	69	94	68	-1
Padres	636	646	84	78	80	82	4
Giants	649	697	75	87	75	87	0
Reds	689	691	74	88	81	81	-7
Astros	605	717	65	97	67	95	-2

The National League figures from last year are also very stable. Only two clubs were off by more than three victories. The Padres, minus-six in 1990, had their luck even out in '91; they won four more than expected by the formula. The Reds' performance, however, wasn't nearly as bad as it seemed. A .500 club based on their runs scored/allowed ratio of 689/691, Cincinnati won only 74 games. One would think that Cincinnati would be a strong candidate for a 1992 comeback.

Understand that the formula is based on **last** year's numbers. It can't take into consideration trades, free agent signings, new managers, youngsters coming on or players growing old, and a lot of other things. What it does take into account is a normal run of luck. Even that doesn't always even out over a two year period, but there's a strong chance that it will.

DOES SWITCHING SKIPPERS IN MIDSEASON EVER WORK?

The 1991 season can be remembered for many things, but most people would probably prefer to forget that it was the "year of the managerial change." Over the course of the season, six clubs switched skippers, and for a while changing managers became a daily ritual. Let's see, first Hal McRae replaced Frank Robinson and then Jim Fregosi replaced Don Zimmer and then Billy Martin took over for Yogi Berra, or was it Bob Lemon? If we seem a little mixed up, you can probably understand why; there were a **lot** of changes. And though some clubs made some moderate improvement, for the most part, the switches didn't change things much.

But of course, changing managers in midseason does occasionally work, sometimes dramatically. Some of these switches are the stuff of baseball legend. The Cubs won two pennants in the 1930s by changing managers in midseason (from Rogers Hornsby to Charlie Grimm in 1932, and from Grimm to Gabby Hartnett in 1938); the 1978 Yankees roared to a championship after bouncing Martin and hiring Lemon; and as recently as 1989, the Blue Jays won a division title after replacing Jimy Williams with Cito Gaston. We thought it might be fun to look at the managers who coaxed the biggest improvements out of their clubs after taking over in midyear. Let's restrict the study to cases where both the old and new managers worked at least 50 games. These skippers brought about the largest increase in winning percentages (Note: *Total Baseball* is the source for these figures; if there were interim managers, we added those totals to the old manager's figures):

Midseason Managerial Changes
Biggest Improvement in Winning Percentage

Yr/Team	Old Manager	W-L	Pct	Pos	New Manager	W-L	Pct	Pos	Pct Chg
52 Phi-N	E. Sawyer	28-35	.444	6	S. O'Neill	59-32	.648	4	204
86 Oak-A	J. Moore	31-52	.373*	7	T. LaRussa	45-34	.570	3	197
38 Det-A	M. Cochrane	47-50	.485	5	D. Baker	37-19	.661	4	176
78 NY-A	B. Martin	52-43	.547*	4	B. Lemon	48-20	.706	1	159
76 Cal-A	D. Williams	39-57	.406	6	N. Sherry	37-29	.561	4	155
77 Tex-A	F. Lucchesi	34-35	.493*	5	B. Hunter	60-33	.645	2	152
61 StL-N	S. Hemus	33-41	.446	6	J. Keane	47-33	.587	5	141
32 Chi-N	R. Hornsby	53-46	.535	2	C. Grimm	37-18	.673	1	138
50 Bos-A	J. McCarthy	31-28	.525	4	S. O'Neill	63-32	.663	3	138
22 Pit-N	G. Gibson	32-33	.492	5	B. McKechnie	53-36	.596	3	134

*includes interim manager games

Too bad Steve O'Neill's been dead for 30 years; he was the undisputed king of the midyear takeover. In 1935 O'Neill got his first managerial job by replacing Indians skipper Walter Johnson in midyear; the Tribe, which had played .489 ball under Johnson, went .610 under O'Neill (not quite enought to make the chart). O'Neill repeated that magic with the 1950 Red Sox and the 1952 Phillies (both on the chart). The only time he started a year with a new team, the '43 Tigers, he improved Detroit's record by five games his first season and won the World Series in his third. Steve was apparently a bit of a disagreeable sort, and he usually wore out his welcome within a few seasons. But in 14 years of managing, his clubs posted a .559 winning percentage, and he had a winning record every year. He's probably one of the most underrated managers in history — and the best ever at making order out of midyear chaos.

Looking at the list of managers who brought about the biggest improvement, you'll find only two pennants. Sometimes the change was simply the result of replacing a taskmaster (like Dick Williams) with an easy-going sort (like Norm Sherry); by the next year, the club was back to floundering. But quite often the improvement shown here was no fluke. LaRussa, Baker, Keane and McKechnie would all win pennants with these clubs within three years, and both Lemon and Grimm returned to the World Series within three years (Lemon typically was bounced and rehired by the Yanks between 1978 and 1981).

A curious case here was Billy Hunter. A longtime assistant to Earl Weaver at Baltimore, Hunter won high praise for turning around the crazy 1977 Rangers (he was the club's **fourth** manager that season); Texas finished that year a strong second, with 94 wins. But after leading the Rangers to 86 wins and another second-place finish in '78, Hunter was bounced. He never managed in the majors again. But if some club is floundering in midyear this season . . .

A complete listing for this category can be found on page 250.

WHO TAKES 'EM, WHO SWINGS AT 'EM, WHO FOULS 'EM OFF?

We record the results of every pitch of each major league season, so we can break down everything that happens in minute detail. Let's have some fun and look at the results of our pitch-by-pitch statistics, and the leaders in each category. The chart shows the percentage of time each pitch was taken for a ball or strike, swung at and missed, fouled off, or put into play in each league in 1991. As in 1990, the hitters were a little more patient in the American League:

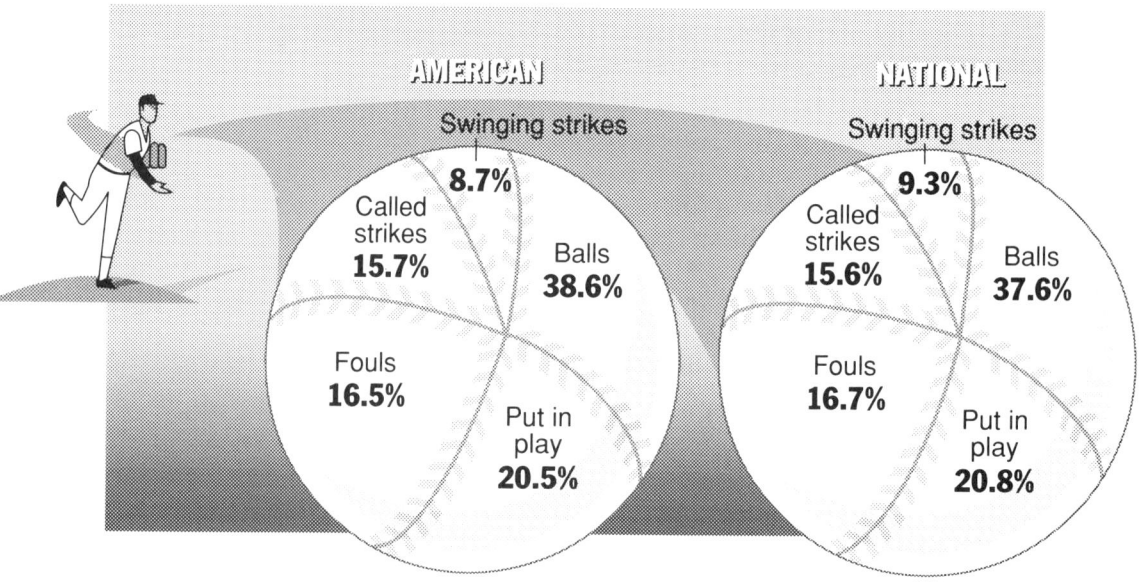

Here are the hitters who took a pitch for a called ball the largest percentage of the time, and the pitchers who most frequently missed the strike zone:

Ball % (Batters)	
Frank Thomas, WSox	46.4
Rickey Henderson, Oak	45.8
Mickey Tettleton, Det	45.1
Lou Whitaker, Det	44.8
Barry Bonds, Pit	44.6

Ball % (Pitchers)	
Jose DeJesus, Phi	43.6
Brian Barnes, Mon	43.3
Randy Johnson, Sea	42.2
Jose Guzman, Tex	42.0
Mike Moore, Oak	41.8

Who takes the most pitches for balls? Power hitters with a good eye, most of them in the American League where the pitchers are less likely to challenge the hitters. No wonder Frank Thomas, who won't swing at pitches out of the strike zone, drew 138 walks. (And no wonder the White Sox would like another power hitter to bat behind him.)

Somewhat surprisingly, the two pitchers who threw the highest percentage of called balls were in the NL . . . but then, truly lousy control has no league identification. Showing this is a pretty consistent category, Henderson, Tettleton, Bonds and Moore all made the top fives both 1990 and 1991.

Called Strike % (Batters)	
Wade Boggs, Bos	22.7
Alex Cole, Cle	22.6
Rickey Henderson, Oak	22.4
Alvin Davis, Sea	22.0
Jody Reed, Bos	21.9

Called Strike % (Pitchers)	
Frank Tanana, Det	19.2
Mike Boddicker, KC	19.1
Mike Morgan, Oak	19.0
Tom Bolton, Bos	18.6
Rod Nichols, Cle	18.6

Which pitchers throw the most pitches for called strikes? Tricky types, who can keep the hitter off stride enough to take one down the middle. Boddicker and Tanana, the kings, ranked one-two in 1990 also, though in the reverse order. Among the hitters, the leaders are mostly guys who hit near the top of the order, and who have great faith in their ability to make contact even when behind in the count. Reed and Boggs are repeaters from 1990; Edgar Martinez and Dave Magadan, who were in the top five in 1990, ranked sixth and seventh in 1991.

Swinging Strike % (Batters)	
Matt Williams, SF	18.1
Cecil Fielder, Det	16.4
Dante Bichette, Mil	15.7
Gary Gaetti, Cal	15.4
Andres Galarraga, Mon	15.3
Rob Deer, Det	15.3

Swinging Strike % (Pitchers)	
Duane Ward, Tor	15.6
Nolan Ryan, Tex	14.9
Juan Guzman, Tor	14.4
David Cone, Mets	13.8
Paul Assenmacher, Cubs	13.6

The swing-and-miss kings among the hitters are familiar to everyone; about the only surprises here were Gaetti (not a major strikeout man) and Deer, whom many would figure to be number one — he isn't because he takes so many pitches for balls). We keep looking for signs that Nolan Ryan is slipping, and here's one: he didn't win the pitcher's swing-and-miss crown last year, as he did in 1990. (On the other hand, his swing-and-miss percentage rose from 14.7 to 14.9. Slipping?)

Foul % (Batters)	
Joe Carter, Tor	23.7
Willie McGee, SF	22.7
Ozzie Guillen, WSox	22.7
Manny Lee, Tor	21.5
Joe Orsulak, Bal	21.2
Terry Pendleton, Atl	21.1
Tony Fernandez, SD	21.1

Foul % (Pitchers)	
Pete Harnisch, Hou	21.3
Mark Leiter, Det	21.1
John Smiley, Pit	20.6
Bret Saberhagen, KC	20.4
Terry Mulholland, Phi	20.2

The modern-day "Luke Appling Trophy" (foul ball king) is a thrilling annual competition between Ozzie Guillen, Joe Carter, and Willie McGee; they ranked in the top five in both 1990 and 1991. Carter, perhaps celebrating his trade to a division champion, won in '91. Pitchers who make batters foul 'em off usually have good stuff, but are not overpowering enough to rank at the top in strikeouts. Harnisch and Mulholland repeat from 1990.

In Play % (Batters)	
Ozzie Guillen, WSox	30.6
Jim Gantner, Mil	29.3
Brian Harper, Min	28.8
Alvaro Espinoza, Yanks	28.7
Mike Greenwell, Bos	28.3

In Play % (Pitchers)	
Bob Tewksbury, StL	27.6
Jeff Ballard, Bal	26.4
Bill Gullickson, Det	26.2
Bryn Smith, StL	25.3
Eric King, Cle	24.6

Contact hitters: Guillen (repeating his 1990 championship) and Brian Harper (third each year). If the game was one strike and you're out, Ozzie might be Ty Cobb. "Contact pitchers" figure they're not going to blow the hitter away anyway, so why not let them hit the ball? It worked for Gullickson (fourth place in 1990, third in '91) to the tune of 20 lucky wins in '91. Expect several more repeats among the "balls in play" leaders before you see Gullickson win 20 again.

A complete listing for this category can be found on page 251.

HOW MUCH DIFFERENCE DOES THE UMPIRE MAKE?

We've been keeping data on umpires for several years, and our annual "umpire report" has become one of the most popular parts of this book. What the data has shown is that the players are exactly right when they say there are "pitcher's umpires" and "hitter's umpires." Are there ever.

What we'd like to do this year is present data on runs per game, walks per game and batting average with each umpire behind the plate. The difference this year is that the data is based on the last three seasons, rather than on just the previous year. Each umpire works the plate about 30-35 times per year; while that is a fair sample, his stats could be skewed a little if he draws a disproportionate number of Astrodome games or Roger Clemens games. Three years of data (generally 90-110 games) eliminates most of the biases.

Here are the top three — and bottom three — American League umpires in scoring, walks, and batting average (minimum 75 games behind the plate in 1989-91):

American League					
Runs per game		Walks per game		Batting average	
Highest:					
Rick Reed	9.84	Derryl Cousins	8.11	Rick Reed	.272
Dale Ford	9.31	Dan Morrison	7.47	Dale Ford	.271
Jim Joyce	9.24	Rocky Roe	7.45	Derryl Cousins	.268
Lowest:					
Larry McCoy	8.16	Greg Kosc	5.99	John Hirschbeck	.251
Mike Reilly	8.09	Tim Welke	5.90	Rick Reilly	.249
Don Denkinger	7.81	Larry McCoy	5.60	Don Denkinger	.244

Though using three years worth of data narrows the difference between top and bottom, it's still amazingly large. With Rick Reed behind the plate, scoring is at a 1920s level — plenty of hitting. But with Don Denkinger working, the scoring level is akin to the pitcher-dominated mid-1960s. Batters in Reed games hit a whopping 28 points higher than batters in Denkinger games. Are these guys using the same rule book?

Here's the National League data:

American League

Runs per game		Walks per game		Batting average	
Highest:					
Dana DeMuth	8.90	Bruce Froemming	7.27	Dana DeMuth	.263
Randy Marsh	8.80	John McSherry	7.17	Tom Hallion	.255
Jerry Crawford	8.72	Jerry Crawford	6.90	John McSherry	.255
Lowest:					
Mark Hirschbeck	7.70	Mark Hirschbeck	5.72	Harry Wendelstedt	.247
Charlie Williams	7.62	Greg Bonin	5.53	Joe West	.247
Greg Bonin	7.39	Bob Davidson	5.43	Charlie Williams	.247

The range in the National League data is somewhat narrower. The difference in scoring between Dana DeMuth games (8.90 runs) and Greg Bonin games (7.39) is still over a run and a half a game, however. A Bonin game is right out of the deadball 1909 National League; a DeMuth game produces scoring at the level of the hit-happy season of 1977.

There's a lot of talk in baseball these days about "the shrinking strike zone." Yet our data makes it clear that some umps have shrunk it a lot more than others. When Larry McCoy was working over the last three years, pitchers allowed only 5.6 walks per game; when Derryl Cousins was behind the plate, they gave up 8.1 — 45 percent more. With McCoy working, it's almost as if every pitch is a strike. Larry not only allowed the fewest walks of any American League umpire; he called the most strikeouts (12.23 per game). Imagine how a hitter must feel, batting with McCoy behind the plate one day and Cousins the next.

This still seems weird to us . . . that both hitters and pitchers have to adapt to strike zones that are, well, in different time zones. But they do. We generally like the modern game just fine. But we wouldn't mind a little more uniformity in umpiring.

A complete listing for this category can be found on page 252.

WHY DON'T THEY PRINT LINEUPS ON SCORECARDS ANY MORE?

I'm probably showing my age by asking this, but do you remember when they used to print the lineups on the scorecards? This quaint habit was still being practiced, in Chicago at least, as recently as the early fifties. In those days, the expectation — and quite often the reality — was that each team would stick with the same batting order, one through eight, day after day.

No more. In the modern era, managers are constantly tinkering with the batting order, shifting the lineup around as one player gets hot and another cools off. And, of course, there are continual injuries, trades and minor league moves that change rosters on practically a daily basis. Know how often the most-used major league lineup (same players in batting positions one through eight in the National League, or one through nine in the American) employed last season? A grand total of 19 times, by the NL East champion Pittsburgh Pirates. Remember it fondly, Pirate fans; now that Bobby Bonilla is a Met, you won't be seeing it again:

The Most Frequently Written Lineup Card of 1991
Pittsburgh Pirates

1.	MERCED, Orlando
2.	BELL, Jay
3.	VAN SLYKE, Andy
4.	BONILLA, Bobby
5.	BONDS, Barry
6.	VARSHO, Gary
7.	LaVALLIERE, Mike
8.	LIND, Jose

This was a **good** lineup, and you can understand why Jim Leyland was fond of using it. Merced could get on base, Bell could bunt him over or even drive the run in himself, the heart of the order was plenty potent, and the 6-7-8 guys were no slouches either. Using this batting order and variations of it, the Pirates wound up scoring 768 runs, tops in the National League.

Given that the division-winning Pirates used the same lineup the most times, you might wonder if lineup stability is a characteristic of winning teams. It is, but only to a degree. Here's how often each club used their most common lineup in 1991, and the number of different lineups they employed over 162 games:

	American League			National League		
Team	# Times	# Used	Team	# Times	# Used
Baltimore	7	132	Atlanta	12	87
Boston	10	106	Chicago	8	102
California	10	127	Cincinnati	4	141
Chicago	7	126	Houston	11	115
Cleveland	4	134	Los Angeles	15	93
Detroit	5	137	Montreal	4	127
Kansas City	7	124	New York	6	127
Milwaukee	9	114	Philadelphia	6	113
Minnesota	12	119	Pittsburgh	19	86
New York	7	106	St. Louis	14	92
Oakland	8	130	San Diego	8	114
Seattle	6	118	San Francisco	15	119
Texas	5	129			
Toronto	6	107			

 # Times = # of games that team's most common lineup used
 # Used = # of different starting lineups used by that team

As you can see, there was more batting order stability in the National League, but that's only because the American League has an extra hitter in the lineup. In the NL the division-winning Braves and Pirates used the fewest number of lineups (87 and 86); the two second-place clubs, the Dodgers and Cardinals, were the only other clubs to use fewer than 100 different lineups over the course of the season. On the other hand, Lou Piniella of the Reds went through 141 different batting order combinations in a frantic effort to find a winning lineup. He never did.

That seems very neat and clean — winning clubs stick with the same lineups, losing clubs experiment. But in the American League, the relationship between winning and batting order stability was a lot less clear. The Red Sox, a good club, used 106 different batting order combinations . . . but so did the hapless Yankees. Was this a reaction to the constant juggling of the Steinbrenner years? If so, it didn't result in victories. Reports have it that George will come back this year and restore his "three lineup system" — one on the way, one playing, one on the way out of town. That's not guaranteed to win either (just look at Cleveland), but things around the Bronx may be a little less dull this summer.

WHY DID MITCH LOVE TO PITCH LAST AUGUST?

There is no player in baseball quite like Mitch Williams, the man who says he pitches "like my hair is on fire." Mitch is always doing something spectacular, which is not always the same as doing something good. Performing true to his ways — both good and bad — Williams almost put the torch to the National League record book last August. In the course of that wondrous month, "Wild Thing" rolled up a total of eight victories. Of course, Williams' four blown saves during the month helped account for a few of those triumphs, but that's just Mitch being Mitch.

However Williams did it, the eight victories were noteworthy even in a season full of outstanding monthly performances. The total was only one win short of the modern National League record shared by two pretty fair pitchers named Christy Mathewson (who won nine games in August of both 1903 and 1904) and Grover Cleveland Alexander (nine victories in May, 1920). And Mitch was only two wins short of the modern major league record, set by another Philadelphia lefthander, Rube Waddell, who was 10-1 in July of 1902. (Williams could probably be compared to the eccentric Waddell in more ways than one.)

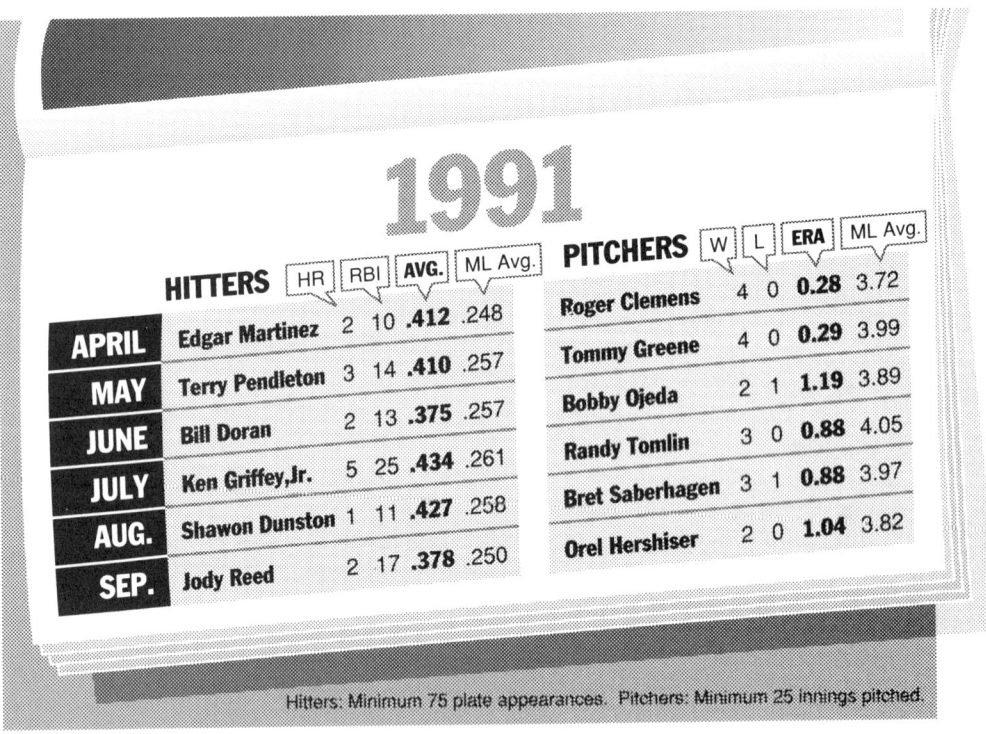

1991

	HITTERS	HR	RBI	AVG.	ML Avg.	PITCHERS	W	L	ERA	ML Avg.
APRIL	Edgar Martinez	2	10	.412	.248	Roger Clemens	4	0	0.28	3.72
MAY	Terry Pendleton	3	14	.410	.257	Tommy Greene	4	0	0.29	3.99
JUNE	Bill Doran	2	13	.375	.257	Bobby Ojeda	2	1	1.19	3.89
JULY	Ken Griffey, Jr.	5	25	.434	.261	Randy Tomlin	3	0	0.88	4.05
AUG.	Shawon Dunston	1	11	.427	.258	Bret Saberhagen	3	1	0.88	3.97
SEP.	Jody Reed	2	17	.378	.250	Orel Hershiser	2	0	1.04	3.82

Hitters: Minimum 75 plate appearances. Pitchers: Minimum 25 innings pitched.

Despite his headline-making work, Williams couldn't make the chart, which lists the best monthly performances of 1991 in terms of batting average and ERA. There are some good stories here. Ken Griffey Jr's great July came in direct response to a midseason column by a Seattle sportswriter who accused him of being an underachiever. (The STATS office people, some of whom have been known to quietly pull for the White Sox, are already drafting our "You're a bum, Frank Thomas" piece.) Shawon Dunston's August was perfectly timed to win him a contract as baseball's highest-paid shortstop (at the time), and Orel Hershiser's September helped convince the Dodgers to re-sign him. Terry Pendleton's May helped put the Braves in the pennant race for good, and Tommy Greene punctuated his own merry month of May by tossing a no-hitter against the Expos.

These players also had months worthy of note:

Rafael Palmeiro	July	.390-8-19, .710 slugging
Robin Ventura	July	.357-12-33, .739 slugging
Joe Carter	June	.352-11-39, .759 slugging
Tom Glavine	May	6-0, 1.76 ERA
Jack Morris	June	6-0, 2.35 ERA

There were many more, of course. Some players, on the other hand, had months they would surely forget:

	Player, Team	HR	RBI	Avg	Pitcher, Team	W	L	ERA
April	Gant, Atl	1	7	.162	Stewart, Oak	2	2	6.75
May	Fletcher, WSox	0	3	.152	Petry, Det	2	2	7.81
June	Downing, Tex	1	7	.119	Leary, Yanks	1	3	8.89
July	Teufel, SD	0	2	.149	Smoltz, Atl	4	2	7.85
Aug.	Davis, Sea	2	8	.104	Johnson, Yanks	1	5	10.87
Sept.	Fisk, WSox	3	8	.129	DeLucia, Sea	1	5	9.64

Can good players have bad months? Sure — just ask Ron Gant, Dave Stewart, Brian Downing, John Smoltz or Carlton Fisk. Or you could ask Frank Viola, who somehow didn't seem to hurt his "free agent salary drive" by going 1-5 with an 8.33 ERA in August.

"I am not a crook, but I am not consistent, either": Otis Nixon batted .391 in May and .363 with a year's best 20 stolen bases in July, but followed that by batting .141 (11 for 78) in August. For Nixon, September would be his Watergate. You probably know why.

A complete listing for this category can be found on page 253.

ARE THE BEST TEAMS GOOD LATE-INNING TEAMS?

As we've argued many times, there are all kinds of "clutch" situations in a game — not just with men in scoring position, not just the late innings. But we can't deny the importance of performing well, both on offense and defense, when the game is nearing its conclusion and the score is close. What we'd like to do here is look at how each team hit last year in the late innings of close games, and how their pitching staffs handled the opposition. One would expect that the winning teams would outhit their opponents in late-and-close situations.

Here's the American League data, and the clubs' won-lost records as a point of reference:

American League — Batting in the Late Innings of Close Games

Team	Avg	Opp Avg	Diff.	W	L
Toronto	.239	.223	16	91	71
Boston	.225	.235	–10	84	78
Detroit	.218	.272	–44	84	78
Milwaukee	.270	.257	13	83	79
New York	.244	.252	–8	71	91
Baltimore	.237	.241	–4	67	95
Cleveland	.218	.266	–48	57	105
Minnesota	.283	.239	44	95	67
Chicago	.264	.231	33	87	75
Texas	.265	.235	30	85	77
Oakland	.241	.251	–10	84	78
Seattle	.246	.246	-----	83	79
Kansas City	.236	.254	–18	82	80
California	.231	.220	11	81	81

In the Western Division, the relationship is fairly neat and clean. The Twins, with the best record, outhit their opponents in the clutch by 44 points; the second place White Sox topped the opposition by 33, the third place Rangers were plus-30. The last-place Angels were plus-11, but California, a .500 club, finished only four games out of third place.

The AL East data, however, is a lot less tidy. The Red Sox, though outhit in the clutch by ten points, finished tied for second with the Tigers, who were outhit by 44! Does this mean that there's no relationship between late-inning clutch performance and playing winning ball? Not necessarily.

The '91 Tigers, we must point out, were a pretty unique club. Overall, Detroit hit .247 last season; the Tigers' opponents hit .281. Yet Detroit outscored its opposition by 23 runs, mostly because the Tigers hit a lot of homers and drew a lot of walks. And indeed, Detroit outhomered its opponents in the clutch last year, 28 to 19. The Bengals are an extreme case, however. For the most part, there seems to be a good relationship between outhitting the opponents in the clutch and playing winning ball.

There seems to be — until we look at the National League data:

National League — Batting in the Late Innings of Close Games

Team	Avg	Opp Avg	Diff.	W	L
Pittsburgh	.248	.252	−4	98	64
St. Louis	.251	.259	−8	84	78
Philadelphia	.235	.237	−2	78	84
Chicago	.257	.269	−12	77	83
New York	.234	.258	−24	77	84
Montreal	.246	.241	5	71	90
Atlanta	.242	.217	25	94	68
Los Angeles	.268	.232	36	93	69
San Diego	.252	.237	15	84	78
San Francisco	.242	.246	−4	75	87
Cincinnati	.236	.269	−33	74	88
Houston	.253	.249	4	65	97

What a mess. Only one NL East club outhit its opponents in the late innings of close games — the last-place Expos, who went 71-90. The West data is a bit more logical . . . until you get to the Astros, who outhit the opposition in the clutch but still won only 65 games.

This suggests a couple of things. One is something we've argued all along — that late-inning clutch performance is important to a club's success, but it's not **all**-important. The other, as the Detroit data demonstrates, is that there are always some limitations to rating by batting average. There are nonetheless some fascinating figures here; doesn't the Twins .283 clutch average jump out at you, or the Braves .217 opponents' average?

A complete listing for this category can be found on page 254.

WHO ARE THE SLOWEST STARTING BATTERIES?

Like player salaries, game times keep going up, up, up, with no end in sight. Twenty years ago, the average nine-inning contest took less than two and a half hours, and even then people complained that the games were too long. They're still complaining, to no avail. Last year the average nine-inning American League game took 2:52; the speedy, no-nonsense NL (right) averaged 2:46. Only one major league team averaged less than two hours and forty minutes for its nine-inning games, the Phillies at 2:39.

Blame for this can be shared by everyone from television networks, with their ever-expanding commercial breaks, to hitters, whose "styling" habits (various forms of mugging for the camera) continue to grow each year. But there's no doubt that a huge part of the blame has to go to the pitchers and catchers, endlessly staring at each other. We now present our annual report on the leading culprits and heroes among those groups. First, the leisurely ones (times here are average for all games, regardless of number of innings; minimum 10 starts for pitchers, 25 for catchers):

Slowest Working Pitchers	Starts	Average
Ramon Garcia, WSox	15	3:22:28
Scott Aldred, Det	11	3:21:16
Kevin Brown, Mil	10	3:19:54

Slowest Working Catchers	Starts	Average
Mike Stanley, Tex	34	3:09:38
Jamie Quirk, Oak	49	3:07:50
Carlton Fisk, WSox	91	3:07:18

White Sox rookie Ramon Garcia, he of the 5.40 ERA, overdid the Andy Warhol bit last year; he made sure he got his three hours and 22 minutes of fame. Among the catchers, Carlton Fisk must be dismayed — he added four minutes to his working time last year, and he still couldn't lead the league. We're sure Pudge will be trying even harder in '92.

The fastest workers:

Fastest Working Pitchers	Starts	Average
Ed Whitson, SD	12	2:34:45
Bob Tewksbury, StL	30	2:35:52
Terry Mulholland, Phi	34	2:37:24

Fastest Working Catchers	Starts	Average
Rich Gedman, StL	27	2:39:15
Joel Skinner, Cle	90	2:42:05
Junior Ortiz, Min	41	2:42:29

The sportswriters' best friends have to be Ed Whitson and Bob Tewksbury, who were among the three fastest workers in both 1990 and '91. When you're Rich Gedman, 32 years old and batting .106, you do everything you can to make people happy. We cracked out the champagne at the STATS office when we heard the Cardinals had signed Gedman for another year.

And now, a double dose of misery (or relief) — the slowest and fastest pitcher-catcher combinations:

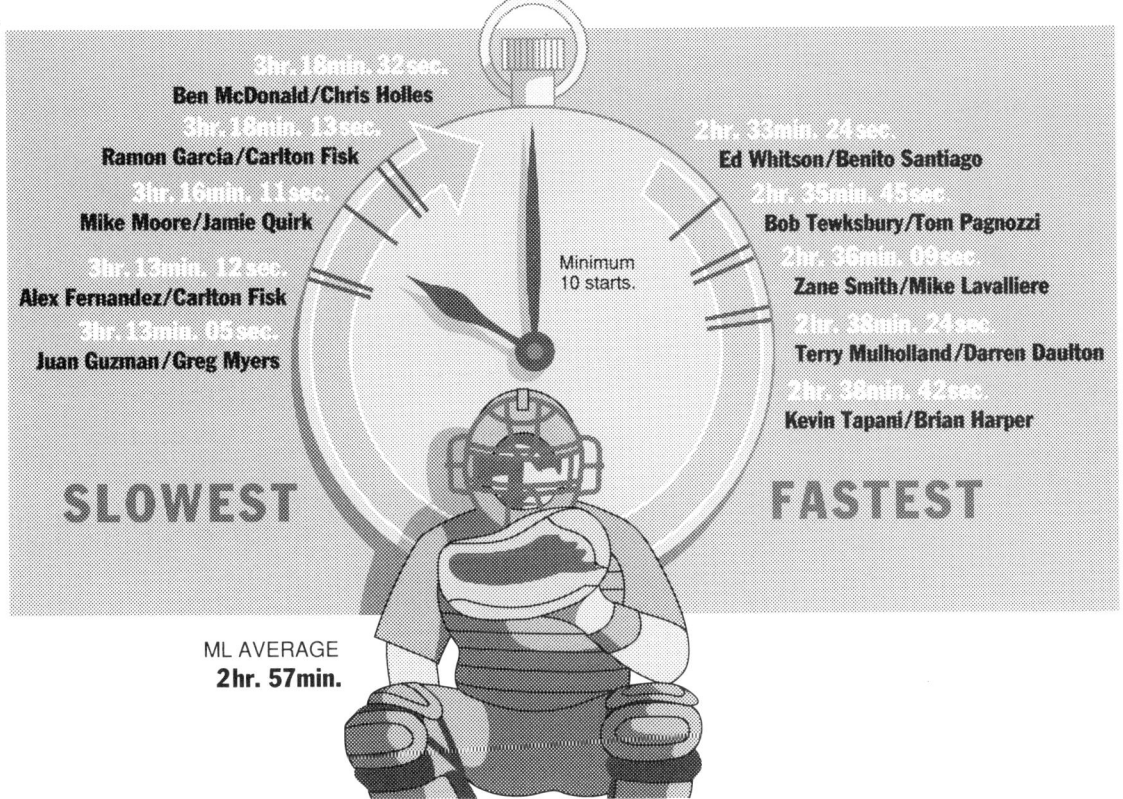

The Fisk-Garcia combination, such an appealing blend of youthful and aged dawdlers, probably won't be working much in '92 since Garcia will probably be in the minors. Pudge will no doubt be working overtime (to say the least) with Alex Fernandez.

Please, dear Lord, let Ed Whitson's arm be healthy in 1992!

A complete listing for this category can be found on page 255.

WHAT KIND OF TEAM CAN'T RALLY IN THE NINTH?

In baseball, nothing seems to fire up a team and its fans like a late-inning, come-from-behind rally. And one reason those rallies seem so special is that they hardly ever happen. Though we won't deny the importance of late-inning clutch performance, the truth is that the club which leads after six innings wins the game over 85 percent of the time. With each passing inning, victory becomes more certain. Here are the numbers from 1991:

Leading After 6, 7 and 8 Innings

1991 Winning Percentages	American League	National League
Leading after six innings	.876	.864
Leading after seven innings	.891	.900
Leading after eight innings	.937	.950

We have an admitted fascination with these stats, and have studied the clubs' records after seven innings in the first two editions of this book. This year we'll do something a little different and look at how the teams performed when ahead, behind or tied after eight innings (the records after six and seven innings are listed in the Appendix). Do some clubs show their spirit by pulling out games in the ninth? Do others show complacency by never rallying? Let's see by scanning the American League data:

AL Records — Ahead/Behind/Tied After 8 Innings

Team	Ahead W	L	Pct	Behind W	L	Pct	Tied W	L	Pct
Orioles	57	5	.919	7	74	.086	3	16	.158
Red Sox	77	8	.906	4	67	.056	3	3	.500
Angels	77	5	.939	0	69	.000	4	7	.364
White Sox	67	4	.944	9	62	.127	11	9	.550
Indians	47	5	.904	5	89	.053	5	11	.313
Tigers	69	3	.958	5	70	.067	10	5	.667
Royals	67	4	.944	6	71	.078	9	5	.643
Brewers	72	4	.947	3	64	.045	8	11	.421
Twins	84	3	.966	5	57	.081	6	7	.462
Yankees	57	4	.934	5	83	.057	9	4	.692
Athletics	70	4	.946	0	68	.000	14	6	.700
Mariners	69	9	.885	5	62	.075	9	8	.529
Rangers	67	4	.944	7	63	.100	11	10	.524
Blue Jays	79	3	.963	4	60	.063	8	8	.500

Why did the Red Sox fail to win the American League East? You might start with those eight games lost when leading after eight innings, a surprising total for a club with a top closer in Jeff Reardon. Those games took an emotional toll; in fact the Sox fell quickly out of the race after blowing a ninth-inning lead to the Yankees on September 22 (on a two-out, game-tying homer by Roberto Kelly). A victory that day would have put Boston in first, but after the devastating loss the BoSox went 3-10 the rest of the way.

The feisty White Sox pulled out eight victories when trailing after eight innings, many of them in dramatic fashion. That's a complete contrast to the Angels and the defending champion A's, both of whom failed to pull out a single victory with a ninth-inning, come-from-behind rally. You can make too much of the "character issue," but this sure looks like the mark of a dead team — something the A's were accused of being last year.

Here's the National League data:

NL Records — Ahead/Behind/Tied After 8 Innings

Team	Ahead			Behind			Tied		
	W	L	Pct	W	L	Pct	W	L	Pct
Braves	81	1	.988	4	60	.063	9	6	.600
Cubs	64	9	.877	5	65	.071	8	9	.471
Reds	65	4	.942	0	79	.000	8	5	.615
Astros	54	6	.900	1	81	.012	10	10	.500
Dodgers	79	2	.975	3	56	.051	11	11	.500
Expos	60	7	.896	2	73	.027	9	10	.474
Mets	64	0	1.000	5	74	.063	7	10	.412
Phillies	60	4	.938	3	70	.041	15	10	.600
Pirates	83	3	.965	6	53	.102	9	8	.529
Cardinals	66	1	.985	7	69	.092	11	8	.579
Padres	76	3	.962	2	65	.030	6	9	.400
Giants	67	3	.957	5	74	.063	3	10	.231

There are some interesting numbers here as well. The Cubs fired two managers last year, but Don Zimmer might still be working in Chicago if Dave Smith & Co. hadn't blown nine ninth-inning leads — five more than the Mets, Cardinals, Braves and Dodgers combined. We saw a lot of those Cub losses, and the carryover effect seemed obvious in the way the club played. Whereas the Braves, 81-1 when leading after eight, must have grown in confidence after nailing down victory after victory.

The National League counterpart to the A's was their 1990 World Series rival, the Cincinnati Reds. It's hard to think that any club managed by Lou Piniella was "dead," but 0-79 when trailing after eight? It's almost unbelievable.

A complete listing for this category can be found on page 256.

ARE THE BRAVES AND ANGELS TOO LOADED WITH LEFTIES?

Astute followers of baseball probably noticed something unusual in the makeup of two 1991 pitching staffs. Both the California Angels (Mark Langston, Chuck Finley, Jim Abbott) and the Atlanta Braves (Tom Glavine, Steve Avery, Charlie Leibrandt) were top-heavy with good left-handed starters. The Angel trio wound up winning 55 games; the Brave threesome won 53. How unusual was that? It turned out that the two clubs ranked among the top teams in modern history in terms of wins by left-handed threesomes (or foursomes, in one case). The following teams posted the most victories by southpaws (three or more), all of whom won at least ten games:

Teams With Three or More Lefties, 10+ Wins Each (Since 1900):

1980 Yankees — 67 wins (Tommy John 22-9, Ron Guidry 17-10, Rudy May 15-5, Tom Underwood 13-9)

1974 Orioles — 56 Wins (Mike Cuellar 22-10, Ross Grimsley 18-13, Dave McNally 16-10)

1991 Angels — 55 Wins (Mark Langston 19-8, Chuck Finley 18-9, Jim Abbott 18-11)

1963 Dodgers — 55 Wins (Sandy Koufax 25-5, Ron Perranoski 16-3, Johnny Podres 14-12)

1932 Athletics — 54 Wins (Lefty Grove 25-10, Rube Walberg 17-10, Tony Freitas 12-5)

1991 Braves — 53 Wins (Tom Glavine 20-11, Steve Avery 18-8, Charlie Leibrandt 15-13)

1979 White Sox — 53 Wins (Ken Kravec 15-13, Rich Wortham 14-14, Ross Baumgarten 13-8, Steve Trout 11-8)

1983 York Yankees — 49 Wins (Ron Guidry 21-9, Dave Righetti 14-8, Shane Rawley 14-14 . . . also Ray Fontenot 8-2 in 15 starts)

1949 Cardinals — 48 Wins (Howie Pollet 20-9, Alpha Brazle 14-8, Harry Brecheen 14-11)

1978 Giants — 48 Wins (Vida Blue 18-10, Bob Knepper 17-11, Gary Lavelle 13-10)

Most of these combinations were made up of starting pitchers, but there a couple of exceptions. The '63 Dodgers got 16 wins from their relief ace, Ron Perranoski; the 1978 Giants got 13 from their southpaw closer, Gary

Lavelle. Rudy May of the 1980 Yankees was also primarily a reliever, but he did make 17 starts.

Last year's Angel club expressed a fear that they were **too** loaded with lefties (late in the year, the Halos recalled another southpaw starter, Kyle Abbott, who has since been traded). Looking at this list, it's hard to see much reason for concern. The 1980 Yankees won a division title, and so did the 1974 Orioles. The '63 Dodgers and '91 Braves won league pennants, with the Dodgers taking the world championship. Among the other clubs, the 1949 Cardinals lost the pennant by one game, the 1932 A's won 94 games while finishing second, the 1978 Giants were a strong third-place club with 89 victories, and the '83 Yankees were also third, with 91 wins.

The only flops on the list were the 1979 White Sox, a fifth-place club with a 73-89 record (Tony LaRussa would soon straighten out **that** mess) and last year's Angels, who were 81-81 while finishing last in the highly competitive American League West. But too much left-handedness was hardly the Angels' problems. The three California lefties went 55-28; the rest of the team went 26-53. What California needs is more pitchers the caliber of Langston, Finley and Abbott . . . whatever side they throw from.

II. QUESTIONS ON OFFENSE

WHY WAS WILL CLARK'S 116 RBI BETTER THAN CECIL FIELDER'S 133?

Ask any knowledgeable fan to identify the RBI champion of 1991, and he'll quickly say, "Cecil Fielder." And there's no denying that Fielder drove home 133 runs last year, 11 more than the number two man, Jose Canseco. But we have our own king: Will Clark, whose RBI count was 116.

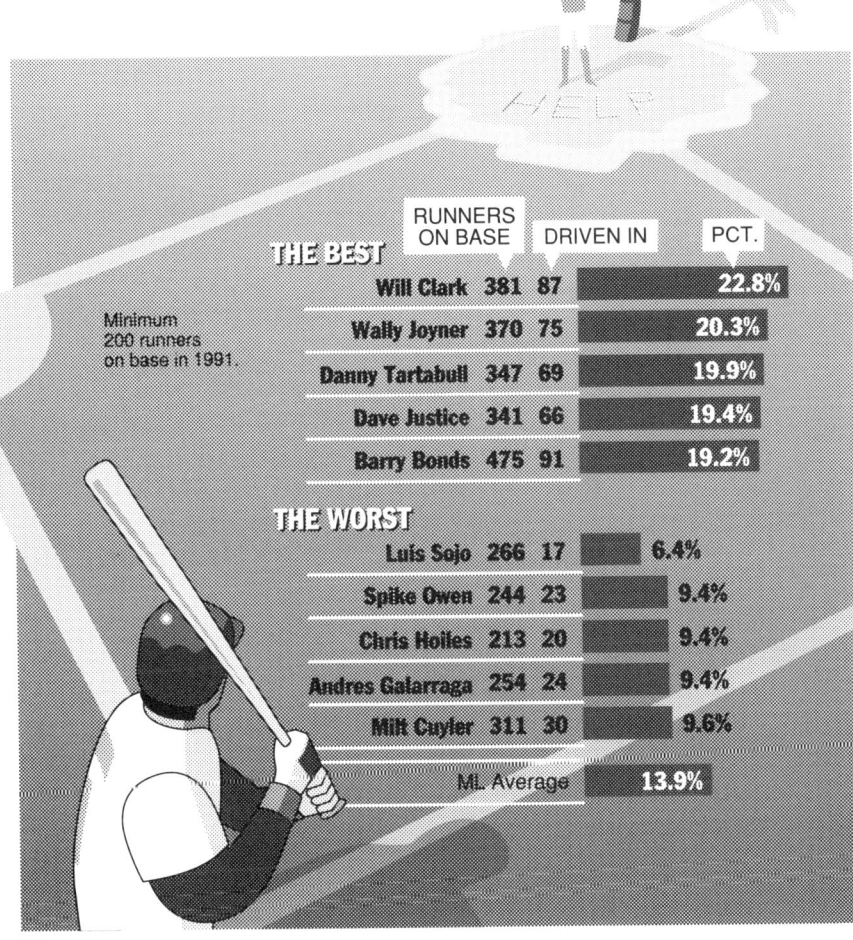

	RUNNERS ON BASE	DRIVEN IN	PCT.
THE BEST			
Will Clark	381	87	22.8%
Wally Joyner	370	75	20.3%
Danny Tartabull	347	69	19.9%
Dave Justice	341	66	19.4%
Barry Bonds	475	91	19.2%
THE WORST			
Luis Sojo	266	17	6.4%
Spike Owen	244	23	9.4%
Chris Hoiles	213	20	9.4%
Andres Galarraga	254	24	9.4%
Milt Cuyler	311	30	9.6%
ML Average			13.9%

Minimum 200 runners on base in 1991.

Our logic is simple. While it's true that Fielder drove home more runs than Clark last year, he also had many more opportunities. Cecil had a total of 487 Detroit runners on base for him; Clark had only 381 San Francisco runners. Clark drove in 87 of his mates, a total of 22.8 percent; Fielder drove in 89 Tiger baserunners, or 18.6 percent. Given Fielder's number of chances, Clark would have had 140 ribbies — 111 teammates driven home, plus his 29 homers. In our book, that makes Will the real champion.

We'd never argue that the RBI is a bad stat; we admire it as much as anyone. But in baseball, it's always useful to examine things in context, and some players simply have more runners on base for them than others do. Here's another comparison; "TBI" is teammates batted in, or RBI minus home runs, a term we believe was first used by Richard Zitrin of SABR:

Player, Team	TBI	Opp	Pct
Harold Baines, Oak	70	376	18.6
Benito Santiago, SD	70	462	15.2

Both Baines and Santiago drove in 70 teammates last season. But Baines was a far more impressive RBI man; he had only 376 runners on base for him, while Santiago had 462.

We think you get the idea. Here are the 1991 leaders in RBI percentage (minimum 200 opportunities):

1991 Leaders — Teammates Batted In per Opportunity

Player, Team	TBI	Opp	Pct
Will Clark, SF	87	381	22.8
Wally Joyner, Cal	75	370	20.3
Danny Tartabull, KC	69	347	19.9
Dave Justice, Atl	66	341	19.4
Barry Bonds, Pit	91	475	19.2
Kent Hrbek, Min	69	361	19.1
Jose Canseco, Oak	78	413	18.9
Pedro Guerrero, StL	62	328	18.9
Albert Belle, Cle	67	356	18.8
Darryl Hamilton, Mil	56	301	18.6
Ruben Sierra, Tex	91	490	18.6
Cal Ripken, Bal	80	431	18.6
Harold Baines, Oak	70	376	18.6

Those of you who are familiar with the first two editions of this book might notice that we've changed this stat a bit this year. Previously we counted runners driven in from scoring position, which certainly is a valid way of identifying clutch hitters. However, that tends to underrate power hitters, who are more likely to bring in a run home from first base with an extra-base hit than a singles hitter is. Indeed, everyone on this list except Daryl Hamilton would be classified as a power hitter. It's certainly an impressive list; Fielder, who ranked 15th, was a top man in this category as well.

Who were the worst performers in this category? Singles hitters, you'd think . . . but you'd only be half right:

1991 Trailers — Teammates Batted In per Opportunity

Player, Team	TBI	Opp	Pct
Luis Sojo, Cal	17	266	6.4
Spike Owen, Mon	23	244	9.4
Chris Hoiles, Bal	20	213	9.4
Andres Galarraga, Mon	24	254	9.4
Milt Cuyler, Det	30	311	9.6
Franklin Stubbs, Mil	27	275	9.8
Robby Thompson, SF	29	294	9.9
Alvaro Espinoza, Yanks	28	282	9.9
Jose Oquendo, StL	25	251	10.0
Leo Gomez, Bal	29	285	10.2

Galarraga and Stubbs are supposed to be RBI men; they weren't last year. Hoiles and Gomez, who have some power, could be forgiven for some rookie jitters with men on base. The most curious case is Robby Thompson: 48 extra-base hits last year, but only 48 RBI (19 homers). By contrast, Baines had 46 extra-base hits, 90 RBI. Thompson has often had poor numbers in clutch categories, and this is yet another example.

A complete listing for this category can be found on page 257.

WHO WAS BASEBALL'S BEST CLEANUP HITTER IN '91?

When the New York Yankees signed Danny Tartabull to a big free agent contract last winter, one thing they were thinking was that they finally had a legitimate cleanup hitter for the first time in years. That was an accurate perception on the part of the often-confused Bombers. We rate cleanup hitters on the basis of slugging percentage — sensible enough, we think, since a number-four hitter's job is to drive runners home with an extra base hit. In the three seasons we've been keeping this stat, the Yanks have yet to rank a cleanup hitter anywhere in the top ten. Where have you gone, Reggie Jackson?

Well, that was then . . . this is now. The Yankees enter 1992 with the knowledge that their new signee, Tartabull, was baseball's most effective cleanup hitter in 1991. The top ten last year, on the basis of slugging average while batting in the number-four position (minimum 150 plate appearances):

Player, Team	Slg	Avg	OBP	AB	H	HR	RBI
Danny Tartabull, KC	.610	.320	.404	444	142	30	95
Howard Johnson, Mets	.592	.303	.384	152	46	10	31
Ron Gant, Atl	.588	.279	.363	226	63	17	55
Joe Carter, Tor	.527	.303	.366	165	50	8	33
Albert Belle, Cle	.526	.275	.320	382	105	22	79
Kevin Mitchell, SF	.524	.263	.346	357	94	26	68
Dave Justice, Atl	.521	.278	.378	338	94	20	75
Paul O'Neill, Cin	.514	.280	.367	214	60	12	37
Cecil Fielder, Det	.513	.261	.347	624	163	44	133
Ruben Sierra, Tex	.513	.294	.354	279	82	13	52

While Tartabull was tops in cleanup slugging percentage last year, he has some competition when it comes to rating as the top number four hitter in baseball. It's hard not to go with Kevin Mitchell, now of the Mariners, who has made the top ten each of the last three seasons (slugging .636, .544 and .524 over the period). Seattle has to be as happy about their acquisition as the Yanks are with theirs.

The only other repeaters on this list from last year are Dave Justice and Cecil Fielder. If you want to argue that Fielder is baseball's best cleanup hitter, we won't complain, either. In 1990 Cecil slugged .585 from the number four slot, with 36 homers and 96 RBI. His slugging mark dropped to .513 in 1991, but Fielder more than made up for that by belting 44 homers with 133 RBI while hitting fourth. The Mets' free agent acquisition, Bobby Bonilla, has also proven himself to be a potent number-four hitter. In 1990 Bonilla drove home 120 runs from the number four spot; in '91 his RBI count was an even 100.

Some players, of course, don't respond to the pressure of the cleanup spot. The following players had the **lowest** slugging percentages while batting fourth in 1991:

Player, Team	Slg	Avg	OBP	AB	H	HR	RBI
Dave Parker, Cal-Tor	.321	.214	.265	234	50	4	24
Ken Caminiti, Hou	.341	.252	.317	258	65	3	29
Tim Wallach, Mon	.343	.236	.299	492	116	11	66
Pedro Guerrero, StL	.363	.273	.328	422	115	8	69
Robin Yount, Mil	.368	.264	.340	318	84	5	48
Eric Davis, Cin	.397	.246	.359	199	49	8	25
Eddie Murray, LA	.399	.255	.317	396	101	12	68
Carlton Fisk, WSox	.400	.236	.291	195	46	7	34
Dave Winfield, Cal	.405	.232	.293	336	78	14	50
Luis Gonzalez, Hou	.415	.236	.307	258	61	8	36

Do you ever wonder why the California Angels have never won a pennant? Well, for about half the season last year, the Halos stuck with ancient Dave Parker as their cleanup hitter, insisting that old Dave was "swinging the bat good." They kept arguing that right up until the day they released him. Now California has neither Parker, nor Dave Winfield, nor Wally Joyner. Who's going to bat fourth for the Angels this year — Gene Autry's horse?

A complete listing for this category can be found on page 259.

Is Wade, Rickey, Paulie or Brett No. 1 at No. 1?

A leadoff hitter has two responsibilities — first, to get on base, and then to move around the bases and score a run, which is why speed is so helpful. The best number-one hitters have both qualities, but the crucial one is the ability to reach first. Last year the speedy Ray Lankford had almost 50 more plate appearances from the number-one spot than the slow-moving Edgar Martinez. Lankford had 23 stolen bases while batting first, Martinez none. Yet Martinez scored 52 runs from the leadoff slot, Lankford only 44.

That's why we rank leadoff hitters by on-base percentage. The following players were tops in OBP while batting first in the lineup in 1991:

Player, Team	OBP	AB	R	H	BB	SB
Wade Boggs, Bos	.440	424	80	147	73	1
Edgar Martinez, Sea	.405	261	52	80	41	0
Rickey Henderson, Oak	.401	464	105	125	97	57
Brett Butler, LA.	.401	614	112	182	108	38
Paul Molitor, Mil	.399	652	132	211	77	19
Lonnie Smith, Atl	.393	130	26	40	15	3
Lenny Dykstra, Phi	.387	242	47	71	36	22
Alex Cole, Cle	.382	373	54	108	57	24
Brian Downing, Tex	.376	348	65	94	52	1
Orlando Merced, Pit	.376	374	77	103	60	7

(Minimum 150 plate appearances while batting leadoff)

Though Boggs gets on base more often than anyone, his lack of speed brings him back to the pack a little. That's also the case with Martinez. Picking the top leadoff man would be a contest among Boggs, Rickey Henderson, Brett Butler and Paul Molitor. Let's list their attributes:

Boggs — In addition to the superior OBP, Wade hits more doubles than anyone. That makes up somewhat for the lack of stolen bases. But of course, driving in Wade Boggs from second is not as easy as scoring Rickey Henderson.

Henderson — Even in a season when he was accused of dogging it, Henderson hit 18 homers, drew 98 walks, stole 58 bases and scored 105 runs in 134 games. A few more underachievers like that, and Oakland would have repeated. Henderson still has a matchless combination of speed, power, and ability to reach base. So is Rickey tops at the top? Well...

Butler — Every time the Cubs played the Dodgers last year, Harry Caray would comment on how Brett Butler was "as good a leadoff man as

Rickey Henderson" — no, better. Then he'd read a list of stats carefully prepared by the Dodger PR staff. Well, here's a few they left out. Butler played 27 more games, but he only scored seven more runs. Henderson stole 58 bases in 76 attempts, a fine 76 percent success rate; Butler stole 38 in 66 attempts, a horrid 58 percent. Henderson had 18 homers and 57 RBI; Butler had two homers and 38 RBI. Better than Rickey? Only in a PR man's dreams.

Molitor — Gets hurt every year, right? Wrong. Molitor has indeed had frequent stints on the disabled list, but last year he played a full season for the third time in four years, and he's stayed healthy enough to record over 2,000 major league hits. Last year was one of his best: 216 hits and 77 walks (no other leadoff man reached base as much), 62 extra-base hits including 13 triples and 17 homers, 75 RBI (while batting leadoff!), 19 stolen bases, a major-league leading 133 runs scored. If Molitor stays healthy two or three more years, we're talking Hall of Fame.

The envelope, please. The Leadoff Trophy — Dick Cramer would want us to call it the Slidin' Billy Hamilton Award — has to go to either Henderson or Molitor. Hmm, Molitor scored a run every 5.6 plate appearances; but Henderson, "underachieving," scored one every 5.5. Still, it's hard to score a run while you're on the disabled list, and Molitor played 24 more games. So, for 1991, the Slidin' Billy Award goes to . . . Paul Molitor! (Standing ovation.)

No trophy to these guys who had the worst on-base percentages from the leadoff spot last year:

Player, Team	OBP	AB	R	H	BB	SB
Jerome Walton, Cubs	.264	196	32	39	15	7
Marquis Grissom, Mon	.278	149	19	35	9	14
Brian McRae, KC	.284	425	59	108	17	18
Bernard Gilkey, StL	.299	143	11	29	19	7
Roberto Kelly, Yanks	.304	168	24	41	14	7
Ray Lankford, StL	.306	321	44	82	23	23
Chico Walker, Cubs	.306	279	42	71	22	10
Mike Felder, SF	.310	260	37	69	17	16
Dan Gladden, Min	.313	444	62	113	34	14
Mike Devereaux, Bal	.316	538	73	139	45	14

Yeah, we know, they're fast. But so is Paul Molitor.

A complete listing for this category can be found on page 260.

WHERE WILL WE FIND THE NEXT JOHNNY BENCH?

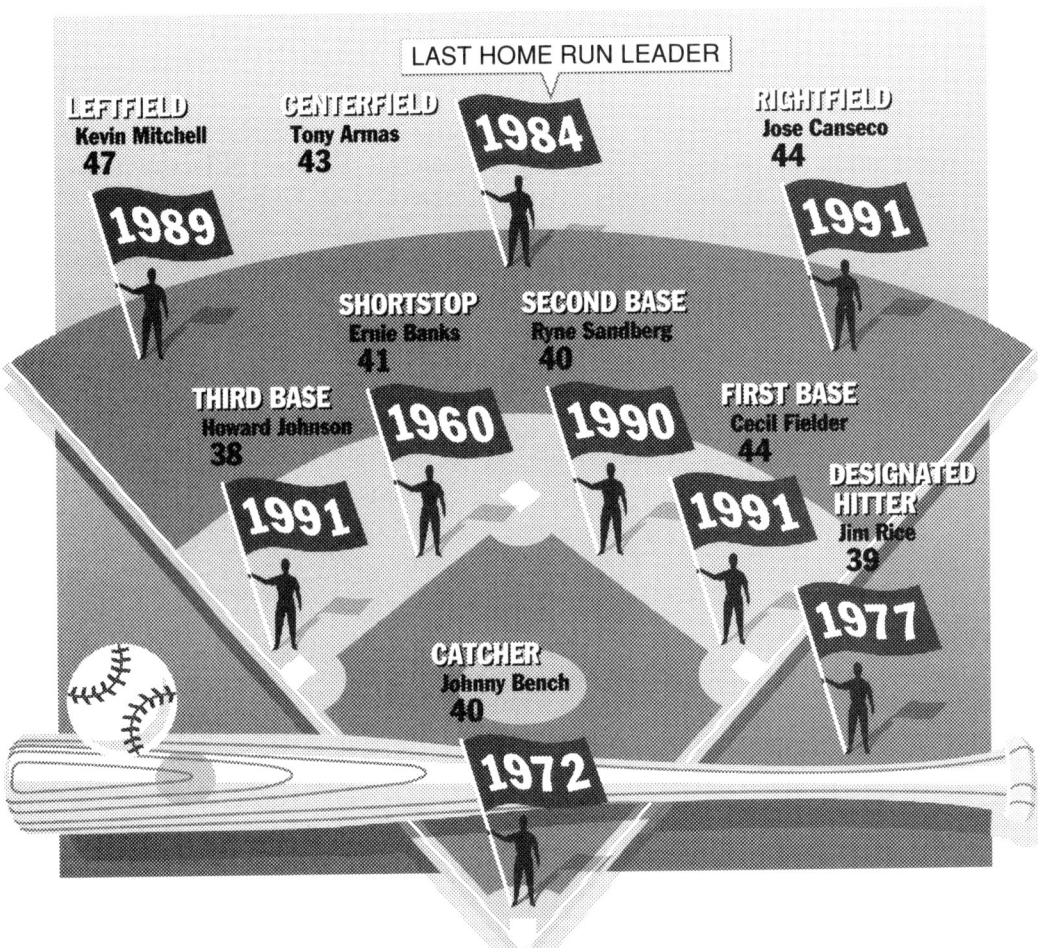

Home run hitters come in all shapes and sizes, but in recent years they've mostly come from certain positions: left field, right field, first base, third base. As baseball has evolved, different positions have come to the fore in regard to producing home run champions. The graphic above shows the last time each position player led his league in home runs. Here's a breakdown by league:

	American League			National League		
Pos	Year	Player	HR	Year	Player	HR
C		Never		1972	J.Bench	40
1B	1991	C.Fielder	44	1982	D.Kingman	37
2B	1981	B.Grich	22	1990	R.Sandberg	40
3B	1976	G.Nettles	32	1991	H.Johnson	38
SS	1945	V.Stephens	24	1960	E.Banks	41
LF	1983	J.Rice	39	1989	K.Mitchell	47
CF	1984	T.Armas	43	1965	W.Mays	52
RF	1991	J.Canseco	44	1988	D.Strawberry	39
DH	1977	J.Rice	39		N/A	

Let's handicap the current positions as far as producing future home run champions:

Catcher: They've had Bill Dickey, Yogi Berra and Carlton Fisk wielding the bat — but never a home run champion? Shame on you, American League! Unless Mickey Tettleton has a career year or Fisk discovers the fountain of youth, the drought figures to continue in 1992. Ditto for the NL, which is still resting on Johnny Bench's laurels. Well, we can always hope that Hector Villanueva is better than we think.

First base: Gee, Cecil Fielder, Frank Thomas, Glenn Davis — the American League is loaded. Not quite so in the NL, which has to hope that Fred McGriff will move up a notch, or that Will Clark will have his career year in 1992.

Second base: What a contrast. The National League has Ryne Sandberg, a threat (especially in Wrigley Field) to lead the league any season. The AL has who — the ever-young Lou Whitaker, maybe?

Third base: HoJo is apparently now an outfielder, but the National League still has Matt Williams. American League long shots: Robin Ventura, Travis Fryman, Leo Gomez. Don't bet on any of them.

Shortstop: The National League, which once had Banks, now thinks of Barry Larkin (20 HR in 1991) as a power guy. That's about it, though, unless Jay Bell begins bunting with power. The AL will seemingly have Ripken — one of the greatest ever at his position — forever.

Left field: Kevin Mitchell is now in the American League, and he's probably the league's big threat at this position (even if Joe Carter plays left this year). The NL responds with either HoJo or Bobby Bonilla (depending on where they play), Barry Bonds, maybe George Bell. Still a slugger's position.

Center Field: Once there was Mays and Mantle. Now there's Ron Gant and Juan Gonzalez. They're still young, but these days center field is primarily a defensive position.

Right Field: Darryl Strawberry. Jose Canseco. Joe Carter. Bonilla or HoJo. David Justice. Danny Tartabull. Ruben Sierra. Jay Buhner. Paul O'Neill. This position is loaded.

Designated Hitter: Frank Thomas is scheduled to be back at first base this year, so the major threats are aging long shots: Jack Clark, Dave Winfield, Chili Davis. Bo Jackson, maybe? Forget it.

CAN WE GO AHEAD AND SAY JOE CARTER IS A CLUTCH HITTER?

There are all kinds of clutch hitting numbers around — batting in the late innings of close games, batting with runners in scoring position, batting from the seventh inning on, and others. No one statistic paints a complete picture, but one we like quite a bit is the "go-ahead RBI." There's no doubt that giving your club the lead in the game — whatever the inning — is an important step toward winning the contest. Among other things, it means that, even if your team goes scoreless the rest of the way, the opposition still has to score two more runs in order to win . . . no easy task. With that introduction, here are the 1991 leaders in go-ahead RBI:

1991 Go-Ahead RBI Leaders

Player, Team	Go Ahead RBI
Fred McGriff, SD	37
Joe Carter, Tor	34
Howard Johnson, Mets	34
Ken Griffey Jr, Sea	33
Ivan Calderon, Mon	32
Jose Canseco, Oak	32
Ron Gant, Atl	32
Ruben Sierra, Tex	32
Darryl Strawberry, LA	31
Will Clark, SF	30

Oddly enough, the two leaders were players who were essentially traded for each other last winter — Fred McGriff and Joe Carter. In the past, McGriff has had a reputation as a poor clutch hitter, mainly because he'd never driven in 100 runs. It didn't help that he had also hit poorly with men in scoring position. After 1991, McGriff has those monkeys off his back, and leading the majors in this category should improve his clutch reputation. Then again, maybe not; people will probably say McGriff hit better last year because he didn't have the pressure of playing for a contender. Unfortunately for him, McGriff won't be able to change that perception until the Padres get into a pennant race.

As for Carter, we've pointed out that his big RBI totals were helped by the fact that he had a very high number of plate appearances with men on base — not that it's easy to drive in 100 runs. But function of opportunity or not, Carter sure drives in a lot of important runs. In 1989, he had 29 go-ahead RBI, the sixth-highest total in baseball, even though he was playing for the lowly (73-89) Indians. In 1990, now with the Padres, he led both leagues in go-ahead RBI with 36. And Carter was the runner-up to McGriff in '91. No other hitter in baseball can match that record, and you have to be impressed.

Is it true that anyone who drives in a lot of runs will end up with a high total of go-ahead RBI? Not really. For example, Barry Bonds, not exactly known as Mr. Clutch after the last two National League Championship Series, drove in 116 runs last year, but only 23 of them gave the Pirates the lead. Nonetheless, it's helpful to rate the hitters on a percentage basis. Since a player can get only one go-ahead RBI per at-bat, we'll figure a percentage based on how many go-ahead RBI he had, versus the number of plate appearances in which he drove in one or more runs. The clutch guys — the ones who drive in their runs when they count most — should have higher percentages. Here are the 1991 leaders (minimum 50 plate appearances with at least one RBI):

1991 Leaders — Go-Ahead RBI Percentage

Player, Team	Plate Appearances with a Go Ahead RBI	Plate Appearances with 1+ RBI	Percent
Ivan Calderon, Mon	32	66	48.5
Fred McGriff, SD	37	81	45.7
Carlos Baerga, Cle	26	57	45.6
Julio Franco, Tex	29	66	43.9
Darryl Strawberry, LA	31	73	42.5
Ken Griffey Jr, Sea	33	79	41.8
Dave Henderson, Oak	25	62	40.3
Jose Canseco, Oak	32	80	40.0
Ron Gant, Atl	32	80	40.0
Don Mattingly, Yanks	24	60	40.0
George Brett, KC	20	50	40.0

It's good to see that Don Mattingly and George Brett, playing at a reduced level because of age and injuries, can gear it up in important situations. McGriff still looks good when the leaders are figured this way, though he yields first place to Ivan Calderon, who was eighth in this category in 1990. We can't jump on Carter much; he missed the top ten, but only by a little at 38.2%. Barry Bonds? Way down at 25.6%. Bonds was even worse in 1990, at 21%. Hmmm . . .

Who were the players who drove in a decent number of runs (at least 60), but hardly ever one that gave their club a lead? We thought you'd never ask:

1991 Trailers — Go-Ahead RBI Percentage

Player, Team	Plate Appearances with a Go Ahead RBI	Plate Appearances with 1+ RBI	Percent
Jay Bell, Pit	6	54	11.1
Brian McRae, KC	6	51	11.8
Brian Harper, Min	8	50	16.0
John Olerud, Tor	10	59	16.9
Kevin Mitchell, SF	10	51	19.6

Jay Bell and Brian McRae are top-of-the order guys. But John Olerud? Kevin Mitchell? We'll be watching how they do in 1992.

A complete listing for this category can be found on page 261.

DO WE REALLY KNOW "WHO CAN POP IN THE CLUTCH"?

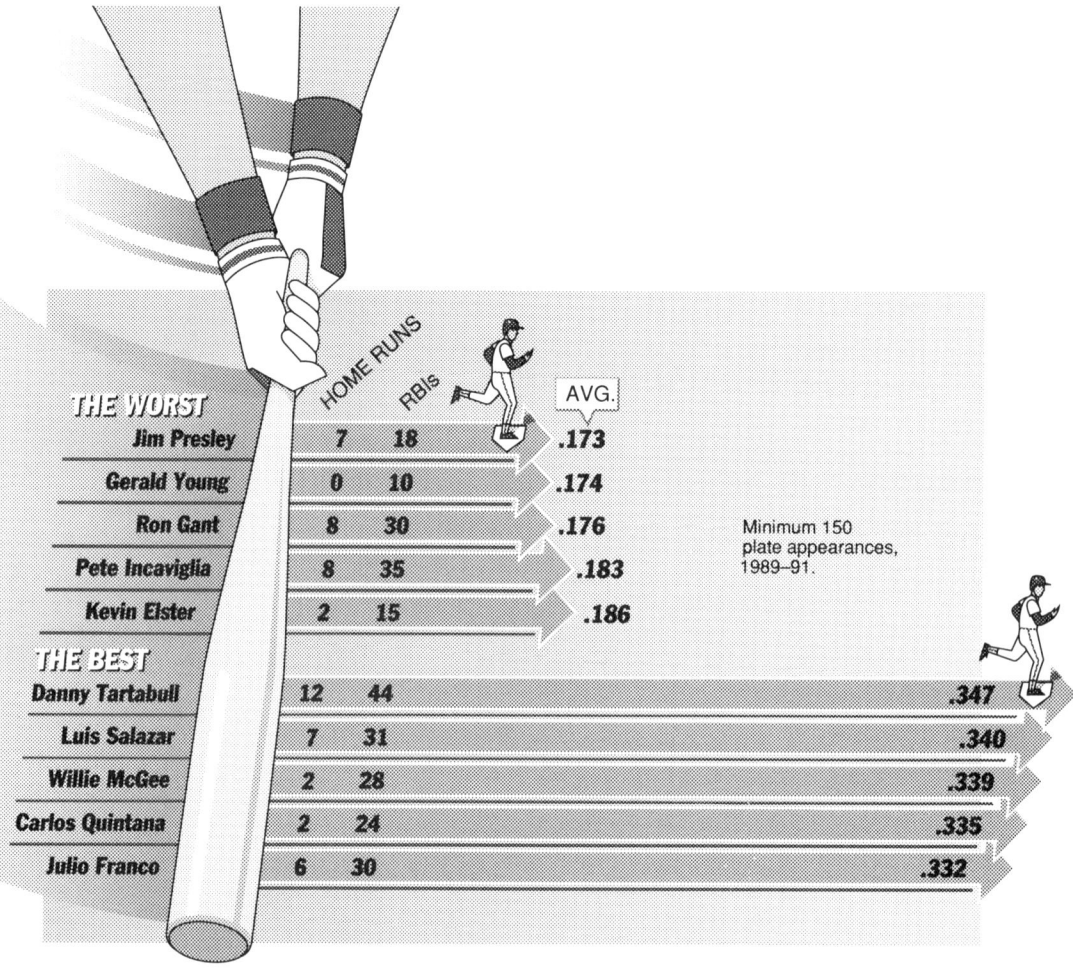

	HOME RUNS	RBIs	AVG.
THE WORST			
Jim Presley	7	18	.173
Gerald Young	0	10	.174
Ron Gant	8	30	.176
Pete Incaviglia	8	35	.183
Kevin Elster	2	15	.186
THE BEST			
Danny Tartabull	12	44	.347
Luis Salazar	7	31	.340
Willie McGee	2	28	.339
Carlos Quintana	2	24	.335
Julio Franco	6	30	.332

Minimum 150 plate appearances, 1989–91.

Like everyone else, we're fascinated by the subject of clutch hitting, and we do our best to measure it statistically. But we'd be the first to acknowledge that there are difficulties. There are many "clutch situations" in a game — not just in the late innings, not just with men in scoring position or whatever. Some games — a World Series game, a late-season contest against a chief rival — are clearly more important than others, and filled with more pressure. Leaders lists for clutch hitting are usually based on sketchy data (60 at-bats or so), and players are usually rated on the basis of batting average, a limited stat. Not surprisingly, there's little continuity among the leaders from year to year, which causes people to question the whole endeavor.

So what we'd like to do here is present data which eliminates some of those weaknesses. The figures here are based on the last three seasons, not just 1991, so the hitters have a more significant amount of at-bats (at least 150 plate appearances). We think the specific subject — batting in the late innings of close games, using essentially the same standards that are used to define a "save situation" — is a useful one, and well worth looking at. And in addition to measuring players by batting average, we rank the leaders in other important offensive categories, to give you a more complete picture. We don't pretend the figures will tell you everything about who the clutch hitters are. But we do think we're giving you more meaningful information than you usually see.

Here then, are the leading hitters in the late innings of close games over the last three seasons, ranked in several categories:

Player	Avg	OBP	Slg	AB	H	HR	RBI
Danny Tartabull	.347	.423	.632	190	66	12	44
Luis Salazar	.340	.381	.497	197	67	7	31
Willie McGee	.339	.386	.431	218	74	2	28
Carlos Quintana	.335	.385	.415	164	55	2	24
Julio Franco	.332	.406	.448	277	92	6	30
Kent Hrbek	.326	.402	.560	184	60	11	36
Tony Gwynn	.325	.384	.394	289	94	2	29
Benito Santiago	.323	.362	.471	257	83	8	38
Otis Nixon	.322	.393	.374	171	55	0	14
Harold Reynolds	.315	.382	.398	279	88	2	47
Kirby Puckett	.315	.376	.480	254	80	8	44
Brian Harper	.315	.336	.453	203	64	6	39

Home Run Leaders: Kevin Mitchell 16, Jack Clark 15, Howard Johnson 15, Kevin McReynolds 15, Andre Dawson 14.

RBI Leaders: Will Clark 59, Ruben Sierra 57, George Bell 52, Howard Johnson 51, Kevin McReynolds 49.

Slugging Leaders: Danny Tartabull .632, Kent Hrbek .560, Kevin Mitchell .542, Cal Ripken .507, Frank Thomas .504.

On-Base Percentage Leaders: Frank Thomas .456, Edgar Martinez .449, Rickey Henderson .443, Randy Ready .428, Randy Milligan .426.

Who have the best clutch hitters been over the last three years? Danny Tartabull (just in time to cash in, Dan!), certainly Kevin Mitchell, who hit only .280, but with great power. Will Clark, the RBI leader. Howard Johnson, whose .250 average gives no indication of the heavy bat he swung. Frank Thomas, who's slugged .504 with a .456 on-base average. Ruben Sierra (57 RBI, .500 Slg). Kent Hrbek, a bust in postseason play last year, showed he's been very reliable in clutch situations over the longer haul. All in all, it's a very impressive leaders list.

Who have the been the duds? One big surprise, Ron Gant, and at least a few guys who are on the way out of baseball (or maybe already gone):

Player	Avg	OBP	Slg	AB	H	HR	RBI
Jim Presley	.173	.205	.346	156	27	7	18
Gerald Young	.174	.262	.198	167	29	0	10
Ron Gant	.176	.264	.324	204	36	8	30
Pete Incaviglia	.183	.229	.337	246	45	8	35
Kevin Elster	.186	.267	.262	183	34	2	15
Tom Pagnozzi	.187	.240	.224	134	25	0	11
Dave Valle	.188	.278	.300	160	30	3	11
Cory Snyder	.191	.223	.288	215	41	3	11
Lance Parrish	.195	.271	.323	220	43	8	21
Jesse Barfield	.196	.345	.349	209	41	8	27
Luis Rivera	.196	.255	.291	148	29	2	11

Don't bother cheering for Jim Presley when the game is on the line; he's already left the baseball world. He may have taken Gerald Young, Pete Incaviglia and Cory Snyder with him.

So do we **really** know who the clutch hitters are? Not completely. But we know a lot more than we did before, and that's a start.

A complete listing for this category can be found on page 262.

WHY DOES JOE CARTER LOVE SKYDOME... AND PAUL O'NEILL THE RIVERFRONT?

Even casual fans now know that Wrigley Field is a great home run park, and that the Astrodome is a slugger's nightmare. Over the past 15 years, starting with Bill James, there has been a steady stream of data to identify pitchers' parks, hitters' parks, good home run parks and bad ones. We've presented some of that data ourselves, and it's helped people understand that some hitters work under more ideal conditions than others.

But hitters are either right or left-handed, and a place like Fenway Park can present a different challenge for a righty swinger than it does for a lefty. Even symmetrical parks often present differing conditions to righties and lefties due to prevailing wind currents, the presence of a big scoreboard, skyboxes or something else. We thought it would make sense to try to answer a simple question: what are the best home run parks for right-handed hitters, and the best for lefties?

To find the answers, we need to do a little mathematical work. Simply counting the number of homers hit by righties, and the number by lefties, won't work; overall there are more righty swingers than lefties, and the number will vary greatly from team to team. So this is what we do, using the Baltimore Orioles as an example. Over the last three seasons, there were 181 home runs hit by left-handed batters in Orioles home games over 6,965 at-bats, or one HR for every 38.481 AB; that's both by the O's and their opponents. In Orioles road games, lefty swingers hit 126 homers in 5,744 at-bats, or one per every 45.587 AB. We divide the road ratio by the home ratio (45.587 by 38.481) and come up with a Baltimore park index of 1.18 for lefty hitters. We then do the index for righty swingers, and so on for each team. An index of 1.000 would indicate a neutral park, one above 1.000 a park favorable for that type of hitter, one below 1.000 a park which is tougher than normal.

We used three-year data in most cases; the exceptions were clubs which got new ballparks, or changed their dimensions significantly. Thus, for the Amercian League, the Toronto data is for 1990-91, and the Chicago, Cleveland and Seattle figures are for 1991 only:

American League

Park	For LHB	For RHB
Baltimore Orioles	1.18	.92
Boston Red Sox	1.01	1.09
California Angels	1.14	1.15
Chicago White Sox *	1.09	1.14
Cleveland Indians *	.38	.54
Detroit Tigers	1.20	1.09

American League		
Park	For LHB	For RHB
Kansas City Royals	.63	.84
Milwaukee Brewers	1.04	1.00
Minnesota Twins	.87	.94
New York Yankees	1.18	.94
Oakland Athletics	.76	.99
Seattle Mariners *	1.46	.91
Texas Rangers	1.07	1.02
Toronto Blue Jays **	1.03	1.54

* one-year data   ** two-year data

Ah, Skydome. Joe Carter got traded to Toronto last year and couldn't say enough good things about his wonderful new country. And why not? With the Padres in 1990, Carter hit 24 homers — 12 at home, 12 on the road. But with the Jays in 1991, Carter hit 33 — 23 at home, 10 on the road. Carter's stats underscore the fact that Skydome is the best park in baseball for a right-handed power hitter. But it's a fairly neutral park for lefties, which explains why John Olerud hasen't gone crazy there.

This is interesting data. Fenway, supposedly a righty power hitters' paradise, does benefit righties, but not to the extent that Toronto, California or the new Comiskey Park do. Cecil Fielder is helped by Tiger Stadium, but not like he'd be if he batted lefty. The changes in Seattle seem to have produced a wide split; it's now a very good park for lefties, but a tougher-than-average park for righties. Would George Brett have been a home run champion if he had played in the current Kingdome?

Here is the National League data; once again we use three-year figures, with the exception of Houston (1991 only):

National League		
Park	For LHB	For RHB
Atlanta Braves	1.27	1.19
Chicago Cubs	1.10	1.16
Cincinnati Reds	1.40	1.37
Houston Astros *	.56	.52
Los Angeles Dodgers	.91	.99
Montreal Expos	.78	.85
New York Mets	1.08	.84
Philadelphia Phillies	1.14	.91
Pittsburgh Pirates	.93	1.02
St. Louis Cardinals	.67	.90
San Diego Padres	1.11	1.04
San Francisco Giants	1.15	1.01

* one-year data

Riverfront Stadium in Cincinnati is not generally known as a great home run park, but since the Reds lowered their fences a few years ago, it's become the son of Crosley Field: the best park in the National League for both lefties and righties. Paul O'Neill, in particular, ought to say thanks. The Reds' lefty-swinging outfielder has hit 75 homers over the last four years; 53 of them (71 percent) have come in Cincinnati.

Most of the National League parks are fairly even to righties and lefties. But there are a few surprises. Shea Stadium in New York is a good home run park for lefties, a bad one for righties. The St. Louis park, which will have shorter dimensions this year, has been tough on all power hitters, but a little more giving to righty swingers; that helps explain why Jack Clark was able to hit a fair number of homers there. And one wonders why the Phillies, with a park very good for a lefty, haven't imported a left-handed pull hitter to see what he could do at the Vet.

WHY PLAY FOR ONE RUN?

Simplifying matters a bit, you could say that there have been two schools of thought when it comes to baseball strategy. The John McGraw School stressed pitching, defense and playing for one run — the bunt, the stolen base and the hit-and-run were big items on the menu. The Babe Ruth School said forget that; when you can outslug the opposition, why waste your outs on bunts and runners caught stealing?

To look at strategic styles, we use a stat called "outs invested in one-run strategies." If you want to get one run, the building blocks are the sacrifice bunt and the stolen base. The drawback is that you invest an out for certain when you bunt, and risk giving up an out when you try to steal. Let's rate the clubs according to their outs invested in those one-run strategies by adding the runners caught stealing to the sacrifice hits. In this study, there's a big American/National League differential. National League teams play in generally-bigger ballparks, and in addition their pitchers have to bat; as a result, NL teams are going to be playing for one run more often. So let's separate the data by leagues. For reasons we'll explain in a minute, we include the total runs scored by each team, the runs allowed, and the difference between the two. First, the American League:

Outs Invested in One-run Strategies

American League	CS	SH	Outs	Runs	Opp. Runs	Diff.
New York	36	37	73	674	777	−103
Baltimore	33	47	80	686	796	−110
Detroit	47	38	85	817	794	23
Boston	39	50	89	731	712	19
Seattle	44	55	99	702	674	28
Oakland	64	41	105	760	776	−16
Toronto	53	56	109	684	622	62
Texas	50	59	109	829	814	15
Minnesota	68	44	112	776	652	124
California	56	63	119	653	649	4
Milwaukee	68	52	120	799	744	55
Cleveland	58	62	120	576	759	−183
Kansas City	68	53	121	727	722	5
Chicago	74	76	150	758	681	77

You might wonder why teams like the Yankees and Orioles, with less-than-great offenses, didn't play for one run more often. The answer is that they were usually being outscored, often by a considerable margin.

When you're down by two or three runs, there's not much point in bunting, and usually not much in stealing (unless you're very sure you'll be safe). Teams which have the lead — in the unbalanced AL, 10 of the 14 clubs outscored their opponents — are much more likely to give up an out in an effort to get an extra run. The oddball club here was (big surprise) Cleveland. The Tribe was outscored by 183 runs, but they still kept bunting and trying to steal. We'll explain their logic in a minute . . . not that we buy it.

Here's the National League data:

Outs Invested in One-run Strategies

National League	CS	SH	Outs	Runs	Opp. Runs	Diff.
Philadelphia	30	52	82	629	680	−51
Cincinnati	56	72	128	689	691	−2
New York	70	60	130	640	646	−6
Houston	68	63	131	605	717	−112
Chicago	64	75	139	695	734	−39
San Diego	64	78	142	636	646	−10
Pittsburgh	46	99	145	768	632	136
San Francisco	57	90	147	649	697	−48
Atlanta	76	86	162	749	644	105
Los Angeles	68	94	162	665	565	110
Montreal	100	64	164	579	655	−76
St. Louis	110	58	168	651	648	3

National League clubs, for the reasons stated, are much more likely to play for one run. Only four of the twelve NL teams outscored the opposition, and all of them ranked near the bottom — in other words, they were more apt to play for one run, which is logical. The oddball club in this league is the Expos — outscored by a considerable margin, but still bunting and stealing. There is probably a ballpark factor at work here, which would partially explain what the Indians were doing. In the cavernous Big O, as with Cleveland Stadium in last year's configuration, you're not going to hit a lot of homers. So there is more of a tendency to go for one run. We still think the Expos (and the Tribe) were overdoing it.

IS PITTSBURGH'S BUNT-IN-THE-FIRST STRATEGY WORTH IT?

Jim Leyland of the Pirates is widely considered one of the best managers in baseball, and we admire his work as much as anyone. However, Leyland has one bit of strategy that is almost unique in baseball today. When the Pirate leadoff man reaches first, Leyland invariably will have his number-two man, Jay Bell, bunt him over to second. How unusual is that? The Pirates sacrificed 16 times in the first inning last year; the number two team, the Toronto Blue Jays, sacrificed only seven. The world champion Minnesota Twins utilized the sacrifice bunt only twice in the first inning, and two teams (the Padres and Phillies) never bunted at all in the first.

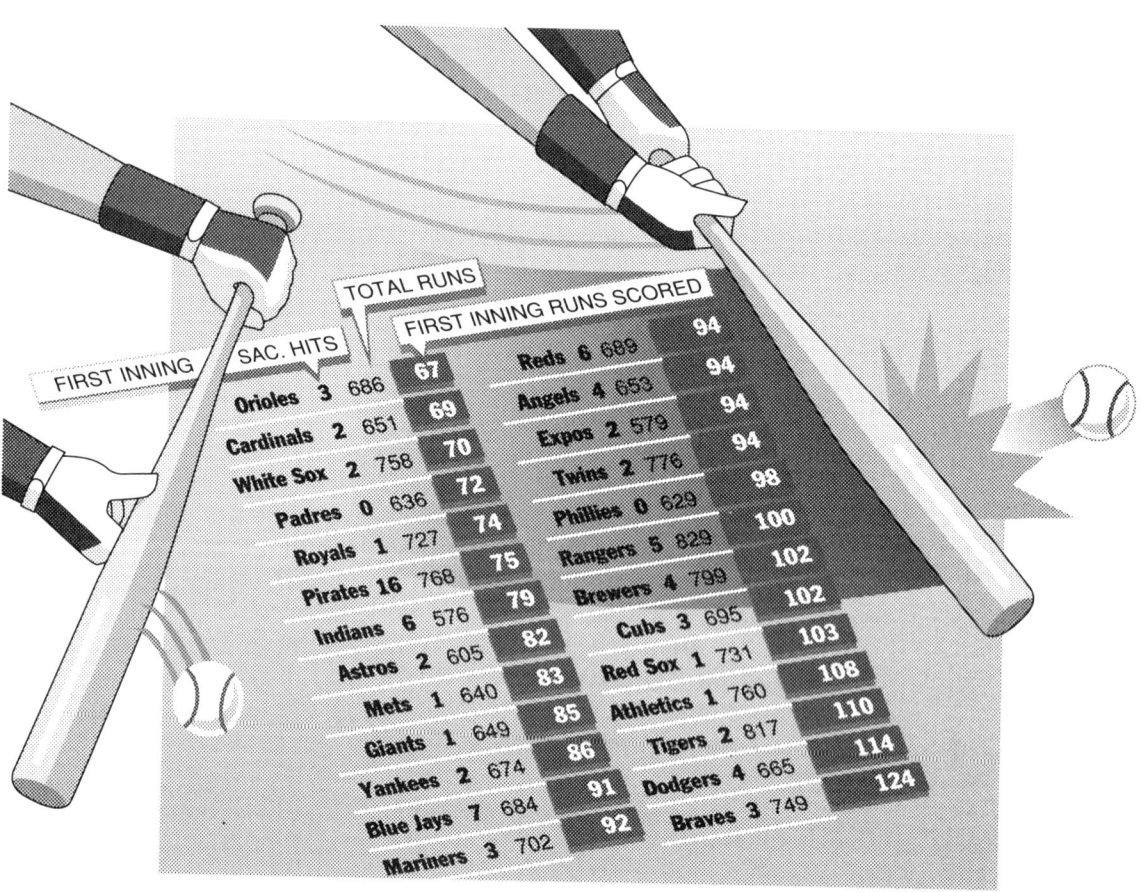

	FIRST INNING SAC. HITS	TOTAL RUNS	FIRST INNING RUNS SCORED		
Orioles	3	686	67	Reds 6 689	94
Cardinals	2	651	69	Angels 4 653	94
White Sox	2	758	70	Expos 2 579	94
Padres	0	636	72	Twins 2 776	94
Royals	1	727	74	Phillies 0 629	98
Pirates	16	768	75	Rangers 5 829	100
Indians	6	576	79	Brewers 4 799	102
Astros	2	605	82	Cubs 3 695	102
Mets	1	640	83	Red Sox 1 731	103
Giants	1	649	85	Athletics 1 760	108
Yankees	2	674	86	Tigers 2 817	110
Blue Jays	7	684	91	Dodgers 4 665	114
Mariners	3	702	92	Braves 3 749	124

Why would Leyland adopt this unorthodox strategy? There are several justifications:

1. Bunting the man over gets a runner into scoring position for the heart of the Pirate order, one of the best in baseball last year (Van Slyke, Bonilla, Bonds).

2. It gives the Pirates an excellent chance to take an early lead. This is no small consideration, as the club which scores first goes on to win the game about 65 percent of the time.

3. One of the drawbacks in attempting to sacrifice is that many players are poor bunters; they wind up forcing the lead runner, giving up an out for no gain. But Bell is one of the most adept bunters in baseball, and he's almost always able to get the runner over.

That all seems reasonable. However, the main drawback to the sacrifice is that it's a "one-run" strategy — it dramatically lessens the chance for a big inning. To see the consequences on the Pirate attack, we ranked the clubs, from low to high, according to first-inning runs last season. We also included how often each team sacrificed in the first, and the total number of runs they scored during the season (see chart).

As you can see, only five major league clubs scored fewer first-inning runs than the Pirates did last year. However, those teams would figure to score fewer; they all had less potent offenses than Pittsburgh, which led the National League in runs scored. Now look at the teams who scored **more** first-inning runs than the Pirates. Over the course of the season, the Bucs outscored the Montreal Expos by 189 runs, over one run a game. But during the first inning, the punchless Expos outscored the Pirates by 19.

A compelling argument against bunting in the first inning is this: it's the only frame in which your offense is guaranteed to be set up exactly as written on the lineup card. Time to go for broke, especially when you consider that, in the first, many pitchers struggle to find their rhythm. The "Pittsburgh strategy" may gain some things for the Pirates — but we think the strategy gives up even more.

WHO'S THE BEST BUNTER: BELL, BUTLER, CUYLER, FINLEY OR NIXON?

Who's the best bunter in baseball? Looking at the 1991 data, five players stand out: Jay Bell, Brett Butler, Milt Cuyler, Steve Finley and Otis Nixon. Bell (the sacrifice king) and Butler (Mr. Bunt-for-a-Hit) are generally considered the best at their respective specialties; the others are notable for being good at both. We'll look at some sacrifice data first. The following players had the best success rates in sacrifice attempts last year (minimum 10 sacrifice attempts):

Bunting For A Sacrifice

Player, Team	SH	Failed SH	Pct
B.J. Surhoff, Mil	13	0	100.0
Jerry Browne, Cle	12	0	100.0
Luis Rivera, Bos	12	0	100.0
Milt Cuyler, Det	12	0	100.0
Mike Sharperson, LA	10	0	100.0
Steve Finley, Hou	10	0	100.0
Lenny Harris, LA	12	1	92.3
Bruce Hurst, SD	12	1	92.3
Jay Bell, Pit	30	3	90.9
Manuel Lee, Tor	10	1	90.9
Tom Browning, Cin	10	1	90.9
Dave Gallagher, Cal	10	1	90.9
Dennis Martinez, Mon	10	1	90.9

A number of players had perfect records in sacrifice attempts last year, including our boys Cuyler and Finley. So did Otis Nixon who was 7-for-7. Butler, a leadoff man, wasn't asked to sacrifice much: he was 4-for-5. Still, it's hard to argue with the notion that Bell is the master of the sacrifice. One thing our data shows pretty clearly is that the more a bunt is expected, the harder it is to lay it down successfully. Bell, asked to sacrifice much more than anyone else in baseball (nobody else had even 20 sacrifice attempts), succeeded 30 of 33 times. He wins this round, closely followed by Cuyler and Finley.

Here are the players who were most successful at bunting for a hit (again, minimum 10 attempts):

Bunting For A Hit

Player, Team	Bunt Hits	Att.	Avg
Dante Bichette, Mil	8	10	.800
Shawon Dunston, Cubs	10	13	.769
Ivan Calderon, Mon	8	11	.727
Carlos Baerga, Cle	8	11	.727
Roberto Alomar, Tor	7	11	.636
Harold Reynolds, Sea	10	16	.625
Luis Sojo, Cal	13	22	.591
Vince Coleman, Mets	8	14	.571
Steve Finley, Hou	16	30	.533
Devon White, Tor	9	17	.529
Omar Vizquel, Sea	9	17	.529

You'll notice that less familiar names are at the top of the list — Bichette, Dunston, etc. (Jay Bell, incidentally, was 2-for-2). Again, there's a law of diminishing returns here, as the players who bunt frequently lose the element of surprise. You can see this by looking at the list of players who had 20 bunt attempts for hits last year:

Players with 20 or more Bunt Attempts for Hits

Player, Team	Bunt Hits	Att.	Pct
Luis Sojo, Cal	13	22	.591
Steve Finley, Hou	16	30	.533
Brett Butler, LA	21	41	.512
Milt Cuyler, Det	15	32	.469
Otis Nixon, Atl	23	52	.442
Luis Polonia, Cal	10	23	.435
Mike Felder, SF	9	21	.429
Brian McRae, KC	5	22	.227

Finley, Butler, Cuyler and Nixon all succeeded nearly half the time, even though they had to face defenses stacked to stop them. While we admire Brett Butler's performance enormously, we're even more impressed with Steve Finley's. Of all the players considered, Finley and Bell are the only ones who play on turf fields ... and turf is considered much harder to bunt on than grass. Bell, who lacks Finley's great speed, simply can't compete when it comes to bunting for hits. We think Steve Finley was the best bunter of 1991.

A complete listing for this category can be found on page 263.

WHO ARE BASEBALL'S TABLE SETTERS?

For many of us, the baseball announcer of our youth was Curt Gowdy. Who can forget Curt saying such unforgettable things as, "His whole future is ahead of him"? One phrase that Curt used really stuck with us. Whenever Pete Rose or Joe Morgan came to bat for the great Reds teams of the seventies, Curt would say, "They're the table setters." Meaning that Rose and Morgan's job was to get on base for Johnny Bench, Tony Perez and company.

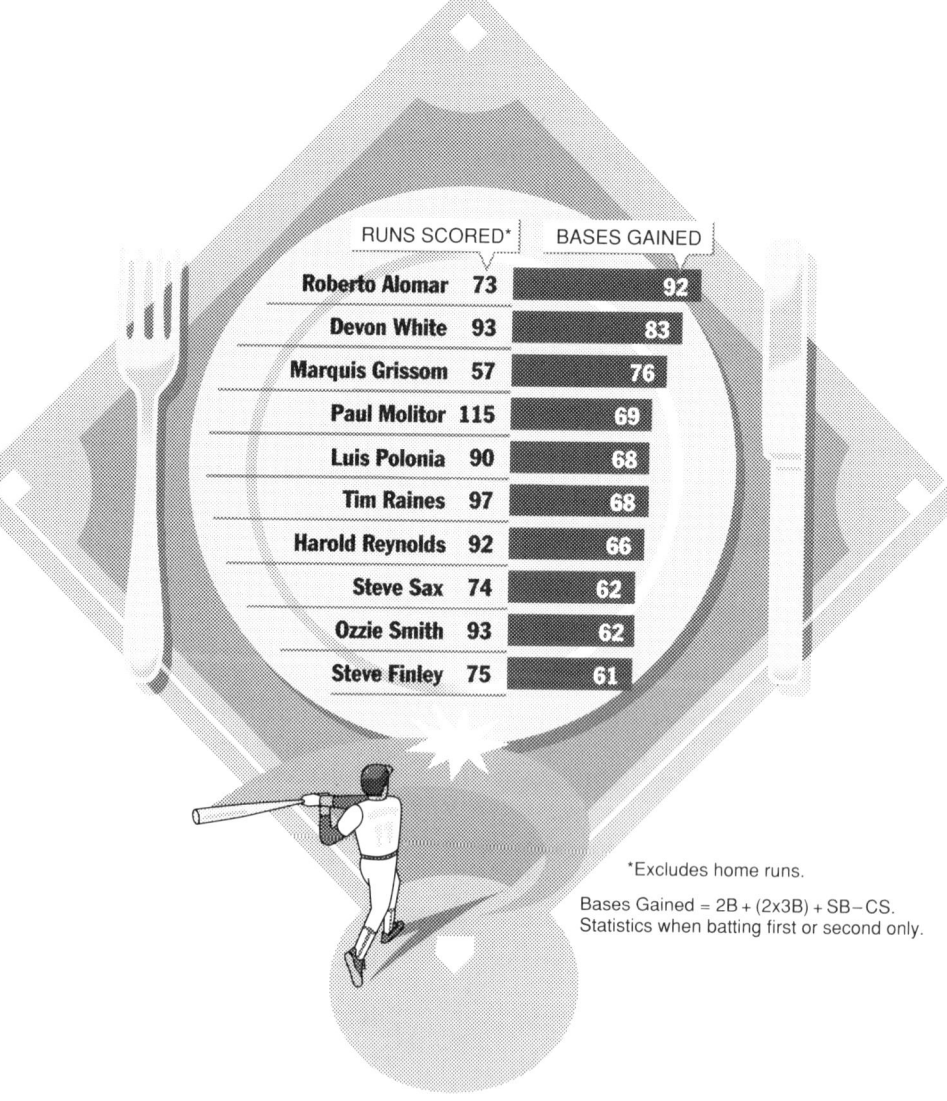

	RUNS SCORED*	BASES GAINED
Roberto Alomar	73	92
Devon White	93	83
Marquis Grissom	57	76
Paul Molitor	115	69
Luis Polonia	90	68
Tim Raines	97	68
Harold Reynolds	92	66
Steve Sax	74	62
Ozzie Smith	93	62
Steve Finley	75	61

*Excludes home runs.
Bases Gained = 2B + (2x3B) + SB − CS.
Statistics when batting first or second only.

Curt had it right. Setting the table for the RBI men is the best way for a team to score runs. We already know the players who get on base the most, and more specifically the leadoff men. But how about the players who **really** set the table — the ones who put themselves in scoring position, where a single will usually bring them home?

For that, we've developed a new stat for number one and two hitters called "bases gained." Don't feel intimidated, because it's pretty simple. All it does is to count the times each player gets into scoring position, with extra credit for getting to third. The formula is

$$\text{Bases Gained} = 2B + (2 \times 3B) + SB - CS$$

For purposes of context, the runs scored in the chart exclude home runs — in other words, the runs scored due to teammates driving the player in. The top 10 leaders are shown in the chart.

As you would think, this is primarily a speed category. Everyone on the list can run pretty well — they steal bases (usually without getting caught too often), and they stretch singles into doubles. It's certainly not a complete portrait of a "table setter." Someone like Wade Boggs (36 bases gained) suffers in this category; Wade reaches base more than anyone, but he usually reaches **first** base, where it ordinarily takes two players to drive him in. A player like Brett Butler also suffers; he's primarily a singles hitter, and though he stole a lot of bases last year (38), he was caught stealing 28 times, negating most of the advantage.

The leader — one who really shouldn't surprise you, if you think about it — is Roberto Alomar of the Blue Jays. What a superb young player (still only 24) this is. Alomar is a consistent hitter for average (.295, .287, .295 the last three years), and he draws more walks than the average youngster (a career-high 57 last year). But two things really set him apart in this category. Alomar is a great base stealer: 53 steals in 64 attempts last year. Even more importantly, he has great extra-base power, with 41 doubles and 11 triples in 1991. It seemed like every time Joe Carter looked up last year, Alomar was in scoring position — which is one reason Carter drove home more than 100 runs again.

Among the other players, there's a pleasing blend of youth (Devon White, Marquis Grissom, Luis Polonia, Steve Finley and company) and heady veterans (Paul Molitor, Tim Raines, Steve Sax, Ozzie Smith, etc.). The hitters must get hungry just looking at this list.

A complete listing for this category can be found on page 264.

FOR WHOM DOES CRIME PAY?

	STOLEN BASES	CAUGHT STEALING	PCT.
Eric Davis	247	37	87.0%
Tim Raines	685	121	85.0%
Marquis Grissom	99	19	83.9%
Willie Wilson	632	124	83.6%
Henry Cotto	91	19	82.7%
Barry Larkin	133	29	82.1%
Vince Coleman	586	129	82.0%
Rickey Henderson	994	229	81.3%
Len Dykstra	190	45	80.9%
Ozzie Smith	499	120	80.6%

Minimum 100 stolen base attempts.

Since World War II, the biggest changes in baseball strategy have probably been the increased usage of relief pitchers and the renewed emphasis on the stolen base. The steal was popular in the deadball era, of course, but the difference between then and now is that today's players don't get tossed out nearly as much. In 1920, for example, when the stolen base was still a much more popular weapon than the home run, the major league success rate was only a little over fifty percent. In fact, the World Champion Cleveland Indians of that year were 73 for 165 (44 percent) in steal attempts. That Tribe club boasted such basepath nifties as Larry Gardner (3 for 23!), Charlie Jamieson (2 for 11) and Bill Wambsganss (9 for 27). Tris Speaker, the Indians' player-manager and a man considered one of the smartest players of all time, hardly set much of an example by going 10 for 23. Yeah, we know, Gramps, the pitchers knew how to hold runners then and the catchers all had cannons for arms, but still . . .

So let us praise the modern ballplayer: he knows how to steal successfully (in more ways than one, some would say). The National League success rate in recent seasons has often been over 70 percent, and even those poky American Leaguers are always over 65. Today's best base stealers have a much higher success rate than that — much, much higher. The three best percentage stealers of all time (minimum 200 lifetime steals), with success rates well over 80 percent, were all active in 1991: Eric Davis, Tim Raines and Willie Wilson. Those three have lots of company, however, when it comes to high percentage stealing. The chart above lists the lifetime leaders among active players with at least 100 steal attempts.

When Rickey Henderson gave his "Today I'm the greatest of all time" speech after breaking the stolen base record, he rubbed a lot of people the wrong way, but he was also telling the truth. Henderson has not only stolen more bases than Lou Brock; he's stolen them at a much higher success rate — 81.3% for Rickey, 75.3 for Lou. Others have higher percentages than Henderson, but they've all stolen a lot fewer bases.

One can't look at the lifetime percentage leaders without wondering where the heir apparents to Rickey Henderson and Vince Coleman are. Among the current crop of younger base thieves, there's no one who seems a legitimate threat for a 100-steal season. There's been talk for several years that baseball isn't luring the top athletes the way it did a few years ago — that baseball is now competing with football, basketball, soccer, and other sports at the youth level — and the stolen base percentage figures seem to give evidence of that. Most of the leaders are veterans — all except Grissom and Larkin. It may also be significant that the National League success rate declined last year, from 71 percent in 1990 to 67 percent in '91. More emphasis on controlling the running game? Perhaps. But perhaps we're also beginning to see fewer great all-around athletes. We shouldn't lose hope, though. Baseball is still producing multi-dimensional stars in the likes of Ron Gant, Howard Johnson, Barry Bonds and Jose Canseco; players who may not have made the very top of the list, but are perennial names among the leaders in both homers and steals.

They had larceny in their hearts (as Bugs Baer once put it), but their feet were honest; these players have the **worst** lifetime stolen base percentages among active players:

Lifetime Stolen Base % — 1991 Active Players

Player	SB	CS	Pct
Tim Wallach	48	59	.449
Tom Brunansky	64	59	.520
Hubie Brooks	60	52	.536
Jack Clark	76	60	.559
Scott Fletcher	57	44	.564

Would Tim Wallach have been a "base stealing terror" for the 1920 Indians?

A complete listing for this category appears on page 265.

ARE SOME BASERUNNERS SIMPLY TOO AGGRESSIVE?

Everyone loves aggressiveness on the bases. The ability to steal or take the extra base can mean added runs over the course of a season. But often there's a price, in the form of being tossed out. Let's look at the players who made the most baserunning outs in 1991. We'll add up times caught stealing, times picked off and what we call "outs advancing" (OAD), or outs trying to take an extra base. We'll also look at how many bases each player stole, and since many, if not most, OADs are the result of trying to stretch singles into doubles or doubles into triples, we'll list the players' doubles and triples counts. This is not an exact times-safe vs. times-out comparison, but it is a decent baserunning profile. Here's the top 15:

Most Times Thrown Out on the Bases — 1991

	Outs				Safe			
Runner, Team	CS	Pck Off	OAD	Tot	SB	2B	3B	Tot
Brett Butler, LA	28	2	6	36	38	13	5	56
Luis Polonia, Cal	23	4	8	35	48	28	8	84
Delino DeShields, Mon	23	3	5	31	56	15	4	75
Ray Lankford, StL	20	2	5	27	44	23	15	82
Otis Nixon, Atl	21	1	4	26	72	10	1	83
Alex Cole, Cle	17	3	4	24	37	7	5	49
Roberto Alomar, Tor	11	4	9	24	53	41	11	105
Howard Johnson, Mets	16	1	6	23	30	34	4	68
Ivan Calderon, Mon	16	2	5	23	31	22	3	56
Rickey Henderson, Oak	18	1	3	22	58	17	1	76
Steve Finley, Hou	18	0	4	22	34	28	10	72
Ron Gant, Atl	15	1	5	21	34	35	3	72
Marquis Grissom, Mon	17	0	3	20	76	23	9	118
Ozzie Guillen, WSox	15	0	5	20	21	20	3	44
Brian McRae, KC	11	1	7	19	20	28	9	57

For players who steal a lot of bases, or pile up a high number of doubles and triples, ranking among the leaders in baserunning outs is not a major concern. A perfect example is Roberto Alomar. Traded to the American League before the '91 campaign, Alomar stepped up his aggressiveness on the bases. The result was a big increase in bases gained:

Roberto Alomar	CS	SB	2B	3B
1990	7	24	27	5
1991	11	53	41	11

But for others, the price paid for bases gained is harder to justify. Ozzie Guillen of the White Sox has an all-out approach on the bases. But getting thrown out 15 times while stealing only 21 bases, as he did last year, wound up costing his club runs. Another example: Luis Polonia more than doubled his stolen base total last year, from 21 to 48. But Polonia was caught stealing 23 times, which virtually negated the effect of the steals. Polonia also had a career-high 28 doubles last year, but paid a big price with eight outs advancing.

Brett Butler, the leader in baserunning outs, is often praised for his aggressive approach. But Butler is now nearly 35 years old, and it seems obvious that he's lost speed. Look at his figures from 1990 and 1991:

Brett Butler	CS	SB	2B	3B
1990	19	51	20	9
1991	28	38	13	5

Butler ran with his usual aggressiveness in 1991; the difference is that he was getting thrown out a lot more. It might be time for him to start exercising more caution.

Another player who might have to face up to his advancing years is Boston's Tony Pena. Pena still has some baserunning smarts, as is indicated by his 1991 stolen base record of eight steals in 11 attempts. However, Pena was also thrown out nine times trying to take an extra base — more than anyone in baseball, except for the much speedier Alomar. Though Pena did have 23 doubles last year, he ran himself into an unacceptable number of outs.

A complete listing for this category can be found on page 266.

ARE POWER HITTERS PULL HITTERS?

This is a slight oversimplification, but you could say that, in modern baseball, there are two schools of hitting. The Ted Williams school teaches a slight uppercut swing and pulling the ball with power. The Charlie Lau school stresses a more level swing and using the whole field. The Lau school has been criticized for making punch-and-judy hitters out of legitimate sluggers; the Williams school has been criticized for producing hitters who are one-dimensional and easy to defense. But both schools have produced many successful hitters.

PULLING POWER	Percentage of pulled home runs	Total home runs
Ron Gant	100%	73
Lou Whitaker	100%	69
Kevin McReynolds	100%	62
Alvin Davis	100%	50
Carlton Fisk	100%	49
ML average	86.7%	

OPPOSITE FIELD POWER	Percentage of pulled home runs	Total home runs
Bo Jackson	60.3%	63
Kal Daniels	56.3%	48
Robin Yount	56.3%	48
Harold Baines	44.2%	52
Roberto Kelly	40.9%	44
ML average	13.3%	

Minimum 40 home runs hit from 1989 through 1991.

It would seem that the Williams School would produce more sluggers — that is, home run hitters are more likely to be pull hitters. Indeed, only 13.3 percent of all homers over the past three seasons have gone to the opposite field. But what about the elite sluggers? Over the past three seasons, only eight players have averaged at least 30 homers a season. It's no shock that all of them pull most of their home runs. But it might surprise you that six of the eight homer to the opposite field more than the average major leaguer:

Opposite Field Homers: 1989-1991
(Minimum 25 HRs Total)

Batter	All HRs	Opposite Field HRs	Percent
Kevin Mitchell	109	21	19.3
Fred McGriff	102	32	31.4

Jose Canseco	98	21	21.4
Howard Johnson	97	3	3.1
Ryne Sandberg	96	4	4.2
Cecil Fielder	95	15	15.8
Mark McGwire	94	20	21.4
Darryl Strawberry	94	20	21.4
Group total	**785**	**136**	**17.3**

What this suggests is that, as a rule, the great sluggers are not "pull-crazy." While they love to pull the ball, they probably get a lot of pitches on the outside part of the plate — away from their power. These hitters are powerful enough to take the ball out of the yard, even when going to the opposite field.

Another way of examining this question is to look at the players who have homered to the opposite field most often over the last three seasons (minimum 25 homers total):

Opposite Field Homers: 1989-1991
(Minimum 25 HRs Total)

Batter	All HRs	Opposite Field HRs	Percent
Bo Jackson	63	38	60.3
Kal Daniels	48	27	56.3
Robin Yount	48	27	56.3
Julio Franco	39	19	48.7
Harold Baines	52	23	44.2
Roberto Kelly	44	18	40.9
Kirby Puckett	36	14	38.9
Jack Howell	36	14	38.9
George Brett	36	14	38.9
Pete Incaviglia	56	21	37.5

This group has produced some 30-homer seasons (Jackson, Baines, Puckett, Brett, Incaviglia), but only sporadically. Except for the oft-injured Jackson, there's no one here who's put up impressive home run totals year after year. That's one of the criticisms of the Lau school: many people argue that Baines and Puckett, to name two, would hit a lot more homers if they pulled the ball more often. The evidence suggests that there's some validity to the argument. But we won't be the ones to say that a group which includes Puckett, Baines, Robin Yount, George Brett and Julio Franco needs a new theory of hitting.

Are power hitters pull hitters? Yes — but not as much as you might think.

A complete listing for this category can be found on page 267.

WHO HAS THE BEST "HEART OF THE ORDER"?

Ask any manager what would top his fantasy list, and he might say, "Give me Ruth, Gehrig and Meusel (1927 Yankees) in the middle of my batting order." Or Frank Robinson, Brooks Robinson and Boog Powell (1966 Orioles). Or how about Joe Morgan, Johnny Bench and Tony Perez (1975 Reds)? One can picture all the runs crossing the plate as the great 3-4-5 combinations — what we call the "heart of the order" — slug them home.

No modern-day manager has a heart of the order quite like the legendary ones listed above, but there are some pretty solid threesomes working today. How about the Texas Rangers, with Rafael Palmeiro, Ruben Sierra and Juan Gonzalez (with Julio Franco in reserve)? Or the Atlanta Braves, with Terry Pendleton, Ron Gant and Dave Justice? Or the world champion Twins, with Kirby Puckett, Kent Hrbek and Chili Davis? Alas, two of the best combinations of recent years are no longer intact. San Francisco's need for pitching broke up the great Will Clark-Kevin Mitchell-Matt Williams trio, and Pittsburgh couldn't ante up the bucks to keep Bobby Bonilla together with Andy Van Slyke and Barry Bonds.

If we want to rate the best 3-4-5 combinations, we need to look at several stats. Home runs, RBI and slugging percentage are the figures we usually scan first when we're rating power hitters; that's how we'll rank the hearts of the order. Here are the top five clubs in each category; note that these figures are for **all** hitters who batted in the 3-4-5 slots in 1991:

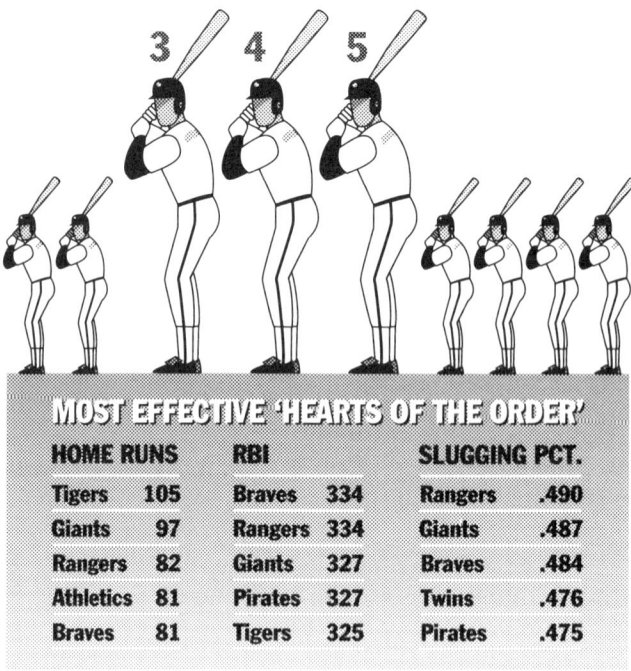

MOST EFFECTIVE 'HEARTS OF THE ORDER'

HOME RUNS		RBI		SLUGGING PCT.	
Tigers	105	Braves	334	Rangers	.490
Giants	97	Rangers	334	Giants	.487
Rangers	82	Giants	327	Braves	.484
Athletics	81	Pirates	327	Twins	.476
Braves	81	Tigers	325	Pirates	.475

There's no single stickout here, but let's try to rank the 1991 hearts of the order as well as we can:

1. San Francisco. Second in slugging, second in homers, tied for third in RBI . . . that's impressive. What's even more impressive is that the Giant trio played in the lower-scoring National League, and in a park that's less-than-great for hitters. The Giants will miss Kevin Mitchell plenty this year, but they're happy to still have Clark and Williams.

2. Texas. The Rangers scored more runs than any club in the majors last year, and the heart of their order was a key reason. Few clubs have not just three, but four outstanding hitters to fill the three spots. They're all pretty young, too. It should be fun times again in Arlington this year.

3. Atlanta. Dave Justice and Ron Gant are two of the best young power hitters in baseball, and Terry Pendleton is the National League's Most Valuable Player. The Braves tied the Rangers for most RBI from the 3-4-5 slots, so we could have ranked them first as easily as third. Our only quibble is that Pendleton had a career year in 1991, and he'll have to prove that he can do it again.

How about the clubs with the worst hearts of the order? It's easy to jump on Houston, Montreal, Cleveland and St. Louis, but those teams play in parks that are notoriously tough for power hitters. Considering the handicaps they were under, the Indians (with Carlos Baerga and Albert Belle), the Cardinals (with Todd Zeile, Felix Jose and Pedro Guerrero, when healthy), and the Astros (with the developing Jeff Bagwell, Luis Gonzalez and Ken Caminiti) weren't all that bad. It makes more sense to pick a club which plays in the American League, in a super hitters' park, and which still has a popgun attack. Yes, we mean . . .

Toronto. How can you play in SkyDome, begin your attack with Devon White, Roberto Alomar and Joe Carter — and yet still rank eleventh in the American League in runs scored? The Blue Jays managed to do that, and we don't think "character" had anything to do with it. Nothing wrong with Carter, but Kelly Gruber had a weak, injury-riddled season last year, and John Olerud has yet to prove himself as a power hitter. Maybe the Blue Jays should spend less time looking in the mirror, and more time looking at ways to improve their power slots.

A complete listing for this category can be found on page 268.

WHO WENT TO THE MOON IN 1991?

If there were no baseball statistics, just stories about players passed down in verse by roving troubadours, the song of 1991 might well have been the "Saga of Jeff Buhner." During the Mariners' East Coast road trip last July, Buhner crushed a ball off Jay Ballard in Baltimore that was estimated — conservatively — at 460 feet. Buhner was just warming up. Five days later, in Yankee Stadium, Buhner crushed a pitch from Wade Taylor which bounced off the Ruth, Gehrig and Huggins monuments, soared out of the Stadium, clanged off both roofs of the World Trade Center, knocked off part of the crown from the Statue of Liberty and wound up on the deck of a schooner steaming for Cadiz. Well, we're exaggerating a little, but not as much as the New York media did. It was a shot.

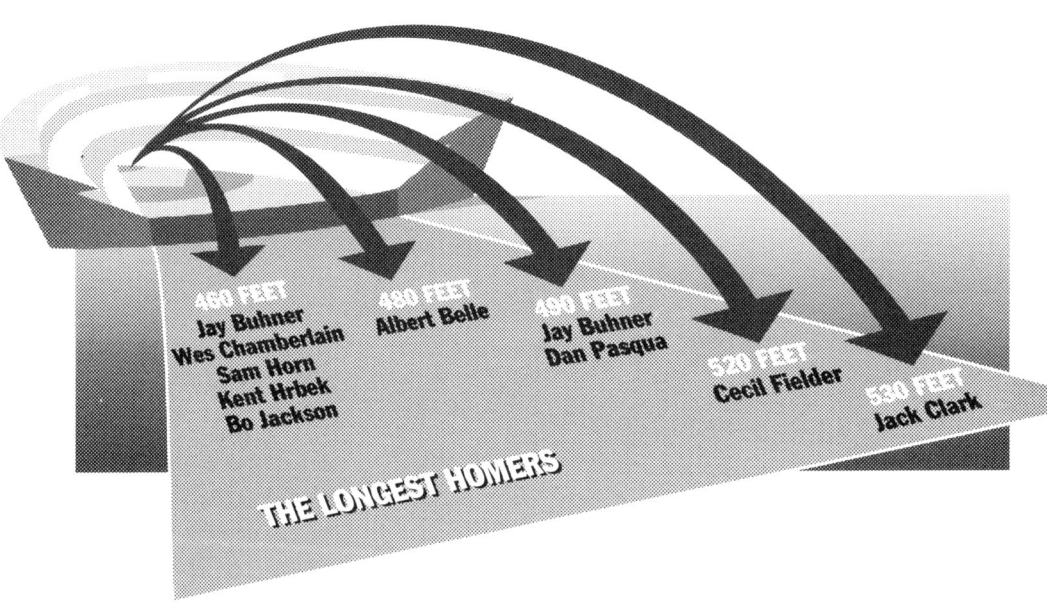

This — our estimate of the longest home runs of 1991 — is strictly for fun. We try to be as exact as possible in our measurements, but cheerily admit that there's some degree of subjectivity involved. I was in Comiskey Park last April when Dan Pasqua hit his mighty right field shot off Eric Plunk of the Yankees (or was it a mighty plunk?), one estimated by the White Sox at 488 feet. I was also in Comiskey in July, when Jack Clark of Boston went to the left field stratosphere against Chicago's Greg Hibbard. Each homer mightily frightened fans lined up at the respective outfield concession stands, but the consensus in the press box was that Clark's went a little farther. Nonetheless the White Sox/IBM estimate of Clark's homer was 420 feet, nearly 70 feet less than Pasqua's. I will say this: both shots were creamed.

Clark wasn't complete short-changed, however; we credit him with the longest homer of 1991, a 530-foot poke at Fenway off the Tigers' Walt Terrell. Even so, the Mr. Longball award would probably have to go to Buhner for his two mighty wallops; Fielder was the only other play with two 450-foot homers. Eat your heart out, Jack.

For the record, we estimate a total of 19 home runs that travelled at least 450 feet, a considerable decline from 1990 when the figure was 32. This is probably a pretty good estimate. Home run production was down in the National League last year, but up in the American. And nine of our ten 460-foot-or-more homers were belted in the American League.

A complete listing for this category can be found on page 269.

WHY SHOULD YOU TAKE A SECOND(ARY) LOOK AT ROB DEER?

A few years ago, Bill James invented the concept of "secondary average." Bear with us if you know about it, but Bill's idea was to create a batting average-like figure to reflect contributions the traditional batting average doesn't reveal — namely walks, extra-base hits and stolen bases.

As usual, Bill knew what he was doing. What secondary average does, very beautifully, is to identify some unsung heroes. Jack Clark, for example, a low average hitter who hits with great power and draws a lot of walks, comes to the fore in secondary average. So does Rickey Henderson, with his great speed, excellent power and superior ability to reach base. The 1991 secondary average leaders — Barry Bonds and Frank Thomas — can't really be considered "unsung heroes," except maybe by some of the MVP voters. But a few others could well be considered in that category. Here is the top ten (minimum 250 plate appearances):

Player, Team	Secondary Average
Barry Bonds, Pit	.490
Frank Thomas, WSox	.479
Jose Canseco, Oak	.462
Rickey Henderson, Oak	.449
Howard Johnson, Mets	.440
Mickey Tettleton, Det	.429
Fred McGriff, SD	.420
Danny Tartabull, KC	.417
Jack Clark, Bos	.412
Lou Whitaker, Det	.406

A typical secondary average star might be Mickey Tettleton. The Mick batted only .263 last year, and he struck out 131 times. But he had 31 homers, and he drew 101 walks. The primary average gives no clue to his true value; the secondary average does, and that's what it was meant to do.

An even better case is a player who just missed the top ten in secondary average — Tettleton's Detroit teammate, Rob Deer. In the course of one of the more unique seasons in major league history, Deer batted .179 last year, the lowest average ever for a hitter with at least 400 at-bats in a season. He also struck out 175 times, which made him the butt of even more jokes. But take a look at his other numbers. Deer belted 25 homers in those 448 at-bats, and he drew 89 walks. Both his on-base percentage (.314) and slugging average (.386) were only a little below the league average. When we say that Deer had a .402 secondary average, we're not implying he had a great, or even a good year. No one has a good year batting .179. What the secondary average points out is that he had considerable value the primary average never indicated.

As we say, secondary average paints a more complete picture of a player's offensive contributions. It works for Deer, and also, in the opposite sense, for someone like Ozzie Guillen. Guillen usually hits for a decent batting average (.273 last year). But with no power, hardly any walks and a stolen base record that works against his team (21 for 36 in 1991), the primary average ridiculously overrates his offensive contributions. Secondary average puts him in his place — Guillen, as usual, ranked among the worst last year, along with the familiar group of light-hitting middle infielders and catchers:

Player, Team	Secondary Average
Mike Bordick, Oak	.085
Alfredo Griffin, LA	.094
Bill Ripken, Bal	.094
Ozzie Guillen, WSox	.099
Mark Lewis, Cle	.102
Joel Skinner, Cle	.102

To make the point once more, secondary average is a tool to be used along-side of, not in place of, batting average. Guillen's batting average is worth something to his team . . . but so is Deer's power and ability to draw walks, which is the point of the whole exercise.

Formula for Secondary Average:

Secondary Average = (2B + 3Bx2 + HRx3 + BB + SB - CS)/ AB

The major league secondary average last year was .238 (.242 for non-pitchers).

A complete listing for this category appears on page 270.

WHO ARE THE "HUMAN AIR CONDITIONERS"?

What a consistent ballplayer that Cecil Fielder is. For two straight years Cecil has won a little-noted (except by us) "triple crown:" he's led the American League in home runs, runs batted in . . . and swings-and-misses. Let's see, there were 51 dingers, 132 ribbies and 465 missed swings in 1990. In 1991, Fielder came through with 44 HR, 133 RBI and 438 swings-and-misses. The Tigers will gladly accept the overall results, and Detroit might consider the following advertising campaign: Come See Cecil — Baseball's Leading Practitioner of S&M!

All kidding aside, the chart shows that swinging-and-missing is no disgrace — as long as you can produce when you do connect. The three leaders in total swings and misses were Fielder, Matt Williams and Jose Canseco, and you won't find three better power hitters in baseball. They pay on the basis of results, and there's no reason for these three to change their style. As for Rob Deer, well at least he's helping Cecil keep Tiger Stadium cool.

A purer way of evaluating the swing-and-miss kings is on a percentage basis. Looked at this way, the undisputed champion is another Tiger, Pete Incaviglia, who was also the 1990 percentage champion:

Highest % of Swings that Missed — 1991

Batter	Swung	Missed	Percent
Pete Incaviglia, Det	683	250	36.6
Sammy Sosa, WSox	698	249	35.7
Andujar Cedeno, Hou	554	196	35.4
Rob Deer, Det	1012	351	34.9
Sam Horn, Bal	705	244	34.6
Hensley Meulens, Yanks	570	194	34.0
Dean Palmer, Tex	584	191	32.7
Jesse Barfield, Yanks	593	189	31.9
Cecil Fielder, Det	1375	438	31.9
Danny Tartabull, KC	1001	319	31.9

(Minimum 500 pitches swung at)

Like we said, they pay on the basis of results, but unfortunately there aren't a lot of them among this group . . . not until you get down to Fielder and Danny Tartabull. You can see some troubled young hitters here — Andujar Cedeno, Hensley Meulens, Dean Palmer and Sammy Sosa, a repeater in the top five from 1990. Let's get real here. If you're going to hit 30-plus homers a year, as Fielder, Canseco and Williams do, it's acceptable to swing from the heels as often as you'd like. The same thinking doesn't apply at all to Sosa, who'd amaze everyone if he walloped 25. The jury is still out on the promising, young Cedeno (nine

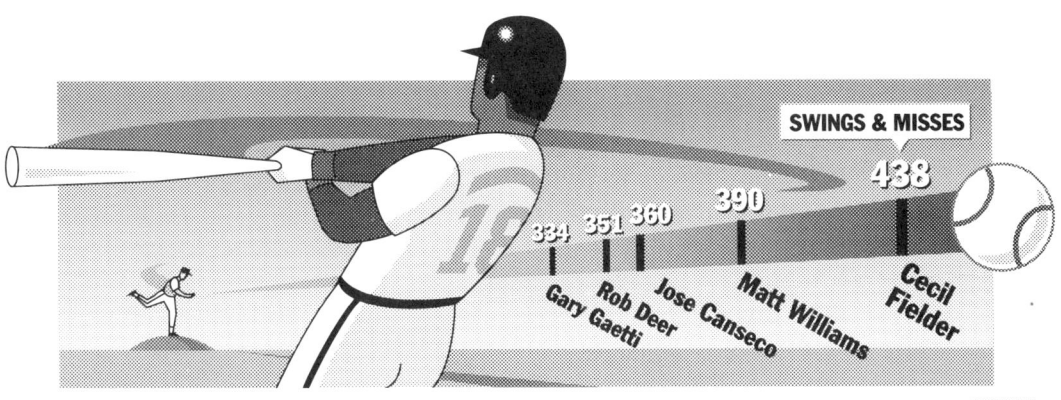

HRs in 251 AstroDome at-bats last year), but it might be past time for the rest of that group to consider cutting down on their swings.

On the other hand, as Randy Travis puts it, there's a golden band: the guys who don't intend to swing at a pitch unless they're going to hit it. These fellows mean exactly that:

Lowest % of Swings that Missed — 1991

Batter	Swung	Missed	Percent
Wade Boggs, Bos	892	45	5.0
Felix Fermin, Cle	732	49	6.7
Tony Gwynn, SD	844	58	6.9
Chuck Knoblauch, Min	888	68	7.7
Jody Reed, Bos	1010	80	7.9
Luis Sojo, Cal	636	52	8.2
B.J. Surhoff, Mil	774	65	8.4
Don Mattingly, Yanks	908	77	8.5
Ozzie Smith, StL	937	82	8.8
Dave Magadan, Mets	732	66	9.0

Wade Boggs, who actually swung and missed 84 times while suffering through a lowly .302 season in 1990, must have spent the winter cleaning up his act. On the whole, you could say there's more Judy than Punch among this group . . . at least when you compare it with Fielder, Canseco and company. But if you think we're going to criticize Boggs and Tony Gwynn, think again.

Don Mattingly, if your back is okay, maybe you could try swinging a bit harder.

A complete listing for this category can be found on page 271.

WHAT KIND OF HITTERS HAVE BIG PLATOON DIFFERENTIALS?

It's well-known that hitters generally perform better against opposite-hand pitchers — right-handed hitters hit lefties better, left-handed hitters hit righties better. Some players have really extreme biases, however . . . 75 points or more difference in their left/right splits. What kind of hitters produce such extreme platoon differentials? The natural tendency would be to think this is a severe sign of weakness, the province of part-time performers. A really good hitter, you'd suppose, wouldn't bat 85 points lower against one kind of pitching.

Let's see what the evidence shows. Because one year's worth of left/right data is based on a pretty limited number of at-bats, we'll use figures for the last three seasons (1989-91). Here are the players with the biggest bias toward lefthanders (minimum 750 plate appearances):

Biggest Bias Toward Lefites (1989-91)

| Player | vs. LHP | | | | vs. RHP | | | | BA |
	Avg	Slg	AB	HR	Avg	Slg	AB	HR	Diff
Mariano Duncan	.349	.536	427	11	.224	.346	599	14	125
Jack Clark	.323	.542	356	19	.223	.457	914	60	100
Frank Thomas	.386	.656	241	16	.291	.495	509	23	95
Cecil Fielder	.335	.733	337	38	.243	.479	860	57	92
Joe Oliver	.278	.445	108	14	.190	.299	395	8	88
Dave Henderson	.328	.556	448	24	.241	.388	1153	36	87
Greg Olson	.303	.461	254	7	.221	.304	101	6	82
Bob Melvin	.286	.388	381	4	.207	.254	426	3	79
Carlos Quintana	.336	.461	369	8	.258	.350	698	10	78
Chris Sabo	.331	.552	507	23	.253	.427	946	34	78

Weak hitters? Oh yeah — Jack Clark, Frank Thomas, Cecil Fielder, Dave Henderson, Carlos Quintana, Chris Sabo. More like an All-Star team, we'd say. Most of these guys absolutely murder lefties, and have a range of skills against righties; Thomas, however, was the only one who could top the .260 mark against right-handed pitching. If Cecil Fielder faced only righthanders, he'd still be a fine slugger. What makes him an exceptional one is the way he creams lefties.

The second group of hitters represents the opposite extreme — much better versus righties:

Biggest Bias Toward Righties (1989-91)

Player	vs. LHP				vs. RHP				BA
	Avg	Slg	AB	HR	Avg	Slg	AB	HR	Diff
Hal Morris	.239	.311	180	1	.350	.531	625	20	−111
Brady Anderson	.138	.211	152	1	.243	.341	604	8	−105
Jack Howell	.145	.216	227	2	.245	.428	804	34	−100
Dave Bergman	.183	.237	93	0	.274	.392	691	16	−91
Scott Bradley	.160	.180	50	0	.245	.314	153	4	−85
Paul O'Neill	.211	.336	464	10	.292	.504	999	49	−81
Lou Whitaker	.197	.319	345	9	.274	.495	1106	60	−77
Terry Kennedy	.185	.284	81	1	.259	.350	748	9	−74
Steve Lyons	.183	.237	131	1	.257	.348	670	6	−74
Dwight Smith	.214	.357	70	2	.288	.426	730	16	−74

There are some fine hitters in this group as well — Hal Morris, Paul O'Neill, Lou Whitaker. But overall it's a decidedly inferior list of players; most of them, in fact, have been reduced to part-time duty. Though the left/right splits are similar in terms of total point differential, the numbers are really quite different. Except for Morris (the only one over .300), no one in this group clobbers righties the way the first group belts lefties; and most of them are pretty pathetic vs. southpaws (seven of them below .200).

There is an explanation for this, a kind of built-in mathematical bias. Most pitchers are right-handed, and hitters who can't bat .200 against righties end up logging fewer total at-bats than hitters who are below .200 vs. lefties. That eliminates a lot of poor hitters who lacked the plate appearances to qualify for the first group. In addition, it's easier to hit .330 over 300 at-bats (the first group vs. lefties), than it is to maintain that figure over 600 AB or more (the second group vs. righties). So lower averages from the second group could be predicted.

That said, it's obvious from the study that even very good hitters can have severe platoon differentials. Who wouldn't want Jack Clark or Hal Morris swinging the bat for them?

A complete listing for this category can be found on page 273.

WHY DON'T MORE CLUBS PLATOON?

Platooning, we suggested a year ago, seems to be out of fashion these days. Nothing that happened in 1991 changed that observation. Less than a dozen legitimate left/right platoons were in operation last year, and most of them were used for only part of the season. We're as surprised by that as ever. Almost every club has several combinations of a lefty swinger who hits much better against righthanders, a right-handed hitter who does better against southpaws. As Earl Weaver used to point out, platooning not only can make a weak position strong, but can also keep the bench players strong by giving them frequent action.

We found a half dozen 1991 platoons which functioned very well. We think it's significant that all six of them came from clubs which won at least 90 games: the Pirates, the Braves, the Dodgers and the Twins. The figures listed are the players' stats (against both lefties and righties) when playing that position only.

Pittsburgh Pirates — C	AB	H	HR	RBI	Avg
Mike LaValliere	333	97	3	40	.291
Don Slaught	206	63	1	26	.306

This platoon, effective in 1990, was even better in '91. It's a natural; LaValliere, the better defensive player, has always had problems with lefties, and platooning him with the good-hitting Slaught keeps both catchers fresh. As we stated last year, catcher is the position where managers are most likely to platoon. Since few receivers are capable of catching every day, that makes perfect sense.

Atlanta Braves — 1B	AB	H	HR	RBI	Avg
Sid Bream	256	62	9	42	.242
Brian Hunter	249	64	11	46	.257

This is a classic old-style platoon, the type you'd think would be used a lot more often. Bream, a veteran lefty swinger, hit .271 vs. righties last year, only .150 (6 for 40) against lefties. Alternating him with the rookie Hunter gave the youngster experience in situations where he was more likely to be successful. When Bream got hurt, Hunter got everyday work. He didn't do badly, but he still hit 40 points higher against lefties.

Atlanta Braves — 2B	AB	H	HR	RBI	Avg
Jeff Treadway	292	94	3	32	.322
Jeff Blauser	89	29	5	28	.326

Atlanta manager Bobby Cox is one of the few who still takes advantage of platooning. As the stats indicate, this one worked beautifully from an offensive standpoint. The weakness is that neither of the Jeffs is a good glove man, and Cox eventually turned to Mark Lemke, not as good a hitter but much stronger afield. You can expect both Treadway and Blauser to get a lot of action this year, however; they both hit too well to sit on the bench. Blauser also has the advantage of being able to play other positions.

Minnesota Twins — 3B	AB	H	HR	RBI	Avg
Mike Pagliarulo	359	101	6	36	.281
Scott Leius	151	43	5	18	.285

Any doubts about the effectiveness of this platoon should have disappeared in the postseason, when both Pagliarulo and Leius came through with key home runs. Again it's a case of a veteran lefty swinger platooning with a young righty — often the ideal way to get the best out of both.

Los Angeles Dodgers — 3B	AB	H	HR	RBI	Avg
Lenny Harris	313	88	2	27	.281
Mike Sharperson	150	45	2	13	.300

This platoon has functioned well for two years, giving the Dodgers adequate defense and high-average hitting at a position where they had a gaping hole. The knock against it is that both Harris and Sharperson lack power. The Dodgers may try someone new at the position for that reason, but they have this reliable duo to fall back on.

Los Angeles Dodgers — C	AB	H	HR	RBI	Avg
Mike Scioscia	337	88	8	38	.261
Gary Carter	204	16	6	23	.265

Another natural platoon, this one of two veteran receivers. Carter has moved on to the Expos, but there's little doubt that Tom Lasorda will find another mate for Scioscia, who has been platooned virtually his entire career.

SHOULD KEVIN McREYNOLDS BE KNOWN AS "MR. AVERAGE"?

You might not be aware of this, but every winter in baseball, they give two State of the Union speeches. This year American League President Dr. Bobby Brown (he spoke first; his guys won the Series) was simply glowing as he spoke of his league's prowess. "The great American League has advanced to the point where Harold Reynolds — the great Harold Reynolds! — is now merely an average performer. Not to mention so fine an American as Brian Downing." The applause was deafening. Things were a little more subdued as NL President Bill White took the podium. With a wistful look in his eye (some said visions of Dan Gladden were dancing in his head), White went right to the heart of the matter. "We're going to miss Kevin," was all he said. He did not elaborate, but everyone knew what he meant.

We give this speech every year as well: in baseball, everything has to be put in context. It's such a simple point that you'd think people would grasp it without thinking, but even the Hall of Fame voters don't quite get it. A Nellie Fox, the dominant player at his position for over a decade, needs to depend on the kindness of the Veterans Committee to get in — he didn't have the offensive numbers of those outfielders who always sail in. Meanwhile, Fred Lindstrom, a .300 hitter in an era when that was only a little above average, has been in the Hall for years. Hey, he hit .300!

So this is a sort of consumers guide — what the average numbers were at each major league position last year. To give you some context, we also list the players whose figures were closest to the average:

1991 American League (per 600 PA)

Pos	Avg	OBP	Slg	HR	RBI	Most Typical Performer
C	.252	.307	.374	12	67	Chris Hoiles
1B	.264	.344	.417	17	75	Randy Milligan
2B	.268	.338	.365	6	52	Harold Reynolds
3B	.259	.327	.387	13	60	Mike Pagliarulo
SS	.255	.310	.352	7	56	Luis Rivera
LF	.261	.330	.398	14	68	Candy Maldonado
CF	.272	.332	.405	12	61	Mike Devereaux
RF	.258	.325	.436	20	78	Dan Pasqua
DH	.257	.345	.424	19	73	Brian Downing

1991 National League (per 600 PA)

Pos	Avg	OBP	Slg	HR	RBI	Most Typical Performer
C	.244	.305	.353	10	61	Greg Olson
1B	.267	.341	.411	15	74	Eddie Murray
2B	.258	.334	.371	10	54	Juan Samuel
3B	.264	.324	.408	15	70	Ken Caminiti
SS	.256	.314	.361	8	50	Dickie Thon
LF	.260	.330	.409	16	72	Kevin McReynolds
CF	.259	.330	.377	10	48	Ray Lankford
RF	.268	.335	.423	16	74	Dale Murphy
P	.138	.178	.167	2	27	

Some of these names are a little shocking . . . Eddie Murray, an average performer? Well, with 19 homers and 96 RBI, Murray was well above the norm, but his other figures (lowered due to a rib injury) were in fact a little below the NL average at his position. The decline of Juan Samuel and Dale Murphy should not be so surprising; they have not performed at their peak levels for several years.

Mr. Average: We've been keeping these figures for three seasons now, and some names keep showing up again and again. Mike Devereux, Harold Reynolds, Ken Caminiti and Dickie Thon are all two-time "most typical" honorees. Well, when you hit .260 every year, that'll happen.

The true master, however, and the man who brought a tear to President White's eye was Kevin McReynolds. Three years in a row, his numbers have been closer than anyone's to the average National League left fielder. Last year he outdid himself. The typical NL left fielder hit .260, slugged .409 and had a .330 on-base percentage with 16 homers and 74 RBI. Kevin's 1991 numbers: .259 Avg, .416 Slg, .322 OBP, 16 HR, 72 RBI. Now that he's in Kansas City, how will National League left fielders know how to perform?

A complete listing for this category can be found on page 274.

WHAT'S AN AVERAGE LINEUP (1991 VERSION)?

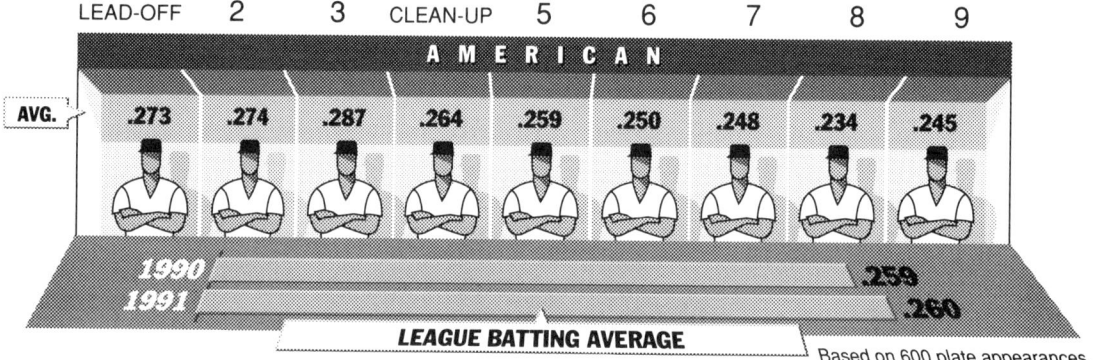

A useful way to measure average major league production is by batting order position. If your club's "nifty leadoff man" finishes the season with 68 runs scored and a .310 on-base average — sounds like Dan Gladden every year — the team is giving away runs at the top of the order. (Yeah, we know, you can't measure "heart." We're working on it.) On the other hand, if your cleanup hitter is a legitimate 30-homer, 100-RBI guy, your production at that spot is well above average.

Here's how each lineup spot performed, by leagues, in 1991:

1991 American League — Batting by Lineup Position per 600 Plate Appearances

	Avg	AB	H	HR	RBI	BB	K	SB
Batting #1	.273	528	144	10	48	60	77	24
Batting #2	.274	533	146	10	62	52	68	13
Batting #3	.287	532	153	18	82	55	78	10
Batting #4	.264	527	139	22	88	62	100	5
Batting #5	.259	532	138	18	77	57	95	6
Batting #6	.250	537	134	16	70	52	102	6
Batting #7	.248	539	134	13	64	47	103	7
Batting #8	.234	538	126	8	53	45	94	6
Batting #9	.245	536	131	5	50	44	88	13

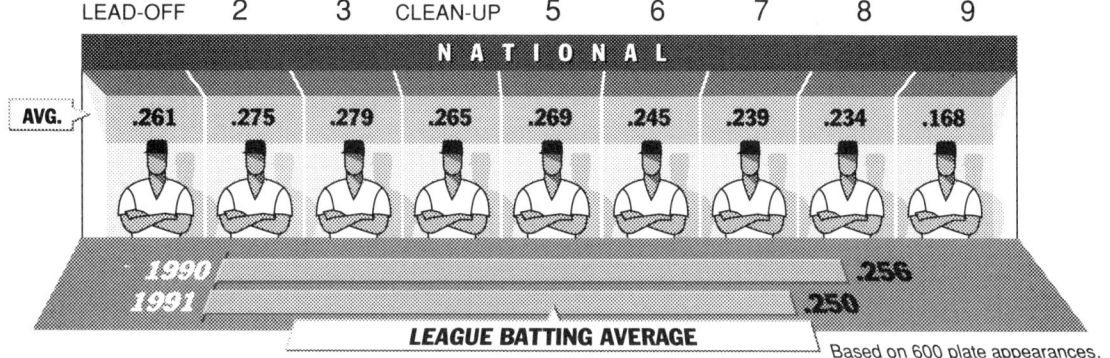

Based on 600 plate appearances.

1991 National League — Batting by Lineup Position per 600 Plate Appearances

	Avg	AB	H	HR	RBI	BB	K	SB
Batting #1	.261	535	140	7	40	57	84	32
Batting #2	.275	532	146	8	52	53	75	19
Batting #3	.279	532	149	15	77	56	80	16
Batting #4	.265	529	140	22	88	60	92	9
Batting #5	.269	536	144	18	84	54	93	12
Batting #6	.245	542	133	14	62	47	93	11
Batting #7	.239	540	129	9	59	47	94	8
Batting #8	.234	538	126	6	48	49	86	6
Batting #9	.168	523	88	4	35	35	154	3

When we examined this subject last year, we noted the surge in offensive production in the National League. The league batting average rose ten points from 1989 to 1990, with a surge in power as well. Except for pitchers' hitting, the NL outproduced the AL offensively in 1990; for each of the first four batting order slots, the Senior Circuit was superior.

That trend did not continue in 1991. Scoring was down in both leagues last year, but particularly in the National; in addition, the NL league batting average dropped six points. Comparing the leagues by batting order position, the only slot where the NL had an edge last year was the number five position. By the time the World Series ended, talk about "National League superiority," so prevalent in 1990, had pretty much disappeared.

Other batting order notes:

1. The National League remains the stolen base league. For each of the first seven batting order slots, the NL stole more bases — 25 percent more at the crucial number one spot.

2. The American League is striking out more, particularly in the power slots. Except for the NL's number nine hitters, the only batting spot to average more than 100 strikeouts in 1990 was the American League at the number four position. But in '91 American League hitters were over the century mark at three different spots in the order — fourth, sixth and seventh. Is this some sort of Fielder-induced fad?

3. The power spot, of course, is the cleanup spot. But in keeping with baseball tradition, the best overall offensive performer hits third. We don't know exactly why this is, but we do like Bobby Bragan's explanation of why he moved Henry Aaron to the third spot: "I want to make sure my best hitter comes up in the first inning."

4. As we noted last year, all this whining about how hard it is to bat eighth in a National League lineup just seems like a crock. American League number-eight hitters are about as unproductive as the National Leaguers are. It's not that those National Leaguers can't hit because they're batting eighth; they're batting eighth because they can't hit.

A complete listing for this category can be found on page 275.

CAN AGGRESSIVE BASERUNNING HELP WIN CHAMPIONSHIPS?

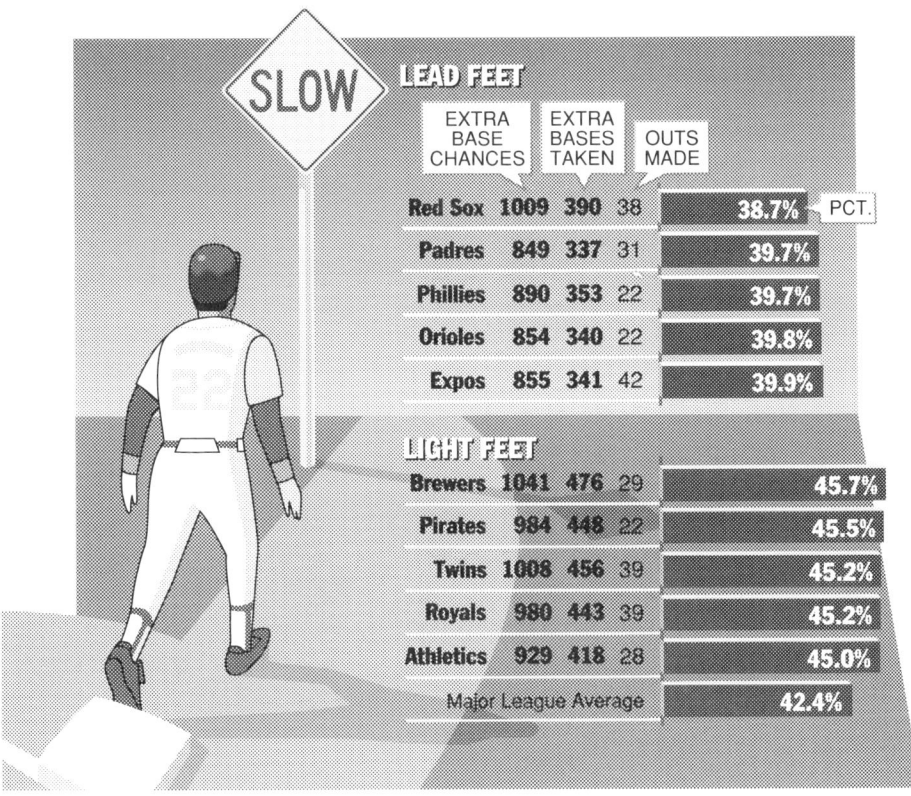

The 1991 World Series might never have ended were it not for the Twins' Dan Gladden. Leading off the bottom of the tenth inning of Game Seven, Gladden aggressively legged out a double on a medium-range outfield gapper. Two batters later, he was crossing home plate with the run that meant the world championship.

Anyone who watched the Series knows that Gladden's take-the-extra-base style was typical of both the Twins and Braves; in fact, risk-taking was one of the factors that made the contests so exciting. Did the clubs show that same kind of aggressiveness during the season? We keep track of how often each club's baserunners, given the opportunity, take an extra base.

We can't measure the aggressiveness of batters (like Gladden) who stretch singles into doubles, but the data gives a very good picture of which teams like to take chances. Here's how the teams ranked in 1991; we include the number of times their runners were thrown out, an important factor:

Team	Extra Base Chances	Extra Bases Taken	Extra Base Pct	Outs
American League				
Milwaukee	1,041	476	45.7	29
Minnesota	1,008	456	45.2	39
Kansas City	980	443	45.2	39
Oakland	929	418	45.0	28
Seattle	951	420	44.2	30
Chicago	945	415	43.9	29
Detroit	832	355	42.7	28
Texas	988	421	42.6	28
New York	911	386	42.4	36
Toronto	916	387	42.2	38
Cleveland	941	392	41.7	39
California	945	379	40.1	33
Baltimore	854	340	39.8	22
Boston	1,009	390	38.7	38
AL Total	13,250	5,678	42.9	456
National League				
Pittsburgh	984	448	45.5	22
Atlanta	958	429	44.8	42
Chicago	872	381	43.7	28
Los Angeles	910	386	42.4	45
New York	877	365	41.6	33
Houston	904	373	41.3	38
San Francisco	828	339	40.9	28
Cincinnati	871	353	40.5	30
St. Louis	979	396	40.4	36
Montreal	855	341	39.9	42
Philadelphia	890	353	39.7	22
San Diego	849	337	39.7	31
NL Total	10,777	4,501	41.8	397

You're probably impressed, as we were, that the champion Twins had the second-best extra-base percentage in the American League, and that the two top National League clubs were the division-winning Pirates and Braves. More important than where the Twins and Braves ranked, however, was how much they improved. The Braves were the **least** aggressive team in the National League in 1990, while the Twins ranked tenth in the American. The improvement on the bases obviously didn't win the pennant for either club, but it seems fairly certain that it helped.

Ballparks play a factor in how aggressive a club is, of course, as does the club's personnel. Playing at Fenway would keep any club from taking many chances on the bases; the sluggish Red Sox, thrown out nine times more than the Brewers while taking 86 fewer bases, have reason to be cautious. But one would think that the Orioles and especially the Phillies, ranking near the bottom of their leagues in percentage while being tossed out only 22 times each, could afford to take more chances. Underscoring this is the fact that the Phils, who had the highest stolen base percentage in the National League (.754), were dead last in steals with 92. There's no excuse for that, not even the loss of Lenny Dykstra.

The best club on the bases had to be the Pirates, who had the second best extra-base percentage in the majors (45.5), were thrown out only 22 times (tying Baltimore and Philadelphia for the lowest total), and had a .729 stolen base percentage, second only to the Phils.

DOES PATIENCE LEAD TO SLUGGING?

By taking pitches and fouling off offerings they don't like, hitters exert a lot of control over how long a plate appearance will last. A Rickey Henderson is notorious for stretching things out; he'll take a walk if he can get it. An Ozzie Guillen, on the other hand, can't ever stop swinging the bat. Which hitters use the most pitches per plate appearances? It's a group with a mixture of skills:

1991 Leaders — Pitches Seen per Plate Appearance

Player, Team	Plate Appearances	Pitches Seen	Pitches per PA
Rickey Henderson, Oak	578	2,511	4.34
Frank Thomas, WSox	701	3,018	4.31
Gary Pettis, Tex	343	1,460	4.26
Jack Clark, Bos	587	2,502	4.26
Rob Deer, Det	539	2,294	4.26
Delino DeShields, Mon	673	2,856	4.24
Orlando Merced, Pit	478	2,021	4.23
Jesse Barfield, Yanks	321	1,352	4.21
Brian Downing, Tex	476	2,006	4.21
Brett Butler, LA	730	3,066	4.20

(Minimum 250 plate appearances)

There are several leadoff men here: Henderson, Pettis, DeShields, Merced, Downing (who batted leadoff at least some of the time), Butler. It would figure that a good leadoff man would look at a lot of pitches. But there are also some power hitters on the list: Thomas, Clark, Deer, Barfield, Downing, Henderson. These hitters look for a pitch to drive, and will also take a walk if need be. All in all, it's a very impressive group of hitters.

Not so impressive is the opposite group, the players who used the fewest pitches per PA last year:

1991 Trailers — Pitches Seen per Plate Appearance

Player, Team	Plate Appearances	Pitches Seen	Pitches per PA
Ozzie Guillen, WSox	555	1,581	2.85
Alvaro Espinoza, Yanks	509	1,496	2.94
Dickie Thon, Phi	570	1,687	2.96
Jim Gantner, Mil	567	1,703	3.00
Mike Greenwell, Bos	598	1,796	3.00
Brook Jacoby, Cle-Oak	453	1,376	3.04
Lance Johnson, WSox	624	1,919	3.08
Ricky Jordan, Phi	322	994	3.09
Rafael Belliard, Atl	385	1,193	3.10
Bill Ripken, Bal	315	981	3.11

Middle infielders predominate here, along with an occasional Greenwell or Jordan — some power there, but not like the first group. Would these guys hit better with a little more patience? It's tough for a hitter to change his style — indeed that's often a sign of desperation — but it's clear that lack of selectivity has really hampered many of the members of this group.

How do the great sluggers rate in this category? Here are the figures for the 12 players who hit 30 or more homers last year. Keep in mind that the average hitter last year used 3.65 pitches/PA:

Player, Team	HR	Pitches per PA
Jose Canseco, Oak	44	3.97
Cecil Fielder, Det	44	3.75
Howard Johnson, Mets	38	3.78
Cal Ripken, Bal	34	3.31
Matt Williams, SF	34	3.39
Joe Carter, Tor	33	3.69
Ron Gant, Atl	32	3.76
Frank Thomas, WSox	32	4.31
Andre Dawson, Cubs	31	3.49
Fred McGriff, SD	31	3.88
Danny Tartabull, KC	31	3.93
Mickey Tettleton, Det	31	4.15

Nine of the 12 hitters were above-average in pitches per plate appearance, and most were well above-average. The only exceptions were Ripken, Williams and Dawson. Once again, it seems pretty obvious that patient hitting pays off.

A complete listing for this category can be found on page 276.

IS PATIENCE A VIRTUE?

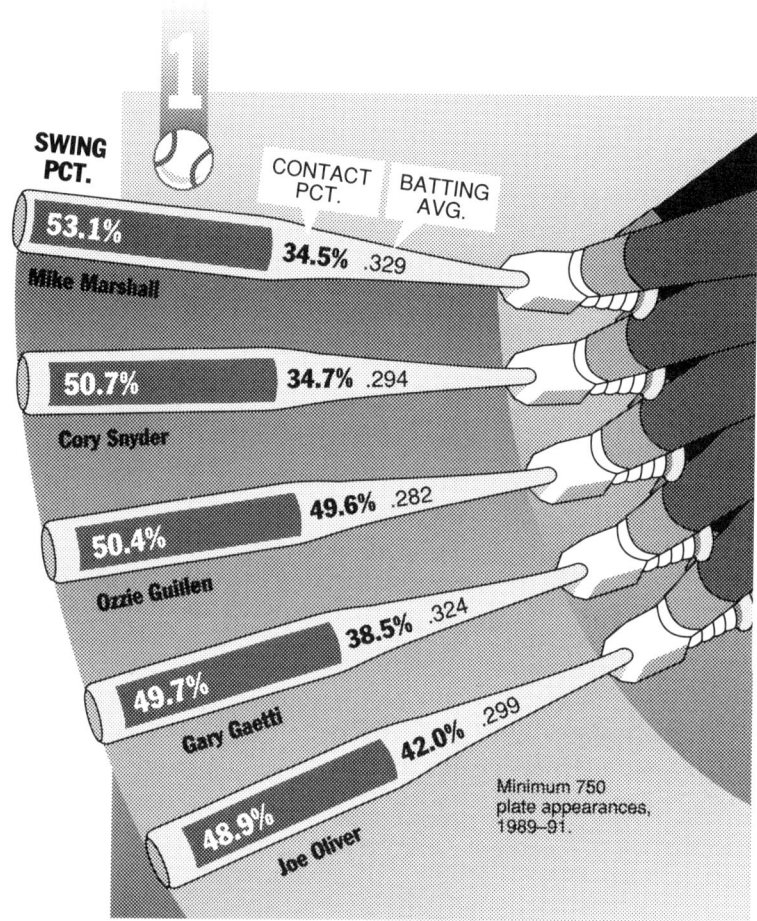

Imagine you're at your high school sock hop, waiting with your buddies for the girls to come out of the ladies room. Your friend Mike, who's known as a "real swinger," can't control himself — he wants to grab the first woman who shows her face. "The first one who comes out is usually pretty good," he says. "Who knows if we'll find anything better?" But your other buddy Wade — he's so cool — just sneers and says, "Let's look over a few. We'll probably find a better one that way . . . and if we don't, it's a nice night for a walk." They both sound pretty convincing. What's a fellow to do?

Regardless of their exploits with women, over the past three seasons, Wade Boggs and the now-departed Mike Marshall represented opposite philosophies when it came to hitting major league pitchers. Marshall loved to swing at the first offering, jumping on it over half the time. Boggs almost always let it go by, swinging at the first pitch in only six percent of his plate appearances.

Is going after the first pitch good strategy? There's a certain logic which would indicate that it is. The pitcher is probably trying to throw a strike, and the chances of getting a fastball are excellent. Indeed, major league hitters bat over .300, with good power, when they put the first pitch in play. But there are negatives as well. It's true that you might get a good pitch; but if you wait and can work the count in your favor, you might get an even better one. And when you swing at the first pitch, you're sacrificing the chance to draw a walk. If you swing and miss or foul the pitch off, you're behind in the count.

If first-pitch swinging is smart strategy, one would expect to find a lot of great hitters doing it. Let's see some results. Here is the top ten in first-pitch swinging over the last three seasons (750 plate appearances):

Swinging at the First Pitch — 1989-91 (Active in 1991)

Name	First Pitches	Swung	Swing %	When First Pitch in Play				
				Avg	Slg	AB	H	HR
Mike Marshall	774	411	53.1	.329	.493	140	46	4
Cory Snyder	1,163	590	50.7	.294	.467	197	58	8
Ozzie Guillen	1,785	899	50.4	.282	.364	412	116	3
Gary Gaetti	1,802	896	49.7	.324	.503	330	107	14
Joe Oliver	832	407	48.9	.299	.473	167	50	6
Alvaro Espinoza	1,526	729	47.8	.305	.382	361	110	2
Matt Williams	1,607	768	47.8	.319	.559	279	89	15
Bo Jackson	1,123	529	47.1	.345	.761	142	49	17
Kirby Puckett	1,933	906	46.9	.367	.529	444	163	11
Don Slaught	890	415	46.6	.357	.538	182	65	4

Are there solid major league hitters in the group? Yes — Matt Williams and Kirby Puckett are outstanding, and Slaught is pretty good. And there's Bo, who when last healthy, hit .272 and slugged .523 for the 1990 Royals. On the other hand, check out the faded careers: Gary Gaetti, Joe Oliver, Cory Snyder, and of course Marshall, who will spend 1992 swinging at the first offerings of Japanese League hurlers. (We understand there's no truth to the rumor that Marshall swings at the first pitch so he can get back to the disabled list more quickly).

Did swinging at the first pitch pay off? No doubt it paid handsome dividends for Puckett, Slaught and Jackson, and produced good results for

Williams and Gaetti . . . when they succeeded in putting the first pitch in play. That happened less than half the time for everyone except Espinoza, who got 53.1% of his first-pitch swings into play. On the other hand, Jackson swung at 529 first pitches, but only 27.4 percent of those swings resulted with the ball in play. The rest of the time, of course, it was strike one.

Even when the hitters did get the first offering into play, their batting average was also their on-base percentage. Thus the overall results are a lot less than they seem at first glance. Would Joe Oliver be a better hitter if he tried to work the count a little more? We'll never know unless he tries.

Now look at the players who swung at the first pitch **least** often:

Swinging at the First Pitch — 1989-91 (Active in 1991)

Name	First Pitches	Swung	Swing %	When First Pitch in Play				
				Avg	Slg	AB	H	HR
Wade Boggs	2,050	123	6.0	.369	.508	65	24	0
Randy Ready	809	75	9.3	.333	.400	30	10	0
Rickey Henderson	1,968	218	11.1	.258	.472	89	23	5
Brian Downing	1,447	171	11.8	.360	.640	75	27	5
Alvin Davis	1,697	209	12.3	.294	.471	102	30	4
Don Mattingly	1,712	226	13.2	.336	.493	134	45	3
Frank Thomas	912	128	14.0	.518	.750	56	29	3
Edgar Martinez	1,379	194	14.1	.322	.437	87	28	1
Jody Reed	2,006	318	15.9	.314	.497	153	48	4
Barry Larkin	1,571	255	16.2	.321	.455	134	43	3

Wade Boggs, Rickey Henderson, Brian Downing, Don Mattingly, Frank Thomas, Edgar Martinez, Jody Reed, Barry Larkin? That's an awfully impressive group of hitters, one clearly superior to the first group. Is patience in laying off the first pitch a factor in their overall performance? It would be hard to argue otherwise. So when you're in that sock hop line, don't listen to impatient Mikey. Wait!

A complete listing for this category can be found on page 277.

CAN YOU BE AN MVP, AND YET NOT CREATE RUNS?

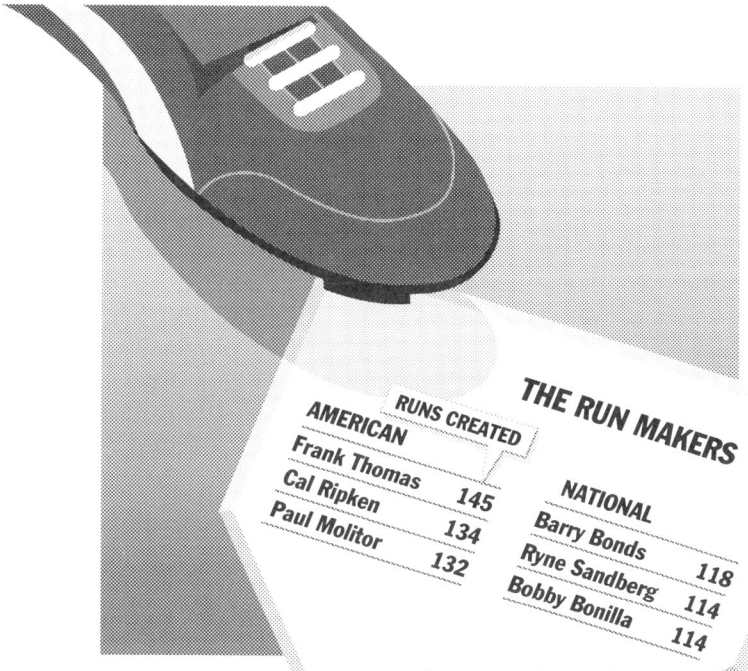

THE RUN MAKERS

AMERICAN	RUNS CREATED	NATIONAL	
Frank Thomas	145	Barry Bonds	118
Cal Ripken	134	Ryne Sandberg	114
Paul Molitor	132	Bobby Bonilla	114

Back in 1960, when the Pittsburgh Pirates were roaring to their first National League pennant in 33 years, their star shortstop, Dick Groat, was the easy winner of the National League's Most Valuable Player Award. Why did 16 of the 22 voters put Groat first on their ballot? It seemed easy:

1. Groat was the National League batting champion with a .325 average.
2. He was the Pirates' captain and team leader.
3. He played a key defensive position, shortstop, and played it very well.

Down in tenth place, an afterthought for most voters (one fourth place vote was his high), was Milwaukee Braves third baseman Eddie Mathews. Mathews hit only .277, well below Groat, but look at his other figures. Mathews hit 39 homers, third in the National League; Groat hit two. Mathews drove in 124 runs, second in the league (to teammate Hank Aaron); Groat drove in 50. Mathews scored 112 runs, again the second-highest total in the league; Groat was far back with 85. Mathews drew 111 walks, once more the league's second-best total; Groat drew 39.

Mathews had a .401 on-base percentage (third best) and a .551 slugging average (sixth best); Groat (.372 OBP and .394 SLG) was not among the leaders in either category. Leadership? Mathews, unlike Groat, would become a major league manager, and his Braves finished in second place, seven games back of Pittsburgh, despite no bullpen and a gaping hole at second base. Defense? Like Groat, Mathews was regarded as one of the best in the league at his position. Mathews even stole ten bases in ten attempts; Groat was 0-for-2.

If we'd had Bill James' "runs created formula" back then, we could have summed all those stats up by saying that Mathews created more runs (128) in 1960 than any player in baseball. Runs created is an estimate of how many runs each player contributes to his team's attack. Though most MVP voters don't know the stat, we've noticed that players with a breadth of offensive skills — like Mathews in 1960 — are no longer ignored; in fact, like Robin Yount in 1989, they often win it. In 1990, the leaders in runs created were Rickey Henderson and Barry Bonds, both MVPs.

Which leads us to '91. Here are the major league leaders in runs created; let's play "find the MVP":

1991 Leaders — Runs Created

Player, Team	Runs Created
Frank Thomas, WSox	145
Cal Ripken, Bal	134
Paul Molitor, Mil	132
Rafael Palmeiro, Tex	129
Ken Griffey Jr, Sea	118
Barry Bonds, Pit	118
Julio Franco, Tex	118
Ruben Sierra, Tex	117
Jose Canseco, Oak	116
Danny Tartabull, KC	116

The American League MVP, Cal Ripken, was second to Frank Thomas, but given that the average first baseman or DH creates many more runs than the average shortstop — and given that Ripken had a superb year in the field while Thomas spent most of the year at DH, nursing a sore arm, the choice makes sense. But where's National League MVP Terry Pendleton? Not that far back, but still only fifth-best in the NL (after Bonds, Ryne Sandberg, Bobby Bonilla and Will Clark) with 107 runs created. Both Pendleton and Bonds played for division champions, and since the voting took place before the playoffs, that was a wash. Defense? Bonds was the one who won the Gold Glove. We can only conclude that while the concept of runs created has gained credibility, it hasn't advanced enough to make up for being perceived as a malcontent.

****

Coupled with runs created is "offensive winning percentage," a James estimate of what a club's winning percentage would be if it consisted of nothing but Frank Thomases (or whatever player we're considering). The 1991 leaders:

1991 Leaders — Offensive Winning Percentage

Player, Team	Off. Win %
Frank Thomas, WSox	.822
Danny Tartabull, KC	.801
Barry Bonds, Pit	.795
Ken Griffey Jr, Sea	.762
Barry Larkin, Cin	.762
Will Clark, SF	.762
Fred McGriff, SD	.754
Bobby Bonilla, Pit	.751
Julio Franco, Tex	.748
Cal Ripken, Bal	.747

(Minimum 300 plate appearances)

Thomas and Bonds are again the leaders. Pendleton was very good, at .710, but again not where you'd think an MVP would be.

The trailers in offensive winning percentage are the usual gaggle of middle infielders and catchers (and one very confused Sammy Sosa):

1991 Trailers — Offensive Winning Percentage

Player, Team	Off. Win %
Bill Ripken, Bal	.139
Scott Fletcher, WSox	.210
Dave Valle, Sea	.218
Sammy Sosa, WSox	.230
Manuel Lee, Tor	.253

Are we sure Bill and Cal are really brothers?

A complete listing for this category can be found on page 278.

WHO ARE THE ROSES AND AARONS OF TOMORROW?

"The Favorite Toy," invented by Bill James a number of years ago, is a favorite of ours as well as Bill's . . . and, judging by the response to our article on the subject last year, it's one of yours as well. The idea is to project, using a player's age and established level of performance (based on his last three seasons, with the most recent one given the heaviest weight), what his chances are to achieve milestones like 500 homers or 3,000 hits. We had so much fun with this last year that we've created a separate article for pitchers' milestones.

We'll dispense with the formula this year since we carried it a year ago (that edition is still available, if you call or write us); the one thing we forgot to note last year is that the formula factors in a three percent chance per season to a sudden end in a player's productivity. At any rate, let's get to the meat of the matter with first a look at the players who have at least a 15% chance to reach 3,000 hits:

Chances For 3,000 Hits

Player	Opening Day Age	Current Total	Projected Total	Chance
Robin Yount	36.6	2,878	3,180	93.9
George Brett	38.9	2,836	3,054	82.9
Ruben Sierra	26.5	993	2,536	26.9
Julio Franco	30.6	1,605	2,655	25.3
Eddie Murray	36.1	2,502	2,876	25.1
Dave Parker	40.8	2,712	2,926	24.3
Cal Ripken	31.6	1,762	2,680	24.2
Roberto Alomar	24.2	685	2,401	24.1
Kirby Puckett	31.1	1,602	2,609	22.0
Steve Sax	32.2	1,781	2,655	21.7
Ken Griffey Jr.	22.4	478	2,267	20.9
Wade Boggs	33.8	1,965	2,659	17.1
Tony Gwynn	31.9	1,699	2,557	15.9
Rafael Palmeiro	27.5	805	2,232	15.0

You can see that though Yount and Brett are projected (as they should be) to get over 3,000, the chance of injury, etc. reduces their percentage of actually achieving it to a little less than 100%; a player that age can fall apart pretty quickly (just ask Dave Parker). No one else is remotely close, but the odds are very great that one or two of them will make it. Don't you like the chances of Roberto Alomar (so good at such a young age) and Kirby Puckett (so determined, such a steady producer)?

How about 4,000 hits? Pete Rose doesn't need to worry too much. Only Alomar (1.8%), Sierra (1.3) and Griffey (0.8) have even faint blips on the radar screen. No one has even a one percent chance to break Rose's record.

Let's shift now to the home run race, and a chart we ran last year — the players with the best chances for 500 homers (at right). Shown below are the projected career totals:

Player	Projected Total
Canseco	481
Strawberry	465
Fielder	394
McGriff	386
Williams	354
McGwire	381

HOME 500 RUNS

	AGE	CHANCE	HOME RUNS
Jose Canseco	27	44%	209
Darryl Strawberry	30	34%	280
Cecil Fielder	28	22%	126
Fred McGriff	28	17%	156
Matt Williams	26	13%	101
Mark McGwire	28	13%	178

Those of you who remember this chart from last you will be aware how much the probabilities can change from year to year. After his big 1991 season, Canseco's chances have risen from 28% to 43; Strawberry's have slipped from 42% to 34. Mark McGwire's chances tumbled from 31% to 13. This is definitely a game of "What have you done for me lately," which is why Fielder, McGriff and Williams are new players on the list. Fans of Cecil should note that Bill's studies indicate that players with his type of body often fade out early; on the other hand, Babe Ruth wasn't exactly Mr. Ultra Slim-Fast.

How about the chances for 600 homers? Canseco is far ahead at 19.6%; Strawberry (7.8), Fielder (6.5) and McGriff (1.8) are the only others with even a one percent chance. Canseco is the only one with a remote chance at 700 homers (5.4%); Henry Aaron can rest easy, as no active player is closer to breaking his record than we are to putting a man on Pluto.

HOW IMPORTANT ARE GOOD PINCH HITTERS?

Bench players are still an important part of a club's success. That goes for pinch hitters, even though the DH rule has lessened their usage in the American League. The club with the best pinch hitting corps in baseball was the world champion Minnesota Twins, who had a nifty .304 average. You could even say that pinch hitting was directly responsible for Minnesota's title. It was a pinch single by Gene Larkin which drove in the only run of Game Seven of the World Series.

Because American League clubs generally hit for a higher average than their National League rivals, it's necessary to evaluate the pinch hitting corps on a league-by-league basis. Here's the American League data:

American League Club Pinch Hitting — 1991

Team	AB	H	HR	RBI	Avg	OBP	Slg	Won-Lost
Minnesota	158	48	6	30	.304	.390	.456	95-67
New York	113	30	4	18	.265	.384	.416	71-91
Seattle	181	47	0	23	.260	.333	.320	83-79
Milwaukee	62	66	0	6	.258	.403	.306	83-79
Baltimore	181	46	7	30	.254	.328	.409	67-95
Kansas City	193	49	5	23	.254	.321	.378	82-80
Oakland	148	37	3	19	.250	.309	.365	84-78
Boston	100	24	1	15	.240	.303	.300	84-78
Toronto	123	29	1	21	.236	.327	.301	91-71
Cleveland	120	28	1	9	.233	.329	.275	57-105
California	74	17	2	10	.230	.269	.351	81-81
Chicago	166	36	6	29	.217	.313	.386	87-75
Texas	207	44	3	33	.213	.279	.314	85-77
Detroit	129	23	5	27	.178	.264	.318	84-78

Milwaukee's infrequent, and ineffective, use of the pinch hitter is remarkable. California was almost as bad but did manage two pinch-hit home runs. You have to appreciate the way Tom Kelly handled his bench. He platooned at third base (Mike Pagliarulo/Scott Leius), gave frequent playing time to his second-string catcher (Junior Ortiz), got Randy Bush and Gene Larkin into the lineup enough to keep them fresh, and even got some useful work from Al Newman. Leius wound up batting .440 as a pinch hitter (11 for 25), and Bush (13 for 34, .382, with two homers and eight RBI) was probably the most effective pinch swinger in the league. That certainly wasn't enough by itself to mean a championship. But it helped.

National League Club Pinch Hitting — 1991

Team	AB	H	HR	RBI	Avg	OBP	Slg	Won-Lost
St. Louis	209	53	2	38	.254	.332	.344	84-78
Philadelphia	245	59	2	33	.241	.321	.318	78-84
Montreal	213	51	5	25	.241	.310	.357	71-90
Atlanta	253	59	3	26	.233	.301	.312	94-68
Chicago	223	52	7	35	.233	.289	.390	77-83
Pittsburgh	217	49	6	29	.226	.324	.364	98-64
Cincinnati	234	52	6	22	.222	.278	.333	74-88
San Francisco	259	56	0	26	.216	.298	.266	75-87
New York	231	49	8	28	.212	.298	.329	77-84
Houston	274	50	3	35	.182	.292	.259	71-90
Los Angeles	305	55	4	42	.180	.251	.266	93-69
San Diego	238	42	4	28	.176	.243	.277	84-78

In the National League, there was a significant difference between the pinch hitting corps of Western division rivals Los Angeles and Atlanta. The Braves had the most effective group of pinch swingers in the division; Bobby Cox even got some useful work from unlikely sources like the presumably-washed-up Danny Heep, who went 6 for 13. The Dodgers, whose pinch hitters batted nearly 60 points lower than Atlanta's, got some nice work from Chris Gwynn (13 pinch hits, 13 RBI), Dave Hansen (10 for 32, .313) and a couple of others. But the LA totals were dragged down by Tommy Lasorda's frequent usage of ineffective players like Stan Javier (5 for 52, .096), Gary Carter (2 for 27, .074) and Lenny Harris (3 for 24, .125). Would LA have made up that one game difference if they'd kept ace pinch swinger Mickey Hatcher (14 for 47 in pinch roles in 1990, with 10 RBI) around for another year? That seems quite possible.

A complete listing for this category can be found on page 279.

WILL THE ORIOLES DRIVE MERCEDES TO A WINNING RECORD?

Who will be the Bagwells and Knoblauchs of 1992? No one knows for sure, of course; heralded phenoms often flop, and little known players sometimes turn into stars. We'll leave evaluations of "intangibles" to other people; what we present here are minor league and 1991 winter league stats for four players (one in each division), along with projections known as "major league equivalents." As we explain elsewhere, the MLE, a tool designed by Bill James, estimates major league performance based on minor league stats. The crucial thing it does is to make an adjustment for league and ballpark, so that players from the low-average Southern League (league average .245) are on more equal footing with those from the hit-happy Pacific Coast League (.284). Here are the four, each a player who might be considered a "sleeper":

Luis Mercedes, 24, Baltimore, OF

	AB	R	H	2B	3B	HR	BI	BB	SO	SB	Avg	OBP	Slg
91 AAA Rochester	428	68	136	16	5	2	38	69	72	23	.318	.415	.393
MLE	357	53	108	12	3	1	28	50	66	16	.303	.388	.361
Avg Min Lg Year	365	62	115	12	5	2	33	41	61	27	.314	.387	.388
91 Winter League	171	35	57	7	1	1	21	35	34	18	.333	.452	.404

Less of a sleeper than the others, Mercedes is the only one of the four with any major league experience. But there are still some doubts about him, even though the Orioles need both outfield and leadoff help. Those doubts have little to do with his hitting skills, which were on display during both the summer and winter of 1991. The numbers seem to be for real, as he's had a good hitting record throughout his minor league career.

The major obstacle facing Mercedes seems to be his fiery temper. Luis' Rochester season ended early when he was suspended after hitting an opposing player in the face with a batting helmet. Mercedes supposedly has a new attitude, but even if he's another Albert (don't call me Joey) Belle, he could still win himself a major league job. The talent is obviously there.

Chad Curtis, 23, California, OF-3B

	AB	R	H	2B	3B	HR	BI	BB	SO	SB	Avg	OBP	Slg
91 AAA Edmont'n	431	81	136	28	7	9	61	51	58	46	.316	.389	.476
MLE	405	58	110	21	3	7	44	36	60	26	.272	.331	.390
Avg Min Lg Year	374	68	114	21	4	9	52	43	57	44	.305	.382	.458
91 Winter League	195	35	66	16	8	1	37	47	16	18	.338	.470	.518

Whitey Herzog loves hard-working Chad Curtis, so you have to figure Curtis has an excellent chance to stick with the Angels this year. The new California GM had third sacker Curtis learning the outfield in Venezuela this winter in order to better fit in with the '92 Halos. Wherever he plays, Curtis looks a fine hitting prospect. After a solid season at AAA Edmonton, he was the MVP of the Venezuelan league, leading the league in batting, RBI, extra-base hits, doubles, triples, on-base percentage, and slugging percentage. Big pluses for Curtis are his abilities to walk and steal bases, which make him ideal at the top of the order. His power looks like the doubles variety, at best.

Herzog has already stated that Junior Felix will have to fight off Curtis for the center field spot. The contrast might work in Curtis' favor; Herzog loves hustling ballplayers, and that term fits Curtis a lot better than it does the moody Felix. Curtis jumped all the way from A-ball to a full season of AAA last year; making the final step to the bigs this year would not be a surprise.

Juan Guerrero, 25, Astros, 3B-OF

	AB	R	H	2B	3B	HR	BI	BB	SO	SB	Avg	OBP	Slg
91 AA Shreveport	479	78	160	40	2	19	94	46	88	14	.334	.395	.545
MLE	456	61	137	35	1	14	73	30	94	9	.300	.344	.474
Avg Min Lg Year	349	53	98	21	2	12	56	28	71	7	.282	.340	.460
91 Winter League	138	14	38	4	0	1	12	12	23	2	.275	.338	.326

Now **here's** a sleeper. Guerrero spent 1991 with San Francisco's AA club at Shreveport, and his numbers were far superior to such top Giant prospects as Royce Clayton, Steve Hosey and John Patterson. Nonetheless San Francisco left Guerrero off their 40-man roster, and he was snapped up by the Astros in the Rule 5 draft. According to Rule 5, Guerrero must spend his entire 1992 season with the Astros; they can't send him to the minors without first giving the Giants a chance to take him back for $25,000. So, unless he's a real disappointment, he figures to stick with Houston.

Why didn't the Giants protect Guerrero? The primary reason was his age; at 25, he's yet to play above AA ball, and that's unusual for a top prospect. Guerrero had never hit higher than .281 prior to last season, so there's a tendency to question those '91 figures. In addition, Guerrero has yet to settle at a defensive position. He's played second, third and the outfield, and he's had his problems at each spot. Still, those 1991 numbers are awfully impressive, and the Astros need help just about everywhere. This is one long shot who could pan out.

Matt Stairs, 23, Expos, 2B-3B

	AB	R	H	2B	3B	HR	BI	BB	SO	SB	Avg	OBP	Slg
91 AA Harrisburg	505	87	168	30	10	13	78	66	47	23	.333	.411	.509
MLE	486	73	149	27	7	9	65	46	50	17	.307	.367	.447
Avg Min Lg Year	421	61	124	23	5	8	57	52	53	16	.295	.375	.430
91 Winter League	264	53	91	9	3	12	55	30	21	26	.345	.403	.538

Wow, another Expo second baseman. Last year Montreal had Delino DeShields as the regular, the promising Bret Barberie as an occasional backup, the .312-hitting Todd Haney at AAA Indianapolis, and Stairs at AA Harrisburg. No wonder there was talk of trading DeShields.

Though Stairs has made five different minor league stops with varying degrees of succes in his short three-year career, his stock is soaring after the year he had at Harrisburg in '91. He followed that up with an outstanding season of winter ball. He has fine power for a middle infielder, and he's always had a good batting eye. Stairs is not considered a great defensive player, but he's adequate, and he can play other positions besides second. He's also Canadian. The consensus is that the Expos will find a spot for Stairs. But for him to be a regular in '92, a trade of DeShields or someone else will probably be necessary.

IS HE THE NEXT VINCE COLEMAN ... OR THE NEXT DONELL NIXON?

Does anyone out there recall the "Great Stolen Base Race" of 1983? That year two 21-year olds dueled all summer long in a quest to set the all-time professional baseball stolen base record. Mariner farmhand Donell Nixon, playing for Bakersfield in the Class A California League, wowed the baseball world by swiping 144 bases. But on the other coast, at Class A Macon of the South Atlantic League, Cardinal prospect Vince Coleman did Nixon one better. Exactly one, and Coleman's 145 steals still ranks as the top mark.

The fortunes of Coleman and Nixon since then point out that it ain't easy being a stolen base king . . . if that's basically all you can do. After beginning his major league career with three straight 100-steal seasons, Coleman has seen both his numbers and his reputation decline in recent years. At least Coleman **had** a reputation, which is more that you can say for Nixon. Donell warmed major league benches for four seasons until 1991, when he slipped completely into obscurity (or was it Japan?).

Is there another Coleman or Rickey Henderson just waiting to be uncovered . . . or another Herb Washington (the first and only "designated runner") waiting to be exposed? Here are the '91 leaders, with their 1992 ages, organizations and other "leadoff man" stats:

1991 Stolen Base Leaders (AA and AAA)

Player, Team	Age	League	Org.	SB	Avg	OBP
Eric Young, San Antonio	25	Texas	LA	71	.280	.373
Will Taylor, Las Vegas	23	Pacific Coast	SD	62	.259	.336
Rodney Lofton, Hagerstown	24	Eastern	Bal	56	.284	.357
Lee Tinsley, Canton	23	Eastern	Cle	54	.247	.356
Jim Walewander, Columbus	31	International	Yanks	54	.225	.342
Vince Harris, Wichita	24	Texas	SD	48	.286	.387
Tom Goodwin, Albuquerque	23	Pacific Coast	LA	48	.273	.349
Chad Curtis, Edmonton	23	Pacific Coast	Cal	46	.316	.389
Wayne Housie, Pawtucket	27	International	Bos	45	.285	.364
Andres Santana, Phoenix	24	Pacific Coast	SF	45	.316	.370
Shawn Gilbert, Orlando	27	Southern	Min	43	.255	.332
Darrell Sherman, Wichita	24	Texas	SD	43	.295	.391
Lou Frazier, London	27	Eastern	Det	42	.239	.353
Tito Navarro, Williamsport	21	Eastern	Mets	42	.288	.380

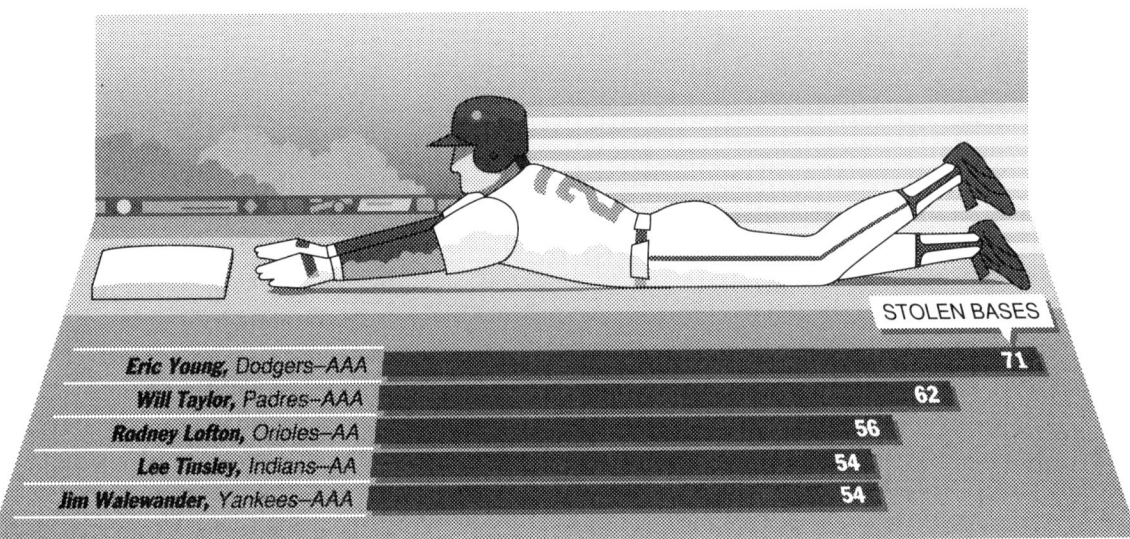

One thing you'll notice in this list is that, for the most part, the on-base averages are excellent. A lot of stolen base kings — Coleman has been one of them — are anxious hitters, swinging at bad pitches while lacking the patience to draw a walk. Their OBPs, as a result, are unacceptably low. The new crop of stolen base kings seems to be more patient . . . which greatly improves their major league chances.

Just looking at the figures, one would think that players like Eric Young, Chad Curtis, Andres Santana and Darrell Sherman, with impressive figures in all three categories (SB, Avg, OBP) would be lead-pipe cinches to succeed at the major league level. But there's no guarantee of that. If a player can steal bases in the minors, he'll probably be able to steal them in the majors . . . but then, merely being able to steal didn't help Donell Nixon much. Batting average and OBP are more important, and those numbers can be inflated by playing in a hitter's league or ballpark.

To remedy that, we use a tool familiar to many of you: Bill James' "major league equivalents." The formula is complicated, but what it does is realistically project how a player would hit in the majors after adjusting his minor league numbers for league and park. Year after year, this system works remarkably well in separating the duds from the real prospects.

The following stolen base kings had the best major league equivalents in 1991:

Player	1991 Minors	MLE
Wade Housie	.285	.282
Chad Curtis	.316	.272
Tito Navarro	.288	.266
Rodney Lofton	.284	.263
Andres Santana	.316	.262

Though predicting is always risky, one would think that Housie and Curtis have the best chance for major league success in 1992. Not only do they have good MLEs, Housie will be playing for Butch Hobson, who managed him in the minors, and Curtis for Buck Rodgers, who loves the stolen base.

WILL THE LINEOUTS OF '91 BECOME THE LINE HITS OF '92?

Is there such a thing as a "tough luck" hitter? Certainly it's true that some players hit into more line drive outs than others do. So for the third year in a row, we'll imagine all those line drive outs were hits and present a new list of the batting leaders; "New Avg" is what the players would have hit if all their lineouts had fallen for hits. You could justifiably say that this is a list of the players who hit the ball hard most consistently in 1991:

1991 Batting Leaders (If Lineouts were Hits)

Player, Team	AB	H	Avg	LO	New Avg
Wade Boggs, Bos	546	181	.332	44	.412
Tony Gwynn, SD	530	168	.317	46	.404
Julio Franco, Tex	589	201	.341	23	.380
Hal Morris, Cin	478	152	.318	29	.379
Paul Molitor, Mil	665	216	.325	32	.373
Cal Ripken, Bal	650	210	.323	32	.372
Ken Griffey Jr., Sea	548	179	.327	21	.365
Edgar Martinez, Sea	544	167	.307	31	.364
Frank Thomas, WSox	559	178	.318	23	.360
Brett Butler, LA	615	182	.296	39	.359

It's quite a list, with Wade Boggs and Tony Gwynn beating out the regular batting champions, Franco and Morris. Not many people would argue with the notion that Boggs and Gwynn have long been the most consistent line drive hitters in the game. Our numbers agree completely. In the three years we've been keeping this figure, Boggs would have finished 2nd-3rd-1st in the American League batting races, an improvement each year over his actual batting race finishes (3rd-5th-2nd), if everyone's liners had dropped in. Gwynn would have finished 1st-2nd-1st in the National League, instead of 1st-6th-3rd. Even the great ones, it seems, have their share of tough luck.

But does that luck tend to even out over time? A year ago, we detected that possibility. The players who had averaged the most lineouts per at-bat in 1989 ("unlucky" hitters) tended to increase their averages in 1990; the ones who had averaged the fewest lineouts in 1989 ("lucky" hitters) tended to post lower averages in '90.

After looking at another year's worth of data, the trend is still there but not as strong. Four of the ten lineout leaders from 1990 had **lower** averages in '91; injuries were a factor for some of them, but Dave Magadan dropped 70 points, Jerry Browne 39, Scott Fletcher 36. The other list, the "lucky" players who had hit the fewest lineouts per AB in '90, was truer to form, with seven of the ten declining in average last year. However, Devon White (a 65 point increase) and Mickey Tettleton (plus 40-points) didn't perform at all as expected.

Here are the players who averaged the most lineouts per AB in 1991. These guys are good candidates for higher batting averages next year:

Most Lineouts per At-Bat — 1991

American League	LO/AB	National League	LO/AB
Wade Boggs, Bos	.081	Tony Gwynn, SD	.087
Felix Fermin, Cle	.078	Jeff Treadway, Atl	.075
Joe Orsulak, Bal	.074	Casey Candaele, Hou	.071
Tom Brunansky, Bos	.072	Mickey Morandini, Phi	.071
Alan Trammell, Det	.072	Jerome Walton, Cubs	.070
Luis Rivera, Bos	.072		

However, what we may not have considered is that many of these players are pure line drive hitters; guys like Boggs and Gwynn are going to hit into a lot of lineouts **every** year. Whereas the second list — the players who lined out with the lowest frequency last year — tends to be dominated by power hitters, flyball hitters and guys who strike out a lot:

Fewest Lineouts per At-Bat — 1991

American League	LO/AB	National League	LO/AB
Dean Palmer, Tex	.015	Dave Justice, Atl	.020
Jose Canseco, Oak	.019	Ron Gant, Atl	.021
Mark McGwire, Oak	.019	Barry Larkin, Cin	.022
Jay Buhner, Sea	.020	Daryl Boston, Mets	.024
Albert Belle, Cle	.020	Eric Davis, Cin	.025

Someone like McGwire doesn't line out much because he doesn't hit many line drives, period. If this group has a lot of batting average decliners, it might simply be that players with extreme uppercut swings are better candidates to go into a slump than the Boggs/Gwynn type. That knowledge might give you a little edge in predicting players whose averages are reasonable bets to fall in 1992. (Can Mark McGwire drop even further?!)

A complete listing for this category can be found on page 281.

IS McGWIRE UPPERCUTTING HIMSELF TO OBLIVION?

In another section of this book, we discuss the prevailing theories of hitting, espoused mainly by Ted Williams (pull/uppercut) and Charlie Lau (all fields/more level). It seems fairly logical that home run hitters would have uppercut swings and produce more flyballs. Let's test it out by looking at two types of hitters. The first consists of the flyball hitters — the players who have the lowest groundball-to-flyball ratio over the last three seasons:

Lowest Groundball/Flyball Ratios (1989-91)

Player	GB	FB	Ratio	HR	Avg
Howard Johnson	388	690	0.56	97	.263
Mark McGwire	359	619	0.58	94	.223
Tom Brunansky	414	584	0.71	52	.241
Kevin Mitchell	404	556	0.73	109	.282
Kevin McReynolds	466	641	0.73	62	.266
Joe Carter	545	737	0.74	92	.249
Chris Sabo	449	566	0.79	57	.280
Alvin Davis	445	549	0.81	50	.271
George Bell	545	661	0.82	64	.283
Ron Gant	423	514	0.82	73	.259

(All players active in 1991; minimum 750 balls in play)

This is familiar territory for those who have seen our stats on this subject in the past: McGwire, Johnson, Brunansky, McReynolds and Mitchell were the top five for the 1990 season. Are they home run hitters? They sure are, averaging 25 home runs per year over the past three seasons.

That group is a big contrast to the leading groundball hitters over the same period. We're talking "singles city" here:

Lowest Groundball/Flyball Ratios (1989-91)

Player	GB	FB	Ratio	HR	Avg
Willie McGee	690	191	3.61	10	.306
Felix Fermin	719	242	2.97	1	.251
Steve Sax	1066	382	2.79	19	.294
Milt Thompson	608	242	2.51	16	.271
Lance Johnson	633	254	2.49	1	.282
Tony Gwynn	845	361	2.34	12	.321
Brett Butler	836	363	2.30	9	.296
Luis Polonia	668	294	2.27	7	.308
Lenny Harris	605	266	2.27	8	.279
Bip Roberts	579	260	2.23	15	.298

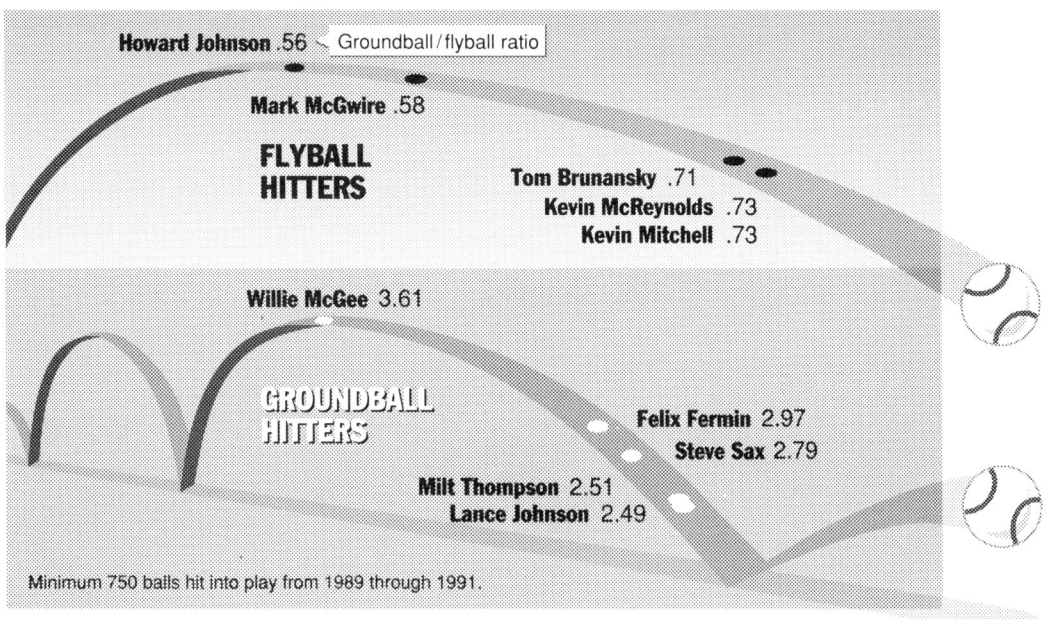

The second group averages only three homers a season, though it obviously includes some very good, high average hitters. For the most part, this group has speed as a primary asset, and hitting the ball on the ground takes advantage of that strength.

So you have to be a flyball hitter to belt homers, right? Not so fast. Check out the ratios of Darryl Strawberry (1.00), Andre Dawson (1.11), Fred McGriff (1.18), Cal Ripken (1.26) and Ryne Sandberg (1.27). These players have more average ground/fly ratios, but still belt the long ball.

Which brings us to Mark McGwire. We suggested a year ago that McGwire might be uppercutting the ball too much, and that the change in his swing might have caused his 1989-90 slump. The slump was even worse in 1991. But McGwire's ground-to-fly ratio was unchanged from '90:

McGwire	Avg	HR	G/F
1989	.231	33	0.65
1990	.235	39	0.54
1991	.201	22	0.55

Compare McGwire to Howard Johnson, who hit the ball in the air even more than McGwire did — while increasing his production:

Johnson	Avg	HR	G/F
1990	.244	23	0.61
1991	.259	38	0.46

McGwire may well be uppercutting too much. But that kind of swing hasn't seemed to hurt HoJo. McGwire's problems may not be so easily solved.

A complete listing for this category can be found on page 282.

DO CLUTCH HITTERS GEAR UP WITH RUNNERS IN SCORING POSITION AND TWO OUT?

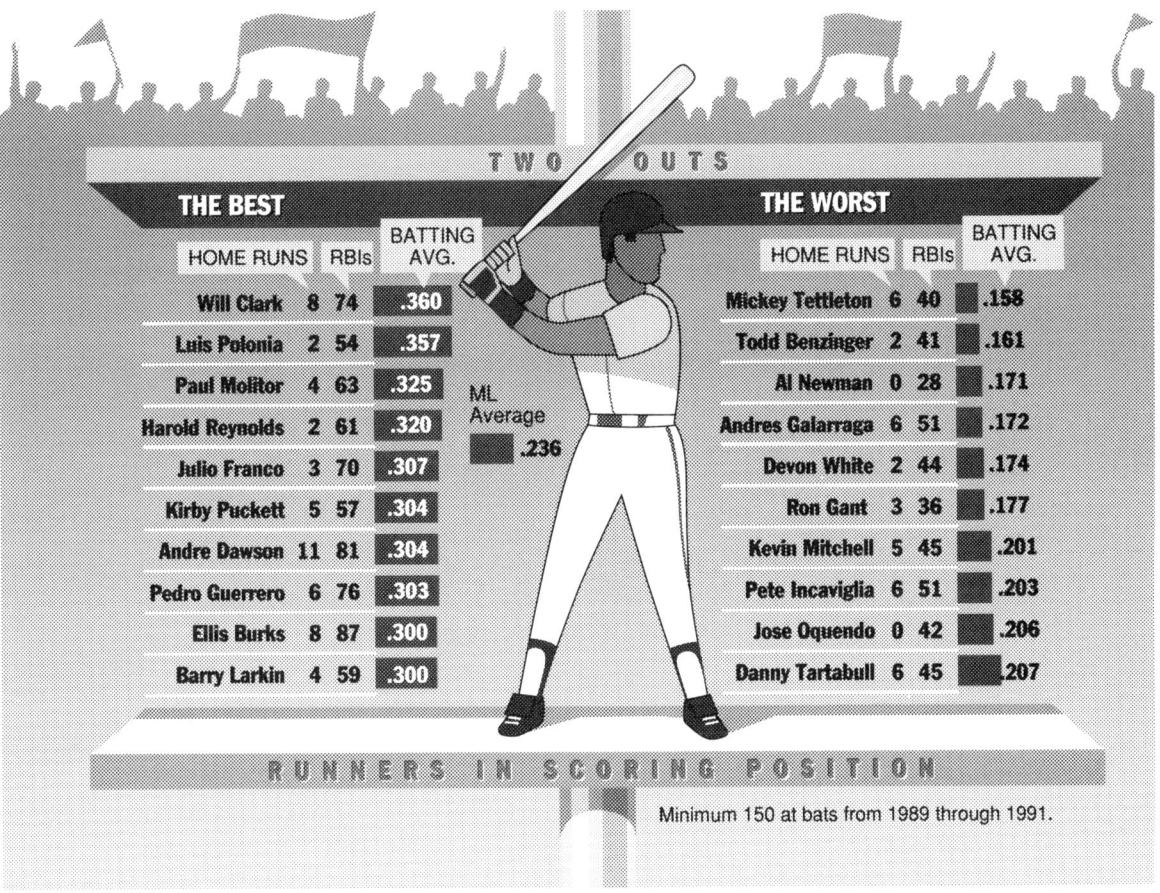

Minimum 150 at bats from 1989 through 1991.

Of all the clutch-hitting statistics, the most widely accepted has been batting average with runners in scoring position. Almost everyone agrees that coming to bat with men on second and/or third is usually a pressure situation. In addition, a full-time player will usually get at least 125 scoring-position at-bats over the course of a season; that makes this figure more valid statistically than, say, batting average in the late innings of close games, which is based on far fewer at-bats.

There is a further refinement of this stat, one we haven't examined until now: batting with runners in scoring position AND two out. If coming up with men in scoring position is a pressure situation, than having two outs, in theory, greatly increases the pressure; if the batter is retired, the inning is over and the scoring opportunity is lost. However, this specialized situation doesn't occur much over the course of a season. For example, in 1990 Jose Canseco had 481 total at-bats, but only 46 of them were with runners in scoring position and two out. It's hard to draw any valid conclusions from such a small sample . . . not that people don't try to do it anyway.

A possible way to give the figure more validity is to look at it over a longer period — say three seasons, where players will have 150 at-bats or so with two outs and men in scoring position. Here are the top ten in batting average in that situation for 1989-91; for basis of comparison, we include the hitters' figures with runners in scoring position and **less** than two out, along with the difference between the two figures:

Leaders — Batting with Runners in Scoring Position and Two Out — 1989-91

Player	2 Out					Less than 2 Out					Diff
	Avg	AB	H	HR	RBI	Avg	AB	H	HR	RBI	
Will Clark	.360	150	54	8	74	.324	318	103	15	169	36
Luis Polonia	.357	154	55	2	54	.278	180	50	0	65	79
Dave Magadan	.353	136	48	1	58	.304	171	52	3	85	49
Paul Molitor	.325	166	54	4	63	.322	171	55	1	67	3
Harold Reynolds	.320	181	58	2	61	.289	201	58	1	79	31
Lonnie Smith	.316	114	36	1	40	.318	170	54	4	78	-2
Alvin Davis	.309	149	46	4	60	.297	212	63	7	111	12
Julio Franco	.307	205	63	3	70	.373	228	85	7	121	-66
Kirby Puckett	.304	171	52	5	57	.334	296	99	4	142	-30
Andre Dawson	.303	201	61	11	81	.286	217	62	11	121	17
Pedro Guerrero	.303	221	67	6	76	.363	251	91	6	152	-60

(Minimum 300 plate appearances with runners in scoring position)

This is a very appealing leaders list, isn't it? Especially Will Clark with that mighty .360 average. Everyone on the list also comes through with men in scoring position and less than two out. But Clark, Polonia, Magadan and Reynolds seem to respond better to the two-out pressure. Does that make them the cream of the clutch hitters?

Before we say yes, take a look at another list. This one consists of the players with the **lowest** averages in the scoring position/two-out situation. But before we label them chokers, examine their figures with men in scoring position and less than two out:

Trailers — Batting with Runners in Scoring Position and Two Out — 1989-91

Player	2 Out					Less than 2 Out					Diff
	Avg	AB	H	HR	RBI	Avg	AB	H	HR	RBI	
Spike Owen	.153	137	21	1	24	.278	158	44	1	57	−125
Mickey Tettleton	.158	158	25	6	40	.262	172	45	12	93	−104
Todd Benzinger	.161	223	36	2	41	.324	188	61	6	108	−163
Rafael Ramirez	.168	143	24	2	31	.325	166	54	0	63	−157
Al Newman	.171	152	26	0	28	.279	136	38	0	55	−108
Andres Galarraga	.172	204	35	6	51	.285	207	59	7	93	−113
Ron Gant	.177	181	32	3	36	.304	191	58	6	93	−127
Glenn Davis	.178	135	24	6	35	.329	143	47	6	70	−151
Billy Doran	.179	140	25	0	24	.333	156	52	4	77	−154
Jerry Browne	.188	128	24	0	32	.335	161	54	2	76	−147

Do these guys fold under pressure? Well, we've already said that a scoring position at-bat — none out, one out or two — is generally a pressure situation. Does it make sense to say that just about everyone on this list responds beautifully to scoring position pressure . . . unless there are two out, at which point he falls apart completely? That defies all logic. It's much more likely that (one year or three) this is just a random statistical occurrence.

Don't get us wrong. We admire Will Clark as much as anyone, and it may well be that he concentrates better with two out. But you can't really conclude that from this data, and you especially can't conclude that Spike Owen and company "choke." We think Clark's overall performance with men in scoring position — a .335 average over the last three years — is quite enough to admire.

A complete listing for this category can be found on page 284.

WILL COMISKEY BE "THE HOUSE THAT FRANK BUILT"?

Not yet 24 years old, Frank Thomas might be the most exciting young slugger in baseball. Thomas not only has a world of talent and a great attitude, but he may have something else going for him: a home ballpark which seems to be ideal for him. Project Thomas' 1991 Comiskey Park stats over a whole season, and it's "move over, Babe Ruth and Ted Williams." How does a .371 average with 48 homers and 122 RBI grab you?

Unfortunately, Thomas had to go on the road occasionally last year, and his stats there were more mortal: .271, 8 HR, 48 RBI. It still added up to a tremendous year . . . and anyway, there's nothing wrong with taking full advantage of your home ballpark. Thomas was one of a half-dozen players who batted at least 100 points higher at home than on the road (minimum 250 plate appearances). The players who had the biggest home bias:

Players Who Love Home Cooking

Player, Team	At Home			On The Road			BA Diff
	Avg	HR	RBI	Avg	HR	RBI	
Joey Cora, WSox	.319	0	10	.165	0	8	+154
Mo Vaughn, Bos	.320	1	16	.210	3	16	+110
Wade Boggs, Bos	.389	6	32	.282	2	19	+107
Mariano Duncan, Cin	.311	10	25	.205	2	15	+106
Chris James, Cle	.290	1	21	.185	4	20	+105
Frank Thomas, WSox	.371	24	61	.271	8	48	+100
Craig Biggio, Hou	.343	0	24	.245	4	22	+98
Mike Sharperson, LA	.330	1	9	.235	1	11	+95
Chuck Knoblauch, Min	.328	1	26	.234	0	24	+94
Harold Reynolds, Sea	.299	1	27	.208	2	30	+91
Greg Olson, Atl	.287	6	31	.196	0	13	+91

Before we mark down Thomas for a Comiskey-driven Hall of Fame career, we need to point out that few players take advantage of their home park year after year the way Wade Boggs (.381 lifetime at Fenway) does. Many players have outstanding success at home one season, but return to earth the next. Check the 1990-91 figures of Ryne Sandberg and Kelly Gruber:

	At Home			On The Road			BA
Player, Team	Avg	HR	RBI	Avg	HR	RBI	Diff
Ryne Sandberg — 1990	.357	25	62	.255	15	38	+102
Ryne Sandberg — 1991	.309	15	54	.272	11	46	+37
Kelly Gruber — 1990	.292	23	62	.254	8	56	+38
Kelly Gruber — 1991	.262	8	31	.240	12	34	+22

What happened to Sandberg and Gruber in 1991? Most likely, nothing. Each seemed to be in a groove at their home parks in 1990, hitting more homers than ever before; they returned to a more normal level in '91, while continuing to perform better at home. So Thomas will probably continue to love Comiskey, but his home/road splits will very likely be less extreme in 1992.

Every year there are always some players who love life on the road:

Players Who Are At Home On The Road

	At Home			On The Road			BA
Player, Team	Avg	HR	RBI	Avg	HR	RBI	Diff
Gerald Perry, StL	.185	1	15	.304	5	21	−119
Jeff Treadway, Atl	.264	1	12	.381	2	20	−117
Andy Van Slyke, Pit	.226	9	46	.310	8	37	−84
Dean Palmer, Tex	.140	6	11	.221	9	26	−81
Kevin Maas, Yanks	.178	8	25	.258	15	38	−80
Willie McGee, SF	.270	2	20	.345	2	23	−75
Jeff Huson, Tex	.177	1	15	.252	1	11	−75
Alfredo Griffin, LA	.203	0	11	.276	0	16	−73
Tom Pagnozzi, StL	.226	2	23	.298	0	34	−72
Luis Polonia, Cal	.261	1	20	.332	1	30	−71

Sometimes there's a logical reason why a player struggles in his home confines. Willie McGee, an extreme groundball hitter, figured to have problems with the long Candlestick Park grass last year, and he did. Andy Van Slyke may have been pressing in an effort to justify his lucrative new contract to the home folks; in 1990, Van Slyke had batted .288 at Three Rivers Stadium. And the pressure of being considered a top prospect may have affected Dean Palmer and Kevin Maas, both of whom had problems in front of the home fans. Expect more normal home performances from most of these players in 1992.

A complete listing for this category can be found on page 285.

WHO ARE THE BEST TWO-STRIKE HITTERS?

We're not saying anything you haven't heard before, but maybe we ought to say it anyway: in baseball, it's three strikes and you're out. We repeat that old adage because, when the count got to strike two in the old days, even mighty sluggers would shorten up their stroke and concentrate on just hitting the ball. That's how Joe DiMaggio hit 361 homers while striking out just 369 times over his long career (see another essay on that topic in this book).

No more. These days, two-strike hitters are pretty much separated by hitting style. The ones with the best two-strike averages are, usually, smart singles hitters. Here are the top ten two-strike hitters over the past three seasons (minimum 600 plate appearances with two strikes):

The Best Two-Strike Hitters — 1989-91

Batter	AB	H	Avg
Tony Gwynn	556	162	.291
Luis Polonia	650	178	.274
Wade Boggs	869	230	.265
Willie Randolph	531	139	.262
Rickey Henderson	776	201	.259
Dave Magadan	558	143	.256
Edgar Martinez	565	142	.251
Gregg Jefferies	619	155	.250
Brett Butler	875	218	.249
Barry Larkin	572	141	.247

"Round up the usual suspects." You'd expect to find Tony Gwynn, Wade Boggs, Willie Randolph, Dave Magadan, Edgar Martinez and Brett Butler on this list . . . they're intelligent hitters, singles types but with traditionally high batting averages. Luis Polonia might be a bit of a surprise; he doesn't walk much, so he's thought of as something of a wild swinger. But Luis knows better than to lash out wildly with two strikes. Rickey Henderson, Gregg Jefferies and Barry Larkin have more power than most of the hitters on the list, but it's more of the old-style "selective" power: with two strikes, they're not looking to drive the ball out of the yard, even though they're capable of doing just that.

The best two-strike hitters were who you'd expect: heady players who know better than to try to do too much when their backs are against the wall. On the other hand, you'd figure that the **worst** two-strike hitters would be, for the most part, oafish brutes who are totally lacking in subtlety. Hey, you smart guy, you'd be right again:

The Worst Two-Strike Hitters — 1989-91

Batter	AB	H	Avg
Cory Snyder	539	65	.121
Rob Deer	778	99	.127
Mark McGwire	651	85	.131
Jack Howell	480	64	.133
Pete Incaviglia	650	89	.137
Dale Murphy	713	103	.144
Sammy Sosa	535	79	.148
Jesse Barfield	738	110	.149
Candy Maldonado	557	83	.149
Junior Felix	514	77	.150

Poor Cory Snyder — he makes every one of these "most stupid hitters" lists, doesn't he? Give the man a break; we don't know whether Cory was smart or dumb, but we do know that in this sort of shorten-up-the-bat situation, Cory was Cory, swinging away like he did when he hit those 33 homers. (That was in 1987, Cory. Everybody hit homers then.)

Cory's got some company when it comes to lost careers. Dale Murphy has had a long and brilliant run, and Jesse Barfield doesn't need to apologize; probably old age and lost bat speed accounts for their presence on this list. Jack Howell, Pete Incaviglia, Candy Maldonado — what might have been? It's still not too late for the still-young Sammy Sosa and Junior Felix, but the clock is ticking. You could write a book on what's happened to Mark McGwire, and somebody probably will.

A complete listing for this category can be found on page 286.

WHAT KIND OF HITTERS MAKE "PRODUCTIVE" OUTS?

It's a close game. There's a man on second with nobody out. The batter grounds out to the second basemen, but it enables the runner to advance to third. The announcer says, "He really did his job. You won't see that in the box score tomorrow!"

Not true anymore! You may have noticed a new category in many box scores throughout the country. It's called "Runners Moved Up" and it is now available in STATS-generated box scores. It was designed by STATS' Dick Cramer because he got tired of hearing that phrase! Look for it in your local newspapers this season. (Note: The Associated Press uses STATS box scores but are only using Runners Moved Up in what they call their expanded box score, normally available for the local team boxes only.)

What kind of hitters move up the most baserunners with their outs? One has the image of Pete Rose, hitting behind the runner and moving him up. Let's look at a list of the players who had the best advance percentages on their outs in 1991. In the table below, "one-out at-bats" means plate appearances with at least one runner on base which produce one out — double plays are excluded, as are sacrifices, since those outs are already kept in the records. "Advance" means the player moved one or more runners up (one "advance" per at-bat credited, regardless of the total number of runners moved up). Here are the leaders (50 or more one-out at-bats):

Players with the Best Percentage of Advancing Runners on Outs — 1991

Player, Team	1-Out At-Bats	Adv	Pct
B.J. Surhoff, Mil	79	41	51.9
Harold Baines, Oak	71	30	42.3
Carlos Quintana, Bos	86	36	41.9
Tony Gwynn, SD	80	33	41.3
Jim Gantner, Mil	68	28	41.2
Kent Hrbek, Min	76	30	39.5
Will Clark, SF	109	43	39.5
Mark Grace, Cubs	94	37	39.4
Pete O'Brien, Sea	69	27	39.1
Mark Lemke, Atl	50	19	38.0

This is a fairly distinctive group of hitters, all of them well above the 1991 major league advance average of 24.0 percent. They're all good contact hitters — it's difficult to advance a runner with a strikeout. They are also primarily groundball or line-drive hitters, not the type who hit long, lazy flies.

But the most distinctive characteristic about the group is a more obvious one: eight of the ten bat left-handed. Of the other two, Lemke is a switch-hitter, and Quintana is a non-power hitting righty who hits a lot of balls to the opposite field. Left-handed hitters have an easier time hitting a ball to right field than most righty swingers do. And a ball hit to the right side has a far, far easier chance of advancing a runner than a ball hit to the left side.

Now let's look at the list of hitters with the **worst** advance percentages:

Players with the Worst Percentage of Advancing Runners on Outs — 1991

Player, Team	1-Out At-Bats	Adv	Pct
Rob Deer, Det	94	6	6.4
Jay Buhner, Sea	66	5	7.6
Travis Fryman, Det	86	7	8.1
Eric Davis, Cin	52	5	9.6
Tom Brunansky, Bos	82	8	9.8
Luis Rivera, Bos	63	7	11.1
Gary Pettis, Tex	52	6	11.5
Juan Gonzalez, Tex	94	11	11.7
Gary Gaetti, Min	84	10	11.9
Greg Gagne, Min	66	8	12.1

Rob Deer, Mr. "Unproductive Out" himself, unsurprisingly leads the way. This group contains more power hitters than the first one, and also more players (like Deer) who strike out a lot. But it's no coincidence at all that every player on the list bats righty; right-handed swingers deal with a huge natural handicap when it comes to advancing runners. So a player may be a "gamer," a "we ballplayer," a "team player." But if he's a right-handed hitter, he's going to have a lot of trouble advancing baserunners.

A complete listing for this category can be found on page 287.

WHO ARE THE RALLY KILLERS?

If the double play is a "pitcher's best friend," then it would also figure to be a hitter's — and an offense's — worst enemy. In the course of a few seconds, you erase both the runner and the batter, and often end the inning completely. Pretty depressing stuff . . . the stuff of losers, right?

Guess again. The club which led the major leagues in grounding into double plays last year was (of course!) the World Champion Minnesota Twins. The club which grounded into the fewest was the Cincinnati Reds, fifth place with a 74-88 record. And if you look at the hitters who have grounded into twin killings at the highest rate (GDP per GDP opportunity; an opportunity is a plate appearance with a runner on first and none or one out) over the last three seasons, you'll find some pretty fair ballplayers:

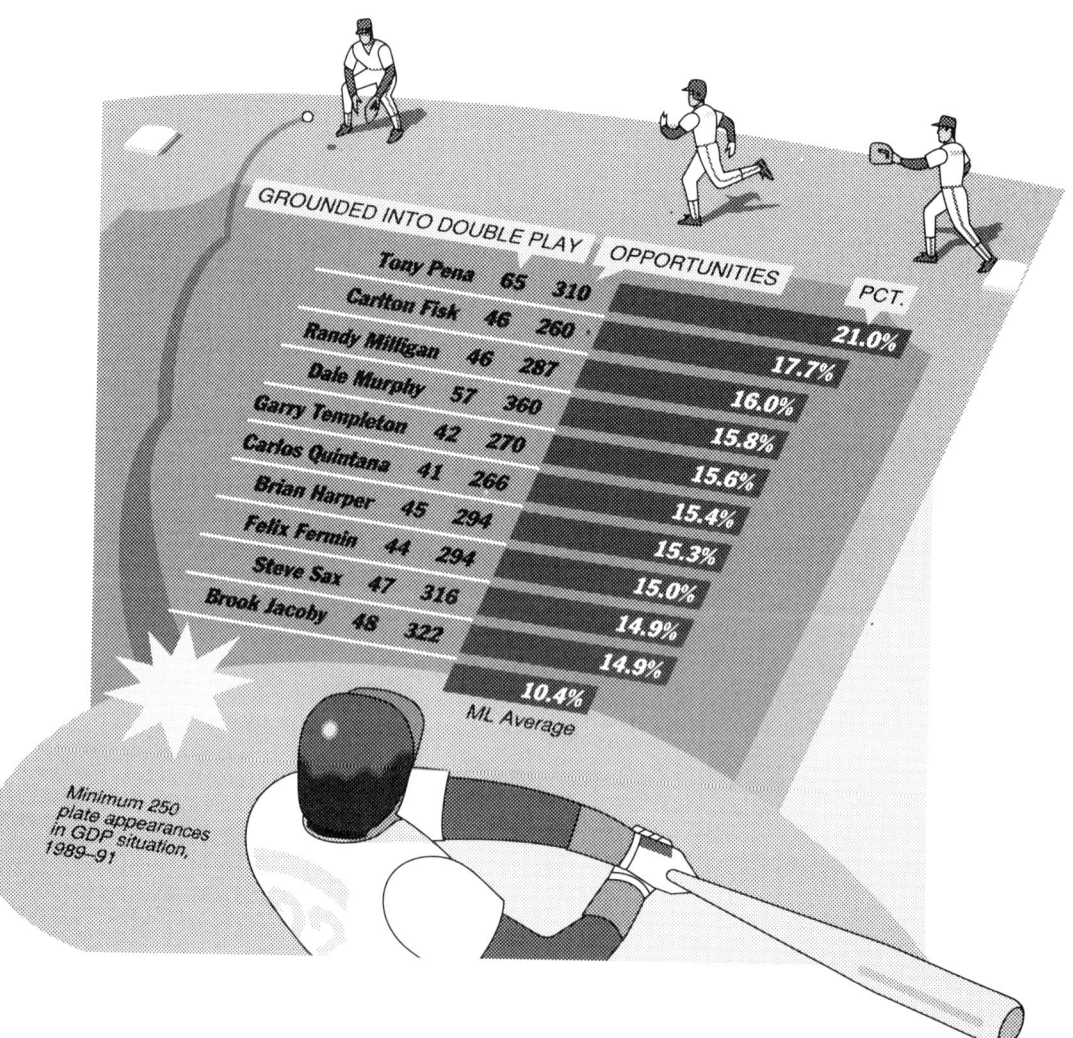

	GROUNDED INTO DOUBLE PLAY	OPPORTUNITIES	PCT.
Tony Pena	65	310	21.0%
Carlton Fisk	46	260	17.7%
Randy Milligan	46	287	16.0%
Dale Murphy	57	360	15.8%
Garry Templeton	42	270	15.6%
Carlos Quintana	41	266	15.4%
Brian Harper	45	294	15.3%
Felix Fermin	44	294	15.0%
Steve Sax	47	316	14.9%
Brook Jacoby	48	322	14.9%
ML Average			10.4%

Minimum 250 plate appearances in GDP situation, 1989–91

These were probably not your top ten fantasy league choices this spring, although it might have been in 1982. But it's not at all a bad list, especially Fisk, Quintana, Harper and Sax. Except for being overaged (Carlos Quintana is one of those "old" young guys), what traits do these players share?

1. Nine of ten are right-handed hitters (all except Templeton, a switch-hitter). Righties have a farther distance to first base than lefties, and the momentum of their swing is toward third base, not toward first as it is with lefty swingers. Thus righties are much easier to double up.

2. They generally hit the ball hard . . . except maybe for Fermin. A hard-hit ball gives the fielders more time to turn the DP.

3. They are either very slow runners (Pena, Fisk, Harper) or, if not slow, very pronounced ground ball hitters (Fermin, Sax).

4. They usually make contact, striking out at a low rate.

Except for lack of speed, this is a fairly good combination of talents. It's just that the talents combine to produce a big negative — the double play — along with the positives.

Now here are the hitters who have grounded into double plays at the **lowest** rate:

**Fewest GDPs per GDP Opportunity —
1989-91**

Batter	GDP	GDP Opp	Pct
Rob Deer	11	306	3.6
Howard Johnson	15	383	3.9
Will Clark	18	416	4.3
Ron Gant	14	284	4.9
Darryl Strawberry	17	328	5.2

Four big stars, and Rob Deer. What traits do these players have? They hit the ball in the air (often over the fence). Except for Clark, they strike out a lot . . . whatever you think about a strikeout, it generally only produces one out. And with the exception of Deer (who seems to either strike out or hit a fly ball every time up), they have good-to-excellent speed. The first combination of talents is good; this combination — especially since speed is so important in baseball — is a better one.

A complete listing for this category can be found on page 289.

WHERE HAVE YOU GONE, JOE DiMAGGIO?

One of the big changes in baseball over the years has come in the makeup of power hitters. As late as the 1950s, it was reasonably common to be both a home run hitter and a contact hitter, one who struck out 50 times a year or less. Let's look at the all-time list of the power hitters (at least 200 home runs, lifetime) with the lowest ratios of strikeouts to homers. The leader, Joe DiMaggio, is well known for his unique prowess in this category. You've undoubtedly heard of the others; you may not know how good they were in this particular category:

	HOME RUNS	STRIKEOUTS	RATIO
THE BEST			
Joe DiMaggio	361	369	1.02
Yogi Berra	358	414	1.16
Ted Kluszewski	279	365	1.31
Ted Williams	521	709	1.36
Bill Dickey	289	202	1.38
THE WORST			
Rick Monday	241	1513	6.28
Bobby Grich	224	1278	5.71
Deron Johnson	245	1318	5.38
Larry Parrish	256	1359	5.31
Bobby Bonds	332	1757	5.29

Even if you're familiar with DiMaggio's numbers — 361 homers, only 369 strikeouts — you have to marvel at them. Some of DiMag's year-by-year figures are truly amazing: 1937, 46 homers, only 37 strikeouts; 1941, 30 homers, 13 (!) strikeouts; 1948, 39 homers, 30 strikeouts. As a rookie in 1936, DiMaggio fanned 39 times (with 29 homers). The 39 Ks were Joe's **career high.**

There was no one else quite as good as DiMaggio as a contact-home run man, but there were a few contenders. The great Yogi Berra, who never fanned more than 38 times in a season, had 28 homers with only 12 strikeouts in 1950. Ted Kluszewski, now all but forgotten, fanned only 35 times while hitting 49 homers for the 1954 Reds. Stan Musial is seventh on the all-time list with only 1.47 strikeouts per home run. His seasonal high in whiffs was 46; in 1948 the Man had 39 homers, 34 Ks. Ted Williams, shame on him, actually fanned as many as 64 times in a season, but that was as a rookie in 1939. Ted quickly learned not to be such a wild swinger (by his standards, anyway) and never had as many as 50 strikeouts after 1942. In 1957, when he turned 39 and was presumably losing his reflexes, The Kid had 38 homers, 43 strikeouts.

Those figures should boggle the mind of the modern fan, who's used to seeing sluggers like Cecil Fielder (44 homers, 151 strikeouts last year) and Jose Canseco (44 HR, 152 Ks in '91) either go downtown or fan the breeze. For historical perspective, consider that Canseco (209 HR, 870 K lifetime) had surpassed DiMaggio's career strikeout total by April of 1988, when he was just beginning his third full season!

What happened? Even in the 1920s and '30s there were sluggers who struck out a lot. Babe Ruth fanned as many as 93 times in a season, a huge number in 1923, and Jimmie Foxx whiffed 119 times (with 41 homers) in 1936. Mickey Mantle had his career-high 126 strikeouts (31 homers) in 1959. However, the floodgates really opened in the 1960s. Hitters such as Dick Allen, Frank Howard, Harmon Killebrew, Willie Stargell and Reggie Jackson re-defined the notion of the home run hitter; people began to feel that it didn't matter how often you struck out, as long as you got your dingers. But what that meant was that the high-average home run hitter, so common throughout baseball history, became rarer and rarer. (It's possible, of course, to hit for a good average while striking out well over 100 times a year. But it makes the task a lot more difficult.)

Along the way, the "contact-home run" type of hitter began to disappear. The only one left, really, is Don Mattingly (178 career homers, 300 career strikeouts), and Mattingly's back problems seem to have cost him his home run stroke. These days, good strikeout-to-homer ratios are represented by hitters like George Brett, Kent Hrbek, Cal Ripken and Eddie Murray, all of whom have fanned around three times as much as they have homered during their careers. Good, but not in the class of such recent heroes as Henry Aaron (1.83 career ratio) or Willie Mays (1.86)

Has the game changed so much that we won't see this type of hitter again? Perhaps we shouldn't despair. Last year Ripken quietly had the kind of figures that wouldn't have looked out of place in Stan Musial's career: 34 homers, 46 strikeouts (and, not coincidentally, a .323 batting average). We'll never see another Joe DiMaggio, but there's no reason why we can't see a few more home run-contact men.

A complete listing for this category can be found on page 290.

WILL THE REAL ALAN TRAMMELL PLEASE STAND UP?

We suggested last year that investing in ballplayers — whether you're a general manager, a fantasy player, or simply a fan with an emotional investment — is more than a little like playing the stock market. There are the blue chips, the Wade Boggses and Tony Gwynns, who prove to be a good value even when they have an off-year. Then there the purely speculative stocks, like Bill Ripken — way up one year, way down the next. Most players are somewhere in the middle: fairly predictable, but with occasional fluctuations usually caused by injury, aging or a change of scenery.

We therefore present our annual Investors Guide. First, the bull market, players who were unusually hot last year compared to 1990:

Batting Average Improved Most

Player, Team	1990	1991	Change
Terry Pendleton, Atl	.230	.319	+ 89
Milt Thompson, StL	.218	.307	+ 89
Cal Ripken, Bal	.250	.323	+ 73
Willie Randolph, Mil	.260	.327	+ 67
Devon White, Tor	.217	.282	+ 65
Carlos Martinez, Cle	.224	.284	+ 60
Larry Walker, Mon	.241	.290	+ 49
Danny Tartabull, KC	.268	.316	+ 48
Steve Buechele, Tex-Pit	.215	.262	+ 47
Otis Nixon, Atl	.251	.297	+ 46

Players (and teams) who surge one year, Bill James once pointed out, tend to fall back the next; that's the nature of statistical variations. So it's risky to think that Cal Ripken, who last year hit .300 for the first time since 1984, will hit as high as .323 again. Or that Otis Nixon, whose previous career high was .263, suddenly found the secret of success last year at age 32. (Nixon's drug problems make him an even riskier bet). Sometimes a change to a better hitters' ballpark can help a player; that was the key for Pendleton and White last year. They should be expected to slip this year, but probably not to their 1990 level.

Pop quiz time. Say you're a major league team and you see a player post the following averages over a four year period: .274, .268, .268, .316. Which is his real level of ability, the place where his numbers figure to settle in year five? Well, of course, at .316 . . . that's the way you think if you own the New York Yankees, and the player is Danny Tartabull. Right.

Now here's the bear market, players who slumped in 1991. They should be available at bargain rates. But will they bounce back?

Batting Average Declined Most

Player, Team	1990	1991	Change
Bill Ripken, Bal	.291	.216	−75
George Brett, KC	.329	.255	−74
Darren Daulton, Phi	.268	.196	−72
Tim Wallach, Mon	.296	.225	−71
Eddie Murray, LA	.330	.260	−70
Dave Magadan, Mets	.328	.258	−70
Brook Jacoby, Cle-Oak	.293	.224	−69
Alvin Davis, Sea	.283	.221	−62
Chris James, Cle	.299	.238	−61
Rickey Henderson, Oak	.325	.268	−57

Another pop quiz. Say you've had a catcher for a long while, and his averages have gone like this: .204, .225, .194, .208, .201, .268. What kind of hitter has he shown himself to be? Why, a .268 hitter, of course, you say if you're the Philadelphia Phillies, and the player is Darren Daulton. The Phils gave Daulton a big contract last year, then just couldn't believe it when he batted .196.

Bets to rebound in 1992: Rickey Henderson (he'll have something to prove), George Brett (assuming he has even marginal health), Dave Magadan (no .258 hitter), Alvin Davis (the Mariners gave up on him; a change of scenery should help his average, if not his power). Risky bets: Chris James (the .299 was the illusion), Bill Ripken (see below), Eddie Murray (still a great player, but entering the New York Zoo at age 36. We can hear the boos already).

Who is the most unpredictable hitter? It could be Ron Gant, who's hit .259, .177, .303 and .251 the last four years. Or Murray, .284, .247, .330 and .260 over the same period. Or Billy Rip, whose year-by-year numbers are .308, .207, .239, .291, .216.

The king, though, is Alan Trammell, who's arguably been a Hall-of-Famer when healthy, but a lot less than that when hurting. Trammell since 1984: .314, .258, .277, .343, .311, .243, .304, .248. Watch those Tiger injury reports this spring.

A complete listing for this category appears on page 292.

WHO WINS THE "GAME OF THE STATES"?

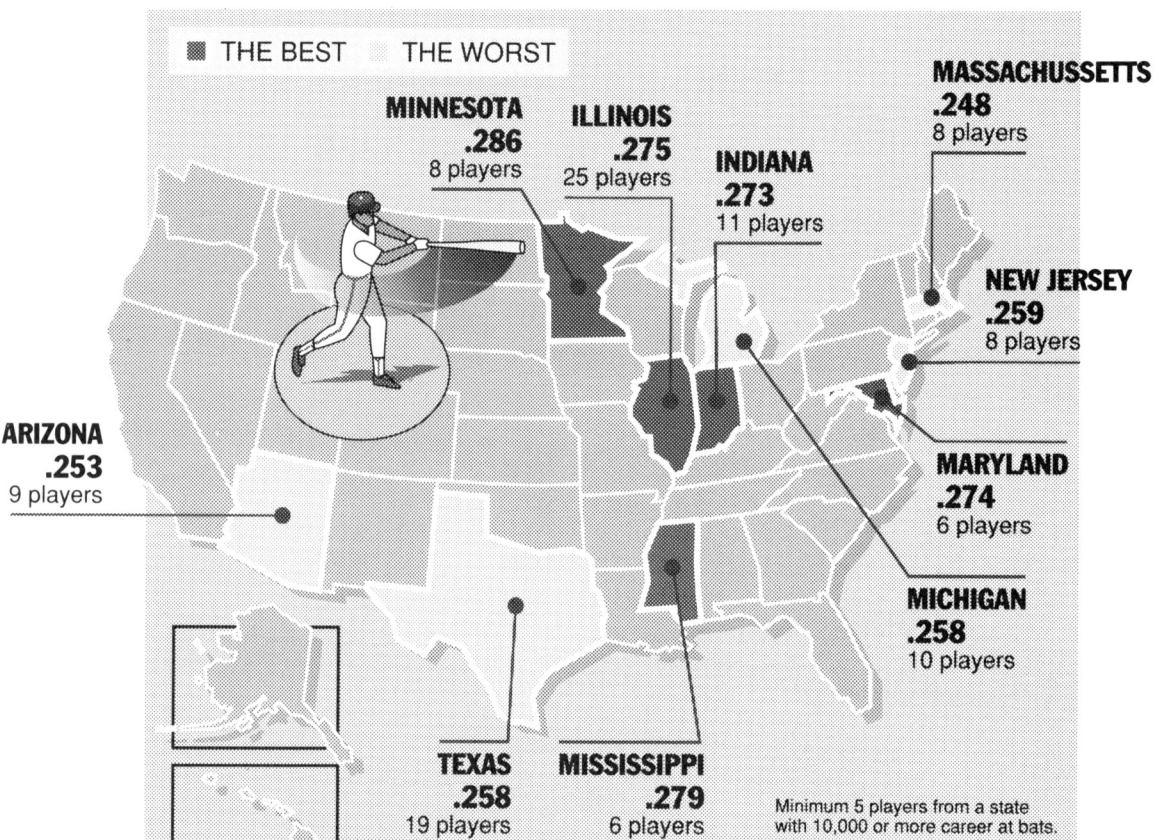

"We, the people of baseball, in order to form a more perfect game, invite players from 50 states and numerous countries to try out for the several teams." So, we believe, begins the preamble to the constitution of baseball. Prejudices naggingly remain, but (unlike in 1946) if you can play the game, you'll probably get your shot . . . wherever you're from, and whoever you are.

Let's imagine baseball as a regional conflict, with each player (hitters only) performing for the state, Canadian province or foreign country in which he was born. Where do the best players come from? As the graphic shows, the best in terms of batting average (five players minimum) are Minnesota, Mississippi, Illinois, Maryland and Indiana.

Minnesota (.286). The Gopher State is on a roll. Minnesota not only produced the 1991 World Champs; it's produced a crop of hitters that include Paul Molitor (.302 lifetime), Kent Hrbek (.289), Dave Winfield

(.285), Jim Eisenreich (.279) and Terry Steinbach (.270). Even the Minnesotan with the **lowest** average, the Braves' Greg Olson (.250), is no slouch.

Mississippi (.279). How did a state whose six players include Barry Lyons (.236 lifetime), Chico Walker (.237), Charlie Hayes (.247) and Dave Clark (.250) rate so highly? Simple; the other two Mississippians are Dave Parker (.290 in 9500 at-bats) and Ellis Burks (.283). The Mudcat State's ranking will sink like a stone, however, if Parker can't find a major league job this year. An entire state depends on you, Dave!

Illinois (.275). Illinois has produced 25 players, with quality as well as quantity. How about Kirby Puckett (.320), Kevin Seitzer (.294), Rickey Henderson (.291), Lonnie Smith (.291) and Robin Yount (.288)? Of course, there's also a few guys like Tom Prince (.179) and Darrin Fletcher (.228), but all in all, the Cubs and White Sox should have this much talent.

Maryland (.274). This is another state dominated by two performers. But when their names are Harold Baines (.289) and Cal Ripken (.279), a state can get away with that. If only brother Bill (.247) and Brady Anderson (.219) could pad their averages a little . . .

Indiana (.273). This is beginning to look like a Midwest convention, isn't it? Indiana is like Mississippi and Maryland, only more so. Only one of the Hoosier State's 11 players has a career average above .265; but, Don Mattingly (.314) makes up for a lot of Jeff Kings (.229) and Brian Dorsetts (.198).

Those are the best states. How about the worst ones?

Massachusetts (.248). How can the state which boasts the Red Sox also "boast" Junior Ortiz (.275) as its second-best hitter? But then, the BoSox traded away the state's number-one man, Jeff Bagwell (.294). Is some kind of witch's curse still at work?

Arizona (.253). Except for the Cactus League, there's no major league baseball tradition here. Maybe someday they'll produce a better hitter than Billy Hatcher (.265).

Michigan (.258) and **Texas** (.258). For shame, for shame! Would you believe the Michigander with the highest lifetime average is Chris Sabo (.278)? Texas' best is Chuck Knoblauch (.281), a rookie last year. Sorry, guys, you can't talk about Nolan Ryan.

New Jersey (.259). Not as bad as it looks, just a lot of fellows like Joe Orsulak (.277) and Dave Gallagher (.275), dragged down by the the likes of Ron Karkovice (.222). Baseball's version of the New Jersey Nets.

A complete listing for this category can be found on page 293.

IS THERE SUCH A THING AS A "TURF HITTER"?

Artificial turf — "If a horse can't eat it, I don't want to play on it," said Dick Allen, and many players would echo that sentiment. Yet there are a lot of misconceptions about plastic grass. We always hear that artificial turf shortens careers, but the only player to win batting titles in three different decades, George Brett, has played most of his games on turf. And we used to hear that turf would raise batting averages by 20-30 points, but there's been no real evidence of that, either.

Another thing we hear is that there are "turf hitters," players whose hitting style is designed for the fast surface. A profile of a turf hitter would include excellent running speed, a tendency to hit the ball on the ground, and little home run power.

Let's see if we can shed some light on the existence of turf hitters. We'll lump all the "turf hitters" together and look at their stats. If there is a particular advantage in playing on an artificial field, we should find that these guys have much better stats on turf than on grass. Here's how we'll isolate the turf hitters (based on the last three years of statistics):

1) They run fast — they must average at least 20 stolen bases plus triples per 600 at-bats.

2) They hit the ball on the ground — they must average at least 1.5 groundballs per flyball. This is well above the major league average of 1.3 groundballs per flyball over the last three years.

3) The don't hit home runs — they must average less than 15 home runs per 600 at-bats.

Using these parameters, we get all the guys known as the classical "turf hitters", including Willie McGee, Vince Coleman, Willie Wilson and Luis Polonia. Here are the results:

	"Turf Hitters"			
Category	AB	H	Avg	Slg
On Grass	37,131	10,176	.274	.359
On Turf	25,820	6,952	.269	.379

Based on these results, the "turf hitter" is a mythological character. The batting average for "turf hitters" actually **drops** five points when they play on turf. The slugging percentage does go up a bit (20 points); the carpet helps turn some singles into doubles/triples. Doubles are up 13% and triples are up 30%.

What about the non-turf hitters (all the rest of the guys)?

	"Non-Turf Hitters"			
Category	AB	H	Avg	Slg
On Grass	220,613	56,695	.257	.394
On Turf	132,696	34,140	.257	.397

The non-turf hitters perform virtually the same on both grass and turf. Slugging percentage is up slightly, three points, with similar increases in doubles and triples on turf as the turf hitters.

For further evidence, let's look at some individual performances. If the theory that turf hitters do exist is valid, then the players who have the biggest turf-over-grass advantages should show those tendencies. Using three years worth of data (1989-91), here are the hitters with the largest bias toward turf (minimum 750 plate appearances):

Players with the Biggest Turf Bias — 1989-91

	On Grass				On Turf				BA
Player	Avg	Slg	AB	HR	Avg	Slg	AB	HR	Diff
Bob Melvin	.227	.293	683	6	.339	.452	124	1	−112
Stan Javier	.238	.301	631	3	.335	.488	164	2	−97
Dave Bergman	.251	.357	673	14	.333	.477	111	2	−82
Glenn Braggs	.229	.343	668	16	.310	.488	410	19	−81
Wally Joyner	.273	.424	1,225	37	.354	.524	229	8	−81
Dave Winfield	.254	.433	882	36	.323	.627	161	13	−69
Brady Anderson	.210	.291	609	7	.272	.415	147	2	−62
Kevin Bass	.236	.378	505	16	.295	.426	383	6	−59
Delino DeShields	.220	.316	313	5	.279	.379	749	9	−59
Mike LaValliere	.242	.315	219	2	.300	.382	586	6	−58

Speedy turf hitters, right? — Bob Melvin, Dave Bergman, Wally Joyner, Dave Winfield, Mike LaValliere. We'll grant you that some of the players fit the profile, but even Delino DeShields, who would seem to be Mr. Turf, doesn't hit an exceptional number of groundballs. Neither does Stan Javier, who, like DeShields, possesses good speed. You could pick a random group of players, and not find as sketchy a group of supposed "turf hitters" as this.

Let's see if the list of players with the biggest grass bias fits the profile any better:

Players with the Biggest Grass Bias — 1989-91

Player	On Grass				On Turf				BA Diff
	Avg	Slg	AB	HR	Avg	Slg	AB	HR	
Frank Thomas	.339	.583	611	34	.245	.388	139	5	94
Dave Henderson	.276	.452	1,364	55	.203	.338	237	5	73
Bill Spiers	.271	.367	963	12	.201	.270	159	2	70
Otis Nixon	.301	.342	392	1	.231	.271	498	0	70
Dwight Smith	.303	.443	544	13	.234	.371	256	5	69
Brook Jacoby	.277	.415	1,247	30	.209	.262	244	1	68
Robby Thompson	.267	.440	1,133	36	.200	.337	404	11	67
Carlos Quintana	.297	.394	873	12	.232	.361	194	6	65
Jerry Browne	.283	.374	1,168	11	.219	.279	233	1	64
Jay Buhner	.299	.541	281	17	.236	.463	492	26	63

Most of these players fit the turf/grass profile better: Frank Thomas, Dave Henderson, Brook Jacoby, Carlos Quintana and Jay Buhner, especially. Yet what is Otis Nixon doing here, or Jerry Browne? Again it's an inexact match, and you'd be stretching things a lot to say that this is a definitive list of "grass hitters." In fact, a more powerful factor at work here may be that the home field of most of these guys is grass. They simply like their home stadiums better. This is especially true for the number-one guy on the list, Frank Thomas (.371 at home vs. 271 on the road in 1991).

The truth is that it's never been proven that grass and turf surfaces produce sharply defined statistical differences. Indeed, some teams cut their grass very short; others try to aid groundball pitchers by letting the grass grow high. And older Astroturf often plays much differently than a field which is newly installed. Some people may continue to think that there are "grass" and "turf" hitters — but the statistical evidence to back those claims has yet to surface.

A complete listing for this category can be found on page 294.

III. QUESTIONS ON PITCHING

DO MINOR LEAGUE STRIKEOUT KINGS MAKE GOOD MAJOR LEAGUE PROSPECTS?

	W–L	ERA	STRIKEOUTS PER 9 INNINGS
Mo Sanford, Reds–AA	10–4	2.44	11.30
Wilson Alvarez, White Sox–AA	10–6	1.83	9.75
Arthur Rhodes, Orioles–AA	7–4	2.70	9.70
Archie Corbin, Royals–AA	8–8	4.66	9.56
Roger Salkeld, Mariners–AAA	10–9	3.28	9.36

Minimum 109 innings pitched.

Since we know many of you are interested in the minor leagues — particularly in trying to identify the best prospects — we thought we'd present some minor league stats this year. Since study after study has shown that power pitchers are better longterm prospects than finesse pitchers, we'll look at the Class AA and AAA leaders in strikeouts per nine innings. There's a good reason why we skip the Class A and Rookie League numbers: they're unreliable predictors of the future, mostly because the level of competition is low. Class AA and AAA numbers can be deceiving, also, but striking out a lot of batters at those levels is a lot more meaningful.

Here are the AA and AAA starters with the highest ratios of strikeouts per nine innings in 1991:

Most Strikeouts per Nine Innings — Starters (AA and AAA 1991)

Starters	Age	Organization	League	K per 9 IP
Mo Sanford, Nashville	25	Cincinnati	American Assn	11.30
Wilson Alvarez, Birmingham	22	White Sox	Southern	9.75
Arthur Rhodes, Hagerstown	22	Baltimore	Eastern	9.70
Archie Corbin, Memphis	24	Kansas City	Southern	9.56
Roger Salkeld, Calgary	21	Seattle	Pacific Coast	9.36
Pat Mahomes, Portland	21	Minnesota	Pacific Coast	9.32
John DeSilva, Toledo	24	Detroit	International	9.25
Lance Dickson, Iowa	22	Cubs	American Assn	8.97
Kevin Coffman, Jackson	27	Astros	Texas	8.94
Willie Smith, Albany	24	Yankees	Eastern	8.64

If you study the organizational reports at all, you're familiar with a lot of these names. Pitchers like Alvarez, Rhodes, Salkeld and Mahomes are considered to be among the top prospects in all of baseball. But not everyone here is so highly rated. When a player is older than 25 and is still laboring at the AA level — like Kevin Coffman — his chances of making it the majors are a lot lower than if he were 21 or 22. The younger, the better, in other words. It's also true that some organizations (the Reds and Mariners, to name two), have a better record in developing power pitchers than others do. A few clubs, most notably the Yankees, show little patience with youthful control problems. Roger Salkeld, in other words, should have an easier path to the majors than Willie Smith will.

These are the AA and AAA relief pitchers who averaged the most strikeouts per nine innings in 1991:

Most Strikeouts per Nine Innings — Relievers (AA and AAA 1991)

Relievers	Age	Organization	League	K per 9 IP
Rudy Seanez, Col. Springs	23	Cleveland	Pacific Coast	14.87
Doug Piatt, Indianapolis	26	Montreal	American Assn	11.68
Tim Fortugno, Denver	30	Milwaukee	American Assn	11.24
Kurt Knudsen, Toledo	25	Detroit	International	10.80
Angel Miranda, Denver	22	Milwaukee	American Assn	10.47
Dana Ridenour, Indianapolis	26	Montreal	American Assn	10.38
Mark Wohlers, Richmond	22	Atlanta	International	10.30
Darren Hall, Knoxville	27	Toronto	Southern	10.13
Matt Grott, Harrisburg	24	Expos	Eastern	9.99
Dave Richards, Jackson	24	Astros	Texas	9.84

Predicting success for relief pitchers is somewhat trickier than it is for starters. A lot of them are in the bullpen because they have shaky control, and there's no better example of that than the leader here, Rudy Seanez. Seanez was up and down with the Indians over the last few years, with discouraging results: 34 games, 37.1 innings, 38 strikeouts, 36 walks, a 6.75 ERA. Even the pitching-poor Tribe got tired of waiting for Rudy to learn control, and he now belongs to the Dodgers. All winter we've heard exciting reports from the winter leagues on the progress Seanez has made. We'll see.

Many of the same rules we applied to the starters also apply to the relievers. That includes the "age barrier." It may well be that Tim Fortugno, who turns 30 on April 11, could make it as a major league reliever. His stats over the last couple of years, recorded while working in the notorious hitters' parks at El Paso and Denver, have been very impressive. Over his minor league career, Fortugno has struck out 620 batters in 485.1 innings! But most clubs figure a guy like this is "too old," and won't even give him a chance. We'll see what happens with a new team; he was picked up by the Angels in the Rule 5 draft over the winter.

WHOSE HEATER IS THE HOTTEST?

No matter what you hear, one axiom that remains true year after year is this one: the best pitch in baseball is the fastball. There's a famous story from the seventies about how Johnny Sain, the wise old White Sox pitching coach, took the young Goose Gossage aside and said, "Rich, you can't throw the fastball past major league hitters." And Gossage just smiled and thought, "Well, maybe **you** couldn't." The Goose, of course, was right. No knock against Johnny Sain, who had a fine major league career, but Gossage is the one who's going to have the plaque hanging in Cooperstown.

It is indeed true that you can throw the fastball past major league hitters; the catch is that you have to throw it hard enough. As we pointed out a couple of years ago, nowadays a lot of the pitchers who throw the hardest are shifted to the bullpen, where they don't have to worry about pacing themselves and can simply air it out pitch after pitch. As has been true for awhile, the list of leaders in strikeouts per nine innings was dominated by short relievers (both leagues in 1991):

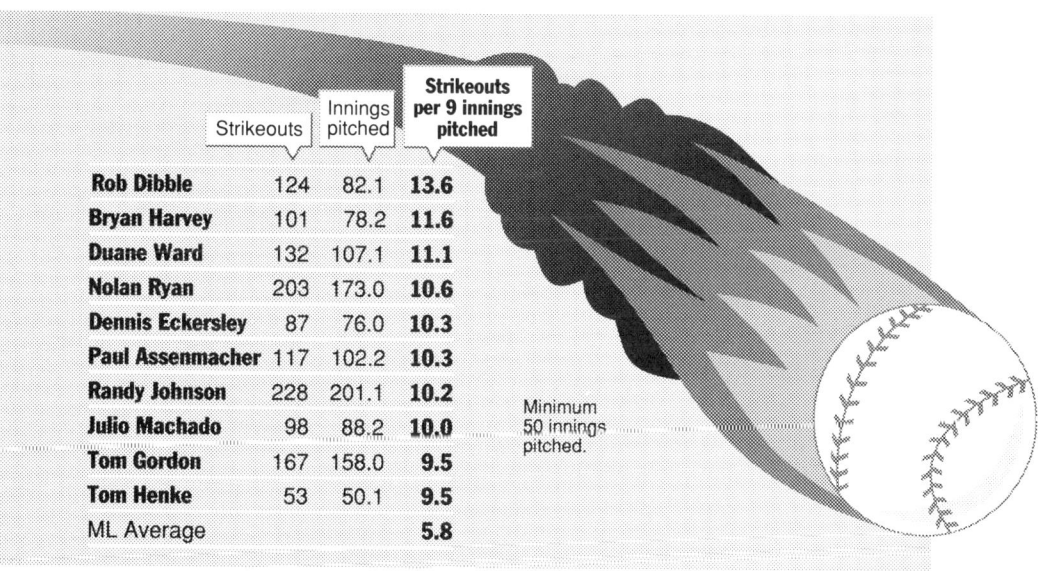

	Strikeouts	Innings pitched	Strikeouts per 9 innings pitched
Rob Dibble	124	82.1	**13.6**
Bryan Harvey	101	78.2	**11.6**
Duane Ward	132	107.1	**11.1**
Nolan Ryan	203	173.0	**10.6**
Dennis Eckersley	87	76.0	**10.3**
Paul Assenmacher	117	102.2	**10.3**
Randy Johnson	228	201.1	**10.2**
Julio Machado	98	88.2	**10.0**
Tom Gordon	167	158.0	**9.5**
Tom Henke	53	50.1	**9.5**
ML Average			**5.8**

Minimum 50 innings pitched.

There are a few starters on this list — Randy Johnson, Tom Gordon, the eternal Nolan Ryan — but the top three are all relievers, and short men dominate the list. Not everyone is exclusively a fastball pitcher; Assenmacher and Gordon are primarily breaking ball pitchers, and several others rely on more than one pitch. But the fastball is king here, and everyone on the list can make the batter swing and miss, which is the point of the whole exercise.

The opposite side of the coin is represented by the pitchers who fanned the fewest batters per nine innings in 1991. It's quite a contrast:

Pitcher, Team	IP	K	K/9 IP
Dave Eiland, Yanks	72.2	18	2.2
Jeff Ballard, Bal	123.2	37	2.7
Roy Smith, Bal	80.1	25	2.8
John Barfield, Tex	83.1	27	2.9
John Cerutti, Det	88.2	29	2.9

(Minimum 50 innings pitched)

Another old axiom — Johnny Sain might have invented this one — is, "Don't be afraid to use your fielders." This theory is clearly espoused by Eiland and company; the problem is that most of their teams were afraid to use **them**. The lowest ERA in the bunch was Barfield's 4.54.

* * * * * * * * * * * *

We thought you might be interested in the list of active lifetime leaders in strikeouts per nine innings. This one is not yet reliever-dominated:

Pitcher	IP	K	K/9 IP
Tom Henke	567.1	649	10.3
Nolan Ryan	5,163.1	5,511	9.6
Lee Smith	992.1	990	9.0
Bobby Witt	980.0	951	8.7
Tom Gordon	532.0	513	8.7
Mitch Williams	511.0	486	8.6
David Cone	1,017.1	966	8.6
Randy Johnson	607.2	577	8.6
Sid Fernandez	1,256.1	1,184	8.5
Roger Clemens	1,784.1	1,665	8.4

(Minimum 500 innings pitched lifetime)

The changing game — the list will change considerably once relievers Ward (491.0 lifetime innings), Myers (458.2), Dibble (338.2) and Harvey

(279.0) work another year or two. These days, the heat is hottest in the bullpen.

A few pitchers survive, some of them barely, strictly on finesse. The lifetime leaders in fewest strikeouts per nine innings:

Pitcher	IP	K	K/9 IP
Jeff Ballard	695.1	217	2.8
Doug Sisk	523.1	195	3.4
Bob Tewksbury	551.1	214	3.5
Bill Swift	759.0	292	3.5
Greg Hibbard	542.1	218	3.6
Allan Anderson	818.2	339	3.7

(Minimum 500 innings pitched lifetime)

So you don't need a good fastball? Don't tell that to Anderson, Sisk or Ballard, who spent their winter months scanning the want ads. Perhaps sensing the trend, Billy got Swifter last year, averaging 4.8 strikeouts per nine.

A complete listing for this category appears on page 295.

WILL THEY KEEP 'EM OFF BASE IN '92 LIKE THEY DID IN 1991?

It's no great revelation that pitchers who can keep runners off base will usually have superior stats across the board. Most fantasy leagues use baserunners per inning or per nine innings as a key factor in identifying the best hurlers, and they have the right idea. Occasionally you'll find someone like Pete Vuckovich in 1982 who posts good overall numbers despite allowing a lot of runners, but those are very rare cases. Keeping the bases empty is one of the unmistakable signs of outstanding pitching.

Here are the 1991 leaders in fewest baserunners per nine innings (minimum 81 innings pitched). We add the pitcher's earned run average to show the strong relationship between the two stats:

Fewest Baserunners per Nine Innings — 1991

Pitcher, Team	IP	BR/9	ERA
Mark Eichhorn, Cal	81.2	8.60	1.98
Todd Frohwirth, Bal	96.1	8.78	1.87
Nolan Ryan, Tex	173.0	9.31	2.91
Jeff Innis, Mets	84.2	9.46	2.66
John Habyan, Yanks	90.0	9.50	2.30
Roger Clemens, Bos	271.1	9.59	2.62
Duane Ward, Tor	107.1	9.64	2.77
Mike Maddux, SD	98.2	9.67	2.46
Carl Willis, Min	89.0	9.71	2.63
Greg W. Harris, SD	133.0	9.74	2.23

Clearly, everyone on this list pitched extremely well last year. But can we expect them to repeat their good work in 1992? The answer is a split decision. Most of the pitchers on this list are relievers, specifically middle relievers. Will Mark Eichhorn, Todd Frohwirth, John Habyan, Mike Maddux and Carl Willis continue to post dominant numbers in 1992? Maybe they will, but you'll have to prove it to all the clubs who gave up on them in the past. The problem is that most of them have to depend on control rather than power in order to succeed. And that type has big problems posting two good seasons in a row; among other things, they often don't get enough work to stay sharp. Witness the up-and-down career of Mark Eichhorn, one of the more talented members of the bunch:

Mark Eichhorn

Year	BR/9	ERA
1986	9.00	1.72
1987	11.84	3.17
1988	15.12	4.18
1989	11.85	4.35
1990	13.50	3.08
1991	8.60	1.98

The moral is that it's very risky to depend on continued success for a reliever lacking overpowering stuff. Starters, however, are a much safer bet. Let's expand the list to include the other starters (minimum 162 IP) who, along with Clemens and Ryan, made up the top ten last year:

Pitcher, Team	IP	BR/9	ERA
Jose Rijo, Cin	204.1	9.82	2.51
Kevin Tapani, Min	244.0	9.85	2.99
Tom Glavine, Atl	246.2	9.92	2.55
Mike Morgan, LA	236.1	9.94	2.78
Scott Sanderson, Yanks	208.0	10.04	3.81
Bret Saberhagen, KC	196.1	10.04	3.07
Dennis Martinez, Mon	222.0	10.26	2.39
Andy Benes, SD	223.0	10.37	3.03

Can this group — plus Clemens and Ryan — be expected to repeat its success in 1992? It seems fairly likely, since most of them had good seasons in both 1990 and '91. Certainly some of them are going to slip (Scott Sanderson, an aging finesse pitcher, is the most obvious candidate). But on the whole, it's far more likely that Kevin Tapani will have a good 1992 than Jeff Innis will.

These pitchers allowed the most baserunners per nine innings in 1991. Without a doubt, their careers will be on the line this year:

Most Baserunners per Nine Innings — 1991

Pitcher, Team	IP	BR/9	ERA
Dave Johnson, Bal	84.0	16.61	7.07
Bobby Witt, Tex	88.2	16.14	6.09
Wade Taylor, Yanks	116.1	15.78	6.27
Tim Leary, Yanks	120.2	15.74	6.49
Jose Mesa, Bal	123.2	15.72	5.97

This is pretty sad, especially if you're not too young to remember when the Orioles and Yankees used to dominate the American League with their great pitching staffs.

A complete listing for this category can be found on page 297.

WHO PITCHED BETTER IN 1991 — BILL GULLICKSON OR FRANK VIOLA?

More than ten years after Bill James invented it, the concept of "run support" — how many runs a club scores for a starting pitcher — finally seems to be getting some acceptance. Following the 1991 season, the Cincinnati Reds made a big trade for Cleveland lefthander Greg Swindell, whose record last season was only 9-16. (Will the loser in this trade consider itself "swindelled"?) Soon afterward the Boston Red Sox gave a big free agent contract to another lefty, Frank Viola, who was coming off a lowly 13-15 campaign. Both the Reds and Red Sox knew that their acquisitions had pitched better than their records last year, that one of their biggest problems was lack of support. Otherwise, why did Viola get all that money?

Swindell and Viola are two of the featured players this year in our annual "who pitched better" comparison. The idea is to match pitchers who have very similar earned run averages, but very different won-loss records. The difference was not in how they pitched; it was in how many runs their offenses provided. The pairings:

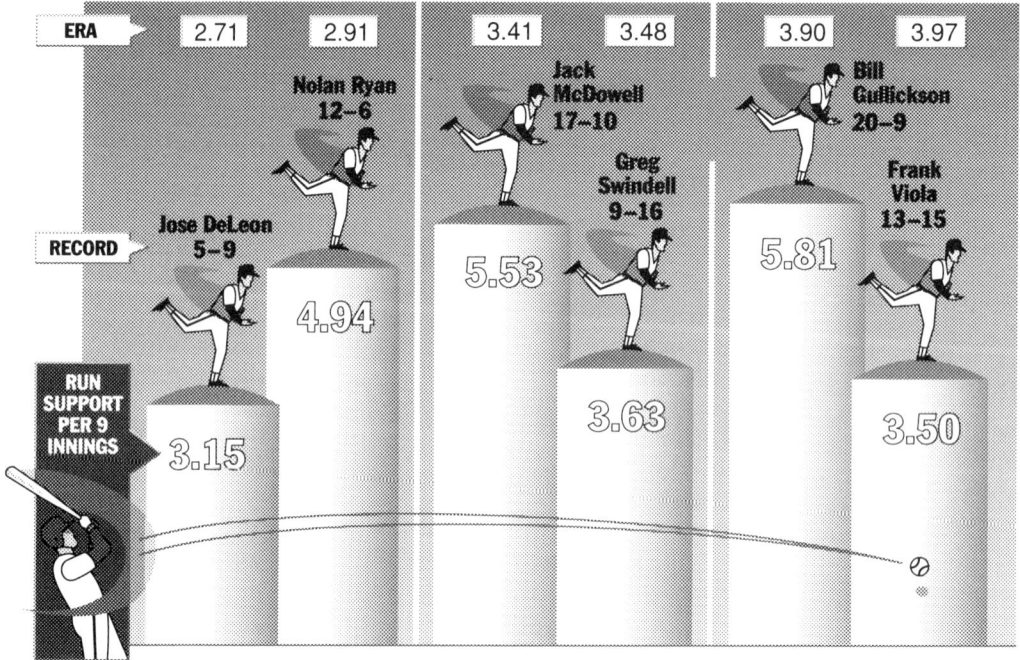

Did we say the notion of run support is gaining acceptance? Well, maybe a little. Bill Gullickson, the hollowest 20-game winner around (check out his .288 opponents' batting average, along with the 3.90 ERA) was considered a "Cy Young Award candidate" by some people. As far as we can see, Gullickson's only qualification is that he may have pitched against Cy Young. But then, Bob Welch — 27 wins, mostly due to 5.90 runs a game worth of support — won the Cy Young in 1990. So why not Gullickson?

What the comparisons show is something the Gullickson crowd still hasn't quite grasped: that it's a lot easier to win a game if your team scores five runs than it is if they only score three — no matter how well or how badly you pitch. Jose DeLeon may or may not be an "underachiever," but it's easier to underachieve when your club only scores 3.15 runs a game for you.

****

The subject of run support often comes up in regard to DeLeon, whom some people are convinced simply "can't win." The subject also applies in the opposite sense to Dwight Gooden, who was blessed by good offense the last two years while DeLeon was being snakebit:

	Won	Lost	ERA	Run Support
Gooden	32	14	3.73	6.03
DeLeon	12	28	3.62	3.05

Despite a lower ERA, DeLeon's record is almost the opposite of Gooden's. Is it because he's a "loser" and Gooden's a "winner" . . . or because Gooden's teammates have averaged almost twice as many runs per game? Before you start dumping on DeLeon, consider that in 1989, when the Cardinals managed to score 3.79 runs per game for him — almort one run per game more than in 1990 and '91, but a figure still below the National League average — Jose's record was 16-12.

A complete listing for this category can be found on page 298.

CAN ANYONE HIT NOLAN RYAN — NOW OR EVER?

Opponents' batting average, a fairly new stat, wasn't invented by Nolan Ryan's press agent, but it should have been. Last year, along with throwing his customary no-hitter, Nolan held the opposition to a .172 average, a full 40 points below any other starting pitcher in baseball. Houston's Pete Harnisch, who was born 12 days after Ryan made his major league debut on September 11, 1966, was a distant number two at .212.

Since Ryan does the spectacular on a regular basis, few people noticed that the .172 mark was the third-lowest one-season opponents' batting average of all time. Only Luis Tiant in 1968 (.168) and Ryan himself in 1972 (.171) had better marks, but you could argue convincingly that Ryan's 1991 effort was the best ever. When Tiant posted that .168 mark in pitcher-dominated 1968, the American League average was only 62 points higher at .230. And when the young Ryan held opponents to that .171 average in 1972, another pitchers' season, the league figure was 68 points higher at .239. But Ryan's 1991 figure was an enormous 88 points below the AL average of .260. No one else has ever bettered the league norm by such a huge margin; as we pointed out a couple of years ago, the old record was 80 points (.183 to .263), set by the wild Yankee lefty, Tommy Byrne, in 1949.

You're probably wondering if Ryan is the best ever when it comes to career opponent batting average. He is. Batters faced and opposition at-bats haven't been kept throughout baseball history, so we don't know, for example, exactly what Cy Young's opponents' average was. But you can make a close estimate using hits allowed and innings pitched, and it's clear that no one can surpass Nolan. For purposes of this leaders list, we restrict the stats only to seasons where we have the actual figures. For all intents and purposes, the only pitcher affected is Big Ed Walsh, who has data missing from three years. For the years the data exists, Walsh's opponent batting average is .217; our friends at *Total Baseball*, who estimate the at-bats for the missing seasons, have Walsh at .218, which doesn't affect his place on the list. Larger blocks of data are missing for Ed Daily, Toad Ramsey, Elton Chamberlain (all 19th century pitchers) and Rube Waddell (1897-1910), all of whom had a theoretical chance at the leaders list. However, the hits and innings pitched for the missing years make it clear that Waddell is the only one who could possibly qualify for the top 20; *Total Baseball* estimates Waddell's opponent batting average at .228. At any rate, here is the all-time leaders list (minimum 4,000 opponent at-bats):

Lowest Opponents' Batting Average — All-Time

Pitcher	Opp. AB	Hits	Opp. Batting Average
Nolan Ryan	18,444	3,731	.202
Sid Fernandez	4,547	930	.205
Sandy Koufax	8,547	1,754	.205
J.R. Richard	5,790	1,227	.212
Andy Messersmith	8,106	1,719	.212
Sam McDowell	9,060	1,948	.215
Hoyt Wilhelm	8,127	1,757	.216
Ed Walsh *	8,839	1,920	.217
Joe Wood	5,171	1,138	.220
Mario Soto	6,336	1,395	.220
Bob Turley	6,200	1,366	.220
Babe Ruth	4,404	974	.221
Don McMahon	4,763	1,054	.221
Orval Overall	5,539	1,232	.222
Jeff Tesreau	6,067	1,350	.223
Jose DeLeon	5,773	1,286	.223
Pete Richert	4,295	959	.223
Ed Reulbach	9,454	2,117	.224
Jim Maloney	6,776	1,518	.224
Tom Seaver	17,605	3,971	.226
Roger Clemens	6,629	1,500	.226

* Three seasons missing

People are always using stats to bash modern ballplayers, so what can they say about this list, which is dominated by pitchers active since the mid-fifties? Maybe they'll just say it proves how lousy modern hitters are. We won't . . . but we **will** say that this is not the primary way we'd rate the greatest pitchers of all time. What kind of pitchers have low opponents' averages? Overpowering ones, usually with great fastballs. But they may also have control problems, or be plagued by injuries. Sid Fernandez, obviously, qualifies on both counts.

Nonetheless, there are some truly great pitchers here — like Koufax, Seaver, Clemens, and of course Ryan. And it's fascinating to see Babe Ruth's name . . . another reminder of what a superb all-around athlete he was.9

A complete listing for this category can be found on page 299.

HOW IMPORTANT IS IT TO "HOLD THE FORT"?

When it comes to getting respect, middle relief pitchers might want to walk up to Rodney Dangerfield and shake his hand. We know how they feel. A few years ago we defined a stat called a "hold" — a save opportunity preserved and passed on to a subsequent reliever — but not a lot of people paid attention to this unglamorous number. In 1989, Rick Honeycutt of the Athletics was the leader in holds with 24; we guess people assumed it was sheer coincidence that Dennis Eckersley had one of the greatest relief seasons ever (33 saves, 1.56 ERA) as the A's closer. In 1990 the hold leaders were Barry Jones of the White Sox (30) and Honeycutt (27); the save leaders were Bobby Thigpen of the ChiSox (an all-time record 57) and Eckersley (48). Big surprise.

Fast-forward to 1991, and who was the American League leader in saves? Bryan Harvey of the Angels with his break-through season of 46 saves. But who was the leader in holds? None other than Mark Eichhorn of those same Angels (25). Meanwhile the White Sox traded away Jones, and Thiggy's save total tumbled from his record 57 to 30. Coincidence again?

Not really. Having looked at this number for three years, we're extremely confident that the hold is a valid stat, one which not only helps identify the best middle relievers, but one which plays a significant part in producing the best closers. This is especially true in the American League. Without having to worry about pitchers hitting, AL managers can "layer" their relief staff pretty exactly, bringing in the set-up man first (to get the hold) and then the closer (to get the save). Here are the major league leaders in holds for 1991:

HOLDING THE FORT — HOLDS

Pitcher	Holds
Mark Eichhorn	25
John Habyan	20
John Candelaria	19
Jeff Gray	19
Tony Fossas	18
Duane Ward	17
Joe Klink	16
Mark Lee	15
Scott Radinsky	15
Mike Stanton	15
Scott Terry	15

Not surprisingly, seven of the eight leaders came from American League teams. It's also not surprising that such closers as Steve Farr of the Yankees, Jeff Reardon of the Red Sox and Tom Henke of the Blue Jays came through with outstanding performances. We hesitate to criticize the Cardinals, but didn't Scott Terry (not offered a Redbird contract as this book went to press) have more than a little to do with Lee Smith's league-record 47 saves? Here are the team hold totals:

Relief Pitcher Holds — 1991

Team	Holds
American League	
Athletics	65
Red Sox	56
Yankees	51
Mariners	49
Orioles	47
Brewers	46
Blue Jays	44
Angels	42
White Sox	41
Rangers	35
Twins	29
Tigers	25
Royals	23
Indians	10
National League	
Dodgers	54
Cardinals	49
Pirates	45
Expos	44
Astros	43
Padres	41
Cubs	38
Braves	37
Giants	35
Phillies	29
Reds	23
Mets	21

These figures have to be interpreted in a different way than individual hold totals. A team which records a high number of holds probably has a good relief staff. But as in the case of the Yankees, the total can be partly due to a club which has weak starters. One always has to view stats in their context — but pay attention to this one when looking at those ace closers!

A complete listing for this category can be found on page 300.

WAS BILL SWIFT THE BEST "TOTAL RELIEVER" OF 1991?

There are a number of stats to evaluate the work of relief pitchers, and three of the ones we like are the save, the save opportunity (saves plus blown saves) and the hold (a save opportunity preserved and passed on to the next reliever). Holds credit the work of good middle relievers, and the "save percentage" (saves per opportunity) is a good stat for identifying the best closers.

But as we pointed out last year, those stats can still obscure the work of middle relief pitchers. The hold, good as it is, doesn't indicate blown opportunities. And when you rank relievers by save percentage, middle men often look worse than they really are; the reason is that they get blown saves the same as closers do, but when they're successful, they usually wind up with a hold instead of a save.

So what we've done is create a "hold plus save percentage." We add up each pitcher's total of holds plus saves, then divide by the number of opportunities (holds plus saves plus blown saves). This works pretty neatly, because a "blown hold" is, in actuality, a blown save. Anyway, here are the 1991 leaders in hold plus save percentage (minimum 20 opportunities). You might recall that when we listed the leaders a year ago, we separated them by leagues; we didn't feel that was necessary for 1991, as the National League success rate (81 percent) was nearly the same as the American League's (83):

Pitcher, Team	Holds	Saves	H+S Opp	Hold+ Save Pct
Bill Swift, Sea	13	17	31	96.7
Juan Berenguer, Atl	4	17	22	95.5
Tony Fossas, Bos	18	1	20	95.0
John Habyan, Yanks	20	2	24	91.7
Tom Henke, Tor	2	32	37	91.9
Duane Ward, Tor	17	23	44	90.9
Jay Howell, LA	2	16	20	90.0
Joe Klink, Oak	16	2	20	90.0
Mark Eichhorn, Cal	25	1	29	89.7
Lee Smith, StL	0	47	53	88.7

What we like about this stat is that gives credit to both superior closers, like Tom Henke, and outstanding middle men, like Tony Fossas. It also credits the unsung heroes who have shown they can handle both roles — like Bill Swift and Duane Ward.

Swift, now of the Giants, is one of the most versatile pitchers in baseball. His job with the Mariners was usually to work as a set-up man for Mike Schooler, but when Schooler got injured, Swift showed that he could finish games himself. Last year he recorded 13 holds and 17 saves while only blowing one lead all season — a truly superior performance. The Giants admired Swift's versatility so much that they figure he can do anything; they have him penciled in for a starting role this year.

You could argue, we suppose, that this stat gives **too** much credit to middle relievers . . . a hold, after all, is not quite as good as a save. We'll buy that, but we'll also submit that the middle man who records a hold is doing his job just the same as a closer is. And as we show elsewhere, the middle men often face more pressure situations (coming in with men on base, in particular) than the closers do. It's time to give them credit.

And time to assess some blame, also. These pitchers had the **lowest** hold-plus-save percentages in 1991:

Pitcher, Team	Holds	Saves	H+S Opp	Hold+ Save Pct
Tim Burke, Mon-Mets	10	6	26	61.5
Barry Jones, Mon	5	13	26	69.2
Al Osuna, Hou	10	12	31	71.0
Mark Lee, Mil	15	1	22	72.7
Mike Jackson, Sea	9	14	31	74.2
Jeff Russell, Tex	0	30	40	75.0
Dave Smith, Cubs	2	17	25	76.0
Alejandro Pena, Mets-Atl	1	15	21	76.2
Paul Assenmacher, Cubs	14	15	38	76.3
Scott Radinsky, WSox	15	8	30	76.7

A couple of mild surprises here — Alejandro Pena and Scott Radinsky (though Pena was a perfect 11-for-11 with the Braves). The difficulties of most of the others were well-documented. Better luck in '92, guys.

A complete listing for this category can be found on page 301.

DID LEE SMITH TAKE A SHORT CUT TO THE SAVE CROWN?

To say the least, not all save situations are alike. One reliever can come in to start the ninth with a three-run lead, give up several hits and a couple of runs . . . and still be credited with the save if he manages to finish the inning with the lead intact. Another fireman might come in with the bases loaded, none out, and a one-run lead; if he yields even a sacrifice fly, he's hit with a "blown save." It's not always fair, but that's the way the save stats are kept.

So last year we presented a sort of consumer's guide to save situations. We started by separating them into "tough," "regular," and "cheap." We'll change the name of the last category to "easy" this year — we don't want to be too negative — but the definitions remain the same:

- **Easy Save:** first batter faced is not the tying run AND reliever pitches one inning or less. Example: Lee Smith comes in with a 5-3 lead and no one on base to start the ninth. Under the current rules, this is a Save Opportunity. We call it an Easy Save Opportunity.

- **Tough Save:** reliever comes in with the tying run anywhere on base. Example: Smith comes in with a 5-3 lead, two outs and the bases loaded in the ninth. This is a Tough Save Opportunity.

- **Regular Save:** All other saves fall into the "Regular" Category.

A pitcher with an "easy" situation has plenty of leeway; he can give up a run, sometimes two, and still get the save. A pitcher with a "tough" opportunity has almost no leeway at all, since the tying run is already on base. The data bears this out. As was the case in 1990, major league relievers converted over 90 percent of their Easy Save Opportunities in '91; they converted less than half of their Tough Opportunities:

League	Easy Sv	Op	%	Regular Sv	Op	%	Tough Sv	Op	%	Total Sv	Op	%
AL Average	212	225	94	326	439	75	80	200	40	618	864	72
NL Average	137	157	87	283	370	76	94	211	45	514	738	70
MLB Average	349	382	91	609	809	74	174	411	42	1132	1602	71

Before we go look at individual relievers, we want to make a couple of comments about the league data:

1. National League relievers earn their saves more than their American League counterparts do; they get fewer Easy Save Opportunities, and more Tough ones. (The difference is even more dramatic than it looks from the totals because the 12 NL teams play about 14 percent fewer total games than the 14 AL teams do.) As we pointed out last year, there is a logical reason for this: American League pitchers don't have to bat. Unless they want to let the pitcher hit, NL managers are often faced with having to use up a position player — either as a pinch-hitter, or in a double-switch — in order to get a reliever into the game. As a result, they tend to hold back their aces for situations where they're really needed.

2. Despite the rules difference, National League managers used their relievers in Easy situations much more in 1991 (157 times) than they did in 1990 (104). We think we know the reason for this, but we'll get into that when we discuss the NL leaders.

Let's look at the American League save leaders for 1991. How were they used?

Reliever	Easy			Regular			Tough			Total		
	Sv	Op	%	Sv	Op	%	Sv	Op	%	Sv	Op	%
Bryan Harvey, Cal	17	18	94	22	26	85	7	8	88	46	52	89
Dennis Eckersley, Oak	15	16	94	25	30	83	3	5	60	43	51	84
Rick Aguilera, Min	16	17	94	19	24	79	7	10	70	42	51	82
Jeff Reardon, Bos	19	20	95	17	23	74	4	6	67	40	49	82
Jeff Montgomery, KC	16	16	100	11	15	73	6	8	75	33	39	85
Tom Henke, Tor	16	17	94	13	14	93	3	4	75	32	35	91
Gregg Olson, Bal	17	18	94	11	17	65	3	4	75	31	39	79
Bobby Thigpen, WSox	13	13	100	14	20	70	3	6	50	30	39	77
Jeff Russell, Tex	13	15	87	15	20	75	2	5	40	30	40	75
Duane Ward, Tor	9	9	100	13	15	87	1	3	33	23	27	85
Steve Farr, Yanks	9	9	100	10	14	71	4	6	67	23	29	79

As you can see, the American League save leaders didn't get many Tough opportunities; the vogue in baseball today is to bring in the ace at the start of the ninth, with a little leeway. Bryan Harvey of the Angels deserved his ranking as the league's (and probably baseball's) top reliever: his seven Tough saves (in only eight opportunities) were as many as any relief ace in baseball.

Now let's look at the National League save leaders:

Reliever	Easy			Regular			Tough			Total		
	Sv	Op	%	Sv	Op	%	Sv	Op	%	Sv	Op	%
Lee Smith, StL	20	20	100	24	28	86	3	5	60	47	53	89
Rob Dibble, Cin	7	7	100	17	21	81	7	8	88	31	36	86
John Franco, Mets	11	12	92	16	19	84	3	4	75	30	35	86
Mitch Williams, Phi	11	11	100	16	22	73	3	6	50	30	39	77
Dave Righetti, SF	9	9	100	9	13	69	6	7	86	24	29	82
Craig Lefferts, SD	8	8	100	9	10	90	6	12	50	23	30	77
Juan Berenguer, Atl	2	2	100	12	13	92	3	3	100	17	18	94
Bill Landrum, Pit	5	5	100	5	8	63	7	9	78	17	22	77
Dave Smith, Cubs	5	6	83	8	12	67	4	5	80	17	23	74
Jay Howell, LA	7	7	100	7	8	88	2	3	67	16	18	89
Stan Belinda, Pit	4	4	100	9	10	90	3	6	50	16	20	80

It's clear that NL relievers don't get those Easy opportunities the way their AL counterparts do . . . that's the biggest reason why the National League doesn't produce as many 40-save guys. However, this may be changing. Lee Smith of the Cardinals had more Easy opportunities than any pitcher in baseball. Not coincidentally, Smith was managed by Joe Torre, who'd spent the previous few years in the American League as an Angel broadcaster. In baseball, success breeds imitation. Our feeling is that Torre's usage of Smith was copied by other NL managers last year — whether it cost the use of a position player or not. The NL "easy" save total should continue to rise in 1992 — and so should the save totals of the league leaders.

It's also evident from looking at the NL data that Smith was really no better last year than Cincinnati's Rob Dibble, who had 16 fewer saves. Dibble was superior to Smith when it came to the tough opportunities; the difference is that he didn't get the easy chances Smith did.

A complete listing for this category can be found on page 302.

WILL MIDDLE RELIEF BE THE WHITE SOX' HIDDEN ADVANTAGE AGAIN IN '92?

Gene Lamont, who's taking over as the White Sox manager in 1992, has to feel pretty good about things. Lamont is blessed with a promising offense led by Frank Thomas and Robin Ventura; great defensive players in Ventura, Ozzie Guillen, Lance Johnson and Ron Karkovice; a starting staff which figures to improve; and a top closer in Bobby Thigpen. But Lamont has another big asset, one which many fans fail to consider — a middle relief corps which was the best in baseball in 1991.

When people talk "bullpen," they usually mean the late-inning relief aces, the ones who get the saves and the big salaries. But in the modern game, starters often leave in the sixth or seventh inning, and it's up to the middle men to preserve the lead until the closer comes in to nail it down. Sometimes disaster strikes and the starter gets knocked out early; when that happens, a good middle relief corps can contain the damage and give a team a chance to get back into the game.

Let's look at how the clubs rank in this vital category. Defining exactly what constitutes middle relief is a matter of debate, but we think this is a reasonable definition: any relief appearance from the first through the eighth inning. "Closers" often appear before the ninth, of course, and "middle men" can be used in extra innings, but from the ninth on is now-or-never time, and that's a closer's domain. Here are the 1991 middle relief numbers:

1991 Relief ERA — 1st through 8th Innings

Team	IP	ER	ERA
Chicago White Sox	306.1	99	2.91
Seattle Mariners	331.0	114	3.10
Los Angeles Dodgers	291.1	105	3.24
San Diego Padres	298.2	108	3.25
Baltimore Orioles	405.2	150	3.33
Chicago Cubs	337.0	125	3.34
New York Mets	282.1	109	3.47
New York Yankees	408.0	154	3.40
San Francisco Giants	362.1	139	3.45
Minnesota Twins	314.2	119	3.40
Cincinnati Reds	337.0	129	3.45
Boston Red Sox	327.0	132	3.63
California Angels	271.1	109	3.62
Atlanta Braves	303.2	128	3.79
Kansas City Royals	313.0	131	3.77
Pittsburgh Pirates	309.2	131	3.81
Philadelphia Phillies	349.2	148	3.81
Toronto Blue Jays	291.0	127	3.93
Montreal Expos	302.0	131	3.90
Houston Astros	349.0	155	4.00
Cleveland Indians	291.0	136	4.21
St. Louis Cardinals	304.0	153	4.53
Milwaukee Brewers	341.0	171	4.51
Texas Rangers	360.2	183	4.57
Detroit Tigers	349.0	200	5.16
Oakland Athletics	320.2	183	5.14

The White Sox, as we've said, were the best, but a surprise was the number-two rated Seattle club; because of Mike Schooler's injury, the Mariners' pen was underrated last year. The Ms will have to do without Bill Swift this year, and they'll also have to do without manager Jim LeFebvre. It'll be interesting to see what LeFebvre, who's shown a real ability to handle a pitching staff, will do with the Cubs this year. The Cubbies already had a decent middle relief staff in '91.

On the other hand, Cardinal manager Joe Torre will be working hard to shore up his middle relief staff this year. In 1991, Torre had the second-best starting corps in the NL East, and closer Lee Smith had his greatest season (47 saves). But middle relief was the Redbirds' undoing:

Cardinals Pitching 1991

Corps	ERA
Starters	3.54
Middle Relief	4.53
Closers *	2.84

* Smith and others

Improvement in middle relief could make the Cards genuine contenders in 1992.

HOW IMPORTANT IS IT TO GET THE FIRST BATTER?

Over the last few years, we've developed some new stats to evaluate the work of relief pitchers — among them save percentage, holds, inherited runners scored. Another stat, one we've run in all three editions of this book, is "first batter efficiency." It's simply opponents' batting average versus the first batter faced by each reliever. Since relievers usually come in during important situations, retiring the first hitter can be vitally important.

Which relievers had the best record against the first batter faced in 1991? Here is the top ten (minimum 30 batters faced):

1991 Leaders — First Batter Efficiency

Player, Team	Avg	AB	H	HR	BB	K
Wally Ritchie, Phi	.063	32	2	0	3	5
Dave Righetti, SF	.071	56	4	0	4	16
Todd Frohwirth, Bal	.109	46	5	1	3	6
Carl Willis, Min	.114	35	4	0	2	6
Stan Belinda, Pit	.120	50	6	1	10	17
Rick Aguilera, Min	.127	55	7	0	8	9
Tony Fossas, Bos	.130	54	7	0	5	10
Steve Bedrosian, Min	.135	52	7	2	3	9
Dan Petry, Det-Atl-Bos	.138	29	4	1	3	7
Doug Henry, Mil	.143	28	4	1	3	7

Most of these pitchers are middle relievers, which is why they may not be big names to you. But that hardly means their work wasn't vital to their teams. For a middle man, giving up a hit to the first batter usually won't directly lose a game . . . but it can help put it out of reach.

You'll notice the presence of three Minnesota relievers on the leaders lists. That's no coincidence. Over the last three seasons, Tom Kelly has had six different relievers appear on our top ten lists. Kelly seems to have a real knack for handling his bullpen, getting the absolute most out of marginal talents like Carl Willis. It's paid off in two world championships during the last five seasons.

Can you have a great year in relief while doing less-than-brilliant work against first batters? Yes, to a degree. Lee Smith has probably been the best closer in the National League over the last two seasons, but his averages against first batters (.300 and .259) were less than stellar. With most closers now coming in at the start of an inning, they often have more of a margin for error than the middle men do. But that's all they have — a **little** margin.

You can see that in the work of the White Sox' Bobby Thigpen. Thigpen didn't have the same great season in 1991 that he did in 1990, and one of his weaknesses was a tendency to get lit up by the first batter. Though his opponents' average against first batters was fine (.220), Thigpen yielded four first-batter homers, tying the Cubs' Paul Assenmacher for the major league lead in that dubious category. That's more of a margin than a top closer can afford.

These fellows were a first batter's dream come true — they had the worst opponents batting averages against the first man they faced:

1991 Trailers — First Batter Efficiency

Player, Team	Avg	AB	H	HR	BB	K
Darren Holmes, Mil	.400	35	14	1	4	6
Curt Schilling, Hou	.396	48	19	0	8	8
Jeff Russell, Tex	.390	59	23	1	7	7
Dave Smith, Cubs	.375	32	12	2	3	5
Steve Olin, Cle	.375	40	15	1	7	6
Kevin Gross, LA	.375	32	12	2	4	6
Melido Perez, WSox	.371	35	13	1	2	8
John Cerutti, Det	.360	25	9	2	4	0
Roger McDowell, Phi-Atl	.354	65	23	0	5	10
Paul Gibson, Det	.350	60	21	0	6	6

If you think first batter efficiency is unimportant for a closer, check with the Astros and Cubs. The weakness of Curt Schilling and Dave Smith in this category has caused them to experiment with other pitchers in the closer's role.

A complete listing for this category can be found on page 303.

WHY DID ATLANTA BUY 'LECKI (AND HIS 4.46 ERA)?

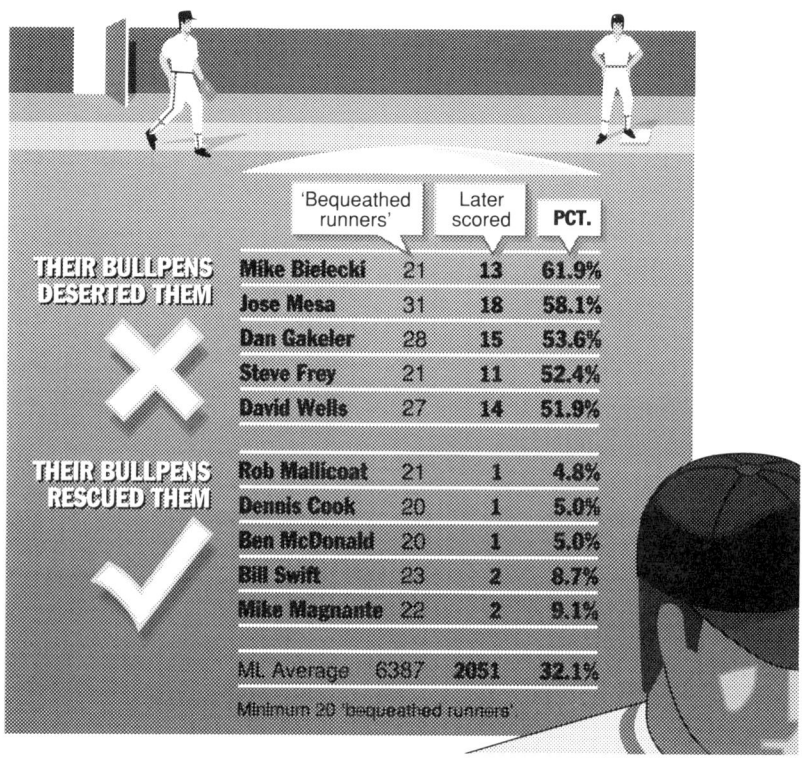

In one of the more curious deals of 1991, the Atlanta Braves made a last-week trade with their superstation rivals, the Chicago Cubs. The Braves surrendered minor leaguers Turk Wendell and Yorkis Perez. (Perez stopped off in Chicago only long enough to catch a flight to the Japanese League.) In return Atlanta received sore-armed catcher Damon Berryhill, and the key man, pitcher Mike Bielecki.

Why would the Braves want Bielecki, who, despite his 13-11 record, finished the year with a 4.46 earned run average? Maybe because Atlanta understood the concept of "bequeathed runners" and how it applied to Bielecki in 1991. Pitchers frequently leave games with runners on base, "bequeathing" them to the reliever (for the relief pitcher, it becomes an "inherited" runner). As we discussed last year, some pitchers are victimized by their relievers, who allow most of the runners to score, thus jacking up the bequeathing pitcher's ERA. Others benefit from a miserly bullpen which prevents the runners from scoring — and preserves the bequeathing pitcher's ERA.

As it turned out, Bielecki was victimized by his relievers more than any pitcher who left at least 20 runners to his bullpen last year. Mike bequeathed 21 runners to his relievers, and the careless Cubbies allowed 13 of them to score (61.9%, when the major league average was only 32.1%). By contrast, Rob Mallicoat of the Astros also left 21 runners to his subsequent relievers, and the Houston bullpenners permitted only one to score. The chart lists the leaders in each category — the unlucky ones first, then the lucky.

If Bielecki had been as blessed by excellent bullpen work as Mallicoat was last year, he would have allowed 12 fewer earned runs; instead of having a 4.46 ERA, his figure would have been a more respectable 3.83. (Did the Braves take this into consideration? It's possible, but very unlikely.) Conversely, if Mallicoat had been victimized the way Bielecki was, he would have given up 12 more earned runs. His ERA, lofty to begin with at 5.48, would have been up in the stratosphere at 7.74. The two represent extreme cases, of course. But with so many pitching changes taking place with men on base, one can see how each pitcher is dependent on his relievers for part of his ERA.

Which pitchers bequeath the most runners? Not surprisingly, it's left-handed relievers, who frequently come in to face one or two lefties, but leave when a righthander comes to the plate. Mike Jeffcoat (47 bequeathed runners), Kenny Rogers (44), Al Osuna (42), Russ Swan (42), Mark Lee (41), Tony Fossas (40) and Scott Ruskin (40), lefties all, left the most runners to their relievers last year. Except for Osuna, whose relievers allowed 17 to score, they were a pretty fortunate bunch. That too would figure. Given their usually-brief action, southpaws are more likely to leave runners on first base than anywhere else — and it's easier for a reliever to strand a runner at first than one at second or third.

A complete listing for this category appears on page 304.

WHICH SOUTHPAWS EAT LEFTIES?

The Left-Handed Gun was a moody, quirky cult film from the late 1950s starring the young Paul Newman as Billy the Kid. Baseball has its own left-handed guns: they're the southpaw relievers who travel from team to team, lasting as long as they can still retire left-handed hitters. If there was a movie about this breed, surely Steve Howe would be Billy the Kid — enormously talented, enormously self-destructive, destined to die young. John Candelaria, meanwhile, would be the aging drifter who's always one step ahead of his past, the one with all the notches on his revolver. Have gun, will travel.

Appealingly enough, Howe and Candelaria were the two toughest lefties in baseball against left-handed hitters. What a strange pair. At 34, Howe has pitched in only seven seasons and worked just 427.2 innings; his lifetime ERA is a brilliant 2.59, but his continual drug problems have wrecked his career time and again. The Candy man, though only four years older than Howe, has logged over twice as many seasons (17) and pitched almost six times as many innings (2,481.1). And oh, yes, he's modeled a few uniforms (eight at last count, including both New York teams, both Canadian teams and both Los Angeles-area teams). That's the nature of this breed.

Here are the lefthanders who had the greatest success against lefty swingers in 1991 (minimum 40 AB vs. LHB):

Pitcher, Team	vs. LHB				vs. RHB			
	Avg	AB	H	HR	Avg	AB	H	HR
Steve Howe, Yanks	.128	47	6	0	.256	129	33	1
John Candelaria, LA	.138	58	8	1	.354	65	23	2
Wally Ritchie, Phi	.161	62	10	1	.270	126	34	3
Dave Righetti, SF	.167	72	12	0	.267	195	52	4
Trevor Wilson, SF	.169	160	27	1	.252	580	146	12
Kevin Brown, Mil	.170	47	8	1	.294	197	58	5
Chuck McElroy, Cubs	.172	122	21	3	.231	225	52	4
Randy Tomlin, Pit	.172	134	23	1	.275	535	147	8
Lee Guetterman, Yanks	.175	97	17	2	.305	243	74	4
Paul Assenmacher, Cubs	.179	134	24	1	.247	247	61	9

Not all these pitchers are relievers, and not all of them have the checkered pasts of Howe and Candelaria. What sets the good ones like Candelaria apart is an ability to handle lefties year after year. That's not always easy, as the following pitchers discovered in 1991:

Pitcher	1990 vs. LHB	1991 vs. LHB
Dan Plesac	.161	.297
Don Carman	.175	.300
Randy Myers	.181	.287
Ken Patterson	.194	.270

So consistency is important, but so is an ability to be at least marginally successful against righties. Candelaria's poor second half last year was due to his inability to handle righthanders; even spotted as carefully as he was (59 games, only 33.2 innings), he faced more righties than he did lefties. He'll have to do better against righthanders if he wants to keep pitching.

The following pitchers, though left-handed, got torched by lefty swingers last season:

Pitcher, Team	vs. LHB				vs. RHB			
	Avg	AB	H	HR	Avg	AB	H	HR
Neal Heaton, Pit	.354	82	29	2	.239	180	43	4
Paul Gibson, Det	.345	113	39	6	.277	264	73	4
John Franco, Mets	.340	53	18	0	.250	172	43	2
Mark Guthrie, Min	.337	86	29	4	.293	297	87	7
Bob MacDonald, Tor	.325	77	25	2	.208	125	26	3
Bob Kipper, Pit	.321	78	25	4	.255	161	41	3
Bill Krueger, Sea	.307	140	43	2	.284	532	151	13
Mark Lee, Mil	.304	92	28	3	.272	162	44	7
Dave Otto, Cle	.304	69	21	0	.278	313	87	7
Mark Davis, KC	.304	56	17	0	.220	173	38	6

For Neal Heaton, this is getting old; he was .311 vs. LHB in 1990. The disturbing name on the list for Met fans is their relief ace, John Franco. However, Franco has always handled lefties in the past, and as a closer he faces far more righties than lefties. There's no reason to be disturbed — yet.

A complete listing for this category can be found on page 305.

IS IT EASIER TO STEAL OFF A LEFTY?

Maury Wills, who probably did more than anyone to revive the stolen base, always used to claim that it was easier for him to steal bases off lefthanders than against righties. Though lefties have the apparent advantage of facing first base from the stretch position, Wills thought that made them easier for him to read. Knowledge is power, in other words.

Was Wills right? Let's examine the issue from a few different perspectives. First, the basic question: is it easier for runners in general to steal off lefties? The answer is a resounding no; it's much easier for the average player to steal off a righty:

	vs LHP			vs RHP		
	SB	CS	Pct	SB	CS	Pct
All Players, 1989-91	2,826	1,600	.638	6,700	2,918	.697

Okay, but Wills was no average base stealer. How about the elite runners? Here's how the top 15 stealers of the last three years compare vs. lefties and righties:

Top 15 Basestealers — 1989-91

	vs LHP			vs RHP		
Runner	SB	CS	Pct	SB	CS	Pct
Marquis Grissom	47	6	.887	52	13	.800
Vince Coleman	63	13	.829	116	28	.806
Rickey Henderson	60	14	.811	140	28	.833
Roberto Alomar	25	6	.806	94	29	.764
Otis Nixon	64	16	.800	95	30	.760
Devon White	30	10	.750	68	22	.756
Tim Raines	38	13	.745	103	27	.792
Steve Sax	39	14	.736	78	23	.772
Howard Johnson	31	13	.705	74	19	.796
Roberto Kelly	33	14	.702	76	24	.760
Delino DeShields	33	14	.702	65	31	.677
Barry Bonds	39	17	.696	88	19	.822
Juan Samuel	31	14	.689	72	26	.735
Gary Pettis	38	22	.633	72	21	.774
Brett Butler	39	29	.574	81	34	.714

Sorry, Maury, 10 of the 15 steal better against righthanders; the five who preferred southpaws were Marquis Grissom (extraordinary, in that nearly half his steals have come against lefthanders), Vince Coleman, Roberto Alomar, Otis Nixon, and Delino DeShields. Ordinarily, the ones who are better against lefties aren't a **lot** better; it could merely be due to chance. Wills appears to have been an exceptional case.

There is, however, a group of players who do steal very well against southpaws. Who are they, and do they show a real preference for lefthanders, or are they just good overall? Here are the top 10 percentage stealers against lefties over the last three years (15 attempts vs. LHP):

Top Percentage Basestealers vs. Lefties — 1989-91

Runner	vs LHP			vs RHP		
	SB	CS	Pct	SB	CS	Pct
Marquis Grissom	47	6	.887	52	13	.800
Barry Larkin	22	3	.880	42	13	.764
Kirk Gibson	13	2	.867	43	7	.860
Jose Gonzalez	13	2	.867	7	2	.778
Jose Canseco	16	3	.842	35	16	.686
Billy Hatcher	25	5	.833	40	21	.656
Vince Coleman	63	13	.829	116	28	.806
Eddie Murray	14	3	.824	11	7	.611
Willie Wilson	18	4	.818	50	13	.794
Rickey Henderson	60	14	.811	140	28	.833

Nine of the top ten are better against southpaws (all but Henderson), and in some cases the difference is pronounced. But of course, the number of attempts is pretty low, and again it's very possible this is just a random effect. Grissom, Larkin, and Hatcher, however, seem to be in the Wills camp — they pretty clearly do better against lefthanders. Some runners, however, can't seem to steal against lefties at all:

Worst Percentage Basestealers vs. Lefties — 1989-91

Runner	vs LHP			vs RHP		
	SB	CS	Pct	SB	CS	Pct
Tony Phillips	6	11	.353	26	11	.703
Mike Gallego	6	9	.400	12	10	.545
Ozzie Guillen	16	22	.421	54	27	.667
Ellis Burks	7	9	.438	29	18	.617
Jay Bell	7	8	.467	18	7	.720
Bobby Bonilla	7	8	.467	7	7	.500
Mike Devereaux	17	18	.486	34	14	.708
Lonnie Smith	10	10	.500	34	17	.667
Bill Pecota	9	8	.529	20	4	.833
Felix Jose	13	10	.565	19	9	.679

Why do Tony Phillips, Ozzie Guillen, Ellis Burks, etc. have so many problems with southpaws? It's not like they're raw rookies. Whatever the case, Wills' assertion may have been true for him, though we don't really know that. Most runners steal much better against righthanders.

A complete listing for this category can be found on page 306.

WHERE WILL WE FIND THE NEXT DON ROBINSON?

One of the better moments of the unforgettable 1991 World Series came in Game Three when Twins manager Tom Kelly sent his relief ace, Rick Aguilera, up to pinch-hit. Kelly was ridiculed as a push-button American League manager who'd let himself run out of players, and certainly a lot of the criticism was valid. But as Tim McCarver pointed out at the time, the move wasn't as crazy as it looked. Aguilera was a hitting star in amateur ball, and he swung a mean stick (for a pitcher, anyway) in his days with the Mets. Among active pitchers, in fact, Aguilera has the fourth-highest lifetime average:

Best Hitting Pitchers — Active Career Leaders

Pitcher	Avg	AB	H	2B	3B	HR	RBI
Dan Schatzeder	.240	242	58	8	2	5	29
Don Robinson	.227	613	139	20	0	13	68
Tim Leary	.221	163	36	6	0	1	19
Rick Aguilera	.203	138	28	3	0	3	11
Fernando Valenzuela	.202	807	163	22	1	8	72
Sid Fernandez	.197	390	77	11	2	1	29
Dennis Rasmussen	.193	259	50	8	0	0	14
Orel Hershiser	.193	487	94	17	2	0	31
Dwight Gooden	.189	576	109	10	2	4	45
Greg Maddux	.187	402	75	7	0	1	21

(150 PA Minimum Lifetime)

When we looked at the leader board a year ago, we commented on how long in the tooth most of the leaders were; we probably could have sneaked Warren Spahn and Bob Lemon onto the list, and they wouldn't have looked out of place. Well, these guys ain't getting any younger. Schatzeder and Leary are currently looking for teams; Rasmussen is barely hanging onto his major league career; Robinson has at least temporarily hung up his bat by signing with an American League team; Fernandez, Hershiser and Gooden, though younger, are battling back from serious injuries. And of course, Aguilera now only gets to hit in the World Series. Things have gotten so bad that even Robinson, once the king, has been slumping. A .267 lifetime hitter after the 1986 season, he was only 43 for 254, .169, the last five years. And when Don Robinson can't hit any more, what pitcher can?

Greg Maddux can, for one. Only 26 this year, Maddux carries on the tradition of the good-hitting pitcher, along with the presumably-healthy Fernandez, Hershiser and Gooden. This short list may soon be getting longer. The 1991 crop of National League pitchers included some impressive hitting numbers:

Best Hitting Pitchers — 1991

Pitcher	Avg	AB	H	2B	3B	HR	RBI
Chris Hammond, Cin	.353	34	12	3	0	0	1
Kip Gross, Cin	.280	25	7	1	0	0	3
Tommy Greene, Phi	.268	71	19	2	0	2	7
Orel Hershiser, LA	.258	31	8	2	0	0	2
Bryn Smith, StL	.246	65	16	1	0	0	8
Dwight Gooden, Mets	.238	63	15	3	0	1	6
Trevor Wilson, SF	.235	51	12	1	0	1	5
Tom Glavine, Atl	.230	74	17	1	0	0	6
Omar Olivares, StL	.226	53	12	3	0	0	6
Steve Avery, Atl	.215	79	17	1	1	0	2
Jose Rijo, Cin	.209	67	14	0	0	0	5
Bob Walk, Pit	.205	39	8	1	0	1	5
Greg Maddux, Cubs	.205	88	18	2	0	1	7

(25 PA Minimum)

As we pointed out a year ago, one reason pitchers don't hit much any more is that organizations don't consider it important. The American League doesn't have to bother, of course, and only the Mets and Dodgers in the National have seemed interested in refining their pitchers' hitting skills. That may be changing. The Reds, under Lou Piniella, had three pitchers who batted over .200 last year, a rare feat in this era. Piniella considers his pitchers athletes, to the extent that Jose Rijo was injured last year trying to steal a base. The Braves seem to have the same philosophy. Tom Glavine and Steve Avery really work on their hitting, and it shows; those kind of work habits often rub off on other pitchers. There may be a few young successors to "Dangerous Don" Robinson after all.

A complete listing for this category can be found on page 307.

IS THE NEXT BOB LEMON SOMEWHERE IN YOUR OUTFIELD?

Does the name "Mel Queen" mean anything to you? Probably not, unless (like us) you routinely recall all the obscure players of the 1960s. In 1966 Melvin Douglas Queen was a struggling Cincinnati outfielder with a .127 batting average. But he had a strong throwing arm, and his father (also named Mel) had been a major league pitcher in the forties and early fifties. "Why not try Mel on the mound?" the Reds thought. They worked him into seven contests that year, and Queen showed enough promise to make a full-time shift to pitching in 1967. Talk about a great move: Queen went 14-8 in '67 with a 2.76 ERA.

Mel Queen is a footnote to a changing game. As far as we know, he's the last position player to make a successful shift to the pitching mound at the major league level. That's strange, because this move has often been spectacularly successful. Bucky Walters, a weak hitting third baseman-outfielder in the 1930s, wound up winning 198 games after being shifted to the mound. Jack Harshman, a slugging first baseman with big holes in his swing, became a very successful hurler for several major league clubs in the fifties. There are others, most notably Bob Lemon, who went on to a Hall of Fame career after the Indians made a pitcher out of him.

These days, when a position player becomes a pitcher, it's in the eighth inning of a game your team is losing 16-0. Usually, it's good for a few laughs on the ESPN highlights, but sometimes these makeshift pitchers show surprising stuff. Who was the best pitcher on the Chicago Cub staff last year? Why, outfielder Doug Dascenzo, of course — a 0.00 ERA in three emergency appearances. A total of 23 active position players have worked on the mound at some point during their careers. While Dascenzo is the unquestioned ace of this staff, several others have shown definite promise. Here are their records — good, bad and indifferent:

They Laughed When I Took the Mound . . .

Player	W	L	IP	H	BB	K	ERA
Vance Law	0	0	8.0	9	3	2	3.38
Jose Oquendo	0	1	6.0	10	9	2	12.00
Doug Dascenzo	0	0	5.0	3	2	2	0.00
Danny Heep	0	0	3.0	6	0	0	9.00
Steve Lyons	0	0	3.0	4	4	2	3.00
John Moses	0	0	3.0	5	3	0	9.00
Darrin Jackson	0	0	2.0	3	2	0	9.00
Paul O'Neill	0	0	2.0	2	4	2	13.50

They Laughed When I Took the Mound...

Player	W	L	IP	H	BB	K	ERA
Rick Cerone	0	0	2.0	0	1	1	0.00
Bill Pecota	0	0	2.0	4	0	0	4.50
Dan Gladden	0	0	2.0	2	1	0	4.50
Tim Wallach	0	0	2.0	3	0	0	4.50
Luis Salazar	0	0	2.0	2	1	0	4.50
Rick Dempsey	0	0	2.0	3	1	0	4.50
Jeff Hamilton	0	1	1.2	2	1	2	5.40
Tim Jones	0	0	1.1	1	2	0	6.75
Greg Litton	0	0	1.0	1	3	0	9.00
Jim Gantner	0	0	1.0	2	0	0	0.00
Donnie Hill	0	0	1.0	0	1	1	0.00
Alvaro Espinoza	0	0	0.2	0	0	0	0.00
Junior Noboa	0	0	0.2	0	1	0	0.00
Tom Foley	0	0	0.1	1	0	0	27.00
Dave Martinez	0	0	0.1	2	2	0	54.00
John Russell	0	0	0.1	0	0	0	0.00
TOTAL	0	2	52.1	65	41	14	5.85

Are there any future Bob Lemons in this group? Probably not, but you have to admit there are some guys with promise. Dascenzo's no joke; he has tricky left-handed stuff, and could likely fashion a better mound career than Hal Jeffcoat, a Cub outfielder-turned-pitcher in the mid-1950s. Steve Lyons is always begging to pitch, and he's made the most of his few opportunities. The Yankees' Alvaro Espinoza turned a few heads in a brief 1991 appearance against the White Sox. They say if Jeff Hamilton could ever stay healthy, he could throw some serious heat.

The most frustrating case for those who love mid-career position shifts has to be Vance Law. Never more than a mediocre infielder (.256 lifetime average), Vance looked like a natural whenever he took the mound — check out that 3.38 ERA. Of course, he had the bloodlines: his father, Vern, was a Cy Young Award winner. Alas, Vance is now 35, probably too old to become the next Bucky Walters.

How about this for a staff of young, hard-throwing aces: Rick Cerone (0.00 ERA), Jim Gantner (0.00), Luis Salazar (4.50) and Rick Dempsey (4.50)? All in all, Mel Queen has to feel fairly secure about his niche in baseball history.

WHO ARE THE HIDDEN RELIEF STARS?

With teams now using several relief pitchers a game as a matter of course, how those pitchers handle their "inherited runners" is crucial to a club's success. Inherited runners are men left on base by the previous pitcher when a reliever comes into the game; if they score, the new pitcher's earned run average is unaffected, but of course the runs count all the same. It's possible for a pitcher to perform miserably in inherited runner situations, but still have a good ERA. Managers and clubs aren't fooled, however, and such pitchers often find themselves out of a job.

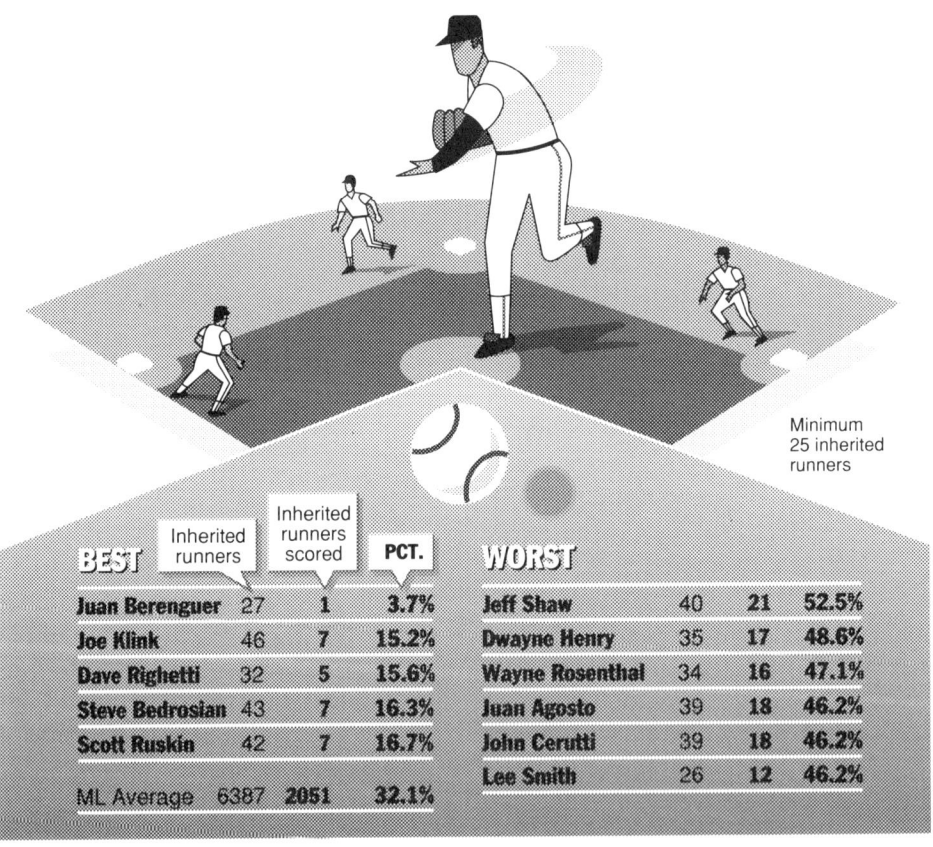

Minimum 25 inherited runners

BEST	Inherited runners	Inherited runners scored	PCT.	WORST	Inherited runners	Inherited runners scored	PCT.
Juan Berenguer	27	1	3.7%	Jeff Shaw	40	21	52.5%
Joe Klink	46	7	15.2%	Dwayne Henry	35	17	48.6%
Dave Righetti	32	5	15.6%	Wayne Rosenthal	34	16	47.1%
Steve Bedrosian	43	7	16.3%	Juan Agosto	39	18	46.2%
Scott Ruskin	42	7	16.7%	John Cerutti	39	18	46.2%
ML Average	6387	2051	32.1%	Lee Smith	26	12	46.2%

The graphic shows the best and worst relievers of 1991 at preventing inherited runners from scoring (minimum 25 inherited runners). As we've pointed out in the past, this is primarily a middle relievers' category. Most managers now try bring in their closers with the bases empty, preferably at the start of an inning. A lot of late relievers, as a result, don't meet or just barely meet our 25-runner minimum. Such stars as Tom Henke (15 inherited runners), Mitch Williams (24), John Franco (25) and Lee Smith (26) seldom had to come into a game with men on base last season; conversely, middle men such as Tony Fossas (71 inherited runners), Paul Gibson (71), Mark Williamson (62) and Bill Swift (61) were constantly brought in with bases occupied. So how come the late relievers are considered the pressure performers?

The truth is, middle relievers often have to respond in crucial situations, and that's why we like to point out some hidden gems. Joe (Colonel) Klink of the A's, for example, has gotten little recognition for his relief work, but over the last two years he's kept those prison doors locked, allowing only 11 of 77 inherited runners (14.3%) to score. Think that didn't help win a few games? Middle men such as Steve Bedrosian, Scott Ruskin and Kenny Rogers continually pitched out of jams when brought in last year; their high ERAs give no hint of their full value. On the other hand, Jeff Shaw and Duane Henry looked like good relievers when judged by their ERAs (3.36 and 3.19). What the ERAs don't show is that Shaw and Henry were letting other pitchers' runners score like crazy. That's a big reason why the Astros left Henry off their winter roster.

It would figure that clubs whose relievers don't let in many inherited runners would also have good team ERAs. The match is pretty good, but as you can see, it's not perfect:

American League

Team	Runners Inherited	Runners Scored	Scored Percent	ERA
Twins	193	47	24.4	3.69
Mariners	280	72	25.7	3.79
Angels	239	65	27.2	3.69
White Sox	307	90	29.3	3.79
Brewers	270	82	30.4	4.14
Yankees	249	80	32.1	4.42
Orioles	326	106	32.5	4.59
Athletics	289	95	32.9	4.57
Tigers	323	107	33.1	4.51
Royals	211	71	33.7	3.92
Rangers	317	112	35.3	4.47
Red Sox	295	107	36.3	4.01
Blue Jays	217	80	36.9	3.50
Indians	287	120	41.8	4.23

National League

Team	Runners Inherited	Runners Scored	Scored Percent	ERA
Dodgers	255	66	25.9	3.06
Giants	194	52	26.8	4.03
Padres	203	55	27.1	3.57
Pirates	194	58	29.9	3.44
Expos	240	73	30.4	3.64
Braves	198	62	31.3	3.49
Phillies	192	61	31.8	3.86
Reds	219	71	32.4	3.83
Astros	240	79	32.9	4.00
Cardinals	203	70	34.5	3.69
Mets	175	64	36.6	3.56
Cubs	271	106	39.1	4.03

The Toronto Blue Jays, tops in the American League in overall ERA, undoubtedly would have had a truly dominant pitching staff if not for the shaky middle relief clearly revealed here. (Maybe the Jays' problems go beyond "character.") And the Mets should be ashamed of themselves. As recently as 1989, New York had Roger McDowell, Julio Machado and Rick Aguilera as part of a very deep bullpen, but dealt away all three (and Terry Leach as well). Now the Mets are hurting between their starters and closer John Franco, and losing games in the process.

A complete listing for this category can be found on page 308.

CAN YOU PITCH YOURSELF INTO A HOLE BUT STILL SURVIVE?

THE WORST

LEADOFF SITUATIONS		WALKS	PCT.
Randy Johnson	642	106	16.5%
Jose DeJesus	343	55	16.0%
Pat Combs	310	45	14.5%
Matt Young	380	54	14.2%
Trevor Wilson	365	50	13.7%

THE BEST

LEADOFF SITUATIONS		WALKS	PCT.
Pascual Perez	303	8	2.6%
Greg Swindell	693	21	3.0%
Rick Reuschel	328	10	3.0%
Jimmy Key	622	19	3.1%
Bob Tewksbury	389	12	3.1%

Minimum 300 batters faced, 1989–1991.

One of the top items on any pitching coach's list of do's and don'ts is, "Don't walk the leadoff man!" You can see the logic of this immediately. With the bases empty, a walk does the same amount of damage as a single. And with none out there's no reason to be pitching around anybody. So go right after the hitter and let the guy hit his way on. Once in a while you'll give up a home run, but with the bags empty, the damage is minimal.

But of course, some pitchers can't seem to avoid getting themselves into trouble, which is one reason why managers and coaches get grey hair. We wondered which pitchers walked the leadoff man most often — and whether they could be successful despite continually being in hot water. Over the last three years, these hurlers were the ones who most often tested their managers' patience:

Most Walks Allowed per Batter Faced
In Leadoff Situation — 1989-91

Pitcher	BFP	BB	Pct
Randy Johnson	642	106	16.5
Jose DeJesus	343	55	16.0
Pat Combs	310	45	14.5
Matt Young	380	54	14.2
Trevor Wilson	365	50	13.7
Bobby Witt	541	73	13.5
Danny Jackson	329	43	13.1
Ken Hill	493	57	11.6
Mark Langston	757	87	11.5
Alex Fernandez	301	34	11.3

(minimum 300 Batters Faced)

Does the word "underachiever" mean anything to you? There's some talented arms in this group, but except for Langston, you'd be going out on a limb drafting any of these guys for your fantasy league team . . . and even Langston suffered through a 10-17 season in 1990. When you have as much stuff as Randy Johnson or Bobby Witt, you can pitch yourself out of jams more easily than most people can. But — and we're surely not the first people to make this observation — why do the opposition any favors by getting yourself into trouble? Johnson went 13-10 last year despite leading both leagues in walks. But he's capable of doing a lot better, and so are most of the pitchers on this list.

Now let's look at the opposite extreme, the pitchers who walk the leadoff man **least** often. We think you'll see the contrast:

Least Walks Allowed per Batter Faced
In Leadoff Situation — 1989-91

Pitcher	BFP	BB	Pct
Pascual Perez	303	8	2.6
Greg Swindell	693	21	3.0
Rick Reuschel	328	10	3.0
Jimmy Key	622	19	3.1
Bob Tewksbury	389	12	3.1
Kevin Tapani	476	15	3.2
Ed Whitson	557	18	3.2
Mike Witt	375	12	3.2
Bill Swift	327	11	3.4
Scott Sanderson	605	22	3.6

(minimum 300 Batters Faced)

There's talent in this group as well, especially Swindell and Tapani. But when you think of pitchers like Jimmy Key and Bob Tewksbury and Ed Whitson and Scott Sanderson, it's hard not use the word "overachiever": these are pitchers who make the absolute most of their talent. Just missing the top ten were Zane Smith, Dennis Martinez, Tom Browning and Bryn Smith. Smart pitchers . . . guys who don't get themselves into trouble very often.

So is it important to avoid walking the leadoff man? You bet it is.

A complete listing for this category can be found on page 309.

DO WORKHORSE STARTERS STILL EXIST?

Back in the good old days, pitchers labored nine innings every four days — and of course, they worked in the bullpen between starts. Not to mention pitching batting practice. If they only threw 300 innings a year, it was because their arms were sore. So we've heard, anyway. There were indeed workhorse pitchers 15-30 years ago, but not very many, and many of them wound up with sore arms. These days starters are expected to go all out from the first pitch, and the complete game is no longer a major goal. Which is not to say that the "workhorse" has disappeared.

We count pitches, and one way to measure the hardest workers is by pitches per start. Though most clubs have several excellent relievers able to step in during the late innings, a number of pitchers don't need much help. Here are the 1991 leaders in most pitches per start; we also include the number of times they threw 130 or more pitches, generally considered the benchmark of a heavy workload:

Most Pitches per 9 Innings — 20+ Starts

Pitcher, Team	GS	130+ Pitch Games	Pitches per Start
Roger Clemens, Bos	35	7	115.2
Tom Candiotti, Cle-Tor	34	4	114.6
Randy Johnson, Sea	33	4	112.6
Dave Stewart, Oak	35	6	112.6
Chuck Finley, Cal	34	8	112.1
Jose Guzman, Tex	25	4	110.5
Mark Langston, Cal	34	4	110.2
David Cone, Mets	34	7	110.1
Jack McDowell, WSox	35	3	109.5
Dennis Martinez, Mon	31	4	108.2
Mike Moore, Oak	33	5	107.2

As critics who have pointed out the danger of high pitch totals to young arms, we find it interesting that the youngest pitcher in this group is Jack McDowell, who was 25 in 1991. The hurlers who throw the most pitches per start are usually in their late twenties or older, and they've shown that their arms can handle a heavy workload. Of course, they're also pitchers with a history of winning records — meaning that their managers are likely to stick with them longer.

Another way to evaluate pitchers' workloads is by the number of pitches they toss per inning. The leaders list here is somewhat different:

Most Pitches per Inning — 20+ Starts

Pitcher, Team	GS	Pitches per Inning	130+ Pitch Games	Pitches per Start
Randy Johnson, Sea	33	18.5	4	112.6
Dave Stewart, Oak	35	17.4	6	112.6
Wade Taylor, Yanks	22	17.3	0	91.0
Jose DeJesus, Phi	29	17.1	4	105.5
Jim Deshaies, Hou	28	17.0	1	97.5
Mike Moore, Oak	33	16.8	5	107.2
Jose Mesa, Bal	23	16.8	0	90.5
Chuck Finley, Cal	34	16.8	8	112.1
Juan Guzman, Tor	23	16.7	0	100.7
Mark Gubicza, KC	26	16.6	0	85.0

A lot of the pitchers on this list aren't exactly workhorses — guys like Taylor, Deshaies, Mesa and Gubicza threw a lot of pitches per inning, but they were usually gone by the time they'd reached the 100-pitch mark. Poor control was the most common problem. You can be successful pitching this way; Johnson, DeJesus, Moore, Finley and Guzman all posted winning records last year. But it's sort of doing it the hard way.

These pitchers throw strikes and get out of there — they averaged the fewest pitches per inning last year:

Fewest Pitches per Inning — 20+ Starts

Pitcher, Team	GS	Pitches per Inning	130+ Pitch Games	Pitches per Start
Bob Tewksbury, StL	30	13.0	0	82.7
Bryn Smith, Mon	31	13.4	0	86.0
Greg Swindell, Cle	33	13.7	0	98.5
Bill Gullickson, Det	35	13.8	0	89.3
Bruce Hurst, SD	31	13.8	1	98.9
Greg Maddux, Cubs	37	13.9	0	98.9

It's hard to quibble with success — the average pitcher on this list won 16 games.

A complete listing for this category can be found on page 310.

DID CLEMENS SACRIFICE SOME QUALITY FOR QUANTITY?

Still reviled by some, the "quality start" has earned increased respect as a useful measure of consistent starting pitching. While the minimum qualifications for a Quality Start — at least six innings pitched, no more than three earned runs — might seem easy to achieve, major league starters turn in a quality start only a little more than half the time (52.6% last year). More to the point, there is a high correlation between making a quality start and winning the game; when one starter turns in a QS and the other doesn't, the quality starter's team wins the game over 90 percent of the time.

Here are the 1991 leaders in highest percentage of quality starts:

Pitcher, Team	GS	QS	Pct
Jose Rijo, Cin	30	25	83.3
Greg Harris, SD	20	16	80.0
Tom Candiotti, Cle-Tor	34	27	79.4
Mark Langston, Cal	34	26	76.5
Jose Guzman, Tex	25	19	76.0
Andy Benes, SD	33	25	75.8
Bob Ojeda, LA	31	23	74.2
Tom Glavine, Atl	34	25	73.5
Jim Abbott, Cal	34	25	73.5
Mike Morgan, LA	33	24	72.7
Pete Harnisch, Hou	33	24	72.7
Tim Belcher, LA	33	24	72.7

(Minimum 20 games started)

Jose Rijo's brilliant season (15-6, 2.51) was cut short by injury, but when healthy, Rijo was the most consistent starter in the major leagues: five of every six times out, Rijo kept the Reds in an excellent position to win the game — and that's very impressive. Greg Harris of the Padres still has to prove himself as a starter over the long haul, but he was excellent in his 20 starts last year; with Andy Benes, Harris and Bruce Hurst (67.7%), San Diego has the foundation for a very fine starting rotation.

You might wonder, when looking at the leaders list, where some famous names were: Roger Clemens, Nolan Ryan and Jack Morris, to name three. Ryan's low percentage (59.3) was due to injuries rather than ineffectiveness. Nolan had only one really bad start all year (1.2 innings, four runs), but sometimes had to leave early because of back or shoulder problems. At 45, Ryan can still be as overpowering as any pitcher in baseball ... but his advanced age catches up to even him at times.

Though Morris (57.1%) finished 1991 in a blaze of glory, he had his ups and downs during the regular season. Morris gave up five runs or more in eight of his starts, and seven runs or more four separate times. The Twins defense didn't always help him, but Morris righted himself at the end of the campaign when it counted most.

Clemens, though, is the most interesting case. Roger just missed the top ten at 71.4%, but his quality start percentage wasn't nearly as high as in 1991 when he led both leagues with 87.1% (27 of 31). This may have been somewhat by design, however. In 1990 Clemens went all-out almost every time out, but wound up with arm trouble during the crucial September stretch run. In '91 he seemed to pace himself a little more, as perhaps Morris does. The result was an increase in subpar outings, but like Morris, Clemens was brilliant down the stretch. He wound up working 271.1 innings, the second-highest total of his career. And it's important to note that Clemens' 25 total quality starts were surpassed only by Tom Candiotti and Mark Langston. The Red Sox — and the Cy Young voters — weren't complaining.

Lack of quality is represented by this group, which had the lowest percentage of quality starts:

Pitcher, Team	GS	QS	Pct
Mark Gubicza, KC	26	6	23.1
Wally Whitehurst, Mets	20	6	30.0
Jose Mesa, Bal	23	7	30.4
Bob Walk, Pit	20	7	35.0
Mike Gardiner, Bos	22	8	36.4
Jack Armstrong, Cin	24	9	37.5
Greg Hibbard, WSox	29	11	37.9
Ben McDonald, Bal	21	8	38.1
Dan August, Mil	23	9	39.1
Jeff Johnson, Yanks	23	9	39.1

(Minimum 20 games started)

Some sore arms (Gubicza, McDonald) here, but mostly it was a case of finesse pitchers who were off their game in 1991. Better luck this year, guys.

A complete listing for this category appears on page 311.

DO PITCHERS COAST WITH A BIG LEAD?

When a pitcher gets a big lead — say three runs or more — managers and broadcasters begin to recite a familiar litany: "Throw strikes... make 'em hit their way on... go right after the hitters... don't walk anybody." Endless variations on the same theme, which is that a pitcher with a comfortable lead doesn't need to aim for the corners.

But do pitchers follow the advice and work differently when they have a big lead? We separated all 1991 plate appearances into those in which the pitcher had at least a three-run lead, and those in which the lead was two runs or less. As you can see, there are some mighty big differences:

Working With a Big Lead — 1991

Situation	Avg	Slg	OBP	SB%	Per 100 Plate Appearances			
					HR	SB	BB	K
American League								
Three run or more lead	.265	.412	.318	77%	2.65	0.48	7.01	14.72
Two runs or less	.260	.393	.327	66%	2.20	1.84	9.12	14.91
National League								
Three run or more lead	.252	.388	.304	88%	2.40	0.92	6.83	15.05
Two runs or less	.250	.371	.318	66%	1.90	2.39	8.69	15.64

Some highlights of the data:

1. It's very clear that pitchers with a big lead do indeed go right after the hitters. And the hitters love it. Their batting averages go up slightly, and their slugging averages go up significantly.

2. With pitchers grooving more offerings down the middle, the home run rate jumps up — a 20 percent increase in the American League, a 26 percent rise in the National.

3. The pitchers do listen to their managers and cut down on those walks; the base on balls rate drops by almost one-forth when the lead is three runs or more. More importantly, despite the batting average increase, opponent on-base average decreases significantly meaning that the pitchers **are** getting more outs.

4. The strikeout rate also drops, although only by two to four percent. The pitchers are clearly more content to let the batters hit the ball.

5. The stolen base success rate goes way up — with a big lead, pitchers don't waste a lot of energy holding baserunners. However, the increased success rate doesn't hurt the pitchers much; the trailing team seldom risks

sending its runners, stealing only about a third as many bases as they do when the lead is two runs or less.

This data does explain a bit what you might call the "Bill Gullickson syndrome." Gullickson had a curious season last year, going 20-9 but with a relatively high ERA (3.90). Outstanding run support was the primary reason why he had such a good record; the Tigers scored nearly six runs a game when Gully was on the mound. But since it's pretty likely that Gullickson found himself coasting with a big lead on more than one occasion last year, you could say that his ERA, along with his record, was a little deceptive. Working with smaller leads, Gullickson wouldn't have challenged the hitters as much, and as a result the figure might have been lower. How much lower is anybody's guess, but the Tiger run support probably helped tack a couple of tenths, at least, onto Gullickson's ERA.

Don't get us wrong. In Gullickson's case, there may be a dual deception (won-lost record and ERA), but the primary deception is still in the won-lost record. Overall, Gullickson just didn't pitch well enough to go 20-9 without extraordinary support. But because he got that support, his ERA was a little higher than it might have been otherwise.

ARE CLEMENS AND GOODEN ON THE TRACK TO IMMORTALITY?

Dwight Gooden and Roger Clemens . . . watching their careers, one can relate to the youngsters of 80 years ago, thrilling to the youthful performances of Walter Johnson and Grover Cleveland Alexander. Or the kids of 25 seasons past (hey, that was us!) wondering how many games Bob Gibson and Juan Marichal would end up winning.

There's no question that Gooden and Clemens are something special. At the age of 29, Clemens has amassed a career record of 134-61, one of the best in modern history for a pitcher his age. Gooden, two years younger, is well ahead of that pace, with a record of 132-53.

What's the future hold for these two aces? No one knows for sure, of course. At Gooden's age, Denny McLain had a record of 117-62 — but his overused right arm had only 14 more victories left in it. On the other hand, Phil Niekro, that slow, sleepy kid in the back of the classroom, had amassed a grand total of six victories by the time he was 27; Niekro would win a total of 318. Even so, the past is some guide for what will happen in the future. And it seems to indicate that the future's brighter for Clemens than it is for Gooden.

We'll begin by looking for pitchers who had records similar to Dwight's at the same age — at least 130 wins, and a .600 winning percentage. We'll restrict the study to post-1920 pitchers, since the frequent 30-win seasons in pre-World War I days make comparisons with modern pitchers impossible. This is a very exclusive list:

Most Wins at Age 27 (since 1920)*

Pitcher	Career through	W	L	Pct	Career Record W	L	Pct
Dizzy Dean	1937	134	75	.641	150	83	.644
Dwight Gooden	1991	132	53	.714	???	???	???

*Pitcher's age calculated as of July 1 of each season

That's how extraordinary Gooden has been — only one pitcher in the last 70-plus years had a record similar to his at the same age. At age 27, the last eight 300-game winners had the following win totals: Don Sutton 102, Tom Seaver 95, Nolan Ryan 91, Steve Carlton 77, Early Wynn 64, Warren Spahn 44, Gaylord Perry 24, Phil Niekro 6.

That would indicate Gooden is well on the path to 300. However, the 300-game winners tended to be late starters, not given heavy usage in their

20s and then coming on after their 30th birthday. That's not the case with Doc, a teenage prodigy who is now recovering from a torn rotator cuff. We also know that many pitchers with exceptional records at this young age had an early end to their careers. Included would be McLain, Don Gullett (105-48 at 27, only four victories afterward), and of course Dean, who was basically finished after the '37 season. Rotator cuff surgery has advanced greatly in the last few years, and Gooden is expected to resume pitching this year. There's hope for Doc in Jim Palmer's record (100-48 at this point). Palmer also had arm problems early in his career (though earlier than Gooden), but recovered to have a brilliant career. One hopes Gooden doesn't become the next Dizzy Dean ... but it's possible.

At this point, Clemens' arm appears to be in much better shape than Gooden's is, though Roger has also had bouts of arm trouble. How does Clemens' record compare with others at the same age? The following pitchers all had amassed at least 130 wins, with a .600 winning percentage, by the age of 29 (again, since 1920):

Pitchers with 130+ wins and a .600 Winning Percentage at Age 29 (since 1920)

Pitcher	Career through	W	L	Pct	Career Record W	L	Pct
Wes Ferrell	1936	161	96	.626	193	128	.626
Robin Roberts	1955	160	102	.611	286	245	.539
Bob Feller	1947	158	83	.656	266	162	.621
Waite Hoyt	1928	155	99	.610	237	182	.566
Dizzy Dean	1937	147	80	.648	150	83	.644
Jim Palmer	1974	139	69	.652	268	152	.638
Lefty Gomez	1937	135	69	.662	189	102	.649
Dave McNally	1971	135	69	.662	184	119	.607
Tom Seaver	1973	135	76	.640	311	205	.603
Roger Clemens	1991	134	61	.687	???	???	???
Juan Marichal	1966	132	53	.714	243	142	.631

It's easy to see the brilliant Clemens finishing up with a career record similar to Palmer's, Marichal's or even Seaver's. But like many of the pitchers on this list, Roger has been worked very hard in his career; will he turn out like Lefty Gomez or Dave McNally, who had done most of their good pitching by this age? Our own hunch is that Clemens has an excellent chance to wind up with 250 victories or more. Like everyone else, we'll have to monitor Gooden's recovery before we can be too optimistic about his future.

A complete listing for this category can be found on page 312.

Is Fading in the Stretch a Fatal Weakness?

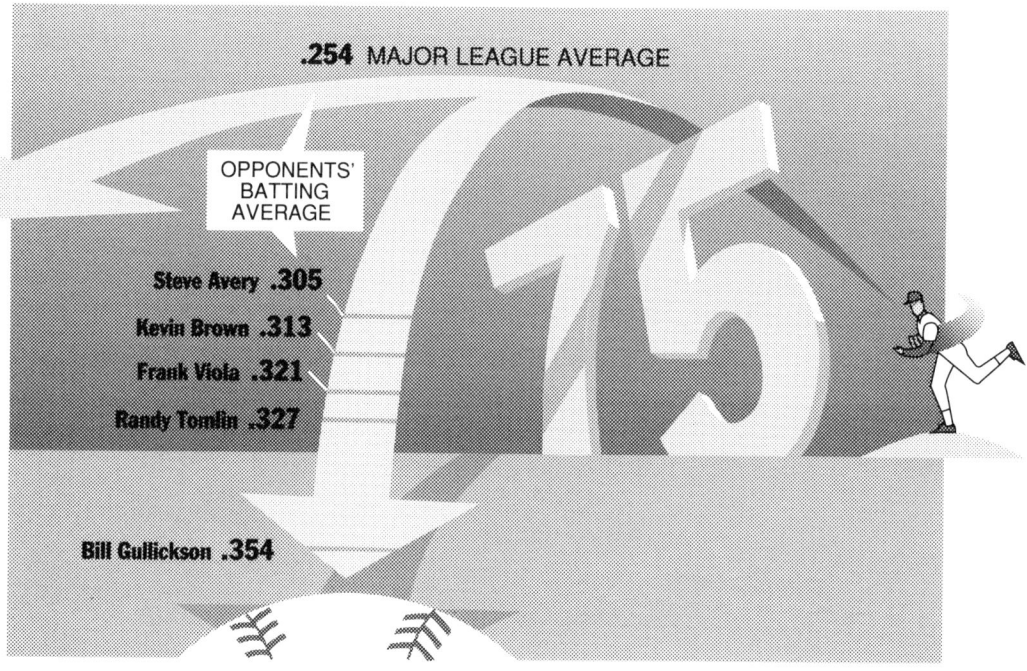

May it rest in peace: the complete game. Not that long ago, a pitcher was expected to be able to finish what he started — no excuses. When Vernon Law, a former Cy Young Award winner, returned to the 1962 Pirates after missing almost all of the previous season with serious arm problems, Sporting News stories didn't want to know whether Law could still be effective; they asked, "Can Vernon go nine?" As recently as 1975, Catfish Hunter threw 30 complete games for the Yankees (while working 328 innings), and Billy Martin's 1980 A's had a staff total of 94 complete games, 28 of them by Rick Langford. It might as well have happened in 1880, the way baseball has changed since then. Last year the entire **National League** — all 12 teams — totaled 150 complete games.

So the complete game is dead, and maybe that's just as well; a lot of those "workhorse starters," including the entire 1980 Oakland starting rotation, wound up with arm problems and shortened careers. In today's game bullpens are layered — middle men, set-up man, closer — and a pitcher is expected to go all out for six innings, maybe seven, before turning the game over to the relievers.

Some pitchers can't even do that. We keep pitch counts, and for most hurlers an inning's work consists of about 15 pitches. One thing we've noticed is that some pitchers seriously begin to lose their stuff after they've reached the 75-pitch mark, which is roughly five innings or even a little less. That would seem to be the mark of a very poor workman, but in fact the list includes some fine pitchers:

Endurance Problems

Pitcher	After Pitch 75			Overall Record			
	AB	H	Avg	GS	W	ERA	Avg
Bill Gullickson, Det	181	64	.354	35	20-9	3.90	.288
Randy Tomlin, Pit	159	52	.327	27	8-7	2.98	.254
Frank Viola, Mets	271	87	.321	35	13-15	3.97	.286
Kevin Brown, Tex	246	77	.313	33	9-12	4.40	.284
Steve Avery, Atl	197	60	.305	35	18-8	3.38	.240
Jaime Navarro, Mil	285	85	.298	34	15-12	3.92	.261
Doug Drabek, Pit	248	74	.298	35	15-14	3.07	.274
Jim Abbott, Cal	293	86	.294	34	18-11	2.89	.244
Walt Terrell, Det	219	64	.292	33	12-14	4.24	.301
Mark Gardner, Mon	162	47	.290	27	9-11	3.85	.230

(minimum 150 batters faced after 75 pitches)

Losing it after 75 pitches, you can see, is hardly fatal for a modern-day pitcher. Seven of these ten had winning records, including a 20-game winner, two 18-game winners and two 15-game winners. The overall record for the group was a fine 137-113. Despite their late-inning problems, two of the ten finished with ERAs under 3.00, and only two were above 4.00. Do these pitchers wind up with a lot of no-decisions because they turn so many games over to their bullpens? Not really, except for Tomlin and Brown.

Naturally, they didn't hit the wall in the sixth inning every time out. Often they pitched well for quite a bit longer than that; when they did lose it early the damage tended to be minimized, since modern managers have no qualms about removing a pitcher when he begins to lose his stuff. What this suggests is that, to a surprising degree, being able to pitch five good innings will take you a long way.

Of course, if you **do** have endurance, so much the better. The pitchers who performed best after after 75 pitches are a very elite group:

	Endurance Kings After Pitch 75			Overall Record			
Pitcher	AB	H	Avg	GS	W	ERA	Avg
Nolan Ryan, Tex	177	26	.147	27	12-6	2.91	.236
Trevor Wilson, SF	160	30	.188	29	13-11	3.56	.234
Pete Harnisch, Hou	237	46	.194	33	12-9	2.70	.212
Jose Rijo, Cin	195	38	.195	30	15-6	2.51	.219
Ramon Martinez, LA	258	52	.202	33	17-13	3.27	.229
Juan Guzman, Tor	145	30	.207	23	10-3	2.99	.197
Roger Clemens, Bos	362	76	.210	35	18-10	2.62	.221
Scott Sanderson, Yanks	180	38	.211	34	16-10	3.81	.252
Tom Candiotti, Cle-Tor	317	69	.218	34	13-13	2.65	.228
Jose Guzman, Tex	220	48	.218	25	13-7	3.08	.239

(minimum 150 batters faced after 75 pitches)

Nolan Ryan, Pete Harnisch, Jose Rijo, Ramon Martinez, Roger Clemens, Tom Candiotti, the Guzmans . . . a superior group of pitchers. Eight of the ten had ERAs under 3.30, and all ten had winning records; the overall won-lost mark was 139-88. Old-timers who like to sneer at the modern game will be comforted to know that even this group didn't "go nine"; the leader in complete games was Clemens with 13. The main reason for that, however, was that, with today's deep bullpens, pitching complete games is no longer essential.

A complete listing for this category appears on page 313.

HOW IMPORTANT IS GOOD CONTROL?

WALKS PER 9 INNINGS PITCHED		ERA
Mitch Williams	6.76	3.33
Bobby Witt	6.26	4.63
Eric Plunk	5.75	4.11
Randy Johnson	5.55	4.01
Tom Gordon	4.72	3.79
1991 ML AVERAGE	3.33	3.91

Minimum 500 innings pitched lifetime.

In another essay we examined how important it was not to walk the leadoff man — pretty darned important, as it turned out. For the most part, the pitchers who struggled in this category were younger hurlers like Randy Johnson, Jose DeJesus, Pat Combs and Alex Fernandez. That data was based on statistics for the last three seasons. Now let's expand the study to look at control overall, and examine its importance to a pitcher's career expectations. Let's look at two groups of pitchers, comparing the ones who have walked the most batters per nine innings over their careers with the ones who have walked the fewest. First, the wild ones:

The Walk Kings	IP	BB	BB/9 IP	H/9 IP	ERA
Mitch Williams	511.0	384	6.76	6.46	3.33
Bobby Witt	980.0	682	6.26	7.72	4.63
Eric Plunk	582.0	372	5.75	7.92	4.11
Randy Johnson	607.2	375	5.55	7.33	4.01
Tom Gordon	532.0	279	4.72	7.77	3.79
Nolan Ryan	5163.1	2686	4.68	6.50	3.15
Doug Sisk	523.1	267	4.59	9.06	3.27
Juan Berenguer	1127.2	568	4.53	7.64	3.79
Jeff M. Robinson	626.2	311	4.47	8.46	4.74
Calvin Schiraldi	553.1	267	4.34	8.49	4.28

We often hear that a pitcher can't succeed in major league baseball unless he can get the ball over the plate. That's not really true. Mitch Williams, who's permitted more walks than hits during his six-year career, has now had two 30-save seasons, including 1991 when he walked 62 men in 88.1 innings. Randy Johnson has won 25 games for a mediocre Seattle club over the last two seasons. Juan Berenguer has lasted 14 seasons now, and of course Nolan Ryan is a certified immortal. How do pitchers like this succeed? Primarily by being very tough to hit. Every pitcher on this list except Doug Sisk (Doug Sisk?) has given up less than a hit per inning during his career. Williams, Witt, Johnson, Gordon, Ryan and Berenguer all have lifetime opponents' batting averages of .235 or less, which means they're very tough indeed.

Yet, as we commented in the essay on pitchers who walk the leadoff man, the word that comes to mind with at least some of these guys is "underachiever." That term would clearly apply to Witt, Plunk, Robinson and Schiraldi, all of whom will be lucky to find major league work in 1992. So yes, you can succeed with poor control, but only if you give up a very low number of hits. Even then, you're apt to have a very up-and-down career.

Contrast that list with this one, the pitchers with the best records of control over their major league careers:

The Control Kings	IP	BB	BB/9 IP	H/9 IP	ERA
Bret Saberhagen	1660.1	331	1.79	8.41	3.21
Bob Tewksbury	551.1	116	1.89	9.97	3.67
Greg Swindell	1043.0	226	1.95	9.14	3.84
John Candelaria	2481.1	570	2.07	8.54	3.30
Dennis Eckersley	2891.1	668	2.08	8.36	3.47
Jimmy Key	1479.0	345	2.10	8.63	3.41

Bill Wegman	914.0	216	2.13	9.37	4.25
Bryn Smith	1740.1	416	2.15	8.57	3.43
Bill Gullickson	2063.1	503	2.19	9.11	3.66
Scott Sanderson	2034.1	507	2.24	8.72	3.61

Another misconception a lot of people have is that control pitchers are soft-tossers, "finesse hurlers." That term might apply to half this group: Tewksbury, Key, Wegman, Smith and Sanderson. Saberhagen, Swindell and Eckersley, however, are most definitely power pitchers; Candelaria still gets a lot of strikeouts even at age 38, and Gullickson, now a finesse type, was a hard thrower in his younger days. These pitchers allow more hits than the first group, possibly sacrificing a little power for the sake of control. They're a more successful group, as well, with generally lower career ERAs.

One thing that might occur to you, though, is that a lot of big names are missing from **both** these groups. Somewhere in the middle — with varying degrees of control — are Roger Clemens (2.47 walks per nine innings), Frank Viola (2.55), Dwight Gooden and Orel Hershiser (both 2.65), Dennis Martinez (2.66), Dave Stieb (3.17), Jack Morris (3.22) and Dave Stewart (3.44). Good control, we conclude, is an important factor in a pitcher's makeup, but it's certainly possible to succeed with a good deal less than that . . . if you have the ability to overpower the hitters. The worse your control, however, the more overpowering you have to be.

A complete listing for this category can be found on page 314.

WILL IT BE DR. TREVOR... OR MR. WILSON?

Some pitchers are the steady types, your June Cleavers: always that dependable smile on their faces, always that nice hot dinner at 7:00. Others are like Moody Pam, a friend of mine from long ago: on her good days, she was the happiest, sexiest woman on earth ... but if she got up on the wrong side of bed, you'd better start looking for your suit of armor.

Earned run average is a terrific stat, and still the best number for evaluating pitchers. But it's just that, an average — it doesn't tell you how the hurler's performance fluctuates from one appearance to the next. So using three years worth of data, a more reliable sample, we decided to examine those fluctuations. What we did was to separate starters' appearances between their winning and losing efforts — basically the good ones from the bad ones. Not surprisingly, the average pitcher performs a lot better when he wins (1.94 ERA) than he does when he loses (6.57 ERA).

These starters were the steady ones — they had the smallest ERA differences between their winning and losing efforts (1989-1991):

Smallest Difference Between Winning/Losing Efforts

Pitcher	W	IP	ERA	L	IP	ERA	Diff
Orel Hershiser	23	176.1	1.99	18	116.0	4.11	2.12
Dennis Martinez	40	315.2	1.74	28	183.1	4.22	2.48
John Cerutti	20	134.2	2.74	24	144.2	5.23	2.49
Charlie Hough	31	226.0	2.55	35	228.0	5.13	2.58
Jose Rijo	36	261.1	1.62	20	117.1	4.30	2.68
John Smiley	40	289.2	2.36	26	152.1	5.20	2.84
Roger Clemens	56	444.2	1.68	27	183.1	4.66	2.98
Frank Tanana	32	229.0	2.55	34	208.2	5.56	3.01
Chris Bosio	33	245.2	1.80	29	191.2	4.84	3.04
Doug Drabek	50	385.2	1.73	32	197.2	4.78	3.05

(minimum 45 starts in 1989-91)

Who else would be leading this list but Mr. Perfect himself, Orel Hershiser. ("Why don't you have more friends like Orel?" your mom says. "Even when he loses, he's so **nice** about it.") Another Mr. Perfect (in more ways than one), Dennis Martinez, ranks second, and most of this group is fairly predictable — down to the aptly named John "Smiley." Even in their losing efforts they keep their team in the game, and you can't ask any more than that. A couple of names surprise us, however. Charlie Hough is a knuckleballer, and you'd think he'd get hammered on the days when his best pitch wasn't knuckling. Relative to other pitchers, that isn't so. Frank Tanana, strictly a finesse pitcher for a long time, wouldn't be expected to have much stuff on his bad days. But he has a lot more than most.

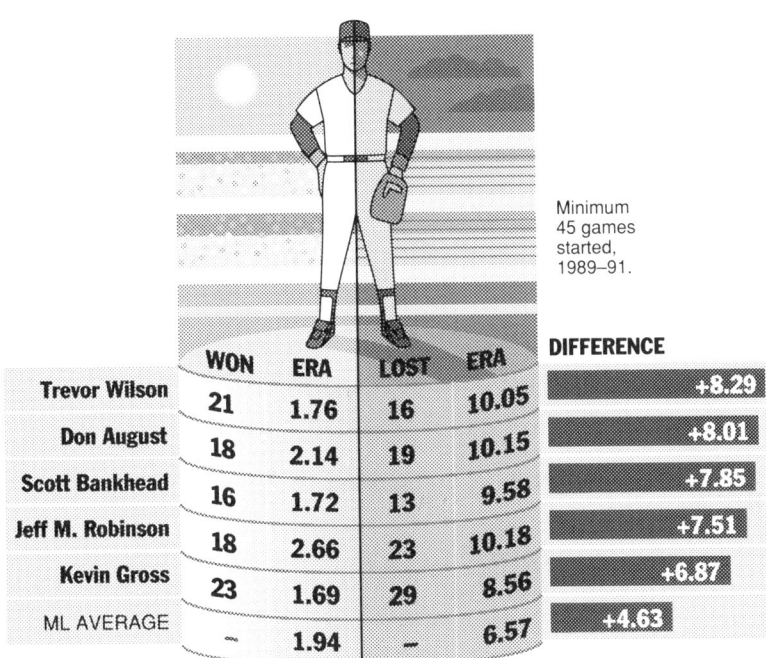

Minimum 45 games started, 1989–91.

The other group is totally unpredictable. On their good days, you can forget it — the other team doesn't have much of a chance. But on their bad days, not even the '27 Yankee offense would help you pick up many wins:

Largest Difference Between Winning and Losing Efforts

Pitcher	W	IP	ERA	L	IP	ERA	Diff
Trevor Wilson	21	153.0	1.76	16	62.2	10.05	8.29
Don August	18	122.0	2.14	19	78.0	10.15	8.01
Scott Bankhead	16	115.0	1.72	13	57.1	9.58	7.85
Jeff M. Robinson	18	128.1	2.66	23	89.1	10.18	7.51
Kevin Gross	23	170.0	1.69	29	143.0	8.56	6.87
Andy Hawkins	24	180.0	1.95	33	162.1	8.65	6.70
Scott Garrelts	27	197.0	1.51	17	74.2	8.20	6.69
Steve Avery	21	153.0	1.59	18	76.2	8.10	6.51
David West	14	99.1	2.27	17	78.0	8.77	6.50
Don Robinson	27	210.0	1.59	25	119.2	7.90	6.31

Trevor Wilson has exasperated Roger Craig and the Giants over the last couple of years. He has Sandy Koufax stuff when he's right, but when he doesn't, it's batting practice time. Even so, no one epitomizes this group better than the enigmatic David West of the Twins — one hit and no runs allowed over 5.2 innings in last year's playoffs, but two hits, four walks and no batters (none) retired in two World Series appearances. No wonder most of these pitchers are in and out of their clubs' starting rotations.

A complete listing for this category can be found on page 315.

DID MORE THROWS TO FIRST HELP DWIGHT GOODEN?

> "They all laughed at John Dewan and Zminda
> When they counted throws to first . . ."
>
> — with apologies to Ira Gershwin

When you're a new face in any established business, people are going to look at you with a skeptical eye. When you're a new face in the baseball business, people are going to dangle you, feet first, from the press box window for three or four seasons . . . just to see if your brains fall out, we guess. We here at STATS seem to be surviving our initiation period (baseball looks great upside down), for a couple of simple reasons: our work makes sense, and it helps people learn some things about this wonderful game.

To our surprise, the most controversial thing we've done has been to count pitchers' throws to first. Even Fay Vincent commented on it with such emotion that we thought he was going to cry; maybe Fay's going to pass a rule against it. But ho ho ho, who's got the last laugh now? Though we reported the figure with our usual light touch, it was obvious from the very beginning that there was a clear relationship between throwing to first and reducing the chance of a successful steal. They'd never credit us, of course, but the major league teams seem to be getting the message; the number of throws to first went up last year, while the stolen base rate, and the number of attempts, went down:

Season	Pickoff Throws	SB Attempts	SB Percentage
1990	23,905	4,800	68.5%
1991	25,044	4,687	66.6%

So when we present the list of 1991 leaders in number of pickoff throws, remember that we're doing more than giving David Cone a claim to fame. We're identifying some pitchers who are doing something concrete to reduce the stolen base damage:

1991 Leaders — Pickoff Throws

Pitcher, Team	Pickoff Throws Total	Pickoff Throws Per 9	Stolen Bases SB	Stolen Bases CS	Stolen Bases SB/9
David Cone, Mets	408	15.8	27	13	1.04
John Burkett, SF	344	15.0	17	16	0.74
Charlie Hough, WSox	317	14.3	10	9	0.45
Jim Deshaies, Hou	295	16.5	21	14	1.17
Bud Black, SF	266	11.2	14	11	0.59
Trevor Wilson, SF	242	10.8	8	12	0.36
Tom Glavine, Atl	240	8.8	18	10	0.66
Charlie Leibrandt, Atl	231	9.1	35	11	1.37
Frank Tanana, Det	215	8.9	17	14	0.70
Dwight Gooden, Mets	215	10.2	33	16	1.56

Teams that have gotten that pickoff religion include the Mets, Braves and Giants — they clearly have instructed their pitchers to throw to first more. The majority have excellent results. Six of the ten pitchers allowed well below the major league average of 0.744 steals per nine innings, and most of them had excellent throw-out rates, as well.

But if you're a power pitcher with a high leg kick, and are often throwing to catchers who couldn't toss out your grandmother, what you're practicing is "damage control." That brings us to the Mets' David Cone and Doc Gooden. Cone, the worthy successor to Jim Deshaies and Charlie Hough as the winner of the Pickoff Trophy (well we had a trophy, but someone stole it) has tripled his throw-to-first rate over the last three years, with modest results. Cone has, however, reduced his stolen base success rate from 73% in 1989 to 68% in 1991. That might be not very significant statistically, but Cone is surely grateful to make some progress.

Gooden, however, is a better story. Always notoriously easy to steal on, he made significant progress last year — with the help of more pickoff throws:

	Pickoff Throws per 9 IP	Stolen Bases per 9 IP
Gooden, 1990	7.9	2.32
Gooden, 1991	10.2	1.56

For Doc, that's a big, big improvement.

A complete listing for this category can be found on page 316.

IS HOLDING RUNNERS OVERRATED?

You always hear how important it is for pitchers to hold runners close to first base; otherwise, every runner on first will quickly become a runner on second, and then a run. Ergo, pitchers who can't hold runners are losers. We can't really argue with the neat logic of that argument. But what seems so clear in theory is anything but clear in practice.

Last year, for example, the leaders list of best pitchers against the stolen base included the likes of Jeff Pico, Mike Jeffcoat, Dave Johnson (the pitcher, not the manager) and John Mitchell (the pitcher, not the Attorney General). Meanwhile, the "easy to steal on" group included Dwight Gooden, Mike Scott, Rob Dibble, Jack Morris and Lee Smith. You can, we think, see a bit of a problem here.

Okay, that was one year's worth of evidence; maybe it was a fluke. Let's move on to the figures from 1991. Here's the first group, the pitchers who were toughest to steal on (in terms of stolen bases allowed per nine innings):

Pitcher, Team	T	SB	CS	PK	SB%	SB/9	ERA
Greg Harris, Bos	R	1	6	3	14.3	.05	3.85
Jeff Ballard, Bal	L	1	4	0	20.0	.07	5.60
Kenny Rogers, Tex	L	1	3	2	25.0	.08	5.42
Bill Swift, Sea	L	1	1	0	50.0	.10	1.99
Jose Melendez, SD	R	1	6	0	14.3	.10	3.27
John Barfield, Tex	L	1	3	1	25.0	.11	4.54
Storm Davis, KC	R	2	2	0	50.0	.16	4.96
Scott Erickson, Min	R	4	10	0	28.6	.18	3.18
Brian Holman, Sea	R	4	5	1	44.4	.18	3.69
Rich DeLucia, Sea	R	4	9	1	30.8	.20	5.09

(Minimum 81 Innings Pitched)

Once again, this will be no one's list of the best pitchers in baseball, though there's nothing wrong with Bill Swift or Scott Erickson. But come on — Jeff Ballard, John Barfield, Storm Davis, Rich DeLucia? If holding runners is so important, why do these people have so much trouble holding a job? (We'll admit, however, that the presence of Kenny "You Got to Know When to Hold 'Em" Rogers is perfect from an aesthetic point of view.)

The most interesting thing about the list, actually, might be the presence of three Seattle pitchers. That's a credit to Mariner catcher Dave Valle, but also to former manager Jim Lefebvre, who insisted his pitchers improve their ability to hold runners. Expect Lefebvre's Cubs to do a better job of controlling the running game this year.

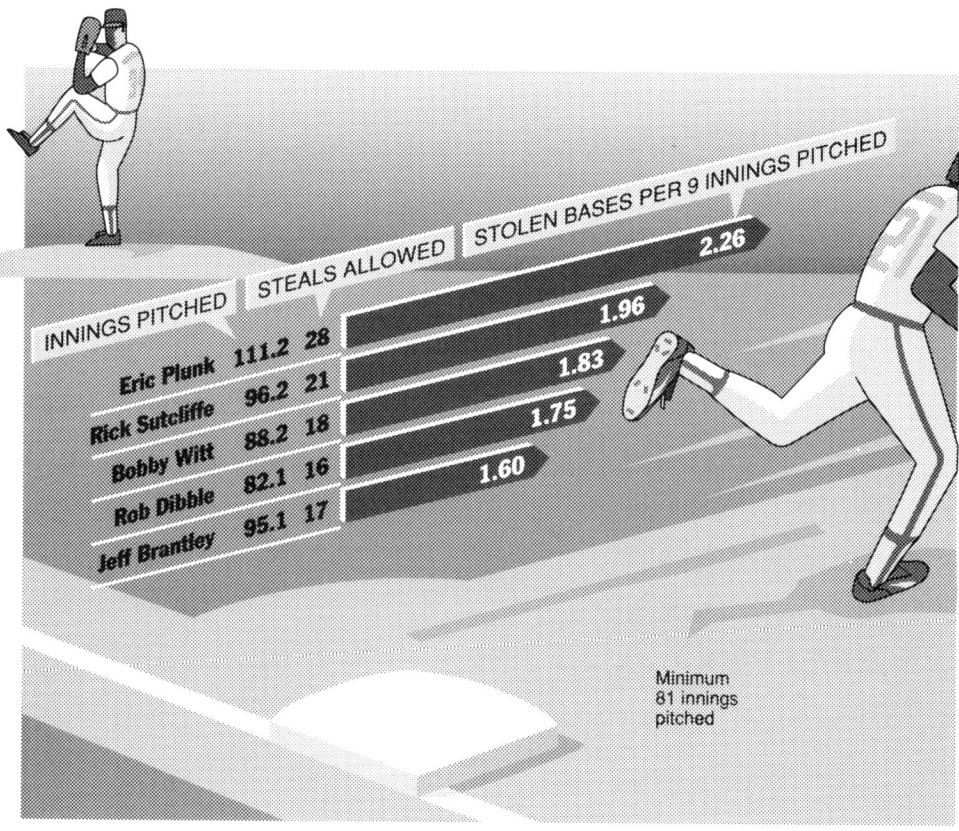

Okay, now let's look at the second group, the pitchers who were the **easiest** to run on. The chart below expands on the data from the graphic:

Pitcher, Team	T	SB	CS	PK	SB%	SB/9	ERA
Eric Plunk, Yanks	R	28	3	1	90.3	2.26	4.76
Rick Sutcliffe, Cubs	R	21	2	0	91.3	1.96	4.10
Bobby Witt, Tex	R	18	4	0	81.8	1.83	6.09
Rob Dibble, Cin	R	16	5	0	76.2	1.75	3.17
Jeff Brantley, SF	R	17	2	0	89.5	1.60	2.45
Dwight Gooden, Mets	R	33	16	0	67.4	1.56	3.60
Bill Sampen, Mon	R	16	8	0	66.7	1.56	4.00
Mike Hartley, LA-Phi	R	13	1	0	92.9	1.40	4.21
Charlie Leibrandt, Atl	L	35	11	4	76.1	1.37	3.49
Dennis Rasmussen, SD	L	21	6	0	77.8	1.29	3.74

Ordinarily, the pitchers who have the most trouble holding runners are hard throwers with high leg kicks. That certainly applies to Plunk, Witt, Dibble and Gooden. (And to Nolan Ryan and Mitch Williams, who just missed the bottom ten.) Pitchers with shaky control (Plunk, Witt, Brantley, Sampen and Hartley) are also often pretty easy to run on. At the same time, however, they weren't all that easy to beat. While the group wasn't full of dazzling ERAs, the only ones who got hammered were Plunk and Witt. Once again, we're forced to conclude that controlling the running game is overrated — the crucial factor is retiring the hitter.

In looking at these lists, you may also have noted that the "tough to steal on" group is dominated by American League hurlers (nine of the ten). The "easy to steal on" category is dominated by National Leaguers (eight of ten). This suggests American League pitchers do a better job of holding runners, but that's misleading; the big factor is that they run a lot less in the American League. In looking at these figures, as with so many others, context is very important.

A complete listing for this category appears on page 317.

IS "UNEARNED RUN AVERAGE" A LEADING INDICATOR?

In this space a year ago, we presented a modest little stat called "unearned average." The idea was fairly simple. ERA subtracts the unearned runs caused by inept defense, but those runs cross the plate anyway, endangering the pitcher's won-lost record and perhaps his confidence as well. What we wanted to do, more than anything, was to identify which pitchers had been victimized by their defenses, and which ones hadn't.

Simple enough. But when we looked at that list of pitchers a year later, we found something fairly interesting: a lot of the hurlers who were victimized in 1990 found plenty of good fortune in 1991. Scott Erickson, the leading victim of 1990, was a 20-game winner in 1991 . . . some would say a lucky 20-game winner. Bill Gullickson was the same — the fates frowned on him in '90, but smiled on him in '91 (also to the tune of 20 wins). Greg Maddux, a .500 pitcher in 1990, returned to his winning ways in Chicago; ditto for Bryn Smith in St. Louis. Bill Krueger had his best major league season, by far, for Seattle, and Krueger's Mariner teammate Billy Swift also had the best year of his career. Charlie Leibrandt was smiled upon, also . . . at least during the regular season. The fates didn't do much for Tom Gordon, Mike Witt or Dennis Rasmussen in '91, but those guys always seem to have a dark cloud over their heads.

So when we present the 1991 leaders in "unearned average" — most unearned runs allowed per nine innings — remember that their luck has a good chance of evening out in 1992:

Their Defenses Deserted Them

Pitcher, Team	IP	R	UER	E	UERA	W	L	ERA
Dan Petry, Det-Atl-Bos	101.1	69	14	16	1.24	2	3	4.88
Kenny Rogers, Tex	109.2	80	14	12	1.15	10	10	5.42
Darryl Kile, Hou	153.2	81	18	21	1.05	5	10	6.64
Jeff Ballard, Bal	123.2	91	14	17	1.02	6	12	5.60
Chuck McElroy, Cubs	101.1	33	11	5	0.98	6	2	1.98
Bob Scanlan, Cubs	111.0	60	12	14	0.97	7	8	3.89
Randy Tomlin, Pit	175.0	75	17	20	0.87	8	7	2.98
Eric Plunk, Yanks	111.2	69	10	11	0.81	2	5	4.76
Bob Tewksbury, StL	191.0	86	17	12	0.80	11	12	3.25
Dennis Rasmussen, SD	146.2	74	13	15	0.80	6	13	3.74

UER=Un-Earned Runs Allowed
E=Errors Committed while Pitching

We don't know how much the fates will smile on Dan Petry, Jeff Ballard, Eric Plunk or the twice-cursed Dennis Rasmussen in 1992 — for them,

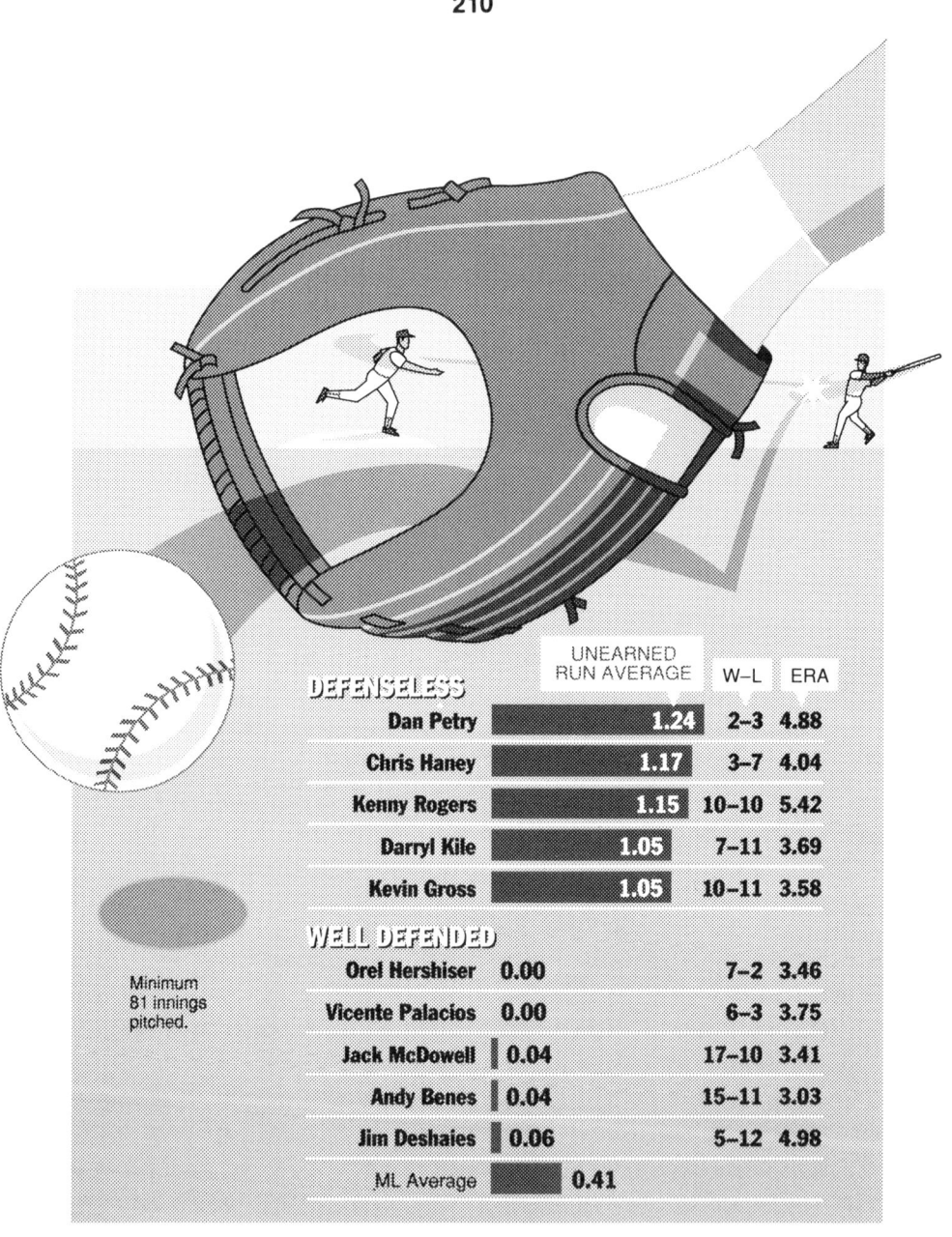

"good luck" will begin with finding a major league employer. But if you wanted a decent long-shot rotisserie pick, you could do worse than gamble on Randy Tomlin or Bob Tewksbury; with a reasonable run of luck this year, they figure to win a lot more games.

The "least-victimized" pitchers in 1990 included Dave Johnson and Tom Bolton, who fell upon hard times in '91, and Tom Browning, who had his worst season since 1987. We can't really predict these pitchers will fall apart in 1992 — but with a more normal run of luck (as you'd expect), their won-lost records figure to decline:

Their Defenses Supported Them

Pitcher, Team	IP	R	UER	E	UERA	W	L	ERA
Orel Hershiser, LA	112.0	43	0	5	0.00	7	2	3.46
Jack McDowell, WSox	253.2	97	1	8	0.04	17	10	3.41
Andy Benes, SD	223.0	76	1	13	0.04	15	11	3.03
Jim Deshaies, Hou	161.0	90	1	15	0.06	5	12	4.98
Nolan Ryan, Tex	173.0	58	2	10	0.10	12	6	2.91
Kevin Tapani, Min	244.0	84	2	11	0.11	16	9	2.99
Melido Perez, WSox	135.2	49	2	15	0.13	8	7	3.12
Oil Can Boyd, Mon-Tex	182.1	96	3	10	0.15	8	15	4.59
Tim Leary, Yanks	120.2	89	2	7	0.15	4	10	6.49
Bruce Ruffin, Phi	119.0	52	2	9	0.15	4	7	3.78

The antidote to worse luck is simply pitching better, and that's what a presumably-healthy Orel Hershiser intends to do this season . . . and what the amazing Nolan Ryan intends to do every season. But did Jack McDowell, Andy Benes and Kevin Tapani "mature" last year, or were their good records partially due to good fortune? All three are very talented, but a decline in their records this year wouldn't surprise us at all.

"Timothy Leary's dead," sang the Moody Blues 20 years ago. They may finally be right, at least in the baseball sense. And if this category is any indicator, the Can can't (pitch winning ball any more).

A complete list for this category can be found on page 318.

WHICH STARTING STAFFS STAR, AND WHICH RELIEF STAFFS REEK?

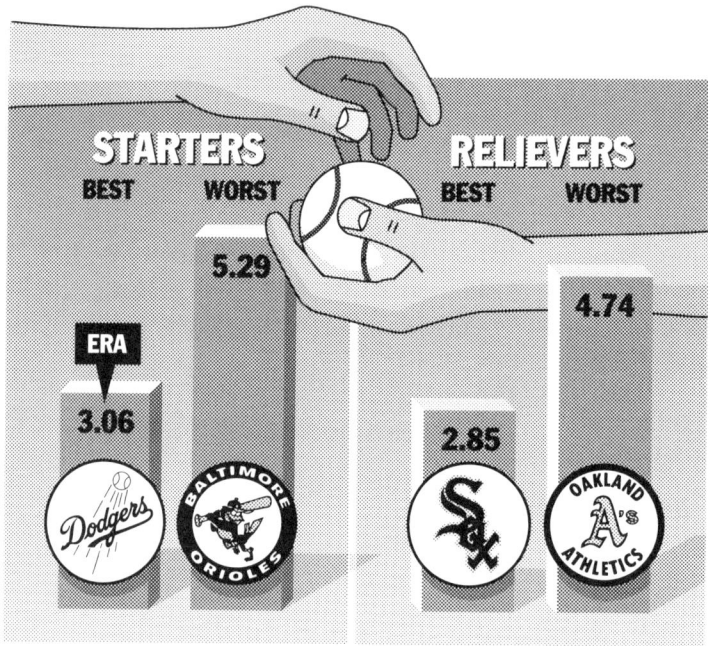

If you don't think baseball is an unpredictable game, you might want to talk to Tony LaRussa. A year ago at this time, LaRussa's A's were gunning for a fourth straight American League pennant. Though repeating was hardly certain, LaRussa had to feel secure about his strong, deep bullpen. Led by the great Dennis Eckersley, the A's 1990 relief corps had been the best in baseball — by a margin of more than half a run a game — with a minuscule earned run average of 2.35.

But when 1991 arrived, the A's relief corps collapsed completely. First Rick Honeycutt got hurt, then Gene Nelson. Eckersley started pitching like a human being again after two years of unbelievable pitching. Younger pitchers couldn't take up the slack, and it didn't help that the A's starting corps was struggling as well, increasing the load on the bullpen. The result? Oakland's bullpen ERA more than doubled, to a lofty 4.74. The best in baseball in 1990, it was the worst in the majors in 1991. The way things unfolded, the A's had to feel lucky to finish with 84 wins.

With today's pitching staffs so specialized that the starters and relievers form two distinct corps — and the bullpen itself layered into distinctive roles — things can quickly fall apart, like a complicated car slipping out of tune. The Red Sox, who had the best starters' ERA in the majors in 1990, couldn't repeat the magic in '91 . . . and couldn't repeat as AL East champions, either. The Reds' bullpen, second only to Oakland in 1990, slipped to the middle of the National League pack in 1991, and so did the club's won-lost record. On the other hand, a few clubs each year find youngsters improving. Or they get help from some new pitchers acquired through trades or free agency. That's what happened to the Braves who, thanks to Mike Stanton, Kent Mercker, Juan Berenguer, Alejandro Pena and others, improved their relief ERA from 5.01 in 1990 (worst in the majors) to 3.57 in 1991.

Let's look at each pitching staff's 1991 figures, separated into starting and relief numbers. First, the American League:

AL Starters	W	L	ERA	IP
Blue Jays	67	50	3.49	1,014.2
Twins	71	51	3.77	1,000.2
Angels	70	67	3.81	1,042.0
Royals	63	59	3.98	1,002.2
Mariners	60	59	4.11	974.2
Brewers	62	52	4.17	974.2
Indians	42	79	4.21	1,032.1
Red Sox	65	61	4.22	984.1
White Sox	54	55	4.23	1,014.1
Tigers	60	60	4.48	961.1
Athletics	56	56	4.50	986.2
Rangers	52	53	4.63	948.0
Yankees	45	68	5.07	892.0
Orioles	42	69	5.29	900.0

AL Relievers	W	L	ERA	IP
White Sox	33	20	2.85	463.2
Mariners	23	20	3.16	489.2
Angels	11	14	3.38	399.2
Yankees	26	23	3.41	552.0
Orioles	25	26	3.45	557.2
Twins	24	16	3.53	448.2
Blue Jays	24	21	3.54	448.0
Red Sox	19	17	3.58	455.1
Royals	19	21	3.81	463.1
Brewers	21	27	4.18	489.0
Rangers	33	24	4.19	531.0
Indians	15	26	4.31	409.0
Tigers	24	18	4.66	489.0
Athletics	28	22	4.74	457.2

You can't underestimate the importance of a good starting rotation; last year the best two starting staffs in the AL were represented by the division champions, Toronto and Minnesota. No one knows what will happen in '92, but with the Twins losing Jack Morris and the Royals Bret Saberhagen, there's bound to be a lot of upheaval in the staff rankings. The club to watch might well be the Red Sox, who have added a solid number two man, Frank Viola, behind baseball's best starter, Roger Clemens. Oakland's experience last year underscores how difficult it is to predict what will happen to the league's relief staffs. But one has to think that LaRussa and his longtime pitching coach, Dave Duncan, will be able to get the A's relief corps out of last place in '92.

Here are the National League figures for 1991:

NL Starters	W	L	ERA	IP
Dodgers	65	48	3.06	1,023.0
Pirates	67	44	3.27	1,005.0
Braves	72	49	3.46	1,009.0
Cardinals	54	57	3.54	1,001.1
Expos	49	59	3.56	998.2
Padres	65	61	3.68	1,011.1
Mets	57	65	3.71	1,017.2
Reds	59	65	3.98	966.0
Phillies	51	63	3.98	964.0
Astros	45	63	4.07	956.1
Giants	54	63	4.18	945.0
Cubs	48	54	4.35	957.0

NL Relievers	W	L	ERA	IP
Dodgers	28	21	3.08	435.0
Mets	20	19	3.22	419.2
Padres	19	17	3.36	441.1
Cubs	29	29	3.46	499.2
Reds	15	23	3.53	474.0
Braves	22	19	3.57	443.2
Phillies	27	21	3.64	499.0
Giants	21	24	3.75	497.0
Expos	22	31	3.83	441.2
Pirates	31	20	3.83	451.2
Astros	20	34	3.86	496.2
Cardinals	30	21	4.02	434.0

The importance of a good starting rotation is also obvious from the

National League numbers. The three best teams in the league last year were the Braves, Pirates and Dodgers, and those were also the teams with the best starting staffs. That makes one wonder why the Mets — with Dwight Gooden and Sid Fernandez both coming back from injuries — let Viola leave via free agency. We know money was involved, and that they've added Bret Saberhagen, but do they know how rare a pitcher like Viola — injury-free year after year, 13 wins even in a bad (for him) season — really is? We think they'll miss him plenty. Among the relief staffs, a club to watch might be San Diego. Greg Riddoch has shown a real ability to handle a bullpen, and he's added Randy Myers, a dominant closer prior to '91.

One last comment about this start/relief stuff. Until pretty recently, it used to be that when a starter began having troubles, he was shifted to the bullpen until he got his game in order. Young pitchers would break in as long relievers, and if they showed promise, they'd be moved into the rotation. This sort of thing still happens now and then, but with the roles so specialized, it's becoming rarer and rarer. When a staff gets out of sync now, all a club can do is make a deal, sign a free agent, or try to bring in some fresh help from the minors. It's another reason why predicting who'll have the best pitching is so difficult nowadays.

A complete listing for this category can be found on page 319.

WHY DO THE METS LET THEIR ACES THROW SO MANY PITCHES?

Ah, the modern game. Ball one. Ball two . . . ball two? The pitcher steps off the mound to argue with the umpire. Strike one. Strike two . . . strike two? Now the batter is arguing. After each pitch, of course, the hitter steps out of the batter's box, adjusts his equipment, communes with himself. (Did you know this is a recent phenomenon, continually stepping out of the box? George Foster started it the mid-1970s. Drove everybody crazy.) Hitter steps back in. Fouls one off. Fouls another one off. The pitcher steps off the mound, rubs up the ball, communes with himself. He throws. Ball three . . . ball three, you're thinking? Yet another full count. You'd like to leave early, but you're a Real Fan. You'll just go without sleep one more night.

This is not something you're imagining. The games **do** take longer, the pitchers **do** throw more pitches. Usually several hurlers share the workload — aren't all those pitching changes fun? — but now and then a starter will stick around, throwing 145 pitches or more. You have to be a pretty good pitcher to be allowed to last that long, as you'll instantly see by scanning this list:

Most Pitches in a Game — 1991

Pitcher, Team	Date Opp	W Fin L	IP	H	R	ER	BB	K	# Pit
Andy Benes, SD	4/16 Cin	0-1 L	8.1	4	1	1	3	13	154
Mike Moore, Oak	6/21 @Bos	2-3 L	8.0	7	3	3	7	2	154
Frank Tanana, Det	9/21 Mil	2-5 L	8.2	8	5	4	5	5	151
Jose DeJesus, Phi	8/31 Atl	5-0 W	8.0	3	0	0	6	13	150
Dave Stewart, Oak	5/31 @Chi	4-5 L	8.0	10	4	4	6	5	150
Roger Clemens, Bos	7/22 @Tex	1-2 L	8.0	7	2	2	4	4	150
Dwight Gooden, Mets	4/13 Mon	5-3 W	9.0	7	3	3	3	14	149
Frank Tanana, Det	6/18 Oak	2-0 W	8.2	4	0	0	4	5	149
David Cone, Mets	6/04 @Cin	4-2 W	8.0	4	2	0	5	13	148
Frank Viola, Mets	6/06 @Cin	3-5 L	8.0	9	5	5	4	4	146

The story here is the Mets, with three pitchers in the top ten. Buddy Harrelson took a lot of heat for letting Doc Gooden throw 149 pitches on a cold April day. The Mets came up with a unique solution to stifling the criticism — stop giving out the pitch count. Stubborn to the end, Harrelson never backed off from leaving his starters out there, even after Gooden blew out his shoulder. David Cone, in particular, toted that barge and lifted that bale: 148 pitches against Cincinnati, 137 against Pittsburgh, 138 against St. Louis, 139 against Houston, 141 against Philadelphia. The last one, which came after Harrelson was fired, was his 19-strikeout game, so it was understandable. But all the others?

One pitcher conspicuously absent from this list was the Dodgers' Ramon Martinez. You might recall that, a year ago, we criticized Tom Lasorda for letting his slim young ace work so many high-pitch outings. We can't take credit (or can we?), but the Dodgers were somewhat more careful with Martinez last year, never letting him throw more than 135 pitches in a game. Ramon nonetheless threw more than 120 pitches on 12 different occasions, and it was no surprise to us that he wore down in the second half.

With pitch counts rising, the hurler who can toss a complete game in less than 100 pitches is becoming increasingly rare. Last year we awarded the "Red Barrett Trophy" — named for an old Brave pitcher who once tossed a 58-pitch complete game — to the Cardinals' Bob Tewskbury, who completed a game in only 76 pitches. No one was quite that economical in 1991. The Barrett winner, Chris Bosio, can nonetheless be proud of his 82-pitch gem; you kind of have to imagine the trophy, Chris, but imagine a really big one:

Least Pitches in a Game — 1991

Pitcher, Team	Date Opp	Fin	W L	IP	H	R	ER	BB	K	# Pit
Chris Bosio, Mil	9/17 @NY	2-0	W	9.0	2	0	0	1	1	82
Jack McDowell, WSox	7/14 @Mil	15-1	W	9.0	1	1	1	1	4	83
Greg Swindell, Cle	6/1 Det	3-1	W	9.0	5	1	0	0	6	90
Kevin Tapani, Min	8/11 @Sea	5-2	W	9.0	4	2	2	1	3	91
Mike Boddicker, KC	4/9 Cle	1-2	L	9.0	5	2	1	0	3	92
Bob Welch, Oak	5/20 Tor	0-1	L	9.0	4	1	1	1	3	93
Greg Swindell, Cle	9/7 Tor	1-4	L	9.0	9	4	4	0	3	93
Greg Hibbard, WSox	6/29 @Min	8-4	W	9.0	7	4	4	1	1	94
Greg Swindell, Cle	8/3 KC	3-1	W	9.0	7	1	1	0	4	94
Joe Slusarski, Oak	7/27 @Bal	9-1	W	9.0	2	1	1	2	2	95

We trust we're not alone in saying Greg Swindell is our kind of guy. But another endangered species surfaces here — the sub-two hour game. The quickest contest in this group was Swindell's June 1 win against the Tigers, in 2:02. George Foster, it's all your fault.

A complete listing for this category can be found on page 320.

WHO'S WORST IN THE FIRST?

"If we're gonna get this guy," managers and broadcasters always say about someone else's ace pitcher, "we have to get him early. After that, he settles down." It makes sense that many pitchers would be vulnerable early in the game, when they're still trying to develop their rhythm. But which pitchers are the easiest prey in the first inning: good pitchers, bad pitchers, power pitchers, finesse pitchers?

This is a fairly straightforward exercise. Here are the starters who had the highest ERAs in the first inning in 1991, along with other pertinent stats (minimum 20 first innings):

The Worst in the First

Pitcher, Team	IP	ERA	HR	Avg
Jim Deshaies, Hou	27.0	10.67	6	.360
Jeff Ballard, Bal	21.2	8.31	1	.333
Rich DeLucia, Sea	31.0	8.13	7	.320
Jose Mesa, Bal	23.0	7.83	1	.315
Trevor Wilson, SF	29.0	7.45	3	.288
Dennis Rasmussen, SD	23.2	7.23	3	.355
Jack Armstrong, Cin	24.0	7.13	4	.323
Charles Nagy, Cle	33.0	7.09	3	.333
Shawn Boskie, Cubs	20.1	7.08	2	.346
Dave Stewart, Oak	35.0	6.94	3	.352

Most of these pitchers struggled in just about every inning, so it's no shock to see they had problems in the first. (Dave Stewart — how the mighty have fallen!) But lest you think Trevor Wilson (13-11, 3.56) is the rare talented pitcher with first-inning problems, guess again. The following pitchers weren't all that far off the worst-in-the-first list: Chuck Finley (6.15 ERA), Bob Tewksbury (6.00, .395 opponents' average), Jack Morris (5.91, .313 average), Orel Hershiser (5.14) and Doug Drabek (4.63, .319 average). Overall, finesse pitchers seem to have more first-inning problems than power pitchers, but it's not a hard-and-fast rule.

What kind of pitchers performed the best in the first inning? This is a very interesting list:

The Best in the First

Pitcher, Team	IP	ERA	HR	Avg
Frank Viola, Mets	35.0	1.03	0	.197
Bret Saberhagen, KC	28.0	1.61	0	.233
Mike Gardiner, Bos	22.0	1.64	1	.122
Kirk McCaskill, Cal	30.0	1.80	1	.221
Mike Morgan, LA	33.0	1.91	0	.195
John Smiley, Pit	32.0	1.97	1	.207
Chris Bosio, Mil	32.0	2.25	1	.217
Oil Can Boyd, Mon-Tex	31.0	2.32	0	.255
Mark Langston, Cal	34.0	2.38	3	.207
Kevin Tapani, Min	34.0	2.38	1	.213

Frankie Vee — if he'd pitched as well in every inning as he did in the first he's probably still be a Met. Those sly New Yorkers were clever enough to replace Viola with Bret Saberhagen. Mike Gardiner, Kirk McCaskill and Oil Can Boyd are other starters who couldn't sustain their first inning brilliance last year; in Boyd's case, there's a question of whether he now wears down too quickly to be a starter any more (if he can find a major league job, that is.) Overall, these pitchers are vastly superior to the first group, which is no major shock. But it's interesting that most of them have more than just a great fastball — the pitch you figure most hitters would be looking for in the first inning.

You wonder why Mark Langston, the Angel lefty, is so great in the first (2.38 ERA), while Chuck Finley, a southpaw teammate with many similar skills, gets pounded (6.15). Differences in warmup, maybe?

A complete listing for this category can be found on page 321.

IV. QUESTIONS ON DEFENSE

DO GOOD-THROWING CATCHERS INTIMIDATE BASERUNNERS?

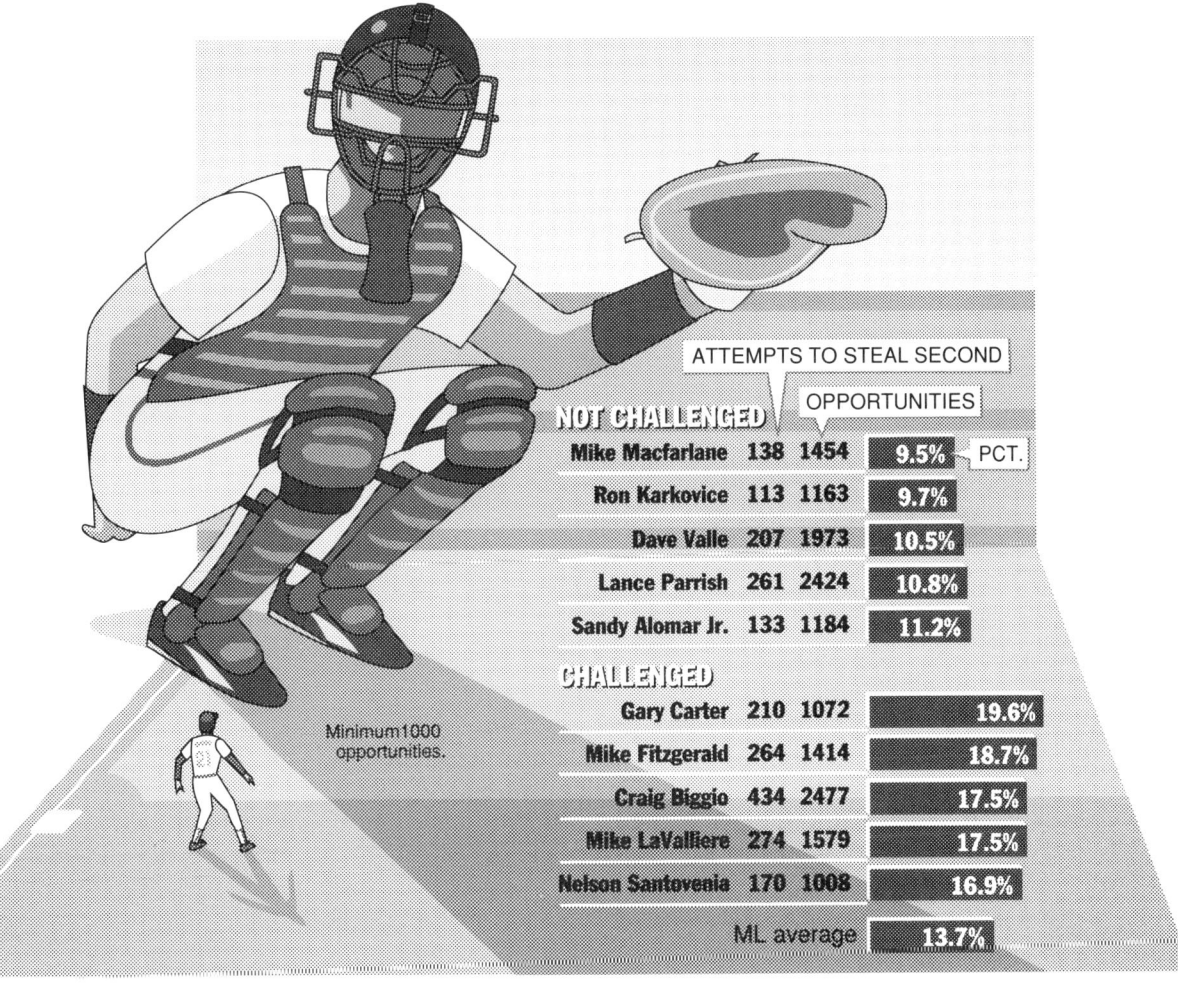

Some catchers have arms which might make Rickey Henderson pause; others throw the sort of rainbows which could tempt Cecil Fielder to go out and get that first major league steal. (Well, maybe with Zminda or Dewan behind the plate . . .) Instinctively this seems right, that everyone runs with a rag-arm behind the plate, but only the bold take off against a guy with a cannon. But is it really true, or is stealing more a function of league, ballpark, playing surface and opposing pitching staff? To find the answer, we've rated catchers on the number of times runners take off for second against them versus the number of "stolen base opportunities" — that is, a runner on first with second base unoccupied. To be more statistically precise, we'll separate the date by leagues (if catchers played in both leagues, we put them in the league where they played the most) and use three years worth of data (1989-91). Here are the AL leaders (we'll lower the league minimums to 500 opportunities; this shows you how impressive the young Ivan Rodriguez is already). The last column represents the catcher's throw-out rate:

Fewest Steal Attempts per Opportunity — AL
1989-91

Catcher	Opp	Att	Att%	CS%
Mike Macfarlane	1454	138	9.5	28.9
Ron Karkovice	1163	113	9.7	47.3
Dave Valle	1973	207	10.5	36.9
Lance Parrish	2424	261	10.8	39.7
Ivan Rodriguez	570	62	10.9	48.6
Sandy Alomar Jr	1184	133	11.2	34.6
Mickey Tettleton	1961	221	11.3	32.2
Joel Skinner	1310	151	11.5	33.5
B.J. Surhoff	2480	291	11.7	26.9
Terry Steinbach	1862	219	11.8	34.0

This is a somewhat bewildering list. Expected names are there — Karkovice, Valle, Parrish, Rodriguez, Alomar, Skinner, Steinbach. Yet the leader, Mike Macfarlane, is not known for his great arm, and Mickey Tettleton and B.J. Surhoff are also curious members of this group. Perhaps we'll discover more by looking at the trailers (we should note that we're eliminating Rick Cerone, Ernie Whitt and Ron Hassey, who saw considerable time in both leagues over the period, from this group):

Most Steal Attempts per Opportunity — AL
1989-91

Catcher	Opp	Att	Att%	CS%
Matt Nokes	1496	219	14.6	32.3
Brian Harper	2138	298	13.9	30.5
Geno Petralli	1250	174	13.9	33.9
Jamie Quirk	723	98	13.6	42.2
Greg Myers	1075	145	13.5	31.7

Interesting. Quirk is respected for his arm; the others are not, though their throw-out percentages are plenty respectable. Nokes throws out more runners than Mike Macfarlane, yet they run much more often on Nokes.

Perhaps one difference is that more marginal (i.e., slow) runners take off against Nokes and company.

Here are the National League leaders:

Fewest Steal Attempts per Opportunity — NL
1989-91

Catcher	Opp	Att	Att%	CS%
Benito Santiago	2394	273	11.4	37.6
Damon Berryhill	898	108	12.0	33.6
Mark Parent	604	75	12.4	29.4
Kirt Manwaring	779	98	12.6	35.2
Steve Lake	797	104	13.0	44.3
Darren Daulton	2201	291	13.2	29.2
Joe Girardi	1366	180	13.2	36.3
Don Slaught	1464	203	13.9	36.1
Mike Scioscia	2267	323	14.2	31.2
Greg Olson	1321	189	14.3	26.0

They run a lot more in the National League (2.53 SB attempts per game last year, vs. 1.96 in the AL), so the difference between best and worst should be more evident. It is. Catchers we'd expect show up on this list (Santiago, Manwaring, Lake, Scioscia). However, you'll also note the predominance of players from home run parks (San Diego, Atlanta, Chicago). Why run when you can hit a home run?

The NL trailers in this category:

Most Steal Attempts per Opportunity — NL
1989-91

Catcher	Opp	Att	Att%	CS%
Mackey Sasser	986	194	19.7	29.4
Gary Carter	1072	210	19.6	28.8
Mike Fitzgerald	1414	264	18.7	23.5
Barry Lyons	581	104	17.9	22.9
Craig Biggio	2477	434	17.5	22.8

There are no real surprises in this group. Mackey Sasser doesn't have the greatest arm, and he's not helped by a staff of power pitchers. But in a way, that's the most important thing that one can gain from this study. Runners try to steal for a variety of reasons: the league, the park, the surface, the pitcher, the catcher. The figures strongly suggest that the catcher is probably one of the least important among all those factors.

A complete listing for this category can be found on page 322.

WHAT DO YOU SACRIFICE FOR A GOOD-THROWING CATCHER?

In baseball today, particularly in the National League, the stolen base has become a vital part of most clubs' attacks. As a consequence, stopping the stolen base is now a major part of each team's defense. Unlike pro football, you can't bring in a good-throwing catcher on "stolen base downs"; you have to put up with catchers who can't hit and pitching staffs which can't hold runners. (God bless baseball).

So when you rate catchers on the basis of their throwing arms alone, be prepared to accept a lot of excess baggage. With that caveat, we present the 1991 catching leaders in caught stealing percentage. We list their percentages, their catchers' pickoff totals, and their average of stolen bases allowed per nine innings (minimum 300 innings caught):

Catcher, Team	SB	CS	CS%	PK	SB/9
Gil Reyes, Mon	38	39	50.6	5	.60
Ron Tingley, Cal	20	19	48.7	0	.56
Ivan Rodriguez, Tex	36	34	48.6	2	.47
Tom Pagnozzi, StL	86	68	44.2	0	.67
Junior Ortiz, Min	15	11	42.3	1	.36
Mike Macfarlane, KC	21	15	41.7	1	.33
Rick Cerone, Mets	39	24	38.1	1	.61
Ron Karkovice, WSox	25	15	37.5	1	.49
Andy Allanson, Det	20	12	37.5	1	.45
Carlton Fisk, WSox	54	32	37.2	0	.61

Now 28 years old, Gilberto Reyes was considered an outstanding thrower when he was a teenager coming up through the Dodger system. However, Reyes is a terrible hitter (.202 lifetime major league average), and he's had a number of "personal problems" as well. Merely having a great throwing arm won't guarantee him a job in 1992 — and the same goes for Tingley, Ortiz, Cerone or Allanson. Ivan Rodriguez, only 20 years old, is considered the most exciting catching prospect in baseball. However, Rodriguez will have to improve his batting eye if he wants to be known as a good all-around catcher.

The following catchers had the poorest percentage against opposing runners in 1991:

Catcher, Team	SB	CS	CS%	PK	SB/9
Mike Stanley, Tex	34	5	12.8	0	.86
Scott Bradley, Sea	36	6	14.3	0	.80
Mike Fitzgerald, Mon	61	12	16.4	0	1.30
Darren Daulton, Phi	84	17	16.8	0	1.05
Greg Myers, Tor	68	15	18.1	0	.81
Brian Harper, Min	98	22	18.3	0	.89
Greg Olson, Atl	95	22	18.8	0	.85
Mike Scioscia, LA	82	24	22.6	0	.81
Mike Heath, Atl	44	13	22.8	1	1.22
Damon Berryhill, Cubs	33	10	23.3	0	.85

People say they steal on the pitcher, not the catcher, and there's a lot of truth to that ... but they always seems to steal on Mike Stanley and Mike Fitzgerald, don't they? Some of the others, however, were undoubtedly victimized by their pitching staffs. Before we decide that Mike Scioscia can't throw any more, remember that people were whispering the same thing about Carlton Fisk a few years ago. The White Sox had their pitchers work on holding baserunners a little better, and suddenly Fisk's throwing figures returned to their previous respectable level. The same may well happen to Scioscia.

Those who insist a great-throwing catcher is vital to a club's success will have a tough time explaining the presence of Brian Harper and Greg Olson, last year's World Series opponents, among the worst throwers. Olson clearly has other attributes, including durability and skill at handling a pitching staff. He seems to be in solid with the Braves. But despite Minnesota's world championship, the Twins seemed to have a difficult time deciding whether or not they wanted to re-sign Harper. Tom Kelly will be comforted in the knowledge that Brian doesn't have to come out on hitting downs.

Technical note: These ratings are based on excluding runners caught stealing by a pitcher's throw to the base. As mentioned in last year's essay, there are good reasons both for including and excluding these when evaluating a catcher's arm. The appendix shows the complete detail for both techniques of calculating catchers' caught stealing.

A complete listing for this category can be found on page 323.

CAN A CATCHER HELP A PITCHER'S ERA?

Some catchers are known for their great arms — Johnny Bench from our youth, for example, or Benito Santiago in modern times. Others are clearly playing because of their bats — Smokey Burgess clearly comes to mind. But a few defy reality. Ron Hassey turned 38 last year, and he has about as much mobility as your great-grandmother. Over the last two seasons, Hassey has batted .213 and .227. Yet he's had no trouble finding work. What's the explanation? Hassey seems to know how to handle pitchers. Look at his teams' ERAs when he was catching, vs. their ERAs with other receivers, over that time period:

	ERA with Hassey	ERA without Hassey	Difference
1990	2.89	3.32	– 0.43
1991	2.69	3.87	– 1.18

Can Hassey handle pitchers? Well, in his three seasons with Oakland (1988-90), he was Bob Welch's personal catcher, and Welch won a total of 61 games, with a Cy Young award in 1990. Last year Hassey left for Montreal, and without him, Welch went 12-13 with a 4.58 ERA.

We know it's not perfect, but we like the concept of "catcher's ERA" as a way of identifying receivers who are good at handling pitchers. Here are the catchers who produced the greatest difference in ERA between when they were catching, and when the club's other receivers were working in 1991 (minimum 300 innings caught):

Catcher, Team	Innings Caught	Own ERA	Others' ERA	Diff
Darren Fletcher, Phi	334.0	2.96	4.13	– 1.17
Hector Villanueva, Cubs	400.0	3.44	4.28	– 0.84
Chris Hoiles, Bal	728.2	4.19	4.99	– 0.80
Don Slaught, Pit	509.0	3.04	3.66	– 0.62
Lance Parrish, Cal	912.2	3.50	4.02	– 0.52
Greg Olson, Atl	1010.1	3.35	3.83	– 0.48
Damon Berryhill, Cubs	349.2	3.58	4.09	– 0.51
Jeff Reed, Cin	690.2	3.60	4.05	– 0.45
Steve Decker, SF	578.1	3.77	4.21	– 0.44
Jamie Quirk, KC	436.2	4.27	4.71	– 0.44
Sandy Alomar Jr, Cle	395.1	3.92	4.36	– 0.44

There are some surprises here — Hector Villanueva, for example. Hector can't move very well behind the plate, and he doesn't have a great arm. The Cubs have experimented with using him at other positions. But his work last year indicates that Villanueva knows how to handle pitchers; maybe he goes to the mound and says, "I'm going to hit a three-run homer my next time up." Obviously Villanueva's 400 innings is not a full season, and obviously there are some other biases at work — for instance, a club may have **two** great receivers, which would cut down on the ERA difference between one catcher and the next. Nonetheless, we feel the stat has merit, and major league clubs indicate they agree. Just ask the man who cashes Ron Hassey's paychecks.

On the other hand, there are catchers who seem to make their pitchers worse. Here are the receivers who had the highest negative ERA differentials when they were working in 1991:

Catcher, Team	Innings Caught	Own ERA	Others' ERA	Diff
Rick Wilkins, Cubs	539.1	4.81	3.60	+ 1.21
Ron Tingley, Cal	323.1	4.20	3.54	+ 0.66
Terry Kennedy, SF	390.1	4.50	3.86	+ 0.64
Steve Lake, Phi	403.0	4.22	3.73	+ 0.49
Bob Melvin, Bal	580.2	4.87	4.40	+ 0.47
Gil Reyes, Mon	568.1	3.86	3.50	+ 0.36
Scott Bradley, Sea	404.2	4.05	3.69	+ 0.36
Darren Daulton, Phi	717.0	4.04	3.69	+ 0.35
Nelson Santovenia, Mon	176.0	3.94	3.60	+ 0.34
Terry Steinbach, Oak	949.1	4.69	4.35	+ 0.34

If you were Rick Wilkins' agent, or Ron Tingley's, you might say: "Hey, I'm new to the major leagues. Give me more of a chance." Fair enough. As for the more experienced catchers, we'll agree it's dangerous to go on one year's worth of data. But if you look at the trailers on this list, and then scan the list of catchers trying to find an employer this spring, we think you'll find some correlation.

A complete listing for this category appears on page 324.

SHOULD YOU GUARD THE LINE IN THE LATE INNINGS?

It's the top of the eighth in an important game. The home nine is protecting a one-run lead, and at some point during the leadoff man's at-bat, the TV camera flashes to the first and third basemen. "Smith and Jones are guarding the lines," the announcer notes. "Yes, they have to protect against the chance of an extra-base hit," his color man says. The game goes on, and the batter rips a scorcher down the third base line. The third baseman, only a step from the bag, grabs it and turns the play into a quick out. "That's the advantage of guarding the line," the color man intones as the crowd cheers. "If Smith isn't playing there, the tying run is on second."

It's all so pat, a part of major league strategy that is only occasionally questioned. Asked why his third baseman was guarding the line in the late innings of a World Series game, Whitey Herzog looked incredulously at his questioner and said, "Well, they've been doing it that way for a hundred years." That's a reasonable answer, but not a completely satisfactory one. Jim Palmer, one of the more thoughtful baseball commentators, once brought up the seldom-noted disadvantage of guarding the line. "If I'm pitching, I want my fielders playing where the batter is likely to hit the ball," Palmer said during another World Series broadcast. And sure enough, the batter hit the ball to the third baseman's left for a single — a ball that would have been an easy out with normal defensive positioning.

Since our scoring system provides pretty exact data on where each ball is hit, we thought we'd examine this strategy and hopefully shed some light on how effective it is. We assume, to begin with, that teams would only guard the lines in the late innings of a close game; it doesn't make a lot of sense to do it any other time. We also assume that a base hit down the line becomes a double. That's not true 100% of the time, but it's very close. We would expect teams to record more outs on balls hit down the line in late-and-close situations ("line-guarding" situations) than they do normally. That's exactly what happens:

Balls Hit Down the Line — 1991

	Late & Close	Other Situations
Number of Balls Hit	653	4,124
Number of Outs	531	2,891
Percent Turned into Outs	81.3%	70.1%

There's a significant difference here. In the late-and-close "line-guarding" situations, teams record a little over 10 percent more outs on balls hit down the line. You can easily calculate how many doubles that saved. If the clubs had been in normal positioning in the late-and-close situations, they would have recorded 458 outs (.701 x 653) instead of 531. Thus guarding the line "saved" 73 doubles. (Note: for this essay, we define "late-and-close" to be one-run games in the seventh inning or later.)

But of course, as Palmer says, you also allow more singles by guarding the lines. How many more? Our coding system allows us to count the number of balls that go through for hits; in the following chart we're counting any ball hit within 30 feet or so of the line, excluding balls hit down the line. Here's the data:

Balls Hit In and Near Normal 1B and 3B Zones* — 1991

	Late & Close	Other Situations
Number of Balls Hit	1,997	13,927
Number of Outs	1,518	11,456
Percent Turned into Outs	76.0%	82.3%

* excluding balls hit down the line

There are about six percent fewer outs recorded on balls hit through the normal zones in the late innings of close games, when teams tend to guard the lines. Assuming those hits to be singles, how many additional hits would that be? Our calculations tell us they would have recorded 1,644 outs (.823 x 1,997) instead of 1,518. Thus guarding the line "costs" 126 singles.

The bottom line is this: by guarding the lines, the teams saved 73 doubles, but allowed 126 more singles. This makes it look like a break-even strategy. Guarding the line will give the opposing team the potential to score more runs in aggregate because of the extra baserunners that reach base; however, as a one-run strategy, which is primarily how guarding the line is used, it does appear to be somewhat beneficial because of the reduction in extra-base hits. Without going into all the calculations, we used a run-scoring chart from John Thorn and Pete Palmer's *Hidden Game of Baseball* to analyze this data. It led us to the following conclusions:

1) Guarding the lines lowers the opposing team's chances of scoring one run by a small amount, but at the same time raises the total number of runs expected to score by a small amount.

2) Guarding the lines becomes a better one-run strategy as the number of outs go up, but it's still a marginally beneficial strategy even with no outs.

The answer is: Yes, you probably should guard the lines in the late innings of a one-run game, but even if you don't, it won't make that much difference.

WHO LED THE LEAGUE IN FUMBLES?

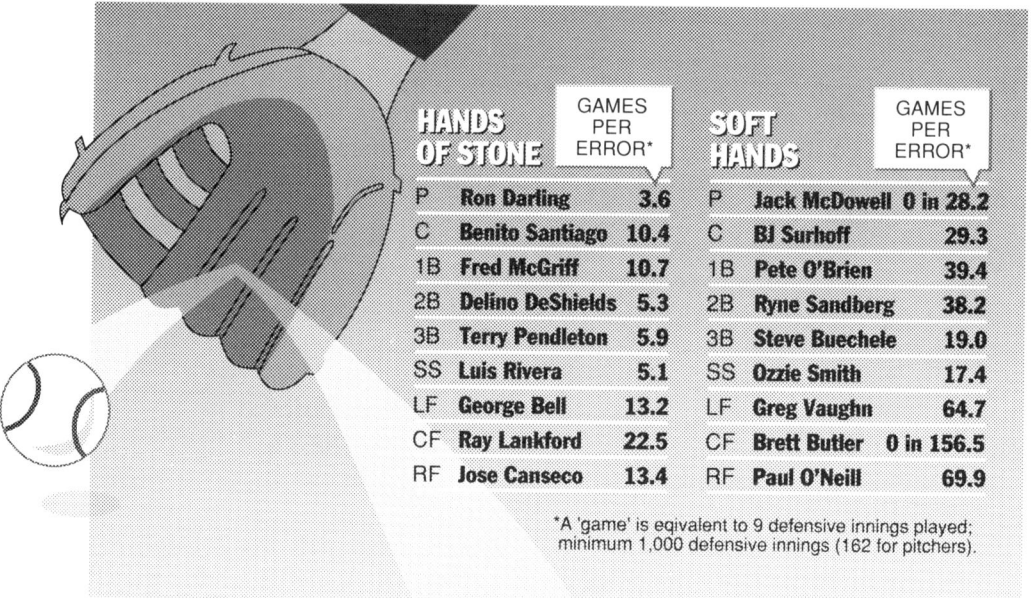

	HANDS OF STONE	GAMES PER ERROR*		SOFT HANDS	GAMES PER ERROR*
P	Ron Darling	3.6	P	Jack McDowell	0 in 28.2
C	Benito Santiago	10.4	C	BJ Surhoff	29.3
1B	Fred McGriff	10.7	1B	Pete O'Brien	39.4
2B	Delino DeShields	5.3	2B	Ryne Sandberg	38.2
3B	Terry Pendleton	5.9	3B	Steve Buechele	19.0
SS	Luis Rivera	5.1	SS	Ozzie Smith	17.4
LF	George Bell	13.2	LF	Greg Vaughn	64.7
CF	Ray Lankford	22.5	CF	Brett Butler	0 in 156.5
RF	Jose Canseco	13.4	RF	Paul O'Neill	69.9

*A 'game' is eqivalent to 9 defensive innings played; minimum 1,000 defensive innings (162 for pitchers).

What a bad year 1991 was for fans of fumble-fingered fielding. Andres Thomas, the "error-apparent" to Rafael Ramirez when it came to shortstop butchery, got released by the Braves, and no one picked him up. (There's no truth to the rumor that Thomas spent the spring serving as Saddam Hussein's Minister of Defense.) Ramirez himself barely saw enough action to join Alfredo Griffin in the coveted "300 Error Club" (that's lifetime; it only seems like they commit 300 errors each season). Jack Clark spent the season as a designated hitter — a complete waste of error-making talent. Even Matt Young proved to be a free agent flop. Signed to a rich contract by the Red Sox and hyped as The Worst Fielding Pitcher Ever by the Beantown press, Matt choked completely, committing only one error all season. (At least his pitching was good for a few laughs.)

We know who to blame for this turn of events: Ted Turner. For years, any time you wanted to see some awesomely bad glove work, all you had to do was tune in a Braves game. There was Ramirez or his young sidekick, Thomas, at shortstop. Bob Horner or Jim Presley at third. Lonnie Smith in left. It was awesome. But that was the old Ted Turner, Captain Outrageous. Now he's so . . . respectable. Marry Jane Fonda, win the Time magazine "Man of the Year" award, get guys who can catch the ball. Gee, Ted, we remember when you were fun.

Fortunately, there's one club which still believes in the old values: the booted grounder, the dropped fly ball, the ball heaved into the stands. Butter-fingered baseball like it oughta be — the New York Mets. The Mets have bad defense down to a science: they round up every bad fielder they can find, then shift him to another position where he can do even worse. Who else would they put Vince Coleman in center? Who else has a catcher (Mackey Sasser) who can't even throw the ball back to the pitcher? Who else has a man with the versatility of Howard Johnson, able to butcher plays wherever he's needed (18 errors at third base last year, 11 at shortstop, 2 in right field). All we can say for 1992 is: welcome aboard, Bobby Bonilla!

****

All kidding aside, our annual "Hands of Stone/Soft Hands" comparison shows how much difference there is between the surest-handed fielders and the shakiest at each position. Delino DeShields is young enough to improve at second base, but last year he erred seven times as often as Ryne Sandberg. Among left fielders, George Bell is five times as likely to boot one as Greg Vaughn is. The Cubs, unfortunately, can't hide Bell at DH.

The chart also shows that there's more to fielding than simply avoiding errors. Terry Pendleton did not have a vintage year with the glove last year (24 errors), but with his great range, he made the Atlanta pitchers feel a lot more confident. And though it's laudable that Brett Butler went the whole year without committing an error, most people would rather have Devon White or Kirby Puckett roaming center field.

A complete listing for this category can be found on page 325.

WHO'S BEST IN THE INFIELD ZONE?

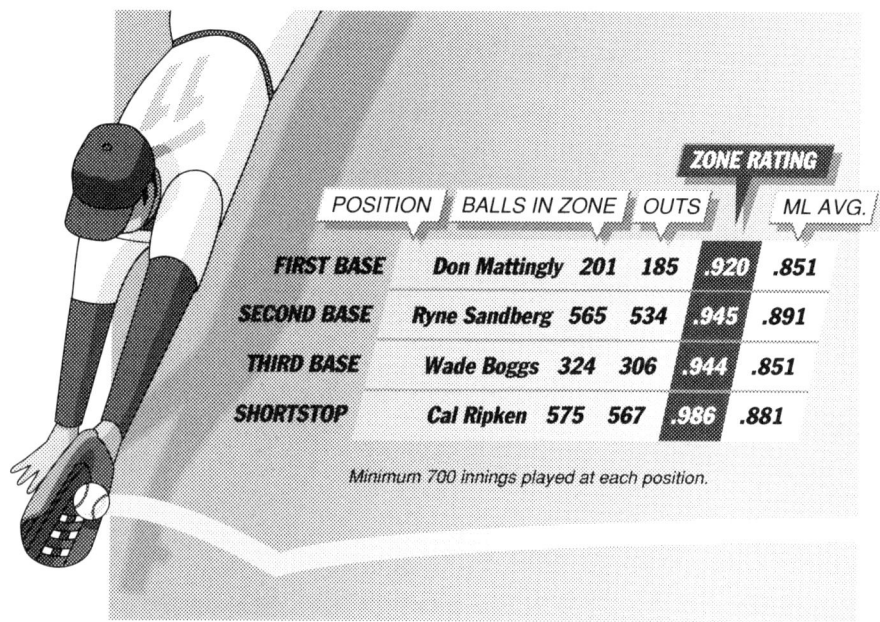

POSITION	BALLS IN ZONE	OUTS	ZONE RATING	ML AVG.
FIRST BASE	Don Mattingly 201	185	.920	.851
SECOND BASE	Ryne Sandberg 565	534	.945	.891
THIRD BASE	Wade Boggs 324	306	.944	.851
SHORTSTOP	Cal Ripken 575	567	.986	.881

Minimum 700 innings played at each position.

The problem with new statistics, Bill James once observed, is that people expect them to be perfect. Let's say baseball was invented in 1951, and you came up with this nifty stat called "earned run average." It seemed like a good idea, measuring the runs allowed by a pitcher (after eliminating the ones caused by errors) per nine innings pitched. Everybody loved it, in theory. So you kept track of the figures all season, and when the year ended, you proudly proclaimed that the earned run champions were Chet Nichols of the Braves and Saul Rogovin of the White Sox. Who? The Lords of Baseball would have tossed you out of the press box, and "earned run average" would have been forgotten forever.

Well, fortunately that didn't happen, and those of us who are in the business of inventing some new stats are still around. We're up front in saying that everything we do isn't perfect, and that you can't learn everything by looking at numbers . . . theirs, ours, anyone's. But we're secure enough about our work to say that we believe in it with great confidence, and that if you approach it with an open mind, you can learn a little about this great game from us. We feel that's the case with one of our babies, zone ratings. Almost everyone would agree with the theory behind it: measure all the balls hit in the area where a fielder can reasonably be expected to record an out, and then count the percentage of outs actually made. The problem is that people don't always agree with the results. To which we say: Remember Chet Nichols!

With no apologies, we present the leaders and trailer in Zone Ratings at each infield position for 1991 (minimum 600 innings), and for the last three seasons (1989-91; minimum 1,200 innings):

First Basemen Zone Ratings

1991		1989-91	
Don Mattingly, Yanks	.920	Kent Hrbek	.899
John Olerud, Tor	.912	John Olerud	.898
Calro Quintana, Bos	.912	Franklin Stubbs	.898
Mark McGwire, Oak	.908	Don Mattingly	.896
Franklin Stubbs, Mil	.898	Mark McGwire	.891
Worst			
Orlando Merced, Pit	.779	Pedro Guerrero	.747

Who's the best-fielding first sacker? Judging from the zone ratings over the last three seasons, it's a photo finish. But Don Mattingly has led the American League in Zone Ratings each of the last two seasons, and we'd have to pick him the best. All the players on the leaders list are American Leaguers; the top National Leaguers last year were Mark Grace, Eddie Murray and John Kruk, but Dave Magadan has ranked the best over the last three years, ahead of Kruk and Grace. Those wily Mets, masters of defensive thinking, are switching Magadan to third this year.

Second Basemen Zone Ratings

1991		1989-91	
Ryne Sandberg	.945	Tony Phillips	.962
Mike Gallego, Oak	.942	Jose Oquendo	.937
Jose Oquendo, StL	.932	Mike Gallego	.935
Jody Reed, Bos	.931	Lou Whitaker	.926
Luis Sojo, Cal	.928	Bill Ripken	.922
Worst			
Julio Franco, Tex	.842	Terry Shumpert	.843

Gallego and Sandberg both have excellent defensive stats overall, so it's not surprising that they rank first and second in the 1991 zone ratings. Sandberg just missed the top five in the three-year rankings, and there seems little to choose between him and Jose Oquendo among NL second basemen; Tony Phillips, first overall in the three-year rankings, played fewer than 300 innings at second last year. But where was Roberto Alomar? In the middle of the pack all three years we've been keeping these stats. We have eyes, and we're big fans of Alomar, too. But he's never led a major league in any category except errors, which is curious, almost unprecedented, for someone considered a dominant fielder. Of course, Alomar is still very young.

Third Basemen Zone Ratings

1991		1989-91	
Wade Boggs, Bos	.944	Gary Gaetti	.901
Mike Pagliarulo, Min	.927	Robin Ventura	.889
Robin Ventura, WSox	.894	Matt Williams	.889
Gary Gaetti, Cal	.892	Ken Caminiti	.883
Ken Caminiti, Hou	.891	Steve Buechele	.875
Worst			
Howard Johnson, Mets	.738	Jim Presley	.738

Lots of good ones here, and it's not easy picking the best-fielding third baseman. Terry Pendleton, who just missed the top five in both the one- and three-year rankings, should also be considered. Robin Ventura and Matt Williams deserved last year's Gold Gloves, but hitting prowess helped both clinch the award. We admire both, but we also like Gary Gaetti, Mike Pagliarulo, Steve Buechele, Ken Caminiti and the underrated Wade Boggs.

Shortstops Zone Ratings

1991		1989-91	
Cal Ripken, Bal	.986	Cal Ripken	.957
Travis Fryman, Det	.978	Dick Schofield	.942
Alan Trammell, Det	.948	Alan Trammell	.935
Rafael Belliard, Atl	.928	Ozzie Guillen	.921
Bill Spiers, Mil	.921	Rafael Belliard	.921
Worst			
Jay Bell, Pit	.829	Rafael Ramirez	.792

Cal Ripken has found the Fountain of Youth. Not only is his hitting getting better, but so is his defense. Ripken's superior Zone Rating in 1991 moved him to the top of the three-year rankings, and he clearly deserved his Gold Glove. Ozzie Smith, just off the leaders list in both one- and three-year rankings, has a legitimate rival for NL shortstop supremacy in Rafael Belliard.

And now, the not-based-on-hitting STATS infield Gold Gloves:

First Base: Don Mattingly, AL, Mark Grace, NL. Mattingly is an obvious choice, and Grace's main National League rival, Dave Magadan, doesn't have Grace's defensive reputation. We don't expect that Magadan will be winning any awards at third base.

Second Base: Mike Gallego, AL, and Ryne Sandberg, NL. We'd love to get on the Alomar bandwagon, but the defensive numbers just aren't there. Gallego's are, and have been. Sandberg gets a narrow National League decision over Jose Oquendo, who played only 118 games at second last year.

Third Base: Wade Boggs, AL, and Steve Buechele, NL. Buechele could have won either league's award and gets the nod over Terry Pendleton and Ken Caminiti due to his superior fielding percentage. In the AL, Peter Gammons has long argued that Boggs deserved a Gold Glove. He might not have been thinking of the STATS version, but there you go, Wade.

Shortstop: Cal Ripken, AL, and Ozzie Smith, NL. Like you, we're still waiting for Ozzie to grow old; he hasn't and he gets the choice over Belliard. Cal, you deserve this one (and not for your hitting)!

Technical note: Our thanks to Pete Palmer and Craig S. Tyle who pointed out a problem of double counting in our 1989 and 1990 zone ratings. The error did not significantly affect the overall rankings for those years. The three-year ratings in this book were recalculated with the 1989 and 1990 numbers restated.

A complete listing for this category appears on page 327.

WHO'S BEST IN THE OUTFIELD ZONE?

Having explained our fielding stats for three years now (also see the infield ratings essay in this book), we will assume you are reasonably familiar with Zone Ratings. To be brief, Zone Ratings measure the number of outs a fielder records per number hit in his fielding area. Here are the 1991 Zone Ratings leaders (and the trailer) at each of the outfield spots (minimum 600 innings played); we also include the leaders and trailer over the last three seasons (1989-91; minimum 1,200 innings):

Left Field Zone Ratings

1991		1989-91	
Bernard Gilkey, Stl	.901	Rickey Henderson	.838
Luis Gonzalez, Hou	.865	Glenn Braggs	.835
Dan Gladden, Min	.864	Candy Maldonado	.833
K. McReynolds, Mets	.851	Kirk Gibson	.831
Ivan Calderon, Mon	.827	Vince Coleman	.826
Worst			
Mike Greenwell, Bos	.711	Mike Greenwell	.742

You could say, in looking at the outfield positions, that left field is the speed position, right field the strength position, and center field is a combination of both — the reason why the best athletes play center. Though of lot of heavy-legged guys wind up in left, the best left fielders are the ones who can run down a lot of balls. Two swift rookies lead the 1991 ratings, and the primary asset of most of the players on the list is speed. The three-year leaders are different because Gilkey and Gonzalez didn't meet the 1200-inning minimum, Coleman was a center fielder in '91, and Maldonado didn't log 600 innings in left during 1991.

Center Field Zone Ratings

1991		1989-91	
Lance Johnson, WSox	.873	Devon White	.869
Devon White, Tor	.872	Mike Devereaux	.858
Mike Devereaux, Bal	.866	Lance Johnson	.854
Darrin Jackson, SD	.865	Dave Gallagher	.853
Brett Butler, LA	.849	Darryl Boston	.851
Worst			
Ray Lankford, StL	.770	Ray Lankford	.772

A crowd at the top: there seems little to choose between Lance Johnson, Devon White and Mike Devereaux when it comes to American League center field supremacy. (There's nothing wrong with Milt Cuyler or Gary Pettis, either). In the National League, Darrin Jackson led the Zone

Ratings, but it's hard to pick him over Brett Butler, who has outstanding range and played errorless ball in 161 games last year. Andy Van Slyke always ranks low in our stats, and Ken Griffey Jr. hasn't fared well either. We stand by our figures.

Right Field Zone Ratings

1991		1989-91	
Joe Carter, Tor	.889	Felix Jose	.875
Felix Jose, StL	.883	Von Hayes	.860
Larry Walker, Mon	.882	Larry Walker	.842
Paul O'Neill, Cin	.844	Sammy Sosa	.834
Jesse Barfield, Yanks	.833	Ruben Sierra	.833
Worst			
Danny Tartabull, KC	.737	Dave Winfield	.752

Joe Carter has spent the last several years shifting between left, center and right fields. Put in right by the Blue Jays last year, he was outstanding. Who knows, he might get to play there two years in a row. In the National League, Tony Gwynn fell out of the top five last year, possibly because knee problems have slowed him down. Von Hayes was hurt last year, leaving the field to Felix Jose, Larry Walker and Paul O'Neill.

And now, the STATS outfield Gold Glove winners — picked on the basis of both statistics and observation:

Left Field: AL Dan Gladden, NL Bernard Gilkey. Two unconventional choices, but these are two players who can track down a ball. That's the most important factor in left field, and the reason they get our vote.

Center Field: AL Devon White, NL Brett Butler. White was a tough choice over Lance Johnson (who got the Chicago vote) and Mike Devereaux. All had outstanding stats . . . but we have to go with White, who won the "other" Gold Glove and has the best throwing arm of the three. We simply can't go against Butler's superior numbers in the National League.

Right Field: AL Joe Carter, NL Larry Walker. Walker over Jose was probably our single most difficult choice; Felix has a slight edge in the Zone Ratings, but he's also known to lose his head from time to time. We went with the steadier Walker. Jesse Barfield is still considered the king of American League right fielders, but he was injured for much of 1991. That's why we chose Carter.

A complete listing for this category can be found on page 329.

WHO ARE THE PRIME PIVOT MEN?

We're always trying to refine our statistics, and one of those refinements comes this year in our analysis of the best second basemen on the double play. The system itself — rating pivot men on the basis of DPs turned per opportunity — has worked very well, with excellent year-to-year consistency. But one thing that we didn't consider is that there is a significant difference between the leagues.

Most people don't know this, but double plays are a lot more frequent in American League games than they are in National League contests. Last year, the NL averaged 1.57 double plays a game, the AL 1.95 — a full 24 percent more. This happens every year; the difference in DP rates is about as reliable as a Rob Deer strikeout. The main reason is that the stolen base, a real DP eliminator, is much more prevalent in the National League. However, even in a double play-pivot situation — runner on first with less than two out, grounder hit to another infielder, second baseman takes the throw — they still turn more DPs in the American League. This is due to a combination of circumstances (more sacrifice bunts, faster runners, more hit-and-runs). Whatever the reasons, the difference is significant:

1991 Second Base DP Opportunities

League	Opp	DP	Pct
American League	1462	908	62.1
National League	1077	544	50.5

So our 1991 rankings will be separated by leagues. Here are the American League second basemen who turned the pivot on at least 20 DPs last year:

Player, Team	Opp	DP	Pct
Willie Randolph, Mil	80	59	73.8
Juan Bell, Bal	39	28	71.8
Carlos Baerga, Cle	58	39	67.2
Jody Reed, Bos	101	67	66.3
Lou Whitaker, Det	74	49	66.2
Terry Shumpert, KC	74	48	64.9
Bill Ripken, Bal	68	44	64.7
Luis Sojo, Cal	72	45	62.5
Chuck Knoblauch, Min	85	53	62.4
Harold Reynolds, Sea	107	66	61.7
Scott Fletcher, WSox	57	35	61.4
Roberto Alomar, Tor	75	44	58.7
Steve Sax, Yanks	94	55	58.5

Jim Gantner, Mil	35	20	57.1
Tony Phillips, Det	36	20	55.6
Mike Gallego, Oak	65	33	50.8
Julio Franco, Tex	76	38	50.0

Willie Randolph is considered the active master of the double play, and our stats agree completely; Randolph has ranked at or near the top all three years we've kept this stat. Jody Reed and Bill Ripken also are familiar faces to those who have studied these figures, whereas Julio Franco consistently brings up the rear. Can you be a great second baseman while not being outstanding on the DP pivot? Yes — if you have great range. Roberto Alomar and Harold Reynolds would certainly be in that category.

A lot of National League teams juggled their second basemen last year, so not many turned the required 20 DPs. Here are the ones who did:

Player, Team	Opp	DP	Pct
Bill Doran, Cin	42	29	69.1
Casey Candaele, Hou	50	33	66.0
Robby Thompson, SF	85	49	57.7
Delino DeShields, Mon	71	39	54.9
Jose Oquendo, StL	52	27	51.9
Ryne Sandberg, Cubs	63	31	49.2
Mark Lemke, Atl	49	24	49.0
Mickey Morandini, Phi	54	26	48.2
Jose Lind, Pit	89	40	44.9
Juan Samuel, LA	94	41	43.6

As with Alomar and Reynolds, Ryne Sandberg and Jose Lind are great second sackers who are not outstanding at turning the DP. Robby Thompson is probably the most dependable on the double play in the NL.

Fans who are familiar with this category might be asking, "Where's Jefferies?" Gregg didn't get many pivot opportunities last year, but he was dismal as ever (6 for 26). Don't be tempted to try him at second, Kansas City.

A complete listing for this category can be found on page 331.

WHICH OUTFIELDERS HAVE THE CANNONS?

Fielding stats have always been the poor relations of baseball statistics. Mike Schmidt's eight home run championships identify him as a great power hitter. But to some people, Schmidt's equally impressive fielding championships — leading the National League seven times in assists, six times in total chances, six times in double plays — are "meaningless." Yeah, right. The simple truth is that the basic fielding stats are quite useful.

Even so, we are the first to admit that the basic numbers have their weaknesses. That's why we're working on developing some new ones. One of the weaknesses comes in the category of outfield assists. As we pointed out last year, it is simply not true that "they don't run on the great throwing arms." They do, which is why people like Roberto Clemente and Jesse Barfield have won so many assist titles. But there's a catch. The catch is that assist totals are much more meaningful for right fielders (where the outfielder has the longest throw) than they are for center or — least of all — left fielders. Here are the major league leaders in outfield assists for 1991, separated by position:

Outfield Assist Leaders

Right Field		Center Field		Left Field	
Dante Bichette, Mil	14	Ken Griffey Jr., Sea	15	Joe Orsulak, Bal	13
Jay Buhner, Sea	14	Kirby Puckett, Min	13	Barry Bonds, Pit	13
Felix Jose, StL	14	Marquis Grissom, Mon	12	Tim Raines, WSox	12
Ruben Sierra, Tex	14	Steve Finley, Hou	11	R. Henderson, Oak	11
Mark Whiten, Tor-Cle	13	Lance Johnson, WSox	11	Kal Daniels, LA	9
Paul O'Neill, Cin	13	Mike Devereaux, Bal	9	Mike Greenwell, Bos	9

(Note: in case of ties, players are ranked by innings played)

If you had to rank the right fielders on the basis of their throwing arms, this list would look perfectly reasonable: Bichette, Buhner, Jose, Sierra. Even so, Jesse Barfield (10 assists in only 81 games) and Mark Whiten (13 assists in 105 games) would be short-changed. The center fielder list — Griffey, Puckett, Grissom, Finley — is also pretty good, but take it from us: Lance Johnson does not have a good arm. The left fielders are a real problem, however. Tim Raines, Rickey Henderson, Kal Daniels? Everyone who's watched them knows they don't have good arms. (Heck, if they had good arms, they wouldn't be playing left field.) Granted, they may get off the ball quickly, but often it's a case of runners simply challenging weak throwers more often.

So what STATS has done is to rate outfielders on the basis of a "hold percentage" — extra bases prevented versus opportunities to take the extra base. That should identify the fielders who intimidate runners from taking

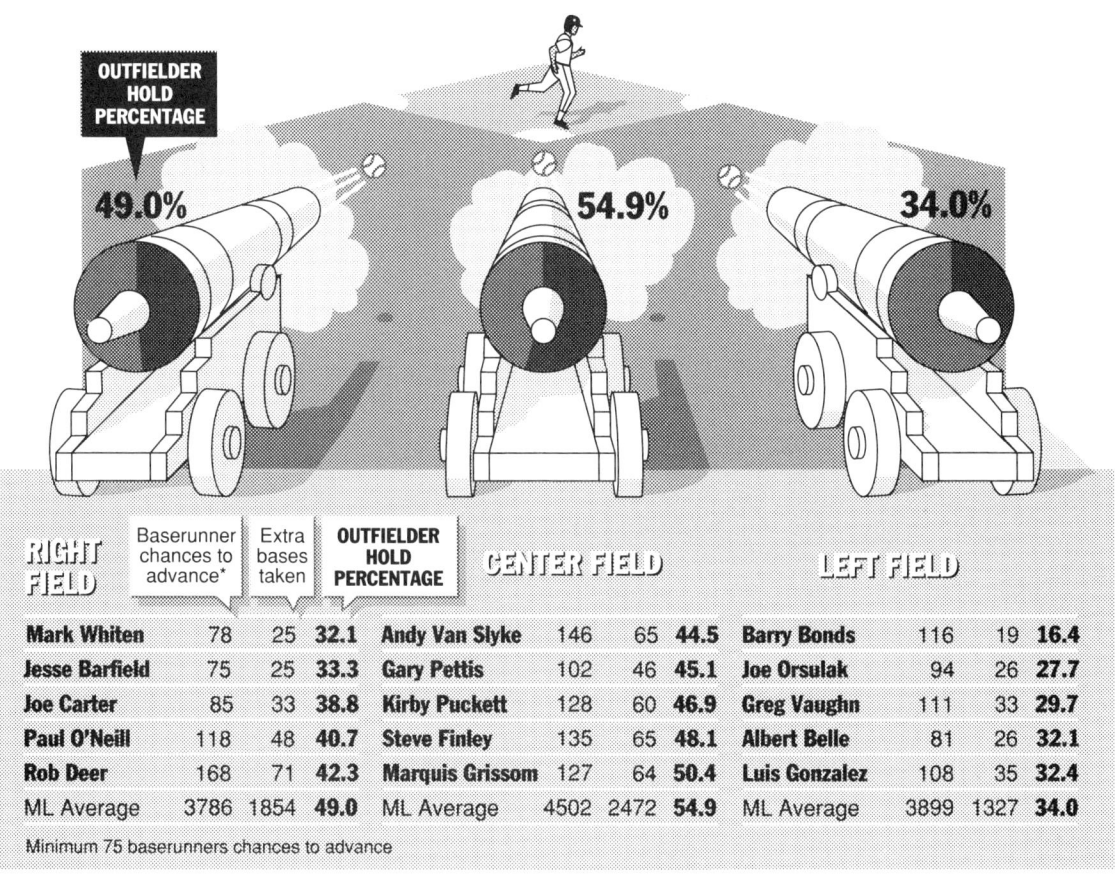

a chance, and fielders who simply throw out a few of the many runners who took a chance against them.

The chart rates outfielders by "hold percentage" at each position, and as you can quickly see, it's pretty good. Barry Bonds, Joe Orsulak and Greg Vaughn lead the left fielders, and there's not a rag-arm in the bunch; much farther down the list are Raines, Daniels and Henderson. The center field leaders are Andy Van Slyke, Gary Pettis and Kirby Puckett, and there's nothing wrong with that list, either. Mark Whiten, Jesse Barfield, and Joe Carter are tops in right; Sammy Sosa, who would have been fourth, didn't have enough opportunities, and Rob Deer and Andre Dawson were fifth and sixth.

We think that's pretty darn good, and helpful to your understanding of identifying the best fielders.

A complete listing for this category can be found on page 332.

WHAT MAKES FOR AN EFFICIENT DEFENSE?

Most of us know that fielding average is an unreliable indicator of who the best glove men are. That goes double in trying to identify the best-fielding **teams**. The Baltimore Orioles had a .985 fielding average last year, tying the Twins for the best mark in baseball. Yet hardly anyone would consider the O's, with limited range at a number of positions, to be one of baseball's best defensive clubs. Unfortunately, total chances can't be used in evaluating a club's range; even the slowest teams record three outs an inning.

In order to fill that void, Bill James invented a tool called the Defensive Efficiency Record. The idea is pretty simple. First, count the number of balls put into play against each defensive team. Then count of number of times the defense turns those balls into outs. Finally, figure a percentage by dividing the second figure by the first. You could argue that some balls just can't be turned into outs, and you'd be right. But of course, many balls thrown by pitchers can't be turned into hits, but we still keep batting averages. As with any such formula, this one is not perfect, but as Bill observed back in 1982, "teams which have high DER win a great deal more often than teams which have low DER." That alone, we think, makes it worth examining.

We'll look at the DER data on a league-by-league basis. First, the American League:

American League	DER	Fld Avg
Chicago White Sox	.704	.982
Toronto Blue Jays	.701	.980
Minnesota Twins	.690	.985
California Angels	.685	.984
Oakland Athletics	.683	.982
Seattle Mariners	.682	.983
Boston Red Sox	.676	.981
Milwaukee Brewers	.675	.981
Detroit Tigers	.673	.983
Kansas City Royals	.672	.980
Baltimore Orioles	.672	.985
Texas Rangers	.670	.979
Cleveland Indians	.663	.976
New York Yankees	.662	.979

As you can see, the AL figures do indeed indicate a strong relationship between DER and winning; the three winningest clubs were the Twins, Blue Jays and White Sox, and those were also the top clubs in DER (though not in the same order). As Bill observed in '82, "the one defensive characteristic associated with high DER seems to be speed in the outfield." The White Sox with a regular outfield of Tim Raines, Lance Johnson and Sammy Sosa obviously qualify, and the other top clubs are characterized by speed in left and center fields. We've pointed out in the past that a speedy left fielder is an underrated asset; here's more evidence.

Here's the National League data:

National League	DER	Fld Avg
Montreal Expos	.696	.979
Philadelphia Phillies	.695	.981
Atlanta Braves	.694	.978
St. Louis Cardinals	.693	.982
Los Angeles Dodgers	.690	.980
San Diego Padres	.688	.982
Chicago Cubs	.685	.982
Cincinnati Reds	.682	.979
San Francisco Giants	.682	.982
Pittsburgh Pirates	.682	.981
Houston Astros	.682	.974
New York Mets	.671	.977

Did we speak too soon in relating DER to playing winning ball? Maybe so; the Expos were the second-worst club in the league, but first in DER. However, Montreal's weak offense (second-lowest in runs scored) was the primary reason for their poor showing. As in the American League, the top clubs in DER fit the "speed" profile, and the Braves' good defense — not at all apparent from their low fielding average — really shows up here. So does the weakness of the New York Mets. DER is not a perfect tool; among other things, we are somewhat at a loss in explaining Pittsburgh's poor showing. Nonetheless, we think it's useful in evaluating team defense, and far superior to fielding average.

A complete listing for this category can be found on page 333.

APPENDIX

In the Introduction to this book, we stated that we thought this edition of the Scoreboard was the best ever. We have the same feeling about this year's Appendix. We've made every effort to make the 77 data charts, player lists, and statistical summations in the following pages easy to decipher, easy to peruse, and, most importantly, easy to read. For some of the Essays, (24 to be exact) all of the figures used for that particular study appear in the Essay itself. In such cases, there is no additional data back here. While the number of appendices has remained constant from last year, we've expanded the total pages by seven. This way we've been able to list more players in many lists when we thought there would be sufficent interest (like career opponent batting average for pitchers with 2,000 opponent at-bats, rather than 4,000, or strikeout to home run ratios for all players in major league history with 200 home runs, rather than 350.)

Each Appendix is keyed twice. The "Title" key serves as a reminder as to what topic is being covered, and corresponds to the title in the Table of Contents. The "Page" key refers to the page where you'll find the appropriate essay. In addition, each Appendix is accompanied by a label describing how the list has been ordered, a "minimum requirement" telling how much of what a player needed to make the list, and a key for deciphering any obscure abbreviations.

As in the previous editions of this book, we've attempted to give you all the data which we used for the Essay — plus a little more. This way, if you'd like to pursue your own statistical investigations, you're free to do so. (If you'd like even **more** numbers than what's back here, feel free to drop us a line with your inquiry. Our address and phone number can be found at the end of this book.)

Fans of the previous editions of the Scoreboard have been very helpful (and constructively critical) in their comments concerning the contents of the book as a whole, and specifically about the organization of this Appendix. As always, we've made every effort to incorporate the best of their suggestions. For one, this means making sure every chart has an "Average" line, so that you can quickly gauge a player's performance in that category. Another is listing the players in alphabetical order, as the majority of these charts are, so that a favorite player can be found quickly.

The team abbreviation following a player's name refers to the team with which he finished the season. Here are the abbreviations:

American League Teams		National League Teams	
Bal	Baltimore Orioles	Atl	Atlanta Braves
Bos	Boston Red Sox	ChN	Chicago Cubs
Cal	California Angels	Cin	Cincinnati Reds
ChA	Chicago White Sox	Hou	Houston Astros
Cle	Cleveland Indians	LA	Los Angeles Dodgers
Det	Detroit Tigers	Mon	Montreal Expos
KC	Kansas City Royals	NYN	New York Mets
Mil	Milwaukee Brewers	Phi	Philadelphia Phillies
Min	Minnesota Twins	Pit	Pittsburgh Pirates
NYA	New York Yankees	StL	St. Louis Cardinals
Oak	Oakland Athletics	SD	San Diego Padres
Sea	Seattle Mariners	SF	San Francisco Giants
Tex	Texas Rangers		
Tor	Toronto Blue Jays		

HOW DOES THE WIND AFFECT RUN-SCORING AT WRIGLEY? (p. 6)

Cubs Home Games: 1990-91

Wind Direction	AB	R	H	2B	3B	HR	R/G	Avg	SLG
Not Recorded	575	81	165	28	2	13	10.13	.287	.410
Out to Left	1109	182	307	61	7	35	11.38	.277	.439
Out to Center	1143	191	328	47	6	51	11.94	.287	.472
Out to Right	1806	278	508	95	13	56	11.12	.281	.441
Left to Right	1795	237	484	73	12	47	9.12	.270	.402
In from Left	923	88	235	52	6	14	6.77	.255	.369
In from Center	1576	175	401	68	8	25	7.61	.254	.355
In from Right	1244	176	326	42	11	42	9.78	.262	.415
Right to Left	1292	183	370	57	13	33	9.63	.286	.427

WAS SCORING POSITION THE KEY FOR THE TWINS AND BRAVES? ? (p. 8)

1991 Team Batting and Pitching — Runners In Scoring Position

American League Batting

Team	Avg	OBP	Slg	AB	H	2B	3B	HR	BB	K
Baltimore	.252	.338	.391	1265	488	319	62	9	32	175
Boston	.264	.356	.400	1437	592	379	80	7	34	231
California	.275	.344	.387	1354	526	372	66	7	24	150
Chicago	.272	.368	.409	1406	592	382	64	12	35	224
Cleveland	.254	.322	.347	1278	473	325	54	8	16	135
Detroit	.257	.352	.422	1345	577	345	65	7	48	217
Kansas City	.290	.374	.422	1412	592	409	73	12	30	209
Milwaukee	.283	.362	.438	1449	683	410	64	23	38	209
Minnesota	.262	.343	.400	1433	599	376	66	10	37	191
New York	.257	.334	.389	1296	512	333	66	3	33	160
Oakland	.261	.357	.419	1354	596	353	52	11	47	217
Seattle	.265	.352	.387	1340	542	355	62	9	28	201
Texas	.274	.359	.435	1454	626	398	66	12	48	202
Toronto	.247	.337	.373	1369	524	338	74	9	27	203

American League Pitching

Team	Avg	OBP	Slg	AB	H	2B	3B	HR	BB	K
Baltimore	.303	.379	.460	1340	439	406	79	10	37	186
Boston	.253	.345	.395	1359	411	344	74	10	33	206
California	.253	.336	.406	1267	358	321	67	6	38	167
Chicago	.257	.342	.396	1249	367	321	49	7	37	181
Cleveland	.273	.344	.403	1423	461	389	70	11	31	177
Detroit	.288	.380	.418	1413	487	407	64	13	31	239
Kansas City	.262	.340	.380	1473	440	386	67	13	27	178
Milwaukee	.280	.352	.421	1409	428	394	65	7	40	169
Minnesota	.236	.318	.358	1314	375	310	55	8	30	173
New York	.280	.357	.441	1416	424	396	76	15	41	180
Oakland	.279	.370	.435	1409	414	393	70	18	38	219
Seattle	.246	.351	.360	1342	420	330	58	10	25	229
Texas	.254	.350	.379	1505	498	383	72	5	35	233
Toronto	.247	.337	.374	1273	364	314	48	6	34	187
AL Total	**.265**	**.350**	**.400**							

National League Batting

Team	Avg	OBP	Slg	AB	H	2B	3B	HR	BB	K
Atlanta	.285	.367	.427	1445	594	412	79	9	36	205
Chicago	.249	.318	.398	1286	522	320	51	9	41	146
Cincinnati	.255	.337	.393	1312	504	334	56	15	32	177
Houston	.255	.341	.367	1350	508	344	66	11	21	189
Los Angeles	.259	.354	.382	1323	545	342	42	11	33	212
Montreal	.244	.328	.343	1354	459	330	58	10	19	182
New York	.256	.345	.362	1357	503	347	68	5	22	202
Philadelphia	.239	.314	.362	1316	493	315	66	6	28	160
Pittsburgh	.270	.355	.413	1449	609	391	72	14	36	217
St. Louis	.272	.360	.376	1424	550	387	67	26	10	214
San Diego	.267	.347	.412	1302	515	348	54	13	36	169
San Francisco	.243	.326	.359	1297	476	315	42	14	27	168

National League Pitching

Team	Avg	OBP	Slg	AB	H	2B	3B	HR	BB	K
Atlanta	.259	.341	.405	1295	346	336	60	13	34	169
Chicago	.276	.353	.409	1448	451	399	62	19	31	199
Cincinnati	.270	.351	.379	1334	426	360	65	9	21	192
Houston	.259	.359	.399	1439	434	373	76	10	35	246
Los Angeles	.232	.325	.320	1323	332	307	42	12	17	194
Montreal	.248	.341	.387	1377	402	341	63	15	33	198
New York	.255	.327	.372	1367	371	348	42	13	31	159
Philadelphia	.240	.337	.366	1458	428	350	76	10	29	233
Pittsburgh	.268	.334	.389	1314	345	352	60	9	27	137
St. Louis	.266	.343	.407	1280	362	341	71	11	29	166
San Diego	.251	.327	.361	1205	337	302	44	7	25	153
San Francisco	.273	.358	.402	1375	406	376	60	15	29	195
NL Total	**.258**	**.341**	**.380**							

WHY THROW TO FIRST? (p. 16)

1991	No Throws Made			Throws Made		
Runner, Team	SB	CS	%	SB	CS	%
Alomar R, Tor	15	6	71	17	4	81
Biggio, Hou	7	1	87	9	5	64
Bonds, Pit	12	5	71	21	7	75
Briley, Sea	8	4	67	12	6	67
Butler, LA	18	9	67	18	19	49
Calderon, Mon	16	3	84	12	10	55
Canseco, Oak	14	2	87	7	4	64
Carter J, Tor	10	4	71	8	5	62
Cole, Cle	10	5	67	12	10	55
Coleman, NYN	15	3	83	16	8	67
Cuyler, Det	12	3	80	19	6	76
DeShields, Mon	13	7	65	35	11	76
Devereaux, Bal	6	3	67	7	5	58
Dunston, ChN	11	0	100	7	4	64
Dykstra, Phi	8	2	80	11	2	85
Felder, SF	7	2	78	13	4	76
Fernandez T, SD	11	2	85	8	7	53
Finley S, Hou	14	2	87	18	11	62
Franco Ju, Tex	16	1	94	16	5	76
Gant, Atl	9	8	53	23	7	77
Grissom, Mon	21	5	81	37	9	80
Guillen, ChA	12	6	67	9	9	50
Henderson R, Oak	24	3	89	13	9	59
Jefferies, NYN	13	1	93	10	3	77
Johnson H, NYN	15	5	75	8	10	44
Johnson L, ChA	15	2	88	9	9	50
Jose, StL	11	1	92	7	10	41
Kelly, NYA	9	1	90	19	8	70
Knoblauch, Min	21	3	87	4	2	67
Landrum C, ChN	4	0	100	14	5	74
Lankford, StL	15	4	79	26	13	67
Larkin B, Cin	6	3	67	8	3	73
McGee, SF	8	1	89	6	8	43
McRae B, KC	10	6	62	10	4	71
Molitor, Mil	9	3	75	7	3	70
Nixon O, Atl	24	4	86	35	15	70
Pettis, Tex	7	2	78	17	7	71
Polonia, Cal	17	7	71	14	12	54
Raines, ChA	27	4	87	22	11	67
Reynolds H, Sea	14	1	93	10	7	59
Roberts Bip, SD	8	4	67	18	6	75
Sabo, Cin	9	2	82	7	3	70
Samuel, LA	12	4	75	11	4	73
Sandberg, ChN	11	3	79	11	5	69
Sax S, NYA	11	4	73	15	5	75
Shumpert, KC	4	3	57	10	6	62
Smith O, StL	14	1	93	18	7	72
Thompson M, StL	8	4	67	7	4	64
White D, Tor	6	3	67	22	7	76
Wilson W, Oak	6	4	60	12	1	92
Zeile, StL	13	3	81	4	7	36
MLB Average	1436	560	72	1255	786	61

Note: Steals of second with second base open only

DOES A HOT START MEAN A HAPPY FINISH? (p. 26)

Team Records in April: 1987 through 1991

American League	1987 W-L	Pct	1988 W-L	Pct	1989 W-L	Pct	1990 W-L	Pct	1991 W-L	Pct	1987-1991 W-L	Pct
Baltimore	9-12	.429	2-22	.083	12-12	.500	9-11	.450	6-12	.333	38-69	.355
Boston	9-13	.409	14-6	.700	10-12	.455	11-8	.579	11-7	.611	55-46	.545
California	12-11	.522	10-13	.435	15-10	.600	8-11	.421	10-10	.500	55-55	.500
Chicago	6-12	.333	11-10	.524	8-16	.333	10-6	.625	11-6	.647	46-50	.479
Cleveland	8-14	.364	16-6	.727	9-13	.409	9-9	.500	7-10	.412	49-52	.485
Detroit	9-12	.429	13-9	.591	8-14	.364	8-12	.400	10-9	.526	48-56	.462
Kansas City	9-10	.474	12-10	.545	16-8	.667	6-12	.333	8-11	.421	51-51	.500
Milwaukee	18-3	.857	9-11	.450	10-12	.455	12-6	.667	10-9	.526	59-41	.590
Minnesota	12-9	.571	8-13	.381	10-12	.455	7-12	.368	9-11	.450	46-57	.447
New York	14-7	.667	16-7	.696	12-12	.500	7-10	.412	6-11	.353	55-47	.539
Oakland	9-14	.391	16-7	.696	18-8	.692	14-5	.737	13-7	.650	70-41	.631
Seattle	12-11	.522	10-14	.417	11-15	.423	8-12	.400	10-11	.476	51-63	.447
Texas	8-11	.421	8-13	.381	17-5	.773	11-9	.550	8-8	.500	52-46	.531
Toronto	12-8	.600	9-13	.409	9-16	.360	12-9	.571	12-9	.571	54-55	.495

National League	1987 W-L	Pct	1988 W-L	Pct	1989 W-L	Pct	1990 W-L	Pct	1991 W-L	Pct	1987-1991 W-L	Pct
Atlanta	9-12	.429	3-16	.158	10-15	.400	4-13	.235	8-10	.444	34-66	.340
Chicago	10-10	.500	10-12	.455	12-11	.522	8-11	.421	10-11	.476	50-55	.476
Cincinnati	15-7	.682	11-11	.500	13-9	.591	13-3	.813	11-8	.579	63-38	.624
Houston	12-9	.571	14-7	.667	11-14	.440	9-10	.474	8-11	.421	54-51	.514
Los Angeles	12-11	.522	13-7	.650	11-13	.458	11-10	.524	10-10	.500	57-51	.528
Montreal	8-12	.400	9-11	.450	13-11	.542	10-9	.526	7-13	.350	47-56	.456
New York	11-9	.550	15-6	.714	12-10	.545	9-10	.474	12-8	.600	59-43	.578
Philadelphia	7-13	.350	7-12	.368	11-12	.478	10-9	.526	9-12	.429	44-58	.431
Pittsburgh	8-11	.421	16-6	727	10-14	.417	14-6	.700	13-7	.650	61-44	.581
St. Louis	12-8	.600	8-14	.364	13-9	.591	9-11	.450	13-8	.619	55-50	.524
San Diego	6-17	.261	9-12	.429	14-12	.538	9-10	.474	11-10	.524	49-61	.445
San Francisco	16-7	.696	11-12	.478	12-12	.500	8-12	.400	8-12	.400	55-55	.500

DOES SWITCHING SKIPPERS IN MIDSEASON EVER WORK?
(p. 30)

Best "Takeover" Percentage for Manager
(minimum 1/3 of total team's games managed and .550 winning percentage)

Year	Team-Lg	Manager	W-L	Pct	Start	Finish
1978	NY-A	Bob Lemon	48-20	.706	4	1
1932	Chi-N	Charlie Grimm	37-18	.673	2	1
1950	Bos-A	Steve O'Neill	63-32	.663	4	3
1938	Det-A	Del Baker	37-19	.661	5	4
1919	Cle-A	Tris Speaker	40-21	.656	3	2
1952	Phi-N	Steve O'Neill	59-32	.648	6	4
1977	Tex-A	Billy Hunter	60-33	.645	5	2
1940	StL-N	Billy Southworth	69-40	.633	7	3
1956	Mil-N	Fred Haney	68-40	.630	5	2
1985	NY-A	Billy Martin	91-54	.628	7	2
1982	Mil-A	Harvey Kuenn	72-43	.626	5	1
1905	Chi-N	Frank Chance	55-33	.625	4	3
1975	KC-A	Whitey Herzog	41-25	.621	2	2
1938	Chi-N	Gabby Hartnett	44-27	.620	3	1
1989	Tor-A	Cito Gaston	77-49	.611	6	1
1983	Phi-N	Paul Owens	47-30	.610	1	1
1935	Cle-A	Steve O'Neill	36-23	.610	5	3
1947	Brk-N	Burt Shotton	92-60	.605	1	1
1974	Atl-N	Clyde King	38-25	.603	4	3
1972	Chi-N	Whitey Lockman	39-26	.600	4	2
1988	Bos-A	Joe Morgan	46-31	.597	4	1
1922	Pit-N	Bill McKechnie	53-36	.596	5	3
1990	NY-N	Bud Harrelson	71-49	.592	4	2
1967	Min-A	Cal Ermer	66-46	.589	6	2
1961	StL-N	Johnny Keane	47-33	.587	6	5
1968	Bal-A	Earl Weaver	48-34	.585	3	2
1904	Chi-A	Fielder Jones	66-47	.584	4	3
1988	SD-N	Kack McKeon	67-48	.583	5	3
1933	StL-N	Frankie Frisch	36-26	.581	5	5
1979	NY-A	Billy Martin	55-40	.579	4	4
1976	Cle-A	Dave Garcia	38-38	.576	6	6
1913	Bos-A	Bill Carrigan	40-30	.571	5	4
1986	Oak-A	Tony LaRussa	45-34	.570	7	3
1902	Cin-N	Joe Kelley	34-26	.567	6	4
1976	Cal-A	Norm Sherry	37-29	.561	6	4
1970	SF-N	Charlie Fox	67-53	.558	4	3
1925	StL-N	Rogers Hornsby	64-51	.557	8	4
1976	Bos-A	Don Zimmer	42-34	.553	5	3
1915	Buf-F	Harry Lord	60-49	.550	8	6
1959	Bos-A	Billy Jurges	44-36	.550	8	5

WHO TAKES 'EM, WHO SWINGS AT 'EM, WHO FOULS 'EM OFF? (p. 32)

The tables below show how hitters reacted to pitches thrown based on the count in 1991.

Listed by League — All Teams Included

	American League							National League					
Count	Total	Ball	Taken Strike	Swing-ing Strike	Foul	In Play	Count	Total	Ball	Taken Strike	Swing-ing Strike	Foul	In Play
0-0	87177	38997	22448	5086	9195	11451	0-0	73299	31672	18259	4903	8196	10269
Pct	100	45	26	6	11	13	Pct	100	43	25	7	11	14
0-1	36690	16481	3890	3473	5716	7130	0-1	31324	13489	3377	3270	5089	6099
Pct	100	45	11	9	16	19	Pct	100	43	11	10	16	19
0-2	15637	7942	713	1632	2508	2842	0-2	14091	6653	768	1686	2355	2629
Pct	100	51	5	10	16	18	Pct	100	47	5	12	17	19
1-0	38932	13791	8092	3108	6160	7781	1-0	31589	11040	6539	2709	5009	6292
Pct	100	35	21	8	16	20	Pct	100	35	21	9	16	20
1-1	33630	12547	3734	3343	6289	7717	1-1	27583	9964	2943	2964	5272	6440
Pct	100	37	11	10	19	23	Pct	100	36	11	11	19	23
1-2	26730	10111	1149	3410	5539	6521	1-2	22428	8163	1105	2877	4720	5563
Pct	100	38	4	13	21	24	Pct	100	36	5	13	21	25
2-0	13726	4400	3422	872	2071	2961	2-0	10970	3640	2930	692	1596	2112
Pct	100	32	25	6	15	22	Pct	100	33	27	6	15	19
2-1	18817	5648	1895	1849	4221	5204	2-1	15108	4405	1517	1521	3281	4384
Pct	100	30	10	10	22	28	Pct	100	29	10	10	22	29
2-2	23561	7074	1072	2913	5605	6897	2-2	18955	5400	822	2500	4572	5595
Pct	100	30	5	12	24	29	Pct	100	29	4	13	24	30
3-0	4368	1664	2295	70	153	186	3-0	3623	1373	1920	49	119	162
Pct	100	38	53	2	4	4	Pct	100	38	53	1	3	4
3-1	8430	2353	1187	598	1699	2593	3-1	6756	1875	1049	469	1293	2070
Pct	100	28	14	7	20	31	Pct	100	28	16	7	19	31
3-2	14446	3210	587	1533	3968	5148	3-2	11370	2450	462	1208	3172	4078
Pct	100	22	4	11	27	36	Pct	100	22	4	11	28	36

HOW MUCH DIFFERENCE DOES THE UMPIRE MAKE? (p. 36)

Home Plate Umpires — Listed Alphabetically by League
(minimum 10 home plate games from 1989 through 1991)

1991 American League Umpires

Umpire	G	R/G	BB/G	K/G	Avg
Barnett, Larry	104	8.6	6.7	11.4	.259
Brinkman, Joe	109	8.8	7.1	11.3	.264
Cedarstrom, Gary	38	8.2	6.5	10.4	.258
Clark, Al	105	8.4	6.8	11.0	.256
Coble, Drew	110	8.8	6.4	11.5	.254
Cooney, Terry	92	9.1	6.8	11.4	.260
Cousins, Derryl	106	9.2	8.1	11.2	.268
Craft, Terry	39	9.0	6.6	10.4	.261
Denkinger, Don	98	7.8	6.8	10.5	.244
Evans, Jeff	37	9.5	6.3	10.5	.268
Evans, Jim	114	8.8	6.3	10.9	.265
Ford, Dale	111	9.3	7.1	11.0	.271
Garcia, Rich	107	8.7	6.4	10.9	.262
Hendry, Ted	97	8.9	6.6	11.8	.259
Hickox, Dan	21	10.1	5.6	11.3	.280
Hirschbeck, John	113	8.5	6.6	11.7	.251
Johnson, Mark	100	8.7	6.8	11.2	.256
Joyce, Jim	89	9.2	6.6	11.5	.267
Kaiser, Ken	81	8.7	6.7	11.0	.266
Kosc, Greg	107	8.3	6.0	12.2	.255
McClelland, Tim	109	8.9	7.0	11.0	.261
McCoy, Larry	104	8.2	5.6	12.2	.254
McKean, Jim	110	8.6	6.0	11.2	.266
Meriwether, Chuck	50	9.0	6.9	10.5	.273
Merrill, Durwood	108	8.8	6.5	10.9	.257
Morrison, Dan	108	9.8	7.5	11.0	.265
Palermo, Steve	80	8.5	6.9	12.0	.252
Phillips, Dave	104	9.0	6.8	10.8	.267
Reed, Rick	105	9.8	7.2	11.0	.272
Reilly, Mike	104	8.1	6.8	10.9	.249
Roe, Rocky	107	9.1	7.4	11.0	.258
Scott, Dale	89	8.5	6.7	11.3	.250
Shulock, John	107	9.1	7.1	11.0	.265
Tschida, Tim	83	8.2	6.5	11.8	.258
Voltaggio, Vic	88	8.5	6.6	11.4	.258
Welke, Tim	107	8.8	5.9	11.9	.256
Young, Larry	93	8.7	6.7	11.2	.259
AL Average	**3400**	**8.7**	**6.7**	**11.2**	**.260**

1991 National League Umpires

Umpire	G	R/G	BB/G	K/G	Avg
Barnes, Ron	14	7.5	5.9	9.9	.256
Bonin, Greg	106	7.4	5.5	11.7	.248
Crawford, Jerry	111	8.7	6.9	11.8	.254
Darling, Gary	106	8.4	6.4	12.1	.252
Davidson, Bob	111	7.8	5.4	12.6	.242
Davis, Gerry	106	8.1	6.5	11.8	.250
DeMuth, Dana	110	8.9	6.9	11.4	.263
Froemming, Bruce	111	7.9	7.3	11.1	.248
Gregg, Eric	94	8.5	6.1	12.2	.254
Hallion, Tom	89	8.6	6.7	11.9	.255
Harvey, Doug	109	8.0	6.1	11.8	.248
Hirschbeck, Mark	90	7.7	5.7	12.2	.245
Hohn, Bill	89	8.5	6.4	11.2	.253
Layne, Jerry	88	7.6	6.7	11.7	.249
Marsh, Randy	110	8.8	6.8	11.5	.249
McSherry, John	108	8.1	7.2	10.5	.255
Montague, Ed	104	7.7	6.6	12.0	.248
Pulli, Frank	107	7.8	6.3	11.9	.253
Quick, Jim	105	8.2	6.4	12.2	.245
Rapuano, Ed	45	9.1	5.9	11.8	.272
Reliford, Charlie	49	8.9	7.3	10.6	.257
Rennert, Dutch	97	8.3	6.6	11.7	.254
Rippley, Steve	110	8.9	6.7	11.2	.253
Runge, Paul	85	7.8	6.2	12.0	.249
Tata, Terry	111	8.4	6.0	12.6	.248
Wendelstedt, H	103	7.7	6.1	11.9	.247
West, Joe	108	8.2	6.7	11.4	.247
Williams, Charlie	102	7.6	5.9	11.4	.247
Winters, Mike	74	8.9	7.2	12.0	.261
NL Average	**2915**	**8.2**	**6.4**	**11.7**	**.251**

WHY DID MITCH LOVE TO PITCH LAST AUGUST? (p. 40)

The Top Batting and Pitching Months of 1991

Batting (75 or more Plate Appearances)

Player	Month	AVG	SLG	OBP	AB	R	H	2B	3B	HR	RBI	SB	BB
Griffey Jr, Sea	July	.434	.735	.489	83	16	36	8	1	5	25	3	9
Dunston, ChN	August	.427	.610	.438	82	14	35	6	3	1	11	5	4
Boggs W, Bos	July	.415	.598	.495	82	21	34	10	1	1	8	0	15
Martinez E, Sea	April	.412	.574	.551	68	17	28	5	0	2	10	0	18
Pendleton, Atl	May	.410	.651	.446	83	17	34	7	2	3	14	1	7
Baines, Oak	May	.397	.654	.505	78	20	31	5	0	5	19	0	17
Nixon O, Atl	May	.391	.464	.463	69	20	27	5	0	0	5	12	10
Palmeiro, Tex	July	.390	.710	.456	100	18	39	6	1	8	19	0	11
Henderson D, Oak	April	.387	.747	.453	75	17	29	9	0	6	18	0	9
Smith O, StL	May	.387	.441	.467	93	17	36	5	0	0	13	11	14
Sierra, Tex	May	.386	.561	.445	114	27	44	4	2	4	21	8	13
Spiers, Mil	August	.386	.500	.450	88	21	34	3	2	1	17	5	11
Orsulak, Bal	August	.384	.495	.419	99	17	38	9	1	0	11	2	6
Briley, Sea	August	.382	.500	.427	68	7	26	8	0	0	5	5	6
Justice, Atl	May	.381	.629	.450	97	19	37	9	0	5	28	4	11
Reed Jd, Bos	September	.378	.541	.492	98	22	37	10	0	2	17	1	20
Tartabull, KC	July	.378	.797	.489	74	20	28	7	0	8	19	1	17
Bonilla B, Pit	August	.377	.604	.465	106	21	40	13	1	3	20	0	19
Griffey Jr, Sea	August	.377	.660	.447	106	19	40	12	0	6	17	5	14
Walker L, Mon	August	.376	.624	.427	101	17	38	13	0	4	12	1	7
Franco Ju, Tex	August	.376	.473	.458	93	17	35	1	1	2	15	4	14
Doran, Cin	June	.375	.528	.459	72	14	27	3	1	2	13	1	12
Reynolds H, Sea	May	.373	.445	.427	110	21	41	6	1	0	9	4	12
Thomas F, ChA	August	.373	.682	.481	110	19	41	8	1	8	27	0	24
Randolph, Mil	August	.371	.440	.449	116	15	43	6	1	0	17	1	18
Ripken C, Bal	June	.371	.603	.417	116	23	43	10	1	5	16	2	9
Larkin B, Cin	June	.370	.717	.496	92	24	34	5	0	9	23	13	23

Pitching (25 or more Innings Pitched)

Pitcher	Month	ERA	W	L	S	IP	H	R	ER	BB	K
Clemens, Bos	April	0.28	4	0	0	32.0	17	1	1	5	34
Greene, Phi	May	0.29	4	0	0	31.0	12	1	1	11	30
Viola, NYN	April	0.86	3	0	0	31.1	28	3	3	5	17
Tomlin R, Pit	July	0.88	3	0	0	30.2	23	7	3	11	17
Saberhagen, KC	August	0.88	3	1	0	41.0	20	4	4	7	31
Belcher, LA	April	0.91	3	1	0	29.2	20	10	3	7	21
Hershiser, LA	September	1.04	2	0	0	26.0	17	3	3	3	17
Harnisch, Hou	April	1.05	1	0	0	25.2	14	3	3	17	21
Aquino, KC	July	1.09	4	1	2	33.0	28	7	4	4	25
Belcher, LA	August	1.16	2	1	0	46.2	34	7	6	11	37
Ojeda, LA	June	1.19	2	1	0	30.1	22	6	4	7	17
Krueger, Sea	July	1.19	4	0	0	37.2	33	8	5	11	24
Ryan, Tex	June	1.20	1	0	0	30.0	17	5	4	6	30
Tanana, Det	June	1.21	3	2	0	44.2	29	8	6	14	30
Benes, SD	September	1.23	4	0	0	36.2	26	5	5	7	28
Martinez De, Mon	April	1.23	3	2	0	36.2	23	6	5	11	23
Candiotti, Tor	April	1.24	2	1	0	29.0	21	5	4	8	19
Martinez R, LA	July	1.24	4	2	0	43.2	36	9	6	8	21
Rijo, Cin	September	1.36	4	1	0	33.0	31	8	5	8	24
Erickson S, Min	May	1.36	5	0	0	46.1	35	9	7	13	29
Martinez De, Mon	June	1.37	3	1	0	46.0	38	9	7	15	27
Frohwirth, Bal	June	1.40	2	1	0	25.2	18	4	4	12	20
Smoltz, Atl	August	1.41	4	1	0	44.2	28	7	7	10	37
Morgan M, LA	April	1.42	2	2	0	31.2	20	8	5	6	12
Nagy, Cle	July	1.42	3	1	0	38.0	34	8	6	10	9
Belcher, LA	June	1.45	2	0	0	43.1	32	8	7	17	36

ARE THE BEST TEAMS GOOD LATE-INNING TEAMS? (p. 42)

1991 Team Batting and Pitching — Late & Close

American League Batting

Team	AVG	OBP	SLG	AB	H	2B	3B	HR	BB	K
Baltimore	.237	.305	.364	970	110	230	30	3	29	93
Boston	.225	.303	.307	805	80	181	33	3	9	87
California	.231	.297	.316	746	65	172	23	1	13	67
Chicago	.264	.340	.390	1109	153	293	45	7	27	124
Cleveland	.218	.279	.286	1043	99	227	28	5	11	84
Detroit	.218	.308	.355	911	119	199	38	1	28	115
Kansas City	.236	.319	.349	938	101	221	37	12	15	114
Milwaukee	.270	.342	.391	960	144	259	37	8	21	103
Minnesota	.283	.355	.421	769	128	218	34	3	22	81
New York	.244	.318	.381	881	114	215	35	1	28	89
Oakland	.241	.329	.384	843	134	203	33	5	26	107
Seattle	.246	.320	.378	928	122	228	51	6	20	100
Texas	.265	.340	.404	993	143	263	36	3	32	109
Toronto	.239	.323	.347	980	110	234	50	7	14	118

American League Pitching

Team	AVG	OBP	SLG	AB	H	2B	3B	HR	BB	K
Baltimore	.241	.315	.355	912	69	220	44	6	16	96
Boston	.235	.317	.369	839	73	197	42	10	17	95
California	.220	.287	.325	861	72	189	26	1	21	81
Chicago	.231	.319	.348	985	91	228	33	2	26	121
Cleveland	.266	.340	.372	927	84	247	45	4	15	105
Detroit	.272	.346	.391	882	100	240	36	6	19	105
Kansas City	.254	.321	.344	934	78	237	31	4	15	86
Milwaukee	.257	.330	.409	930	94	239	33	0	36	101
Minnesota	.239	.307	.357	852	71	204	39	5	17	81
New York	.252	.323	.365	819	67	206	34	4	17	80
Oakland	.251	.335	.406	914	91	229	41	7	29	106
Seattle	.246	.319	.354	956	80	235	40	6	17	99
Texas	.235	.322	.370	1036	105	243	43	5	29	129
Toronto	.223	.297	.316	1029	76	229	23	5	21	106

National League Batting

Team	AVG	OBP	SLG	AB	H	2B	3B	HR	BB	K
Atlanta	.242	.327	.345	823	115	199	34	6	13	100
Chicago	.257	.321	.382	1134	142	292	49	7	26	101
Cincinnati	.236	.308	.327	890	91	210	25	7	14	90
Houston	.253	.322	.330	988	118	250	40	3	10	96
Los Angeles	.268	.355	.367	961	142	258	36	7	15	128
Montreal	.246	.322	.347	1060	113	261	39	7	18	115
New York	.234	.328	.368	913	115	214	44	3	24	128
Philadelphia	.235	.305	.343	1099	119	258	44	6	21	110
Pittsburgh	.248	.338	.374	855	121	212	41	5	19	117
St. Louis	.251	.332	.344	926	115	232	34	7	13	110
San Diego	.252	.319	.369	932	122	235	31	6	22	89
San Francisco	.242	.327	.352	918	125	222	35	9	16	115

National League Pitching

Team	AVG	OBP	SLG	AB	H	2B	3B	HR	BB	K
Atlanta	.217	.290	.306	903	71	196	31	5	13	89
Chicago	.269	.346	.402	1083	130	291	44	11	26	126
Cincinnati	.269	.345	.371	825	73	222	33	6	13	97
Houston	.249	.345	.368	951	80	237	45	7	18	140
Los Angeles	.232	.311	.326	969	96	225	39	8	12	110
Montreal	.241	.322	.336	1044	111	252	47	8	12	119
New York	.258	.308	.362	921	73	238	36	7	15	67
Philadelphia	.237	.341	.345	1028	84	244	48	3	19	156
Pittsburgh	.252	.321	.367	979	91	247	34	3	24	91
St. Louis	.259	.328	.382	930	72	241	34	10	20	93
San Diego	.237	.302	.323	972	88	230	33	3	15	93
San Francisco	.246	.335	.362	894	87	220	28	2	24	118

	AVG	OBP	SLG
AL Total	.244	.319	.360
NL Total	.257	.341	.377

WHO ARE THE SLOWEST STARTING BATTERIES? (p. 44)

Average game time for starting pitchers (minimum 15 games started) and starting catchers (minimum 54 games started)

1991 Both Leagues — Listed Alphabetically

Pitcher, Team	GS	Time	Pitcher, Team	GS	Time	Pitcher, Team	GS	Time
Abbott, Cal	34	2:54	Hershiser, LA	21	3:12	Stottlemyre, Tor	34	2:49
Anderson A, Min	22	2:49	Hesketh, Bos	17	3:03	Sutcliffe, ChN	18	2:57
Appier, KC	31	2:58	Hibbard, ChA	29	3:12	Swindell, Cle	33	2:40
Aquino, KC	18	3:02	Hill K, StL	30	2:51	Tanana, Det	33	3:03
Armstrong, Cin	24	2:49	Holman B, Sea	30	2:41	Tapani, Min	34	2:40
August, Mil	23	2:56	Hough, ChA	29	2:58	Taylor W, NYA	22	2:57
Avery, Atl	35	2:54	Hurst, SD	31	2:44	Terrell, Det	33	3:03
Ballard, Bal	22	2:56	Johnson J, NYA	23	2:50	Tewksbury, StL	30	2:35
Barnes B, Mon	27	2:59	Johnson R, Sea	33	3:04	Tomlin R, Pit	27	3:01
Belcher, LA	33	3:03	Jones Jim, Hou	22	2:48	Viola, NYN	35	2:47
Benes, SD	33	2:46	Key, Tor	33	2:49	Walk, Pit	20	2:59
Bielecki, Atl	25	2:48	Kile, Hou	22	3:00	Wegman, Mil	28	2:48
Black, SF	34	2:44	King E, Cle	24	2:56	Welch, Oak	35	2:54
Boddicker, KC	29	2:52	Krueger, Sea	25	2:54	Wells, Tor	28	2:50
Bolton, Bos	19	2:58	Langston, Cal	34	2:49	Whitehurst, NYN	20	2:54
Bosio, Mil	32	2:47	Leary, NYA	18	3:09	Wilson Tr, SF	29	2:53
Boskie, ChN	20	2:47	Leibrandt, Atl	36	2:46	Witt B, Tex	16	3:13
Boyd, Tex	31	2:53	Leiter M, Det	15	3:11	Young Mt, Bos	16	3:07
Brown Kev, Tex	33	3:05	Maddux G, ChN	37	2:46			
Browning, Cin	36	2:40	Martinez De, Mon	31	2:52	**Catcher, Team**	**GS**	**Time**
Burkett, SF	34	2:46	Martinez R, LA	33	2:54	Biggio, Hou	131	2:53
Candiotti, Tor	34	2:52	McCaskill, Cal	30	2:45	Borders, Tor	71	2:53
Castillo F, ChN	18	2:51	McDonald, Bal	21	3:13	Carter G, LA	55	3:01
Clemens, Bos	35	3:00	McDowell J, ChA	35	2:55	Cerone, NYN	63	2:49
Cone, NYN	34	2:55	Mesa, Bal	23	3:07	Daulton, Phi	80	2:51
Cox, Phi	17	2:58	Milacki, Bal	26	2:57	Decker S, SF	65	2:50
Darling, Oak	32	2:54	Moore M, Oak	33	3:10	Fisk, ChA	91	3:07
DeJesus J, Phi	29	2:54	Morgan M, LA	33	2:49	Harper B, Min	114	2:48
DeLeon J, StL	28	2:43	Morris Jk, Min	35	2:43	Hoiles, Bal	80	3:01
Delucia, Sea	31	2:54	Morton, Bos	15	2:59	LaValliere, Pit	100	2:48
Deshaies, Hou	28	2:56	Mulholland, Phi	34	2:37	Macfarlane, KC	66	2:50
Drabek, Pit	35	2:47	Nabholz, Mon	24	2:50	Manwaring, SF	57	2:49
Erickson S, Min	32	2:44	Nagy, Cle	33	2:46	Mayne, KC	63	2:57
Fernandez A, ChA	32	3:10	Navarro, Mil	34	2:49	Melvin, Bal	67	3:02
Finley C, Cal	34	2:56	Nichols Rod, Cle	16	2:46	Myers G, Tor	91	2:56
Garcia R, ChA	15	3:22	Ojeda, LA	31	2:59	Nokes, NYA	112	2:58
Gardiner, Bos	22	2:56	Olivares, StL	24	2:44	O'Brien C, NY	56	2:59
Gardner M, Mon	27	2:47	Portugal, Hou	27	2:43	Oliver, Cin	78	2:46
Glavine, Atl	34	2:48	Rasmussen D, SD	24	2:44	Olson Greg, Atl	113	2:51
Gooden, NYN	27	2:56	Rijo, Cin	30	2:45	Pagnozzi, StL	133	2:46
Greene, Phi	27	2:51	Robinson D, SF	16	2:53	Parrish Ln, Cal	102	2:51
Gubicza, KC	26	2:56	Robinson JM, Bal	19	3:02	Pena T, Bos	132	2:59
Gullickson, Det	35	3:04	Ruffin, Phi	15	2:48	Reed Jf, Cin	77	2:49
Guzman J, Tor	23	3:06	Ryan, Tex	27	3:09	Reyes, Mon	63	2:58
Guzman, Tex	25	2:50	Saberhagen, KC	28	2:50	Rodriguez I, Tex	81	3:00
Hammond, Cin	18	2:45	Sanderson, NYA	34	2:57	Santiago, SD	148	2:47
Haney, Mon	16	3:12	Slusarski, Oak	19	3:02	Scioscia, LA	104	2:57
Hanson, Sea	27	2:54	Smiley, Pit	32	2:42	Skinner J, Cle	90	2:42
Harnisch, Hou	33	2:56	Smith B, StL	31	2:49	Steinbach, Oak	108	2:59
Harris GA, Bos	21	2:50	Smith Z, Pit	35	2:46	Surhoff BJ, Mil	118	2:56
Harris GW, SD	20	2:50	Smoltz, Atl	36	2:51	Tettleton, Det	116	3:06
Hawkins, Oak	17	2:57	Stewart D, Oak	35	3:07	Valle, Sea	106	2:57
						Wilkins R, ChN	54	2:57
						AL Avg—2:58	**NL Avg—2:51**	

WHAT KIND OF TEAM CAN'T RALLY IN THE NINTH? (p. 46)

1991 records when Ahead/Behind/Tied after 6/7 innings

Teams' Records when Ahead/Behind/Tied After 6 and 7 Innings

Record After 6 Innings

American League	Ahead W	L	Pct	Behind W	L	Pct	Tied W	L	Pct
Orioles	49	11	.817	6	71	.078	12	13	.480
Red Sox	71	9	.887	9	59	.132	4	10	.286
Angels	68	10	.872	3	63	.045	10	8	.556
White Sox	58	9	.866	14	60	.189	15	6	.714
Indians	42	9	.824	6	78	.071	9	18	.333
Tigers	65	7	.903	5	65	.071	14	6	.700
Royals	64	5	.928	9	60	.130	9	15	.375
Brewers	67	11	.859	10	59	.145	6	9	.400
Twins	72	5	.935	12	51	.190	11	11	.500
Yankees	51	8	.864	11	76	.126	9	7	.563
Athletics	67	8	.893	6	61	.090	11	9	.550
Mariners	61	11	.847	14	61	.187	8	7	.533
Rangers	65	9	.878	7	57	.109	13	11	.542
Blue Jays	69	11	.863	11	48	.186	11	12	.478
AL Total	869	123	.876	123	869	.124	142	142	.500

National League	Ahead W	L	Pct	Behind W	L	Pct	Tied W	L	Pct
Braves	74	7	.914	11	52	.175	9	9	.500
Cubs	55	13	.809	10	56	.152	12	14	.462
Reds	58	8	.879	5	66	.070	11	14	.440
Astros	45	15	.750	6	66	.083	14	16	.467
Dodgers	68	8	.895	9	51	.150	16	10	.615
Expos	51	12	.810	9	59	.132	11	19	.367
Mets	58	12	.829	8	62	.114	11	10	.524
Phillies	51	8	.864	8	62	.114	19	14	.576
Pirates	78	8	.907	9	48	.158	11	8	.579
Cardinals	58	8	.879	14	59	.192	12	11	.522
Padres	58	7	.892	13	58	.183	13	13	.500
Giants	55	6	.902	10	70	.125	10	11	.476
NL Total	709	112	.864	112	709	.136	149	149	.500

Record After 7 Innings

American League	Ahead W	L	Pct	Behind W	L	Pct	Tied W	L	Pct
Orioles	53	8	.869	8	71	.101	6	16	.273
Red Sox	74	9	.892	5	65	.071	5	4	.556
Angels	72	8	.900	3	64	.045	6	9	.400
White Sox	62	9	.873	13	56	.188	12	10	.545
Indians	44	8	.846	6	87	.065	7	10	.412
Tigers	67	6	.918	7	68	.093	10	4	.714
Royals	63	5	.926	8	64	.111	11	11	.500
Brewers	74	7	.914	6	61	.090	3	11	.214
Twins	74	8	.902	11	53	.172	10	6	.625
Yankees	54	6	.900	7	78	.082	10	7	.588
Athletics	65	9	.878	6	62	.088	13	7	.650
Mariners	64	11	.853	10	62	.139	9	6	.600
Rangers	64	8	.889	10	58	.147	11	11	.500
Blue Jays	73	9	.890	11	54	.169	7	8	.467
AL Total	903	111	.891	111	903	.109	120	120	.500

National League	Ahead W	L	Pct	Behind W	L	Pct	Tied W	L	Pct
Braves	76	4	.950	9	55	.141	9	8	.529
Cubs	59	12	.831	7	60	.104	11	11	.500
Reds	59	6	.908	3	73	.039	11	9	.550
Astros	52	13	.800	5	73	.064	8	11	.421
Dodgers	73	4	.948	10	57	.149	10	8	.556
Expos	54	11	.831	7	69	.092	10	10	.500
Mets	59	7	.894	8	68	.105	9	9	.500
Phillies	60	8	.882	5	67	.069	13	9	.591
Pirates	81	4	.953	10	49	.169	7	11	.389
Cardinals	64	5	.928	10	62	.139	10	11	.476
Padres	70	7	.909	4	60	.063	10	10	.500
Giants	60	4	.938	7	74	.086	8	9	.471
NL Total	767	85	.900	85	767	.100	116	116	.500

WHY WAS WILL CLARK'S 116 RBI BETTER THAN CECIL FIELDER'S 133? (p. 51)

Both Leagues — Listed Alphabetically
(minimum 100 RBI Opportunities)

Player, Team	RBI	Opp	Pct	Player, Team	RBI	Opp	Pct	Player, Team	RBI	Opp	Pct
Alomar R, Tor	60	394	15.2	Cole, Cle	21	201	10.4	Gonzalez J, Tex	75	445	16.9
Anderson B, Bal	25	165	15.2	Cora, ChA	18	152	11.8	Gonzalez L, Hou	56	381	14.7
Baerga, Cle	58	391	14.8	Cuyler, Det	30	311	9.6	Grace, ChN	50	378	13.2
Bagwell, Hou	67	405	16.5	Daniels, LA	56	352	15.9	Grebeck, ChA	25	163	15.3
Baines, Oak	70	376	18.6	Dascenzo, ChN	17	158	10.8	Greenwell, Bos	74	459	16.1
Barfield Je, NYA	31	200	15.5	Daulton, Phi	30	199	15.1	Griffey Jr, Sea	78	431	18.1
Bass K, SF	30	271	11.1	Davis A, Sea	57	333	17.1	Griffin Alf, LA	27	237	11.4
Bell Geo, ChN	61	389	15.7	Davis C, Min	64	427	15.0	Grissom, Mon	33	299	11.0
Bell Jay, Pit	51	404	12.6	Davis E, Cin	22	208	10.6	Gruber, Tor	45	318	14.2
Belle, Cle	67	356	18.8	Dawson, ChN	73	408	17.9	Guerrero, StL	62	328	18.9
Belliard, Atl	27	228	11.8	Decker S, SF	19	162	11.7	Guillen, ChA	46	335	13.7
Benzinger, KC	48	317	15.1	Deer, Det	39	342	11.4	Gwynn T, SD	58	328	17.7
Bichette, Mil	44	321	13.7	DeShields, Mon	41	295	13.9	Hall M, NYA	61	396	15.4
Biggio, Hou	42	320	13.1	Devereaux, Bal	40	297	13.5	Hamilton, Mil	56	301	18.6
Blauser, Atl	43	266	16.2	Doran, Cin	29	207	14.0	Harper B, Min	59	337	17.5
Boggs W, Bos	43	312	13.8	Downing, Tex	32	257	12.5	Harris L, LA	35	313	11.2
Bonds, Pit	91	475	19.2	Duncan, Cin	28	184	15.2	Hatcher B, Cin	37	236	15.7
Bonilla B, Pit	82	472	17.4	Dunston, ChN	38	287	13.2	Hayes C, Phi	41	299	13.7
Borders, Tor	31	198	15.7	Eisenreich, KC	45	274	16.4	Hayes V, Phi	21	185	11.4
Braggs, Cin	28	178	15.7	Elster, NYN	30	245	12.2	Henderson D, Ok	60	404	14.9
Bream, Atl	34	208	16.3	Espinoza, NYA	28	282	9.9	Henderson R, Ok	39	294	13.3
Brett, KC	51	335	15.2	Evans Dw, Bal	32	223	14.3	Herr, SF	20	168	11.9
Briley, Sea	24	223	10.8	Felder, SF	18	162	11.1	Hoiles, Bal	20	213	9.4
Brooks, NYN	34	284	12.0	Felix, Cal	24	150	16.0	Horn, Bal	38	217	17.5
Browne J, Cle	28	208	13.5	Fermin, Cle	31	283	11.0	Howard D, KC	16	164	9.8
Brunansky, Bos	54	384	14.1	Fernandez T, SD	34	295	11.5	Howard T, SD	18	176	10.2
Buechele, Pit	63	413	15.3	Fielder, Det	89	487	18.3	Howell Jk, SD	15	150	10.0
Buhner, Sea	50	324	15.4	Finley S, Hou	46	288	16.0	Hrbek, Min	69	361	19.1
Burks, Bos	42	364	11.5	Fisk, ChA	56	376	14.9	Huff, ChA	22	170	12.9
Butler, LA	36	303	11.9	Fletcher S, ChA	27	150	18.0	Hunter B, Atl	38	212	17.9
Calderon, Mon	56	328	17.1	Franco Ju, Tex	63	400	15.8	Huson, Tex	24	198	12.1
Caminiti, Hou	67	435	15.4	Fryman T, Det	70	436	16.1	Incaviglia, Det	27	255	10.6
Candaele, Hou	46	319	14.4	Gaetti, Cal	48	365	13.2	Jackson Dar, SD	28	213	13.1
Canseco, Oak	78	413	18.9	Gagne, Min	34	296	11.5	Jacoby, Oak	40	291	13.7
Carreon, NYN	17	197	8.6	Galarraga, Mon	24	254	9.4	James C, Cle	36	273	13.2
Carter G, LA	20	184	10.9	Gallagher, Cal	29	179	16.2	Jefferies, NYN	53	336	15.8
Carter J, Tor	75	443	16.9	Gallego, Oak	37	301	12.3	Johnson H, NYN	79	450	17.6
Cedeno A, Hou	27	168	16.1	Gant, Atl	73	446	16.4	Johnson L, ChA	49	386	12.7
Cerone, NYN	14	164	8.5	Gantner, Mil	45	338	13.3	Jordan, Phi	40	229	17.5
Chamberlain, Phi	37	255	14.5	Gibson K, KC	39	285	13.7	Jose, StL	69	409	16.9
Clark Je, SD	37	263	14.1	Gilkey, StL	15	198	7.6	Joyner, Cal	75	370	20.3
Clark Jk, Bos	59	439	13.4	Gladden, Min	46	281	16.4	Justice, Atl	66	341	19.4
Clark W, SF	87	381	22.8	Gomez L, Bal	29	285	10.2	Kelly, NYA	49	327	15.0

Player, Team	RBI	Opp	Pct	Player, Team	RBI	Opp	Pct	Player, Team	RBI	Opp	Pct
Kelly P, NYA	20	183	10.9	Olson Greg, Atl	38	260	14.6	Sierra, Tex	91	490	18.6
Knoblauch, Min	49	332	14.8	Oquendo, StL	25	251	10.0	Skinner J, Cle	23	194	11.9
Kruk, Phi	71	396	17.9	Orsulak, Bal	38	307	12.4	Slaught, Pit	28	175	16.0
Lankford, StL	60	357	16.8	Owen S, Mon	23	244	9.4	Smith Lo, Atl	37	229	16.2
Larkin B, Cin	48	301	15.9	Pagliarulo, Min	30	237	12.7	Smith O, StL	47	332	14.2
Larkin G, Min	17	177	9.6	Pagnozzi, StL	55	338	16.3	Sojo, Cal	17	266	6.4
LaValliere, Pit	38	253	15.0	Palmeiro, Tex	62	439	14.1	Sosa, ChA	23	209	11.0
Lee M, Tor	29	275	10.5	Palmer Dn, Tex	22	166	13.3	Spiers, Mil	46	283	16.3
Lemke, Atl	21	196	10.7	Parker D, Tor	48	343	14.0	Stanley M, Tex	22	154	14.3
Lewis M, Cle	30	219	13.7	Parrish Ln, Cal	32	254	12.6	Steinbach, Oak	61	347	17.6
Lind, Pit	51	374	13.6	Pasqua, ChA	48	345	13.9	Stillwell, KC	45	297	15.2
Maas, NYA	40	364	11.0	Pecota, KC	39	278	14.0	Strawberry, LA	71	395	18.0
Macfarlane, KC	28	200	14.0	Pena T, Bos	43	344	12.5	Stubbs, Mil	27	275	9.8
Mack, Min	56	322	17.4	Pendleton, Atl	64	410	15.6	Surhoff BJ, Mil	63	368	17.1
Magadan, NYN	47	309	15.2	Perry G, StL	30	179	16.8	Sveum, Mil	39	215	18.1
Maldonado, Tor	36	217	16.6	Pettis, Tex	19	198	9.6	Tabler, Tor	20	151	13.2
Martinez Crl, Cle	25	158	15.8	Phillips, Det	55	315	17.5	Tartabull, KC	69	347	19.9
Martinez Cm, Cin	26	182	14.3	Polonia, Cal	48	344	14.0	Templeton, NYN	23	188	12.2
Martinez Da, Mon	35	230	15.2	Puckett, Min	74	421	17.6	Tettleton, Det	58	385	15.1
Martinez E, Sea	38	353	10.8	Quinones L, Cin	16	172	9.3	Teufel, SD	32	248	12.9
Mattingly, NYA	59	382	15.4	Quintana, Bos	60	388	15.5	Thomas F, ChA	77	449	17.1
Mayne, KC	28	167	16.8	Raines, ChA	45	315	14.3	Thompson M, StL	28	230	12.2
McClendon, Pit	17	150	11.3	Ramirez R, Hou	19	153	12.4	Thompson R, SF	29	294	9.9
McGee, SF	39	275	14.2	Randolph, Mil	54	354	15.3	Thon, Phi	35	304	11.5
McGriff F, SD	75	444	16.9	Ready, Phi	19	158	12.0	Trammell, Det	46	302	15.2
McGwire, Oak	53	402	13.2	Reed Jd, Bos	55	429	12.8	Treadway, Atl	29	184	15.8
McRae B, KC	56	348	16.1	Reed Jf, Cin	28	174	16.1	Valle, Sea	24	226	10.6
McReynolds, NY	58	339	17.1	Reimer, Tex	49	301	16.3	Van Slyke, Pit	66	357	18.5
Melvin, Bal	22	160	13.8	Reynolds H, Sea	54	405	13.3	Vaughn G, Mil	71	420	16.9
Merced, Pit	40	233	17.2	Riles, Oak	27	200	13.5	Vaughn M, Bos	28	167	16.8
Meulens, NYA	23	179	12.8	Ripken B, Bal	14	171	8.2	Ventura, ChA	77	425	18.1
Milligan, Bal	54	371	14.6	Ripken C, Bal	80	431	18.6	Vizquel, Sea	40	291	13.7
Mitchell K, SF	42	275	15.3	Rivera L, Bos	32	291	11.0	Walker C, ChN	28	209	13.4
Molitor, Mil	58	381	15.2	Roberts Bip, SD	29	188	15.4	Walker L, Mon	48	315	15.2
Morandini, Phi	19	172	11.0	Rodriguez I, Tex	24	169	14.2	Wallach, Mon	60	400	15.0
Morris H, Cin	45	326	13.8	Sabo, Cin	62	403	15.4	Webster M, LA	17	151	11.3
Moseby, Det	29	180	16.1	Salazar L, ChN	24	197	12.2	Whitaker, Det	55	355	15.5
Mulliniks, Tor	22	163	13.5	Samuel, LA	46	398	11.6	White D, Tor	43	355	12.1
Murphy Dl, Phi	63	414	15.2	Sandberg, ChN	74	411	18.0	Whiten, Cle	36	275	13.1
Murray E, LA	77	454	17.0	Santiago, SD	70	462	15.2	Williams B, NYA	31	193	16.1
Myers G, Tor	28	222	12.6	Sasser, NYN	30	156	19.2	Williams MD, SF	64	418	15.3
Newman A, Min	19	187	10.2	Sax S, NYA	46	347	13.3	Wilson M, Tor	26	186	14.0
Nixon O, Atl	26	187	13.9	Schofield, Cal	31	284	10.9	Wilson W, Oak	28	191	14.7
Nokes, NYA	53	337	15.7	Scioscia, LA	32	257	12.5	Winfield, Cal	58	394	14.7
O'Brien P, Sea	71	442	16.1	Segui, Bal	20	150	13.3	Yelding, Hou	19	153	12.4
O'Neill, Cin	63	417	15.1	Seitzer, KC	24	167	14.4	Yount, Mil	67	406	16.5
Olerud, Tor	51	343	14.9	Sharperson, LA	18	161	11.2	Zeile, StL	70	401	17.5
Oliver, Cin	30	169	17.8	Shumpert, KC	29	259	11.2	**ML Average**			13.6

WHO WAS BASEBALL'S BEST CLEANUP HITTER IN '91? (p.54)

Both Leagues — Listed Alphabetically
(Players with 100+ Plate Appearances batting Cleanup)

Player, Team	Slg	AB	H	2B	3B	HR	RBI	AB/RBI
Baines, Oak	.462	433	125	22	1	17	82	5.3
Bell Geo, ChN	.434	267	73	7	0	12	38	7.0
Belle, Cle	.526	382	105	26	2	22	79	4.8
Bonilla B, Pit	.494	575	174	44	6	18	100	5.8
Brooks, NYN	.412	119	29	5	0	5	15	7.9
Buhner, Sea	.505	101	28	5	0	6	16	6.3
Caminiti, Hou	.341	258	65	10	2	3	29	8.9
Carter J, Tor	.527	165	50	13	0	8	33	5.0
Clark Jk, Bos	.462	439	111	18	1	24	77	5.7
Davis C, Min	.483	201	51	10	0	12	41	4.9
Davis E, Cin	.397	199	49	6	0	8	25	8.0
Davis G, Bal	.425	146	31	7	0	8	24	6.1
Dawson, ChN	.462	316	81	12	1	17	57	5.5
Fielder, Det	.513	624	163	25	0	44	133	4.7
Fisk, ChA	.400	195	46	11	0	7	34	5.7
Franco Ju, Tex	.495	198	66	12	1	6	29	6.8
Gant, Atl	.588	226	63	15	2	17	55	4.1
Gonzalez L, Hou	.415	258	61	16	3	8	36	7.2
Gruber, Tor	.453	117	29	4	1	6	17	6.9
Guerrero, StL	.363	422	115	12	1	8	69	6.1
Hall M, NYA	.421	280	80	13	2	7	37	7.6
Horn, Bal	.468	203	47	12	0	12	35	5.8
Hrbek, Min	.473	357	107	17	0	15	71	5.0
Johnson H, NYN	.592	152	46	14	0	10	31	4.9
Justice, Atl	.521	338	94	20	1	20	75	4.5
Kruk, Phi	.498	313	93	20	2	13	52	6.0
Maas, NYA	.498	201	55	7	1	12	27	7.4
Martinez Crl, Cle	.381	97	28	3	0	2	8	12.1
McGriff F, SD	.486	486	134	18	0	28	95	5.1
McReynolds, NYN	.427	328	87	21	1	10	48	6.8
Mitchell K, SF	.524	357	94	13	1	26	68	5.3
Murphy Dl, Phi	.422	211	54	8	0	9	27	7.8
Murray E, LA	.399	396	101	19	1	12	68	5.8
O'Brien P, Sea	.438	258	71	16	1	8	50	5.2
O'Neill, Cin	.514	214	60	14	0	12	37	5.8
Olerud, Tor	.429	219	56	17	0	7	30	7.3
Parker D, Tor	.321	234	50	11	1	4	24	9.8
Pasqua, ChA	.490	261	72	15	4	11	45	5.8
Sabo, Cin	.712	118	45	16	1	7	28	4.2
Sierra, Tex	.513	279	82	16	3	13	52	5.4
Strawberry, LA	.503	193	52	9	0	12	40	4.8
Stubbs, Mil	.313	115	23	7	0	2	10	11.5
Tartabull, KC	.610	444	142	33	3	30	95	4.7
Vaughn G, Mil	.392	125	27	4	0	6	22	5.7
Wallach, Mon	.343	492	116	20	0	11	66	7.5
Williams MD, SF	.500	148	39	8	0	9	29	5.1
Winfield, Cal	.405	336	78	14	1	14	50	6.7
Yount, Mil	.368	318	84	14	2	5	48	6.6
Zeile, StL	.400	110	31	7	0	2	16	6.9
AL Composite	.445	625	165	31	2	26	103	6.1
NL Composite	.441	617	163	30	2	25	102	6.1

IS WADE, RICKEY, PAULIE OR BRETT NO. 1 AT NO. 1? (p. 56)

Both Leagues — Listed Alphabetically
(Players with 100+ Plate Appearances batting Leadoff in 1991)

Player, Team	OBP	AB	R	H	BB	HBP	SB
Anderson B, Bal	.369	87	17	24	13	1	6
Boggs W, Bos	.440	424	80	147	73	0	1
Boston, NYN	.380	122	22	37	15	0	6
Briley, Sea	.259	102	6	23	5	0	6
Butler, LA	.401	614	112	182	108	1	38
Cole, Cle	.382	373	54	108	57	0	24
Coleman, NYN	.349	276	45	71	39	0	37
Cuyler, Det	.320	153	28	36	16	3	10
Dascenzo, ChN	.371	135	23	40	15	1	8
DeShields, Mon	.350	459	72	108	81	2	45
Devereaux, Bal	.316	538	73	139	45	2	14
Doran, Cin	.370	184	30	54	23	0	4
Downing, Tex	.376	348	65	94	52	8	1
Dykstra, Phi	.387	242	47	71	36	1	22
Felder, SF	.310	260	37	69	17	0	16
Finley S, Hou	.334	349	52	103	21	1	16
Gibson K, KC	.337	83	10	17	16	1	4
Gilkey, StL	.299	143	11	29	19	1	7
Gladden, Min	.313	444	62	113	34	5	14
Grissom, Mon	.278	149	19	35	9	0	14
Hatcher B, Cin	.252	124	11	26	5	2	3
Henderson R, Oak	.401	464	105	125	97	7	57
Hill G, Cle	.336	97	11	26	10	0	4
Howard T, SD	.311	97	13	26	6	0	5
Huff, ChA	.350	153	29	35	26	3	10
Kelly, NYA	.304	168	24	41	14	1	7
Lankford, StL	.306	321	44	82	23	1	23
Larkin B, Cin	.351	101	14	29	10	0	5
Lewis D, SF	.357	213	40	53	34	2	12
Martinez E, Sea	.405	261	52	80	41	4	0
McRae B, KC	.284	425	59	108	17	2	18
Merced, Pit	.376	374	77	103	60	1	7
Miller K, NYN	.316	198	21	52	13	3	8
Molitor, Mil	.399	652	132	211	77	6	19
Nixon O, Atl	.368	387	76	115	45	0	70
Pettis, Tex	.296	91	11	15	17	0	6
Phillips, Det	.368	491	73	138	69	2	10
Polonia, Cal	.354	597	92	178	52	1	47
Raines, ChA	.361	604	102	163	83	5	51
Redus, Pit	.325	213	37	55	20	3	15
Reed Jd, Bos	.361	153	18	47	12	1	1
Reynolds H, Sea	.321	192	27	43	27	2	8
Roberts Bip, SD	.339	412	66	115	35	4	26
Sabo, Cin	.322	134	17	34	13	1	6
Sax S, NYA	.344	285	38	87	16	2	17
Smith Lo, Atl	.393	130	26	40	15	4	3
Thompson Ro, SF	.307	90	20	20	9	2	3
Thurman, KC	.357	105	12	33	6	1	5
Walker C, ChN	.306	279	42	71	22	0	10
Walton, ChN	.264	196	32	39	15	3	7
White D, Tor	.342	642	110	181	55	7	33
Williams B, NYA	.328	210	31	46	33	1	7
Yelding, Hou	.248	124	8	27	5	0	5
AL Team Avg	.349	672	106	183	76	5	30
NL Team Avg	.332	665	103	173	70	3	40

CAN WE GO AHEAD AND SAY JOE CARTER IS A CLUTCH HITTER? (p. 61)

1991 Both Leagues — Listed Alphabetically
(minimum 50 RBI total in 1991)

Player, Team	GA RBI	RBI Occ	All RBI	%	Player, Team	GA RBI	RBI Occ	All RBI	%
Alomar R, Tor	16	55	69	29	Lankford, StL	17	57	69	30
Baerga, Cle	26	57	69	46	Larkin B, Cin	20	55	69	36
Bagwell, Hou	15	64	82	23	Maas, NYA	13	47	63	28
Baines, Oak	20	65	90	31	Mack, Min	12	51	74	24
Bell Geo, ChN	24	69	86	35	Mattingly, NYA	24	60	68	40
Bell Jay, Pit	6	54	67	11	McGriff F, SD	37	81	106	46
Belle, Cle	25	67	95	37	McGwire, Oak	13	51	75	25
Bichette, Mil	11	41	59	27	McRae B, KC	6	51	64	12
Bonds, Pit	23	90	116	26	McReynolds, NYN	17	54	74	31
Bonilla B, Pit	23	80	100	29	Milligan, Bal	12	55	70	22
Brett, KC	20	50	61	40	Mitchell K, SF	10	51	69	20
Brunansky, Bos	9	52	70	17	Molitor, Mil	15	61	75	25
Buechele, Pit	18	57	85	32	Morris H, Cin	12	53	59	23
Buhner, Sea	17	60	77	28	Murphy Dl, Phi	20	67	81	30
Burks, Bos	12	42	56	29	Murray E, LA	26	73	96	36
Calderon, Mon	32	66	75	48	Nokes, NYA	13	54	77	24
Caminiti, Hou	21	59	80	36	O'Brien P, Sea	19	72	88	26
Canseco, Oak	32	80	122	40	O'Neill, Cin	18	61	91	30
Carter J, Tor	34	89	108	38	Olerud, Tor	10	59	68	17
Clark Jk, Bos	19	60	87	32	Pagnozzi, StL	10	46	57	22
Clark W, SF	30	85	116	35	Palmeiro, Tex	20	71	88	28
Daniels, LA	16	52	73	31	Parker D, Tor	17	51	59	33
Davis A, Sea	14	52	69	27	Pasqua, ChA	12	47	66	26
Davis C, Min	24	70	93	34	Pendleton, Atl	23	70	86	33
Dawson, ChN	24	72	104	33	Phillips, Det	14	61	72	23
Deer, Det	12	43	64	28	Puckett, Min	26	78	89	33
Devereaux, Bal	11	48	59	23	Quintana, Bos	10	52	71	19
Fielder, Det	28	88	133	32	Reed Jd, Bos	13	50	60	26
Fisk, ChA	15	51	74	29	Reimer, Tex	8	46	69	17
Franco Ju, Tex	29	66	78	44	Reynolds H, Sea	9	47	57	19
Fryman T, Det	15	69	91	22	Ripken C, Bal	24	90	114	27
Gaetti, Cal	15	54	66	28	Sabo, Cin	20	65	88	31
Gant, Atl	32	80	105	40	Samuel, LA	15	44	58	34
Gibson K, KC	11	42	55	26	Sandberg, ChN	27	75	100	36
Gonzalez Juan, Tex	23	66	102	35	Santiago, SD	18	70	87	26
Gonzalez L, Hou	16	57	69	28	Sax S, NYA	13	51	56	25
Grace, ChN	12	51	58	24	Sierra, Tex	32	85	116	38
Greenwell, Bos	19	63	83	30	Steinbach, Oak	15	56	67	27
Griffey Jr, Sea	33	79	100	42	Strawberry, LA	31	73	99	42
Gruber, Tor	18	49	65	37	Surhoff BJ, Mil	18	58	68	31
Guerrero, StL	13	61	70	21	Tartabull, KC	25	77	100	32
Gwynn T, SD	20	55	62	36	Tettleton, Det	19	62	89	31
Hall M, NYA	23	61	80	38	Thomas F, ChA	24	82	109	29
Hamilton, Mil	12	47	57	26	Trammell, Det	12	43	55	28
Harper B, Min	8	50	69	16	Van Slyke, Pit	22	70	83	31
Henderson D, Oak	25	62	85	40	Vaughn G, Mil	22	71	98	31
Henderson R, Oak	13	41	57	32	Ventura, ChA	22	74	100	30
Horn, Bal	12	41	61	29	Walker L, Mon	16	49	64	33
Hrbek, Min	22	64	89	34	Wallach, Mon	22	60	73	37
Jefferies, NYN	12	52	62	23	Whitaker, Det	15	58	78	26
Johnson H, NYN	34	95	117	36	White D, Tor	11	53	60	21
Jose, StL	16	56	77	29	Williams MD, SF	18	78	98	23
Joyner, Cal	21	70	96	30	Winfield, Cal	21	66	86	32
Justice, Atl	26	66	87	39	Yount, Mil	24	63	77	38
Kelly, NYA	13	53	69	25	Zeile, StL	23	65	81	35
Kruk, Phi	25	73	92	34	**MLB Average**	3730	13547	17048	28

DO WE REALLY KNOW WHO CAN POP IN THE CLUTCH? (p. 64)

1989-1991 Both Leagues — Listed Alphabetically
(minimum 250 plate appearances Late & Close from 1989 through 1991)

Player, Team	AVG	AB	H	HR	RBI	Player, Team	AVG	AB	H	HR	RBI
Alomar R, Tor	.276	304	84	3	34	Johnson H, NYN	.250	292	73	15	51
Baines, Oak	.260	208	54	9	30	Johnson L, ChA	.237	232	55	0	20
Barfield Je, NYA	.196	209	41	8	27	Kelly, NYA	.284	271	77	12	40
Bell Geo, ChN	.262	286	75	13	52	Kruk, Phi	.284	218	62	6	37
Bell Jay, Pit	.271	218	59	3	28	Lind, Pit	.260	281	73	0	17
Benzinger, KC	.197	239	47	4	26	Mattingly, NYA	.276	246	68	10	46
Biggio, Hou	.250	296	74	3	36	McGriff F, SD	.250	248	62	10	33
Blauser, Atl	.232	233	54	8	28	McGwire, Oak	.247	194	48	12	46
Boggs W, Bos	.285	270	77	2	20	McReynolds, NY	.288	281	81	15	49
Bonds, Pit	.277	260	72	6	33	Mitchell K, SF	.280	225	63	16	39
Bonilla B, Pit	.239	285	68	10	42	Molitor, Mil	.278	212	59	6	26
Brett, KC	.256	215	55	5	26	Murphy Dl, Phi	.212	288	61	10	44
Brooks, NYN	.270	237	64	9	36	Murray E, LA	.255	286	73	8	37
Browne J, Cle	.285	246	70	3	21	O'Brien P, Sea	.206	248	51	3	28
Brunansky, Bos	.229	240	55	3	25	O'Neill, Cin	.249	233	58	4	24
Burks, Bos	.250	228	57	6	26	Oquendo, StL	.295	241	71	1	15
Butler, LA	.287	296	85	3	30	Owen S, Mon	.249	261	65	7	28
Calderon, Mon	.288	278	80	7	32	Palmeiro, Tex	.269	290	78	11	38
Caminiti, Hou	.251	311	78	6	27	Parker D, Tor	.228	228	52	7	23
Carter J, Tor	.201	338	68	10	46	Pena T, Bos	.215	246	53	1	18
Clark Jk, Bos	.209	225	47	15	38	Pendleton, Atl	.256	270	69	3	31
Clark W, SF	.289	273	79	12	59	Phillips, Det	.239	230	55	5	21
Davis A, Sea	.232	237	55	10	37	Puckett, Min	.315	254	80	8	44
Davis C, Min	.265	211	56	5	26	Raines, ChA	.286	308	88	5	43
Dawson, ChN	.237	266	63	14	41	Ramirez R, Hou	.258	248	64	1	33
Devereaux, Bal	.263	228	60	7	24	Randolph, Mil	.274	230	63	2	23
Doran, Cin	.222	225	50	4	21	Reed Jd, Bos	.273	242	66	1	29
Downing, Tex	.282	227	64	8	30	Reynolds H, Sea	.315	279	88	2	47
Dunston, ChN	.305	279	85	6	32	Ripken C, Bal	.290	286	83	13	40
Dykstra, Phi	.308	221	68	2	25	Sabo, Cin	.221	217	48	9	26
Evans Dw, Bal	.269	245	66	11	48	Samuel, LA	.282	238	67	6	37
Fernandez T, SD	.287	254	73	1	18	Sandberg, ChN	.282	301	85	13	48
Fisk, ChA	.255	231	59	11	45	Santiago, SD	.323	257	83	8	38
Fletcher S, ChA	.222	225	50	1	20	Sax S, NYA	.294	289	85	3	32
Franco Ju, Tex	.332	277	92	6	30	Seitzer, KC	.278	216	60	1	19
Gaetti, Cal	.214	248	53	10	32	Sierra, Tex	.297	296	88	13	57
Galarraga, Mon	.239	309	74	9	39	Smith O, StL	.262	240	63	0	30
Grace, ChN	.291	285	83	5	32	Stillwell, KC	.212	217	46	1	10
Greenwell, Bos	.288	250	72	5	32	Strawberry, LA	.215	261	56	11	39
Griffey Jr, Sea	.242	248	60	8	33	Surhoff BJ, Mil	.264	227	60	3	33
Griffin Alf, LA	.234	231	54	0	11	Templeton, NYN	.220	255	56	3	27
Gruber, Tor	.256	254	65	8	47	Tettleton, Det	.231	238	55	13	38
Guerrero, StL	.263	228	60	4	44	Thompson M, StL	.267	232	62	2	29
Guillen, ChA	.290	328	95	1	39	Thompson R, SF	.250	256	64	7	31
Gwynn T, SD	.325	289	94	2	29	Thon, Phi	.278	277	77	5	25
Hatcher B, Cin	.248	234	58	1	19	Van Slyke, Pit	.230	244	56	6	34
Hayes C, Phi	.275	247	68	8	29	Wallach, Mon	.262	344	90	7	42
Hayes V, Phi	.250	212	53	7	19	Whitaker, Det	.207	227	47	12	38
Henderson D, Oak	.262	244	64	6	31	White D, Tor	.243	280	68	3	20
Henderson R, Oak	.300	210	63	10	37	Wilson M, Tor	.253	237	60	1	27
Herr, SF	.230	239	55	2	28	Yount, Mil	.270	244	66	5	46
Incaviglia, Det	.183	246	45	8	35	AL Avg	.244				
Jacoby, Oak	.236	263	62	7	28	NL Avg	.246				
James C, Cle	.224	232	52	2	20						
Jefferies, NYN	.244	262	64	2	25						

WHO'S THE BEST BUNTER: BELL, BUTLER, CUYLER, FINLEY OR NIXON? (p. 74)

The following table shows how batters fared in two aspects of bunting. Sacrificing (**SH** = Sac Hits; **FSH** = Failed Sac Hits), and Bunting for a Hit (**BH**= Bunt Hits; **FBH** = Failed Bunt Hits).

Both Leagues — Listed Alphabetically (minimum 10 bunts in play)

Batter, Team	SH	FSH	%	BH	FBH	%
Alomar R, Tor	16	3	84	7	4	64
Anderson B, Bal	11	3	79	4	6	40
Baerga, Cle	4	0	100	8	3	73
Barnes B, Mon	3	6	33	2	1	67
Bell Jay, Pit	30	3	91	2	0	100
Belliard, Atl	7	4	64	0	3	0
Bichette, Mil	1	1	50	8	2	80
Biggio, Hou	5	0	100	6	9	40
Bordick, Oak	12	2	86	2	1	67
Browne J, Cle	12	0	100	3	0	100
Browning, Cin	10	1	91	0	1	0
Buechele, Pit	11	3	79	4	0	100
Burkett, SF	9	1	90	0	0	0
Butler, LA	4	1	80	21	20	51
Calderon, Mon	1	0	100	8	3	73
Charlton, Cin	4	3	57	0	3	0
Cole, Cle	4	1	80	7	9	44
Coleman, NYN	1	1	50	8	6	57
Cone, NYN	6	4	60	0	0	0
Cora, ChA	8	2	80	2	1	67
Cuyler, Det	12	0	100	15	17	47
Dascenzo, ChN	6	1	86	1	8	11
Deshaies, Hou	8	2	80	0	0	0
DeShields, Mon	8	0	100	5	6	45
Dunston, ChN	4	1	80	10	3	77
Espinoza, NYA	9	2	82	1	1	50
Felder, SF	4	3	57	9	12	43
Fermin, Cle	13	3	81	0	1	0
Fernandez T, SD	7	1	88	4	7	36
Finley S, Hou	10	0	100	16	14	53
Gallagher, Cal	10	1	91	3	3	50
Gallego, Oak	10	2	83	2	4	33
Gantner, Mil	7	3	70	2	1	67
Gladden, Min	5	1	83	2	2	50
Glavine, Atl	15	3	83	3	0	100
Gonzales R, Tor	6	2	75	1	2	33
Gooden, NYN	8	3	73	1	0	100
Grace, ChN	4	0	100	1	5	17
Griffey Jr, Sea	4	0	100	6	1	86
Griffin Alf, LA	7	2	78	8	10	44
Guillen, ChA	13	3	81	1	3	25
Hamilton, Mil	7	2	78	3	7	30
Harnisch, Hou	7	7	50	0	1	0
Harris L, LA	12	1	92	2	2	50
Hatcher B, Cin	4	2	67	3	3	50
Howard D, KC	9	1	90	3	6	33
Howard T, SD	2	1	67	4	5	44
Hudler, StL	2	0	100	5	6	45
Huff, ChA	6	1	86	1	2	33
Hurst, SD	12	1	92	1	0	100
Huson, Tex	9	0	100	4	3	57
Johnson L, ChA	6	3	67	8	8	50
Karkovice, ChA	9	1	90	3	0	100
Kelly P, NYA	2	0	100	4	9	31
Landrum C, ChN	3	0	100	3	6	33
Lankford, StL	4	1	80	2	4	33
Larkin B, Cin	3	2	60	2	4	33
Lee M, Tor	10	1	91	2	4	33
Leibrandt, Atl	12	3	80	0	0	0
Lewis D, SF	7	1	88	2	5	29
Lyons S, Bos	3	1	75	1	5	17
Maddux G, ChN	11	2	85	2	0	100
Martinez De, Mon	10	1	91	0	0	0
Martinez E, Sea	2	0	100	5	3	63
Martinez R, LA	8	2	80	0	1	0
McGee, SF	8	0	100	2	1	67
McRae B, KC	3	3	50	5	17	23
Miller K, NYN	0	0	0	8	7	53
Morandini, Phi	6	2	75	4	1	80
Morgan M, LA	8	3	73	0	0	0
Mulholland, Phi	5	6	45	0	0	0
Newman A, Min	5	1	83	3	3	50
Nixon O, Atl	7	0	100	23	29	44
Pendleton, Atl	7	0	100	6	0	100
Pettis, Tex	6	4	60	3	5	38
Polonia, Cal	2	0	100	10	13	43
Puckett, Min	8	1	89	8	1	89
Raines, ChA	9	0	100	8	7	53
Reed Jd, Bos	11	4	73	3	1	75
Reynolds H, Sea	14	2	88	10	6	63
Rijo, Cin	9	0	100	1	1	50
Ripken B, Bal	11	2	85	2	3	40
Ripken C, Bal	0	0	0	4	6	40
Rivera L, Bos	12	0	100	1	4	20
Roberts Bip, SD	4	1	80	3	5	38
Samuel, LA	10	2	83	5	2	71
Sax S, NYA	5	2	71	1	2	33
Schaefer, Sea	6	2	75	3	0	100
Schofield, Cal	7	3	70	3	1	75
Sharperson, LA	10	0	100	0	1	0
Shumpert, KC	10	3	77	6	3	67
Slaught, Pit	5	0	100	3	2	60
Smith O, StL	6	0	100	5	3	63
Smith Z, Pit	13	3	81	0	0	0
Sojo, Cal	19	2	90	13	9	59
Spiers, Mil	10	3	77	3	6	33
Surhoff BJ, Mil	13	0	100	1	5	17
Tewksbury, StL	7	3	70	0	0	0
Thompson R, SF	11	2	85	1	3	25
Tomlin R, Pit	13	2	87	1	0	100
Valle, Sea	6	1	86	2	2	50
Varsho, Pit	1	2	33	4	5	44
Ventura, ChA	8	0	100	5	4	56
Viola, NYN	10	2	83	0	0	0
Vizquel, Sea	8	1	89	9	8	53
Walker C, ChN	1	0	100	3	6	33
Walton, ChN	3	2	60	3	6	33
Webster M, LA	2	0	100	1	8	11
White D, Tor	5	0	100	9	8	53
Williams B, NYA	2	1	67	2	8	20
Yelding, Hou	3	1	75	5	2	71
ML Average	**1624**	**353**	**82**	**665**	**662**	**50**

WHO ARE BASEBALL'S TABLE SETTERS? (p. 76)

The table below lists Bases Gained (**BG**): **2B+(2x3B)+SB-CS**; **R** = runs scored minus home runs while batting first and second.

Both Leagues 1991— Listed Alphabetically
(minimum 15 bases gained batting first and second)

Batter	BG	2B	3B	SB	CS	R	Batter	BG	2B	3B	SB	CS	R
Alomar R, Tor	92	37	10	45	10	73	McGee, SF	40	28	3	13	7	57
Anderson B, Bal	21	12	3	8	5	30	McRae B, KC	52	27	8	20	11	75
Bell Jay, Pit	52	32	8	10	6	79	Merced, Pit	24	17	2	7	4	68
Biggio, Hou	22	10	3	9	3	43	Miller K, NYN	31	22	1	10	3	32
Boggs W, Bos	36	33	2	1	2	73	Molitor, Mil	69	32	13	19	8	115
Boston, NYN	20	14	3	6	6	22	Morandini, Phi	28	8	4	13	1	34
Butler, LA	33	13	5	38	28	110	Nixon O, Atl	60	8	1	70	20	77
Cole, Cle	32	17	3	24	15	54	Orsulak, Bal	19	13	1	4	0	30
Coleman, NYN	40	7	5	37	14	44	Owen S, Mon	17	11	2	2	0	16
Cotto, Sea	16	6	1	11	3	23	Palmeiro, Tex	29	26	1	3	2	41
Cuyler, Det	17	6	2	10	3	28	Pendleton, Atl	18	10	2	5	1	26
DeShields, Mon	56	15	4	56	23	73	Phillips, Det	38	25	4	10	5	66
Devereaux, Bal	54	27	10	16	9	63	Polonia, Cal	68	28	8	47	23	90
Downing, Tex	17	13	2	1	1	50	Raines, ChA	68	20	6	51	15	97
Dykstra, Phi	40	12	5	22	4	44	Randolph, Mil	15	11	2	2	2	45
Felder, SF	34	9	6	18	5	41	Redus, Pit	28	12	2	15	3	31
Fernandez T, SD	44	24	5	18	8	69	Reed Jd, Bos	45	41	2	5	5	81
Finley S, Hou	61	26	10	33	18	75	Reynolds H, Sea	66	34	6	28	8	92
Franco Ju, Tex	26	8	2	15	1	35	Roberts Bip, SD	34	13	3	26	11	63
Gibson K, KC	36	16	5	14	4	53	Samuel, LA	37	17	4	19	7	49
Gladden, Min	37	14	9	14	9	56	Sandberg, ChN	18	15	1	4	3	34
Grace, ChN	19	13	4	1	3	51	Sax S, NYA	62	38	2	31	11	74
Grissom, Mon	76	20	8	54	14	57	Smith O, StL	62	30	3	35	9	93
Hatcher B, Cin	20	14	3	7	7	27	Thompson Ro, SF	20	12	3	4	2	30
Henderson D, Oak	25	24	0	4	3	44	Treadway, Atl	15	11	2	2	2	29
Henderson R, Oak	58	17	1	57	18	87	Ventura, ChA	21	21	1	0	2	58
Huff, ChA	18	6	1	12	2	31	Walton, ChN	15	7	1	7	1	29
Joyner, Cal	16	14	0	2	0	23	Whitaker, Det	28	22	2	3	1	60
Knoblauch, Min	55	24	6	24	5	73	White D, Tor	83	40	10	33	10	93
Landrum C, ChN	17	2	1	17	4	13	Williams B, NYA	25	15	3	8	4	32
Lankford, StL	38	16	7	23	15	36	Wilson W, Oak	19	8	2	12	5	23
Larkin B, Cin	22	12	1	10	2	28							
Lewis D, SF	16	5	3	12	7	39							
Martinez E, Sea	23	23	1	0	2	48							

FOR WHOM DOES CRIME PAY ? (p. 78)

Both Leagues — Listed Alphabetically
(1991 active players with a minimum of 100 stolen base attempts lifetime)

Player, Team	SB	Att	Pct.	Player, Team	SB	Att	Pct.
Alomar R, Tor	143	184	.777	McGee, SF	294	390	.754
Backman, Phi	116	168	.690	McReynolds, NYN	82	111	.739
Barfield Je, NYA	65	111	.586	Molitor, Mil	381	490	.778
Bass K, SF	120	172	.698	Moseby, Det	280	372	.753
Bernazard, Det	113	168	.673	Moses, Det	101	158	.639
Bonds, Pit	212	276	.768	Murphy Dl, Phi	161	229	.703
Boston, NYN	85	122	.697	Murray E, LA	86	120	.717
Brett, KC	186	272	.684	Newman A, Min	82	131	.626
Brooks, NYN	60	112	.536	Nixon O, Atl	264	349	.756
Browne J, Cle	62	103	.602	Oberkfell, Hou	62	108	.574
Brunansky, Bos	64	123	.520	Orsulak, Bal	77	122	.631
Burks, Bos	88	130	.677	Owen S, Mon	65	111	.586
Butler, LA	396	584	.678	Parker D, Tor	154	267	.577
Calderon, Mon	92	137	.672	Pena T, Bos	75	131	.573
Canseco, Oak	122	168	.726	Pendleton, Atl	109	159	.686
Carter J, Tor	169	217	.779	Perry G, StL	137	204	.672
Clark Jk, Bos	76	136	.559	Pettis, Tex	340	440	.773
Coleman, NYN	586	715	.820	Phillips, Det	85	141	.603
Cotto, Sea	91	110	.827	Polonia, Cal	144	205	.702
Daniels, LA	87	111	.784	Puckett, Min	100	158	.633
Davis C, Min	113	193	.585	Puhl, KC	217	316	.687
Davis E, Cin	247	284	.870	Raines, ChA	685	806	.850
Dawson, ChN	304	408	.745	Ramirez R, Hou	112	187	.599
DeShields, Mon	98	143	.685	Randolph, Mil	270	361	.748
Doran, Cin	201	290	.693	Redus, Pit	307	382	.804
Duncan, Cin	124	162	.765	Reynolds H, Sea	213	321	.664
Dunston, ChN	131	179	.732	Roberts Bip, SD	107	155	.690
Dykstra, Phi	190	235	.809	Sabo, Cin	104	143	.727
Espy, Pit	95	130	.731	Salazar L, ChN	116	166	.699
Evans Dw, Bal	78	137	.569	Samuel, LA	341	456	.748
Felder, SF	129	162	.796	Sandberg, ChN	297	381	.780
Fernandez T, SD	161	232	.694	Santiago, SD	60	101	.594
Finley S, Hou	73	103	.709	Sax S, NYA	407	570	.714
Fisk, ChA	125	182	.687	Schofield, Cal	98	128	.766
Fletcher S, ChA	57	101	.564	Shelby, Det	98	138	.710
Franco Ju, Tex	219	301	.728	Sheridan, NYA	86	121	.711
Gaetti, Cal	79	128	.617	Sierra, Tex	74	103	.718
Gagne, Min	73	121	.603	Smith Lo, Atl	356	492	.724
Gant, Atl	99	148	.669	Smith O, StL	499	619	.806
Gantner, Mil	131	207	.633	Strawberry, LA	201	284	.708
Gibson K, KC	253	317	.798	Surhoff BJ, Mil	69	112	.616
Gladden, Min	210	296	.709	Templeton, NYN	242	371	.652
Griffey, Sea	200	283	.707	Thompson M, StL	173	224	.772
Griffin Alf, LA	189	322	.587	Thompson Ro, SF	82	126	.651
Grissom, Mon	99	118	.839	Thon, Phi	149	205	.727
Guerrero, StL	95	140	.679	Trammell, Det	210	308	.682
Guillen, ChA	135	213	.634	Uribe, SF	71	115	.617
Gwynn T, SD	246	346	.711	Van Slyke, Pit	208	262	.794
Hatcher B, Cin	192	258	.744	Wallach, Mon	48	107	.449
Hayes V, Phi	242	333	.727	Webster M, LA	144	204	.706
Henderson R, Oak	994	1223	.813	Whitaker, Det	128	196	.653
Herr, SF	188	252	.746	White D, Tor	156	208	.750
Hudler, StL	75	105	.714	Wilson M, Tor	327	425	.769
Jackson B, ChA	81	111	.730	Wilson W, Oak	632	756	.836
Johnson H, NYN	191	255	.749	Winfield, Cal	216	305	.708
Johnson L, ChA	90	129	.698	Winningham, Cin	99	147	.673
Kelly, NYA	123	166	.741	Yelding, Hou	86	125	.688
Lansford, Oak	217	319	.680	Young G, Hou	147	216	.681
Larkin B, Cin	133	162	.821	Yount, Mil	247	344	.718
Martinez Da, Mon	95	136	.699				

ARE SOME BASERUNNERS SIMPLY TOO AGGRESSIVE? (p. 80)

The table shows the total number of outs on the bases (**Outs**) made by each player, which is the sum of his Caught Stealings (**CS**), times Picked Off (**Pk**), and Outs Advancing on hits or outs (**OAD**).

Both Leagues — Listed Alphabetically
(minimum 10 outs made on the bases)

Player, Team	Outs	CS	Pk	OAD	Player, Team	Outs	CS	Pk	OAD
Alomar R, Tor	24	11	4	9	Jose, StL	18	12	2	4
Bell Geo, ChN	11	6	1	4	Justice, Atl	14	8	0	6
Bell Jay, Pit	11	6	2	3	Kelly, NYA	10	9	0	1
Benzinger, KC	10	6	1	3	Knoblauch, Min	10	5	3	2
Bichette, Mil	10	8	1	1	Lankford, StL	27	20	2	5
Biggio, Hou	12	6	0	6	Mack, Min	13	9	0	4
Blauser, Atl	10	6	2	2	Martinez Da, Mon	14	7	4	3
Bonds, Pit	15	13	0	2	McGee, SF	15	9	2	4
Boston, NYN	10	8	0	2	McRae B, KC	19	11	1	7
Briley, Sea	16	11	1	4	Milligan, Bal	10	5	2	3
Burks, Bos	13	11	1	1	Molitor, Mil	13	8	0	5
Butler, LA	36	28	2	6	Nixon O, Atl	26	21	1	4
Calderon, Mon	23	16	2	5	O'Neill, Cin	11	7	1	3
Carter J, Tor	14	9	1	4	Owen S, Mon	10	6	0	4
Cole, Cle	24	17	3	4	Pagnozzi, StL	17	13	0	4
Coleman, NYN	17	14	2	1	Pecota, KC	10	7	0	3
Cuyler, Det	12	10	0	2	Pena T, Bos	13	3	1	9
Dascenzo, ChN	10	7	1	2	Perry G, StL	13	8	0	5
Davis C, Min	16	6	2	8	Pettis, Tex	16	13	1	2
DeShields, Mon	31	23	3	5	Phillips, Det	10	5	0	5
Devereaux, Bal	15	9	2	4	Polonia, Cal	35	23	4	8
Dunston, ChN	11	6	0	5	Puckett, Min	12	5	0	7
Fernandez T, SD	15	9	1	5	Raines, ChA	16	15	1	0
Finley S, Hou	22	18	0	4	Reynolds H, Sea	14	8	3	3
Franco Ju, Tex	14	9	3	2	Roberts Bip, SD	15	11	0	4
Gagne, Min	13	9	1	3	Sabo, Cin	16	6	3	7
Gallagher, Cal	10	4	0	6	Samuel, LA	11	8	0	3
Gallego, Oak	12	9	0	3	Sandberg, ChN	15	8	2	5
Gant, Atl	21	15	1	5	Santiago, SD	15	10	1	4
Gilkey, StL	10	8	2	0	Sax S, NYA	16	11	1	4
Gladden, Min	13	9	3	1	Scioscia, LA	10	3	0	7
Gonzalez L, Hou	10	7	0	3	Shumpert, KC	14	11	1	2
Greenwell, Bos	12	5	3	4	Smith O, StL	16	9	5	2
Grissom, Mon	20	17	0	3	Strawberry, LA	14	8	1	5
Gruber, Tor	10	7	1	2	Surhoff BJ, Mil	12	8	0	4
Guillen, ChA	20	15	0	5	Thompson M, StL	14	9	2	3
Gwynn T, SD	10	8	1	1	Thon, Phi	12	5	1	6
Hamilton, Mil	13	6	3	4	Walker L, Mon	13	9	2	2
Harris L, LA	10	3	1	6	Wallach, Mon	10	4	1	5
Hatcher B, Cin	11	9	0	2	White D, Tor	16	10	4	2
Henderson D, Oak	11	6	1	4	Whiten, Cle	10	3	3	4
Henderson R, Oak	22	18	1	3	Yelding, Hou	13	9	2	2
Hudler, StL	11	8	0	3	Zeile, StL	16	11	1	4
Jefferies, NYN	11	5	2	4					
Johnson H, NYN	23	16	1	6					
Johnson L, ChA	14	11	0	3					

ARE POWER HITTERS PULL HITTERS? (p. 82)

The table below lists the number of opposite field home runs hit (**Op**), the total home runs hit (**HR**), and the percentage hit to the opposite field (%).

1989-1991 Both Leagues — Listed Alphabetically
(minimum 25 home runs hit from 1989 through 1991)

Player, Team	HR	Op	%	Player, Team	HR	Op	%	Player, Team	HR	Op	%
Baines, Oak	52	23	44.2	Galarraga, Mon	52	13	25.0	Nokes, NYA	44	0	0.0
Balboni, NYA	34	0	0.0	Gant, Atl	73	0	0.0	O'Brien P, Sea	34	0	0.0
Barfield Je, NYA	65	12	18.5	Gibson K, KC	33	4	12.1	O'Neill, Cin	59	7	11.9
Bell Geo, ChN	64	1	1.6	Gonzalez Juan, Tex	32	3	9.4	Olerud, Tor	31	8	25.8
Bell Jay, Pit	25	5	20.0	Grace, ChN	30	3	10.0	Palmeiro, Tex	48	3	6.3
Belle, Cle	36	3	8.3	Greenwell, Bos	37	1	2.7	Parker D, Tor	54	3	5.6
Benzinger, KC	25	3	12.0	Griffey Jr, Sea	60	16	26.7	Parrish Ln, Cal	60	12	20.0
Bichette, Mil	33	4	12.1	Gruber, Tor	69	8	11.6	Pasqua, ChA	42	9	21.4
Blauser, Atl	31	1	3.2	Guerrero, StL	38	2	5.3	Pendleton, Atl	41	6	14.6
Bonds, Pit	77	17	22.1	Hall M, NYA	48	1	2.1	Phillips, Det	29	2	6.9
Bonilla B, Pit	74	11	14.9	Hayes C, Phi	30	4	13.3	Presley, SD	32	3	9.4
Braggs, Cin	35	0	0.0	Hayes V, Phi	43	1	2.3	Puckett, Min	36	14	38.9
Bream, Atl	26	3	11.5	Henderson D, Oak	60	6	10.0	Ripken C, Bal	76	1	1.3
Brett, KC	36	14	38.9	Henderson R, Oak	58	3	5.2	Sabo, Cin	57	1	1.8
Brooks, NYN	50	8	16.0	Horn, Bal	37	8	21.6	Salazar L, ChN	35	2	5.7
Brunansky, Bos	52	8	15.4	Howell Jk, SD	36	14	38.9	Samuel, LA	36	7	19.4
Buechele, Pit	45	7	15.6	Hrbek, Min	67	8	11.9	Sandberg, ChN	96	4	4.2
Buhner, Sea	43	11	25.6	Incaviglia, Det	56	21	37.5	Santiago, SD	44	8	18.2
Burks, Bos	47	3	6.4	Jackson B, ChA	63	38	60.3	Scioscia, LA	30	0	0.0
Bush, Min	26	0	0.0	Jackson Dar, SD	28	2	7.1	Sierra, Tex	70	12	17.1
Calderon, Mon	47	7	14.9	Jacoby, Oak	31	5	16.1	Smith Lo, Atl	37	5	13.5
Caminiti, Hou	27	0	0.0	James C, Cle	30	3	10.0	Snyder C, Tor	35	2	5.7
Canseco, Oak	98	21	21.4	Jefferies, NYN	36	1	2.8	Sosa, ChA	29	2	6.9
Carter J, Tor	92	9	9.8	Johnson H, NYN	97	3	3.1	Strawberry, LA	94	20	21.3
Clark Jk, Bos	79	13	16.5	Jordan, Phi	26	3	11.5	Stubbs, Mil	38	3	7.9
Clark W, SF	71	22	31.0	Joyner, Cal	45	7	15.6	Tartabull, KC	64	22	34.4
Daniels, LA	48	27	56.3	Justice, Atl	50	6	12.0	Tettleton, Det	72	14	19.4
Daulton, Phi	32	1	3.1	Kelly, NYA	44	18	40.9	Thomas F, ChA	39	13	33.3
Davis A, Sea	50	0	0.0	Kittle, ChA	31	4	12.9	Thompson Ro, SF	47	3	6.4
Davis C, Min	63	19	30.2	Kruk, Phi	36	13	36.1	Thon, Phi	32	1	3.1
Davis E, Cin	69	19	27.5	Larkin B, Cin	31	4	12.9	Trammell, Det	28	0	0.0
Davis G, Bal	66	9	13.6	Leonard J, Sea	34	3	8.8	Van Slyke, Pit	43	4	9.3
Dawson, ChN	79	9	11.4	Maas, NYA	44	2	4.5	Vaughn G, Mil	49	3	6.1
Deer, Det	78	10	12.8	Mack, Min	26	8	30.8	Ventura, ChA	28	3	10.7
Devereaux, Bal	39	9	23.1	Maldonado, Tor	43	6	14.0	Walker L, Mon	35	12	34.3
Downing, Tex	45	6	13.3	Martinez Crm, Cin	26	0	0.0	Wallach, Mon	47	5	10.6
Duncan, Cin	25	8	32.0	Martinez E, Sea	27	2	7.4	Whitaker, Det	69	0	0.0
Dunston, ChN	38	1	2.6	Mattingly, NYA	37	1	2.7	White D, Tor	40	4	10.0
Elster, NYN	25	1	4.0	McGriff F, SD	102	32	31.4	Williams MD, SF	85	16	18.8
Esasky, Atl	30	4	13.3	McGwire, Oak	94	20	21.3	Winfield, Cal	49	9	18.4
Evans Dw, Bal	39	1	2.6	McReynolds, NYN	62	0	0.0	Worthington, Bal	27	3	11.1
Felix, Cal	26	7	26.9	Milligan, Bal	48	9	18.8	Yount, Mil	48	27	56.3
Fielder, Det	95	15	15.8	Mitchell K, SF	109	21	19.3	Zeile, StL	27	0	0.0
Fisk, ChA	49	0	0.0	Molitor, Mil	40	3	7.5	**Major League Avg**	**9,783**	**1,298**	**13.3**
Franco Ju, Tex	39	19	48.7	Moseby, Det	31	0	0.0				
Fryman T, Det	30	3	10.0	Murphy Dl, Phi	62	17	27.4				
Gaetti, Cal	53	4	7.5	Murray E, LA	65	10	15.4				

WHO HAS THE BEST "HEART OF THE ORDER"? (p. 84)

Team total statistics for the Number 3, 4, and 5 hitters

American League — Listed by Most RBI

Team	Avg	HR	RBI	Slg	Main 3-4-5 Hitters
Texas	.297	82	334	.490	Sierra, Franco, Gonzalez Juan
Detroit	.251	105	325	.466	Trammell, Fielder, Tettleton
Oakland	.265	81	317	.453	Canseco, Baines, Steinbach
Minnesota	.298	72	315	.476	Puckett, Hrbek, Davis C
Chicago	.266	75	309	.447	Thomas F, Pasqua, Fisk
Baltimore	.279	79	296	.469	Ripken C, Horn, Milligan
Milwaukee	.247	46	294	.373	Surhoff BJ, Yount, Vaughn G
Boston	.278	61	292	.436	Quintana, Clark Jk, Greenwell
Seattle	.277	58	288	.427	Griffey Jr, O'Brien P, Davis A
Kansas City	.280	59	280	.450	Brett, Tartabull, Benzinger
New York	.268	71	273	.433	Mattingly, Hall M, Maas
California	.257	64	265	.416	Joyner, Winfield, Parker D
Toronto	.257	65	263	.428	Carter J, Olerud, Olerud
Cleveland	.264	49	242	.395	Baerga, Belle, Whiten
AL Average	**.270**	**68**	**291**	**.436**	

National League — Listed by Most RBI

Team	Avg	HR	RBI	Slg	Main 3-4-5 Hitters
Atlanta	.281	81	334	.484	Pendleton, Justice, Bream
San Francisco	.274	97	327	.487	Clark W, Mitchell K, Williams MD
Pittsburgh	.286	66	327	.475	Van Slyke, Bonilla B, Bonds
Chicago	.276	79	314	.453	Sandberg, Dawson, Bell Geo
Los Angeles	.256	71	293	.416	Strawberry, Murray E, Daniels
San Diego	.283	59	291	.436	Gwynn T, McGriff F, Santiago
Cincinnati	.278	71	282	.459	Larkin B, O'Neill, Sabo
New York	.255	71	279	.431	Jefferies, McReynolds, Johnson H
Philadelphia	.261	59	274	.423	Chamberlain, Kruk, Murphy Dl
St. Louis	.274	32	259	.395	Lankford, Guerrero, Jose
Montreal	.269	49	250	.411	Calderon, Wallach, Walker L
Houston	.263	37	248	.392	Bagwell, Gonzalez L, Caminiti
NL Average	**.271**	**63**	**288**	**.434**	

WHO WENT TO THE MOON IN 1991? (p. 86)

Both Leagues — 1991 Home Runs Listed by Distance (440+ Feet)

Dis	Batter	Pitcher	When?	Where?
530	Clark Jk, Bos	Terrell, Det	07/05	@Bos
520	Fielder, Det	Plesac, Mil	09/14	@Mil
490	Pasqua, ChA	Plunk, NYA	04/27	@ChA
490	Buhner, Sea	Taylor W, NYA	07/25	@NYA
480	Belle, Cle	Aldred, Det	09/24	@Det
460	Jackson B, ChA	Abbott K, Cal	09/21	@ChA
460	Chamberlain, Phi	Smiley, Pit	08/20	@Phi
460	Horn, Bal	Wegman, Mil	08/08	@Bal
460	Hrbek, Min	Holman B, Sea	04/27	@Min
460	Buhner, Sea	Ballard, Bal	07/20	@Bal
450	Tettleton, Det	Nagy, Cle	09/24	@Det
450	Fielder, Det	Wegman, Mil	09/15	@Mil
450	Belle, Cle	Saberhagen, KC	04/08	@KC
450	Mack, Min	Cadaret, NYA	06/24	@NYA
450	Canseco, Oak	Abbott, Cal	04/17	@Cal
450	Tettleton, Det	Navarro, Mil	06/26	@Det
450	Gonzalez Juan, Tex	Erickson S, Min	05/23	@Min
450	Bagwell, Hou	Kipper, Pit	05/05	@Pit
450	Davis C, Min	Cadaret, NYA	06/13	@Min
440	McGriff F, SD	Maddux G, ChN	06/06	@ChN
440	Strawberry, LA	Harris GW, SD	08/20	@LA
440	Fielder, Det	Ballard, Bal	07/02	@Bal
440	Walker L, Mon	Armstrong, Cin	06/22	@Cin
440	Daniels, LA	McElroy, ChN	06/17	@LA
440	Spehr, KC	Abbott, Cal	09/29	@KC
440	Tettleton, Det	Barfield Jn, Tex	07/27	@Tex
440	Baerga, Cle	Taylor W, NYA	07/02	@NYA
440	Winfield, Cal	Guthrie, Min	04/13	@Min
440	Deer, Det	West, Min	07/29	@Min
440	McGriff F, SD	Darling, Oak	07/14	@NYN
440	Hrbek, Min	Robinson JM, Bal	06/03	@Min
440	Davis E, Cin	Robinson D, SF	05/27	@SF
440	Nokes, NYA	Lee, Mil	09/23	@Mil
440	Thomas F, ChA	Knudson, Mil	05/01	@Mil
440	Buechele, Pit	Tapani, Min	05/21	@Min
440	Palmeiro, Tex	Tanana, Det	05/03	@Det
440	Baines, Oak	Ryan, Tex	07/02	@Tex
440	White D, Tor	Johnson J, NYA	08/29	@NYA
440	Martinez Crl, Cle	Klink, Oak	07/24	@Cle
440	Braggs, Cin	Berenguer, Atl	04/13	@Cin
440	Tartabull, KC	Stewart D, Oak	07/07	@KC
440	Vaughn M, Bos	Robinson JM, Bal	06/30	@Bal
440	Palmer Dn, Tex	Abbott, Cal	09/19	@Tex
440	Hrbek, Min	Beasley, Cal	08/12	@Min
440	Martinez C, Bal	Sanderson, NYA	09/09	@Bal

WHY SHOULD YOU TAKE A SECOND(ARY) LOOK AT ROB DEER? (p. 88)

1991 Both Leagues — Listed Alphabetically
(minimum 350 plate appearances in 1991)

Player, Team	SA	Player, Team	SA	Player, Team	SA	Player, Team	SA
Alomar R, Tor	.297	Fernandez T, SD	.211	Larkin B, Cin	.362	Rivera L, Bos	.210
Baerga, Cle	.192	Fielder, Det	.377	LaValliere, Pit	.173	Roberts Bip, SD	.189
Bagwell, Hou	.283	Finley S, Hou	.218	Lee M, Tor	.119	Sabo, Cin	.302
Baines, Oak	.324	Fisk, ChA	.239	Lind, Pit	.139	Salazar L, ChN	.210
Bass K, SF	.241	Franco Ju, Tex	.289	Maas, NYA	.344	Samuel, LA	.226
Bell Geo, ChN	.233	Fryman T, Det	.273	Mack, Min	.305	Sandberg, ChN	.368
Bell Jay, Pit	.250	Gaetti, Cal	.189	Magadan, NYN	.282	Santiago, SD	.172
Belle, Cle	.317	Gagne, Min	.199	Martinez Da, Mon	.197	Sax S, NYA	.204
Belliard, Atl	.105	Galarraga, Mon	.176	Martinez E, Sea	.294	Schofield, Cal	.162
Benzinger, KC	.149	Gallego, Oak	.255	Mattingly, NYA	.187	Scioscia, LA	.267
Bichette, Mil	.218	Gant, Atl	.405	McGee, SF	.181	Shumpert, KC	.203
Biggio, Hou	.200	Gantner, Mil	.125	McGriff F, SD	.420	Sierra, Tex	.298
Blauser, Atl	.301	Gibson K, KC	.346	McGwire, Oak	.377	Smith Lo, Atl	.272
Boggs W, Bos	.289	Gladden, Min	.200	McRae B, KC	.164	Smith O, StL	.280
Bonds, Pit	.490	Gomez L, Bal	.279	McReynolds, NYN	.251	Sojo, Cal	.113
Bonilla B, Pit	.343	Gonzalez J, Tex	.292	Merced, Pit	.290	Spiers, Mil	.215
Brett, KC	.265	Gonzalez L, Hou	.271	Milligan, Bal	.306	Steinbach, Oak	.160
Briley, Sea	.178	Grace, ChN	.212	Mitchell K, SF	.372	Stillwell, KC	.179
Brooks, NYN	.300	Greenwell, Bos	.217	Molitor, Mil	.296	Strawberry, LA	.378
Brunansky, Bos	.266	Griffey Jr, Sea	.352	Morandini, Phi	.191	Stubbs, Mil	.268
Buechele, Pit	.260	Griffin Alf, LA	.094	Morris H, Cin	.270	Surhoff BJ, Mil	.129
Buhner, Sea	.382	Grissom, Mon	.272	Murphy Dl, Phi	.254	Tartabull, KC	.417
Burks, Bos	.243	Gruber, Tor	.275	Murray E, LA	.250	Tettleton, Det	.429
Butler, LA	.239	Guerrero, StL	.180	Nixon O, Atl	.274	Teufel, SD	.320
Calderon, Mon	.326	Guillen, ChA	.099	Nokes, NYA	.259	Thomas F, ChA	.479
Caminiti, Hou	.209	Gwynn T, SD	.179	O'Brien P, Sea	.230	Thompson M, StL	.255
Candaele, Hou	.200	Hall M, NYA	.222	O'Neill, Cin	.372	Thompson Ro, SF	.327
Canseco, Oak	.462	Hamilton, Mil	.180	Olerud, Tor	.328	Thon, Phi	.156
Carter J, Tor	.324	Harper B, Min	.166	Olson Greg, Atl	.212	Trammell, Det	.248
Chamberlain, Phi	.253	Harris L, LA	.170	Oquendo, StL	.240	Valle, Sea	.204
Clark Jk, Bos	.412	Hatcher B, Cin	.161	Orsulak, Bal	.146	Van Slyke, Pit	.340
Clark Je, SD	.211	Hayes C, Phi	.167	Owen S, Mon	.200	Vaughn G, Mil	.327
Clark W, SF	.329	Henderson D, Oak	.290	Pagliarulo, Min	.159	Ventura, ChA	.287
Cole, Cle	.235	Henderson R, Oak	.449	Pagnozzi, StL	.157	Vizquel, Sea	.181
Cuyler, Det	.255	Hoiles, Bal	.220	Palmeiro, Tex	.320	Walker C, ChN	.190
Daniels, LA	.295	Horn, Bal	.397	Parker D, Tor	.191	Walker L, Mon	.265
Davis A, Sea	.229	Hrbek, Min	.323	Parrish Ln, Cal	.256	Wallach, Mon	.192
Davis C, Min	.406	Incaviglia, Det	.240	Pasqua, ChA	.350	Whitaker, Det	.406
Dawson, ChN	.254	Jackson Dar, SD	.295	Pecota, KC	.239	White D, Tor	.294
Deer, Det	.402	Jacoby, Oak	.150	Pena T, Bos	.181	Whiten, Cle	.221
DeShields, Mon	.321	James C, Cle	.119	Pendleton, Atl	.285	Williams B, NYA	.278
Devereaux, Bal	.260	Jefferies, NYN	.243	Phillips, Det	.303	Williams MD, SF	.287
Doran, Cin	.224	Johnson H, NYN	.440	Polonia, Cal	.210	Winfield, Cal	.317
Downing, Tex	.319	Johnson L, ChA	.138	Puckett, Min	.201	Yount, Mil	.227
Duncan, Cin	.192	Jose, StL	.236	Quintana, Bos	.247	Zeile, StL	.253
Dunston, ChN	.224	Joyner, Cal	.285	Raines, ChA	.273	**AL Average**	**.243**
Eisenreich, KC	.149	Justice, Atl	.391	Randolph, Mil	.225	**NL Average**	**.241**
Elster, NYN	.221	Kelly, NYA	.317	Reed Jd, Bos	.197	(excluding pitchers)	
Espinoza, NYA	.127	Knoblauch, Min	.209	Reimer, Tex	.284		
Felder, SF	.193	Kruk, Phi	.327	Reynolds H, Sea	.233		
Fermin, Cle	.104	Lankford, StL	.256	Ripken C, Bal	.332		

WHO ARE THE "HUMAN AIR CONDITIONERS"? (p. 90)

The table below shows swings missed (**Sw**) as a % of total pitches swung at (**Pit**).

1991 Both Leagues — Listed Alphabetically
(minimum 400 plate appearances)

Player, Team	Sw	Pit	%	Player, Team	Sw	Pit	%
Alomar R, Tor	197	1309	15.0	Doran, Cin	83	625	13.3
Baerga, Cle	189	1117	16.9	Downing, Tex	125	751	16.6
Bagwell, Hou	292	1104	26.4	Dunston, ChN	159	958	16.6
Baines, Oak	125	856	14.6	Eisenreich, KC	69	638	10.8
Bass K, SF	118	663	17.8	Espinoza, NYA	130	857	15.2
Bell Geo, ChN	182	1082	16.8	Fermin, Cle	49	732	6.7
Bell Jay, Pit	196	1126	17.4	Fernandez T, SD	155	1140	13.6
Belle, Cle	254	959	26.5	Fielder, Det	438	1375	31.9
Benzinger, KC	159	828	19.2	Finley S, Hou	157	1071	14.7
Bichette, Mil	268	936	28.6	Fisk, ChA	177	871	20.3
Biggio, Hou	150	990	15.2	Franco Ju, Tex	158	1092	14.5
Blauser, Atl	126	626	20.1	Fryman T, Det	295	1165	25.3
Boggs W, Bos	45	892	5.0	Gaetti, Cal	334	1256	26.6
Bonds, Pit	141	986	14.3	Gagne, Min	176	872	20.2
Bonilla B, Pit	185	1106	16.7	Galarraga, Mon	211	775	27.2
Brett, KC	190	980	19.4	Gallego, Oak	162	958	16.9
Briley, Sea	109	692	15.8	Gant, Atl	270	1049	25.7
Brooks, NYN	161	694	23.2	Gantner, Mil	101	911	11.1
Brunansky, Bos	159	824	19.3	Gibson K, KC	226	970	23.3
Buechele, Pit	192	979	19.6	Gladden, Min	108	852	12.7
Buhner, Sea	198	738	26.8	Gomez L, Bal	156	793	19.7
Burks, Bos	175	916	19.1	Gonzalez Juan, Tex	278	1037	26.8
Butler, LA	129	1209	10.7	Gonzalez L, Hou	196	937	20.9
Calderon, Mon	181	934	19.4	Grace, ChN	128	1072	11.9
Caminiti, Hou	203	1063	19.1	Greenwell, Bos	136	962	14.1
Candaele, Hou	115	879	13.1	Griffey Jr, Sea	208	1059	19.6
Canseco, Oak	360	1189	30.3	Grissom, Mon	226	1055	21.4
Carter J, Tor	296	1442	20.5	Gruber, Tor	223	880	25.3
Chamberlain, Phi	181	785	23.1	Guerrero, StL	141	810	17.4
Clark Je, SD	207	766	27.0	Guillen, ChA	116	997	11.6
Clark Jk, Bos	299	1026	29.1	Gwynn T, SD	58	844	6.9
Clark W, SF	201	1075	18.7	Hall M, NYA	125	882	14.2
Cole, Cle	58	630	9.2	Hamilton, Mil	69	732	9.4
Cuyler, Det	171	879	19.5	Harper B, Min	93	754	12.3
Daniels, LA	206	845	24.4	Harris L, LA	117	787	14.9
Davis A, Sea	105	767	13.7	Hatcher B, Cin	130	834	15.6
Davis C, Min	285	1150	24.8	Hayes C, Phi	180	906	19.9
Dawson, ChN	264	1159	22.8	Henderson D, Oak	271	1193	22.7
Deer, Det	351	1012	34.7	Henderson R, Oak	100	845	11.8
DeShields, Mon	260	1109	23.4	Hrbek, Min	125	838	14.9
Devereaux, Bal	237	1126	21.0	Jacoby, Oak	99	666	14.9

Player, Team	Sw	Pit	%	Player, Team	Sw	Pit	%
James C, Cle	124	764	16.2	Polonia, Cal	150	1189	12.6
Jefferies, NYN	88	854	10.3	Puckett, Min	210	1141	18.4
Johnson H, NYN	267	1166	22.9	Quintana, Bos	112	824	13.6
Johnson L, ChA	125	965	13.0	Raines, ChA	121	1092	11.1
Jose, StL	278	1155	24.1	Randolph, Mil	70	719	9.7
Joyner, Cal	158	1027	15.4	Reed Jd, Bos	80	1010	7.9
Justice, Atl	205	853	24.0	Reimer, Tex	205	810	25.3
Kelly, NYA	203	987	20.6	Reynolds H, Sea	104	1027	10.1
Knoblauch, Min	68	888	7.7	Ripken C, Bal	131	1236	10.6
Kruk, Phi	219	988	22.2	Rivera L, Bos	159	856	18.6
Lankford, StL	258	1140	22.6	Roberts Bip, SD	155	857	18.1
Larkin B, Cin	118	816	14.5	Sabo, Cin	175	1165	15.0
Lee M, Tor	196	943	20.8	Samuel, LA	332	1305	25.4
Lind, Pit	129	933	13.8	Sandberg, ChN	200	1054	19.0
Maas, NYA	251	971	25.8	Santiago, SD	306	1194	25.6
Mack, Min	208	877	23.7	Sax S, NYA	105	1076	9.8
Magadan, NYN	66	732	9.0	Schofield, Cal	140	860	16.3
Martinez Da, Mon	108	735	14.7	Scioscia, LA	59	594	9.9
Martinez E, Sea	94	964	9.8	Shumpert, KC	151	750	20.1
Mattingly, NYA	77	908	8.5	Sierra, Tex	196	1199	16.3
McGee, SF	208	1099	18.9	Smith Lo, Atl	194	755	25.7
McGriff F, SD	262	1012	25.9	Smith O, StL	82	937	8.8
McGwire, Oak	256	940	27.2	Sojo, Cal	52	636	8.2
McRae B, KC	237	1231	19.3	Spiers, Mil	95	728	13.0
McReynolds, NYN	125	920	13.6	Steinbach, Oak	178	873	20.4
Merced, Pit	153	760	20.1	Stillwell, KC	107	665	16.1
Milligan, Bal	194	932	20.8	Strawberry, LA	258	1025	25.2
Mitchell K, SF	156	767	20.3	Stubbs, Mil	152	721	21.1
Molitor, Mil	155	1248	12.4	Surhoff BJ, Mil	65	774	8.4
Morris H, Cin	128	887	14.4	Tartabull, KC	319	1001	31.9
Murphy Dl, Phi	264	1054	25.0	Tettleton, Det	270	968	27.9
Murray E, LA	244	1161	21.0	Thomas F, ChA	161	1027	15.7
Nixon O, Atl	94	685	13.7	Thompson Ro, SF	193	1020	18.9
Nokes, NYA	156	904	17.3	Thon, Phi	222	970	22.9
O'Brien P, Sea	95	926	10.3	Trammell, Det	75	630	11.9
O'Neill, Cin	195	938	20.8	Van Slyke, Pit	185	969	19.1
Olerud, Tor	119	808	14.7	Vaughn G, Mil	317	1118	28.4
Olson Greg, Atl	86	680	12.6	Ventura, ChA	127	1028	12.4
Oquendo, StL	77	652	11.8	Vizquel, Sea	72	765	9.4
Orsulak, Bal	121	940	12.9	Walker C, ChN	127	689	18.4
Owen S, Mon	115	723	15.9	Walker L, Mon	300	1061	28.3
Pagnozzi, StL	143	901	15.9	Wallach, Mon	276	1132	24.4
Palmeiro, Tex	138	1083	12.7	Whitaker, Det	103	836	12.3
Parker D, Tor	288	1077	26.7	White D, Tor	323	1303	24.8
Parrish Ln, Cal	226	754	30.0	Whiten, Cle	206	802	25.7
Pasqua, ChA	154	780	19.7	Williams MD, SF	390	1252	31.2
Pecota, KC	98	684	14.3	Winfield, Cal	296	1105	26.8
Pena T, Bos	147	900	16.3	Yount, Mil	164	990	16.6
Pendleton, Atl	152	1137	13.4	Zeile, StL	167	946	17.7
Phillips, Det	175	1020	17.2	**MLB Average**			**19.4**

WHAT KIND OF HITTERS HAVE BIG PLATOON DIFFERENTIALS? (p. 92)

Both Leagues — Listed Alphabetically
(players with 500 plate appearances in 1991 — 1989-1991 data)

Player, Team	LH	RH	Dff	Player, Team	LH	RH	Dff	Player, Team	LH	RH	Dff
Alomar R, Tor	.254	.311	-57	Gibson K, KC	.195	.258	-63	Orsulak, Bal	.227	.287	-60
Baerga, Cle	.295	.271	24	Gladden, Min	.279	.270	9	Pagnozzi, StL	.244	.264	-20
Bagwell, Hou	.320	.279	41	Gonzalez Juan,Tex	.277	.250	27	Palmeiro, Tex	.289	.314	-25
Baines, Oak	.270	.305	-35	Gonzalez L, Hou	.171	.278	107	Parker D, Tor	.243	.274	-31
Bell Geo, ChN	.277	.285	-8	Grace, ChN	.280	.307	-27	Pena T, Bos	.290	.233	57
Bell Jay, Pit	.279	.251	28	Greenwell, Bos	.283	.310	-27	Pendleton, Atl	.266	.279	-13
Biggio, Hou	.255	.289	-34	Griffey Jr, Sea	.286	.304	-18	Phillips, Det	.285	.257	28
Boggs W, Bos	.279	.342	-63	Grissom, Mon	.265	.261	4	Polonia, Cal	.266	.319	-53
Bonds, Pit	.286	.275	11	Guillen, ChA	.247	.279	-32	Puckett, Min	.333	.314	19
Bonilla B, Pit	.258	.307	-49	Gwynn T, SD	.293	.338	-45	Quintana, Bos	.336	.258	78
Brett, KC	.259	.307	-48	Hall M, NYA	.253	.275	-22	Raines, ChA	.284	.277	7
Brunansky, Bos	.257	.233	24	Henderson D,Oak	.328	.241	87	Randolph, Mil	.332	.269	63
Buechele, Pit	.276	.229	47	Henderson R,Oak	.292	.287	5	Reed Jd, Bos	.294	.284	10
Burks, Bos	.281	.284	-3	Hrbek, Min	.279	.282	-3	Reynolds H, Sea	.290	.259	31
Butler, LA	.288	.301	-13	Jefferies, NYN	.270	.272	-2	Ripken C, Bal	.279	.277	2
Calderon, Mon	.323	.266	57	Johnson H, NYN	.245	.274	-29	Sabo, Cin	.331	.253	78
Caminiti, Hou	.287	.228	59	Johnson L, ChA	.278	.284	-6	Samuel, LA	.265	.241	24
Candaele, Hou	.310	.246	64	Jose, StL	.301	.272	29	Sandberg, ChN	.308	.290	18
Canseco, Oak	.262	.272	-10	Joyner, Cal	.259	.300	-41	Santiago, SD	.265	.254	11
Carter J, Tor	.247	.250	-3	Kelly, NYA	.322	.268	54	Sax S, NYA	.328	.278	50
Clark Jk, Bos	.323	.223	100	Knoblauch, Min	.257	.290	-33	Sierra, Tex	.333	.281	52
Clark W, SF	.295	.319	-24	Kruk, Phi	.269	.306	-37	Smith O, StL	.278	.266	12
Cuyler, Det	.276	.250	26	Lankford, StL	.249	.262	-13	Strawberry, LA	.249	.262	-13
Daniels, LA	.256	.275	-19	Larkin B, Cin	.312	.310	2	Surhoff BJ, Mil	.293	.267	26
Davis A, Sea	.274	.270	4	Lind, Pit	.251	.252	-1	Tartabull, KC	.308	.277	31
Davis C, Min	.256	.279	-23	Maas, NYA	.206	.243	-37	Tettleton, Det	.242	.251	-9
Dawson, ChN	.297	.271	26	Magadan, NYN	.253	.311	-58	Thomas F, ChA	.386	.291	95
Deer, Det	.248	.178	69	Martinez E, Sea	.320	.284	36	Thompson R, SF	.287	.230	57
DeShields, Mon	.241	.274	-33	Mattingly, NYA	.293	.282	11	Thon, Phi	.264	.256	8
Devereaux, Bal	.269	.248	21	McGee, SF	.300	.309	-9	Van Slyke, Pit	.234	.279	-45
Dunston, ChN	.280	.259	21	McGriff F, SD	.262	.295	-33	Vaughn G, Mil	.215	.247	-32
Espinoza, NYA	.300	.234	66	McGwire, Oak	.231	.220	11	Ventura, ChA	.244	.274	-30
Fernandez T, SD	.256	.274	-18	McRae B, KC	.312	.242	70	Walker L, Mon	.250	.267	-17
Fielder, Det	.335	.243	92	McReynolds,NY	.262	.269	-7	Wallach, Mon	.266	.267	-1
Finley S, Hou	.220	.286	-66	Milligan, Bal	.252	.272	-20	Whitaker, Det	.197	.274	-77
Fisk, ChA	.287	.264	23	Molitor, Mil	.321	.308	13	White D, Tor	.267	.244	23
Franco Ju, Tex	.315	.319	-4	Morris H, Cin	.239	.350	111	Williams MD, SF	.278	.250	28
Fryman T, Det	.304	.255	49	Murphy Dl, Phi	.285	.221	64	Winfield, Cal	.294	.252	42
Gaetti, Cal	.231	.246	-15	Murray E, LA	.245	.300	-55	Yount, Mil	.292	.271	21
Gallego, Oak	.251	.229	22	O'Brien P, Sea	.246	.247	-1	Zeile, StL	.287	.247	40
Gant, Atl	.262	.257	5	O'Neill, Cin	.211	.292	-81	**AL Avg**	**.265**	**.258**	**–7**
Gantner, Mil	.279	.273	6	Olerud, Tor	.274	.258	16	**NL Avg**	**.252**	**.249**	**–3**

SHOULD KEVIN MCREYNOLDS BE KNOWN AS "MR AVERAGE"? (p. 96)

1991 Composite League Statistics — Per 600 Plate Appearances

American League

Pos	Avg	OBP	Slg	AB	R	H	2B	3B	HR	RBI	BB	K
As c	.252	.307	.374	544	56	137	27	1	12	67	41	88
As 1b	.264	.344	.417	526	70	139	26	2	17	75	63	82
As 2b	.268	.338	.365	529	70	142	25	4	6	52	53	62
As 3b	.259	.327	.387	534	67	138	26	2	13	60	52	82
As ss	.255	.310	.352	539	63	137	24	3	7	56	42	78
As lf	.261	.330	.398	535	75	139	24	4	14	68	53	89
As cf	.272	.332	.405	539	76	147	27	5	12	61	48	94
As rf	.258	.325	.436	536	72	138	26	4	20	78	53	113
As dh	.257	.345	.424	522	73	134	26	3	19	73	69	103
As ph	.242	.324	.354	525	52	127	20	2	12	79	61	120

National League

Pos	Avg	OBP	Slg	AB	R	H	2B	3B	HR	RBI	BB	K
As p	.138	.178	.167	515	29	71	10	0	2	27	24	175
As c	.244	.305	.353	540	49	132	25	2	10	61	46	85
As 1b	.267	.341	.411	530	71	142	24	3	15	74	59	85
As 2b	.258	.334	.371	528	67	136	22	4	10	54	59	83
As 3b	.264	.324	.408	542	66	143	25	3	15	70	47	86
As ss	.256	.314	.361	541	63	138	24	4	8	50	46	84
As lf	.260	.330	.409	532	68	139	23	4	16	72	54	89
As cf	.259	.330	.377	535	79	139	23	6	10	48	55	87
As rf	.268	.335	.423	538	71	144	28	4	16	74	54	94
As ph	.216	.294	.314	530	50	114	18	3	9	67	58	116

WHAT'S AN AVERAGE LINEUP (1991 VERSION)? (p. 98)
1991 Composite League Statistics — Per 600 Plate Appearances

American League

Pos	AVG	OBP	SLG	AB	R	H	2B	3B	HR	RBI	BB	K	SB
Batting #1	.273	.350	.396	528	83	144	25	5	10	48	60	77	24
Batting #2	.274	.341	.393	533	76	146	27	3	10	62	52	68	13
Batting #3	.287	.353	.457	532	78	153	30	3	18	82	55	78	10
Batting #4	.264	.343	.446	528	76	139	27	2	22	88	62	100	5
Batting #5	.259	.332	.416	532	70	138	25	2	18	77	57	95	6
Batting #6	.250	.318	.396	537	65	134	24	4	16	70	52	102	6
Batting #7	.248	.311	.378	539	60	134	26	3	13	64	47	103	7
Batting #8	.234	.295	.328	538	56	126	23	2	8	53	45	94	6
Batting #9	.245	.305	.327	536	59	131	21	4	5	50	44	88	13

National League

Pos	AVG	OBP	SLG	AB	R	H	2B	3B	HR	RBI	BB	K	SB
Batting #1	.261	.334	.359	535	83	140	21	5	7	40	57	84	32
Batting #2	.275	.341	.386	532	79	146	25	4	8	52	53	75	19
Batting #3	.279	.348	.435	532	78	149	25	6	15	77	56	80	16
Batting #4	.265	.341	.445	529	73	140	26	2	22	88	60	92	9
Batting #5	.269	.335	.435	536	69	144	28	3	18	84	54	93	12
Batting #6	.245	.307	.376	542	55	133	22	4	14	62	47	93	11
Batting #7	.239	.301	.347	540	49	129	24	3	9	59	47	94	8
Batting #8	.234	.300	.319	538	49	126	20	4	6	48	49	86	6
Batting #9	.168	.222	.222	523	40	88	13	1	4	35	35	154	3

DOES PATIENCE LEAD TO SLUGGING? (p. 104)

The table below lists the number of pitches seen per plate appearance (P/PA) in 1991.

Both Leagues Listed Alphabetically
(minimum 300 plate appearances in 1991)

Player, Team	P/PA	Player, Team	P/PA	Player, Team	P/PA	Player, Team	P/PA
Alomar R, Tor	3.77	Fermin, Cle	3.16	Lankford, StL	3.82	Reed Jd, Bos	3.75
Anderson B, Bal	4.06	Fernandez T, SD	3.69	Larkin B, Cin	3.94	Reimer, Tex	3.71
Baerga, Cle	3.60	Fielder, Det	3.75	LaValliere, Pit	3.15	Reynolds H, Sea	3.72
Bagwell, Hou	3.75	Finley S, Hou	3.50	Lee M, Tor	3.75	Riles, Oak	3.81
Baines, Oak	3.47	Fisk, ChA	3.64	Lemke, Atl	3.15	Ripken B, Bal	3.11
Barfield Je, NYA	4.21	Franco Ju, Tex	3.84	Lewis M, Cle	3.44	Ripken C, Bal	3.31
Bass K, SF	3.51	Fryman T, Det	3.86	Lind, Pit	3.26	Rivera L, Bos	3.82
Bell Geo, ChN	3.44	Gaetti, Cal	3.43	Maas, NYA	4.13	Roberts Bip, SD	3.70
Bell Jay, Pit	3.62	Gagne, Min	3.71	Mack, Min	3.40	Sabo, Cin	3.70
Belle, Cle	3.67	Galarraga, Mon	3.45	Magadan, NYN	4.00	Salazar L, ChN	3.62
Belliard, Atl	3.10	Gallagher, Cal	3.79	Maldonado, Tor	3.77	Samuel, LA	3.88
Benzinger, KC	3.41	Gallego, Oak	3.80	Martinez Cm, Cin	4.12	Sandberg, ChN	3.97
Bichette, Mil	3.54	Gant, Atl	3.76	Martinez Da, Mon	3.76	Santiago, SD	3.37
Biggio, Hou	3.42	Gantner, Mil	3.00	Martinez E, Sea	4.08	Sax S, NYA	3.47
Blauser, Atl	3.98	Gibson K, KC	4.06	Mattingly, NYA	3.27	Schofield, Cal	3.88
Boggs W, Bos	3.85	Gilkey, StL	3.62	McGee, SF	3.69	Scioscia, LA	3.78
Bonds, Pit	3.75	Gladden, Min	3.85	McGriff F, SD	3.88	Shumpert, KC	3.62
Bonilla B, Pit	3.56	Gomez L, Bal	4.02	McGwire, Oak	3.78	Sierra, Tex	3.64
Borders, Tor	3.36	Gonzalez J, Tex	3.57	McRae B, KC	3.62	Skinner J, Cle	3.60
Brett, KC	3.54	Gonzalez L, Hou	3.56	McReynolds, NY	3.55	Smith Lo, Atl	3.79
Briley, Sea	3.69	Grace, ChN	3.49	Merced, Pit	4.23	Smith O, StL	3.57
Brooks, NYN	3.59	Greenwell, Bos	3.00	Meulens, NYA	3.76	Sojo, Cal	3.23
Browne J, Cle	3.51	Griffey Jr, Sea	3.53	Miller K, NYN	3.58	Sosa, ChA	3.59
Brunansky, Bos	3.72	Griffin Alf, LA	3.13	Milligan, Bal	4.17	Spiers, Mil	3.63
Buechele, Pit	3.74	Grissom, Mon	3.62	Mitchell K, SF	3.66	Steinbach, Oak	3.36
Buhner, Sea	3.85	Gruber, Tor	3.34	Molitor, Mil	3.52	Stillwell, KC	3.49
Burks, Bos	3.92	Guerrero, StL	3.51	Morandini, Phi	3.81	Strawberry, LA	4.05
Butler, LA	4.20	Guillen, ChA	2.85	Morris H, Cin	3.64	Stubbs, Mil	3.75
Calderon, Mon	3.56	Gwynn T, SD	3.37	Murphy Dl, Phi	3.41	Surhoff BJ, Mil	3.16
Caminiti, Hou	3.49	Hall M, NYA	3.18	Murray E, LA	3.51	Sveum, Mil	4.13
Candaele, Hou	3.46	Hamilton, Mil	3.71	Myers G, Tor	3.36	Tartabull, KC	3.93
Canseco, Oak	3.97	Harper B, Min	3.16	Nixon O, Atl	3.37	Tettleton, Det	4.15
Carter J, Tor	3.69	Harris L, LA	3.26	Nokes, NYA	3.29	Teufel, SD	4.17
Chamberlain, Phi	3.60	Hatcher B, Cin	3.35	O'Brien P, Sea	3.69	Thomas F, ChA	4.31
Clark Jk, Bos	4.28	Hayes C, Phi	3.46	O'Neill, Cin	3.71	Thompson M, StL	3.66
Clark Je, SD	3.51	Hayes V, Phi	3.74	Olerud, Tor	3.86	Thompson R, SF	3.86
Clark W, SF	3.54	Henderson D, Oak	3.93	Olson Greg, Atl	3.41	Thon, Phi	2.96
Cole, Cle	3.73	Henderson R, Oak	4.34	Oquendo, StL	3.76	Trammell, Det	3.46
Coleman, NYN	3.96	Hoiles, Bal	3.81	Orsulak, Bal	3.42	Treadway, Atl	3.37
Cuyler, Det	3.68	Horn, Bal	3.96	Owen S, Mon	3.60	Valle, Sea	3.55
Daniels, LA	3.83	Howard T, SD	3.58	Pagliarulo, Min	3.58	Van Slyke, Pit	3.94
Daulton, Phi	4.07	Hrbek, Min	3.55	Pagnozzi, StL	3.37	Vaughn G, Mil	3.79
Davis A, Sea	4.04	Huson, Tex	3.81	Palmeiro, Tex	3.63	Ventura, ChA	3.86
Davis C, Min	3.90	Incaviglia, Det	3.67	Palmer Dn, Tex	4.20	Vizquel, Sea	3.47
Davis E, Cin	4.05	Jackson Dar, SD	3.60	Parker D, Tor	3.61	Walker C, ChN	3.71
Dawson, ChN	3.49	Jacoby, Oak	3.04	Parrish Ln, Cal	3.91	Walker L, Mon	3.62
Deer, Det	4.26	James C, Cle	3.53	Pasqua, ChA	3.75	Wallach, Mon	3.55
DeShields, Mon	4.24	Jefferies, NYN	3.75	Pecota, KC	3.66	Whitaker, Det	3.88
Devereaux, Bal	3.93	Johnson H, NYN	3.78	Pena T, Bos	3.44	White D, Tor	3.87
Doran, Cin	3.67	Johnson L, ChA	3.08	Pendleton, Atl	3.47	Whiten, Cle	3.53
Downing, Tex	4.21	Jordan, Phi	3.09	Pettis, Tex	4.26	Williams B, NYA	3.87
Duncan, Cin	3.32	Jose, StL	3.46	Phillips, Det	3.94	Williams MD, SF	3.39
Dunston, ChN	3.23	Joyner, Cal	3.60	Polonia, Cal	3.74	Wilson W, Oak	3.71
Eisenreich, KC	3.33	Justice, Atl	3.85	Puckett, Min	3.19	Winfield, Cal	3.84
Elster, NYN	3.72	Kelly P, NYA	3.36	Quintana, Bos	3.73	Yount, Mil	3.63
Espinoza, NYA	2.94	Kelly, NYA	3.57	Raines, ChA	3.65	Zeile, StL	4.00
Evans Dw, Bal	3.91	Knoblauch, Min	3.44	Randolph, Mil	3.77	**MLB Average**	**3.65**
Felder, SF	3.57	Kruk, Phi	3.72	Reed Jf, Cin	3.81		

IS PATIENCE A VIRTUE? (p. 106)

The first column shows the percentage of times the batter swung at the first pitch (**S%**); the second, how often he put his first swing in play (**IP%**); the third, how successful he was in terms of batting average (**Avg**).

1989-1991 Both Leagues — Listed Alphabetically
(minimum 500 plate appearances in 1991)

Player, Team	S%	IP%	Avg	Player, Team	S%	IP%	Avg	Player, Team	S%	IP%	Avg
Alomar R, Tor	23.9	40.9	.358	Gibson K, KC	28.3	42.2	.314	Orsulak, Bal	32.3	45.7	.280
Baerga, Cle	23.2	52.9	.345	Gladden, Min	31.7	50.9	.341	Pagnozzi, StL	38.2	45.5	.309
Bagwell, Hou	33.2	39.3	.385	Gonzalez J, Tex	23.2	40.9	.243	Palmeiro, Tex	22.1	55.2	.332
Baines, Oak	38.2	49.3	.384	Gonzalez L, Hou	37.9	41.9	.310	Parker D, Tor	44.2	40.0	.300
Bell Geo, ChN	18.5	49.4	.341	Grace, ChN	36.2	56.1	.329	Pena T, Bos	38.8	45.8	.328
Bell Jay, Pit	29.7	45.0	.309	Greenwell, Bos	38.4	55.9	.337	Pendleton, Atl	38.3	44.5	.321
Biggio, Hou	27.5	46.3	.327	Griffey Jr, Sea	32.8	41.8	.391	Phillips, Det	25.6	49.7	.336
Boggs W, Bos	6.0	53.7	.369	Grissom, Mon	23.5	44.4	.255	Polonia, Cal	33.4	41.2	.335
Bonds, Pit	25.3	47.4	.303	Guillen, ChA	50.4	49.6	.282	Puckett, Min	46.9	50.3	.367
Bonilla B, Pit	38.1	46.4	.349	Gwynn T, SD	19.3	62.7	.340	Quintana, Bos	31.7	52.1	.347
Brett, KC	36.2	46.9	.328	Hall M, NYA	42.2	50.3	.344	Raines, ChA	28.0	52.0	.316
Brunansky, Bos	27.7	47.8	.306	Henderson D, Oak	32.0	35.2	.344	Randolph, Mil	24.5	59.7	.290
Buechele, Pit	27.6	41.3	.293	Henderson R, Oak	11.1	42.2	.258	Reed Jd, Bos	15.9	53.1	.314
Burks, Bos	21.8	47.2	.313	Hrbek, Min	43.0	49.5	.347	Reynolds H, Sea	17.8	57.4	.278
Butler, LA	22.7	49.7	.333	Jefferies, NYN	19.9	52.7	.226	Ripken C, Bal	22.8	49.4	.338
Calderon, Mon	46.6	40.7	.317	Johnson H, NYN	31.2	43.2	.361	Sabo, Cin	28.3	46.3	.345
Caminiti, Hou	36.3	46.3	.314	Johnson L, ChA	39.4	59.1	.346	Samuel, LA	30.4	33.9	.335
Candaele, Hou	31.2	49.4	.291	Jose, StL	43.2	40.8	.365	Sandberg, ChN	18.7	41.8	.406
Canseco, Oak	26.5	31.6	.415	Joyner, Cal	30.7	45.9	.315	Santiago, SD	46.3	42.3	.319
Carter J, Tor	34.6	34.1	.348	Kelly, NYA	31.9	41.6	.350	Sax S, NYA	17.8	51.4	.320
Clark Jk, Bos	35.0	30.3	.373	Knoblauch, Min	24.0	66.7	.304	Sierra, Tex	23.2	50.5	.312
Clark W, SF	40.5	39.3	.367	Kruk, Phi	31.8	44.0	.317	Smith O, StL	24.5	54.6	.330
Cuyler, Det	31.7	46.0	.368	Lankford, StL	27.5	36.4	.325	Strawberry, LA	28.3	40.8	.299
Daniels, LA	26.1	45.8	.388	Larkin B, Cin	16.2	56.5	.321	Surhoff BJ, Mil	21.2	65.6	.338
Davis A, Sea	12.3	51.7	.294	Lind, Pit	23.1	49.9	.273	Tartabull, KC	31.7	34.1	.381
Davis C, Min	40.4	38.6	.356	Maas, NYA	22.5	41.5	.287	Tettleton, Det	19.3	36.8	.310
Dawson, ChN	30.4	43.8	.325	Magadan, NYN	18.4	57.4	.364	Thomas F, ChA	14.0	43.0	.518
Deer, Det	31.2	29.2	.259	Martinez E, Sea	14.1	46.9	.322	Thompson Ro, SF	27.8	40.7	.341
DeShields, Mon	20.6	41.4	.327	Mattingly, NYA	13.2	62.8	.336	Thon, Phi	41.5	48.8	.306
Devereaux, Bal	17.0	52.7	.276	McGee, SF	43.8	34.0	.407	Van Slyke, Pit	28.4	48.6	.342
Dunston, ChN	36.9	39.4	.341	McGriff F, SD	31.1	38.7	.368	Vaughn G, Mil	38.6	41.1	.283
Espinoza, NYA	47.8	53.2	.305	McGwire, Oak	38.0	40.4	.316	Ventura, ChA	18.7	49.8	.274
Fernandez T, SD	35.3	45.3	.334	McRae B, KC	32.8	43.0	.233	Walker L, Mon	43.6	36.0	.323
Fielder, Det	35.8	32.7	.376	McReynolds, NY	25.9	48.7	.316	Wallach, Mon	37.5	43.5	.359
Finley S, Hou	24.4	52.9	.353	Milligan, Bal	25.9	35.0	.331	Whitaker, Det	27.0	47.5	.261
Fisk, ChA	27.2	41.5	.361	Molitor, Mil	34.2	44.4	.344	White D, Tor	29.0	35.7	.316
Franco Ju, Tex	16.2	49.1	.353	Morris H, Cin	32.0	50.4	.370	Williams MD, SF	47.8	37.5	.319
Fryman T, Det	32.8	39.4	.345	Murphy Dl, Phi	42.5	41.3	.309	Winfield, Cal	20.9	42.7	.370
Gaetti, Cal	49.7	38.5	.324	Murray E, LA	42.7	38.7	.333	Yount, Mil	25.6	50.7	.308
Gallego, Oak	32.7	46.3	.294	O'Brien P, Sea	22.8	58.4	.284	Zeile, StL	17.3	44.7	.344
Gant, Atl	30.6	40.3	.340	O'Neill, Cin	32.5	43.8	.355	**MLB Average**	**30.6**	**44.2**	**.314**
Gantner, Mil	37.9	56.3	.296	Olerud, Tor	24.4	50.7	.343				

CAN YOU BE AN MVP, AND YET NOT CREATE RUNS? (p. 109)

1991 Both Leagues — Listed Alphabetically
(minimum 500 plate appearances in 1991)

Player, Team	RC	OW%	Player, Team	RC	OW%	Player, Team	RC	OW%
Alomar R, Tor	107.4	.639	Gibson K, KC	68.3	.554	Orsulak, Bal	55.9	.460
Baerga, Cle	81.9	.553	Gladden, Min	48.6	.375	Pagnozzi, StL	48.8	.427
Bagwell, Hou	98.1	.708	Gonzalez Juan, Tex	81.8	.581	Palmeiro, Tex	128.9	.742
Baines, Oak	89.0	.686	Gonzalez L, Hou	64.8	.566	Parker D, Tor	51.8	.382
Bell Geo, ChN	81.5	.616	Grace, ChN	84.3	.581	Pena T, Bos	39.8	.274
Bell Jay, Pit	84.7	.556	Greenwell, Bos	80.8	.591	Pendleton, Atl	107.4	.729
Biggio, Hou	79.1	.628	Griffey Jr, Sea	118.2	.762	Phillips, Det	96.8	.652
Boggs W, Bos	106.6	.731	Grissom, Mon	68.9	.518	Polonia, Cal	80.5	.522
Bonds, Pit	118.2	.795	Guillen, ChA	48.0	.318	Puckett, Min	90.6	.581
Bonilla B, Pit	114.0	.751	Gwynn T, SD	78.0	.639	Quintana, Bos	74.1	.602
Brett, KC	64.6	.480	Hall M, NYA	71.7	.583	Raines, ChA	85.0	.532
Brunansky, Bos	55.7	.448	Henderson D, Oak	92.5	.625	Randolph, Mil	72.2	.660
Buechele, Pit	74.4	.528	Henderson R, Oak	91.3	.686	Reed Jd, Bos	82.6	.521
Burks, Bos	60.4	.481	Hrbek, Min	78.5	.639	Reynolds H, Sea	77.7	.457
Butler, LA	93.0	.629	Jefferies, NYN	63.8	.557	Ripken C, Bal	133.9	.747
Calderon, Mon	84.7	.702	Johnson H, NYN	106.8	.707	Sabo, Cin	103.1	.710
Caminiti, Hou	64.9	.464	Johnson L, ChA	59.3	.376	Samuel, LA	78.4	.555
Candaele, Hou	55.2	.516	Jose, StL	87.9	.651	Sandberg, ChN	114.2	.743
Canseco, Oak	115.9	.708	Joyner, Cal	97.5	.680	Santiago, SD	60.9	.428
Carter J, Tor	107.1	.635	Kelly, NYA	71.9	.557	Sax S, NYA	92.1	.559
Clark Jk, Bos	86.0	.644	Knoblauch, Min	76.0	.537	Sierra, Tex	117.3	.677
Clark W, SF	110.4	.762	Kruk, Phi	99.0	.727	Smith O, StL	85.7	.647
Cuyler, Det	61.5	.485	Lankford, StL	67.4	.488	Strawberry, LA	91.7	.703
Daniels, LA	65.2	.584	Larkin B, Cin	93.0	.762	Surhoff BJ, Mil	53.9	.385
Davis A, Sea	48.0	.365	Lind, Pit	48.2	.383	Tartabull, KC	115.9	.801
Davis C, Min	107.4	.718	Maas, NYA	72.0	.540	Tettleton, Det	99.2	.703
Dawson, ChN	79.3	.595	Magadan, NYN	62.3	.607	Thomas F, ChA	144.7	.822
Deer, Det	59.7	.478	Martinez E, Sea	99.9	.688	Thompson Ro, SF	81.5	.658
DeShields, Mon	74.3	.519	Mattingly, NYA	75.7	.508	Thon, Phi	52.3	.399
Devereaux, Bal	79.8	.498	McGee, SF	71.1	.613	Van Slyke, Pit	85.1	.685
Dunston, ChN	58.8	.492	McGriff F, SD	107.1	.754	Vaughn G, Mil	82.2	.575
Espinoza, NYA	45.3	.341	McGwire, Oak	65.3	.484	Ventura, ChA	97.2	.603
Fernandez T, SD	69.7	.528	McRae B, KC	64.2	.378	Walker L, Mon	78.0	.662
Fielder, Det	110.1	.654	McReynolds, NYN	69.7	.561	Wallach, Mon	55.7	.381
Finley S, Hou	79.7	.557	Milligan, Bal	70.7	.549	Whitaker, Det	99.0	.739
Fisk, ChA	51.7	.411	Molitor, Mil	131.9	.741	White D, Tor	104.5	.624
Franco Ju, Tex	117.8	.748	Morris H, Cin	89.2	.742	Williams MD, SF	88.0	.620
Fryman T, Det	75.3	.511	Murphy Dl, Phi	66.6	.505	Winfield, Cal	83.7	.556
Gaetti, Cal	62.7	.395	Murray E, LA	72.7	.527	Yount, Mil	63.4	.477
Gallego, Oak	63.2	.483	O'Brien P, Sea	66.0	.441	Zeile, StL	81.6	.600
Gant, Atl	96.5	.670	O'Neill, Cin	89.4	.671			
Gantner, Mil	57.7	.421	Olerud, Tor	72.4	.588			

HOW IMPORTANT ARE GOOD PINCH HITTERS? (p. 114)

1991 Pinch Hitters — Both Leagues combined
(minimum 15 pinch hit at-bats in 1991)

Team	AB	H	2B	3B	HR	RBI	BB	K	AVG	OBP	SLG
Abner, Cal	15	2	0	0	0	0	0	6	.133	.133	.133
Aldrete, Cle	20	2	1	0	0	3	5	3	.100	.280	.150
Alicea, StL	39	8	1	0	0	0	6	10	.205	.311	.231
Anderson D, SF	29	4	1	0	0	2	3	3	.138	.219	.172
Azocar, SD	26	6	1	0	0	5	0	6	.231	.259	.269
Backman, Phi	38	7	4	0	0	8	8	10	.184	.319	.289
Barberie, Mon	16	1	1	0	0	1	2	7	.063	.211	.125
Bass K, SF	24	3	1	1	0	3	3	2	.125	.222	.250
Benzinger, KC	22	3	0	0	0	1	1	3	.136	.167	.136
Bergman, Det	25	3	1	0	0	3	3	9	.120	.207	.160
Berryhill, Atl	17	2	0	0	0	1	0	7	.118	.118	.118
Blauser, Atl	26	6	0	0	0	3	2	5	.231	.286	.231
Borders, Tor	18	5	2	0	1	6	1	3	.278	.300	.556
Boston, NYN	27	6	1	0	0	1	2	4	.222	.276	.259
Bradley S, Sea	25	3	1	0	0	2	2	5	.120	.185	.160
Braggs, Cin	15	4	0	0	2	4	1	7	.267	.313	.667
Briley, Sea	24	7	2	0	0	1	1	6	.292	.320	.375
Browne J, Cle	34	11	0	0	1	3	2	4	.324	.351	.412
Bullock, Mon	48	10	2	0	0	3	7	9	.208	.304	.250
Bush, Min	34	13	2	0	2	8	8	4	.382	.500	.618
Cabrera, Atl	18	3	1	0	0	3	0	8	.167	.167	.222
Candaele, Hou	19	3	0	0	0	3	2	1	.158	.238	.158
Carreon, NYN	35	12	1	0	3	7	4	7	.343	.425	.629
Carter G, LA	27	2	1	0	0	1	4	5	.074	.194	.111
Cochrane, Sea	16	4	2	0	0	1	0	4	.250	.294	.375
Cotto, Sea	15	10	0	1	0	5	0	1	.667	.667	.800
Cromartie, KC	35	8	0	0	1	5	5	7	.229	.325	.314
Dascenzo, ChN	28	3	1	0	0	1	1	4	.107	.167	.143
Daugherty, Tex	15	2	1	0	0	1	3	4	.133	.263	.200
Davidson M, Hou	29	4	0	0	0	3	6	4	.138	.286	.138
Davis A, Sea	16	3	0	0	0	2	0	3	.188	.188	.188
Doran, Cin	15	4	1	1	0	5	4	1	.267	.421	.467
Downing, Tex	24	9	1	0	0	6	1	3	.375	.400	.417
Eisenreich, KC	32	7	2	1	0	2	2	7	.219	.265	.344
Evans Dw, Bal	25	10	2	0	1	6	7	5	.400	.531	.600
Felder, SF	36	10	1	0	0	3	5	1	.278	.366	.306
Gonzalez Jo, Cle	18	0	0	0	0	0	2	9	.000	.100	.000
Gregg, Atl	39	9	4	0	0	2	6	8	.231	.333	.333
Gwynn C, LA	56	13	2	0	2	13	3	10	.232	.279	.375
Hansen, LA	32	10	2	0	1	4	1	5	.313	.333	.469
Harris L, LA	24	3	0	0	0	2	2	1	.125	.192	.125
Hatcher B, Cin	19	3	0	0	0	0	0	5	.158	.158	.158
Herr, SF	28	5	0	0	0	2	5	9	.179	.303	.179
Hill D, Cal	16	3	1	0	0	3	2	1	.188	.278	.250
Horn, Bal	24	7	2	0	3	7	2	9	.292	.346	.750
Howard T, SD	26	3	1	0	1	3	2	8	.115	.179	.269
Howell Jk, SD	15	4	0	0	0	4	2	2	.267	.353	.267
Hudler, StL	27	4	2	0	0	2	3	7	.148	.226	.222
Hunter B, Atl	18	3	1	0	1	3	0	6	.167	.158	.389
Jackson Dar, SD	23	3	0	0	1	2	5	7	.130	.286	.261
Javier, LA	52	5	0	1	0	4	14	.096	.161	.135
Jones Chris, Cin	26	8	0	1	1	3	1	7	.308	.333	.500
Jones Ron, Phi	26	4	2	0	0	3	2	9	.154	.214	.231

Team	AB	H	2B	3B	HR	RBI	BB	K	AVG	OBP	SLG
Jones Tr, Sea	20	6	2	0	0	3	6	4	.300	.481	.400
Jordan, Phi	28	9	3	0	0	6	2	7	.321	.355	.429
Kingery, SF	44	11	0	1	0	7	8	8	.250	.365	.295
Lampkin, SD	24	5	1	1	0	1	2	5	.208	.269	.333
Larkin G, Min	19	3	0	0	0	2	5	2	.158	.333	.158
Leius, Min	25	11	2	0	0	2	5	7	.440	.533	.520
Lemke, Atl	27	9	1	0	0	5	0	4	.333	.333	.370
Leonard M, SF	26	7	2	1	0	5	3	5	.269	.323	.423
Lindeman, Phi	36	13	1	0	0	2	2	5	.361	.395	.389
Lyons S, Bos	21	1	0	0	0	0	0	4	.048	.048	.048
Martinez Crm, Cin	19	5	0	0	3	3	2	3	.263	.333	.737
McClendon, Pit	33	9	1	0	2	8	5	6	.273	.400	.485
Merced, Pit	17	6	0	0	1	3	3	7	.353	.450	.529
Merullo, ChA	41	7	0	0	2	8	1	10	.171	.178	.317
Morris Jn, Phi	28	6	0	0	0	2	2	6	.214	.290	.214
Mulliniks, Tor	19	3	0	0	0	4	3	7	.158	.261	.158
Newman A, Min	21	5	0	0	0	3	1	5	.238	.261	.238
Newson, ChA	22	8	2	0	0	5	6	6	.364	.500	.455
Noboa, Mon	46	14	2	0	1	2	1	6	.304	.319	.413
Nokes, NYA	17	4	0	0	0	1	2	3	.235	.316	.235
Oberkfell, Hou	32	6	2	0	0	8	6	6	.188	.316	.250
Ortiz Ja, Hou	21	5	2	0	0	1	5	2	.238	.385	.333
Perry G, StL	41	11	0	1	1	13	6	8	.268	.354	.390
Petralli, Tex	22	3	1	0	0	1	4	6	.136	.269	.182
Quinones L, Cin	36	6	0	0	1	4	6	5	.167	.279	.250
Quintana, Bos	17	5	1	0	0	4	1	3	.294	.333	.353
Quirk, Oak	17	5	1	0	0	3	0	2	.294	.294	.353
Ramirez R, Hou	39	9	2	0	0	7	5	7	.231	.311	.282
Redus, Pit	31	9	1	0	1	3	5	8	.290	.389	.419
Reimer, Tex	28	8	3	0	2	5	3	7	.286	.355	.607
Riles, Oak	27	4	0	1	0	3	3	7	.148	.233	.222
Rohde, Hou	17	2	0	0	0	0	3	4	.118	.250	.118
Salas, Det	15	1	0	0	1	4	0	5	.067	.167	.267
Sasser, NYN	38	10	0	0	2	7	1	4	.263	.275	.421
Segui, Bal	24	6	0	0	0	3	2	4	.250	.308	.250
Seitzer, KC	20	11	2	1	0	3	2	0	.550	.591	.750
Sharperson, LA	22	6	1	0	0	3	4	4	.273	.385	.318
Sheridan, NYA	25	5	1	0	2	2	6	10	.200	.355	.480
Smith Dw, ChN	45	11	3	1	0	6	2	7	.244	.277	.356
Smith Lo, Atl	22	4	0	0	0	0	1	4	.182	.217	.182
Snyder C, Tor	15	2	1	0	0	1	1	5	.133	.188	.200
Stanley M, Tex	27	6	2	0	0	5	5	9	.222	.333	.296
Stillwell, KC	18	2	0	0	1	1	1	3	.111	.158	.278
Tabler, Tor	21	9	2	0	0	6	9	1	.429	.563	.524
Templeton, NYN	36	4	2	0	1	5	2	5	.111	.158	.250
Thompson M, StL	28	10	0	1	1	6	5	5	.357	.455	.536
Tolentino, Hou	30	6	1	0	1	5	2	6	.200	.242	.333
Varsho, Pit	41	9	2	0	1	6	2	10	.220	.256	.341
Venable, Cal	16	3	0	0	1	1	1	3	.188	.278	.375
Walker C, ChN	32	13	1	0	1	6	6	4	.406	.500	.531
Walton, ChN	25	5	1	0	0	3	1	7	.200	.222	.240
Webster M, LA	35	7	2	1	0	6	6	11	.200	.317	.314
Whitt, Bal	16	4	0	0	0	0	4	4	.250	.400	.250
Wilkerson, Pit	33	7	0	1	1	5	3	4	.212	.270	.364
Wilson C, StL	37	11	2	0	0	11	3	6	.297	.333	.351
Wilson W, Oak	21	6	1	0	0	2	2	3	.286	.348	.333
Winningham, Cin	33	13	0	0	0	2	2	8	.394	.429	.394
Young G, Hou	23	3	0	0	0	0	6	4	.130	.310	.130

WILL THE LINEOUTS OF '91 BECOME THE LINE HITS OF '92? (p. 122)

The following table lists the number of lineouts a player hit into in 1991 (**LO**); his lineouts per at bat, or the number of points his batting average would have gone up if these all had been hits (**Inc**); and his batting average if these all had been hits (**New Avg**).

1991 Both Leagues — Listed Alphabetically
(minimum 500 plate appearances in 1991)

Player, Team	LO	Inc	New Avg	Player, Team	LO	Inc	New Avg	Player, Team	LO	Inc	New Avg
Alomar R, Tor	33	.052	.347	Gibson K, KC	11	.024	.260	Orsulak, Bal	36	.074	.352
Baerga, Cle	28	.047	.336	Gladden, Min	23	.050	.297	Pagnozzi, StL	23	.050	.314
Bagwell, Hou	31	.056	.350	Gonzalez J, Tex	14	.026	.290	Palmeiro, Tex	22	.035	.357
Baines, Oak	18	.037	.332	Gonzalez L, Hou	22	.047	.300	Parker D, Tor	10	.020	.259
Bell Geo, ChN	38	.068	.353	Grace, ChN	39	.063	.336	Pena T, Bos	24	.052	.282
Bell Jay, Pit	23	.038	.308	Greenwell, Bos	30	.055	.355	Pendleton, Atl	20	.034	.353
Biggio, Hou	26	.048	.342	Griffey Jr, Sea	21	.038	.365	Phillips, Det	27	.048	.332
Boggs W, Bos	44	.081	.412	Grissom, Mon	24	.043	.310	Polonia, Cal	29	.048	.344
Bonds, Pit	24	.047	.339	Guillen, ChA	25	.048	.321	Puckett, Min	22	.036	.355
Bonilla B, Pit	19	.033	.334	Gwynn T, SD	46	.087	.404	Quintana, Bos	15	.031	.326
Brett, KC	25	.050	.305	Hall M, NYA	16	.033	.317	Raines, ChA	24	.039	.307
Brunansky, Bos	33	.072	.301	Henderson D, Ok	31	.054	.330	Randolph, Mil	13	.030	.357
Buechele, Pit	22	.042	.304	Henderson R, Oak	28	.060	.328	Reed Jd, Bos	43	.070	.353
Burks, Bos	15	.032	.283	Hrbek, Min	17	.037	.320	Reynolds H, Sea	35	.055	.309
Butler, LA	39	.063	.359	Jefferies, NYN	19	.039	.311	Ripken C, Bal	32	.049	.372
Calderon, Mon	14	.030	.330	Johnson H, NYN	14	.025	.284	Sabo, Cin	20	.034	.335
Caminiti, Hou	27	.047	.300	Johnson L, ChA	37	.063	.337	Samuel, LA	28	.047	.318
Candaele, Hou	33	.072	.334	Jose, StL	23	.040	.345	Sandberg, ChN	31	.053	.344
Canseco, Oak	11	.019	.285	Joyner, Cal	23	.042	.343	Santiago, SD	35	.060	.328
Carter J, Tor	22	.034	.307	Kelly, NYA	18	.037	.305	Sax S, NYA	27	.041	.345
Clark Jk, Bos	21	.044	.293	Knoblauch, Min	24	.042	.324	Sierra, Tex	19	.029	.336
Clark W, SF	31	.055	.356	Kruk, Phi	31	.058	.351	Smith O, StL	28	.051	.336
Cuyler, Det	27	.057	.314	Lankford, StL	25	.044	.295	Strawberry, LA	24	.048	.313
Daniels, LA	22	.048	.297	Larkin B, Cin	10	.022	.323	Surhoff BJ, Mil	29	.057	.347
Davis A, Sea	23	.050	.271	Lind, Pit	19	.038	.303	Tartabull, KC	13	.027	.343
Davis C, Min	20	.037	.315	Maas, NYA	12	.024	.244	Tettleton, Det	18	.036	.299
Dawson, ChN	29	.052	.323	Magadan, NYN	24	.057	.316	Thomas F, ChA	23	.041	.360
Deer, Det	18	.040	.219	Martinez E, Sea	31	.057	.364	Thompson R, SF	20	.041	.303
DeShields, Mon	17	.030	.268	Mattingly, NYA	20	.034	.322	Thon, Phi	36	.067	.319
Devereaux, Bal	22	.036	.296	McGee, SF	18	.036	.348	Van Slyke, Pit	22	.045	.310
Dunston, ChN	27	.055	.315	McGriff F, SD	20	.038	.316	Vaughn G, Mil	22	.041	.284
Espinoza, NYA	17	.035	.292	McGwire, Oak	9	.019	.219	Ventura, ChA	22	.036	.320
Fernandez T, SD	35	.063	.335	McRae B, KC	29	.046	.307	Walker L, Mon	16	.033	.322
Fielder, Det	23	.037	.298	McReynolds, NY	21	.040	.299	Wallach, Mon	26	.045	.270
Finley S, Hou	23	.039	.324	Milligan, Bal	17	.035	.298	Whitaker, Det	28	.060	.338
Fisk, ChA	16	.035	.276	Molitor, Mil	32	.048	.373	White D, Tor	18	.028	.310
Franco Ju, Tex	23	.039	.380	Morris H, Cin	29	.061	.379	Williams MD, SF	23	.039	.307
Fryman T, Det	25	.045	.303	Murphy Dl, Phi	25	.046	.298	Winfield, Cal	20	.035	.298
Gaetti, Cal	16	.027	.273	Murray E, LA	22	.038	.299	Yount, Mil	31	.062	.322
Gallego, Oak	24	.050	.297	O'Brien P, Sea	25	.045	.293	Zeile, StL	14	.025	.304
Gant, Atl	12	.021	.273	O'Neill, Cin	22	.041	.297	**MLB Average**		**.044**	**.300**
Gantner, Mil	31	.059	.342	Olerud, Tor	20	.044	.300				

Is McGwire Undercutting Himself to Oblivion? (p. 124)

The table below lists the number of groundballs hit (**Grd**), the number of flyballs hit (**Fly**), and the ratio of the two (**G/F**).

Both Leagues — Listed Alphabetically
(minimum 600 balls hit in play from 1989 through 1991)

Player, Team	Grd	Fly	G/F	Player, Team	Grd	Fly	G/F
Alomar R, Tor	765	474	1.61	Eisenreich, KC	600	392	1.53
Baines, Oak	565	326	1.73	Elster, NYN	377	380	0.99
Barfield Je, NYA	368	347	1.06	Espinoza, NYA	586	371	1.58
Bass K, SF	360	271	1.33	Evans Dw, Bal	415	401	1.03
Bell Geo, ChN	545	661	0.82	Felder, SF	397	223	1.78
Bell Jay, Pit	513	448	1.15	Felix, Cal	420	247	1.70
Benzinger, KC	503	438	1.15	Fermin, Cle	719	242	2.97
Biggio, Hou	588	426	1.38	Fernandez T, SD	714	479	1.49
Blauser, Atl	376	388	0.97	Fielder, Det	321	362	0.89
Boggs W, Bos	797	411	1.94	Finley S, Hou	544	320	1.70
Bonds, Pit	521	572	0.91	Fisk, ChA	429	416	1.03
Bonilla B, Pit	617	658	0.94	Fletcher S, ChA	527	375	1.41
Braggs, Cin	415	290	1.43	Franco Ju, Tex	723	413	1.75
Brett, KC	610	449	1.36	Gaetti, Cal	572	542	1.06
Briley, Sea	450	294	1.53	Gagne, Min	403	414	0.97
Brooks, NYN	546	423	1.29	Galarraga, Mon	537	339	1.58
Browne J, Cle	591	410	1.44	Gallagher, Cal	369	308	1.20
Brunansky, Bos	414	584	0.71	Gallego, Oak	477	342	1.39
Buechele, Pit	419	374	1.12	Gant, Atl	423	514	0.82
Burks, Bos	534	453	1.18	Gantner, Mil	567	326	1.74
Butler, LA	836	363	2.30	Gibson K, KC	326	324	1.01
Calderon, Mon	655	505	1.30	Gladden, Min	540	458	1.18
Caminiti, Hou	601	504	1.19	Grace, ChN	717	447	1.60
Canseco, Oak	332	393	0.84	Greenwell, Bos	763	516	1.48
Carter J, Tor	545	737	0.74	Griffey Jr, Sea	567	458	1.24
Clark Jk, Bos	337	364	0.93	Griffin Alf, LA	515	364	1.41
Clark W, SF	542	557	0.97	Grissom, Mon	383	247	1.55
Coleman, NYN	549	301	1.82	Gruber, Tor	576	524	1.10
Daniels, LA	417	253	1.65	Guerrero, StL	552	484	1.14
Daulton, Phi	373	373	1.00	Guillen, ChA	723	465	1.55
Davis A, Sea	445	549	0.81	Gwynn T, SD	845	361	2.34
Davis C, Min	560	406	1.38	Hall M, NYA	446	437	1.02
Davis E, Cin	419	328	1.28	Harper B, Min	510	435	1.17
Davis G, Bal	359	378	0.95	Harris L, LA	605	266	2.27
Dawson, ChN	551	497	1.11	Hatcher B, Cin	603	398	1.52
Deer, Det	267	433	0.62	Hayes C, Phi	499	394	1.27
DeShields, Mon	433	206	2.10	Hayes V, Phi	436	393	1.11
Devereaux, Bal	488	435	1.12	Henderson D, Oak	440	523	0.84
Doran, Cin	473	411	1.15	Henderson R, Oak	525	477	1.10
Downing, Tex	436	427	1.02	Herr, SF	575	330	1.74
Duncan, Cin	401	270	1.49	Howell Jk, SD	324	309	1.05
Dunston, ChN	507	504	1.01	Hrbek, Min	532	440	1.21
Dykstra, Phi	529	409	1.29	Incaviglia, Det	415	337	1.23

Player, Team	Grd	Fly	G/F	Player, Team	Grd	Fly	G/F
Jacoby, Oak	550	477	1.15	Reynolds H, Sea	752	562	1.34
James C, Cle	580	417	1.39	Ripken B, Bal	450	237	1.90
Jefferies, NYN	606	531	1.14	Ripken C, Bal	761	606	1.26
Johnson H, NYN	388	690	0.56	Rivera L, Bos	345	318	1.08
Johnson L, ChA	633	254	2.49	Roberts Bip, SD	579	260	2.23
Jordan, Phi	458	334	1.37	Sabo, Cin	449	566	0.79
Jose, StL	428	233	1.84	Salazar L, ChN	382	330	1.16
Joyner, Cal	484	542	0.89	Samuel, LA	594	366	1.62
Kelly, NYA	535	431	1.24	Sandberg, ChN	686	541	1.27
Kruk, Phi	522	319	1.64	Santiago, SD	425	430	0.99
Lansford, Oak	491	279	1.76	Sax S, NYA	1066	382	2.79
Larkin B, Cin	627	404	1.55	Schofield, Cal	369	301	1.23
Larkin G, Min	413	337	1.23	Scioscia, LA	474	390	1.22
Lee M, Tor	482	220	2.19	Seitzer, KC	642	400	1.61
Lind, Pit	727	436	1.67	Sheffield, Mil	353	391	0.90
Magadan, NYN	473	304	1.56	Sierra, Tex	728	571	1.27
Maldonado, Tor	395	371	1.06	Smith Lo, Atl	384	428	0.90
Martinez Da, Mon	413	342	1.21	Smith O, StL	802	429	1.87
Martinez E, Sea	446	357	1.25	Snyder C, Tor	309	325	0.95
Mattingly, NYA	603	580	1.04	Spiers, Mil	458	284	1.61
McGee, SF	690	191	3.61	Steinbach, Oak	504	355	1.42
McGriff F, SD	534	451	1.18	Stillwell, KC	491	438	1.12
McGwire, Oak	359	619	0.58	Strawberry, LA	460	460	1.00
McReynolds, NYN	466	641	0.73	Surhoff BJ, Mil	637	386	1.65
Milligan, Bal	388	362	1.07	Tartabull, KC	390	328	1.19
Mitchell K, SF	404	556	0.73	Templeton, NYN	530	357	1.48
Molitor, Mil	650	490	1.33	Tettleton, Det	381	364	1.05
Moseby, Det	415	345	1.20	Thompson M, StL	608	242	2.51
Murphy Dl, Phi	613	473	1.30	Thompson Ro, SF	477	483	0.99
Murray E, LA	630	568	1.11	Thon, Phi	577	438	1.32
Newman A, Min	518	263	1.97	Trammell, Det	481	448	1.07
Nokes, NYA	358	389	0.92	Treadway, Atl	441	423	1.04
O'Brien P, Sea	573	506	1.13	Uribe, SF	432	340	1.27
O'Neill, Cin	476	456	1.04	Valle, Sea	429	268	1.60
Oquendo, StL	513	452	1.13	Van Slyke, Pit	477	470	1.01
Orsulak, Bal	481	394	1.22	Vaughn G, Mil	290	356	0.81
Owen S, Mon	509	412	1.24	Ventura, ChA	486	329	1.48
Pagliarulo, Min	396	328	1.21	Vizquel, Sea	474	272	1.74
Palmeiro, Tex	653	561	1.16	Wallach, Mon	594	605	0.98
Parker D, Tor	616	491	1.25	Walton, ChN	453	235	1.93
Parrish Ln, Cal	403	390	1.03	Whitaker, Det	455	533	0.85
Pasqua, ChA	279	344	0.81	White D, Tor	618	425	1.45
Pena T, Bos	649	327	1.98	Williams MD, SF	452	499	0.91
Pendleton, Atl	658	489	1.35	Wilson M, Tor	593	287	2.07
Perry G, StL	418	279	1.50	Wilson W, Oak	402	238	1.69
Pettis, Tex	424	196	2.16	Winfield, Cal	412	290	1.42
Phillips, Det	593	423	1.40	Worthington, Bal	377	257	1.47
Polonia, Cal	668	294	2.27	Young G, Hou	365	235	1.55
Presley, SD	314	289	1.09	Yount, Mil	591	571	1.04
Puckett, Min	838	412	2.03	Zeile, StL	445	333	1.34
Quintana, Bos	519	218	2.38	**MLB Avg**			**1.30**
Raines, ChA	669	430	1.56				
Ramirez R, Hou	490	337	1.45				
Randolph, Mil	608	349	1.74				
Reed Jd, Bos	638	544	1.17				

DO CLUTCH HITTERS GEAR UP WITH RUNNERS IN SCORING POSITION AND TWO OUT? (p. 127)

Both Leagues — Listed Alphabetically
(minimum 300 PA w/runners in scoring position from 1989 through 1991)

Player, Team	2 Out	<2 Out	Diff	Player, Team	2 Out	<2 Out	Diff	Player, Team	2 Out	<2 Out	Diff
Alomar R, Tor	.241	.332	91	Griffey Jr, Sea	.280	.341	61	Pasqua, ChA	.267	.283	16
Baines, Oak	.285	.260	25	Griffin Alf, LA	.229	.244	15	Pena T, Bos	.240	.270	30
Barfield Je, NYA	.257	.200	57	Gruber, Tor	.238	.304	66	Pendleton, Atl	.276	.276	0
Bell Geo, ChN	.278	.291	13	Guerrero, StL	.303	.363	60	Perry G, StL	.232	.284	52
Bell Jay, Pit	.240	.361	121	Guillen, ChA	.228	.336	108	Phillips, Det	.285	.275	10
Benzinger, KC	.161	.324	163	Gwynn T, SD	.289	.353	64	Polonia, Cal	.357	.278	79
Biggio, Hou	.268	.283	15	Hall M, NYA	.242	.269	27	Presley, SD	.209	.216	7
Blauser, Atl	.265	.328	63	Harper B, Min	.277	.351	74	Puckett, Min	.304	.334	30
Boggs W, Bos	.293	.363	70	Hatcher B, Cin	.242	.278	36	Quintana, Bos	.302	.264	38
Bonds, Pit	.287	.370	83	Hayes C, Phi	.219	.257	38	Raines, ChA	.275	.343	68
Bonilla B, Pit	.251	.328	77	Hayes V, Phi	.216	.255	39	Ramirez R, Hou	.168	.325	157
Braggs, Cin	.189	.346	157	Henderson D, Oak	.221	.324	103	Randolph, Mil	.291	.306	15
Brett, KC	.252	.332	80	Henderson R, Oak	.212	.281	69	Reed Jd, Bos	.233	.313	80
Brooks, NYN	.220	.291	71	Herr, SF	.230	.251	21	Reynolds H, Sea	.320	.289	31
Browne J, Cle	.188	.335	147	Hrbek, Min	.267	.311	44	Ripken C, Bal	.232	.273	41
Brunansky, Bos	.220	.251	31	Incaviglia, Det	.203	.265	62	Rivera L, Bos	.231	.221	10
Buechele, Pit	.228	.298	70	Jackson B, ChA	.287	.224	63	Sabo, Cin	.245	.309	64
Burks, Bos	.300	.264	36	Jacoby, Oak	.299	.217	82	Samuel, LA	.234	.210	24
Butler, LA	.291	.271	20	James C, Cle	.272	.281	9	Sandberg, ChN	.248	.315	67
Calderon, Mon	.243	.336	93	Jefferies, NYN	.250	.302	52	Santiago, SD	.263	.247	16
Caminiti, Hou	.283	.278	5	Johnson H, NYN	.254	.327	73	Sax S, NYA	.252	.312	60
Canseco, Oak	.286	.278	8	Johnson L, ChA	.287	.302	15	Scioscia, LA	.237	.290	53
Carter J, Tor	.248	.286	38	Jordan, Phi	.210	.319	109	Seitzer, KC	.250	.289	39
Clark Jk, Bos	.252	.269	17	Jose, StL	.274	.382	108	Sheffield, Mil	.273	.262	11
Clark W, SF	.360	.324	36	Joyner, Cal	.269	.338	69	Sierra, Tex	.280	.375	95
Coleman, NYN	.225	.256	31	Justice, Atl	.225	.409	184	Smith Lo, Atl	.316	.318	2
Daniels, LA	.283	.288	5	Kelly, NYA	.274	.278	4	Smith O, StL	.230	.298	68
Daulton, Phi	.231	.307	76	Kruk, Phi	.274	.264	10	Snyder C, Tor	.192	.241	49
Davis A, Sea	.309	.297	12	Lansford, Oak	.256	.281	25	Spiers, Mil	.243	.333	90
Davis C, Min	.272	.291	19	Larkin B, Cin	.300	.302	2	Steinbach, Oak	.233	.333	100
Davis E, Cin	.295	.249	46	Larkin G, Min	.248	.214	34	Stillwell, KC	.267	.284	17
Davis G, Bal	.178	.329	151	Lee M, Tor	.268	.227	41	Strawberry, LA	.215	.314	99
Dawson, ChN	.303	.286	17	Leonard J, Sea	.229	.310	81	Surhoff BJ, Mil	.262	.309	46
Deer, Det	.213	.208	5	Lind, Pit	.234	.308	74	Tabler, Tor	.222	.283	61
Devereaux, Bal	.253	.237	16	Magadan, NYN	.353	.304	49	Tartabull, KC	.207	.344	137
Doran, Cin	.179	.333	154	Maldonado, Tor	.248	.246	2	Templeton, NYN	.228	.257	29
Downing, Tex	.260	.292	32	Martinez E, Sea	.233	.260	27	Tettleton, Det	.158	.262	104
Dunston, ChN	.263	.265	2	Mattingly, NYA	.267	.328	61	Thompson M, StL	.286	.247	39
Eisenreich, KC	.259	.313	54	McGee, SF	.294	.330	36	Thompson Ro, SF	.227	.205	22
Elster, NYN	.234	.303	69	McGriff F, SD	.209	.303	94	Thon, Phi	.247	.287	40
Espinoza, NYA	.252	.265	13	McGwire, Oak	.249	.255	6	Trammell, Det	.269	.345	76
Evans Dw, Bal	.258	.353	95	McReynolds, NYN	.257	.327	70	Treadway, Atl	.266	.351	85
Felix, Cal	.230	.295	65	Milligan, Bal	.287	.272	15	Uribe, SF	.223	.250	27
Fermin, Cle	.210	.264	54	Mitchell K, SF	.201	.288	87	Van Slyke, Pit	.256	.296	40
Fernandez T, SD	.255	.327	72	Molitor, Mil	.325	.322	3	Vaughn G, Mil	.282	.309	27
Fielder, Det	.224	.317	93	Moseby, Det	.244	.233	11	Ventura, ChA	.283	.335	52
Finley S, Hou	.290	.264	26	Murphy Dl, Phi	.282	.259	23	Vizquel, Sea	.235	.226	9
Fisk, ChA	.234	.310	76	Murray E, LA	.248	.309	61	Wallach, Mon	.235	.308	73
Fletcher S, ChA	.245	.260	15	Newman A, Min	.171	.279	108	Whitaker, Det	.266	.271	5
Franco Ju, Tex	.307	.373	66	Nokes, NYA	.239	.299	60	White D, Tor	.174	.224	50
Gaetti, Cal	.270	.247	23	O'Brien P, Sea	.209	.268	59	Williams MD, SF	.257	.262	5
Gagne, Min	.194	.236	42	O'Neill, Cin	.293	.280	13	Wilson M, Tor	.217	.270	53
Galarraga, Mon	.172	.285	113	Oquendo, StL	.206	.308	102	Winfield, Cal	.217	.297	80
Gallego, Oak	.190	.252	62	Orsulak, Bal	.248	.294	46	Worthington, Bal	.220	.300	80
Gant, Atl	.177	.304	127	Owen S, Mon	.153	.278	125	Yount, Mil	.245	.327	82
Gantner, Mil	.221	.298	77	Pagliarulo, Min	.203	.232	29	Zeile, StL	.220	.269	49
Gladden, Min	.237	.259	22	Palmeiro, Tex	.252	.303	51	**MLB Average**	**.236**	**.282**	**46**
Grace, ChN	.261	.319	58	Parker D, Tor	.237	.296	59				
Greenwell, Bos	.211	.328	117	Parrish Ln, Cal	.237	.238	0				

WILL COMISKEY BE "THE HOUSE THAT FRANK BUILT"? (p. 130)

1991 Both Leagues — Listed Alphabetically
(minimum 500 plate apperances in 1991)

Player, Team	Hm	Rd	Dff	Player, Team	Hm	Rd	Dff	Player, Team	Hm	Rd	Dff
Alomar R, Tor	.297	.293	4	Gibson K, KC	.222	.251	-29	Orsulak, Bal	.277	.279	-2
Baerga, Cle	.291	.286	5	Gladden, Min	.266	.226	40	Pagnozzi, StL	.226	.298	-72
Bagwell, Hou	.296	.293	3	Gonzalez J, Tex	.267	.261	6	Palmeiro, Tex	.339	.306	33
Baines, Oak	.264	.322	-58	Gonzalez L, Hou	.273	.236	37	Parker D, Tor	.214	.260	-46
Bell Geo, ChN	.267	.304	-37	Grace, ChN	.289	.256	33	Pena T, Bos	.222	.239	-17
Bell Jay, Pit	.281	.259	22	Greenwell, Bos	.302	.298	4	Pendleton, Atl	.340	.299	41
Biggio, Hou	.343	.245	98	Griffey Jr, Sea	.365	.286	79	Phillips, Det	.295	.272	23
Boggs W, Bos	.389	.282	107	Grissom, Mon	.279	.258	21	Polonia, Cal	.261	.332	-71
Bonds, Pit	.272	.313	-41	Guillen, ChA	.287	.260	27	Puckett, Min	.326	.311	15
Bonilla B, Pit	.309	.295	14	Gwynn T, SD	.307	.325	-18	Quintana, Bos	.292	.298	-6
Brett, KC	.247	.263	-16	Hall M, NYA	.273	.296	-23	Raines, ChA	.254	.280	-26
Brunansky, Bos	.256	.200	56	Henderson D, Oak	.259	.293	-34	Randolph, Mil	.336	.318	18
Buechele, Pit	.275	.251	24	Henderson R, Oak	.278	.257	21	Reed Jd, Bos	.263	.304	-41
Burks, Bos	.267	.236	31	Hrbek, Min	.318	.248	70	Reynolds H, Sea	.299	.208	91
Butler, LA	.312	.281	31	Jefferies, NYN	.295	.248	47	Ripken C, Bal	.286	.358	-72
Calderon, Mon	.308	.293	15	Johnson H, NYN	.268	.250	18	Sabo, Cin	.339	.261	78
Caminiti, Hou	.253	.253	0	Johnson L, ChA	.266	.281	-15	Samuel, LA	.254	.288	-34
Candaele, Hou	.294	.230	64	Jose, StL	.296	.313	-17	Sandberg, ChN	.309	.272	37
Canseco, Oak	.270	.262	8	Joyner, Cal	.276	.325	-49	Santiago, SD	.244	.290	-46
Carter J, Tor	.290	.256	34	Kelly, NYA	.310	.228	82	Sax S, NYA	.291	.317	-26
Clark Jk, Bos	.281	.215	66	Knoblauch, Min	.328	.234	94	Sierra, Tex	.320	.294	26
Clark W, SF	.283	.319	-36	Kruk, Phi	.286	.302	-16	Smith O, StL	.323	.243	80
Cuyler, Det	.244	.268	-24	Lankford, StL	.237	.265	-28	Strawberry, LA	.284	.246	38
Daniels, LA	.248	.251	-3	Larkin B, Cin	.326	.275	51	Surhoff BJ, Mil	.267	.309	-42
Davis A, Sea	.230	.212	18	Lind, Pit	.244	.287	-44	Tartabull, KC	.314	.318	-4
Davis C, Min	.303	.251	52	Maas, NYA	.178	.258	-80	Tettleton, Det	.264	.263	1
Dawson, ChN	.293	.251	42	Magadan, NYN	.243	.273	-30	Thomas F, ChA	.371	.271	100
Deer, Det	.193	.165	28	Martinez E, Sea	.320	.296	24	Thompson R, SF	.295	.231	64
DeShields, Mon	.265	.218	47	Mattingly, NYA	.305	.274	31	Thon, Phi	.270	.234	36
Devereaux, Bal	.252	.267	-15	McGee, SF	.270	.345	-75	Van Slyke, Pit	.226	.310	-84
Dunston, ChN	.295	.227	68	McGriff F, SD	.280	.277	3	Vaughn G, Mil	.246	.241	5
Espinoza, NYA	.248	.265	-17	McGwire, Oak	.185	.217	-32	Ventura, ChA	.289	.278	11
Fernandez T, SD	.292	.254	38	McRae B, KC	.267	.254	13	Walker L, Mon	.273	.300	-27
Fielder, Det	.256	.266	-10	McReynolds, NY	.237	.276	-39	Wallach, Mon	.213	.233	-20
Finley S, Hou	.273	.297	-24	Milligan, Bal	.249	.276	-27	Whitaker, Det	.304	.253	51
Fisk, ChA	.236	.247	-11	Molitor, Mil	.292	.354	-62	White D, Tor	.298	.266	32
Franco Ju, Tex	.344	.339	5	Morris H, Cin	.319	.317	2	Williams MD, SF	.287	.250	37
Fryman T, Det	.249	.267	-18	Murphy Dl, Phi	.280	.223	57	Winfield, Cal	.244	.279	-35
Gaetti, Cal	.275	.219	56	Murray E, LA	.270	.252	18	Yount, Mil	.236	.285	-49
Gallego, Oak	.270	.226	44	O'Brien P, Sea	.238	.259	-21	Zeile, StL	.297	.262	35
Gant, Atl	.279	.228	51	O'Neill, Cin	.284	.227	57	**AL Avg**	**.263**	**.257**	**-6**
Gantner, Mil	.287	.279	8	Olerud, Tor	.270	.241	29	**NL Avg**	**.254**	**.246**	**-8**

WHO ARE THE BEST TWO-STRIKE HITTERS? (p. 132)

1989-1991 Both Leagues Listed Alphabetically
(minimum 500 plate appearances with 2 strikes from 1989 through 1991)

Batter, Team	AB	H	Avg
Alomar R, Tor	828	184	.222
Baines, Oak	558	105	.188
Barfield Je, NYA	738	110	.149
Bell Geo, ChN	719	166	.231
Bell Jay, Pit	704	142	.202
Benzinger, KC	605	103	.170
Biggio, Hou	639	116	.182
Blauser, Atl	573	90	.157
Boggs W, Bos	869	230	.265
Bonds, Pit	652	130	.199
Bonilla B, Pit	750	153	.204
Braggs, Cin	483	75	.155
Brett, KC	551	103	.187
Briley, Sea	466	89	.191
Brooks, NYN	695	136	.196
Browne J, Cle	564	127	.225
Brunansky, Bos	708	128	.181
Buechele, Pit	627	104	.166
Burks, Bos	643	138	.215
Butler, LA	875	218	.249
Calderon, Mon	674	154	.228
Caminiti, Hou	697	130	.187
Canseco, Oak	717	130	.181
Carter J, Tor	881	164	.186
Clark Jk, Bos	703	116	.165
Clark W, SF	760	165	.217
Coleman, NYN	634	134	.211
Daniels, LA	550	97	.176
Daulton, Phi	507	78	.154
Davis A, Sea	640	138	.216
Davis C, Min	675	122	.181
Davis E, Cin	559	85	.152
Davis G, Bal	498	83	.167
Dawson, ChN	643	138	.215
Deer, Det	778	99	.127
DeShields, Mon	533	91	.171
Devereaux, Bal	663	133	.201
Doran, Cin	476	86	.181
Downing, Tex	670	143	.213
Dunston, ChN	621	125	.201
Dykstra, Phi	535	114	.213
Elster, NYN	515	87	.169
Espinoza, NYA	504	97	.192
Evans Dw, Bal	527	95	.180
Felix, Cal	514	77	.150
Fermin, Cle	469	107	.228
Fernandez T, SD	685	146	.213
Fielder, Det	614	109	.178
Finley S, Hou	549	109	.199
Fisk, ChA	567	108	.190
Fletcher S, ChA	508	86	.169
Franco Ju, Tex	775	191	.246
Gaetti, Cal	723	124	.172
Gagne, Min	532	96	.180
Galarraga, Mon	742	125	.168
Gallego, Oak	515	85	.165
Gant, Atl	662	113	.171
Gibson K, KC	482	73	.151
Gladden, Min	584	116	.199
Grace, ChN	587	141	.240
Greenwell, Bos	527	120	.228
Griffey Jr, Sea	701	155	.221
Griffin Alf, LA	510	79	.155
Gruber, Tor	646	125	.193
Guerrero, StL	623	127	.204
Guillen, ChA	555	129	.232
Gwynn T, SD	556	162	.291
Hatcher B, Cin	553	109	.197
Hayes C, Phi	589	115	.195
Hayes V, Phi	620	108	.174
Henderson D, Oak	826	156	.189
Henderson R, Oak	776	201	.259
Herr, SF	548	114	.208
Howell Jk, SD	480	64	.133
Hrbek, Min	429	98	.228
Incaviglia, Det	650	89	.137
Jackson B, ChA	538	92	.171
Jacoby, Oak	488	87	.178
James C, Cle	596	108	.181
Jefferies, NYN	619	155	.250
Johnson H, NYN	743	124	.167
Jose, StL	490	105	.214
Joyner, Cal	575	135	.235
Kelly, NYA	779	175	.225
Kruk, Phi	541	115	.213
Larkin B, Cin	572	141	.247
Lee M, Tor	586	94	.160
Lind, Pit	634	128	.202
Magadan, NYN	558	143	.256
Maldonado, Tor	557	83	.149
Martinez Da, Mon	485	112	.231
Martinez E, Sea	565	142	.251
Mattingly, NYA	486	115	.237
McGee, SF	602	142	.236
McGriff F, SD	760	129	.170
McGwire, Oak	651	85	.131
McReynolds, NYN	648	153	.236
Milligan, Bal	654	134	.205
Mitchell K, SF	607	104	.171
Molitor, Mil	659	160	.243
Moseby, Det	570	108	.189
Murphy Dl, Phi	713	103	.144
Murray E, LA	704	153	.217
O'Brien P, Sea	524	96	.183
O'Neill, Cin	647	108	.167
Oquendo, StL	574	127	.221
Orsulak, Bal	485	98	.202
Owen S, Mon	572	110	.192
Pagliarulo, Min	493	86	.174
Palmeiro, Tex	675	167	.247
Parker D, Tor	694	122	.176
Parrish Ln, Cal	646	109	.169
Pasqua, ChA	449	70	.156
Pena T, Bos	547	97	.177
Pendleton, Atl	643	149	.232
Pettis, Tex	643	109	.170
Phillips, Det	731	148	.202
Polonia, Cal	650	178	.274
Presley, SD	473	72	.152
Puckett, Min	599	134	.224
Quintana, Bos	443	90	.203
Raines, ChA	560	131	.234
Ramirez R, Hou	502	95	.189
Randolph, Mil	531	139	.262
Reed Jd, Bos	743	176	.237
Reynolds H, Sea	676	150	.222
Ripken C, Bal	745	171	.230
Rivera L, Bos	465	95	.204
Roberts Bip, SD	606	142	.234
Sabo, Cin	569	120	.211
Salazar L, ChN	547	112	.205
Samuel, LA	855	146	.171
Sandberg, ChN	754	168	.223
Santiago, SD	552	86	.156
Sax S, NYA	755	183	.242
Schofield, Cal	476	86	.181
Seitzer, KC	596	121	.203
Sierra, Tex	734	153	.208
Smith Lo, Atl	552	115	.208
Smith O, StL	589	124	.211
Snyder C, Tor	539	65	.121
Sosa, ChA	535	79	.148
Steinbach, Oak	519	100	.193
Stillwell, KC	546	98	.179
Strawberry, LA	762	136	.178
Tartabull, KC	641	131	.204
Templeton, NYN	534	88	.165
Tettleton, Det	708	114	.161
Thompson M, StL	523	93	.178
Thompson Ro, SF	731	112	.153
Thon, Phi	571	100	.175
Trammell, Det	517	117	.226
Van Slyke, Pit	677	124	.183
Vaughn G, Mil	487	78	.160
Ventura, ChA	452	93	.206
Wallach, Mon	760	136	.179
Walton, ChN	504	93	.185
Whitaker, Det	626	134	.214
White D, Tor	890	148	.166
Williams MD, SF	647	113	.175
Wilson M, Tor	604	122	.202
Wilson W, Oak	493	93	.189
Winfield, Cal	477	89	.187
Worthington, Bal	569	102	.179
Yount, Mil	690	146	.212
Zeile, StL	525	99	.189
MLB Avg			**.185**

WHAT KIND OF HITTERS MAKE "PRODUCTIVE OUTS"? (p. 134)

1991 Both Leagues — Listed Alphabetically
(minimum 50 at bats)

Player, Team	Outs	Adv	Pct	Player, Team	Outs	Adv	Pct
Alomar R, Tor	86	26	30.2	Eisenreich, KC	58	21	36.2
Baerga, Cle	82	30	36.6	Espinoza, NYA	54	15	27.8
Bagwell, Hou	95	22	23.2	Fermin, Cle	54	20	37.0
Baines, Oak	71	30	42.3	Fernandez T, SD	73	21	28.8
Barfield Je, NYA	53	10	18.9	Fielder, Det	82	14	17.1
Bell Geo, ChN	77	14	18.2	Finley S, Hou	67	16	23.9
Bell Jay, Pit	72	13	18.1	Fisk, ChA	59	10	16.9
Belle, Cle	55	12	21.8	Franco Ju, Tex	86	17	19.8
Benzinger, KC	61	18	29.5	Fryman T, Det	86	7	8.1
Bichette, Mil	67	14	20.9	Gaetti, Cal	84	10	11.9
Biggio, Hou	86	15	17.4	Gagne, Min	66	8	12.1
Blauser, Atl	54	17	31.5	Galarraga, Mon	66	13	19.7
Boggs W, Bos	58	21	36.2	Gallego, Oak	60	11	18.3
Bonds, Pit	78	21	26.9	Gant, Atl	102	15	14.7
Bonilla B, Pit	85	20	23.5	Gantner, Mil	68	28	41.2
Brett, KC	88	32	36.4	Gibson K, KC	70	18	25.7
Briley, Sea	58	19	32.8	Gladden, Min	50	11	22.0
Brooks, NYN	67	20	29.9	Gomez L, Bal	57	12	21.1
Brunansky, Bos	82	8	9.8	Gonzalez Juan, Tex	94	11	11.7
Buechele, Pit	78	14	17.9	Gonzalez L, Hou	83	14	16.9
Buhner, Sea	66	5	7.6	Grace, ChN	94	37	39.4
Burks, Bos	93	17	18.3	Greenwell, Bos	68	23	33.8
Calderon, Mon	81	22	27.2	Griffey Jr, Sea	91	28	30.8
Caminiti, Hou	98	27	27.6	Grissom, Mon	88	25	28.4
Candaele, Hou	65	19	29.2	Gruber, Tor	77	22	28.6
Canseco, Oak	119	21	17.6	Guerrero, StL	60	13	21.7
Carter J, Tor	119	27	22.7	Guillen, ChA	66	24	36.4
Chamberlain, Phi	76	14	18.4	Gwynn T, SD	80	33	41.3
Clark Je, SD	58	14	24.1	Hall M, NYA	85	28	32.9
Clark Jk, Bos	82	13	15.9	Hamilton, Mil	65	19	29.2
Clark W, SF	109	43	39.4	Harper B, Min	52	17	32.7
Cole, Cle	55	14	25.5	Harris L, LA	51	18	35.3
Cuyler, Det	63	16	25.4	Hayes C, Phi	80	18	22.5
Daniels, LA	79	25	31.6	Henderson D, Oak	102	16	15.7
Daulton, Phi	56	12	21.4	Hoiles, Bal	50	8	16.0
Davis A, Sea	67	15	22.4	Hrbek, Min	76	30	39.5
Davis C, Min	78	22	28.2	Incaviglia, Det	55	8	14.5
Davis E, Cin	52	5	9.6	Jacoby, Oak	65	12	18.5
Dawson, ChN	81	23	28.4	James C, Cle	72	17	23.6
Deer, Det	94	6	6.4	Jefferies, NYN	79	26	32.9
DeShields, Mon	58	16	27.6	Johnson H, NYN	108	17	15.7
Devereaux, Bal	60	12	20.0	Johnson L, ChA	82	26	31.7
Downing, Tex	51	9	17.6	Jose, StL	89	13	14.6
Dunston, ChN	74	15	20.3	Joyner, Cal	87	19	21.8

Player, Team	Outs	Adv	Pct	Player, Team	Outs	Adv	Pct
Knoblauch, Min	74	26	35.1	Reynolds H, Sea	104	29	27.9
Kruk, Phi	85	20	23.5	Ripken C, Bal	103	24	23.3
Lankford, StL	94	22	23.4	Rivera L, Bos	63	7	11.1
Larkin B, Cin	75	21	28.0	Sabo, Cin	78	14	17.9
Lee M, Tor	66	17	25.8	Salazar L, ChN	54	16	29.6
Lemke, Atl	50	19	38.0	Samuel, LA	98	22	22.4
Lind, Pit	92	23	25.0	Sandberg, ChN	83	25	30.1
Maas, NYA	92	17	18.5	Santiago, SD	90	11	12.2
Mack, Min	54	15	27.8	Sax S, NYA	73	26	35.6
Magadan, NYN	75	20	26.7	Schofield, Cal	75	22	29.3
Martinez Da, Mon	51	14	27.5	Shumpert, KC	63	13	20.6
Martinez E, Sea	63	16	25.4	Sierra, Tex	111	31	27.9
Mattingly, NYA	105	23	21.9	Smith Lo, Atl	55	17	30.9
McGee, SF	57	15	26.3	Smith O, StL	80	27	33.8
McGriff F, SD	76	23	30.3	Sosa, ChA	51	12	23.5
McGwire, Oak	94	15	16.0	Spiers, Mil	55	16	29.1
McRae B, KC	84	25	29.8	Steinbach, Oak	61	12	19.7
McReynolds, NYN	73	9	12.3	Stillwell, KC	70	16	22.9
Milligan, Bal	68	14	20.6	Strawberry, LA	94	16	17.0
Mitchell K, SF	60	8	13.3	Stubbs, Mil	64	10	15.6
Molitor, Mil	77	16	20.8	Surhoff BJ, Mil	79	41	51.9
Morris H, Cin	72	24	33.3	Tartabull, KC	62	13	21.0
Murphy Dl, Phi	87	20	23.0	Tettleton, Det	75	12	16.0
Murray E, LA	89	24	27.0	Thomas F, ChA	95	16	16.8
Myers G, Tor	54	16	29.6	Thompson M, StL	63	19	30.2
Nixon O, Atl	54	19	35.2	Thompson Ro, SF	77	14	18.2
Nokes, NYA	59	15	25.4	Thon, Phi	84	14	16.7
O'Brien P, Sea	69	27	39.1	Trammell, Det	83	23	27.7
O'Neill, Cin	84	17	20.2	Van Slyke, Pit	104	28	26.9
Olerud, Tor	54	16	29.6	Vaughn G, Mil	87	14	16.1
Orsulak, Bal	84	27	32.1	Ventura, ChA	92	29	31.5
Owen S, Mon	55	10	18.2	Vizquel, Sea	53	14	26.4
Pagliarulo, Min	52	12	23.1	Walker L, Mon	63	21	33.3
Pagnozzi, StL	78	18	23.1	Wallach, Mon	76	15	19.7
Palmeiro, Tex	95	33	34.7	Whitaker, Det	80	19	23.8
Parker D, Tor	81	18	22.2	White D, Tor	69	18	26.1
Parrish Ln, Cal	53	7	13.2	Whiten, Cle	62	13	21.0
Pasqua, ChA	78	11	14.1	Williams MD, SF	94	20	21.3
Pecota, KC	68	18	26.5	Wilson W, Oak	52	19	36.5
Pena T, Bos	66	18	27.3	Winfield, Cal	83	14	16.9
Pendleton, Atl	113	40	35.4	Yount, Mil	80	12	15.0
Pettis, Tex	52	6	11.5	Zeile, StL	77	17	22.1
Phillips, Det	66	17	25.8	**ML Avg**	**21255**	**5094**	**24.0**
Polonia, Cal	80	24	30.0				
Puckett, Min	102	27	26.5				
Quintana, Bos	86	36	41.9				
Raines, ChA	58	19	32.8				
Randolph, Mil	63	21	33.3				
Reed Jd, Bos	93	23	24.7				
Reimer, Tex	56	10	17.9				

WHO ARE THE RALLY KILLERS? (p. 136)

The following table lists the number of double play opportunities (a man on first base and less than two out) for each batter from 1989 through 1991 (**Opp**), the number of doubles plays hit into (**GDP**), and the percentage (**Pct**).

1989-1991 Both Leagues — Listed Alphabetically
(minimum 250 plate appearances in a GDP situation from 1989-1991)

Batter, Team	Opp	GDP	Pct	Batter, Team	Opp	GDP	Pct	Batter, Team	Opp	GDP	Pct
Alomar R, Tor	370	31	.084	Greenwell, Bos	420	51	.121	Owen S, Mon	257	28	.109
Baines, Oak	324	44	.136	Griffey Jr, Sea	351	26	.074	Palmeiro, Tex	424	60	.142
Barfield Je, NYA	285	25	.088	Gruber, Tor	317	34	.107	Parker D, Tor	348	48	.138
Bell Geo, ChN	316	42	.133	Guerrero, StL	298	43	.144	Parrish Ln, Cal	285	30	.105
Bell Jay, Pit	363	38	.105	Guillen, ChA	315	21	.067	Pena T, Bos	310	65	.210
Benzinger, KC	257	15	.058	Gwynn T, SD	405	36	.089	Pendleton, Atl	385	44	.114
Biggio, Hou	344	20	.058	Hall M, NYA	258	22	.085	Phillips, Det	294	35	.119
Blauser, Atl	251	15	.060	Harper B, Min	294	45	.153	Puckett, Min	456	63	.138
Boggs W, Bos	352	49	.139	Hayes C, Phi	259	31	.120	Quintana, Bos	266	41	.154
Bonds, Pit	305	24	.079	Hayes V, Phi	323	23	.071	Raines, ChA	255	24	.094
Bonilla B, Pit	380	34	.089	Henderson D, Oak	345	26	.075	Randolph, Mil	291	38	.131
Brett, KC	376	55	.146					Reed Jd, Bos	412	46	.112
Brooks, NYN	326	35	.107	Herr, SF	276	24	.087	Reynolds H, Sea	336	24	.071
Browne J, Cle	260	26	.100	Hrbek, Min	341	38	.111	Ripken C, Bal	442	53	.120
Brunansky, Bos	376	32	.085	Incaviglia, Det	325	36	.111	Samuel, LA	319	23	.072
Buechele, Pit	272	40	.147	Jacoby, Oak	322	48	.149	Sandberg, ChN	391	26	.066
Burks, Bos	344	33	.096	James C, Cle	314	40	.127	Santiago, SD	300	34	.113
Calderon, Mon	386	53	.137	Jefferies, NYN	317	41	.129	Sax S, NYA	316	47	.149
Caminiti, Hou	360	40	.111	Johnson H, NYN	383	15	.039	Scioscia, LA	251	20	.080
Canseco, Oak	336	29	.086	Jordan, Phi	277	39	.141	Seitzer, KC	261	31	.119
Carter J, Tor	417	25	.060	Joyner, Cal	302	36	.119	Sierra, Tex	446	39	.087
Clark Jk, Bos	320	39	.122	Kelly, NYA	295	30	.102	Smith O, StL	287	26	.091
Clark W, SF	416	18	.043	Kruk, Phi	299	32	.107	Snyder C, Tor	252	28	.111
Davis A, Sea	332	32	.096	Lansford, Oak	255	31	.122	Steinbach, Oak	276	40	.145
Davis C, Min	349	44	.126	Larkin B, Cin	277	28	.101	Stillwell, KC	294	22	.075
Davis E, Cin	273	26	.095	Larkin G, Min	253	29	.115	Strawberry, LA	328	17	.052
Dawson, ChN	320	38	.119	Leonard J, Sea	271	32	.118	Surhoff BJ, Mil	310	37	.119
Deer, Det	306	11	.036	Lind, Pit	365	52	.142	Tartabull, KC	253	30	.119
Dunston, ChN	273	25	.092	Magadan, NYN	252	17	.067	Templeton, NYN	270	42	.156
Eisenreich, KC	270	26	.096	Martinez E, Sea	265	35	.132	Tettleton, Det	326	27	.083
Espinoza, NYA	318	37	.116	Mattingly, NYA	384	49	.128	Thompson M, StL	277	20	.072
Evans Dw, Bal	323	41	.127	McGriff F, SD	350	35	.100	Thompson R, SF	308	20	.065
Fermin, Cle	294	44	.150	McGwire, Oak	381	49	.129	Thon, Phi	294	29	.099
Fernandez T, SD	330	37	.112	McReynolds, NY	283	24	.085	Trammell, Det	379	27	.071
Fielder, Det	273	32	.117	Milligan, Bal	287	46	.160	Van Slyke, Pit	351	24	.068
Fisk, ChA	260	46	.177	Mitchell K, SF	330	21	.064	Wallach, Mon	350	45	.129
Franco Ju, Tex	366	52	.142	Molitor, Mil	259	29	.112	Whitaker, Det	357	20	.056
Gaetti, Cal	372	47	.126	Moseby, Det	255	25	.098	White D, Tor	337	24	.071
Gagne, Min	275	30	.109	Murphy Dl, Phi	360	57	.158	Williams MD, SF	296	29	.098
Galarraga, Mon	298	32	.107	Murray E, LA	398	48	.121	Yount, Mil	372	29	.078
Gallego, Oak	257	31	.121	O'Brien P, Sea	280	36	.129	**MLB Average**			**.109**
Gant, Atl	284	14	.049	O'Neill, Cin	301	27	.090				
Grace, ChN	362	28	.077	Oquendo, StL	266	24	.090				
				Orsulak, Bal	286	25	.087				

WHERE HAVE YOU GONE, JOE DiMAGGIO? (p. 138)

The table below lists all the players in baseball history who have hit 200 or more home runs, their total Home Runs (**HR**), career strikeouts (**K**), and their strikeouts per home run (**K/HR**).

Player	K	HR	K/HR	Player	K	HR	K/HR
Aaron, Hank	1383	755	1.8	Cooper, Cecil	911	241	3.8
Adcock, Joe	1059	336	3.2	Dawson, Andre	1279	377	3.4
Allen, Dick	1556	351	4.4	DeCinces, Doug	904	237	3.8
Allison, Bob	1033	256	4.0	Dickey, Bill	289	202	1.4
Alou, Felipe	706	206	3.4	DiMaggio, Joe	369	361	1.0
Armas, Tony	1201	251	4.8	Doby, Larry	1011	253	4.0
Averill, Earl	518	238	2.2	Doerr, Bobby	608	223	2.7
Baines, Harold	956	225	4.2	Downing, Brian	1069	265	4.0
Baker, Dusty	926	242	3.8	Ennis, Del	719	288	2.5
Bando, Sal	923	242	3.8	Evans, Darrell	1410	414	3.4
Banks, Ernie	1236	512	2.4	Evans, Dwight	1697	385	4.4
Barfield, Jesse	1207	239	5.1	Fairly, Ron	877	215	4.1
Baylor, Don	1069	338	3.2	Fisk, Carlton	1337	372	3.6
Bell, Buddy	776	201	3.9	Foster, George	1419	348	4.1
Bell, George	625	227	2.8	Foxx, Jimmie	1311	534	2.5
Bell, Gus	636	206	3.1	Freehan, Bill	753	200	3.8
Bench, Johnny	1278	389	3.3	Gaetti, Gary	981	219	4.5
Berger, Wally	693	242	2.9	Gamble, Oscar	546	200	2.7
Berra, Yogi	414	358	1.2	Garvey, Steve	1003	272	3.7
Bonds, Bobby	1757	332	5.3	Gehrig, Lou	789	493	1.6
Bottomley, Jim	591	219	2.7	Gibson, Kirk	1056	208	5.1
Boyer, Ken	1017	282	3.6	Gordon, Joe	702	253	2.8
Brett, George	772	291	2.7	Gordon, Sid	356	202	1.8
Brunansky, Tom	975	240	4.1	Goslin, Goose	585	248	2.4
Burroughs, Jeff	1135	240	4.7	Greenberg, Hank	844	331	2.5
Callison, Johnny	1064	226	4.7	Grich, Bobby	1278	224	5.7
Camilli, Dolf	961	239	4.0	Guerrero, Pedro	837	214	3.9
Campanella, Roy	501	242	2.1	Hartnett, Gabby	697	236	3.0
Canseco, Jose	870	209	4.2	Hebner, Richie	741	203	3.7
Carter, Gary	960	319	3.0	Hendrick, George	1013	267	3.8
Carter, Joe	742	208	3.6	Hodges, Gil	1137	370	3.1
Carty, Rico	663	204	3.3	Horner, Bob	512	218	2.3
Cash, Norm	1091	377	2.9	Hornsby, Rogers	679	301	2.3
Cepeda, Orlando	1169	379	3.1	Horton, Willie	1313	325	4.0
Cey, Ron	1235	316	3.9	Howard, Frank	1460	382	3.8
Clark, Jack	1354	335	4.0	Hrbek, Kent	657	243	2.7
Clemente, Roberto	1230	240	5.1	Jackson, Reggie	2597	563	4.6
Colavito, Rocky	880	374	2.4	Johnson, Bob	851	288	3.0

Player	K	HR	K/HR	Player	K	HR	K/HR
Johnson, Deron	1318	245	5.4	Ripken, Cal	747	259	2.9
Kaline, Al	1020	399	2.6	Robinson, Brooks	990	268	3.7
Killebrew, Harmon	1699	573	3.0	Robinson, Frank	1532	586	2.6
Kiner, Ralph	749	369	2.0	Ruth, Babe	1330	714	1.9
Kingman, Dave	1816	442	4.1	Sandberg, Ryne	875	205	4.3
Klein, Chuck	521	300	1.7	Santo, Ron	1343	342	3.9
Kluszewski, Ted	365	279	1.3	Sauer, Hank	714	288	2.5
Lemon, Chet	1024	215	4.8	Schmidt, Mike	1883	548	3.4
Luzinski, Greg	1495	307	4.9	Scott, George	1418	271	5.2
Lynn, Fred	1116	306	3.6	Sievers, Roy	920	318	2.9
Mantle, Mickey	1710	536	3.2	Simmons, Al	737	307	2.4
Maris, Roger	733	275	2.7	Simmons, Ted	694	248	2.8
Mathews, Eddie	1487	512	2.9	Singleton, Ken	1246	246	5.1
Matthews, Gary	1125	234	4.8	Skowron, Bill	870	211	4.1
May, Lee	1570	354	4.4	Smith, Reggie	1030	314	3.3
Mayberry, John	810	255	3.2	Snider, Duke	1237	407	3.0
Mays, Willie	1526	660	2.3	Stargell, Willie	1936	475	4.1
McCovey, Willie	1550	521	3.0	Staub, Rusty	888	292	3.0
Medwick, Joe	551	205	2.7	Stephens, Vern	685	247	2.8
Mincher, Don	668	200	3.3	Strawberry, Darryl	1085	280	3.9
Mize, Johnny	524	359	1.5	Stuart, Dick	957	228	4.2
Monday, Rick	1513	241	6.3	Tenace, Gene	998	201	5.0
Morgan, Joe	1015	268	3.8	Thomas, Frank	894	286	3.1
Murcer, Bobby	841	252	3.3	Thomas, Gorman	1339	268	5.0
Murphy, Dale	1720	396	4.3	Thompson, Jason	862	208	4.1
Murray, Eddie	1150	398	2.9	Thomson, Bobby	804	264	3.0
Musial, Stan	696	475	1.5	Thornton, Andre	851	253	3.4
Nettles, Graig	1209	390	3.1	Torre, Joe	1094	252	4.3
Nicholson, Bill	828	235	3.5	Trosky, Hal	440	228	1.9
Oglivie, Ben	852	235	3.6	Wagner, Leon	656	211	3.1
Oliva, Tony	645	220	2.9	Wertz, Vic	842	266	3.2
Oliver, Al	756	219	3.5	White, Bill	927	202	4.6
Ott, Mel	896	511	1.8	Williams, Billy	1046	426	2.5
Patko, Andy	477	213	2.2	Williams, Cy	721	251	2.9
Parker, Dave	1537	339	4.5	Williams, Ted	709	521	1.4
Parrish, Lance	1372	304	4.5	Wilson, Hack	713	244	2.9
Parrish, Larry	1359	256	5.3	Winfield, Dave	1414	406	3.5
Pepitone, Joe	526	219	2.4	Wynn, Jimmy	1427	291	4.9
Perez, Tony	1867	379	4.9	Yastrzemski, Carl	1393	452	3.1
Petrocelli, Rico	926	210	4.4	York, Rudy	867	277	3.1
Pinson, Vada	1196	256	4.7	Yount, Robin	1176	235	5.0
Post, Wally	813	210	3.9	Zernial, Gus	755	237	3.2
Powell, Boog	1226	339	3.6	Zisk, Richie	910	207	4.4
Rice, Jim	1423	382	3.7				

WILL THE REAL ALAN TRAMMELL PLEASE STAND UP? (p. 140)

Both Leagues — Listed Alphabetically
(minimum 350 PA in 1990 and 1991)

Player, Team	90	91	Dff	Player, Team	90	91	Dff	Player, Team	90	91	Dff
Alomar R, Tor	.287	.295	8	Griffin Alf, LA	.210	.243	33	Palmeiro, Tex	.319	.322	3
Baines, Oak	.284	.295	11	Gruber, Tor	.274	.252	-22	Parker D, Tor	.289	.239	-50
Bell Geo, ChN	.265	.285	20	Guerrero, StL	.281	.272	-9	Parrish Ln, Cal	.268	.216	-52
Bell Jay, Pit	.254	.270	16	Guillen, ChA	.279	.273	-6	Pena T, Bos	.263	.231	-32
Benzinger, KC	.253	.262	9	Gwynn T, SD	.309	.317	8	Pendleton, Atl	.230	.319	89
Biggio, Hou	.276	.295	19	Hall M, NYA	.258	.285	27	Phillips, Det	.251	.284	33
Blauser, Atl	.269	.259	-10	Harper B, Min	.294	.311	17	Polonia, Cal	.335	.296	-39
Boggs W, Bos	.302	.332	30	Harris L, LA	.304	.287	-17	Puckett, Min	.298	.319	21
Bonds, Pit	.301	.292	-9	Hatcher B, Cin	.276	.262	-14	Quintana, Bos	.287	.295	8
Bonilla B, Pit	.280	.302	22	Hayes C, Phi	.258	.230	-28	Raines, ChA	.287	.268	-19
Brett, KC	.329	.255	-74	Henderson D, Oak	.271	.276	5	Randolph, Mil	.260	.327	67
Brooks, NYN	.266	.238	-28	Henderson R, Oak	.325	.268	-57	Reed Jd, Bos	.289	.283	-6
Brunansky, Bos	.255	.229	-26	Hrbek, Min	.287	.284	-3	Reynolds H, Sea	.252	.254	2
Burks, Bos	.296	.251	-45	Jacoby, Oak	.293	.224	-69	Ripken C, Bal	.250	.323	73
Butler, LA	.309	.296	-13	James C, Cle	.299	.238	-61	Roberts Bip, SD	.309	.281	-28
Calderon, Mon	.273	.300	27	Jefferies, NYN	.283	.272	-11	Sabo, Cin	.270	.301	30
Caminiti, Hou	.242	.253	9	Johnson H, NYN	.244	.259	15	Samuel, LA	.242	.271	29
Canseco, Oak	.274	.266	-8	Johnson L, ChA	.285	.274	-11	Sandberg, ChN	.306	.291	-15
Carter J, Tor	.232	.273	41	Jose, StL	.265	.305	40	Sax S, NYA	.260	.304	44
Clark W, SF	.295	.301	6	Justice, Atl	.282	.275	-7	Sierra, Tex	.280	.307	27
Daniels, LA	.296	.249	-47	Kelly, NYA	.285	.267	-18	Smith Lo, Atl	.305	.275	-30
Davis A, Sea	.283	.221	-62	Kruk, Phi	.291	.294	3	Smith O, StL	.254	.285	31
Davis C, Min	.265	.277	12	Larkin B, Cin	.301	.302	1	Spiers, Mil	.242	.283	39
Dawson, ChN	.310	.272	-38	Lee M, Tor	.243	.234	-9	Steinbach, Oak	.251	.274	23
Deer, Det	.209	.179	-30	Lind, Pit	.261	.265	4	Stillwell, KC	.249	.265	16
DeShields, Mon	.289	.238	-51	Magadan, NYN	.328	.258	-70	Strawberry, LA	.277	.265	-12
Devereaux, Bal	.240	.260	20	Martinez Da, Mon	.279	.295	16	Stubbs, Mil	.261	.213	-48
Doran, Cin	.300	.280	-20	Martinez E, Sea	.302	.307	5	Surhoff BJ, Mil	.276	.289	13
Dunston, ChN	.262	.260	-2	Mattingly, NYA	.256	.288	32	Tettleton, Det	.223	.263	40
Eisenreich, KC	.280	.301	21	McGee, SF	.324	.312	-12	Thompson Ro, SF	.245	.262	17
Espinoza, NYA	.224	.256	32	McGriff F, SD	.300	.278	-22	Thon, Phi	.255	.252	-3
Fermin, Cle	.256	.262	6	McGwire, Oak	.235	.201	-34	Trammell, Det	.304	.248	-56
Fernandez T, SD	.276	.272	-4	McReynolds, NYN	.269	.259	-10	Van Slyke, Pit	.284	.265	-19
Fielder, Det	.277	.261	-16	Milligan, Bal	.265	.263	-2	Vaughn G, Mil	.220	.244	24
Finley S, Hou	.256	.285	29	Mitchell K, SF	.290	.256	-34	Ventura, ChA	.249	.284	35
Fisk, ChA	.285	.241	-44	Molitor, Mil	.285	.325	40	Walker L, Mon	.241	.290	49
Franco Ju, Tex	.296	.341	46	Murphy Dl, Phi	.245	.252	7	Wallach, Mon	.296	.225	-71
Gaetti, Cal	.229	.246	17	Murray E, LA	.330	.260	-70	Whitaker, Det	.237	.279	42
Gagne, Min	.235	.265	30	Nokes, NYA	.248	.268	20	White D, Tor	.217	.282	65
Galarraga, Mon	.256	.219	-37	O'Brien P, Sea	.224	.248	24	Williams MD, SF	.277	.268	-9
Gallego, Oak	.206	.247	41	O'Neill, Cin	.270	.256	-14	Winfield, Cal	.267	.262	-5
Gant, Atl	.303	.251	-52	Olerud, Tor	.265	.256	-9	Yount, Mil	.247	.260	13
Gladden, Min	.275	.247	-28	Oquendo, StL	.252	.240	-12	Zeile, StL	.244	.280	36
Grace, ChN	.309	.273	-36	Orsulak, Bal	.269	.278	9	**AL Avg**	**.263**	**.256**	**-7**
Greenwell, Bos	.297	.300	3	Owen S, Mon	.234	.255	21	**NL Avg**	**.267**	**.262**	**-5**
Griffey Jr, Sea	.300	.327	27	Pagliarulo, Min	.254	.279	25				

WHO WINS THE "GAME OF THE STATES"? (p. 142)

Batting Average by State/Province/Country (career)

State	#Pl	Avg	OBP	Slg	AB	R	H	HR	RBI	BB	K	SB
AK	1	.257	.332	.414	5815	869	1494	169	737	616	1135	280
AL	7	.268	.331	.373	21440	3185	5739	278	1983	1999	3084	1651
AR	2	.267	.324	.447	4647	630	1240	184	701	407	594	83
Austrla.	1	.237	.265	.287	160	15	38	1	12	4	26	0
AZ	9	.253	.318	.369	13030	1571	3298	242	1364	1206	1928	396
Brit.Col	1	.262	.335	.433	953	122	250	35	119	96	227	36
Belize	1	.269	.303	.514	216	32	58	13	33	11	51	1
CA	130	.265	.336	.411	232678	31483	61689	6657	29788	24281	37479	5646
CO	1	.167	.262	.241	54	9	9	1	1	6	7	3
CT	4	.251	.329	.389	3330	420	836	84	405	387	552	23
Cuba	3	.278	.344	.476	6751	995	1876	303	1097	661	1278	152
DC	1	.280	.338	.382	2774	367	777	33	241	235	459	173
DE	2	.256	.345	.406	3880	525	995	108	480	491	702	130
DomRp	37	.267	.317	.381	64659	8054	17260	1149	6981	4613	9474	1997
FL	35	.269	.336	.417	64480	8987	17316	1796	7989	6428	10631	2368
GA	16	.269	.342	.398	23096	3093	6223	522	2808	2545	3482	583
Germ.	1	.203	.270	.304	217	21	44	6	25	19	66	1
HI	1	.246	.356	.347	268	46	66	4	27	40	54	14
Hondu.	1	.249	.332	.306	1679	235	418	3	105	210	193	147
ID	1	.256	.326	.376	3802	453	972	71	442	408	602	34
IL	25	.275	.344	.415	59687	8561	16408	1519	7052	6114	9002	2155
IN	11	.273	.328	.434	13814	1797	3774	472	1892	1130	2015	246
Jamac.	2	.264	.331	.421	8127	1183	2142	261	1053	833	1621	269
KS	3	.251	.329	.384	4809	635	1205	109	515	551	850	166
KY	7	.261	.319	.399	12185	1550	3177	305	1547	1019	2191	261
LA	6	.287	.351	.471	5192	779	1492	194	850	502	933	77
MA	8	.248	.306	.400	10239	1226	2537	296	1223	824	1963	98
MD	6	.274	.339	.433	15668	2123	4298	503	2180	1547	2159	129
ME	1	.182	.242	.261	165	12	30	2	15	12	50	1
Mexico	6	.240	.292	.324	179	16	43	1	12	14	34	0
MI	10	.258	.328	.415	15333	2150	3957	494	1924	1550	2705	519
MN	8	.286	.353	.453	27150	4072	7778	899	3876	2814	3649	715
MO	9	.230	.304	.301	3130	386	720	24	278	331	441	115
MS	6	.279	.329	.442	15303	2020	4262	494	2224	1122	2536	306
NC	10	.262	.335	.369	10500	1351	2752	186	1120	1163	1555	502
NE	2	.341	.431	.466	5828	1015	1987	80	648	940	465	16
Neth.A	1	.223	.286	.333	399	51	89	9	40	29	130	4
NH	2	.264	.329	.377	793	117	209	16	93	76	168	12
NJ	8	.259	.316	.361	13432	1538	3485	190	1435	1097	1560	155
NM	1	.133	.235	.133	15	0	2	0	0	2	5	0
NY	28	.265	.331	.403	41609	5649	11015	1021	5041	4071	6395	998
OH	23	.264	.327	.385	28238	3525	7441	583	3239	2643	4253	733
OK	8	.245	.315	.416	9555	1259	2341	365	1339	922	2031	212
Ontario	1	.247	.324	.341	299	47	74	2	30	35	83	8
OR	8	.261	.339	.405	18894	2693	4935	552	2303	2210	3176	556
PA	20	.270	.345	.417	41562	5523	11211	1197	5423	4811	6451	674
Pan.	1	.282	.336	.422	1697	239	479	46	192	127	344	123
PueR	27	.262	.323	.391	35802	4425	9363	822	4320	3227	5694	704
Sask.	1	.280	.349	.388	4855	676	1361	62	435	505	507	217
SC	8	.270	.342	.360	16915	2417	4565	159	1483	1832	2226	762
SD	1	.226	.304	.339	62	1	14	1	4	5	12	0
TN	5	.238	.312	.349	7478	859	1779	141	773	810	1182	109
TX	19	.258	.312	.383	24398	2971	6293	503	2695	1874	3698	560
VA	5	.242	.285	.306	3661	394	886	20	292	212	598	83
Venez.	14	.262	.301	.364	17579	1952	4610	278	1832	917	2641	374
VI	1	.269	.347	.350	2093	298	564	14	182	254	225	62
VT	1	.270	.342	.461	8515	1262	2303	372	1305	824	1337	125
WA	3	.278	.338	.428	8997	1340	2498	255	1057	827	1386	337
WI	3	.273	.319	.353	6365	753	1738	50	591	400	551	150
WV	3	.305	.377	.485	11642	1809	3547	360	1835	1400	1217	232
WY	1	.251	.306	.393	1463	196	367	39	160	116	243	54

IS THERE SUCH A THING AS A "TURF HITTER"? (p. 144)

The table below lists 1991 active players Batting Average on Grass (**G**) and on Turf (**T**) from 1989 through 1991, and the difference (**Dff**) between the two.

Both Leagues — Listed Alphabetically
(minimum 500 plate appearances in 1991)

Player, Team	G	T	Dff	Player, Team	G	T	Dff	Player, Team	G	T	Dff
Alomar R, Tor	.267	.314	-47	Gibson K, KC	.261	.222	39	Orsulak, Bal	.281	.262	18
Baerga, Cle	.295	.247	48	Gladden, Min	.239	.253	-14	Pagnozzi, StL	.266	.263	3
Bagwell, Hou	.278	.301	-23	Gonzalez J, Tex	.282	.188	94	Palmeiro, Tex	.333	.263	70
Baines, Oak	.301	.265	36	Gonzalez L, Hou	.250	.255	-5	Parker D, Tor	.233	.265	-32
Bell Geo, ChN	.290	.272	18	Grace, ChN	.283	.247	36	Pena T, Bos	.226	.253	-27
Bell Jay, Pit	.237	.281	-43	Greenwell, Bos	.299	.304	-5	Pendleton, Atl	.326	.300	26
Biggio, Hou	.243	.319	-76	Griffey Jr, Sea	.277	.357	-80	Phillips, Det	.283	.289	-6
Boggs W, Bos	.330	.337	-7	Grissom, Mon	.260	.271	-11	Polonia, Cal	.278	.383	105
Bonds, Pit	.280	.296	-16	Guillen, ChA	.274	.267	7	Puckett, Min	.323	.317	6
Bonilla B, Pit	.284	.308	-24	Gwynn T, SD	.321	.308	13	Quintana, Bos	.291	.313	-22
Brett, KC	.251	.259	-8	Hall M, NYA	.283	.294	-11	Raines, ChA	.277	.211	66
Brunansky, Bos	.216	.287	-72	Henderson D, Oak	.287	.214	73	Randolph, Mil	.330	.313	17
Buechele, Pit	.267	.248	19	Henderson R, Oak	.270	.255	15	Reed Jd, Bos	.287	.261	26
Burks, Bos	.247	.267	-20	Hrbek, Min	.258	.300	-42	Reynolds H, Sea	.197	.288	-91
Butler, LA	.304	.274	30	Jefferies, NYN	.277	.254	23	Ripken C, Bal	.315	.370	-55
Calderon, Mon	.295	.302	-7	Johnson H, NY	.255	.268	-13	Sabo, Cin	.284	.308	-24
Caminiti, Hou	.260	.249	11	Johnson L, ChA	.277	.256	21	Samuel, LA	.269	.278	-9
Candaele, Hou	.237	.273	-36	Jose, StL	.270	.319	-49	Sandberg, ChN	.303	.261	42
Canseco, Oak	.257	.305	-48	Joyner, Cal	.294	.346	-52	Santiago, SD	.277	.237	40
Carter J, Tor	.263	.279	-16	Kelly, NYA	.284	.193	91	Sax S, NYA	.299	.330	-31
Clark Jk, Bos	.247	.264	-17	Knoblauch, Min	.241	.306	-65	Sierra, Tex	.302	.333	-31
Clark W, SF	.295	.316	-21	Kruk, Phi	.261	.305	-44	Smith O, StL	.197	.313	116
Cuyler, Det	.245	.307	-62	Lankford, StL	.273	.243	30	Strawberry, LA	.270	.254	16
Daniels, LA	.249	.250	-1	Larkin B, Cin	.266	.315	-49	Surhoff BJ, Mil	.298	.236	62
Davis A, Sea	.209	.229	-20	Lind, Pit	.277	.260	17	Tartabull, KC	.317	.316	1
Davis C, Min	.271	.281	-10	Maas, NYA	.210	.271	-61	Tettleton, Det	.271	.224	47
Dawson, ChN	.277	.259	18	Magadan, NYN	.247	.288	-41	Thomas F, ChA	.343	.191	152
Deer, Det	.183	.160	23	Martinez E, Sea	.288	.320	-32	Thompson R, SF	.273	.231	42
DeShields, Mon	.202	.254	-52	Mattingly, NYA	.293	.262	31	Thon, Phi	.245	.255	-10
Devereaux, Bal	.251	.301	-50	McGee, SF	.284	.388	104	Van Slyke, Pit	.277	.261	16
Dunston, ChN	.280	.216	64	McGriff F, SD	.287	.255	32	Vaughn G, Mil	.256	.173	83
Espinoza, NYA	.258	.247	11	McGwire, Oak	.205	.181	24	Ventura, ChA	.284	.284	0
Fernandez T, SD	.276	.263	13	McRae B, KC	.270	.255	15	Walker L, Mon	.288	.290	-2
Fielder, Det	.260	.270	-10	McReynolds, NY	.244	.292	-48	Wallach, Mon	.236	.221	15
Finley S, Hou	.328	.266	62	Milligan, Bal	.252	.324	-72	Whitaker, Det	.295	.186	109
Fisk, ChA	.247	.203	44	Molitor, Mil	.318	.358	-40	White D, Tor	.255	.299	-44
Franco Ju, Tex	.342	.336	6	Morris H, Cin	.369	.299	70	Williams MD, SF	.284	.221	63
Fryman T, Det	.261	.247	14	Murphy Dl, Phi	.204	.271	-67	Winfield, Cal	.251	.323	-72
Gaetti, Cal	.248	.232	16	Murray E, LA	.277	.217	60	Yount, Mil	.259	.267	-8
Gallego, Oak	.251	.228	23	O'Brien P, Sea	.280	.229	51	Zeile, StL	.268	.284	-16
Gant, Atl	.260	.227	33	O'Neill, Cin	.286	.243	43	**AL Avg**	**.259**	**.262**	**-3**
Gantner, Mil	.288	.250	38	Olerud, Tor	.256	.255	1	**NL Avg**	**.252**	**.249**	**3**

WHOSE HEATER IS THE HOTTEST? (p. 151)

1991 Both Leagues — Listed Alphabetically
(minimum 81 innings pitched or 50 relief games)

Pitcher, Team	K	IP	K/9	Pitcher, Team	K	IP	K/9
Abbott, Cal	158	243.0	5.9	Drabek, Pit	142	234.2	5.4
Acker, Tor	44	88.1	4.5	Eckersley, Oak	87	76.0	10.3
Agosto, StL	34	86.0	3.6	Eichhorn, Cal	49	81.2	5.4
Aguilera, Min	61	69.0	8.0	Erickson S, Min	108	204.0	4.8
Alexander G, Tex	50	89.1	5.0	Farr, NYA	60	70.0	7.7
Anderson A, Min	51	134.1	3.4	Fassero, Mon	42	55.1	6.8
Appier, KC	158	207.2	6.8	Fernandez A, ChA	145	191.2	6.8
Aquino, KC	80	157.0	4.6	Finley C, Cal	171	227.1	6.8
Armstrong, Cin	93	139.2	6.0	Flanagan, Bal	55	98.1	5.0
Assenmacher, ChN	117	102.2	10.3	Fossas, Bos	29	57.0	4.6
August, Mil	62	138.1	4.0	Franco Jn, NYN	45	55.1	7.3
Avery, Atl	137	210.1	5.9	Frohwirth, Bal	77	96.1	7.2
Ballard, Bal	37	123.2	2.7	Gardiner, Bos	91	130.0	6.3
Barfield Jn, Tex	27	83.1	2.9	Gardner M, Mon	107	168.1	5.7
Barnes B, Mon	117	160.0	6.6	Gibson P, Det	52	96.0	4.9
Bedrosian, Min	44	77.1	5.1	Glavine, Atl	192	246.2	7.0
Belcher, LA	156	209.1	6.7	Gooden, NYN	150	190.0	7.1
Belinda, Pit	71	78.1	8.2	Gordon, KC	167	158.0	9.5
Benes, SD	167	223.0	6.7	Gott, LA	73	76.0	8.6
Bielecki, Atl	75	173.2	3.9	Gray, Bos	41	61.2	6.0
Black, SF	104	214.1	4.4	Greene, Phi	154	207.2	6.7
Boddicker, KC	79	180.2	3.9	Gross K, LA	95	115.2	7.4
Boever, Phi	89	98.1	8.1	Gross Kip, Cin	40	85.2	4.2
Bolton, Bos	64	110.0	5.2	Gubicza, KC	89	133.0	6.0
Bosio, Mil	117	204.2	5.1	Guetterman, NYA	35	88.0	3.6
Boskie, ChN	62	129.0	4.3	Gullickson, Det	91	226.1	3.6
Boyd, Tex	115	182.1	5.7	Guthrie, Min	72	98.0	6.6
Brantley J, SF	81	95.1	7.6	Guzman, Tex	125	169.2	6.6
Brown Kev, Tex	96	210.2	4.1	Guzman J, Tor	123	138.2	8.0
Browning, Cin	115	230.1	4.5	Habyan, NYA	70	90.0	7.0
Burke, NYN	59	101.2	5.2	Hammond, Cin	50	99.2	4.5
Burkett, SF	131	206.2	5.7	Haney, Mon	51	84.2	5.4
Cadaret, NYA	105	121.2	7.8	Hanson, Sea	143	174.2	7.4
Candelaria, LA	38	33.2	10.2	Harnisch, Hou	172	216.2	7.1
Candiotti, Tor	167	238.0	6.3	Harris GA, Bos	127	173.0	6.6
Carpenter, StL	47	66.0	6.4	Harris GW, SD	95	133.0	6.4
Castillo F, ChN	73	111.2	5.9	Hartley, Phi	63	83.1	6.8
Cerutti, Det	29	88.2	2.9	Harvey, Cal	101	78.2	11.6
Charlton, Cin	77	108.1	6.4	Hawkins, Oak	45	89.2	4.5
Chitren, Oak	47	60.1	7.0	Henneman, Det	61	84.1	6.5
Clancy, Atl	50	89.2	5.0	Henry, Hou	51	67.2	6.8
Clemens, Bos	241	271.1	8.0	Hershiser, LA	73	112.0	5.9
Cone, NYN	241	232.2	9.3	Hesketh, Bos	104	153.1	6.1
Cox, Phi	46	102.1	4.0	Hibbard, ChA	71	194.0	3.3
Crews, LA	53	76.0	6.3	Hill K, StL	121	181.1	6.0
Crim, Mil	39	91.1	3.8	Hillegas, Cle	66	83.0	7.2
Darling, Oak	129	194.1	6.0	Holman B, Sea	108	195.1	5.0
Davis Storm, KC	53	114.1	4.2	Hough, ChA	107	199.1	4.8
DeJesus J, Phi	118	181.2	5.8	Hurst, SD	141	221.2	5.7
DeLeon J, StL	118	162.2	6.5	Innis, NYN	47	84.2	5.0
Delucia, Sea	98	182.0	4.8	Jackson M, Sea	74	88.2	7.5
Deshaies, Hou	98	161.0	5.5	Jeffcoat, Tex	43	79.2	4.9
Dibble, Cin	124	82.1	13.6	Johnson D, Bal	38	84.0	4.1
Downs, SF	62	111.2	5.0	Johnson J, NYA	62	127.0	4.4

Pitcher, Team	K	IP	K/9	Pitcher, Team	K	IP	K/9
Johnson R, Sea	228	201.1	10.2	Power, Cin	51	87.0	5.3
Jones Ba, Mon	46	88.2	4.7	Radinsky, ChA	49	71.1	6.2
Jones Jim, Hou	88	135.1	5.9	Rasmussen D, SD	75	146.2	4.6
Key, Tor	125	209.1	5.4	Reardon, Bos	44	59.1	6.7
Kile, Hou	100	153.2	5.9	Righetti, SF	51	71.2	6.4
King E, Cle	59	150.2	3.5	Rijo, Cin	172	204.1	7.6
Kipper, Pit	38	60.0	5.7	Robinson D, SF	78	121.1	5.8
Klink, Oak	34	62.0	4.9	Robinson JM, Bal	65	104.1	5.6
Krueger, Sea	91	175.0	4.7	Rodriguez Rich, SD	40	80.0	4.5
Lamp, Bos	57	92.0	5.6	Rogers, Tex	73	109.2	6.0
Lancaster, ChN	102	156.0	5.9	Ruffin, Phi	85	119.0	6.4
Landrum B, Pit	45	76.1	5.3	Ruskin, Mon	46	63.2	6.5
Langston, Cal	183	246.1	6.7	Russell Jf, Tex	52	79.1	5.9
Leach T, Min	32	67.1	4.3	Ryan, Tex	203	173.0	10.6
Leary, NYA	83	120.2	6.2	Saberhagen, KC	136	196.1	6.2
Lee, Mil	43	67.2	5.7	Sampen, Mon	52	92.1	5.1
Lefferts, SD	48	69.0	6.3	Sanderson, NYA	130	208.0	5.6
Leibrandt, Atl	128	229.2	5.0	Scanlan, ChN	44	111.0	3.6
Leiter M, Det	103	134.2	6.9	Schilling, Hou	71	75.2	8.4
Machado, Mil	98	88.2	9.9	Schourek, NYN	67	86.1	7.0
Maddux G, ChN	198	263.0	6.8	Scudder, Cin	51	101.1	4.5
Maddux M, SD	57	98.2	5.2	Slocumb, ChN	34	62.2	4.9
Martinez De, Mon	123	222.0	5.0	Slusarski, Oak	60	109.1	4.9
Martinez R, LA	150	220.1	6.1	Smiley, Pit	129	207.2	5.6
McCaskill, Cal	71	177.2	3.6	Smith B, StL	94	198.2	4.3
McDonald, Bal	85	126.1	6.1	Smith Le, StL	67	73.0	8.3
McDowell J, ChA	191	253.2	6.8	Smith Z, Pit	120	228.0	4.7
McDowell R, LA	50	101.1	4.4	Smoltz, Atl	148	229.2	5.8
McElroy, ChN	92	101.1	8.2	Stanton M, Atl	54	78.0	6.2
Melendez J, SD	60	93.2	5.8	Stewart D, Oak	144	226.0	5.7
Mesa, Bal	64	123.2	4.7	Stottlemyre, Tor	116	219.0	4.8
Milacki, Bal	108	184.0	5.3	Sutcliffe, ChN	52	96.2	4.8
Montgomery, KC	77	90.0	7.7	Swan, Sea	33	78.2	3.8
Moore M, Oak	153	210.0	6.6	Swift, Sea	48	90.1	4.8
Morgan M, LA	140	236.1	5.3	Swindell, Cle	169	238.0	6.4
Morris Jk, Min	163	246.2	5.9	Tanana, Det	107	217.1	4.4
Morton, Bos	45	86.1	4.7	Tapani, Min	135	244.0	5.0
Mulholland, Phi	142	232.0	5.5	Taylor W, NYA	72	116.1	5.6
Murphy R, Sea	34	48.0	6.4	Terrell, Det	80	218.2	3.3
Mussina, Bal	52	87.2	5.3	Terry, StL	52	80.1	5.8
Myers R, Cin	108	132.0	7.4	Tewksbury, StL	75	191.0	3.5
Nabholz, Mon	99	153.2	5.8	Thigpen, ChA	47	69.2	6.1
Nagy, Cle	109	211.1	4.6	Timlin, Tor	85	108.1	7.1
Navarro, Mil	114	234.0	4.4	Tomlin R, Pit	104	175.0	5.3
Nichols Rod, Cle	76	137.1	5.0	Viola, NYN	132	231.1	5.1
Ojeda, LA	120	189.1	5.7	Walk, Pit	67	115.0	5.2
Olivares, StL	91	167.1	4.9	Ward D, Tor	132	107.1	11.1
Oliveras, SF	48	79.1	5.4	Wegman, Mil	89	193.1	4.1
Olson Gregg, Bal	72	73.2	8.8	Welch, Oak	101	220.0	4.1
Osuna, Hou	68	81.2	7.5	Wells, Tor	106	198.1	4.8
Otto, Cle	47	100.0	4.2	Whitehurst, NYN	87	133.1	5.9
Palacios, Pit	64	81.2	7.1	Williams Mitch, Phi	84	88.1	8.6
Pall, ChA	40	71.0	5.1	Williamson, Bal	53	80.1	5.9
Patterson B, Pit	57	65.2	7.8	Willis, Min	53	89.0	5.4
Pena A, Atl	62	82.1	6.8	Wilson Tr, SF	139	202.0	6.2
Perez M, ChA	128	135.2	8.5	Witt B, Tex	82	88.2	8.3
Petry, Bos	39	101.1	3.5	Young Mt, Bos	69	88.2	7.0
Plesac, Mil	61	92.1	5.9	**MLB Avg**			**5.8**
Plunk, NYA	103	111.2	8.3				
Portugal, Hou	120	168.1	6.4				

WILL THEY KEEP 'EM OFF BASE IN '92 LIKE THEY DID IN '91? (p. 154)

The table lists the number of baserunners allowed (**BR**) — hits plus walks plus hit batsmen — per nine innings pitched (**IP**) under the **BR/9** column.

Both Leagues Listed Alphabetically
(minimum 125 Innings Pitched in 1991)

Pitcher, Team	BR/9	IP	BR	Pitcher, Team	BR/9	IP	BR
Abbott, Cal	11.11	243.0	300	Key, Tor	10.92	209.1	254
Anderson A, Min	13.06	134.1	195	Kile, Hou	13.70	153.2	234
Appier, KC	11.61	207.2	268	King E, Cle	12.72	150.2	213
Aquino, KC	11.64	157.0	203	Krueger, Sea	13.27	175.0	258
Armstrong, Cin	13.79	139.2	214	Lancaster, ChN	11.71	156.0	203
August, Mil	14.05	138.1	216	Langston, Cal	10.52	246.1	288
Avery, Atl	11.00	210.1	257	Leibrandt, Atl	10.66	229.2	272
Barnes B, Mon	12.66	160.0	225	Leiter M, Det	12.10	134.2	181
Belcher, LA	11.44	209.1	266	Maddux G, ChN	10.40	263.0	304
Benes, SD	10.37	223.0	257	Martinez D, Mon	10.26	222.0	253
Bielecki, Atl	11.87	173.2	229	Martinez R, LA	10.87	220.1	266
Black, SF	11.59	214.1	276	McCaskill, Cal	13.27	177.2	262
Boddicker, KC	12.95	180.2	260	McDonald, Bal	12.11	126.1	170
Bosio, Mil	11.13	204.2	253	McDowell J, ChA	10.57	253.2	298
Boskie, ChN	14.44	129.0	207	Milacki, Bal	11.20	184.0	229
Boyd, Tex	12.49	182.1	253	Moore M, Oak	12.26	210.0	286
Brown Kev, Tex	14.35	210.2	336	Morgan M, LA	9.94	236.1	261
Browning, Cin	11.76	230.1	301	Morris Jk, Min	11.79	246.2	323
Burkett, SF	12.76	206.2	293	Mulholland, Phi	10.98	232.0	283
Candiotti, Tor	10.63	238.0	281	Myers R, Cin	13.43	132.0	197
Clemens, Bos	9.59	271.1	289	Nabholz, Mon	11.30	153.2	193
Cone, NYN	10.91	232.2	282	Nagy, Cle	12.78	211.1	300
Darling, Oak	12.27	194.1	265	Navarro, Mil	12.15	234.0	316
DeJesus J, Phi	13.82	181.2	279	Nichols Rod, Cle	11.86	137.1	181
DeLeon J, StL	11.67	162.2	211	Ojeda, LA	12.07	189.1	254
Delucia, Sea	12.76	182.0	258	Olivares, StL	11.51	167.1	214
Deshaies, Hou	12.80	161.0	229	Perez M, ChA	10.88	135.2	164
Drabek, Pit	11.89	234.2	310	Portugal, Hou	11.98	168.1	224
Erickson S, Min	11.74	204.0	266	Rasmussen, SD	12.64	146.2	206
Fernandez A, Ch	12.96	191.2	276	Rijo, Cin	9.82	204.1	223
Finley C, Cal	12.43	227.1	314	Ryan, Tex	9.31	173.0	179
Gardiner, Bos	12.95	130.0	187	Saberhagen, KC	10.04	196.1	219
Gardner M, Mon	11.66	168.1	218	Sanderson, NYA	10.04	208.0	232
Glavine, Atl	9.92	246.2	272	Smiley, Pit	10.44	207.2	241
Gooden, NYN	11.56	190.0	244	Smith B, StL	10.87	198.2	240
Gordon, KC	12.53	158.0	220	Smith Z, Pit	10.46	228.0	265
Greene, Phi	10.66	207.2	246	Smoltz, Atl	11.21	229.2	286
Gubicza, KC	14.62	133.0	216	Stewart D, Oak	14.30	226.0	359
Gullickson, Det	12.09	226.1	304	Stottlemyre, Tor	11.55	219.0	281
Guzman, Tex	12.73	169.2	240	Swindell, Cle	10.40	238.0	275
Guzman J, Tor	10.90	138.2	168	Tanana, Det	12.30	217.1	297
Hanson, Sea	12.37	174.2	240	Tapani, Min	9.85	244.0	267
Harnisch, Hou	10.68	216.2	257	Terrell, Det	13.91	218.2	338
Harris GA, Bos	12.02	173.0	231	Tewksbury, StL	11.73	191.0	249
Harris GW, SD	9.74	133.0	144	Tomlin R, Pit	11.83	175.0	230
Hesketh, Bos	11.45	153.1	195	Viola, NYN	12.22	231.1	314
Hibbard, ChA	11.83	194.0	255	Wegman, Mil	10.38	193.1	223
Hill K, StL	10.92	181.1	220	Welch, Oak	13.17	220.1	322
Holman B, Sea	13.18	195.1	286	Wells, Tor	10.85	198.1	239
Hough, ChA	12.28	199.1	272	Whitehurst, NYN	11.54	133.1	171
Hurst, SD	10.68	221.2	263	Wilson Tr, SF	11.36	202.0	255
Johnson J, NYA	13.82	127.0	195	**MLB Average**	**12.26**		
Johnson R, Sea	14.08	201.1	315				
Jones Jim, Hou	13.10	135.1	197				

WHO PITCHED BETTER IN 1991 — BILL GULLICKSON OR FRANK VIOLA? (p. 156)

In the table below, **Sup** stands for Run Support Per Nine Innings. **RS** is the total Runs In Support of that pitcher while he was in the game. Statistics are for pitchers in a starting role only.

1991 Both Leagues — Listed Alphabetically
(minimum 20 games started in 1991)

Pitcher, Team	W/L	ERA	Sup	IP	RS	Pitcher, Team	W/L	ERA	Sup	IP	RS
Abbott, Cal	18-11	2.89	4.70	243.0	127	Armstrong, Cin	7-13	5.51	4.57	134.0	68
Anderson A, Min	5-9	4.80	4.28	120.0	57	Avery, Atl	18-8	3.38	5.39	210.1	126
Appier, KC	13-9	3.37	4.81	200.1	107	Barnes B, Mon	5-8	4.24	3.62	159.1	64
August, Mil	8-7	5.40	6.91	125.0	96	Belcher, LA	10-9	2.62	3.44	209.1	80
Ballard, Bal	6-12	5.48	4.55	116.2	59	Benes, SD	15-11	3.03	3.31	223.0	82
Boddicker, KC	11-12	4.11	4.46	179.2	89	Bielecki, Atl	10-8	4.41	5.01	149.0	83
Bosio, Mil	14-10	3.25	4.62	204.2	105	Black, SF	12-16	3.99	4.03	214.1	96
Boyd, Tex	8-15	4.59	3.85	182.1	78	Boskie, ChN	3-9	5.48	3.44	110.0	42
Brown Kev, Tex	9-12	4.40	4.57	210.2	107	Browning, Cin	14-14	4.18	4.77	230.1	122
Candiotti, Tor	13-13	2.65	3.52	238.0	93	Burkett, SF	12-11	4.21	4.26	205.0	97
Clemens, Bos	18-10	2.62	4.44	271.1	134	Cone, NYN	14-14	3.29	4.18	232.2	108
Darling, Oak	8-15	4.26	3.61	194.1	78	DeJesus J, Phi	10-9	3.43	4.08	178.2	81
Delucia, Sea	11-13	5.18	5.53	177.1	109	DeLeon J, StL	5-9	2.71	3.15	162.2	57
Erickson S, Min	20-8	3.18	5.74	204.0	130	Deshaies, Hou	5-12	4.98	3.35	161.0	60
Fernandez A, ChA	9-13	4.57	3.29	189.0	69	Drabek, Pit	15-14	3.07	4.83	234.2	126
Finley C, Cal	18-9	3.80	5.38	227.1	136	Gardner M, Mon	9-11	3.85	3.37	168.1	63
Gardiner, Bos	9-10	4.85	6.23	130.0	90	Glavine, Atl	20-11	2.55	4.71	246.2	129
Gubicza, KC	9-12	5.68	4.26	133.0	63	Gooden, NYN	13-7	3.60	5.12	190.0	108
Gullickson, Det	20-9	3.90	5.81	226.1	146	Greene, Phi	12-7	3.30	4.55	180.0	91
Guzman, Tex	13-7	3.08	5.20	169.2	98	Harnisch, Hou	12-9	2.70	3.49	216.2	84
Guzman J, Tor	10-3	2.99	5.97	138.2	92	Harris GW, SD	9-5	2.23	3.32	133.0	49
Hanson, Sea	8-8	3.81	5.15	174.2	100	Hershiser, LA	7-2	3.46	6.19	112.0	77
Harris GA, Bos	7-10	4.55	4.55	120.2	61	Hill K, StL	11-10	3.57	3.47	181.1	70
Hibbard, ChA	10-11	4.52	4.86	183.1	99	Hurst, SD	15-8	3.29	4.71	221.2	116
Holman B, Sea	13-14	3.69	3.64	195.1	79	Jones Jim, Hou	5-7	4.35	3.65	128.1	52
Hough, ChA	9-10	3.95	4.18	193.2	90	Kile, Hou	7-9	3.07	4.53	129.0	65
Johnson R, Sea	13-10	3.98	5.01	201.1	112	Leibrandt, Atl	15-13	3.49	4.04	229.2	103
Johnson J, NYA	6-11	5.95	4.18	127.0	59	Maddux G, ChN	15-11	3.35	4.45	263.0	130
Key, Tor	16-12	3.05	4.60	209.1	107	Martinez De, Mon	14-11	2.39	3.69	222.0	91
King E, Cle	6-11	4.55	4.13	148.1	68	Martinez R, LA	17-13	3.27	4.94	220.1	121
Krueger, Sea	10-7	3.50	4.27	151.2	72	Morgan M, LA	14-10	2.81	3.62	234.0	94
Langston, Cal	19-8	3.00	4.57	246.1	125	Mulholland, Phi	16-13	3.61	4.27	232.0	110
McCaskill, Cal	10-19	4.26	3.14	177.2	62	Nabholz, Mon	8-7	3.63	4.51	153.2	77
McDonald, Bal	6-8	4.84	5.06	126.1	71	Ojeda, LA	12-9	3.18	3.42	189.1	72
McDowell J, ChA	17-10	3.41	5.53	253.2	156	Olivares, StL	11-7	3.68	4.30	159.0	76
Mesa, Bal	6-11	5.97	5.46	123.2	75	Portugal, Hou	10-10	4.23	4.56	163.2	83
Milacki, Bal	9-9	4.25	4.03	163.0	73	Rasmussen D, SD	6-13	3.74	3.56	146.2	58
Moore M, Oak	17-8	2.96	4.37	210.0	102	Rijo, Cin	15-6	2.51	5.64	204.1	128
Morris Jk, Min	18-12	3.43	5.14	246.2	141	Smiley, Pit	19-8	3.14	4.82	203.1	109
Nagy, Cle	10-15	4.13	3.41	211.1	80	Smith B, StL	12-9	3.85	5.48	198.2	121
Navarro, Mil	15-12	3.92	4.88	234.0	127	Smith Z, Pit	16-10	3.20	5.13	228.0	130
Ryan, Tex	12-6	2.91	4.94	173.0	95	Smoltz, Atl	14-13	3.80	4.47	229.2	114
Saberhagen, KC	13-8	3.07	4.31	196.1	94	Tewksbury, StL	11-12	3.25	4.38	191.0	93
Sanderson, NYA	16-10	3.81	4.98	208.0	115	Tomlin R, Pit	8-7	3.09	4.47	169.0	84
Stewart D, Oak	11-11	5.18	6.13	226.0	154	Viola, NYN	13-15	3.97	3.50	231.1	90
Stottlemyre, Tor	15-8	3.78	4.52	219.0	110	Walk, Pit	7-2	3.77	5.53	107.1	66
Swindell, Cle	9-16	3.48	3.63	238.0	96	Whitehurst, NYN	5-11	4.53	4.61	107.1	55
Tanana, Det	13-12	3.77	5.18	217.1	125	Wilson Tr, SF	13-8	3.47	4.63	179.0	92
Tapani, Min	16-9	2.99	5.31	244.0	144	**MLB Average**		4.02	4.50		
Taylor W, NYA	7-12	5.82	5.28	116.0	68						
Terrell, Det	11-14	4.23	4.48	215.0	107						
Wegman, Mil	15-7	2.84	5.21	193.1	112						
Welch, Oak	12-13	4.58	4.17	220.0	102						
Wells, Tor	14-10	3.75	4.70	180.0	94						

CAN ANYONE HIT NOLAN RYAN — NOW OR EVER? (p. 158)

The following table lists the Opponent Batting Average (**Avg**) and Opponent At-bats (**AB**) for 1991 active pitchers.

Both Leagues — 1991 Active Pitchers Listed Alphabetically
(minimum 2,000 opponent at-bats lifetime)

Pitcher, Team	AB	Avg	Pitcher, Team	AB	Avg	Pitcher, Team	AB	Avg
Abbott, Cal	2437	.270	Gubicza, KC	5823	.253	Perez M, ChA	2735	.248
Acker, Tor	3300	.265	Gullickson, Det	7932	.263	Perez P, NYA	4696	.249
Agosto, StL	2123	.266	Guzman, Tex	3003	.251	Petry, Bos	7837	.253
Aguilera, Min	2585	.250	Hammaker, SD	4083	.254	Plunk, NYA	2150	.238
Andersen L, SD	3260	.251	Hanson, Sea	2134	.246	Portugal, Hou	2684	.259
Anderson A, Min	3194	.282	Harris GA, Bos	4283	.244	Power, Cin	3851	.263
Bailes, Cal	2260	.274	Hawkins, Oak	5935	.265	Rasmussen D, SD	5233	.256
Ballard, Bal	2759	.294	Heaton, Pit	5538	.273	Reardon, Bos	3725	.228
Bankhead, Sea	2658	.257	Henke, Tor	2059	.212	Reuschel, SF	13578	.264
Bannister, Cal	9022	.253	Hershiser, LA	5940	.232	Righetti, SF	4506	.236
Bedrosian, Min	3959	.230	Hesketh, Bos	2415	.251	Rijo, Cin	4005	.236
Belcher, LA	2977	.228	Hibbard, ChA	2058	.262	Robinson D, SF	7195	.254
Berenguer, Atl	4160	.230	Higuera, Mil	4820	.238	Robinson JD, Cal	3124	.257
Bielecki, Atl	3222	.261	Holman B, Sea	2589	.263	Robinson JM, Bal	2377	.248
Black, SF	6395	.250	Honeycutt, Oak	7513	.265	Robinson R, Mil	2917	.263
Boddicker, KC	7517	.254	Hough, ChA	12201	.230	Ruffin, Phi	3453	.284
Bosio, Mil	3706	.259	Howell Jay, LA	2628	.247	Russell Jf, Tex	3257	.256
Boyd, Tex	5363	.266	Hurst, SD	8251	.263	Ryan, Tex	18444	.202
Brown Kev, Tex	2340	.262	Jackson Dan, ChN	4849	.258	Saberhagen, KC	6267	.247
Browning, Cin	6353	.255	Johnson R, Sea	2209	.224	Sanderson, NYA	7744	.255
Burke, NYN	2424	.236	Jones Jim, Hou	2254	.278	Schatzeder, NYN	4971	.253
Candelaria, LA	9368	.251	Key, Tor	5620	.252	Schiraldi, Tex	2102	.248
Candiotti, Tor	5355	.252	Kilgus, Bal	2007	.263	Schmidt D, Mon	3492	.273
Carman, Cin	3450	.245	King E, Cle	2956	.245	Scott M, Hou	7746	.240
Cerutti, Det	3302	.271	Krueger, Sea	3271	.278	Show, Oak	6184	.247
Clancy, Atl	9639	.261	LaCoss, SF	6603	.270	Smiley, Pit	3217	.245
Clemens, Bos	6629	.226	LaPoint, Phi	5769	.277	Smith B, StL	6609	.251
Cone, NYN	3768	.228	Lamp, Bos	6991	.278	Smith Dv, ChN	2932	.234
Cox, Phi	4102	.265	Lancaster, ChN	2121	.263	Smith Le, StL	3661	.234
Crawford, KC	2218	.290	Langston, Cal	6802	.237	Smith Roy, Bal	2448	.289
Crim, Mil	2038	.267	Leach T, Min	2331	.264	Smith Z, Pit	5064	.264
Darling, Oak	6386	.245	Leary, NYA	4485	.270	Smoltz, Atl	2723	.237
Darwin, Bos	7484	.247	Lefferts, SD	3067	.242	Stewart D, Oak	7765	.248
Davis Mrk, KC	3667	.241	Leibrandt, Atl	7575	.268	Stieb, Tor	10090	.237
Davis S, KC	5939	.267	Long B, Mon	2023	.281	Stottlemyre, Tor	2478	.264
Dayley, Tor	2161	.261	Maddux G, ChN	4472	.257	Sutcliffe, ChN	8345	.252
DeLeon J, StL	5773	.223	Mahler R, Atl	7515	.275	Swift, Sea	2940	.281
Deshaies, Hou	4095	.238	Martinez De, Mon	11185	.257	Swindell, Cle	4015	.264
Downs, SF	2640	.242	Martinez R, LA	2180	.223	Tanana, Det	14479	.253
Drabek, Pit	4623	.246	McCaskill, Cal	4633	.257	Terrell, Det	7090	.272
Eckersley, Oak	10992	.244	McClure, StL	4145	.256	Tewksbury, StL	2150	.284
Eichhorn, Cal	2316	.244	McDowell J, ChA	2400	.235	Valenzuela, Cal	8760	.241
Farr, NYA	2597	.243	McDowell R, LA	2661	.248	Viola, NYN	8992	.260
Fernandez S, NYN	4547	.205	McGaffigan, KC	3134	.247	Walk, Pit	5125	.259
Finley C, Cal	3687	.249	Milacki, Bal	2216	.253	Wegman, Mil	3558	.268
Flanagan, Bal	10419	.265	Moore M, Oak	8013	.258	Welch, Oak	10234	.244
Franco Jn, NYN	2414	.243	Morgan M, LA	5337	.271	Wells, Tor	2129	.245
Fraser, StL	2361	.252	Morris Jk, Min	12357	.242	Whitson, SD	8573	.261
Garrelts, SF	3511	.232	Moyer, StL	2710	.283	Witt B, Tex	3618	.232
Glavine, Atl	3383	.255	Mulholland, Phi	2416	.265	Witt M, NYA	7875	.257
Gooden, NYN	6364	.231	Nelson G, Oak	3683	.253	Young C, Oak	3946	.263
Gossage, Tex	6056	.227	Ojeda, LA	6315	.254	Young Mt, Bos	4012	.265
Gott, LA	3371	.253	Orosco, Cle	3059	.224			
Gross K, LA	6058	.259	Pena A, Atl	3489	.240			

HOW IMPORTANT IS IT TO "HOLD THE FORT"? (p. 160)

A Hold (**H**) is a Save Opportunity passed on to the next pitcher. If a pitcher comes into the game in a Save Situation and leaves the game having gotten at least one out and without having blown the lead, this is a "passed on" Save Opportunity and the pitcher is credited with a Hold.

Both Leagues — Listed By Most Holds
(minumum 1 Hold in 1991)

Pitcher, Team	H	Pitcher, Team	H	Pitcher, Team	H	Pitcher, Team	H
Eichhorn, Cal	25	Crews, LA	7	Alexander G, Tex	4	Crawford, KC	2
Habyan, NYA	20	Fassero, Mon	7	Charlton, Cin	3	Searcy, Phi	2
Gray, Bos	19	Gossage, Tex	7	Schourek, NYN	3	Long B, Mon	1
Candelaria, LA	19	Howe S, NYA	7	Mercker, Atl	3	Olson Gregg, Bal	1
Fossas, Bos	18	Hartley, Phi	7	Mason R, Pit	3	Clark M, StL	1
Ward D, Tor	17	Nelson G, Oak	7	Farr, NYA	3	Castillo T, NYN	1
Klink, Oak	16	Young C, Oak	7	Simons, NYN	3	Gross Kip, Cin	1
Lee, Mil	15	Rojas, Mon	7	Petry, Bos	3	Capel, Hou	1
Radinsky, ChA	15	Ritchie, Phi	7	Henry D, Mil	3	Williams Mitch, Phi	1
Stanton M, Atl	15	Ruskin, Mon	7	Hillegas, Cle	3	Young Mt, Bos	1
Terry, StL	15	Slocumb, ChN	6	Kilgus, Bal	3	Bitker, Tex	1
Chitren, Oak	14	Lamp, Bos	6	Orosco, Cle	3	Robinson D, SF	1
Assenmacher, ChN	14	Harris GA, Bos	6	Lefferts, SD	3	Appier, KC	1
Honeycutt, Oak	14	Acker, Tor	6	Johnston, KC	3	Edwards, ChA	1
Flanagan, Bal	14	Costello, SD	6	Hickey, Bal	3	Burkett, SF	1
Crim, Mil	13	Belinda, Pit	6	Montgomery, KC	3	Henneman, Det	1
Swift, Sea	13	Andersen L, SD	6	Holmes, Mil	3	Christopher, LA	1
Patterson B, Pit	13	Boever, Phi	6	Henry Dw, Hou	3	Cook D, LA	1
Swan, Sea	12	Leach T, Min	5	Wilson Tr, SF	3	Allison, Oak	1
Williamson, Bal	12	Jones Ba, Mon	5	Wells, Tor	3	Aquino, KC	1
Brantley J, SF	12	Gott, LA	5	Whitehurst, NYN	3	Cerutti, Det	1
Carpenter, StL	12	Hernandez X, Hou	5	Wohlers, Atl	3	Weathers, Tor	1
Pall, ChA	12	Robinson JD, Cal	5	Mathews T, Tex	2	Portugal, Hou	1
Cadaret, NYA	11	Heaton, Pit	5	Leiter M, Det	2	Hickerson, SF	1
Mallicoat, Hou	11	Righetti, SF	5	Beasley, Cal	2	Layana, Cin	1
Rogers, Tex	11	Guthrie, Min	5	Plunk, NYA	2	Grahe, Cal	1
Machado, Mil	10	Gleaton, Det	5	Howell Jay, LA	2	Clements P, SD	1
McDowell R, LA	10	Palacios, Pit	5	Rosenthal, Tex	2	Jones Cal, Sea	1
McElroy, ChN	10	MacDonald, Tor	5	Magnante, KC	2	Walton B, Oak	1
Murphy R, Sea	10	Kipper, Pit	5	Melendez J, SD	2	Minutelli, Cin	1
Frohwirth, Bal	10	Ruffin, Phi	5	Sauveur, NYN	2	Plesac, Mil	1
Osuna, Hou	10	Schilling, Hou	5	Rosenberg, SD	2	Fernandez A, ChA	1
Gibson P, Det	10	Willis, Min	5	Smith Dv, ChN	2	Valdez E, Tor	1
Bedrosian, Min	10	Wilson S, LA	5	Lewis Jim, SD	2	Pena A, Atl	1
Burke, NYN	10	Sampen, Mon	5	Scanlan, ChN	2	Jones Jim, Hou	1
Oliveras, SF	10	Sisk, Atl	4	Gakeler, Det	2	Downs, SF	1
Freeman M, Atl	9	Landrum B, Pit	4	Wayne, Min	2	Nunez E, Mil	1
Perez M, ChA	9	Davis Storm, KC	4	Davis Mrk, KC	2	Patterson K, ChA	1
Maddux M, SD	9	Innis, NYN	4	Piatt, Mon	2	Fleming, Sea	1
Jackson M, Sea	9	Frey, Mon	4	Clancy, Atl	2	Harris Ge, Sea	1
Power, Cin	9	Poole, Bal	4	Bell E, Cle	2	Burns, Oak	1
Timlin, Tor	9	Hesketh, Bos	4	Campbell K, Oak	2	Cox, Phi	1
Rodriguez Rich, SD	8	Gross K, LA	4	Perez Mk, StL	2	Beck, SF	1
Myers R, Cin	8	Berenguer, Atl	4	Casian, Min	2	Akerfelds, Phi	1
Agosto, StL	8	Fraser, StL	4	Schooler, Sea	2	Nichols Rod, Cle	1
Jeffcoat, Tex	8	Lancaster, ChN	4	Drahman, ChA	2	Hernandez Jer, SD	1
McClure, StL	8	Gordon, KC	4	Gardner W, KC	2	Terrell, Det	1
Bailes, Cal	8	Rodriguez Ro, Pit	4	Show, Oak	2	Meacham R, Det	1
Guetterman, NYA	8	Corsi, Hou	4	Henke, Tor	2	Horsman, Tor	1

WAS BILL SWIFT THE BEST "TOTAL RELIEVER" OF 1991?
(p. 162)

The table below lists a reliever's Holds (**H**), Saves (**Sv**), Blown Saves (**BS**), and Hold + Save Percentage (**%**), which is (Holds plus Saves) divided by (Holds plus Saves plus Blown Saves).

1991 Both Leagues — Listed Alphabetically
(minimum 5 Holds+Saves+Blown Saves in 1991)

Pitcher	H	Sv	BS	%	Pitcher	H	Sv	BS	%	Pitcher	H	Sv	BS	%
Acker, Tor	6	1	2	78	Guthrie, Min	5	2	0	100	Oliveras, SF	10	3	1	93
Agosto, StL	8	2	5	67	Habyan, NYA	20	2	2	92	Olson Gregg, Bal	1	31	8	80
Aguilera, Min	0	42	9	82	Harris GA, Bos	6	2	3	73	Osuna, Hou	10	12	9	71
Andersen L, SD	6	13	3	86	Hartley, Phi	7	2	2	82	Palacios, Pit	5	3	2	80
Assenmacher, Ch	14	15	9	76	Harvey, Cal	0	46	6	88	Pall, ChA	12	0	1	92
Bailes, Cal	8	0	1	89	Heaton, Pit	5	0	1	83	Patterson B, Pit	13	2	1	94
Bedrosian, Min	10	6	1	94	Henke, Tor	2	32	3	92	Pena A, Atl	1	15	5	76
Belinda, Pit	6	16	4	85	Henneman, Det	1	21	3	88	Perez M, ChA	9	1	4	71
Berenguer, Atl	4	17	1	95	Henry, Hou	3	2	0	100	Plesac, Mil	1	8	4	69
Boever, Phi	6	0	2	75	Henry D, Mil	3	15	1	95	Poole, Bal	4	1	0	100
Brantley J, SF	12	15	4	87	Hernandez X, Hou	5	3	3	73	Power, Cin	9	3	1	92
Burke, NYN	10	6	10	62	Hillegas, Cle	3	7	2	83	Radinsky, ChA	15	8	7	77
Cadaret, NYA	11	3	4	78	Holmes, Mil	3	3	3	67	Reardon, Bos	0	40	9	82
Candelaria, LA	19	2	3	88	Honeycutt, Oak	14	0	4	78	Righetti, SF	5	24	5	85
Capel, Hou	1	3	1	80	Howe S, NYA	7	3	0	100	Ritchie, Phi	7	0	3	70
Carpenter, StL	12	0	0	100	Howell Jay, LA	2	16	2	90	Robinson JD, Cal	5	3	2	80
Cerutti, Det	1	2	3	50	Innis, NYN	4	0	3	57	Rodriguez R, SD	8	0	2	80
Charlton, Cin	3	1	3	57	Jackson M, Sea	9	14	8	74	Rodriguez Ro, Pit	4	6	0	100
Chitren, Oak	14	4	3	86	Jeffcoat, Tex	8	1	4	69	Rogers, Tex	11	5	1	94
Clancy, Atl	2	8	3	77	Jones Ba, Mon	5	13	8	69	Rojas, Mon	7	6	3	81
Corsi, Hou	4	0	3	57	Jones D, Cle	0	7	5	58	Ruffin, Phi	5	0	0	100
Costello, SD	6	0	1	86	Kipper, Pit	5	4	2	82	Ruskin, Mon	7	6	5	72
Crews, LA	7	6	2	87	Klink, Oak	16	2	2	90	Russell Jf, Tex	0	30	10	75
Crim, Mil	13	3	2	89	Lamp, Bos	6	0	0	100	Sampen, Mon	5	0	0	100
Davis Mrk, KC	2	1	1	75	Lancaster, ChN	4	3	3	70	Schilling, Hou	5	8	3	81
Davis Storm, KC	4	2	1	86	Landrum B, Pit	4	17	5	81	Schooler, Sea	2	7	3	75
Dibble, Cin	0	31	5	86	Leach T, Min	5	0	2	71	Schourek, NYN	3	2	1	83
Eckersley, Oak	0	43	8	84	Lee, Mil	15	1	6	73	Slocumb, ChN	6	1	2	78
Eichhorn, Cal	25	1	3	90	Lefferts, SD	3	23	7	79	Smith Dv, ChN	2	17	6	76
Farr, NYA	3	23	6	81	Leiter M, Det	2	1	1	75	Smith Le, StL	0	47	6	09
Fassero, Mon	7	8	3	83	MacDonald, Tor	5	0	4	56	Stanton M, Atl	15	7	3	88
Flanagan, Bal	14	3	2	89	Machado, Mil	10	3	3	81	Swan, Sea	12	2	3	82
Fossas, Bos	18	1	1	95	Maddux M, SD	9	5	2	88	Swift, Sea	13	17	1	97
Franco Jn, NYN	0	30	5	86	Mallicoat, Hou	11	1	0	100	Terry, StL	15	1	2	89
Fraser, StL	4	0	0	100	Mason R, Pit	3	3	0	100	Thigpen, ChA	0	30	9	77
Freeman M, Atl	9	1	0	100	Mathews T, Tex	2	1	2	60	Timlin, Tor	9	3	5	71
Frey, Mon	4	1	1	83	McClure, StL	8	0	4	67	Ward D, Tor	17	23	4	91
Frohwirth, Bal	10	3	2	87	McDowell R, LA	10	10	5	80	Wells, Tor	3	1	1	80
Gakeler, Det	2	2	2	67	McElroy, ChN	10	3	3	81	Williams Mitch, Phi	1	30	9	78
Gibson P, Det	10	8	5	78	Melendez J, SD	2	3	1	83	Williamson, Bal	12	4	3	84
Gleaton, Det	5	2	1	88	Mercker, Atl	3	6	2	82	Willis, Min	5	2	1	88
Gordon, KC	4	1	3	63	Montgomery, KC	3	33	6	86	Wilson S, LA	5	2	0	100
Gossage, Tex	7	1	4	67	Murphy R, Sea	10	4	0	100	Wohlers, Atl	2	2	2	67
Gott, LA	5	2	3	70	Myers R, Cin	8	6	4	78	Young C, Oak	7	0	0	100
Gray, Bos	19	1	3	87	Nelson G, Oak	7	0	5	58	**MLB Average**				82
Gross K, LA	4	3	2	70	Nunez E, Mil	1	8	1	90					
Guetterman, NY	8	6	3	82	Olin, Cle	0	17	5	77					

DID LEE SMITH TAKE A SHORTCUT TO THE SAVE CROWN?
(p. 164)

Both Leagues — Listed Alphabetically
(1991 Relievers with a minimum of 3 Save Opportunities)

Reliever	Easy	Regular	Tough	Reliever	Easy	Regular	Tough
Acker, Tor	1/1	0/2	0/0	Klink, Oak	1/1	0/0	1/3
Agosto, StL	0/0	2/4	0/3	Lancaster, ChN	0/0	3/4	0/2
Aguilera, Min	16/17	19/24	7/10	Landrum B, Pit	5/5	5/8	7/9
Andersen L, SD	4/4	6/8	3/4	Lee, Mil	0/0	1/4	0/3
Aquino, KC	0/0	3/4	0/0	Lefferts, SD	8/8	9/10	6/12
Assenmacher, ChN	3/4	8/10	4/10	Machado, Mil	0/0	3/6	0/0
Bedrosian, Min	1/1	5/5	0/1	Maddux M, SD	1/1	2/2	2/4
Belinda, Pit	4/4	9/10	3/6	Mason R, Pit	0/0	3/3	0/0
Berenguer, Atl	2/2	12/13	3/3	Mathews T, Tex	0/0	1/3	0/0
Brantley J, SF	2/3	7/8	6/8	McDowell R, LA	4/5	5/6	1/4
Burke, NYN	0/2	5/8	1/6	McElroy, ChN	0/0	3/5	0/1
Cadaret, NYA	0/0	3/4	0/3	Melendez J, SD	2/2	1/1	0/1
Candelaria, LA	0/1	1/1	1/3	Mercker, Atl	2/2	3/3	1/3
Capel, Hou	1/1	1/1	1/2	Montgomery, KC	16/16	11/15	6/8
Cerutti, Det	1/1	0/0	1/4	Murphy R, Sea	1/1	3/3	0/0
Charlton, Cin	0/1	1/2	0/1	Myers R, Cin	2/2	3/5	1/3
Chitren, Oak	1/1	2/2	1/4	Nunez E, Mil	4/4	4/5	0/0
Clancy, Atl	2/3	6/6	0/2	Olin, Cle	5/5	11/15	1/2
Crews, LA	2/2	3/4	1/2	Oliveras, SF	0/0	1/2	2/2
Crim, Mil	0/0	2/2	1/3	Olson Gregg, Bal	17/18	11/17	3/4
Davis Storm, KC	0/1	2/2	0/0	Osuna, Hou	2/3	8/9	2/9
Dibble, Cin	7/7	17/21	7/8	Palacios, Pit	1/2	2/2	0/1
Eckersley, Oak	15/16	25/30	3/5	Patterson B, Pit	1/1	1/2	0/0
Eichhorn, Cal	1/1	0/2	0/1	Pena A, Atl	5/5	9/12	1/3
Farr, NYA	9/9	10/14	4/6	Perez M, ChA	0/0	1/1	0/4
Fassero, Mon	0/1	6/8	2/2	Plesac, Mil	4/5	3/3	1/4
Flanagan, Bal	0/0	2/3	1/2	Power, Cin	0/0	2/3	1/1
Franco Jn, NYN	11/12	16/19	3/4	Radinsky, ChA	1/1	6/9	1/5
Frohwirth, Bal	1/1	2/3	0/1	Reardon, Bos	19/20	17/23	4/6
Gakeler, Det	1/1	1/2	0/1	Righetti, SF	9/9	9/13	6/7
Gibson P, Det	0/0	5/8	3/5	Robinson JD, Cal	0/0	3/3	0/2
Gleaton, Det	1/1	0/1	1/1	Rodriguez Ro, Pit	2/2	4/4	0/0
Gordon, KC	0/0	1/1	0/3	Rogers, Tex	1/1	3/4	1/1
Gossage, Tex	0/0	0/0	1/5	Rojas, Mon	2/2	2/4	2/3
Gott, LA	0/0	1/2	1/3	Ruskin, Mon	1/1	4/5	1/5
Gray, Bos	0/0	1/1	0/3	Russell Jf, Tex	13/15	15/20	2/5
Gross K, LA	0/0	3/5	0/1	Schilling, Hou	1/1	5/6	2/4
Guetterman, NYA	2/2	3/4	1/3	Schooler, Sea	5/5	1/3	1/2
Habyan, NYA	1/1	1/2	0/1	Schourek, NYN	0/0	2/2	0/1
Harris GA, Bos	0/0	1/3	1/2	Shaw, Cle	0/0	1/3	0/1
Hartley, Phi	0/0	2/3	0/1	Slocumb, ChN	0/0	0/1	1/2
Harvey, Cal	17/18	22/26	7/8	Smith Dv, ChN	5/6	8/12	4/5
Henke, Tor	16/17	13/14	3/4	Smith Le, StL	20/20	24/28	3/5
Henneman, Det	3/3	12/14	6/7	Stanton M, Atl	2/3	4/5	1/2
Henry D, Mil	5/5	9/9	1/2	Swan, Sea	0/0	1/2	1/3
Hernandez X, Hou	0/0	3/3	0/3	Swift, Sea	4/4	11/11	2/3
Hillegas, Cle	1/1	6/7	0/1	Terry, StL	0/0	1/1	0/2
Holmes, Mil	0/0	3/4	0/2	Thigpen, ChA	13/13	14/20	3/6
Howe S, NYA	1/1	2/2	0/0	Timlin, Tor	0/0	3/6	0/2
Howell Jay, LA	7/7	7/8	2/3	Ward D, Tor	9/9	13/15	1/3
Jackson M, Sea	2/2	7/11	5/9	Williams Mitch, Phi	11/11	16/22	3/6
Jeffcoat, Tex	0/0	1/3	0/2	Williamson, Bal	0/0	4/4	0/3
Jones Ba, Mon	1/3	8/9	4/9	Willis, Min	0/1	2/2	0/0
Jones Cd, Sea	0/0	2/3	0/0	Wohlers, Atl	1/2	0/0	1/2
Jones D, Cle	3/3	4/7	0/2	MLB Average	349/382	609/809	174/411
Kipper, Pit	1/1	3/5	0/0				

HOW IMPORTANT IS IT TO GET THE FIRST BATTER? (p. 170)

1991 Both Leagues — Listed Alphabetically
(minimum 35 first batters faced in relief)

Pitcher, Team	AVG	AB	H	HR	BB	K
Acker, Tor	.205	44	9	2	4	6
Agosto, StL	.322	59	19	0	9	1
Aguilera, Min	.127	55	7	0	8	9
Andersen L, SD	.250	36	9	0	1	6
Assenmacher, Ch	.209	67	14	4	8	25
Bailes, Cal	.194	36	7	0	4	8
Bedrosian, Min	.135	52	7	2	3	9
Belinda, Pit	.120	50	6	1	10	17
Berenguer, Atl	.170	47	8	0	2	12
Boever, Phi	.271	59	16	2	8	13
Brantley J, SF	.190	58	11	1	6	12
Burke, NYN	.308	65	20	3	6	9
Cadaret, NYA	.189	53	10	0	10	10
Candelaria, LA	.179	56	10	0	2	24
Carpenter, StL	.273	55	15	2	3	8
Chitren, Oak	.306	49	15	0	7	5
Clancy, Atl	.239	46	11	2	6	5
Corsi, Hou	.167	42	7	0	5	4
Crews, LA	.250	56	14	2	2	13
Crim, Mil	.333	63	21	2	2	10
Davis Storm, KC	.286	35	10	2	6	2
Dibble, Cin	.259	58	15	0	8	24
Eckersley, Oak	.212	66	14	1	1	18
Eichhorn, Cal	.185	65	12	1	4	11
Farr, NYA	.232	56	13	0	4	13
Fassero, Mon	.200	45	9	0	6	11
Flanagan, Bal	.281	57	16	3	4	12
Fossas, Bos	.130	54	7	0	5	10
Franco Jn, NYN	.200	50	10	0	1	11
Fraser, StL	.289	38	11	0	8	6
Frohwirth, Bal	.109	46	5	1	3	6
Gibson P, Det	.350	60	21	0	6	6
Gleaton, Det	.205	39	8	0	6	5
Gossage, Tex	.325	40	13	2	3	9
Gott, LA	.319	47	15	0	7	15
Gray, Bos	.200	45	9	3	2	8
Gross K, LA	.375	32	12	2	4	6
Guetterman, NYA	.276	58	16	1	5	2
Habyan, NYA	.200	60	12	0	5	15
Hartley, Phi	.255	51	13	1	5	12
Harvey, Cal	.203	64	13	1	3	20
Heaton, Pit	.282	39	11	1	0	1
Henke, Tor	.188	48	9	0	1	11
Henneman, Det	.226	53	12	0	6	14
Henry, Hou	.267	45	12	1	7	11
Hillegas, Cle	.189	37	7	1	9	10
Holmes, Mil	.400	35	14	1	4	6
Honeycutt, Oak	.190	42	8	1	1	12
Howe S, NYA	.167	36	6	0	0	9
Howell Jay, LA	.238	42	10	2	2	9
Innis, NYN	.219	64	14	1	4	15
Jackson M, Sea	.148	61	9	0	8	18
Jeffcoat, Tex	.344	61	21	2	6	5
Jones Ba, Mon	.290	69	20	3	4	9
Kilgus, Bal	.156	32	5	0	5	2
Kipper, Pit	.229	48	11	2	4	9
Klink, Oak	.236	55	13	0	4	11
Lamp, Bos	.261	46	12	1	3	5
Lancaster, ChN	.313	48	15	0	3	5
Landrum B, Pit	.155	58	9	1	3	7
Leach T, Min	.313	48	15	1	0	8
Lee, Mil	.294	51	15	2	10	7
Lefferts, SD	.333	48	16	1	2	7
MacDonald, Tor	.244	41	10	0	3	6
Machado, Mil	.156	45	7	1	9	17
Maddux M, SD	.193	57	11	0	4	9
Magnante, KC	.286	35	10	0	3	7
McClure, StL	.257	35	9	0	6	6
McDowell R, LA	.354	65	23	0	5	10
McElroy, ChN	.246	57	14	1	8	14
Mercker, Atl	.216	37	8	1	9	10
Montgomery, KC	.311	61	19	2	5	12
Murphy R, Sea	.302	53	16	1	2	10
Myers R, Cin	.275	40	11	0	5	8
Nelson G, Oak	.225	40	9	4	3	9
Olin, Cle	.375	40	15	1	7	6
Oliveras, SF	.167	48	8	0	4	9
Olson Gregg, Bal	.182	66	12	0	4	12
Orosco, Cle	.326	43	14	0	1	7
Osuna, Hou	.233	60	14	1	9	7
Pall, ChA	.213	47	10	1	1	4
Patterson B, Pit	.294	51	15	1	2	7
Patterson K, ChA	.270	37	10	1	4	4
Pena A, Atl	.170	53	9	0	4	7
Perez M, ChA	.371	35	13	1	2	8
Plesac, Mil	.188	32	6	1	1	4
Plunk, NYA	.294	34	10	1	1	5
Power, Cin	.262	61	16	1	6	8
Radinsky, ChA	.186	59	11	1	5	15
Reardon, Bos	.222	54	12	0	2	7
Righetti, SF	.071	56	4	0	4	16
Ritchie, Phi	.063	32	2	0	3	5
Robinson JD, Cal	.289	38	11	3	1	9
Rodriguez R, SD	.232	56	13	2	6	6
Rogers, Tex	.196	46	9	0	5	9
Rojas, Mon	.265	34	9	1	2	5
Rosenthal, Tex	.310	29	9	1	7	3
Ruskin, Mon	.186	59	11	1	5	14
Russell Jf, Tex	.390	59	23	1	7	7
Sampen, Mon	.242	33	8	1	2	6
Schilling, Hou	.396	48	19	0	8	8
Simons, NYN	.306	36	11	2	3	7
Slocumb, ChN	.146	41	6	0	8	6
Smith Dv, ChN	.375	32	12	2	3	5
Smith Le, StL	.270	63	17	2	3	13
Stanton M, Atl	.171	70	12	0	4	13
Swan, Sea	.328	58	19	1	2	5
Swift, Sea	.246	65	16	0	4	10
Terry, StL	.298	57	17	0	8	12
Thigpen, ChA	.220	59	13	4	4	8
Timlin, Tor	.294	51	15	0	8	10
Ward D, Tor	.231	78	18	1	1	28
Williams Mitch, Phi	.145	55	8	0	13	10
Williamson, Bal	.263	57	15	2	5	9
Willis, Min	.114	35	4	0	2	6
Young C, Oak	.194	36	7	0	4	4
MLB	**.251**					

WHY DID ATLANTA BUY 'LECKI (AND HIS 4.46 ERA)? (p. 172)

The following table lists the Percentage (%) of baserunners a pitcher "bequeathed" to his bullpen (**Left**), and those that later scored (%).

Both Leagues — Listed Alphabetically (minimum 18 runners bequeathed)

Pitcher	Left	Sc	%	Pitcher	Left	Sc	%	Pitcher	Left	Sc	%
Abbott, Cal	20	6	30.0	Gross K, LA	18	9	50.0	Myers R, Cin	34	8	23.5
Acker, Tor	22	9	40.9	Gubicza, KC	21	5	23.8	Nagy, Cle	27	11	40.7
Agosto, StL	34	10	29.4	Guetterman, NYA	18	8	44.4	Navarro, Mil	25	9	36.0
Alexander G, Tex	19	9	47.4	Gullickson, Det	29	5	17.2	Ojeda, LA	21	2	9.5
Anderson A, Min	18	5	27.8	Guthrie, Min	24	6	25.0	Orosco, Cle	32	8	25.0
Appier, KC	24	11	45.8	Guzman, Tex	22	10	45.5	Osuna, Hou	42	17	40.5
Aquino, KC	18	6	33.3	Habyan, NYA	29	5	17.2	Otto, Cle	18	13	72.2
Armstrong, Cin	18	5	27.8	Hanson, Sea	18	3	16.7	Pall, ChA	37	8	21.6
Assenmacher, ChN	32	10	31.3	Harris GA, Bos	30	10	33.3	Patterson B, Pit	18	3	16.7
August, Mil	21	7	33.3	Hartley, Phi	20	7	35.0	Patterson K, ChA	25	4	16.0
Avery, Atl	23	5	21.7	Henry, Hou	20	3	15.0	Perez M, ChA	26	8	30.8
Bailes, Cal	26	7	26.9	Hesketh, Bos	32	12	37.5	Petry, Bos	24	7	29.2
Ballard, Bal	23	6	26.1	Hibbard, ChA	30	14	46.7	Plunk, NYA	29	7	24.1
Barfield Jn, Tex	27	9	33.3	Hillegas, Cle	20	9	45.0	Power, Cin	26	4	15.4
Barnes B, Mon	19	6	31.6	Holman B, Sea	20	7	35.0	Radinsky, ChA	39	8	20.5
Belcher, LA	28	3	10.7	Holmes, Mil	25	8	32.0	Ritz, Det	18	8	44.4
Benes, SD	20	4	20.0	Honeycutt, Oak	30	9	30.0	Robinson D, SF	20	4	20.0
Bielecki, Atl	21	13	61.9	Hough, ChA	26	5	19.2	Robinson JM, Bal	28	11	39.3
Black, SF	25	6	24.0	Jackson Dan, ChN	20	8	40.0	Rodriguez Rich, SD	29	5	17.2
Boddicker, KC	20	6	30.0	Jackson M, Sea	27	8	29.6	Rogers, Tex	44	14	31.8
Bolton, Bos	26	12	46.2	Jeffcoat, Tex	47	13	27.7	Rosenthal, Tex	20	9	45.0
Bosio, Mil	18	7	38.9	Johnson D, Bal	21	6	28.6	Ruffin, Phi	20	9	45.0
Boskie, ChN	32	11	34.4	Johnson J, NYA	19	9	47.4	Ruskin, Mon	40	7	17.5
Boyd, Tex	18	12	66.7	Johnson R, Sea	31	11	35.5	Schilling, Hou	23	5	21.7
Brown K, Mil	18	7	38.9	Jones Jim, Hou	19	11	57.9	Schourek, NYN	24	5	20.8
Brown Kev, Tex	28	8	28.6	Key, Tor	19	8	42.1	Scudder, Cin	18	9	50.0
Burke, NYN	24	12	50.0	King E, Cle	30	8	26.7	Searcy, Phi	23	10	43.5
Cadaret, NYA	37	7	18.9	Kipper, Pit	21	8	38.1	Shaw, Cle	21	9	42.9
Candelaria, LA	34	7	20.6	Klink, Oak	34	6	17.6	Simons, NYN	25	9	36.0
Cerutti, Det	19	4	21.1	Krueger, Sea	25	9	30.0	Slusarski, Oak	18	11	61.1
Chitren, Oak	25	7	28.0	Lamp, Bos	37	8	21.6	Smiley, Pit	23	4	17.4
Cook D, LA	20	1	5.0	Lancaster, ChN	31	11	35.5	Smith Roy, Bal	24	10	41.7
Crews, LA	25	6	24.0	Langston, Cal	21	3	14.3	Smoltz, Atl	21	7	33.3
Crim, Mil	39	11	28.2	Leach T, Min	23	3	13.0	Stanton M, Atl	22	6	27.3
Davis Storm, KC	19	3	15.8	Leary, NYA	26	13	50.0	Stewart D, Oak	19	5	26.3
DeJesus J, Phi	24	4	16.7	Lee, Mil	41	6	14.6	Stottlemyre, Tor	20	10	50.0
DeLeon J, StL	20	5	25.0	Leibrandt, Atl	26	9	34.6	Swan, Sea	42	10	23.8
Delucia, Sea	22	5	22.7	Leiter A, Det	24	11	45.8	Swift, Sea	23	2	8.7
Deshaies, Hou	19	7	36.8	Lewis S, Cal	19	3	15.8	Tanana, Det	22	5	22.7
Downs, SF	23	9	39.1	MacDonald, Tor	20	1	5.0	Taylor W, NYA	18	9	50.0
Eichhorn, Cal	27	6	22.2	Maddux G, ChN	23	11	47.8	Terrell, Det	32	11	34.4
Fernandez A, ChA	38	10	26.3	Maddux M, SD	20	9	45.0	Terry, StL	22	10	45.5
Finley C, Cal	26	9	34.6	Magnante, KC	22	2	9.1	Timlin, Tor	23	8	34.8
Flanagan, Bal	19	8	42.1	Mallicoat, Hou	21	1	4.8	Tomlin R, Pit	19	6	31.6
Fossas, Bos	40	11	27.5	Mathews T, Tex	20	6	30.0	Welch, Oak	22	7	31.8
Frey, Mon	21	11	52.4	McClure, StL	36	9	25.0	Wells, Tor	27	14	51.9
Frohwirth, Bal	29	4	13.8	McElroy, ChN	37	12	32.4	Williamson, Bal	35	10	28.6
Gakeler, Det	28	15	53.6	Mesa, Bal	31	18	58.1	Wilson Tr, SF	23	10	43.5
Gardiner, Bos	26	11	42.3	Milacki, Bal	26	8	30.8	Young C, Oak	32	15	46.9
Gardner M, Mon	23	7	30.4	Moore M, Oak	26	9	34.6	Young Mt, Bos	31	14	45.2
Gibson P, Det	37	13	35.1	Morgan M, LA	23	7	30.4	**MLB**			**32.9**
Gleaton, Det	24	6	25.0	Morris Jk, Min	21	5	23.8				
Gordon, KC	18	10	55.6	Morton, Bos	22	7	31.8				
Gott, LA	18	9	50.0	Mulholland, Phi	20	6	30.0				
Greene, Phi	20	5	25.0	Murphy R, Sea	27	3	11.1				

WHICH SOUTHPAWS EAT LEFTIES? (p. 174)

1991 Both Leagues — Listed Alphabetically
(minimum 1 relief game in 1991)

Pitcher, Team	Vs. LHB BFP	Vs. LHB Avg	Vs. RHB BFP	Vs. RHB Avg	Pitcher, Team	Vs. LHB BFP	Vs. LHB Avg	Vs. RHB BFP	Vs. RHB Avg
Abbott K, Cal	15	.308	75	.300	Krueger, Sea	154	.307	597	.284
Agosto, StL	122	.271	255	.300	Lee, Mil	106	.304	185	.272
Allison, Oak	22	.421	27	.348	Lefferts, SD	72	.281	218	.286
Anderson A, Min	117	.225	467	.296	Leiter, Tor	7	.333	6	1.000
Assenmacher, ChN	147	.179	280	.247	Lilliquist, SD	19	.333	51	.396
Bailes, Cal	87	.247	132	.198	MacDonald, Tor	90	.325	141	.208
Ballard, Bal	95	.182	445	.328	Magnante, KC	83	.260	153	.263
Bannister F, Cal	35	.258	69	.270	Mallicoat, Hou	45	.263	58	.255
Barfield Jn, Tex	56	.269	305	.293	McClure, StL	73	.230	73	.354
Beatty, NYN	13	.500	29	.154	McElroy, ChN	150	.172	269	.231
Bell E, Cle	24	.045	37	.121	Mercker, Atl	85	.194	221	.216
Bolton, Bos	88	.247	411	.322	Minutelli, Cin	37	.333	87	.273
Brown K, Mil	54	.170	231	.294	Munoz, Det	15	.357	31	.346
Cadaret, NYA	133	.246	384	.246	Murphy R, Sea	79	.203	132	.281
Candelaria, LA	64	.138	74	.354	Myers R, Cin	152	.287	423	.226
Carman, Cin	58	.300	106	.278	Neagle, Min	21	.238	71	.359
Casian, Min	29	.138	58	.480	Nolte, Tex	35	.276	90	.400
Castillo T, NYN	36	.176	112	.340	Orosco, Cle	67	.286	135	.286
Cerutti, Det	82	.188	307	.299	Osuna, Hou	126	.239	227	.179
Charlton, Cin	106	.253	332	.231	Otto, Cle	75	.304	350	.278
Clements P, SD	25	.174	38	.321	Patterson B, Pit	88	.181	182	.310
Cook D, LA	29	.160	40	.235	Patterson K, ChA	77	.270	188	.193
Dalton, Det	15	.286	23	.364	Perez Y, ChN	7	.167	9	.167
Dascenzo, ChN	4	0.000	11	.200	Plesac, Mil	72	.297	330	.255
Davis Mrk, KC	66	.304	210	.220	Poole, Bal	71	.188	95	.203
Dayley, Tor	15	.300	11	.444	Radinsky, ChA	83	.205	206	.207
Drees, ChA	9	.286	28	.364	Remlinger, SF	24	.250	131	.274
Edwards, ChA	32	.308	74	.237	Righetti, SF	76	.167	228	.267
Fassero, Mon	76	.243	147	.171	Ritchie, Phi	70	.161	143	.270
Flanagan, Bal	138	.181	253	.266	Rodriguez Rich, SD	113	.221	222	.241
Fleming, Sea	11	.333	62	.276	Rodriguez Ro, Pit	21	.250	46	.243
Fossas, Bos	96	.190	148	.266	Rogers, Tex	122	.224	389	.298
Franco Jn, NYN	59	.340	188	.250	Rosenberg, SD	14	.308	35	.226
Frey, Mon	65	.268	117	.289	Ruffin, Phi	119	.252	389	.279
Gibson P, Det	127	.345	305	.277	Ruskin, Mon	102	.275	173	.219
Gleaton, Det	83	.263	236	.271	Sauveur, NYN	6	.500	13	.455
Guetterman, NYA	109	.175	267	.305	Schatzeder, NYN	12	.455	25	.316
Gunderson, SF	3	0.000	15	.400	Schourek, NYN	127	.264	258	.240
Guthrie, Min	94	.337	338	.293	Searcy, Phi	84	.242	251	.302
Guzman R, Oak	6	.500	18	.500	Sherill, StL	22	.294	45	.357
Hammond, Cin	113	.184	312	.274	Simons, NYN	98	.195	160	.277
Heaton, Pit	91	.354	202	.239	Stanton M, Atl	113	.194	201	.230
Hesketh, Bos	103	.241	528	.252	Swan, Sea	134	.193	202	.319
Hibbard, ChA	128	.250	678	.269	Tomlin R, Pit	154	.172	582	.275
Hickerson, SF	52	.234	160	.288	Valdez E, Tor	13	.444	14	.083
Hickey, Bal	31	.321	31	.231	Wayne, Min	15	.308	37	.219
Honeycutt, Oak	64	.204	103	.295	Wells, Tor	139	.208	672	.261
Horsman, Tor	5	.333	11	.111	West, Min	41	.343	264	.229
Howe S, NYA	51	.128	138	.256	Williams Mitch, Phi	85	.191	301	.179
Jackson Dan, ChN	75	.300	272	.311	Wilson S, LA	28	.182	53	.204
Jeffcoat, Tex	132	.289	231	.340	Wilson Tr, SF	186	.169	655	.252
Kaiser, Det	9	.375	17	.231	Young Cli, Cal	9	.250	40	.263
Kilgus, Bal	94	.232	173	.270	Young C, Oak	122	.229	184	.312
Kipper, Pit	83	.321	181	.255	Young Mt, Bos	59	.255	345	.268
Kiser, Cle	16	.308	9	.500	**MLB**		**.242**		**.264**
Klink, Oak	111	.224	155	.286					

IS IT EASIER TO STEAL OFF A LEFTY? (p. 176)

Both Leagues — Listed Alphabetically
(players with 25+ stolen base attempts in 1991; 5-yr totals exclude pitchers)

	1991						1987-1991					
	LHP			RHP			LHP			RHP		
Player, Team	SB	CS	Pct	SB	CS	Pct	SB	CS	Pct	SB	CS	Pct
Alomar R, Tor	11	3	78.6	42	8	84.0	32	7	82.1	111	34	76.6
Biggio, Hou	12	1	92.3	7	5	58.3	34	8	81.0	37	13	74.0
Bonds, Pit	14	6	70.0	29	7	80.6	54	23	70.1	122	34	78.2
Briley, Sea	1	1	50.0	22	10	68.8	4	3	57.1	46	18	71.9
Butler, LA	13	13	50.0	25	15	62.5	52	43	54.7	144	56	72.0
Calderon, Mon	8	6	57.1	23	10	69.7	23	17	57.5	61	25	70.9
Canseco, Oak	11	2	84.6	15	4	78.9	39	10	79.6	67	28	70.5
Carter J, Tor	9	1	90.0	11	8	57.9	30	9	76.9	83	22	79.0
Cole, Cle	6	5	54.5	21	12	63.6	19	9	67.9	48	17	73.8
Coleman, NYN	12	5	70.6	25	9	73.5	141	30	82.5	228	60	79.2
Cuyler, Det	8	4	66.7	33	6	84.6	8	5	61.5	34	7	82.9
DeShields, Mon	20	5	80.0	36	18	66.7	33	14	70.2	65	31	67.7
Devereaux, Bal	1	5	16.7	15	4	78.9	18	20	47.4	36	14	72.0
Dunston, ChN	8	3	72.7	13	3	81.3	29	12	70.7	78	22	78.0
Dykstra, Phi	9	2	81.8	15	2	88.2	39	10	79.6	105	26	80.2
Felder, SF	5	1	83.3	16	5	76.2	34	14	70.8	75	16	82.4
Fernandez T, SD	6	2	75.0	17	7	70.8	25	11	69.4	93	34	73.2
Finley S, Hou	12	6	66.7	22	12	64.7	19	7	73.1	54	23	70.1
Franco Ju, Tex	7	4	63.6	29	5	85.3	37	20	64.9	108	22	83.1
Gant, Atl	12	4	75.0	22	11	66.7	34	19	64.2	65	30	68.4
Grissom, Mon	35	5	87.5	41	12	77.4	47	6	88.7	52	13	80.0
Guillen, ChA	2	6	25.0	19	9	67.9	26	28	48.1	94	42	69.1
Henderson R, Oak	8	6	57.1	50	12	80.6	98	26	79.0	236	37	86.4
Jefferies, NYN	9	2	81.8	17	3	85.0	17	6	73.9	46	8	85.2
Johnson H, NYN	12	5	70.6	18	11	62.1	43	18	70.5	117	31	79.1
Johnson L, ChA	7	2	77.8	19	9	67.9	24	14	63.2	66	25	72.5
Jose, StL	10	7	58.8	10	5	66.7	13	10	56.5	20	9	69.0
Kelly, NYA	10	5	66.7	22	4	84.6	37	15	71.2	86	28	75.4
Knoblauch, Min	2	1	66.7	23	4	85.2	2	1	66.7	23	4	85.2
Landrum C, ChN	8	0	100.0	19	5	79.2	8	0	100.0	19	5	79.2
Lankford, StL	20	8	71.4	24	12	66.7	22	8	73.3	30	14	68.2
Larkin B, Cin	8	1	88.9	16	5	76.2	39	7	84.8	86	22	79.6
McGee, SF	6	5	54.5	11	4	73.3	27	13	67.5	86	21	80.4
McRae B, KC	7	1	87.5	13	10	56.5	8	3	72.7	16	11	59.3
Molitor, Mil	6	4	60.0	13	4	76.5	45	17	72.6	105	25	80.8
Nixon O, Atl	22	6	78.6	50	15	76.9	81	25	76.4	126	37	77.3
Pettis, Tex	11	5	68.8	18	8	69.2	57	28	67.1	121	30	80.1
Polonia, Cal	11	5	68.8	37	18	67.3	16	9	64.0	128	52	71.1
Raines, ChA	14	6	70.0	37	9	80.4	51	16	76.1	173	36	82.8
Reynolds H, Sea	5	1	83.3	23	7	76.7	58	31	65.2	121	60	66.9
Roberts Bip, SD	3	3	50.0	23	8	74.2	21	17	55.3	72	19	79.1
Sabo, Cin	7	2	77.8	12	4	75.0	45	12	78.9	59	27	68.6
Samuel, LA	7	3	70.0	16	5	76.2	50	22	69.4	121	43	73.8
Sandberg, ChN	7	5	58.3	15	3	83.3	27	11	71.1	81	21	79.4
Sax S, NYA	12	5	70.6	19	6	76.0	62	21	74.7	134	39	77.5
Shumpert, KC	8	3	72.7	9	8	52.9	11	4	73.3	9	10	47.4
Smith O, StL	11	4	73.3	24	5	82.8	62	16	79.5	134	24	84.8
Thompson M, StL	1	2	33.3	15	7	68.2	8	8	50.0	123	33	78.8
White D, Tor	11	4	73.3	22	6	78.6	43	15	74.1	104	36	74.3
Wilson W, Oak	4	1	80.0	16	4	80.0	29	9	76.3	133	26	83.6
Zeile, StL	8	4	66.7	9	7	56.3	9	5	64.3	10	10	50.0
MLB Average	**900**	**532**	**62.9**	**2220**	**1035**	**78.2**	**4648**	**2559**	**64.5**	**11756**	**4902**	**70.6**

WHERE WILL WE FIND THE NEXT DON ROBINSON? (p. 178)

1991 Active Pitchers — Listed Alphabetically
(minimum 150 plate appearances lifetime)

Pitcher, Team	AVG	AB	H	HR	RBI	Pitcher, Team	AVG	AB	H	HR	RBI
Aguilera, Min	.203	138	28	3	11	LaCoss, SF	.125	481	60	2	19
Armstrong, Cin	.092	119	11	0	5	LaPoint, Phi	.104	251	26	0	15
Avery, Atl	.193	109	21	0	2	Lancaster, ChN	.102	128	13	0	5
Belcher, LA	.114	246	28	1	14	Leach T, Min	.097	72	7	0	3
Benes, SD	.096	146	14	2	5	Lefferts, SD	.150	80	12	1	3
Bielecki, Atl	.074	243	18	0	12	Leibrandt, Atl	.120	209	25	0	10
Black, SF	.183	71	13	0	6	Lilliquist, SD	.213	108	23	2	8
Boskie, ChN	.195	77	15	1	5	Maddux G, ChN	.187	402	75	1	21
Boyd, Tex	.063	95	6	0	2	Maddux M, SD	.068	73	5	0	4
Browning, Cin	.145	539	78	1	26	Mahler R, Atl	.179	581	104	1	37
Burkett, SF	.067	119	8	0	4	Martinez De, Mon	.131	366	48	0	24
Candelaria, LA	.174	596	104	1	48	Martinez R, LA	.124	201	25	1	18
Carman, Cin	.057	209	12	0	5	Morgan M, LA	.098	183	18	0	6
Charlton, Cin	.075	80	6	0	0	Moyer, StL	.139	151	21	0	4
Combs, Phi	.149	87	13	0	2	Mulholland, Phi	.076	211	16	0	3
Cone, NYN	.167	330	55	0	16	Nabholz, Mon	.082	73	6	0	1
Cook D, LA	.250	96	24	1	7	Ojeda, LA	.131	298	39	1	6
Cox, Phi	.110	345	38	0	11	Olivares, StL	.214	70	15	1	10
Darling, Oak	.145	525	76	2	21	Pena A, Atl	.113	177	20	1	7
DeJesus J, Phi	.110	100	11	0	6	Portugal, Hou	.171	146	25	1	10
DeLeon J, StL	.090	387	35	0	8	Power, Cin	.089	157	14	1	7
Deshaies, Hou	.080	338	27	0	12	Rasmussen D, SD	.193	259	50	0	14
Downs, SF	.132	197	26	0	11	Reuschel, SF	.168	1115	187	4	79
Drabek, Pit	.161	380	61	1	20	Rijo, Cin	.167	204	34	1	9
Eckersley, Oak	.133	180	24	3	12	Robinson D, SF	.227	613	139	13	68
Fernandez S, NYN	.197	390	77	1	29	Ruffin, Phi	.080	263	21	0	6
Gardner M, Mon	.105	105	11	0	5	Russell Jf, Tex	.139	79	11	1	10
Garrelts, SF	.125	232	29	1	10	Scott M, Hou	.124	653	81	2	45
Glavine, Atl	.168	279	47	0	20	Scudder, Cin	.113	71	8	1	3
Gooden, NYN	.189	576	109	4	45	Show, Oak	.160	506	81	4	28
Gott, LA	.174	69	12	4	5	Smiley, Pit	.110	254	28	0	15
Greene, Phi	.237	93	22	2	7	Smith B, StL	.156	487	76	3	37
Gross K, LA	.165	485	80	4	26	Smith P, Atl	.107	140	15	0	3
Gullickson, Det	.141	576	81	3	27	Smith Z, Pit	.160	394	63	0	24
Hammaker, SD	.118	305	36	0	10	Smoltz, Atl	.128	218	28	1	13
Harkey, ChN	.236	72	17	0	4	Sutcliffe, ChN	.184	539	99	4	54
Harris GW, SD	.068	74	5	0	2	Terry, StL	.216	97	21	2	7
Heaton, Pit	.171	187	32	0	12	Tewksbury, StL	.148	115	17	0	5
Hershiser, LA	.193	487	94	0	31	Tomlin R, Pit	.143	77	11	0	2
Hill K, StL	.137	131	18	0	7	Viola, NYN	.140	179	25	0	6
Honeycutt, Oak	.133	181	24	0	8	Walk, Pit	.154	409	63	1	44
Hurst, SD	.098	204	20	0	7	Welch, Oak	.151	581	88	2	30
Jackson Dan, ChN	.134	186	25	0	11	Whitson, SD	.125	576	72	1	27
Jones Jim, Hou	.169	148	25	2	7	Wilson Tr, SF	.211	95	20	1	6
Kipper, Pit	.137	95	13	0	2	**MLB 1991**	**.139**	**4008**	**555**	**12**	**214**

WHO ARE THE HIDDEN RELIEF STARS? (p. 182)

The table below shows the percentage (%) of Inherited Runners (**IR**) each relief pitcher allowed to score (**SC**)

Both Leagues — Listed Alphabetically
(minimum 15 inherited runners)

Pitcher, Team	IR	SC	%	Pitcher, Team	IR	SC	%	Pitcher, Team	IR	SC	%
Acker, Tor	31	14	45.2	Gordon, KC	17	6	35.3	Myers R, Cin	38	8	21.1
Agosto, StL	39	18	46.2	Gossage, Tex	53	22	41.5	Nelson G, Oak	46	17	37.0
Aguilera, Min	37	9	24.3	Gott, LA	21	6	28.6	Nichols Rod, Cle	17	11	64.7
Akerfelds, Phi	19	3	15.8	Gray, Bos	36	12	33.3	Olin, Cle	28	12	42.9
Alexander G, Tex	25	9	36.0	Guetterman, NYA	33	10	30.3	Oliveras, SF	31	7	22.6
Allison, Oak	15	4	26.7	Habyan, NYA	49	17	34.7	Olson Gregg, Bal	30	12	40.0
Andersen L, SD	23	6	26.1	Harris GA, Bos	27	9	33.3	Orosco, Cle	60	21	35.0
Aquino, KC	16	7	43.8	Hartley, Phi	38	15	39.5	Osuna, Hou	57	20	35.1
Assenmacher, ChN	51	21	41.2	Harvey, Cal	37	10	27.0	Palacios, Pit	15	9	60.0
Bailes, Cal	33	9	27.3	Henke, Tor	15	3	20.0	Pall, ChA	46	12	26.1
Bannister F, Cal	15	3	20.0	Henneman, Det	41	8	19.5	Patterson B, Pit	29	7	24.1
Barfield Jn, Tex	24	4	16.7	Henry D, Mil	18	3	16.7	Patterson K, ChA	49	14	28.6
Beasley, Cal	20	5	25.0	Henry, Hou	35	17	48.6	Pena A, Atl	28	8	28.6
Bedrosian, Min	43	7	16.3	Hernandez X, Hou	21	7	33.3	Perez M, ChA	36	14	38.9
Belinda, Pit	38	13	34.2	Hesketh, Bos	26	11	42.3	Petry, Bos	35	16	45.7
Berenguer, Atl	27	1	3.7	Hickey, Bal	18	2	11.1	Plesac, Mil	22	4	18.2
Boever, Phi	35	15	42.9	Hillmi, Cin	19	6	31.6	Plunk, NYA	24	11	45.8
Brantley J, SF	39	11	28.2	Hillegas, Cle	46	17	37.0	Poole, Bal	33	9	27.3
Burke, NYN	39	11	28.2	Holmes, Mil	44	16	36.4	Power, Cin	33	9	27.3
Cadaret, NYA	44	14	31.8	Honeycutt, Oak	23	7	30.4	Radinsky, ChA	63	16	25.4
Campbell K, Oak	15	5	33.3	Howe S, NYA	26	5	19.2	Reardon, Bos	18	5	27.8
Candelaria, LA	60	11	18.3	Howell Jay, LA	15	5	33.3	Righetti, SF	32	5	15.6
Capel, Hou	18	5	27.8	Innis, NYN	57	20	35.1	Ritchie, Phi	28	7	25.0
Carman, Cin	18	5	27.8	Irvine, Bos	16	9	56.3	Robinson JD, Cal	37	9	24.3
Carpenter, StL	37	8	21.6	Jackson M, Sea	52	10	19.2	Rodriguez Rich, SD	49	10	20.4
Casian, Min	15	1	6.7	Jeffcoat, Tex	41	16	39.0	Rogers, Tex	50	9	18.0
Cerutti, Det	39	18	46.2	Jones Ba, Mon	51	17	33.3	Rojas, Mon	18	6	33.3
Charlton, Cin	16	12	75.0	Jones Cd, Sea	16	5	31.3	Rosenthal, Tex	34	16	47.1
Chitren, Oak	50	20	40.0	Kiecker, Bos	16	7	43.8	Ruskin, Mon	42	7	16.7
Clancy, Atl	26	7	26.9	Kilgus, Bal	36	11	30.6	Russell Jf, Tex	45	18	40.0
Cook D, LA	29	6	20.7	Kipper, Pit	33	9	27.3	Sampen, Mon	21	7	33.3
Corsi, Hou	22	4	18.2	Kiser, Cle	15	3	20.0	Scanlan, ChN	15	5	33.3
Crawford, KC	22	5	22.7	Klink, Oak	46	7	15.2	Schilling, Hou	29	10	34.5
Crews, LA	49	14	28.6	Lamp, Bos	57	18	31.6	Schourek, NYN	19	9	47.4
Crim, Mil	46	15	32.6	Lancaster, ChN	44	18	40.9	Searcy, Phi	17	6	35.3
Davis Mrk, KC	19	7	36.8	Landrum B, Pit	35	10	28.6	Shaw, Cle	40	21	52.5
Davis Storm, KC	31	11	35.5	Layana, Cin	15	3	20.0	Simons, NYN	17	6	35.3
Dibble, Cin	42	8	19.0	Leach T, Min	38	16	42.1	Slocumb, ChN	40	13	32.5
Downs, SF	32	10	31.3	Lee, Mil	56	18	32.1	Smith Dv, ChN	21	9	42.9
Drahman, ChA	36	10	27.8	Lefferts, SD	30	10	33.3	Smith Le, StL	26	12	46.2
Eckersley, Oak	31	9	29.0	Leiter M, Det	35	14	40.0	Stanton M, Atl	58	16	27.6
Edwards, ChA	18	5	27.8	MacDonald, Tor	49	20	40.8	Swan, Sea	58	11	19.0
Eichhorn, Cal	54	15	27.8	Machado, Mil	54	14	25.9	Swift, Sea	61	17	27.9
Farr, NYA	31	8	25.8	Maddux M, SD	47	9	19.1	Terry, StL	35	12	34.3
Fassero, Mon	38	10	26.3	Magnante, KC	36	10	27.8	Thigpen, ChA	42	12	28.6
Flanagan, Bal	47	12	25.5	Mahler R, Atl	15	7	46.7	Timlin, Tor	44	20	45.5
Fossas, Bos	71	20	28.2	Mallicoat, Hou	20	7	35.0	Ward D, Tor	36	10	27.8
Franco Jn, NYN	25	8	32.0	Mason R, Pit	21	1	4.8	Weathers, Tor	18	7	38.9
Fraser, StL	25	10	40.0	Mathews T, Tex	21	7	33.3	Williams Mitch, Phi	24	6	25.0
Freeman M, Atl	18	7	38.9	McClure, StL	42	12	28.6	Williamson, Bal	62	21	33.9
Frey, Mon	17	8	47.1	McDowell R, LA	43	14	32.6	Willis, Min	28	6	21.4
Frohwirth, Bal	58	18	31.0	McElroy, ChN	58	21	36.2	Wilson S, LA	23	4	17.4
Gakeler, Det	25	6	24.0	Monteleone, NYA	26	9	34.6	Young C, Oak	25	6	24.0
Gibson P, Det	71	26	36.6	Montgomery, KC	41	17	41.5	**MLB Average**			**32.1**
Gleaton, Det	46	11	23.9	Murphy R, Sea	46	15	32.6				

CAN YOU PITCH YOURSELF INTO A HOLE BUT STILL SURVIVE? (p. 185)

The first column lists the number of batters faced in a leadoff situation — none on and none out — (**BFP**), the number of batters that were walked (**BB**), and the percentage that were walked (**Pct**).

Both Leagues — Listed Alphabetically
(minimum 300 first batters faced from 1989 through 1991)

Pitcher, Team	BFP	BB	Pct	Pitcher, Team	BFP	BB	Pct	Pitcher, Team	BFP	BB	Pct
Abbott, Cal	685	48	.070	Gooden, NYN	567	47	.083	Ojeda, LA	537	46	.086
Acker, Tor	300	19	.063	Gordon, KC	532	57	.107	Perez M, ChA	556	61	.110
Anderson A, Min	561	20	.036	Greene, Phi	304	28	.092	Perez P, NYA	303	8	.026
Appier, KC	443	33	.074	Gross K, LA	521	43	.083	Petry, Bos	330	30	.091
Aquino, KC	364	30	.082	Gubicza, KC	503	22	.044	Portugal, Hou	513	49	.096
Armstrong, Cin	382	30	.079	Gullickson, Det	454	19	.042	Rasmussen, SD	571	46	.081
August, Mil	325	18	.055	Guthrie, Min	321	21	.065	Reuschel, SF	328	10	.030
Avery, Atl	338	29	.086	Hanson, Sea	558	36	.065	Rijo, Cin	533	46	.086
Ballard, Bal	523	27	.052	Harnisch, Hou	558	58	.104	Robinson D, SF	512	27	.053
Bankhead, Sea	300	22	.073	Harris GA, Bos	488	49	.100	Robinson JM, Bal	375	37	.099
Belcher, LA	626	46	.073	Harris GW, SD	384	23	.060	Ruffin, Phi	423	42	.099
Benes, SD	525	38	.072	Hawkins, Oak	505	45	.089	Ryan, Tex	651	56	.086
Bielecki, Atl	600	49	.082	Heaton, Pit	388	22	.057	Saberhagen, KC	617	29	.047
Black, SF	692	41	.059	Hershiser, LA	404	18	.045	Sanderson, NYA	605	22	.036
Boddicker, KC	671	43	.064	Hibbard, ChA	590	34	.058	Scott M, Hou	461	27	.059
Bosio, Mil	611	32	.052	Higuera, Mil	364	32	.088	Smiley, Pit	606	32	.053
Boyd, Tex	465	34	.073	Hill K, StL	493	57	.116	Smith B, StL	588	24	.041
Brown Kev, Tex	621	55	.089	Holman B, Sea	624	59	.095	Smith Roy, Bal	450	24	.053
Browning, Cin	778	31	.040	Hough, ChA	657	66	.100	Smith Z, Pit	619	23	.037
Burkett, SF	437	25	.057	Hurst, SD	729	60	.082	Smoltz, Atl	707	57	.081
Cadaret, NYA	359	39	.109	Jackson Dn, ChN	329	43	.131	Stewart D, Oak	807	58	.072
Candiotti, Tor	680	37	.054	Jeffcoat, Tex	350	18	.051	Stieb, Tor	500	51	.102
Cary, NYA	333	27	.081	Johnson D, Bal	397	22	.055	Stottlemyre, Tor	586	37	.063
Cerutti, Det	465	26	.056	Johnson R, Sea	642	106	.165	Sutcliffe, ChN	377	23	.061
Charlton, Cin	371	33	.089	Key, Tor	622	19	.031	Swift, Sea	327	11	.034
Clancy, Atl	321	25	.078	King E, Cle	508	42	.083	Swindell, Cle	693	21	.030
Clemens, Bos	786	52	.066	Knudson, Mil	348	18	.052	Tanana, Det	662	38	.057
Combs, Phi	310	45	.145	Krueger, Sea	419	26	.062	Tapani, Min	476	15	.032
Cone, NYN	706	45	.064	Lancaster, ChN	327	16	.049	Terrell, Det	633	39	.062
Cook D, LA	307	20	.065	Langston, Cal	757	87	.115	Terry, StL	302	21	.070
Darling, Oak	571	27	.047	LaPoint, Phi	311	27	.087	Tewksbury, StL	389	12	.031
Darwin, Bos	348	14	.040	Leary, NYA	582	49	.084	Valenzuela, Cal	426	28	.066
Davis Storm, KC	424	31	.073	Leibrandt, Atl	589	29	.049	Viola, NYN	780	44	.056
DeJesus J, Phi	343	55	.160	Lilliquist, SD	333	19	.057	Walk, Pit	476	30	.063
DeLeon J, StL	636	69	.108	Maddux G, ChN	783	54	.069	Ward D, Tor	322	27	.084
Deshaies, Hou	649	52	.080	Mahler R, Atl	441	19	.043	Welch, Oak	728	49	.067
Drabek, Pit	748	36	.048	Martinez D, Mon	712	26	.037	Wells, Tor	490	37	.076
Erickson S, Min	340	34	.100	Martinez R, LA	590	44	.075	West, Min	314	23	.073
Fernandez A, Ch	301	34	.113	McCaskill, Cal	607	56	.092	Whitson, SD	557	18	.032
Fernandez S, NY	471	28	.059	McDowell J, ChA	493	33	.067	Wilson Tr, SF	365	50	.137
Finley C, Cal	714	50	.070	Milacki, Bal	624	58	.093	Witt B, Tex	541	73	.135
Flanagan, Bal	301	16	.053	Moore M, Oak	696	64	.092	Witt M, NYA	375	12	.032
Gardner M, Mon	370	30	.081	Morgan M, LA	633	29	.046	Young C, Oak	333	26	.078
Garrelts, SF	428	24	.056	Morris Jk, Min	714	57	.080	Young Mt, Bos	380	54	.142
Gibson P, Det	324	31	.096	Mulholland, Phi	562	28	.050	**MLB Avg:**			**.076**
Glavine, Atl	686	30	.044	Navarro, Mil	528	36	.068	1989-1991			

DO WORKHORSE STARTERS STILL EXIST? (p. 188)

Both Leagues — Listed Alphabetically (minimum 15 games started in 1991)

Pitcher, Team	GS	#Pitches	Pit/GS	Pitcher, Team	GS	#Pitches	Pit/GS
Abbott, Cal	34	3579	105	Key, Tor	33	3255	99
Anderson A, Min	22	1808	82	Kile, Hou	22	1997	91
Appier, KC	31	3256	105	King E, Cle	24	2212	92
Aquino, KC	18	1711	95	Krueger, Sea	25	2246	90
Armstrong, Cin	24	2071	86	Langston, Cal	34	3746	110
August, Mil	23	2038	89	Leary, NYA	18	1763	98
Avery, Atl	35	3261	93	Leibrandt, Atl	36	3422	95
Ballard, Bal	22	1686	77	Leiter M, Det	15	1482	99
Barnes B, Mon	27	2556	95	Maddux G, ChN	37	3660	99
Belcher, LA	33	3285	100	Martinez De, Mon	31	3353	108
Benes, SD	33	3449	105	Martinez R, LA	33	3515	107
Bielecki, Atl	25	2239	90	McCaskill, Cal	30	2826	94
Black, SF	34	3188	94	McDonald, Bal	21	2017	96
Boddicker, KC	29	2833	98	McDowell J, ChA	35	3832	109
Bolton, Bos	19	1624	85	Mesa, Bal	23	2081	90
Bosio, Mil	32	2881	90	Milacki, Bal	26	2392	92
Boskie, ChN	20	1812	91	Moore M, Oak	33	3536	107
Boyd, Tex	31	2725	88	Morgan M, LA	33	3279	99
Brown Kev, Tex	33	3354	102	Morris Jk, Min	35	3742	107
Browning, Cin	36	3368	94	Morton, Bos	15	1339	89
Burkett, SF	34	3048	90	Mulholland, Phi	34	3377	99
Candiotti, Tor	34	3897	115	Nabholz, Mon	24	2221	93
Castillo F, ChN	18	1682	93	Nagy, Cle	33	3264	99
Clemens, Bos	35	4031	115	Navarro, Mil	34	3603	106
Cone, NYN	34	3745	110	Nichols Rod, Cle	16	1554	97
Cox, Phi	17	1382	81	Ojeda, LA	31	2968	96
Darling, Oak	32	3074	96	Olivares, StL	24	2412	101
DeJesus J, Phi	29	3060	106	Portugal, Hou	27	2411	89
DeLeon J, StL	28	2533	90	Rasmussen D, SD	24	2225	93
Delucia, Sea	31	2900	94	Rijo, Cin	30	3014	100
Deshaies, Hou	28	2730	98	Robinson D, SF	16	1375	86
Drabek, Pit	35	3509	100	Robinson JM, Bal	19	1703	90
Erickson S, Min	32	2961	93	Ruffin, Phi	15	1324	88
Fernandez A, ChA	32	3137	98	Ryan, Tex	27	2817	104
Finley C, Cal	34	3813	112	Saberhagen, KC	28	2898	104
Garcia R, ChA	15	1284	86	Sanderson, NYA	34	3175	93
Gardiner, Bos	22	2117	96	Slusarski, Oak	19	1683	89
Gardner M, Mon	27	2651	98	Smiley, Pit	32	2949	92
Glavine, Atl	34	3600	106	Smith B, StL	31	2667	86
Gooden, NYN	27	2838	105	Smith Z, Pit	35	3173	91
Greene, Phi	27	2836	105	Smoltz, Atl	36	3449	96
Gubicza, KC	26	2209	85	Stewart D, Oak	35	3940	113
Gullickson, Det	35	3125	89	Stottlemyre, Tor	34	3335	98
Guzman, Tex	25	2763	111	Sutcliffe, ChN	18	1563	87
Guzman J, Tor	23	2317	101	Swindell, Cle	33	3249	98
Hammond, Cin	18	1485	83	Tanana, Det	33	3490	106
Haney, Mon	16	1472	92	Tapani, Min	34	3384	100
Hanson, Sea	27	2821	104	Taylor W, NYA	22	2001	91
Harnisch, Hou	33	3434	104	Terrell, Det	33	3226	98
Harris GA, Bos	21	1885	90	Tewksbury, StL	30	2480	83
Harris GW, SD	20	1899	95	Tomlin R, Pit	27	2492	92
Hawkins, Oak	17	1465	86	Viola, NYN	35	3567	102
Hershiser, LA	21	1627	77	Walk, Pit	20	1610	81
Hesketh, Bos	17	1588	93	Wegman, Mil	28	2731	98
Hibbard, ChA	29	2688	93	Welch, Oak	35	3524	101
Hill K, StL	30	2759	92	Wells, Tor	28	2628	94
Holman B, Sea	30	3060	102	Whitehurst, NYN	20	1593	80
Hough, ChA	29	3076	106	Wilson Tr, SF	29	2776	96
Hurst, SD	31	3065	99	Witt B, Tex	16	1586	99
Johnson J, NYA	23	1996	87	Young Mt, Bos	16	1470	92
Johnson R, Sea	33	3715	113	**MLB Avg**			**95**
Jones Jim, Hou	22	1959	89				

DID CLEMENS SACRIFICE SOME QUALITY FOR QUANTITY?
(p. 190)

Both Leagues — Listed Alphabetically
(minimum 20 games started in 1991)

Player, Team	Games Started	Quality Starts	Pct.	Player, Team	Games Started	Quality Starts	Pct.
Abbott, Cal	34	25	73.5	Jones Jim, Hou	22	11	50.0
Anderson A, Min	22	10	45.5	Key, Tor	33	21	63.6
Appier, KC	31	16	51.6	Kile, Hou	22	15	68.2
Armstrong, Cin	24	9	37.5	King E, Cle	24	13	54.2
August, Mil	23	9	39.1	Krueger, Sea	25	14	56.0
Avery, Atl	35	17	48.6	Langston, Cal	34	26	76.5
Ballard, Bal	22	9	40.9	Leibrandt, Atl	36	22	61.1
Barnes B, Mon	27	13	48.1	Maddux G, ChN	37	23	62.2
Belcher, LA	33	24	72.7	Martinez De, Mon	31	21	67.7
Benes, SD	33	25	75.8	Martinez R, LA	33	21	63.6
Bielecki, Atl	25	12	48.0	McCaskill, Cal	30	15	50.0
Black, SF	34	19	55.9	McDonald, Bal	21	8	38.1
Boddicker, KC	29	15	51.7	McDowell J, ChA	35	25	71.4
Bosio, Mil	32	19	59.4	Mesa, Bal	23	7	30.4
Boskie, ChN	20	10	50.0	Milacki, Bal	26	14	53.8
Boyd, Tex	31	13	41.9	Moore M, Oak	33	22	66.7
Brown Kev, Tex	33	21	63.6	Morgan M, LA	33	24	72.7
Browning, Cin	36	21	58.3	Morris Jk, Min	35	20	57.1
Burkett, SF	34	18	52.9	Mulholland, Phi	34	19	55.9
Candiotti, Tor	34	27	79.4	Nabholz, Mon	24	13	54.2
Clemens, Bos	35	25	71.4	Nagy, Cle	33	19	57.6
Cone, NYN	34	24	70.6	Navarro, Mil	34	20	58.8
Darling, Oak	32	21	65.6	Ojeda, LA	31	23	74.2
DeJesus J, Phi	29	15	51.7	Olivares, StL	24	14	58.3
DeLeon J, StL	28	17	60.7	Portugal, Hou	27	14	51.9
Delucia, Sea	31	15	48.4	Rasmussen D, SD	24	14	58.3
Deshaies, Hou	28	13	46.4	Rijo, Cin	30	25	83.3
Drabek, Pit	35	23	65.7	Ryan, Tex	27	16	59.3
Erickson S, Min	32	21	65.6	Saberhagen, KC	28	19	67.9
Fernandez A, ChA	32	17	53.1	Sanderson, NYA	34	16	47.1
Finley C, Cal	34	21	61.8	Smiley, Pit	32	20	62.5
Gardiner, Bos	22	8	36.4	Smith B, StL	31	17	54.8
Gardner M, Mon	27	18	66.7	Smith Z, Pit	35	20	57.1
Glavine, Atl	34	25	73.5	Smoltz, Atl	36	22	61.1
Gooden, NYN	27	16	59.3	Stewart D, Oak	35	14	40.0
Greene, Phi	27	16	59.3	Stottlemyre, Tor	34	19	55.9
Gubicza, KC	26	6	23.1	Swindell, Cle	33	20	60.6
Gullickson, Det	35	20	57.1	Tanana, Det	33	16	48.5
Guzman, Tex	25	19	76.0	Tapani, Min	34	23	67.6
Guzman J, Tor	23	13	56.5	Taylor W, NYA	22	9	40.9
Hanson, Sea	27	16	59.3	Terrell, Det	33	18	54.5
Harnisch, Hou	33	24	72.7	Tewksbury, StL	30	19	63.3
Harris GA, Bos	21	10	47.6	Tomlin R, Pit	27	17	63.0
Harris GW, SD	20	16	80.0	Viola, NYN	35	20	57.1
Hershiser, LA	21	11	52.4	Walk, Pit	20	7	35.0
Hibbard, ChA	29	11	37.9	Wegman, Mil	28	16	57.1
Hill K, StL	30	19	63.3	Welch, Oak	35	19	54.3
Holman B, Sea	30	14	46.7	Wells, Tor	28	16	57.1
Hough, ChA	29	16	55.2	Whitehurst, NYN	20	6	30.0
Hurst, SD	31	21	67.7	Wilson Tr, SF	29	18	62.1
Johnson J, NYA	23	9	39.1	**MLB**	**4208**	**2212**	**52.6**
Johnson R, Sea	33	19	57.6				

ARE CLEMENS AND GOODEN ON THE TRACK TO IMMORTAILITY? (p. 194)

The years of a player's career to be considered were determined by his birthdate. If a player was born in July through September, then that current season's totals were included. If a player was born in October through June (e.g. Jim Palmer), the season just completed was included.

100 Wins and .600 Win Pct at 29 — Sorted by Winning Percentage

Pitcher	Record through	W-L	Pct	IP	ER	ERA
Bob Caruthers *	1890	198-75	.725	2430.0	722	2.67
Dwight Gooden *	1991	132-53	.714	1713.2	554	2.91
Juan Marchal	1966	130-58	.691	1721.0	508	2.66
Ed Reulbach	1911	125-56	.691	1658.0	374	2.03
Roger Clemens	1991	134-61	.687	1784.1	565	2.85
Don Gullett *	1977	105-48	.686	1346.0	463	3.10
John Clarkson *	1888	170-79	.683	2238.0	620	2.49
Jim Palmer *	1972	100-48	.676	1391.0	420	2.72
Joe Wood *	1916	115-56	.673	1417.1	313	1.99
Grover Alexander	1915	127-63	.668	1714.0	442	2.32
Larry Corcoran *	1886	177-88	.668	2377.1	605	2.29
Lefty Gomez *	1935	101-51	.664	1331.0	475	3.21
Bob Feller *	1945	112-57	.663	1521.0	532	3.15
Kid Nichols *	1896	214-109	.663	2887.2	1004	3.13
Dave McNally	1971	135-69	.662	1887.0	660	3.15
Denny McLain *	1970	117-62	.654	1592.0	554	3.13
Hoss Radbourn	1883	106-56	.654	1431.2	342	2.15
Cy Young *	1893	106-57	.650	1447.0	446	2.77
Addie Joss	1908	141-77	.647	1977.1	415	1.89
Nig Cuppy *	1896	120-66	.645	1646.2	649	3.55
Jesse Tannehill	1903	131-72	.645	1767.2	565	2.88
Christy Mathewson *	1905	128-71	.643	1719.2	397	2.08
Tommy Bond *	1882	180-101	.641	2547.2	605	2.14
Dizzy Dean *	1937	134-75	.641	1737.1	577	2.99
Tom Seaver	1973	135-76	.640	1931.0	511	2.38
Carl Erskine	1955	100-57	.637	1346.0	573	3.83
George Wiltse	1909	100-57	.637	1399.2	357	2.30
Jim Crandall	1916	102-59	.634	1514.0	493	2.93
Wes Ferrell *	1934	116-67	.634	1503.0	612	3.66
Ed Walsh	1909	109-64	.630	1642.0	307	1.68
Clark Griffith	1898	132-78	.629	1847.1	737	3.59
Lon Warneke	1937	118-70	.628	1661.0	570	3.09
Carl Mays	1920	107-65	.622	1535.2	399	2.34
Vida Blue *	1976	110-67	.621	1666.0	517	2.79
John Stivetts *	1894	150-92	.620	2088.1	815	3.51
Jeff Tesreau	1917	111-68	.620	1605.0	434	2.43
Jim Maloney	1968	122-75	.619	1623.0	562	3.12
Gary Nolan	1976	106-66	.616	1618.0	534	2.97
Sandy Koufax	1964	112-70	.615	1666.0	575	3.11
John Ward *	1886	163-102	.615	2461.2	575	2.10
Chief Bender *	1910	123-77	.615	1798.1	463	2.32
Art Nehf	1921	102-65	.611	1529.1	466	2.74
Waite Hoyt	1928	155-99	.610	2250.0	857	3.43
Robin Roberts *	1953	114-73	.610	1670.0	554	2.99
Walter Johnson *	1914	178-115	.608	2447.0	437	1.61
Charles Buffington	1889	182-20	.603	2660.0	844	2.86

* had 100 wins by age 27

IS FADING IN THE STRETCH A FATAL WEAKNESS? (p. 196)

The table below shows how each pitcher was hit (opponent batting average) up through his 75th pitch thrown (**<76**), and after (**76+**); the difference between the two averages (**Diff**) is also shown.

Both Leagues — Listed Alphabetically
(minimum 125 innings pitched)

Pitcher, Team	<76	76+	Diff	Pitcher, Team	<76	76+	Diff	Pitcher, Team	<76	76+	Diff
Abbott, Cal	.221	.294	73	Greene, Phi	.233	.225	-8	Mulholland, Phi	.258	.266	8
Anderson A, Min	.273	.329	56	Gubicza, KC	.300	.359	59	Myers R, Cin	.240	.247	7
Appier, KC	.267	.227	-40	Gullickson, Det	.271	.354	83	Nabholz, Mon	.242	.217	-25
Aquino, KC	.267	.180	-87	Guzman, Tex	.250	.218	-32	Nagy, Cle	.282	.259	-23
Armstrong, Cin	.275	.376	101	Guzman J, Tor	.193	.207	14	Navarro, Mil	.244	.298	54
August, Mil	.313	.250	-63	Hanson, Sea	.287	.224	-64	Nichols Rod, Cle	.289	.209	-80
Avery, Atl	.218	.305	87	Harnisch, Hou	.220	.194	-26	Ojeda, LA	.263	.236	-27
Barnes B, Mon	.225	.260	35	Harris GA, Bos	.234	.306	72	Olivares, StL	.231	.277	46
Belcher, LA	.230	.261	31	Harris GW, SD	.235	.228	-7	Perez M, ChA	.220	.247	27
Benes, SD	.223	.254	31	Hesketh, Bos	.250	.250	0	Portugal, Hou	.265	.224	-41
Bielecki, Atl	.264	.252	-12	Hibbard, ChA	.266	.266	0	Rasmussen, SD	.283	.234	-49
Black, SF	.259	.222	-37	Hill K, StL	.216	.250	34	Rijo, Cin	.227	.195	-32
Boddicker, KC	.266	.286	20	Holman B, Sea	.280	.235	-45	Ryan, Tex	.182	.147	-35
Bosio, Mil	.241	.256	15	Hough, ChA	.230	.226	-4	Saberhagen, KC	.215	.255	40
Boskie, ChN	.295	.286	-9	Hurst, SD	.242	.239	-3	Sanderson, NYA	.263	.211	-52
Boyd, Tex	.266	.321	55	Johnson J, NYA	.302	.316	14	Smiley, Pit	.245	.272	27
Brown Kev, Tex	.271	.313	42	Johnson R, Sea	.188	.259	71	Smith B, StL	.257	.218	-39
Browning, Cin	.268	.257	-11	Jones Jim, Hou	.273	.255	-18	Smith Z, Pit	.265	.280	15
Burkett, SF	.285	.250	-35	Key, Tor	.261	.234	-27	Smoltz, Atl	.242	.245	3
Candiotti, Tor	.233	.218	-15	Kile, Hou	.245	.250	5	Stewart D, Oak	.275	.284	9
Clemens, Bos	.227	.210	-17	King E, Cle	.262	.350	88	Stottlemyre, Tor	.233	.240	7
Cone, NYN	.239	.228	-11	Krueger, Sea	.292	.273	-19	Swindell, Cle	.253	.289	36
Darling, Oak	.261	.234	-27	Lancaster, ChN	.247	.316	69	Tanana, Det	.258	.281	23
DeJesus J, Phi	.226	.221	-5	Langston, Cal	.210	.225	15	Tapani, Min	.241	.260	19
DeLeon J, StL	.235	.254	19	Leibrandt, Atl	.234	.283	49	Terrell, Det	.304	.292	-12
Delucia, Sea	.261	.255	-0	Leiter M, Det	.218	.339	121	Tewksbury, StL	.272	.328	56
Deshaies, Hou	.271	.230	-41	Maddux G, ChN	.226	.265	39	Tomlin R, Pit	.231	.327	96
Drabek, Pit	.265	.298	33	Martinez De, Mon	.215	.247	32	Viola, NYN	.271	.321	50
Erickson S, Min	.250	.242	-8	Martinez R, LA	.242	.202	-40	Wegman, Mil	.230	.271	41
Fernandez A, Ch	.263	.249	-14	McCaskill, Cal	.295	.248	-47	Welch, Oak	.269	.251	-18
Finley C, Cal	.255	.225	-30	McDonald, Bal	.275	.228	-47	Wells, Tor	.244	.277	33
Gardiner, Bos	.251	.347	96	McDowell J, ChA	.218	.247	29	Whitehurst, NYN	.275	.267	-8
Gardner M, Mon	.208	.290	82	Milacki, Bal	.255	.246	-9	Wilson Tr, SF	.247	.188	-59
Glavine, Atl	.213	.244	31	Moore M, Oak	.224	.239	15	**MLB Avg**	**.255**	**.261**	**6**
Gooden, NYN	.246	.281	35	Morgan M, LA	.215	.258	43				
Gordon, KC	.218	.228	10	Morris Jk, Min	.252	.229	-23				

HOW IMPORTANT IS GOOD CONTROL? (p. 199)

Both Leagues — Listed Alphabetically
(minimum 500 Innings Pitched Lifetime)

Pitcher, Team	IP	BB/9	Pitcher, Team	IP	BB/9	Pitcher, Team	IP	BB/9
Abbott, Cal	636.0	3.10	Gullickson, Det	2063.1	2.19	Perez P, NYA	1244.0	2.49
Acker, Tor	873.2	3.27	Guzman, Tex	789.2	3.67	Petry, Bos	2080.2	3.69
Agosto, StL	570.2	3.72	Hammaker, SD	1071.0	2.34	Plunk, NYA	582.0	5.75
Aguilera, Min	683.0	2.67	Hanson, Sea	565.2	2.67	Portugal, Hou	711.2	3.39
Andersen L, SD	866.2	2.77	Harnisch, Hou	521.2	4.18	Power, Cin	1015.0	3.55
Anderson A, Min	818.2	2.32	Harris GA, Bos	1148.1	3.84	Rasmussen D, SD	1379.0	3.21
Bailes, Cal	578.2	3.22	Hawkins, Oak	1558.1	3.53	Reardon, Bos	1003.0	3.01
Ballard, Bal	695.1	2.64	Heaton, Pit	1438.0	3.07	Reuschel, SF	3549.2	2.37
Bankhead, Sea	689.1	2.65	Henke, Tor	567.1	2.79	Righetti, SF	1207.2	3.73
Bannister F, Cal	2350.2	3.16	Hershiser, LA	1594.1	2.65	Rijo, Cin	1076.1	3.80
Bedrosian, Min	1067.0	4.00	Hesketh, Bos	645.2	3.42	Robinson D, SF	1897.2	3.02
Belcher, LA	806.0	2.91	Hibbard, ChA	542.1	2.54	Robinson JD, Cal	823.1	3.38
Berenguer, Atl	1127.2	4.53	Higuera, Mil	1291.1	2.73	Robinson JM, Bal	626.2	4.47
Bielecki, Atl	846.2	3.71	Holman B, Sea	676.2	3.38	Robinson R, Mil	764.2	2.81
Black, SF	1681.0	2.67	Honeycutt, Oak	1959.0	2.76	Ruffin, Phi	889.0	3.63
Boddicker, KC	1983.0	3.04	Hough, ChA	3306.0	4.02	Russell Jf, Tex	857.1	3.45
Bosio, Mil	958.2	2.30	Howell Jay, LA	696.0	3.12	Ryan, Tex	5163.1	4.68
Boyd, Tex	1389.2	2.38	Hurst, SD	2149.1	2.79	Saberhagen, KC	1660.1	1.79
Brown Kev, Tex	610.0	3.36	Jackson Dan, ChN	1277.0	3.67	Sanderson, NYA	2034.1	2.24
Browning, Cin	1669.1	2.40	Johnson R, Sea	607.2	5.55	Schatzeder, NYN	1317.2	3.24
Burke, NYN	656.0	2.76	Jones Jim, Hou	576.0	2.98	Schiraldi, Tex	553.1	4.34
Candelaria, LA	2481.1	2.07	Key, Tor	1479.0	2.10	Schmidt D, Mon	899.0	2.34
Candiotti, Tor	1404.2	2.95	Kilgus, Bal	516.2	3.17	Scott M, Hou	2068.0	2.73
Carman, Cin	919.1	3.70	King E, Cle	784.0	3.50	Show, Oak	1655.0	3.32
Cerutti, Det	861.0	3.04	Kipper, Pit	523.1	3.49	Sisk, Atl	523.1	4.59
Clancy, Atl	2518.2	3.38	Krueger, Sea	845.1	4.02	Smiley, Pit	854.0	2.41
Clemens, Bos	1784.1	2.47	LaCoss, SF	1739.2	3.75	Smith B, StL	1740.1	2.15
Cone, NYN	1017.1	3.09	Lamp, Bos	1803.0	2.70	Smith Dv, ChN	795.1	3.16
Cox, Phi	1088.0	2.78	Lancaster, ChN	555.2	3.06	Smith Le, StL	992.1	3.41
Crawford, KC	562.2	2.98	Langston, Cal	1843.2	4.24	Smith Roy, Bal	618.1	2.94
Crim, Mil	529.2	2.57	LaPoint, Phi	1487.0	3.38	Smith Z, Pit	1344.1	3.11
Darling, Oak	1712.0	3.45	Leach T, Min	610.0	2.58	Smoltz, Atl	733.0	3.34
Darwin, Bos	1981.1	2.71	Leary, NYA	1160.0	2.94	Stewart D, Oak	2053.2	3.43
Davis Mrk, KC	989.2	3.92	Lefferts, SD	831.1	2.61	Stieb, Tor	2726.2	3.17
Davis Storm, KC	1545.1	3.31	Leibrandt, Atl	1964.2	2.61	Stottlemyre, Tor	647.2	3.25
Dayley, Tor	573.0	3.47	Long B, Mon	518.2	2.43	Sutcliffe, ChN	2227.0	3.64
DeLeon J, StL	1579.2	3.97	Maddux G, ChN	1174.0	2.95	Swift, Sea	759.0	3.00
Deshaies, Hou	1109.0	3.49	Mahler R, Atl	1951.1	2.80	Swindell, Cle	1043.0	1.95
Downs, SF	699.2	3.13	Martinez De, Mon	2933.1	2.66	Tanana, Det	3797.1	2.63
Drabek, Pit	1237.2	2.42	Martinez R, LA	589.0	3.04	Terrell, Det	1850.0	3.41
Eckersley, Oak	2891.1	2.08	McCaskill, Cal	1221.0	3.30	Tewksbury, StL	551.1	1.89
Eichhorn, Cal	624.0	2.78	McClure, StL	1098.1	3.83	Valenzuela, Cal	2355.1	3.51
Farr, NYA	697.0	3.47	McDowell J, ChA	645.1	3.25	Viola, NYA	2339.0	2.55
Fernandez S, NYN	1256.1	3.58	McDowell R, LA	712.2	3.27	Walk, Pit	1344.0	3.30
Finley C, Cal	994.1	3.73	McGaffigan, KC	833.1	3.18	Wegman, Mil	914.0	2.13
Flanagan, Bal	2735.1	2.85	Milacki, Bal	587.1	3.23	Welch, Oak	2732.1	2.94
Franco Jn, NYN	651.0	3.44	Moore M, Oak	2108.0	3.45	Wells, Tor	567.1	2.62
Fraser, StL	619.0	3.24	Morgan M, LA	1385.1	3.03	Whitson, SD	2240.2	2.80
Garrelts, SF	959.1	3.87	Morris Jk, Min	3290.0	3.22	Williams Mitch, Phi	511.0	6.76
Glavine, Atl	892.2	2.85	Moyer, StL	700.0	3.63	Williamson, Bal	515.2	3.04
Gooden, NYN	1713.2	2.65	Mulholland, Phi	628.2	2.42	Witt B, Tex	980.0	6.26
Gordon, KC	532.0	4.72	Nelson G, Oak	967.1	3.46	Witt M, NYA	2067.1	3.01
Gossage, Tex	1676.1	3.61	Nunez E, Mil	502.1	3.92	Young C, Oak	1024.2	3.01
Gott, LA	886.2	3.82	Ojeda, LA	1671.2	3.06	Young Mt, Bos	1044.2	4.01
Gross K, LA	1585.0	3.59	Orosco, Cle	836.2	3.75	**MLB Avg**		**3.29**
Gubicza, KC	1540.1	3.40	Pena A, Atl	927.1	2.80			
Guetterman, NYA	518.1	2.74	Perez M, ChA	723.1	3.79			

WILL IT BE DR. TREVOR... OR MR. WILSON? (p. 202)

1989-1991 Both Leagues — Listed Alphabetically
(minimum 45 starts from 1989 through 1991)

Pitcher, Team	W	ERA	L	ERA	W-L	Pitcher, Team	W	ERA	L	ERA	W-L
Abbott, Cal	40	1.94	37	5.63	-3.69	Langston, Cal	45	1.87	39	5.41	-3.54
Anderson A, Min	29	1.77	37	7.77	-6.00	LaPoint, Phi	13	2.75	20	7.10	-4.35
Appier, KC	26	2.08	21	5.43	-3.35	Leary, NYA	20	1.78	40	5.66	-3.88
Armstrong, Cin	21	1.86	25	7.10	-5.24	Leibrandt, Atl	29	1.58	35	6.10	-4.53
August, Mil	18	2.14	19	10.15	-8.01	Lilliquist, SD	13	1.45	22	7.75	-6.30
Avery, Atl	21	1.59	18	8.10	-6.51	Maddux G, ChN	49	1.77	38	5.42	-3.65
Ballard, Bal	25	2.31	30	6.90	-4.59	Magrane, StL	28	1.46	26	5.58	-4.12
Bankhead, Sea	16	1.72	13	9.58	-7.85	Mahler R, Atl	17	2.38	21	6.04	-3.66
Belcher, LA	33	1.01	28	6.27	-5.26	Martinez De, Mon	40	1.74	28	4.22	-2.48
Benes, SD	31	1.73	25	5.74	-4.01	Martinez R, LA	43	1.70	23	6.48	-4.78
Bielecki, Atl	35	2.07	26	7.55	-5.48	McCaskill, Cal	37	1.68	40	6.01	-4.33
Black, SF	35	1.59	38	6.25	-4.66	McDowell J, ChA	31	1.88	19	7.27	-5.40
Blyleven, Cal	25	2.04	12	8.36	-6.32	Milacki, Bal	28	1.94	29	6.75	-4.81
Boddicker, KC	43	2.17	31	6.09	-3.92	Moore M, Oak	49	1.60	34	6.17	-4.56
Bosio, Mil	33	1.80	29	4.84	-3.04	Morgan M, LA	31	1.70	36	4.99	-3.29
Boyd, Tex	21	1.37	23	7.23	-5.86	Morris Jk, Min	39	2.58	44	5.96	-3.38
Brown Kev, Tex	33	2.09	31	7.06	-4.98	Mulholland, Phi	29	1.79	30	5.92	-4.13
Browning, Cin	44	2.27	35	6.73	-4.45	Navarro, Mil	29	2.36	27	6.05	-3.70
Burkett, SF	26	2.18	18	7.27	-5.09	Ojeda, LA	29	1.92	25	6.00	-4.08
Candiotti, Tor	41	1.88	34	5.31	-3.42	Perez M, ChA	25	2.10	32	8.31	-6.22
Cary, NYA	11	1.58	21	6.62	-5.04	Perez P, NYA	11	1.20	18	4.97	-3.77
Cerutti, Det	20	2.74	24	5.23	-2.49	Portugal, Hou	28	2.23	21	6.01	-3.78
Clemens, Bos	56	1.68	27	4.66	-2.98	Rasmussen, SD	27	2.41	38	5.93	-3.52
Combs, Phi	16	2.04	16	7.57	-5.52	Reuschel, SF	20	1.78	15	6.26	-4.48
Cone, NYN	42	1.56	32	6.32	-4.76	Rijo, Cin	36	1.62	20	4.30	-2.68
Darling, Oak	28	1.62	36	5.92	-4.30	Robinson D, SF	27	1.59	25	7.90	-6.31
Davis Storm, KC	28	2.48	22	8.03	-5.55	Robinson JM, Bal	18	2.66	23	10.18	-7.51
DeJesus J, Phi	17	2.05	17	5.75	-3.70	Ruffin, Phi	15	1.57	30	6.45	-4.87
DeLeon J, StL	28	1.59	40	5.72	-4.13	Ryan, Tex	41	1.90	25	5.80	-3.89
Deshaies, Hou	27	1.89	34	7.63	-5.73	Saberhagen, KC	41	1.29	22	4.58	-3.29
Drabek, Pit	50	1.73	32	4.78	-3.05	Sanderson, NYA	43	2.24	28	6.02	-3.77
Erickson S, Min	28	1.55	12	6.05	-4.50	Scott M, Hou	28	1.90	25	7.13	-5.23
Farrell, Cle	13	1.15	19	5.86	-4.72	Smiley, Pit	40	2.36	26	5.20	-2.84
Fernandez A, ChA	14	2.26	18	7.21	-4.95	Smith B, StL	31	1.61	28	5.93	-4.32
Fernandez S, NYN	24	1.27	22	5.28	-4.01	Smith P, Atl	11	2.72	23	7.74	-5.02
Finley C, Cal	52	1.80	27	5.10	-3.29	Smith Roy, Bal	20	2.53	19	7.16	-4.62
Gardner M, Mon	16	1.04	22	7.30	-6.26	Smith Z, Pit	29	1.40	31	5.49	-4.09
Garrelts, SF	27	1.51	17	8.20	-6.69	Smoltz, Atl	40	1.81	35	6.01	-4.21
Glavine, Atl	44	1.81	31	6.58	-4.77	Stewart D, Oak	54	1.83	31	6.24	-4.41
Gooden, NYN	41	2.67	18	7.00	-4.33	Stieb, Tor	39	1.21	17	7.15	-5.95
Gordon, KC	24	1.97	25	8.08	-6.11	Stottlemyre, Tor	35	1.98	31	6.47	-4.48
Gross K, LA	23	1.69	29	8.56	-6.87	Sutcliffe, ChN	22	2.57	18	5.80	-3.23
Gubicza, KC	28	2.18	30	7.09	-4.91	Swindell, Cle	34	1.99	31	6.64	-4.65
Gullickson, Det	30	2.54	23	6.07	-3.53	Tanana, Det	32	2.55	34	5.56	-3.01
Hanson, Sea	35	2.01	22	6.36	-4.35	Tapani, Min	30	1.78	19	6.77	-5.00
Harnisch, Hou	28	2.03	29	6.12	-4.09	Terrell, Det	30	2.28	43	6.61	-4.32
Harris GA, Bos	19	2.04	19	7.27	-5.24	Tewksbury, StL	22	1.48	21	5.21	-3.73
Hawkins, Oak	24	1.95	33	8.65	-6.70	Valenzuela, Cal	23	2.38	28	6.31	-3.92
Hershiser, LA	23	1.99	18	4.11	-2.12	Viola, NYN	46	1.59	44	5.82	-4.22
Hibbard, ChA	30	2.01	27	6.07	-4.05	Walk, Pit	27	2.68	17	6.33	-3.65
Higuera, Mil	23	2.41	18	6.66	-4.25	Welch, Oak	56	1.98	27	6.51	-4.53
Hill K, StL	23	1.80	31	5.66	-3.86	Wells, Tor	24	1.87	15	6.59	-4.71
Holman B, Sea	33	1.79	36	5.72	-3.93	West, Min	14	2.27	17	8.77	-6.50
Hough, ChA	31	2.55	35	5.13	-2.58	Whitson, SD	34	1.69	26	5.20	-3.51
Howell K, Phi	20	2.09	19	6.84	-4.75	Wilson Tr, SF	21	1.76	16	10.05	-8.29
Hurst, SD	41	1.81	28	5.00	-3.19	Witt B, Tex	32	2.14	30	7.94	-5.81
Jackson Dan, ChN	13	2.96	22	7.19	-4.23	Witt M, NYA	14	2.35	22	7.04	-4.69
Johnson D, Bal	19	2.43	24	7.88	-5.45	Young Mt, Bos	11	1.76	26	5.34	-3.59
Johnson R, Sea	34	2.16	34	6.20	-4.04	**MLB Average: 1989-1991**		**1.94**		**6.57**	**-4.63**
Key, Tor	42	2.15	33	6.52	-4.37						
King E, Cle	27	1.87	25	6.29	-4.42						
Krueger, Sea	16	1.78	14	5.53	-3.76						

DID MORE THROWS TO FIRST HELP DWIGHT GOODEN? (p. 204)

1991 Both Leagues — Listed Alphabetically
(minimum 125 innings pitched)

Pitcher	Pickoff Throws Total	Per 9	PO	Stolen Bases SB	Per 9	Pitcher	Pickoff Throws Total	Per 9	PO	Stolen Bases SB	Per 9
Abbott, Cal	180	6.7	1	12	0.4	Key, Tor	102	4.4	0	6	0.3
Anderson A, Min	94	6.3	1	14	0.9	Kile, Hou	79	4.6	0	12	0.7
Appier, KC	166	7.2	0	10	0.4	King E, Cle	126	7.5	0	8	0.5
Aquino, KC	117	6.7	1	10	0.6	Krueger, Sea	164	8.4	4	11	0.6
Armstrong, Cin	204	13.1	6	12	0.8	Lancaster, ChN	124	7.2	1	14	0.8
August, Mil	145	9.4	1	18	1.2	Langston, Cal	171	6.2	4	10	0.4
Avery, Atl	59	2.5	0	21	0.9	Leibrandt, Atl	231	9.1	4	35	1.4
Barnes B, Mon	203	11.4	1	20	1.1	Leiter M, Det	67	4.5	0	6	0.4
Belcher, LA	118	5.1	0	17	0.7	Maddux G, ChN	166	5.7	5	25	0.9
Benes, SD	43	1.7	0	10	0.4	Martinez De, Mon	194	7.9	3	22	0.9
Bielecki, Atl	157	8.1	2	17	0.9	Martinez R, LA	138	5.6	1	16	0.7
Black, SF	266	11.2	1	14	0.6	McCaskill, Cal	142	7.2	1	8	0.4
Boddicker, KC	205	10.2	2	17	0.8	McDonald, Bal	77	5.5	0	14	1.0
Bosio, Mil	135	5.9	2	9	0.4	McDowell J, ChA	200	7.1	5	22	0.8
Boskie, ChN	137	9.6	1	4	0.3	Milacki, Bal	53	2.6	0	12	0.6
Boyd, Tex	66	3.3	0	14	0.7	Moore M, Oak	122	5.2	0	19	0.8
Brown Kev, Tex	194	8.3	3	5	0.2	Morgan M, LA	143	5.4	2	24	0.9
Browning, Cin	118	4.6	1	21	0.8	Morris Jk, Min	43	1.6	0	32	1.2
Burkett, SF	344	15.0	3	17	0.7	Mulholland, Phi	144	5.6	4	6	0.2
Candiotti, Tor	190	7.2	3	26	1.0	Myers R, Cin	96	6.5	0	4	0.3
Clemens, Bos	183	6.1	1	23	0.8	Nabholz, Mon	163	9.5	1	15	0.9
Cone, NYN	408	15.8	1	27	1.0	Nagy, Cle	124	5.3	0	23	1.0
Darling, Oak	213	9.9	4	24	1.1	Navarro, Mil	122	4.7	0	23	0.9
DeJesus J, Phi	37	1.8	0	19	0.9	Nichols Rod, Cle	60	3.9	0	16	1.0
DeLeon J, StL	35	1.9	0	12	0.7	Ojeda, LA	146	6.9	0	23	1.1
Delucia, Sea	92	4.5	1	4	0.2	Olivares, StL	130	7.0	1	10	0.5
Deshaies, Hou	295	16.5	1	21	1.2	Perez M, ChA	131	8.7	1	15	1.0
Drabek, Pit	128	4.9	3	29	1.1	Portugal, Hou	136	7.3	0	12	0.6
Erickson S, Min	75	3.3	0	4	0.2	Rasmussen D, SD	85	5.2	0	21	1.3
Fernandez A, ChA	175	8.2	1	15	0.7	Rijo, Cin	180	7.9	4	16	0.7
Finley C, Cal	54	2.1	0	15	0.6	Ryan, Tex	19	1.0	1	24	1.2
Gardiner, Bos	46	3.2	1	11	0.8	Saberhagen, KC	187	8.6	4	9	0.4
Gardner M, Mon	127	6.8	0	13	0.7	Sanderson, NYA	74	3.2	0	16	0.7
Glavine, Atl	240	8.8	0	18	0.7	Smiley, Pit	109	4.7	0	18	0.8
Gooden, NYN	215	10.2	0	33	1.6	Smith B, StL	76	3.4	0	19	0.9
Gordon, KC	109	6.2	0	9	0.5	Smith Z, Pit	152	6.0	0	26	1.0
Greene, Phi	70	3.0	1	18	0.8	Smoltz, Atl	128	5.0	2	14	0.5
Gubicza, KC	196	13.3	0	18	1.2	Stewart D, Oak	53	2.1	0	23	0.9
Gullickson, Det	75	3.0	1	15	0.6	Stottlemyre, Tor	187	7.7	0	24	1.0
Guzman, Tex	68	3.6	1	12	0.6	Swindell, Cle	146	5.5	2	9	0.3
Guzman J, Tor	137	8.9	1	11	0.7	Tanana, Det	215	8.9	0	17	0.7
Hanson, Sea	63	3.2	0	11	0.6	Tapani, Min	45	1.7	0	18	0.7
Harnisch, Hou	138	5.7	0	27	1.1	Terrell, Det	62	2.6	0	6	0.2
Harris GA, Bos	151	7.9	3	1	0.1	Tewksbury, StL	56	2.6	0	10	0.5
Harris GW, SD	59	4.0	0	13	0.9	Tomlin R, Pit	115	5.9	1	17	0.9
Hesketh, Bos	90	5.3	1	7	0.4	Viola, NYN	207	8.1	0	6	0.2
Hibbard, ChA	146	6.8	0	6	0.3	Wegman, Mil	157	7.3	1	10	0.5
Hill K, StL	95	4.7	0	19	0.9	Welch, Oak	121	4.9	1	12	0.5
Holman B, Sea	110	5.1	1	4	0.2	Wells, Tor	153	6.9	3	8	0.4
Hough, ChA	317	14.3	1	10	0.5	Whitehurst, NYN	138	9.3	0	9	0.6
Hurst, SD	163	6.6	4	11	0.4	Wilson Tr, SF	242	10.8	0	8	0.4
Johnson J, NYA	129	9.1	1	18	1.3	MLB	25044	6.0	172	3120	0.7
Johnson R, Sea	103	4.6	0	18	0.8						
Jones Jim, Hou	98	6.5	0	18	1.2						

Is Holding Runners Overrated? (p. 206)

Both Leagues — Listed Alphabetically
(minimum 125 innings pitched)

Pitcher, Team	SB	CS	SB%	SB/9	PkO	Pitcher, Team	SB	CS	SB%	SB/9	PkO
Abbott, Cal	12	14	46.2	0.44	1	Key, Tor	6	2	75.0	0.26	0
Anderson A, Min	14	6	70.0	0.94	1	Kile, Hou	12	3	80.0	0.70	0
Appier, KC	10	8	55.6	0.43	0	King E, Cle	8	3	72.7	0.48	0
Aquino, KC	10	6	62.5	0.57	1	Krueger, Sea	11	5	68.8	0.57	4
Armstrong, Cin	12	8	60.0	0.77	6	Lancaster, ChN	14	14	50.0	0.81	1
August, Mil	18	4	81.8	1.17	1	Langston, Cal	10	15	40.0	0.37	4
Avery, Atl	21	11	65.6	0.90	1	Leibrandt, Atl	35	11	76.1	1.37	4
Barnes B, Mon	20	8	71.4	1.13	1	Leiter M, Det	6	6	50.0	0.40	0
Belcher, LA	17	10	63.0	0.73	0	Maddux G, ChN	25	7	78.1	0.86	5
Benes, SD	10	11	47.6	0.40	0	Martinez De, Mon	22	4	84.6	0.89	3
Bielecki, Atl	17	9	65.4	0.88	2	Martinez R, LA	16	9	64.0	0.65	1
Black, SF	14	11	56.0	0.59	1	McCaskill, Cal	8	6	57.1	0.41	1
Boddicker, KC	17	10	63.0	0.85	2	McDonald, Bal	14	3	82.4	1.00	0
Bosio, Mil	9	4	69.2	0.40	2	McDowell J, ChA	22	10	68.8	0.78	5
Boskie, ChN	4	2	66.7	0.28	1	Milacki, Bal	12	6	66.7	0.59	0
Boyd, Tex	14	12	53.8	0.69	0	Moore M, Oak	19	12	61.3	0.81	0
Brown Kev, Tex	5	11	31.3	0.21	3	Morgan M, LA	24	7	77.4	0.91	2
Browning, Cin	21	6	77.8	0.82	1	Morris Jk, Min	32	8	80.0	1.17	0
Burkett, SF	17	16	51.5	0.74	0	Mulholland, Phi	6	5	54.5	0.23	4
Candiotti, Tor	26	8	76.5	0.98	3	Myers R, Cin	4	7	36.4	0.27	0
Clemens, Bos	23	16	59.0	0.76	1	Nabholz, Mon	15	11	57.7	0.88	1
Cone, NYN	27	13	67.5	1.04	1	Nagy, Cle	23	7	76.7	0.98	0
Darling, Oak	24	3	88.9	1.11	4	Navarro, Mil	23	7	76.7	0.88	0
DeJesus J, Phi	19	11	63.3	0.94	0	Nichols Rod, Cle	16	8	66.7	1.05	0
DeLeon J, StL	12	12	50.0	0.66	0	Ojeda, LA	23	15	60.5	1.09	0
Delucia, Sea	4	9	30.8	0.20	1	Olivares, StL	10	11	47.6	0.54	1
Deshaies, Hou	21	14	60.0	1.17	1	Perez M, ChA	15	5	75.0	1.00	1
Drabek, Pit	29	15	65.9	1.11	3	Portugal, Hou	12	7	63.2	0.64	0
Erickson S, Min	4	10	28.6	0.18	0	Rasmussen D, SD	21	6	77.8	1.29	0
Fernandez A, ChA	15	11	57.7	0.70	1	Rijo, Cin	16	3	84.2	0.70	4
Finley C, Cal	15	14	51.7	0.59	0	Ryan, Tex	24	8	75.0	1.25	1
Gardiner, Bos	11	5	68.8	0.76	1	Saberhagen, KC	9	9	50.0	0.41	4
Gardner M, Mon	13	17	43.3	0.70	0	Sanderson, NYA	16	7	69.6	0.69	0
Glavine, Atl	18	10	64.3	0.66	0	Smiley, Pit	18	13	58.1	0.78	0
Gooden, NYN	33	16	67.3	1.56	0	Smith B, StL	19	8	70.4	0.86	0
Gordon, KC	9	7	56.3	0.51	0	Smith Z, Pit	26	8	76.5	1.03	0
Greene, Phi	18	7	72.0	0.78	1	Smoltz, Atl	14	13	51.9	0.55	2
Gubicza, KC	18	6	75.0	1.22	0	Stewart D, Oak	23	9	71.9	0.92	0
Gullickson, Det	15	8	65.2	0.60	1	Stottlemyre, Tor	24	3	88.9	0.99	0
Guzman, Tex	12	13	48.0	0.64	1	Swindell, Cle	9	11	45.0	0.34	2
Guzman J, Tor	11	6	64.7	0.71	0	Tanana, Det	17	14	54.8	0.70	0
Hanson, Sea	11	10	52.4	0.57	0	Tapani, Min	18	3	85.7	0.66	0
Harnisch, Hou	27	6	81.8	1.12	0	Terrell, Det	6	5	54.5	0.25	0
Harris GA, Bos	1	6	14.3	0.05	3	Tewksbury, StL	10	10	50.0	0.47	0
Harris GW, SD	13	8	61.9	0.88	0	Tomlin R, Pit	17	12	58.6	0.87	1
Hesketh, Bos	7	8	46.7	0.41	1	Viola, NYN	6	16	27.3	0.23	0
Hibbard, ChA	6	8	42.9	0.28	0	Wegman, Mil	10	7	58.8	0.47	1
Hill K, StL	19	11	63.3	0.94	0	Welch, Oak	12	16	42.9	0.49	1
Holman B, Sea	4	5	44.4	0.18	1	Wells, Tor	8	13	38.1	0.36	3
Hough, ChA	10	9	52.6	0.45	1	Whitehurst, NYN	9	8	52.9	0.61	0
Hurst, SD	11	6	64.7	0.45	4	Wilson Tr, SF	8	12	40.0	0.36	0
Johnson J, NYA	18	4	81.8	1.28	1						
Johnson R, Sea	18	9	66.7	0.80	0	MLB	3120	1567	66.6	0.74	172
Jones Jim, Hou	18	6	75.0	1.20	0						

Is "Unearned Run Average" a Leading Indicator? (p. 209)

In the table below, **UER** stands for unearned runs charged to the pitcher, **Err** is the number of errors committed while he was pitching, and **UERA** is his Un-Earned Run Average.

1991 Both Leagues—Listed Alphabetically
(Minimum 125 Innings Pitched)

Player, Team	IP	R	UER	Err	UERA
Abbott, Cal	243.0	85	7	20	0.26
Anderson A, Mi	134.1	82	8	11	0.54
Appier, KC	207.2	97	18	22	0.78
Aquino, KC	157.0	67	7	12	0.40
Armstrong, Cin	139.2	90	5	10	0.32
August, Mil	138.1	87	3	10	0.20
Avery, Atl	210.1	89	10	19	0.43
Barnes B, Mon	160.0	82	7	17	0.39
Belcher, LA	209.1	76	15	24	0.64
Benes, SD	223.0	76	1	13	0.04
Bielecki, Atl	173.2	91	5	8	0.26
Black, SF	214.1	104	9	14	0.38
Boddicker, KC	180.2	89	7	16	0.35
Bosio, Mil	204.2	80	6	12	0.26
Boskie, ChN	129.0	78	3	10	0.21
Boyd, Tex	182.1	96	3	10	0.15
Brown Kev, Tex	210.2	116	13	22	0.56
Browning, Cin	230.1	124	17	21	0.66
Burkett, SF	206.2	103	7	22	0.30
Candiotti, Tor	238.0	82	12	18	0.45
Clemens, Bos	271.1	93	14	17	0.46
Cone, NYN	232.2	95	10	17	0.39
Darling, Oak	194.1	100	8	18	0.37
DeJesus J, Phi	181.2	74	5	12	0.25
DeLeon J, StL	162.2	57	8	12	0.44
Delucia, Sea	182.0	107	4	11	0.20
Deshaies, Hou	161.0	90	1	15	0.06
Drabek, Pit	234.2	92	12	23	0.46
Erickson S, Mi	204.0	80	8	21	0.35
Fernandez A, C	191.2	100	4	13	0.19
Finley C, Cal	227.1	102	6	11	0.24
Gardiner, Bos	130.0	79	9	13	0.62
Gardner M, Mon	168.1	78	6	13	0.32
Glavine, Atl	246.2	83	13	21	0.47
Gooden, NYN	190.0	80	4	22	0.19
Gordon, KC	158.0	76	8	13	0.46
Greene, Phi	207.2	85	7	12	0.30
Gubicza, KC	133.0	90	6	13	0.41
Gullickson, De	226.1	109	11	17	0.44
Guzman, Tex	169.2	67	9	17	0.48
Guzman J, Tor	138.2	53	7	16	0.45
Hanson, Sea	174.2	82	8	18	0.41
Harnisch, Hou	216.2	71	6	22	0.25
Harris GA, Bos	173.0	79	5	11	0.26
Harris GW, SD	133.0	42	9	8	0.61
Hesketh, Bos	153.1	59	3	11	0.18
Hibbard, ChA	194.0	107	14	17	0.65
Hill K, StL	181.1	76	4	15	0.20
Holman B, Sea	195.1	86	6	10	0.28
Hough, ChA	199.1	98	9	18	0.41
Hurst, SD	221.2	89	8	16	0.32
Johnson J, NYA	127.0	89	6	18	0.43
Johnson R, Sea	201.1	96	7	18	0.31
Jones Jim, Hou	135.1	73	7	16	0.47
Key, Tor	209.1	84	13	25	0.56
Kile, Hou	153.2	81	18	21	1.05
King E, Cle	150.2	83	6	18	0.36
Krueger, Sea	175.0	82	12	12	0.62
Lancaster, ChN	156.0	68	7	9	0.40
Langston, Cal	246.1	89	7	15	0.26
Leibrandt, Atl	229.2	105	16	26	0.63
Leiter M, Det	134.2	66	3	12	0.20
Maddux G, ChN	263.0	113	15	14	0.51
Martinez De, M	222.0	70	11	23	0.45
Martinez R, LA	220.1	89	9	12	0.37
McCaskill, Cal	177.2	93	9	13	0.46
McDonald, Bal	126.1	71	3	6	0.21
McDowell J, Ch	253.2	97	1	8	0.04
Milacki, Bal	184.0	86	4	12	0.20
Moore M, Oak	210.0	75	6	10	0.26
Morgan M, LA	236.1	85	12	24	0.46
Morris Jk, Min	246.2	107	13	8	0.47
Mulholland, Ph	232.0	100	7	21	0.27
Myers R, Cin	132.0	61	9	11	0.61
Nabholz, Mon	153.2	66	4	7	0.23
Nagy, Cle	211.1	103	6	17	0.26
Navarro, Mil	234.0	117	15	21	0.58
Nichols Rod, C	137.1	63	9	13	0.59
Ojeda, LA	189.1	78	11	15	0.52
Olivares, StL	167.1	72	3	13	0.16
Perez M, ChA	135.2	49	2	15	0.13
Portugal, Hou	168.1	91	7	22	0.37
Rasmussen D, S	146.2	74	13	15	0.80
Rijo, Cin	204.1	69	12	20	0.53
Ryan, Tex	173.0	58	2	10	0.10
Saberhagen, KC	196.1	76	9	14	0.41
Sanderson, NYA	208.0	95	7	16	0.30
Smiley, Pit	207.2	78	7	10	0.30
Smith B, StL	198.2	95	10	15	0.45
Smith Z, Pit	228.0	95	14	20	0.55
Smoltz, Atl	229.2	101	4	13	0.16
Stewart D, Oak	226.0	135	5	19	0.20
Stottlemyre, T	219.0	97	5	12	0.21
Swindell, Cle	238.0	112	20	24	0.76
Tanana, Det	217.1	98	9	14	0.37
Tapani, Min	244.0	84	3	11	0.11
Terrell, Det	218.2	115	12	12	0.49
Tewksbury, StL	191.0	86	17	12	0.80
Tomlin R, Pit	175.0	75	17	20	0.87
Viola, NYN	231.1	112	10	17	0.39
Wegman, Mil	193.1	76	15	18	0.70
Welch, Oak	220.0	124	12	18	0.49
Wells, Tor	198.1	88	6	16	0.27
Whitehurst, NY	133.1	67	5	12	0.34
Wilson Tr, SF	202.0	87	7	18	0.31
MLB Average					0.41

WHICH STARTING STAFFS STAR, AND WHICH RELIEF STAFFS REEK? (p. 212)

1991 Team Pitching Statistics — Listed Alphabetically by Team

American League Starters

Team	ERA	W	L	IP	H	R	ER	HR	BB	K	BA
Baltimore	5.29	42	69	900.00	1025	566	529	104	318	479	.288
Boston	4.22	65	61	984.33	984	509	462	103	341	711	.261
California	3.81	70	67	1042.00	1009	480	441	102	404	660	.257
Chicago	4.23	54	55	1014.33	927	516	477	112	411	621	.245
Cleveland	4.21	42	79	1032.33	1124	539	483	77	261	596	.278
Detroit	4.48	60	60	961.33	1074	521	478	99	333	436	.286
Kansas City	3.98	63	59	1002.67	990	496	443	75	327	638	.258
Milwaukee	4.17	62	52	974.67	1012	497	452	88	314	502	.268
Minnesota	3.77	71	51	1000.67	982	459	419	102	324	582	.258
New York	5.07	45	68	892.00	984	532	502	108	304	528	.283
Oakland	4.50	56	56	986.67	965	530	493	98	460	585	.258
Seattle	4.11	60	59	974.67	961	483	445	102	432	688	.262
Texas	4.63	52	53	948.00	968	541	488	92	442	653	.265
Toronto	3.49	67	50	1014.67	913	433	393	86	340	606	.239

National League Starters

Team	ERA	W	L	IP	H	R	ER	HR	BB	K	BA
Atlanta	3.46	72	49	1009.00	897	438	388	80	310	661	.239
Chicago	4.35	48	54	957.00	972	511	463	76	331	542	.266
Cincinnati	3.98	59	65	966.00	930	484	427	94	359	614	.254
Houston	4.07	45	63	956.33	884	473	433	89	402	666	.245
Los Angeles	3.06	65	48	1023.00	926	396	348	62	332	679	.241
Montreal	3.56	49	59	998.67	892	442	395	76	403	622	.241
New York	3.71	57	65	1017.67	1007	467	419	81	277	748	.259
Philadelphia	3.98	51	63	964.00	900	458	426	74	419	631	.249
Pittsburgh	3.27	67	44	1005.00	991	425	365	72	244	594	.260
St. Louis	3.54	54	57	1001.33	942	441	394	82	300	557	.252
San Diego	3.68	65	61	1011.33	978	462	413	112	285	636	.253
San Francisco	4.18	54	63	945.00	933	474	439	94	340	562	.260

American League Relievers

Team	ERA	W	L	IP	H	R	ER	HR	BB	K	BA
Baltimore	3.45	25	26	557.67	509	230	214	43	186	389	.246
Boston	3.58	19	17	455.33	421	203	181	44	189	288	.246
California	3.38	11	14	399.67	342	169	150	39	139	330	.232
Chicago	2.85	33	20	463.67	375	165	147	42	190	302	.225
Cleveland	4.31	15	26	409.00	427	220	196	33	180	266	.270
Detroit	4.66	24	18	489.00	496	273	253	49	260	303	.269
Kansas City	3.81	19	21	463.33	483	226	196	30	202	366	.268
Milwaukee	4.18	21	27	489.00	486	247	227	59	213	357	.263
Minnesota	3.53	24	16	448.67	420	193	176	37	164	294	.250
New York	3.41	26	23	552.00	526	245	209	44	202	408	.252
Oakland	4.74	28	22	457.67	460	246	241	57	195	307	.263
Seattle	3.16	23	20	489.67	426	191	172	34	196	315	.235
Texas	4.19	33	24	531.00	518	273	247	59	220	369	.257
Toronto	3.54	24	21	448.00	388	189	176	35	183	365	.235

National League Relievers

Team	ERA	W	L	IP	H	R	ER	HR	BB	K	BA
Atlanta	3.57	22	19	443.67	407	206	176	38	171	308	.243
Chicago	3.46	29	29	499.67	443	223	192	41	211	385	.240
Cincinnati	3.53	15	23	474.00	442	207	186	33	201	383	.251
Houston	3.86	20	34	496.67	463	244	213	40	249	367	.250
Los Angeles	3.08	28	21	435.00	386	169	149	34	168	349	.240
Montreal	3.83	22	31	441.67	412	213	188	35	181	287	.251
New York	3.22	20	19	419.67	396	179	150	27	133	280	.250
Philadelphia	3.64	27	21	499.00	446	222	202	37	251	357	.240
Pittsburgh	3.83	31	20	451.67	420	207	192	45	157	325	.246
St. Louis	4.02	30	21	434.00	425	207	194	32	154	265	.261
San Diego	3.36	19	17	441.33	407	184	165	27	172	285	.249
San Francisco	3.75	21	24	497.00	464	223	207	49	204	343	.251

WHY DO THE METS LET THEIR ACES THROW SO MANY PITCHES? (p. 216)

Most Pitches In a Game By Starting Pitchers in 1991

Pitcher	Opp	Date	Sc	W/L	IP	H	R	ER	BB	SO	#Pit
Benes, SD	Cin	04/16/1991	0-1	L	8.1	4	1	1	3	13	154
Moore M, Oak	@Bos	06/21/1991	2-3	L	8.0	7	3	3	7	2	154
Tanana, Det	Mil	09/21/1991	2-5	L	8.2	8	5	4	5	5	151
Stewart D, Oak	@ChA	05/31/1991	4-5	L	8.0	10	4	4	6	5	150
Clemens, Bos	@Tex	07/22/1991	1-2	L	8.0	7	2	2	4	4	150
DeJesus J, Phi	Atl	08/31/1991	5-0	W	8.0	3	0	0	6	13	150
Gooden, NYN	Mon	04/13/1991	5-3	W	9.0	7	3	3	3	14	149
Tanana, Det	Oak	06/18/1991	2-0	W	8.2	4	0	0	4	5	149
Cone, NYN	@Cin	06/04/1991	4-2	W	8.0	4	2	0	5	13	148
Viola, NYN	@Cin	06/06/1991	3-5	L	8.0	9	5	5	4	4	146
DeJesus J, Phi	ChN	10/02/1991	0-1	L	9.0	3	1	1	5	4	144
Burkett, SF	SD	07/07/1991	3-0	W	9.0	5	0	0	4	9	143
Candiotti, Tor	Oak	05/17/1991	11-6	W	8.0	11	4	4	1	1	141
Stewart D, Oak	@Mil	06/15/1991	4-6	L	7.0	6	6	6	4	5	141
Clemens, Bos	NYA	06/25/1991	4-6	L	9.0	10	6	3	2	8	141
Finley C, Cal	Tex	06/29/1991	4-7	L	8.0	11	4	4	3	8	141
McDowell J, Ch	Tor	07/24/1991	1-2	L	9.0	10	2	2	0	9	141
Myers R, Cin	LA	08/07/1991	0-2	L	8.0	7	2	2	6	6	141
Hurst, SD	@Hou	08/07/1991	7-4	W	8.2	4	4	3	8	141
Johnson R, Sea	Oak	08/14/1991	4-0	W	9.0	1	0	0	3	12	141
Cone, NYN	@Phi	10/06/1991	7-0	W	9.0	3	0	0	1	19	141
Clemens, Bos	Mil	10/06/1991	3-6	L	9.0	13	6	5	2	10	141
Martinez De, M	Atl	06/15/1991	2-0	W	9.0	8	0	0	2	5	140
Tanana, Det	Oak	09/05/1991	1-4	L	7.0	7	4	4	4	4	140

Fewest Pitches In a Complete Game By Starting Pitchers in 1991

Pitcher	Opp	Date	Sc	W/L	IP	H	R	ER	BB	SO	#Pit
Bosio, Mil	@NYA	09/17/1991	2-0	W	9.0	2	0	0	1	1	82
McDowell J, Ch	@Mil	07/14/1991	15-1	W	9.0	1	1	1	1	4	83
Gullickson, De	@Cle	09/18/1991	2-3	L	8.0	6	3	2	0	4	88
Hibbard, ChA	@Sea	07/04/1991	2-3	L	8.0	6	3	3	0	4	89
Harnisch, Hou	@Pit	05/03/1991	0-1	L	8.0	2	1	1	1	3	89
Smith Z, Pit	@StL	05/29/1991	6-0	W	9.0	1	0	0	1	5	89
Tewksbury, StL	Cin	07/26/1991	5-1	W	9.0	8	1	1	0	3	89
Maddux G, ChN	@Phi	10/02/1991	1-0	W	9.0	3	0	0	0	6	89
King E, Cle	@Tor	07/31/1991	1-3	L	8.0	6	3	2	0	4	90
Swindell, Cle	Det	06/01/1991	3-1	W	9.0	5	1	0	0	6	90
Tapani, Min	@Sea	08/11/1991	5-2	W	9.0	4	2	2	1	3	91
Glavine, Atl	NYN	08/28/1991	3-1	W	9.0	4	1	1	1	4	91
Smith Z, Pit	Hou	05/03/1991	1-0	W	9.0	4	0	0	0	4	92
Gooden, NYN	Hou	06/15/1991	6-0	W	9.0	3	0	0	0	5	92
Boddicker, KC	Cle	04/09/1991	1-2	L	9.0	5	2	1	0	3	92
Jones Jim, Hou	Cin	07/06/1991	3-0	W	9.0	3	0	0	0	6	92
Swindell, Cle	Tor	09/07/1991	1-4	L	9.0	9	4	4	0	3	93
Welch, Oak	Tor	05/20/1991	0-1	L	9.0	4	1	1	1	3	93
Gullickson, De	@Cal	08/28/1991	0-1	L	8.0	5	1	1	0	3	93
Drabek, Pit	@StL	05/27/1991	8-0	W	9.0	1	0	0	0	2	93
Smith B, StL	Mon	09/23/1991	10-1	W	9.0	3	1	1	1	6	94
Hibbard, ChA	@Min	06/29/1991	8-4	W	9.0	7	4	4	1	1	94
Swindell, Cle	KC	08/03/1991	3-1	W	9.0	7	1	0	0	4	94
Gullickson, De	@Cle	06/01/1991	1-3	L	8.0	9	3	3	3	1	95
Slusarski, Oak	@Bal	07/27/1991	9-1	W	9.0	2	1	1	2	2	95
Armstrong, Cin	SF	05/23/1991	6-2	W	9.0	4	2	2	1	5	95
Tewksbury, StL	@SF	09/01/1991	14-1	W	9.0	7	1	1	0	0	95

WHO'S WORST IN THE FIRST? (p. 218)

Both Leagues — Listed Alphabetically
(minimum 10 first innings pitched)

Pitcher	IP	ERA	HR	Pitcher	IP	ERA	HR	Pitcher	IP	ERA	HR
Abbott, Cal	34.0	3.18	2	Gordon, KC	14.0	2.57	1	Myers R, Cin	12.0	8.25	0
Aldred, Det	10.1	6.97	1	Greene, Phi	27.2	2.60	0	Nabholz, Mon	24.0	3.75	0
Anderson A, Min	22.0	6.14	4	Grimsley, Phi	11.1	7.94	0	Nagy, Cle	33.0	7.09	3
Appier, KC	31.0	2.90	0	Gross K, LA	10.0	5.40	0	Navarro, Mil	34.0	2.91	1
Aquino, KC	18.0	4.00	0	Gubicza, KC	25.2	6.31	1	Nichols Rod, Cle	16.0	4.50	1
Armstrong, Cin	24.0	7.13	3	Gullickson, Det	34.0	4.76	5	Ojeda, LA	31.0	3.48	0
August, Mil	23.0	6.65	3	Guthrie, Min	12.0	9.00	4	Olivares, StL	24.0	4.88	3
Avery, Atl	35.0	4.37	4	Guzman, Tex	25.0	3.24	2	Otto, Cle	14.0	5.14	1
Ballard, Bal	21.2	8.31	1	Guzman J, Tor	23.0	5.48	2	Perez P, NYA	13.0	3.46	1
Barnes B, Mon	27.0	2.67	2	Hammond, Cin	18.0	3.00	0	Peterson, SD	11.0	9.00	3
Belcher, LA	32.2	2.76	1	Haney, Mon	16.0	5.63	3	Plesac, Mil	10.0	3.60	1
Benes, SD	33.0	3.55	2	Hanson, Sea	27.0	3.33	5	Portugal, Hou	26.2	6.07	2
Bielecki, Atl	25.0	5.76	5	Harnisch, Hou	33.0	3.00	1	Rasmussen D, SD	23.2	7.23	3
Black, SF	34.0	4.50	3	Harris GA, Bos	21.0	3.86	4	Rijo, Cin	30.0	4.50	1
Boddicker, KC	28.0	3.54	1	Harris GW, SD	19.0	3.79	3	Robinson D, SF	16.0	3.38	0
Bohanon, Tex	11.0	5.73	1	Hawkins, Oak	17.0	6.35	3	Robinson JM, Bal	17.2	12.23	3
Bolton, Bos	19.0	5.68	1	Hershiser, LA	21.0	5.14	1	Ruffin, Phi	15.0	6.60	2
Bones, SD	11.0	4.91	0	Hesketh, Bos	17.0	2.12	1	Ryan, Tex	27.0	3.67	2
Bosio, Mil	32.0	2.25	1	Hibbard, ChA	29.0	4.97	4	Saberhagen, KC	28.0	1.61	0
Boskie, ChN	20.1	7.08	2	Hill K, StL	30.0	2.70	2	Sanderson, NYA	34.0	3.71	2
Boucher, Cle	12.0	6.75	3	Holman B, Sea	30.0	3.60	4	Scanlan, ChN	13.2	5.27	1
Bowen R, Hou	13.0	9.00	1	Hough, ChA	29.0	3.41	4	Scudder, Cin	13.2	7.24	0
Boyd, Tex	31.0	2.32	0	Hurst, SD	31.0	2.61	1	Slusarski, Oak	19.0	3.79	5
Brown K, Mil	10.0	4.50	1	Jackson Dan, ChN	14.0	8.36	3	Smiley, Pit	32.0	1.97	1
Brown Kev, Tex	33.0	4.09	0	Johnson D, Bal	14.0	7.71	5	Smith B, StL	31.0	4.35	4
Browning, Cin	36.0	6.25	6	Johnson J, NYA	23.0	6.65	2	Smith Roy, Bal	14.0	3.86	1
Burkett, SF	34.0	4.76	2	Johnson R, Sea	33.0	3.27	5	Smith Z, Pit	35.0	4.11	3
Candiotti, Tor	33.2	4.01	1	Jones Jim, Hou	22.1	4.43	2	Smoltz, Atl	36.0	4.00	2
Castillo F, ChN	17.0	5.29	1	Key, Tor	33.0	3.82	3	Stewart D, Oak	35.0	6.94	3
Charlton, Cin	11.0	7.36	0	Kile, Hou	22.0	2.86	1	Stottlemyre, Tor	34.0	5.03	7
Clemens, Bos	35.0	4.11	2	King E, Cle	24.0	4.50	1	Sutcliffe, ChN	18.0	7.00	1
Combs, Phi	11.1	12.71	3	Krueger, Sea	25.0	5.04	2	Swindell, Cle	33.0	4.36	4
Cone, NYN	34.0	4.24	5	Langston, Cal	34.0	2.38	3	Tanana, Det	32.2	4.68	6
Cormier, StL	10.0	0.90	0	Leary, NYA	18.0	7.50	3	Tapani, Min	34.0	2.38	1
Cox, Phi	18.0	3.50	2	Leibrandt, Atl	36.0	2.50	4	Taylor W, NYA	21.2	4.57	2
Darling, Oak	32.0	2.81	0	Leiter M, Det	15.1	0.59	0	Terrell, Det	33.0	3.27	1
Darwin, Bos	12.0	3.75	1	Lewis S, Cal	11.0	0.18	1	Tewksbury, StL	30.0	6.00	2
DeJesus J, Phi	29.0	2.79	1	Maddux G, ChN	37.0	2.68	1	Tomlin R, Pit	27.0	3.33	2
DeLeon J, StL	27.2	3.90	3	Martinez De, Mon	31.0	3.48	2	Viola, NYN	35.0	1.03	0
Delucia, Sea	31.0	8.13	7	Martinez R, LA	33.0	3.27	5	Walk, Pit	20.0	6.30	3
Deshaies, Hou	27.0	10.67	6	McCaskill, Cal	30.0	1.80	1	Wegman, Mil	27.2	3.25	2
Downs, SF	10.2	9.28	2	McClellan, SF	12.0	3.75	2	Welch, Oak	35.0	4.11	2
Drabek, Pit	35.0	4.63	1	McDonald, Bal	21.0	5.57	2	Wells, Tor	28.0	2.89	5
Eiland, NYA	13.0	2.08	0	McDowell J, ChA	35.0	3.86	3	West, Min	12.0	3.00	2
Erickson S, Min	31.2	3.13	1	Mesa, Bal	23.0	7.83	1	Whitehurst, NYN	20.0	4.95	2
Fernandez A, ChA	32.0	3.38	2	Milacki, Bal	26.1	5.47	3	Whitson, SD	12.0	6.75	2
Finley C, Cal	33.2	6.15	3	Moore M, Oak	33.0	3.82	2	Wilson Tr, SF	29.0	7.45	3
Garcia R, ChA	14.1	6.91	4	Morgan M, LA	33.0	1.91	0	Witt B, Tex	16.0	3.94	0
Gardiner, Bos	22.0	1.64	1	Morris Jk, Min	35.0	5.91	4	Young Mt, Bos	16.0	2.81	0
Gardner M, Mon	27.0	4.33	4	Morton, Bos	14.2	5.52	2	MLB Avg		4.62	
Glavine, Atl	34.0	4.76	3	Mulholland, Phi	34.0	4.76	2				
Gooden, NYN	27.0	3.67	1	Mussina, Bal	12.0	1.50	1				

DO GOOD-THROWING CATCHERS INTIMIDATE BASERUNNERS? (p. 221)

Opp = opportunities to steal second (runner on first with second base open); **Att** = stolen base attempts; **Att%** = stolen base attempts divided by opportunities; **CS%** = overall percentage of runners caught stealing from 1989 through 1991.

Both Leagues — 1991 Catchers — Listed Alphabetically
(Minimum 100 Opportunities from 1989 through 1991)

Catcher, Team	Opp	Att	Att%	CS%	Catcher, Team	Opp	Att	Att%	CS%
Allanson, Det	990	117	11.8	32.4	Nokes, NYA	1496	219	14.6	32.3
Alomar S, Cle	1184	133	11.2	34.6	O'Brien C, NYN	1303	171	13.1	36.8
Berryhill, Atl	898	108	12.0	33.6	Oliver, Cin	1501	217	14.5	34.0
Biggio, Hou	2477	434	17.5	22.8	Olson Greg, Atl	1321	189	14.3	26.0
Bilardello, SD	291	50	17.2	37.3	Ortiz, Min	1100	140	12.7	31.7
Borders, Tor	1477	197	13.3	38.9	Orton, Cal	458	55	12.0	38.7
Bradley S, Sea	1119	148	13.2	21.8	Pagnozzi, StL	1407	233	16.6	42.0
Cabrera, Atl	111	12	10.8	26.7	Parent, Tex	604	75	12.4	29.4
Carter G, LA	1072	210	19.6	28.8	Parrish Ln, Cal	2424	261	10.8	39.7
Cerone, NYN	1278	185	14.5	37.0	Pena T, Bos	2590	344	13.3	32.7
Daulton, Phi	2201	291	13.2	29.2	Petralli, Tex	1250	174	13.9	33.9
Decker S, SF	552	86	15.6	36.5	Prince, Pit	197	45	22.8	29.4
Dempsey, Mil	869	126	14.5	37.8	Quirk, Oak	723	98	13.6	42.2
Fisk, ChA	1987	249	12.5	36.4	Reed Jf, Cin	1534	250	16.3	30.0
Fitzgerald, Mon	1414	264	18.7	23.5	Reyes, Mon	459	76	16.6	52.4
Fletcher D, Phi	299	47	15.7	23.6	Rodriguez I, Tex	570	62	10.9	48.6
Gedman, StL	976	170	17.4	25.2	Russell Jn, Tex	359	56	15.6	28.4
Geren, NYA	1273	152	11.9	39.8	Salas, Det	367	50	13.6	30.5
Girardi, ChN	1366	180	13.2	36.3	Santiago, SD	2394	273	11.4	37.6
Harper B, Min	2138	298	13.9	30.5	Santovenia, Mon	1008	170	16.9	29.2
Hassey, Mon	989	139	14.1	29.3	Sasser, NYN	986	194	19.7	29.4
Heath, Atl	1798	260	14.5	31.3	Scioscia, LA	2267	323	14.2	31.2
Hoiles, Bal	613	73	11.9	36.1	Sinatro, Sea	220	34	15.5	37.8
Hundley, NYN	248	41	16.5	22.7	Skinner J, Cle	1310	151	11.5	33.5
Karkovice, ChA	1163	113	9.7	47.3	Slaught, Pit	1464	203	13.9	36.1
Kennedy, SF	1586	241	15.2	36.1	Spehr, KC	179	22	12.3	51.9
Kreuter, Tex	468	74	15.8	19.5	Stanley M, Tex	692	88	12.7	20.8
Lake, Phi	797	104	13.0	44.3	Steinbach, Oak	1862	219	11.8	34.0
Lampkin, SD	196	30	15.3	36.1	Surhoff BJ, Mil	2480	291	11.7	26.9
LaValliere, Pit	1579	274	17.4	28.5	Taubensee, Cle	155	20	12.9	13.6
Lyons Bar, Cal	581	104	17.9	22.9	Tettleton, Det	1961	221	11.3	32.2
Macfarlane, KC	1454	138	9.5	28.9	Tingley, Cal	282	36	12.8	48.9
Manwaring, SF	779	98	12.6	35.2	Valle, Sea	1973	207	10.5	36.9
Marzano, Bos	408	53	13.0	37.1	Villanueva, ChN	425	56	13.2	30.2
Mayne, KC	512	68	13.3	29.3	Webster L, Min	129	16	12.4	11.1
Melvin, Bal	1456	180	12.4	29.0	Whitt, Bal	1178	171	14.5	31.4
Merullo, ChA	286	42	14.7	24.4	Wilkins R, ChN	462	61	13.2	39.5
Myers G, Tor	1075	145	13.5	31.7	**MLB Avg:**	88583	12149	13.7	32.3

WHAT DO YOU SACRIFICE FOR A GOOD-THROWING CATCHER? (p. 224)

1991 Both Leagues — Listed Alphabetically
(minimum 250 innings caught)

Catcher, Team	SB	CS	CS%	PkO	SB/9	Pit CS	%
Allanson, Det	20	16	44.4	1	0.45	4	37.5
Alomar S, Cle	21	12	36.4	0	0.48	2	32.3
Berryhill, Atl	33	10	23.3	0	0.85	0	23.3
Biggio, Hou	126	46	26.7	0	0.96	6	24.1
Borders, Tor	50	28	35.9	0	0.64	4	32.4
Bradley S, Sea	36	7	16.3	0	0.80	1	14.3
Carter G, LA	59	28	32.2	0	1.07	3	29.8
Cerone, NYN	39	32	45.1	1	0.61	8	38.1
Daulton, Phi	84	18	17.6	0	1.05	1	16.8
Decker S, SF	49	28	36.4	0	0.76	5	31.9
Dempsey, Mil	29	12	29.3	1	0.64	0	29.3
Fisk, ChA	54	37	40.7	0	0.61	5	37.2
Fitzgerald, Mon	61	21	25.6	0	1.30	9	16.4
Fletcher D, Phi	33	13	28.3	0	0.89	1	26.7
Gedman, StL	30	10	25.0	0	1.08	0	25.0
Geren, NYA	31	14	31.1	0	0.74	2	27.9
Harper B, Min	98	28	22.2	0	0.89	6	18.3
Hassey, Mon	33	9	21.4	0	1.08	0	21.4
Heath, Atl	44	18	29.0	1	1.22	5	22.8
Hoiles, Bal	49	26	34.7	0	0.61	1	33.8
Karkovice, ChA	25	19	43.2	1	0.49	4	37.5
Kennedy, SF	44	35	44.3	0	1.01	9	37.1
Lake, Phi	34	17	33.3	1	0.76	2	30.6
LaValliere, Pit	90	39	30.2	0	0.95	11	23.7
Macfarlane, KC	21	17	44.7	1	0.33	2	41.7
Manwaring, SF	35	20	36.4	0	0.67	4	31.4
Marzano, Bos	16	13	44.8	0	0.51	3	38.5
Mayne, KC	53	23	30.3	0	0.79	2	28.4
Melvin, Bal	48	19	28.4	1	0.74	0	28.4
Myers G, Tor	68	25	26.9	0	0.81	10	18.1
Nokes, NYA	99	36	26.7	2	0.89	6	23.3
O'Brien C, NYN	55	26	32.1	3	1.01	1	31.3
Oliver, Cin	70	28	28.6	1	0.93	6	23.9
Olson Greg, Atl	95	37	28.0	0	0.85	15	18.8
Ortiz, Min	15	13	46.4	1	0.36	2	42.3
Pagnozzi, StL	86	70	44.9	0	0.67	2	44.2
Parrish Ln, Cal	53	39	42.4	0	0.52	8	36.9
Pena T, Bos	81	40	33.1	2	0.63	7	28.9
Petralli, Tex	36	17	32.1	1	0.80	3	28.0
Quirk, Oak	38	24	38.7	0	0.78	2	36.7
Reed Jf, Cin	57	28	32.9	0	0.74	9	25.0
Reyes, Mon	38	43	53.1	5	0.60	4	50.6
Rodriguez I, Tex	36	34	48.6	2	0.47	0	48.6
Santiago, SD	93	57	38.0	1	0.64	13	32.1
Scioscia, LA	82	30	26.8	0	0.81	6	22.6
Skinner J, Cle	54	28	34.1	0	0.62	4	30.8
Slaught, Pit	42	27	39.1	0	0.74	4	35.4
Stanley M, Tex	34	7	17.1	0	0.86	2	12.8
Steinbach, Oak	76	35	31.5	1	0.72	3	29.6
Surhoff BJ, Mil	86	35	28.9	0	0.73	5	25.9
Tettleton, Det	64	40	38.5	0	0.57	15	28.1
Tingley, Cal	20	22	52.4	0	0.56	3	48.7
Valle, Sea	46	31	40.3	2	0.45	6	35.2
Villanueva, ChN	42	16	27.6	0	0.94	3	23.6
Wilkins R, ChN	46	30	39.5	1	0.77	5	35.2
MLB	3120	1567	33.4	32	0.74	269	29.4

CAN A CATCHER HELP A PITCHER'S ERA? (p. 226)

1991 Both Leagues — Listed Alphabetically
(minimum 250 innings caught)

Catcher	Innings	Own ERA	Others ERA	Diff
Allanson, Det	396.2	4.52	4.54	- 0.02
Alomar S, Cle	395.1	3.92	4.36	- 0.44
Berryhill, Atl	349.2	3.58	4.09	- 0.51
Biggio, Hou	1175.1	3.93	4.31	- 0.38
Borders, Tor	700.2	3.42	3.58	- 0.16
Bradley S, Sea	404.2	4.05	3.69	+ 0.36
Carter G, LA	497.1	2.80	3.20	- 0.40
Cerone, NYN	573.0	3.38	3.69	- 0.31
Daulton, Phi	717.0	4.04	3.69	+ 0.35
Decker S, SF	578.1	3.77	4.21	- 0.44
Dempsey, Mil	408.2	4.10	4.21	- 0.11
Fisk, ChA	794.1	3.95	3.62	+ 0.33
Fitzgerald, Mon	421.2	3.84	3.56	+ 0.28
Fletcher D, Phi	334.0	2.96	4.13	- 1.17
Gedman, StL	251.0	3.33	3.76	- 0.43
Geren, NYA	375.2	4.19	4.52	- 0.33
Harper B, Min	990.0	3.75	3.59	+ 0.16
Hassey, Mon	274.1	2.69	3.87	- 1.18
Heath, Atl	324.1	3.66	3.45	+ 0.21
Hoiles, Bal	728.2	4.19	4.99	- 0.80
Karkovice, ChA	455.1	3.66	3.86	- 0.20
Kennedy, SF	390.1	4.50	3.86	+ 0.64
Lake, Phi	403.0	4.22	3.73	+ 0.49
LaValliere, Pit	852.2	3.55	3.29	+ 0.26
Macfarlane, KC	578.2	4.06	3.83	+ 0.23
Manwaring, SF	471.1	3.99	4.05	- 0.06
Marzano, Bos	283.0	4.17	3.98	+ 0.19
Mayne, KC	607.0	3.78	4.02	- 0.24
Melvin, Bal	580.2	4.87	4.40	+ 0.47
Myers G, Tor	752.0	3.57	3.43	+ 0.14
Nokes, NYA	1001.2	4.50	4.27	+ 0.23
O'Brien C, NYN	488.0	3.54	3.57	- 0.03
Oliver, Cin	676.1	3.94	3.74	+ 0.20
Olson Greg, Atl	1010.1	3.35	3.83	- 0.48
Ortiz, Min	370.2	3.64	3.71	- 0.07
Pagnozzi, StL	1156.1	3.75	3.42	+ 0.33
Parrish Ln, Cal	912.2	3.50	4.02	- 0.52
Pena T, Bos	1156.2	3.98	4.17	- 0.19
Petralli, Tex	403.0	4.51	4.46	+ 0.05
Quirk, Oak	436.2	4.27	4.71	- 0.44
Reed Jf, Cin	690.2	3.60	4.05	- 0.45
Reyes, Mon	568.1	3.86	3.50	+ 0.36
Rodriguez I, Tex	684.0	4.39	4.54	- 0.15
Santiago, SD	1305.1	3.58	3.60	- 0.02
Scioscia, LA	907.1	3.19	2.86	+ 0.33
Skinner J, Cle	790.0	4.22	4.27	- 0.05
Slaught, Pit	509.0	3.04	3.66	- 0.62
Stanley M, Tex	356.0	4.65	4.42	+ 0.23
Steinbach, Oak	949.1	4.69	4.35	+ 0.34
Surhoff BJ, Mil	1055.0	4.21	4.10	+ 0.11
Tettleton, Det	1013.2	4.55	4.49	+ 0.06
Tingley, Cal	323.1	4.20	3.54	+ 0.66
Valle, Sea	926.1	3.65	4.03	- 0.38
Villanueva, ChN	400.0	3.44	4.28	- 0.84
Wilkins R, ChN	539.1	4.81	3.60	+ 1.21

WHO LED THE LEAGUE IN FUMBLES? (p. 230)

Both Leagues — Listed by Most games per Error (G/E) — 1991
(minimum 600 defensive innings played)

Name	Inn	E	G/E	Name	Inn	E	G/E
				McGwire, Oak	1262.2	4	35.1
Catchers				O'Brien P, Sea	1063.0	3	39.4
Oliver, Cin	676.1	11	6.8	Kruk, Phi	809.2	2	45.0
Myers G, Tor	752.0	11	7.6	**Second Basemen**			
Rodriguez I, Tex	684.0	10	7.6				
Steinbach, Oak	949.1	13	8.1	Treadway, Atl	629.1	15	4.7
Daulton, Phi	717.0	8	10.0	DeShields, Mon	1297.1	27	5.3
Santiago, SD	1305.1	14	10.4	Randolph, Mil	997.1	20	5.5
Mayne, KC	607.0	6	11.2	Baerga, Cle	633.2	11	6.4
Biggio, Hou	1175.1	10	13.1	Shumpert, KC	1092.2	16	7.6
Harper B, Min	990.0	8	13.7	Knoblauch, Min	1240.1	18	7.7
Scioscia, LA	907.1	7	14.4	Lemke, Atl	605.1	8	8.4
Reed Jf, Cin	690.2	5	15.3	Samuel, LA	1317.2	17	8.6
Valle, Sea	926.1	6	17.2	Reynolds H, Sea	1402.1	18	8.7
Skinner J, Cle	790.0	5	17.6	Sojo, Cal	899.1	11	9.1
Pagnozzi, StL	1156.1	7	18.4	Franco Ju, Tex	1283.1	14	10.2
Nokes, NYA	1001.2	6	18.5	Reed Jd, Bos	1320.2	14	10.5
Tettleton, Det	1013.2	6	18.8	Alomar R, Tor	1420.2	15	10.5
Borders, Tor	700.2	4	19.5	Candaele, Hou	868.0	9	10.7
Fisk, ChA	794.1	4	22.1	Doran, Cin	704.2	7	11.2
Pena T, Bos	1156.2	5	25.7	Jefferies, NYN	611.2	6	11.3
Olson Greg, Atl	1010.1	4	28.1	Thompson Ro, SF	1204.0	11	12.2
Surhoff BJ, Mil	1055.0	4	29.3	Ripken B, Bal	827.0	7	13.1
Parrish Ln, Cal	912.2	2	50.7	Morandini, Phi	766.2	6	14.2
Hoiles, Bal	728.2	1	81.0	Oquendo, StL	904.2	7	14.4
LaValliere, Pit	852.2	1	94.7	Lind, Pit	1242.1	9	15.3
				Gallego, Oak	1073.1	7	17.0
First Basemen				Sax S, NYA	1305.1	7	20.7
Guerrero, StL	922.1	16	6.4	Fletcher S, ChA	647.1	3	24.0
Jordan, Phi	600.1	9	7.4	Whitaker, Det	1063.2	4	29.5
Merced, Pit	870.1	12	8.1	Sandberg, ChN	1374.2	4	38.2
Milligan, Bal	902.0	10	10.0				
Galarraga, Mon	865.1	9	10.7	**Third Basemen**			
McGriff F, SD	1347.0	14	10.7	Kelly P, NYA	661.1	16	4.6
Stubbs, Mil	789.0	8	11.0	Baerga, Cle	698.2	15	5.2
Bagwell, Hou	1331.2	12	12.3	Johnson H, NYN	878.0	18	5.4
Palmeiro, Tex	1366.0	12	12.6	Zeile, StL	1325.1	25	5.9
Morris H, Cin	1067.1	9	13.2	Pendleton, Atl	1283.2	24	5.9
Fielder, Det	1037.0	8	14.4	Harris L, LA	781.2	14	6.2
Quintana, Bos	1042.2	8	14.5	Caminiti, Hou	1308.2	23	6.3
Hrbek, Min	1082.1	8	15.0	Fryman T, Det	702.0	11	7.1
Joyner, Cal	1238.0	8	17.2	Ventura, ChA	1275.2	18	7.9
Benzinger, KC	792.1	5	17.6	Hayes C, Phi	1043.2	14	8.3
Grace, ChN	1404.1	8	19.5	Salazar L, ChN	673.2	9	8.3
Murray E, LA	1301.1	7	20.7	Gruber, Tor	977.1	13	8.4
Magadan, NYN	1029.0	5	22.9	Gaetti, Cal	1339.2	17	8.8
Bream, Atl	640.2	3	23.7	Williams MD, SF	1317.2	16	9.2
Mattingly, NYA	1090.2	5	24.2	Martinez E, Sea	1239.2	15	9.2
Olerud, Tor	1126.1	5	25.0	Pagliarulo, Min	913.1	11	9.2
Clark W, SF	1234.1	4	34.3	Wallach, Mon	1321.1	14	10.5

Name	Inn	E	G/E
Boggs W, Bos	1196.2	12	11.1
Sabo, Cin	1303.1	12	12.1
Gomez L, Bal	915.1	7	14.5
Gantner, Mil	764.0	5	17.0
Buechele, Pit	1195.0	7	19.0
Pecota, KC	762.0	4	21.2

Shortstops

Name	Inn	E	G/E
Griffin Alf, LA	933.2	22	4.7
Rivera L, Bos	1103.2	24	5.1
Fryman T, Det	604.2	12	5.6
Stillwell, KC	911.0	18	5.6
Huson, Tex	765.1	15	5.7
Belliard, Atl	990.0	18	6.1
Bell Jay, Pit	1347.1	24	6.2
Uribe, SF	620.1	11	6.3
Dunston, ChN	1192.0	21	6.3
Espinoza, NYA	1197.0	21	6.3
Lee M, Tor	1155.1	19	6.8
Thon, Phi	1277.0	21	6.8
Guillen, ChA	1286.0	21	6.8
Elster, NYN	865.0	14	6.9
Fernandez T, SD	1262.2	20	7.0
Spiers, Mil	1104.0	17	7.2
Bordick, Oak	683.2	10	7.6
Larkin B, Cin	1032.0	15	7.6
Schofield, Cal	1140.0	15	8.4
Trammell, Det	771.0	9	9.5
Vizquel, Sea	1134.1	13	9.7
Fermin, Cle	1092.1	12	10.1
Gagne, Min	1067.2	9	13.2
Ripken C, Bal	1427.2	11	14.4
Owen S, Mon	1066.0	8	14.8
Smith O, StL	1253.1	8	17.4

Left Fielders

Name	Inn	E	G/E
Belle, Cle	726.2	9	9.0
Bell Geo, ChN	1191.1	10	13.2
Henderson R, Oak	982.1	8	13.6
Mitchell K, SF	824.0	6	15.3
Smith Lo, Atl	725.0	5	16.1
Calderon, Mon	1038.0	7	16.5
Gibson K, KC	759.1	4	21.1
Daniels, LA	1041.1	5	23.1
Gonzalez L, Hou	1084.2	5	24.1
Polonia, Cal	1249.2	5	27.8
Chamberlain, Phi	841.2	3	31.2
Gladden, Min	990.0	3	36.7
Raines, ChA	1165.2	3	43.2
Greenwell, Bos	1219.2	3	45.2
Bonds, Pit	1295.2	3	48.0
McReynolds, NYN	959.1	2	53.3
Vaughn G, Mil	1164.1	2	64.7
Gilkey, StL	604.1	1	67.1
Clark Je, SD	693.0	1	77.0

Name	Inn	E	G/E
Orsulak, Bal	651.1	0	0 in 72.4

Center Fielders

Name	Inn	E	G/E
Cole, Cle	800.0	7	12.7
Pettis, Tex	782.0	6	14.5
Williams B, NYA	754.1	5	16.8
Coleman, NYN	603.0	3	22.3
Lankford, StL	1217.1	6	22.5
Cuyler, Det	1229.1	6	22.8
Davis E, Cin	633.0	3	23.4
Kelly, NYA	641.0	3	23.7
Gant, Atl	1293.1	6	24.0
Gonzalez Juan, Tex	651.0	3	24.1
Grissom, Mon	1140.2	5	25.3
McGee, SF	700.1	3	25.9
Puckett, Min	1216.2	5	27.0
Finley S, Hou	948.0	3	35.1
Griffey Jr, Sea	1271.2	4	35.3
Devereaux, Bal	1261.0	3	46.7
McRae B, KC	1301.1	3	48.2
Yount, Mil	1021.0	2	56.7
Burks, Bos	1074.0	2	59.7
Jackson Dar, SD	654.2	1	72.7
Johnson L, ChA	1332.1	2	74.0
Van Slyke, Pit	1137.1	1	126.4
Henderson D, Oak	1179.1	1	131.0
White D, Tor	1384.0	1	153.8
Butler, LA	1409.0	0	0 in 156.6

Right Fielders

Name	Inn	E	G/E
Sosa, ChA	699.2	6	13.0
Canseco, Oak	1084.1	9	13.4
Whiten, Cle	881.2	7	14.0
Justice, Atl	957.1	7	15.2
Tartabull, KC	1035.2	7	16.4
Brooks, NYN	791.1	5	17.6
Bichette, Mil	981.0	6	18.2
Deer, Det	1146.0	7	18.2
Sierra, Tex	1405.0	7	22.3
Bass K, SF	606.0	3	22.4
Buhner, Sea	1011.1	5	22.5
Strawberry, LA	1185.2	5	26.3
Murphy Dl, Phi	1235.2	5	27.5
Carter J, Tor	871.0	3	32.3
Brunansky, Bos	1099.2	3	40.7
Gwynn T, SD	1175.2	3	43.5
Walker L, Mon	790.0	2	43.9
Dawson, ChN	1192.1	3	44.2
Bonilla B, Pit	810.2	2	45.0
Jose, StL	1308.1	3	48.5
Winfield, Cal	984.0	2	54.7
O'Neill, Cin	1258.2	2	69.9
Barfield Je, NYA	677.2	0	0 in 75.3

WHO'S BEST IN THE INFIELD ZONE? (p. 232)

Zone Ratings — Infielders
(minimum 600 defensive innings in 1991)

FIRST BASE

Player, Team	Innings	1991 In Zone	1991 Outs	1991 Zone Rating	1989-1991 In Zone	1989-1991 Outs	1989-1991 Zone Rating
Mattingly, NYA	1090.2	201	185	.920	627	562	.896
Olerud, Tor	1126.1	216	197	.912	245	220	.898
Quintana, Bos	1042.2	204	186	.912	515	448	.870
McGwire, Oak	1262.2	273	248	.908	743	662	.891
Stubbs, Mil	789.0	176	158	.898	303	272	.898
Hrbek, Min	1082.1	208	185	.889	494	444	.899
Joyner, Cal	1238.0	216	192	.889	590	512	.868
Grace, ChN	1404.1	376	333	.886	1017	890	.875
Murray E, LA	1301.1	274	240	.876	857	735	.858
Palmeiro, Tex	1366.0	259	224	.865	768	652	.849
Kruk, Phi	809.2	155	134	.865	244	214	.877
Fielder, Det	1037.0	187	161	.861	427	357	.836
O'Brien P, Sea	1063.0	207	178	.860	589	510	.866
Clark W, SF	1234.1	253	217	.858	841	717	.853
Benzinger, KC	792.1	169	144	.852	556	467	.840
Magadan, NYN	1029.0	210	177	.843	488	433	.887
Milligan, Bal	902.0	195	164	.841	566	485	.857
Morris H, Cin	1067.1	202	169	.837	307	255	.831
Galarraga, Mon	865.1	173	143	.827	695	590	.849
McGriff F, SD	1347.0	246	203	.825	739	626	.847
Bagwell, Hou	1331.2	283	233	.823	283	233	.823
Bream, Atl	640.2	110	90	.818	315	274	.870
Jordan, Phi	600.1	145	118	.814	528	432	.818
Guerrero, StL	922.1	218	175	.803	734	548	.747
Merced, Pit	870.1	149	116	.779	149	116	.779
				.851			.843

SECOND BASE

Player, Team	Innings	1991 In Zone	1991 Outs	1991 Zone Rating	1989-1991 In Zone	1989-1991 Outs	1989-1991 Zone Rating
Sandberg, ChN	1374.2	565	534	.945	1601	1473	.920
Gallego, Oak	1073.1	416	392	.942	819	766	.935
Oquendo, StL	904.2	395	368	.932	1359	1273	.937
Reed Jd, Bos	1320.2	464	432	.931	1129	1026	.909
Sojo, Cal	899.1	333	309	.928	348	323	.928
Whitaker, Det	1063.2	397	367	.924	1225	1134	.926
Reynolds H, Sea	1402.1	505	458	.907	1626	1462	.899
Lemke, Atl	605.1	228	205	.899	403	371	.921
Randolph, Mil	997.1	406	365	.899	1200	1090	.908
Ripken B, Bal	827.0	305	274	.898	1037	956	.922
Knoblauch, Min	1240.1	502	450	.896	502	450	.896
Treadway, Atl	629.1	235	207	.881	1018	898	.882
Thompson Ro, SF	1204.0	453	399	.881	1435	1299	.905
Sax S, NYA	1305.1	510	449	.880	1526	1381	.905
Samuel, LA	1317.2	516	454	.880	844	731	.866
Jefferies, NYN	611.2	219	192	.877	866	742	.857
Lind, Pit	1242.1	506	443	.875	1500	1316	.877
Morandini, Phi	766.2	289	253	.875	361	318	.881
Alomar R, Tor	1420.2	527	461	.875	1485	1314	.885
Baerga, Cle	633.2	261	228	.874	289	247	.855
Fletcher S, ChA	647.1	201	174	.866	839	737	.878
Candaele, Hou	868.0	342	291	.851	457	395	.864
Doran, Cin	704.2	238	202	.849	1024	868	.848
DeShields, Mon	1297.1	474	400	.844	910	783	.860
Shumpert, KC	1092.2	432	364	.843	517	436	.843
Franco Ju, Tex	1283.1	462	389	.842	1370	1228	.896
				.891			.893

THIRD BASE

		1991			1989-1991		
Player, Team	Innings	In Zone	Outs	Zone Rating	In Zone	Outs	Zone Rating
Boggs W, Bos	1196.2	324	306	.944	974	850	.873
Pagliarulo, Min	913.1	302	280	.927	832	707	.850
Ventura, ChA	1275.2	350	313	.894	738	656	.889
Gaetti, Cal	1339.2	435	388	.892	1151	1037	.901
Caminiti, Hou	1308.2	358	319	.891	1081	954	.883
Pendleton, Atl	1283.2	423	376	.889	1223	1066	.872
Buechele, Pit	1195.0	376	333	.886	897	785	.875
Gantner, Mil	764.0	198	174	.879	224	192	.857
Pecota, KC	762.0	208	182	.875	232	207	.892
Wallach, Mon	1321.1	383	334	.872	1119	963	.861
Sabo, Cin	1303.1	314	273	.869	853	711	.834
Gruber, Tor	977.1	298	257	.862	1016	857	.844
Williams MD, SF	1317.2	356	305	.857	853	758	.889
Martinez E, Sea	1239.2	392	334	.852	812	700	.862
Baerga, Cle	698.2	232	195	.841	369	309	.837
Hayes C, Phi	1043.2	325	272	.837	962	833	.866
Fryman T, Det	702.0	196	164	.837	321	271	.844
Harris L, LA	781.2	217	180	.829	447	364	.814
Zeile, StL	1325.1	390	315	.808	444	356	.802
Gomez L, Bal	915.1	250	199	.796	280	221	.789
Salazar L, ChN	673.2	191	151	.791	552	453	.821
Kelly P, NYA	661.1	218	168	.771	218	168	.771
Johnson H, NYN	878.0	240	177	.738	693	525	.758
				.851			.841

SHORTSTOP

		1991			1989-1991		
Player, Team	Innings	In Zone	Outs	Zone Rating	In Zone	Outs	Zone Rating
Ripken C, Bal	1427.2	575	567	.986	1666	1594	.957
Fryman T, Det	604.2	226	221	.978	287	278	.969
Trammell, Det	771.0	325	308	.948	1238	1158	.935
Belliard, Atl	990.0	418	388	.928	542	499	.921
Spiers, Mil	1104.0	420	387	.921	1135	1033	.910
Schofield, Cal	1140.0	453	416	.918	1117	1052	.942
Vizquel, Sea	1134.1	470	431	.917	1220	1101	.902
Smith O, StL	1253.1	441	404	.916	1447	1324	.915
Guillen, ChA	1286.0	509	465	.914	1641	1511	.921
Bordick, Oak	683.2	256	232	.906	260	235	.904
Fermin, Cle	1092.1	435	394	.906	1552	1389	.895
Espinoza, NYA	1197.0	490	441	.900	1528	1385	.906
Fernandez T, SD	1262.2	509	453	.890	1623	1477	.910
Rivera L, Bos	1103.2	464	408	.879	1142	982	.860
Lee M, Tor	1155.1	446	392	.879	545	488	.895
Gagne, Min	1067.2	434	381	.878	1364	1181	.866
Owen S, Mon	1066.0	445	388	.872	1329	1161	.874
Griffin Alf, LA	933.2	421	367	.872	1287	1110	.862
Uribe, SF	620.1	263	229	.871	1229	1052	.856
Thon, Phi	1277.0	478	416	.870	1442	1276	.885
Larkin B, Cin	1032.0	447	388	.868	1325	1166	.880
Huson, Tex	765.1	334	289	.865	694	598	.862
Dunston, ChN	1192.0	478	404	.845	1395	1215	.871
Stillwell, KC	911.0	335	281	.839	1183	996	.842
Elster, NYN	865.0	374	313	.837	1134	979	.863
Bell Jay, Pit	1347.1	636	527	.829	1471	1254	.852
				.881			.883

WHO'S BEST IN THE OUTFIELD ZONE (p. 236)

Zone Ratings — Outfielders
(minimum 600 defensive innings in 1991)

LEFT FIELD

		1991			1989-1991		
Player, Team	Innings	In Zone	Balls Handled	Zone Rating	In Zone	Balls Handled	Zone Rating
Gilkey, StL	604.1	171	154	.901	221	200	.905
Gonzalez L, Hou	1084.2	334	289	.865	334	289	.865
Gladden, Min	990.0	273	236	.864	915	746	.815
McReynolds, NYN	959.1	268	228	.851	953	758	.795
Calderon, Mon	1038.0	306	253	.827	696	553	.795
Clark Je, SD	693.0	172	142	.826	195	156	.800
Vaughn G, Mil	1164.1	371	306	.825	643	523	.813
Mitchell K, SF	824.0	219	180	.822	960	746	.777
Gibson K, KC	759.1	192	157	.818	360	299	.831
Bonds, Pit	1295.2	378	307	.812	1201	972	.809
Smith Lo, Atl	725.0	164	132	.805	827	659	.797
Polonia, Cal	1249.2	305	241	.790	747	579	.775
Daniels, LA	1041.1	278	218	.784	645	509	.789
Bell Geo, ChN	1191.1	312	244	.782	896	718	.801
Henderson R, Oak	982.1	314	244	.777	1008	845	.838
Raines, ChA	1165.2	345	268	.777	908	725	.798
Chamberlain, Phi	841.2	244	189	.775	266	210	.789
Orsulak, Bal	651.1	206	159	.772	333	259	.778
Belle, Cle	726.2	234	170	.726	266	190	.714
Greenwell, Bos	1219.2	360	256	.711	1022	758	.742
				.804			.800

CENTER FIELD

		1991			1989-1991		
Player, Team	Innings	In Zone	Balls Handled	Zone Rating	In Zone	Balls Handled	Zone Rating
Johnson L, ChA	1332.1	479	418	.873	906	774	.854
White D, Tor	1384.0	499	435	.872	1320	1147	.869
Devereaux, Bal	1261.0	455	394	.866	1009	866	.858
Jackson Dar, SD	654.2	245	212	.865	383	337	.880
Butler, LA	1409.0	437	371	.849	1407	1154	.820
Coleman, NYN	603.0	157	132	.841	157	132	.841
Davis E, Cin	633.0	215	179	.833	747	613	.821
Cuyler, Det	1229.1	496	410	.827	540	447	.828
McRae B, KC	1301.1	483	399	.826	625	517	.827
Pettis, Tex	782.0	294	242	.823	1026	831	.810
Grissom, Mon	1140.2	421	346	.822	568	460	.810
Gonzalez Juan, Tex	651.0	230	189	.822	328	272	.829
Kelly, NYA	641.0	202	165	.817	1118	895	.801
McGee, SF	700.1	228	186	.816	838	669	.798
Henderson D, Oak	1179.1	431	350	.812	1238	1028	.830
Finley S, Hou	948.0	323	262	.811	521	430	.825
Burks, Bos	1074.0	348	281	.807	1068	837	.784
Yount, Mil	1021.0	386	310	.803	1374	1084	.789
Williams B, NYA	754.1	284	227	.799	284	227	.799
Cole, Cle	800.0	301	240	.797	473	378	.799
Puckett, Min	1216.2	437	343	.785	1348	1086	.806
Gant, Atl	1293.1	423	330	.780	832	648	.779
Griffey Jr, Sea	1271.2	460	356	.774	1206	962	.798
Van Slyke, Pit	1137.1	337	260	.772	1159	906	.782
Lankford, StL	1217.1	460	354	.770	565	436	.772
				.820			.816

RIGHT FIELD		1991			1989-1991		
Player, Team	Innings	In Zone	Balls Handled	Zone Rating	In Zone	Balls Handled	Zone Rating
Carter J, Tor	871.0	207	184	.889	208	185	.889
Jose, StL	1308.1	283	250	.883	457	400	.875
Walker L, Mon	790.0	245	216	.882	563	474	.842
O'Neill, Cin	1258.2	352	297	.844	915	758	.828
Barfield Je, NYA	677.2	210	175	.833	930	759	.816
Sosa, ChA	699.2	223	185	.830	604	504	.834
Bass K, SF	606.0	147	121	.823	403	318	.789
Sierra, Tex	1405.0	362	297	.820	1051	876	.833
Murphy Dl, Phi	1235.2	333	273	.820	867	704	.812
Gwynn T, SD	1175.2	355	290	.817	893	742	.831
Whiten, Cle	881.2	285	232	.814	357	291	.815
Bichette, Mil	981.0	310	248	.800	475	387	.815
Dawson, ChN	1192.1	291	232	.797	851	677	.796
Brunansky, Bos	1099.2	332	264	.795	1014	822	.811
Strawberry, LA	1185.2	263	209	.795	893	722	.809
Buhner, Sea	1011.1	296	233	.787	502	386	.769
Bonilla B, Pit	810.2	206	162	.786	543	437	.805
Deer, Det	1146.0	377	296	.785	1014	802	.791
Brooks, NYN	791.1	207	162	.783	804	638	.794
Justice, Atl	957.1	259	201	.776	429	335	.781
Canseco, Oak	1084.1	316	240	.759	686	528	.770
Winfield, Cal	984.0	258	192	.744	468	352	.752
Tartabull, KC	1035.2	255	188	.737	496	374	.754
				.808			.809

WHO ARE THE PRIME PIVOT MEN? (p. 238)

1991 Both Leagues — Listed Alphabetically
All Second Basemen in 1991 with one DP opportunity

Player, Team	DP Opp	DP	Pct.	Player, Team	DP Opp	DP	Pct.
Alicea, StL	1	1	1.000	Lind, Pit	89	40	.449
Alomar R, Tor	75	44	.587	Liriano, KC	3	1	.333
Amaro, Cal	1	1	1.000	Litton, SF	8	5	.625
Anderson D, SF	2	1	.500	Lyons S, Bos	4	4	1.000
Backman, Phi	17	6	.353	Manrique, Oak	2	1	.500
Baerga, Cle	58	39	.672	McLemore, Hou	5	4	.800
Barberie, Mon	9	3	.333	Miller K, NYN	36	17	.472
Barrett M, SD	1	1	1.000	Morandini, Phi	54	26	.481
Bell Ju, Bal	39	28	.718	Mota, SD	5	3	.600
Benavides, Cin	2	1	.500	Mota A, Hou	5	3	.600
Bernazard, Det	3	3	1.000	Newman A, Min	13	7	.538
Biggio, Hou	1	1	1.000	Noboa, Mon	4	1	.250
Blankenship L, Oak	23	14	.609	Oquendo, StL	52	27	.519
Blauser, Atl	15	9	.600	Paredes, Det	5	4	.800
Bordick, Oak	3	2	.667	Pecota, KC	12	4	.333
Brosius, Oak	1	1	1.000	Pena G, StL	23	18	.783
Browne J, Cle	15	9	.600	Perezchica, Cle	2	1	.500
Brumley, Bos	6	6	1.000	Phillips, Det	36	20	.556
Buechele, Pit	4	1	.250	Quinones L, Cin	14	9	.643
Candaele, Hou	50	33	.660	Ramirez R, Hou	5	4	.800
Cora, ChA	31	17	.548	Randolph, Mil	80	59	.738
DeShields, Mon	71	39	.549	Ready, Phi	26	10	.385
Diaz Mar, Tex	8	5	.625	Reed Jd, Bos	101	67	.663
Disarcina, Cal	3	2	.667	Reynolds H, Sea	107	66	.617
Doran, Cin	42	29	.690	Riles, Oak	3	2	.667
Duncan, Cin	26	13	.500	Ripken B, Bal	68	44	.647
Escobar J, Cle	3	2	.667	Roberts Bip, SD	43	17	.395
Faries, SD	17	9	.529	Rohde, Hou	1	1	1.000
Fariss, Tex	2	1	.500	Rose, Cal	4	3	.750
Fletcher S, ChA	57	35	.614	Samuel, LA	94	41	.436
Flora, Cal	4	1	.250	Sandberg, ChN	63	31	.492
Foley T, Mon	1	1	1.000	Sax S, NYA	94	55	.585
Franco Ju, Tex	76	38	.500	Schaefer, Sea	4	4	1.000
Gallego, Oak	65	33	.508	Sharperson, LA	1	1	1.000
Gantner, Mil	35	20	.571	Shipley, SD	4	2	.500
Grebeck, ChA	12	10	.833	Shumpert, KC	74	48	.649
Harris L, LA	10	5	.500	Sojo, Cal	72	45	.625
Hemond, Oak	2	1	.500	Teufel, SD	30	10	.333
Herr, SF	27	16	.593	Thompson Ro, SF	85	49	.576
Hill D, Cal	28	19	.679	Treadway, Atl	37	16	.432
Howard D, KC	10	5	.500	Vizcaino, ChN	3	2	.667
Howell Jk, SD	5	1	.200	Walker C, ChN	3	1	.333
Hulett, Bal	10	5	.500	Whitaker, Det	74	49	.662
Jefferies, NYN	26	6	.231	Wilkerson, Pit	18	7	.389
Kelly P, NYA	13	10	.769	**MLB Avg**	**2539**	**1452**	**.572**
Knoblauch, Min	85	53	.624				
Lemke, Atl	49	24	.490				
Lewis M, Cle	29	19	.655				

WHICH OUTFIELDERS HAVE THE CANNONS? (p. 240)

Both Leagues — 1991 — Listed by Hold Percentage
(minimum 25 baserunner opportunities to advance)

Right Field				Center Field				Left Field			
Player, Team	Opp	XB	Pct	Player, Team	Opp	XB	Pct	Player, Team	Opp	XB	Pct
Whiten, Cle	78	25	32.1	Young G, Hou	49	13	26.5	Bonds, Pit	116	19	16.4
Barfield Je, NYA	75	25	33.3	Winningh'm, Cin	39	16	41.0	Thurman, KC	41	9	22.0
Rhodes, Hou	34	13	38.2	Abner, Cal	55	23	41.8	Carter J, Tor	44	10	22.7
Carter J, Tor	85	33	38.8	Van Slyke, Pit	146	65	44.5	Briley, Sea	62	15	24.2
Finley S, Hou	36	14	38.9	Pettis, Tex	102	46	45.1	Sanders, Atl	28	7	25.0
Briley, Sea	25	10	40.0	Puckett, Min	128	60	46.9	Mack, Min	31	8	25.8
Sosa, ChA	62	25	40.3	Hill G, Cle	25	12	48.0	Moseby, Det	58	15	25.9
O'Neill, Cin	118	48	40.7	McReynolds, NY	27	13	48.1	Shelby, Det	34	9	26.5
Martinez D, Mon	41	17	41.5	Finley S, Hou	135	65	48.1	Kruk, Phi	34	9	26.5
Deer, Det	168	71	42.3	Jackson D, SD	58	29	50.0	James C, Cle	29	8	27.6
Larkin G, Min	30	13	43.3	Grissom, Mon	127	64	50.4	Orsulak, Bal	94	26	27.7
Martinez C, Bal	42	19	45.2	Martinez Da, Mon	27	14	51.9	Anderson B, Bal	47	13	27.7
Dawson, ChN	118	54	45.8	Cole, Cle	100	52	52.0	Gilkey, StL	38	11	28.9
Varsho, Pit	28	13	46.4	Dascenzo, ChN	42	22	52.4	Maldonado, Tor	58	17	29.3
Evans Dw, Bal	69	33	47.8	Griffey Jr, Sea	154	81	52.6	Vaughn G, Mil	111	33	29.7
Buhner, Sea	89	43	48.3	Cuyler, Det	176	93	52.8	Hatcher B, Cin	69	21	30.4
Gwynn T, SD	123	61	49.6	Walton, ChN	68	36	52.9	Belle, Cle	81	26	32.1
Sierra, Tex	159	80	50.3	Huff, ChA	49	26	53.1	Gonzalez L, Hou	108	35	32.4
Canseco, Oak	123	62	50.4	Lankford, StL	135	72	53.3	Braggs, Cin	37	12	32.4
Walker L, Mon	63	32	50.8	Butler, LA	153	82	53.6	Clark Je, SD	55	18	32.7
Orsulak, Bal	49	25	51.0	White D, Tor	144	78	54.2	Thompson M, StL	61	20	32.8
Ward T, Tor	41	21	51.2	Walker C, ChN	44	24	54.5	Greenwell, Bos	140	46	32.9
Strawberry, LA	111	57	51.4	Felder, SF	33	18	54.5	Nixon O, Atl	32	11	34.4
Winfield, Cal	100	52	52.0	Howard T, SD	33	18	54.5	Webster M, LA	29	10	34.5
Eisenreich, KC	25	13	52.0	Burks, Bos	98	54	55.1	Carreon, NYN	26	9	34.6
Brunansky, Bos	103	54	52.4	Johnson L, ChA	125	69	55.2	Gonzalez J, Tex	48	17	35.4
Jose, StL	138	73	52.9	Williams B, NYA	104	58	55.8	Mitchell K, SF	93	33	35.5
Hall M, NYA	41	22	53.7	Dykstra, Phi	64	36	56.3	Hall M, NYA	53	19	35.8
Bichette, Mil	115	63	54.8	Gonzalez J, Tex	88	50	56.8	Raines, ChA	97	35	36.1
Brooks, NYN	93	51	54.8	Devereaux, Bal	151	86	57.0	Chamberlain, Phi	99	36	36.4
Murphy Dl, Phi	116	64	55.2	Venable, Cal	28	16	57.1	Daugherty, Tex	32	12	37.5
Bass K, SF	45	25	55.6	Anderson B, Bal	26	15	57.7	Incaviglia, Det	45	17	37.8
Tartabull, KC	115	64	55.7	Davis E, Cin	81	47	58.0	Polonia, Cal	95	36	37.9
Hamilton, Mil	41	23	56.1	Lyons S, Bos	36	21	58.3	Daniels, LA	87	33	37.9
McGee, SF	39	22	56.4	Kelly, NYA	75	44	58.7	Gladden, Min	79	30	38.0
Justice, Atl	78	44	56.4	Gant, Atl	126	74	58.7	McReynolds, NY	105	40	38.1
Bonilla B, Pit	57	33	57.9	Boston, NYN	56	33	58.9	Kelly, NYA	44	17	38.6
Johnson H, NY	27	16	59.3	McRae B, KC	172	102	59.3	Jones Tr, Sea	30	12	40.0
Mack, Min	43	27	62.8	Gallagher, Cal	32	19	59.4	Henders'n R, Oak	113	46	40.7
Nixon O, Atl	31	20	64.5	McGee, SF	80	48	60.0	Calderon, Mon	81	33	40.7
Newson, ChA	30	20	66.7	Hatcher B, Cin	54	33	61.1	Smith Lo, Atl	53	22	41.5
				Wilson W, Oak	39	24	61.5	Wilson M, Tor	36	15	41.7
			49.0	Felix, Cal	52	33	63.5	Reimer, Tex	64	27	42.2
				Coleman, NY	63	40	63.5	Segui, Bal	40	17	42.5
				Yount, Mil	146	93	63.7	Bell Geo, ChN	129	56	43.4
				Hayes V, Phi	39	25	64.1	Eisenreich, KC	48	21	43.8
				Lewis D, SF	67	43	64.2	Gibson K, KC	83	38	45.8
				Hamilton, Mil	55	36	65.5	Meulens, NYA	59	28	47.5
				Henderson D, Oak	151	100	66.2	Bass K, SF	25	12	48.0
				Cotto, Sea	26	18	69.2				34.0
							54.9				

WHAT MAKES FOR AN EFFICIENT DEFENSE? (p. 242)

The first section of the tables below lists the team's Defensive Efficiency Rating (**DER**), which is the division of the Plays Made (**PM**) by the Balls in Play (**BIP**). The second section shows that team's traditional defensive statistics: Total Chances (**TC**), Errors (**E**), and Fielding Percentage (**Pct**), the latter being the division of (Total Chances minus Errors) by Total Chances.

American League

Team	BIP	PM	DER	TC	E	Pct
Chicago White Sox	4640	3266	.704	6290	116	.982
Toronto Blue Jays	4600	3225	.701	6201	127	.980
Minnesota Twins	4714	3255	.690	6222	95	.985
California Angels	4488	3073	.685	6285	102	.984
Oakland Athletics	4700	3208	.683	6048	107	.982
Seattle Mariners	4585	3126	.682	6286	110	.983
Boston Red Sox	4566	3085	.676	6203	116	.981
Milwaukee Brewers	4871	3290	.675	6279	118	.981
Detroit Tigers	4988	3356	.673	6251	104	.983
Kansas City Royals	4732	3182	.672	6201	125	.980
Baltimore Orioles	4849	3258	.672	6271	91	.985
Texas Rangers	4758	3189	.670	6283	134	.979
Cleveland Indians	4892	3241	.663	6185	149	.976
New York Yankees	4727	3128	.662	6217	133	.979
AL Average	66110	44882	.679	87238	1627	.981

National League

Team	BIP	PM	DER	TC	E	Pct
Montreal Expos	4537	3158	.696	6250	133	.979
Philadelphia Phillies	4633	3221	.695	6131	119	.981
Atlanta Braves	4574	3174	.694	6330	133	.978
St. Louis Cardinals	4677	3243	.693	6102	107	.982
Los Angeles Dodgers	4533	3130	.690	6292	123	.980
San Diego Padres	4700	3235	.688	6202	113	.982
Chicago Cubs	4727	3238	.685	6313	113	.982
Cincinnati Reds	4551	3102	.682	6060	125	.979
San Francisco Giants	4651	3173	.682	6188	109	.982
Pittsburgh Pirates	4699	3206	.682	6336	120	.981
Houston Astros	4543	3099	.682	6137	161	.974
New York Mets	4568	3067	.671	6221	143	.977
NL Average	55393	38046	.687	74562	1504	.980

About STATS, Inc.

It all starts with the **system**. The STATS scoring method, which includes pitch-by-pitch information and the direction, distance, and velocity of each ball hit into play, yields an immense amount of information. Sure, we have all the statistics you're used to seeing, but where other statistical sources stop, STATS is just getting started.

Then, there's the **network**. Our information is timely because our game reporters send their information by computer as soon as the game is over. Statistics are checked, rechecked, updated, and are available daily.

Analysis comes next. STATS constantly searches for new ways to use this wealth of information to open windows into the workings of baseball. Accurate numbers, intelligent computer programming, and a large dose of imagination all help coax the most valuable information from its elusive cover.

Finally, distribution!

For 12 years now STATS has served Major League teams including the White Sox, Athletics and Cubs. The boxscores that STATS provides to the *Associated Press* and *USA Today* have revolutionized what baseball fans expect from a boxscore. *Sports Illustrated* and *The Sporting News* regularly feature STATS, Inc. while *ESPN's* nightly baseball coverage is supported by a full-time STATS statistician. We provide statistics for *Earl Weaver Baseball*, *Rotisserie Baseball*, the syndicated newspaper game *Dugout Derby*, and many other baseball games and fantasy leagues all over the country.

For the baseball fan, STATS publishes monthly and year-end reports on each Major League team. We offer a host of year-end statistical breakdowns on paper or disk that cover hitting, pitching, catching, baserunning, throwing, and more. STATS even produces custom reports on request.

Computer users with modems can access the STATS computer for information with **STATS On-Line**. If you own a computer with a modem, there is no other source with the scope of baseball information that STATS can offer.

STATS and Bill James enjoy an on-going affiliation that has produced several baseball products including the *STATS 1992 Major League Handbook*, the *STATS 1992 Minor League Handbook* and *Bill James Fantasy Baseball*, designed by Bill James himself. This is the ultimate fantasy baseball game, allowing you to manage your own team and compete with other team owners around the country. STATS also produces a similarly-designed head-to-head fantasy football game, *STATS Fantasy Football*.

Always looking for innovative approaches, STATS has other exciting future projects underway for sports fans nationwide. It is the purpose of STATS, Inc. to make the best possible sports information available to all interests: fans, players, teams, or media. For more information write to:

STATS, Inc.
7366 North Lincoln Ave.
Lincolnwood, IL 60646-1708

. . . or call us at 1-708-676-3322. We can send you a STATS brochure, a free Bill James Fantasy Baseball information kit, and/or information on STATS On-Line.

To maintain our information, STATS hires people around the country to cover games using the STATS scoring method. If you are interested in applying for a game reporter's position, please write or call STATS.

For the story behind the players, check out another STATS publication: *The Scouting Report: 1992*. This book combines the observations of baseball's top analysts on the skills and potential of each player with the state-of-the-art statistics of STATS, Inc. Over 700 player scouting reports are detailed. John Dewan and Don Zminda edit this book that baseball fans, players, sportswriters, broadcasters, and general managers can't be without! Look for it at your favorite bookstore or order it directly from STATS with the order form on the last page of this book.

In fact, you can order all of our books, fantasy games or information brochures directly from STATS with the order form in the back.

Index

A

Aaron, Hank
  chance of home run record being
  broken 112
Advancing runners
  moving runners on outs made 34
American League East
  free-agent signings by Boston and
  Toronto 20
  importance of starting pitching in 20
American League West
  improvement vs. the American League
  East 18
April
  team records in from 1987 through
  1991 26
Artificial turf
  batting performance on grass vs. turf 144
  existence of 'turf hitters' examined 144
Astrodome (Houston Astros)
  effects on home runs 67

B

Ballparks
  effects on home runs by left- and
  right-handed batters 67
Base hits
  chances of batters reaching 3,000 and
  4,000 hits 112
  net effects of guarding the line 228
Base stealing
  best and worst percentage base stealers
  lifetime 78
  pitchers holding runners 206
Baseball plays
  occurrences of various events 11
Baserunners
  most and least allowed per nine innings 154
Baserunning
  getting into scoring position ('bases
  gained') 76
  outs made on the bases 80
  teams' ability to take the extra base 101
Basestealing
  effects of pickoff throws on 16
  stolen base attempts per opportunity
  off catchers 221
  success against left- and right-handed
  pitchers 176
Batting (general)
  offensive production by batters
  birthplace 142
Batting (individual)
  advancing baserunners on outs 134
  at home and on the road 130
  average production by lineup position 98
  average production by fielding position.. 96
  best and worst base stealers 78
  best and worst bunters 74
  best and worst cleanup hitters 54
  best and worst leadoff hitters 56
  best and worst monthly performances..... 40
  best hitting pitchers 178
  best middle of the order (3-4-5 hitters) ... 84
  best "pitching" hitters 180
  highest and lowest GDP per GDP
  situation 136
  highest and lowest offensive winning
  percentage 109
  home run leaders by fielding position..... 58
  longest home runs hit in 1991 86
  most go-ahead RBI 61
  most improved 140

most lineouts 122
most runs created....................................109
opposite field home runs hit......................82
percentage of first pitches swung at.......106
percentage of pitches fouled off...............32
percentage of pitches put in play..............32
percentage of pitches swung and
missed..32
percentage of pitches taken for a ball.......32
percentage of pitches taken for a strike....32
performance with runners in scoring
position...127
performance with two strikes 132
pitches seen per plate appearance 104
projection for Cal Ripken.........................14
rated by 'bases gained' into scoring
position...76
RBI per runners on base 51
secondary average 88
strikeout to home run ratio 138
vs. left- and right-handed pitchers............92
Batting (team)
best 'heart of the order' (3-4-5 hitters).....84
pinch hitting... 114
team performance in late & close
situation 42
team performance with runners in
scoring position 8
Batting at home
effects of ballparks on home runs 67
vs. batting on the road 130
Batting average
best and worst with two strikes 132
lowest allowed by pitchers in history.....158
lowest allowed by relievers to first
batter faced 170
increase of when opposing pitcher gets
a big lead 192
Batting on the road
vs. at home..130
Bunting
best and worst at sacrifice bunting...........74
best at bunting for a hit.............................74

C

Catchers
earned run average 226
stolen bases/caught stealing off..............224
time of game when starting 44
Caught stealing
by catchers..224

totals for individual pitchers (vs. stolen
bases)..206
Cleanup hitters
best and worst of 1991 54
Cleveland Stadium (Cleveland Indians)
effects on home runs 67
Clutch hitting
batting with runners in scoring position.127
best and worst late & close hitters 64
most go-ahead RBI...................................61
RBI per runners on base 51

D

Defense
effects of poor defense on pitchers'
ERA..209
team defensive efficiency rating 242
Defensive efficiency
team performance (plays made per
balls in play)...242
Division
American League East free agent
signings of 1991 20
American League West improvement 18
can Pittsburgh, Montreal, etc. compete
with New York and Chicago....................24
chances of Braves repeating in 1992........22
Double plays
batters' rate of GDP per GDP
opportunity 136

E

Earned run average
best and worst team in middle relief 167
catcher ERA 226
effect of getting a big lead on pitchers'
ERA..192
highest and lowest in the first inning 218
starters affected by "bequeathed
runners" scoring......................................172
Errors
effect on pitchers' ERA 209
most and least games per error...............230

F

Fielding
best and worst second basemen at
turning the double play..........................238

catchers throwing out base stealers 224
infielder zone ratings 232
most and least errors per nine innings ... 230
most outfield assists 240
outfielder "baserunner hold percentage" 240
outfielder zone ratings 236

First batter efficiency
lowest batting average allowed to first batters 170

H

Hitting tendencies
batters at home and on the road 130
batters taking the most pitches per plate appearance 104
batters with opposite field home run power 82
batting performance on grass and turf ... 144
best and worst bunters 74
grounding into double plays 136

Holds
combined with Saves (Hold plus Save percentage) 162
most by relievers in 1991 160

Home runs
chances of batter hitting 500, 600, or 700 home runs 112
effects of ballparks on by left- and right-handed batters 67
home run champions by fielding position 58
longest of 1991 86
percentage pulled and hit to the opposite field 82
strikeout/home run ratio for batters 138

I

Inherited runners
most and least allowed to score by relievers 182

L

Late & close
team batting and pitching 42

Leadoff hitters
best and worst of 1991 56
most walks allowed by pitchers in a leadoff situation 185

Lineup
'bases gained' (getting in scoring position) 76
average offensive production from each lineup position 98
best and worst leadoff hitters 56
most frequently used in 1991 38
platooning vs. left- and right-handed pitchers 94
teams rated by number 3-4-5 hitters 84

M

Major league equivalents
as a predictor of major league ability 116

Managers
best records after taking over a team 30

Middle relief
ERA from the first through eighth innings 167

Minor leagues
four potential major league prospects ... 116
stolen base leaders of 1991 119
strikeout leaders and possible major league success 148

N

National League East
ability of "small market" cities to compete 24

National League West
chances of Braves winning second straight title 22

O

Offensive winning percentage
highest and lowest of 1991 109

Outfielders
outfielder Zone Ratings 236
rated by baserunner "hold percentage" . 240

P

Pickoff throws
effects on basestealing 16

Pinch hitting
team performance 199

Pitchers (as batters)
best hitting pitchers, 1991 and career 178

Pitches
  average pitches thrown per start............188
  most and least thrown in a game............216
Pitching (general)
  ability of left-handers to reduce stolen
  base rate..176
  overall pitching performance with a
  3-run lead..192
Pitching (individual)
  "easy," "regular" and "tough" saves........164
  baserunners allowed per nine innings.....154
  bequeathed runners allowed to score
  by relievers...172
  best and worst monthly performances.....40
  best "pitching" hitters.............................180
  first batter efficiency 170
  holding baserunners from stealing 206
  inherited runners allowed to score by
  relievers 182
  left-handed pitchers vs. left-handed
  batters 174
  longest home runs given up by in 1991 ...86
  lowest opponent batting average ever....158
  most and least strikeouts per nine
  innings 151
  most pickoff throws by..........................204
  most and least pitches thrown in a
  game 216
  performance in the first inning...............218
  performance in wins and losses 202
  pitch counts per start 188
  quality starts 190
  run support...156
  stolen base success vs. left- and
  right-handers..176
  stolen bases and caught stealing off.......206
  time of game when starting 44
  un-earned run average 209
  walks allowed in leadoff situations.........185
  walks allowed per nine innings (career) 199
Pitching (team)
  best and worst middle relief ERA 167
  ERA by starters and relievers.................212
Pitching tendencies
  vs. left- and right-handed batters...........174
Platooning
  base stealing off left- and right-handed
  pitchers 176
  batters vs. left- and right-handed
  pitchers 92
  common platoons used in 1991................94
  declining use of as a strategy 94
Player comparison

batting performance by players'
birthplace 142
ERA of teams' catchers..........................226
pitchers compared by ERA and Run
Support 156
team starters and relievers 212
Projections
  batters chances to reach 500 home runs
  and 3000 hits 112
  Cal Ripken career projection....................14
  Favorite Toy to determine chance of
  batter reaching goals..............................112
  major league equivalents for minor
  leaguers..116
  minor league stolen bases as a
  predictor of ability 119
Pull hitting
  percentage of home runs pulled vs.
  opposite field 82

Q

Quality starts
  as percentage of total starts 190

R

Relief pitching
  "easy," "regular," and "tough" saves......164
  bequeathed runners................................172
  best and worst team middle relief
  pitching..167
  first batter efficiency 170
  hold plus save percentage......................162
  inherited runners....................................182
  leaders in Holds for 1991 160
  left-handed relievers vs left-handed
  batters 174
  lowest ERA by relief staffs 212
  position players used as relievers...........180
Ripken, Cal
  career projection......................................14
Riverfront Stadium (Cincinnati Reds)
  effects in home runs 67
Rose, Pete
  chance of hit record being broken..........112
Run support
  most and least for pitchers in 1991 156
Runs batted in
  RBI per runners on base 51
Runs created
  most in 1991 109

Runs scored
  first inning run scored 72

S

Sabermetrics
  offensive winning percentage 109
  pythagorean theorem for 1991 teams 28
  runs created 109
  secondary averages for 1991 88
  team defensive efficiency 242
Sacrifice
  as a first-inning strategy 72
Sacrifice bunt
  as a one-run strategy 70
Saves
  "easy," "regular," and "tough" saves 164
  closers helped by middle relievers
    (Holds) 160
  combined with Holds (Hold plus Save
    percentage) 162
Second basemen
  best and worst at turning the double
    play 238
Secondary average
  batters' records for 1991 88
SkyDome
  effects on home runs 67
Starting pitching
  lowest ERA by starting staffs 212
  percentage of total starts which were
    "quality starts" 190
  victimized by bullpen ('bequeathed
    runners') 172
Stolen bases
  highest stolen base percentage lifetime ... 78
  minor league leaders of 1991 119
  percentage of runners caught stealing
    by catchers 224
  percentage off left- and right-handed
    pitchers 176
  stolen bases/caught stealing off by
    pitchers 204
Strategy
  changing managers in mid-season 30
  guarding the line in the late innings 228
  number of different lineups used 38
  outs invested in one-run strategies 70
  sacrificing in the first inning 72
Strikeouts
  minor league leaders in 1991 148

  most and least per nine innings 151
  strikeout per home run ratio for batters . 138

T

Team performance
  ability to take the extra base 101
  after a managerial change 30
  as predicted by the pythagorean
    theorem 28
  batting and pitching in late & close
    situations 42
  best middle of the order (3-4-5 hitters) ... 84
  number of different lineups used 38
  pinch hitting 114
  records when tied, ahead, or behind
    after 6/7/8 innings 46
  team defensive efficiency rating 242
  team records in April from 1987
    through 1991 26

U

Umpires
  offensive performance with various
    home plate umpires 36
Unearned run average
  highest and lowest for pitchers 209

W

Walks
  allowed in leadoff situations 185
  career walks allowed per nine innings .. 199
Weather
  affects of wind direction on offense
    (Wrigley Field) 6
Wrigley Field (Cubs)
  affects of wind direction on offense 6

ORDER FORM
Mad Aztec Press
1215 Willow View Drive, Kirkwood, MO 63122
NEW Phone: (314) 965-9789

"When James gave up the **Baseball Abstracts,** he released the copyright on his formulas so his work could be continued. This book does just that and does it well." - *Baseball America*

COMPLETE

- Ballpark Adjusted Batting Lines
- Sabermetric Batting Stats
- Sabermetric Pitching Stats
- Ballpark Adjusted Leader Boards
- WAR Ranking Lists of all Players

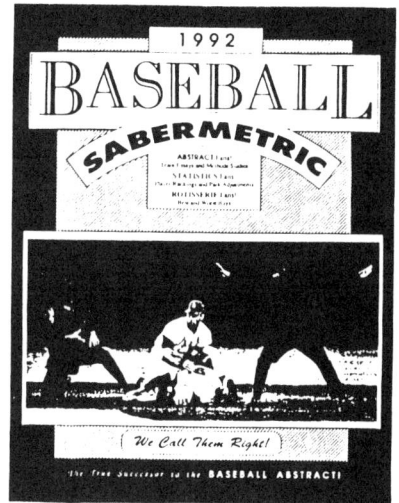

FEATURES

- Team Essays
- Player Rankings by Wins Above Replacement
- Sabermetric Studies
- and the best STAT BOXES in the history of baseball, from Dick Cramer and STATS, Inc.!

The Familiar **BASEBALL ABSTRACT** Format and Features

____ *1992 BASEBALL SABERMETRIC* @ $15.95   = $ _____

____ **1991 BASEBALL SABERMETRIC** @ $15.95   = $ _____

____ **1990 BASEBALL SABERMETRIC** @ $15.95   = $ _____

____ **1989 BASEBALL ABSTRACT** @ $13.95   = $ _____

POSTAGE: $2 for delivery to Canada, or $5 for foreign delivery   = $ _____

GRAND TOTAL: = $ _____

SHIP TO (Please Print):

NAME _____
ADDRESS _____
_____ COUNTRY _____
CITY _____ STATE _____ ZIP _____

Two More Hits from Bill James and STATS, Inc.

Bill James/STATS 1992 Major League Handbook

All New for 1992! **Available now!**

- Exclusive Bill James' Projections for 1992!
- Complete Career Stats of Every Active Major Leaguer
- Lefty/Right Stats — Every 1991 Player
- Unique Leader Boards and Player Profiles

"Statistics [that are] far better than the Baseball Register!" — *Peter Gammons*

Bill James/STATS 1992 Minor League Handbook

New in 1992! **Available now!**

- Exclusive Bill James' Major League Equivalencies
- Official Minor League Stats from Howe Sportsdata International
- Minor League Career Records
- Minor League Leader Boards

"The Next Step for the Serious Baseball Fan!"

Order Now! Use the STATS Order Form on the last page of this book.

Bill James FANTASY BASEBALL

If You Like Fantasy Baseball, You'll Love Bill James Fantasy Baseball...

"Hi. This is Bill James. A few years ago I designed a set of rules for a new fantasy baseball league, which has been updated with the benefit of experience and the input of a few thousand owners.

The idea of a fantasy league, of course, is that it forges a link between you and your ballplayers; YOU win or lose based on how the players that you picked have performed. My goal was to develop a fantasy league based on the simplest and yet most realistic principles possible — a league in which the values are as nearly as possible what they ought to be, without being distorted by artificial category values or rankings, but which at the same time are so simple that you can keep track of how you've done just by checking box scores. There are a lot of different rules around for fantasy leagues, but none of them before this provided exactly what I was looking for. Here's what we want:

1) *We want it to be realistic.* We don't want the rules to make David Cone the MVP because of his strikeouts. We don't want Vince Coleman to be worth more than Bobby Bonilla because he steals lots of bases. We want good ballplayers to be good ballplayers.

2) *We prefer it simple.* We want you to be able to look up your players in the morning paper, and know how you've done.

3) *We want you to have to develop a real team.* We don't want somebody to win by stacking up starting pitchers and leadoff men. We don't want somebody to corner the market on home run hitters.

I made up the rules and I'll be playing the game with you. STATS, Inc. is running the leagues. They'll run the draft, man the computers, keep the rosters straight and provide you with weekly updates. Of course you can make trades, pick up free agents and move players on and off the inactive list; that's not my department, but there are rules for that, too. It all starts with a draft..."

- Draft Your Own Team and Play vs. Other Owners! Play by Mail or With a Computer On-Line!
- Manage Your Roster All Season With Daily Transactions! Live Fantasy Phone Lines Every Day of the Baseball Season!
- Realistic Team and Individual Player Totals That Even Take Fielding Into Account!
- The Best Weekly Reports in the Business!
- Play Against Bill James' Own Drafted Teams!
- Get Discounted Prices by Forming Your Own Private League of 11 or 12 Owners! (Call or write for more information)
- Money-Back Guarantee! Play one month, and if not satisfied, we'll return your franchise fee!

All This, All Summer Long — For Less Than An Average of $5 per week.

Reserve your BJFB team now! Sign up with the STATS Order Form on the next page, or send for additional Free Information.

STATS Order Form

Product	Quantity	Your price	Total
Bill James Fantasy Baseball Franchise		$25 deposit	
STATS 1992 Baseball Scoreboard		$12.95	
Bill James/STATS 1992 Minor League Handbook		17.95	
The Scouting Report: 1992		15.95	
Bill James/STATS 1992 Major League Handbook		17.95	
Discounts on previous editions while supplies last:			
Bill James/STATS 1991 Major League Handbook		9.95	
Bill James/STATS 1990 Major League Handbook		9.95	
STATS 1991 Baseball Scoreboard		9.95	
The STATS Baseball Scoreboard (1990)		7.95	
U.S. – For First Class Mailing – add $2.50 per book		2.50	
Canada – all orders – add $3.50 per book		3.50	
Subtotal			
Subtract $1.00 per book if you order 2 or more		– $1.00	–
Total			

☐ Yes, I can't wait! Sign me up to play Bill James Fantasy Baseball in 1992. Enclosed is my deposit of $25.00 on the franchise fee of $89.00. A processing fee of $1.00 per player is charged during the season for roster moves.

Team Nickname: _____ _____ (example: Dayton Mutants)

Would you like to play in a league with a team drafted by Bill James? Yes No (circle one)

Would you like to receive information on playing BJFB on-line by computer? Yes No (circle one)

Please Rush Me These Free Informational Brochures:

☐ Bill James Fantasy Baseball Info Kit
☐ STATS Fantasy Football Info Kit
☐ STATS On-Line Brochure
☐ STATS Year-End Reports Brochure
☐ STATS Reporter Brochure

Please Print:

Name_____ Phone_____
Address_____
City_____ State_____ Zip_____

Method of Payment (U.S. Funds only):
☐ Check (no Candian checks) ☐ Money Order ☐ Visa ☐ MasterCard

Credit Card Information:
Cardholder Name_____
Visa/MC #_____ Exp. Date_____
Signature_____

Return this form (don't tear your book; copy this page) to:

STATS, Inc.
7366 N. Lincoln Ave
Lincolnwood, IL
60646-1708

For faster credit card service: call 1-800-63-STATS to place your order, or fax this page to 1-708-676-0821.